International Entrepreneur$hip

To my wife, Tina;
my daughters, Kary, Katy, and Kelly;
my son-in-law, Rich; and grandchildren, Rachel and Andrew.
To all your global and entrepreneurial endeavors.

International Entrepreneur$hip

STARTING, DEVELOPING, AND MANAGING A GLOBAL VENTURE

Robert D. Hisrich
Thunderbird School of Global Management

Los Angeles • London • New Delhi • Singapore • Washington DC

For information:

SAGE Publications, Inc.
2455 Teller Road
Thousand Oaks, California 91320
E-mail: order@sagepub.com

SAGE Publications Ltd.
1 Oliver's Yard
55 City Road
London, EC1Y 1SP
United Kingdom

SAGE Publications India Pvt. Ltd.
B 1/I 1 Mohan Cooperative Industrial Area
Mathura Road, New Delhi 110 044
India

SAGE Publications Asia-Pacific Pte. Ltd.
33 Pekin Street #02-01
Far East Square
Singapore 048763

Printed in the United States of America

Library of Congress Cataloging-in-Publication Data

Hisrich, Robert D.
International entrepreneurship : starting, developing, and managing a global venture / Robert D. Hisrich.
    p. cm.
Includes bibliographical references and index.
ISBN 978-1-4129-5798-4 (pbk. : alk. paper)
1. Entrepreneurship. 2. International business enterprises.
3. Entrepreneurship–Case studies. 4. International business enterprises–Case studies. I. Title.
HB615.H576 2009
658'.049–dc22

                    2008034488

This book is printed on acid-free paper.

09 10 11 12 13 10 9 8 7 6 5 4 3 2 1

Acquisitions Editor:	Lisa Cuevas Shaw
Editorial Assistant:	MaryAnn Vail
Production Editor:	Belinda Thresher
Copy Editor:	Christina Quinlan
Typesetter:	Amanda Sylvester
Proofreader:	Lisa Allen
Indexer:	Linda Buskus
Cover Designer:	Gail Buschman
Marketing Manager:	Jennifer Reed Banando

Contents

PART 2. Entering the Global Market

PART 3. Managing the Global Entrepreneurial Enterprise

Preface

S tarting and operating a new venture in one's own country involves considerable risk and energy to overcome all the obstacles involved. These are significantly compounded when one crosses national borders—the fate of the global entrepreneur. This book is designed to help you understand all these international obstacles and to assist you with starting and growing a successful international venture.

To provide an understanding of the person and the process of creating and growing an international venture, this book, *International Entrepreneurship*, is divided into three parts—international entrepreneurship and entrepreneurship opportunities, entering the global market, and managing the global enterprise.

Part 1, International Entrepreneurship and Entrepreneurship Opportunities, deals with the general aspects of being a global entrepreneur and identifying global opportunities. The specific issues covered include the importance of international entrepreneurship, globalization and the international environment, the impact of a culture, the global entrepreneur and his or her venture, and the importance and aspects of the global business.

These chapters describing the general nature and aspects of international entrepreneurship are followed by a discussion of entering a global market in Part 2. The three chapters in Part 2 are extremely important, because without a successful global market selection and entry, obtaining sales and revenues from the global effort becomes very difficult. These three chapters address selecting a business opportunity and its global market, international legal concerns that the global entrepreneur needs to address, and alternative market entry strategies for entrance into the selected market.

The final section of the book, Part 3, deals with all aspects of managing the global enterprise. The specific areas addressed include the global monetary system, global marketing and research and development, global human resource management, and implementing a global strategy and managing the global venture. Because global family businesses comprise the majority of businesses in the world, the book appropriately concludes by addressing this important topic.

To facilitate an understanding of the material and allow the reader to apply it in a global context, original case studies follow each part. These case studies, written by individuals from a wide range of countries, cover global entrepreneurs from these countries who are creating and growing ventures in a wide variety of industries. Each case study is followed by questions that will ensure the most important aspects of the case have been understood.

Acknowledgments

M any individuals—corporate executives, entrepreneurs, small business managers, professors from all over the world, and the publishing staff—have made this book possible. My special thanks goes to four individuals involved with the publishing process for their detailed comments and editorial assistance: Al Bruckner, Editor, Sage Publications; MaryAnn Vail, Sage Publications; Belinda Thresher, Director of Production, Appingo Publishing Services; and Christina Quinlan, Copy Editor, Appingo Publishing Services. My research assistants—Falyne Chave, Michael Cordaro, Erinn Lachner, Rebecca Mitchell, and Elena Ziebarth—provided significant research and editorial assistance. And, my utmost appreciation goes to my administrative assistant, Carol Pacelli, without whom this book would have never been prepared in a timely manner.

I am deeply indebted to my wife, Tina; my daughters, Kary, Katy, and Kelly; my son-in-law, Rich; and my grandchildren, Rachel and Andrew, for their support and understanding of my time commitment in writing this book. It is to them and their generation that this book is particularly dedicated, as the world is truly global.

Part 1

International Entrepreneurship and Entrepreneurship Opportunities

Cases

- Motrada Ltd.

- Parsek LLC

- Beijing Sammies

- TRIMO

Importance of International Entrepreneurship 1

Profile: Ping Fu

GEOMAGIC

Since the mid-1990s, Geomagic has defined and dominated the high-tech field of digital shape sampling and processing, or DSSP, which entails scanning an object with optical beams then rendering it on a computer screen in full three-dimensional fidelity for manufacturing, testing, and inspection purposes. From 2000 to 2005, Geomagic's revenue grew by 2,105%, to around $30 million a year.

DSSP technology holds significant promise because it is universally applicable; any object, animate or inanimate, natural or manmade, of any shape or size, still or, in some cases, moving, can be digitally processed. Within the past few years, DSSP and Geomagic have transformed the hearing aid and dental tech industries, helped digitally preserve the Statue of Liberty, streamlined the manufacturing process for Fisher-Price dollhouses, and re-created engine manifolds for a NASCAR racing team. DSSP crossed into public consciousness by playing a key role in the perilous landing of the space shuttle Challenger. Relying on Geomagic software, NASA engineers scanned and inspected the spacecraft's damaged shuttle tiles with a 10-foot-long robotic arm, and subsequently determined that they could safely withstand the stress of reentry into Earth's atmosphere.

While 2005 represented a breakout year for the company, an even brighter future beckons, and not just for Geomagic, but for manufacturing itself. By the end of the decade, three-dimensional DSSP technology promises to become as common as two-dimensional computer graphics are today. Ping Fu's dream of mass customization, in which DSSP technology allows custom-made, locally produced goods to be manufactured as cheaply as mass-produced outsourced ones, might come to pass.

Ping Fu was forced to leave her homeland, China, in 1981 after being jailed for documenting infanticide in rural China after her research was published by major Chinese newspapers. After learning English at the University of New Mexico, Ping studied computer science as an undergraduate at the University of California at San Diego while working as a programmer for a start-up software design company.

After earning her baccalaureate and starting a doctorate in computer sciences, Ping moved to Illinois in 1986 to work at Bell Labs and study at the University of Illinois and its federally funded National Center for Supercomputing Applications (NCSA). She completed her doctorate while working at NCSA and stayed on as a staff member for a number of years, focusing her work on computer visualization. Among the many products she helped design at NCSA was the animation software used in the film *Terminator 2*. In 1991, Ping married Herbert Edelsbrunner, a professor and expert in algorithms and computational geometry.

In 1991 a friend came to Ping with a problem: Was it possible to digitally compute spaces, as well as shapes and objects? Ping was intrigued. She recalled a Chinese proverb: A house is defined by walls and roofs, but in empty space do people live. But that was as far as she could get with the problem. She took the riddle to her husband, who, it turned out, had already solved it. From those equations Ping conceived an application, a product, a story. Geomagic was born.

In 1997 Ping left NCSA to devote her energies to the start-up Geomagic. She borrowed $500,000 from her sister (who had followed Ping to America and remained under her wing until her marriage to a successful businessman in Phoenix), then traveled to Chicago and wowed an audience of venture capitalists. They invested $1.5 million in Geomagic.

Still, the mechanics of running a company seemed daunting. That feeling is common among engineers and scientists founding start-ups. Like many technologists before and since, Ping hired an experienced chief executive. At the same time, she decided to relocate Geomagic near a university where her husband could teach and continue his research. (Edelsbrunner serves on Geomagic's board and generates the mathematical theories driving the company's products, but is removed from day-to-day business.) Every major research school in the United States was eager to hire Edelsbrunner. He and Ping chose Duke.

In 1999, shortly after the move, Ping made a pitch to Franklin Street Partners. "She came across as extremely intelligent and prepared, and communicated her vision of the company in a gripping manner," recalls Paul Rizzo, former vice chairman of the board at IBM and emeritus dean of the business school at the University of North Carolina, who was present at the meeting and now sits on Geomagic's board. "You could tell she had a strong intuitive sense about what she was doing. And the technology she was talking about was just so interesting that it seemed like it couldn't fail."

Franklin Street invested $6.5 million in the seemingly sure bet, and yet failure very nearly descended. The CEO that Ping had hired had an impressive track record at a large tech company, but had no experience with a small start-up. He spent most of Geomagic's capital, along with most of his salespeople, and brought in virtually no revenue.

"A slow start was pretty much in the cards," Rizzo points out. "Geomagic was introducing what amounted to brand new technology. They had to build a market at the same time that they were building a brand."

The second year turned out to be as dry as the first. By the end of 2000, the money was gone, the tech bubble had burst, and the company still had virtually zero revenue. Ping went to her Franklin Street investors and told them that she wanted to take the reins of the company. It was their money and her family's money that had disappeared, she said, and her employees whose futures were at risk.

Franklin Street agreed to Ping's emergency business plan and she went to talk to her people. The CEO resigned and the salespeople left. (To pay their severance packages, she mortgaged her house.) She asked her remaining employees to give her 3 months to turn Geomagic around. If she failed, she would sell the company and try to help them all keep their jobs.

"I must admit I had my doubts," Rob Black recalls. "If it had been any other boss but Ping, I probably would have bailed. But she communicated such a sense of resolve that I just couldn't help believing in her. Thank goodness I decided to stay."

Ping went into survival mode, a state of mind and being she had developed all too well during her childhood in China. "All of my instincts kicked in," she says. "In a crisis mode, you lose all self-doubt; at least I do. I couldn't afford the luxury of doubt. I had too many people depending on me. I knew I had to make Geomagic's story so compelling that no potential customer could possibly turn me down."

Desperation turned out to be the mother of invention: Ping made a $1.8 million sale to Align Technology (in fairness, the former CEO had established the groundwork for the sale) and convinced customers in the dental tech industry that DSSP could deliver a new age of custom-fit crowns and implants. She decided not to assemble an in-house sales staff, relying instead on resellers, particularly laser-scanner and processor manufacturers. Within the promised 3 months, Ping had stabilized Geomagic, and within a year the company was showing a profit.

"Being so close to failure somehow gave me confidence," says Ping. "Everybody worked together; we reinforced each other. And the crisis committed me to running the company. The experience really opened my eyes about corporate governance. I learned that I must listen very carefully, gather all the information and advice that I can, but in the end I must make the decisions. I know I will make mistakes. But I also learned that, at times, it's more important to be clear than to be right."

Among Geomagic's thousands of clients are NASCAR teams, which use DSSP to streamline the inspection and production of cylinder heads, and the Cleveland Clinic, which has used DSSP to model and test a new artificial heart.

Then there is the Statue of Liberty. After 9/11, the impregnability of American landmarks could no longer be assumed. If a terrorist attack or other catastrophe damaged Lady Liberty, officials would want to rebuild it with maximum fidelity to the original. But certain architectural details—the folds of her robe, the lift of her eyebrows—could not be recast from photographs. So a research team from Texas Tech University spent days laser-scanning the statue, accumulating a total of 16 million data points from which to build a digital model with Geomagic software.

But it is in bread-and-butter manufacturing that Geomagic truly shows its potential. American turbine companies, for instance, use DSSP to perform 100% digital inspections for new parts. In the dental industry, the technology has produced a new generation of implants and bridgework that actually fit. Ditto for hearing aids. Extrapolate as you like. Ping likes to imagine that each of us will soon be in possession of a DSSP model of our feet, and when we need new shoes, we'll transmit that model to a manufacturer, which will make shoes that fit like no off-the-shelf shoes can.

Common to these projects is quality custom work performed by American companies for a domestic market. By their very nature, none of these products could have been satisfactorily delivered by foreign competitors, especially the one that looms the largest: China. It's an important point for Ping. "I don't think having China manufacture all our goods and ship them back over here at a grotesque trade imbalance is a good model for anybody," she says.

"I really believe that this technology is important," Ping continues. "We are just on the edge of it now. I hoped that mass acceptance would have come already, but it takes time. I can honestly say that if in 5 years Geomagic is a highly profitable company, but the DSSP revolution has not arrived, then I would not consider myself a success. By the same token, if we sold the company to a buyer who understands our vision and in 5 years the revolution takes place but Geomagic's contribution is forgotten, I would consider my work accomplished. I am not interested in wealth. I want to produce something of value."

www.geomagic.com/en/about_us/

www.geomagic.com

NOTE: This profile was adapted from Brant, J. (2005, December). The Dimensions of Ping Fu, *Inc. 27*(12), 90–97, 132+.

Chapter Objectives

1. To understand the fundamental importance of the global venture in today's constantly changing world.

2. To introduce the concept of entrepreneurship from a global perspective, crossing national boundaries.

3. To learn the key differences in operating a business in a global environment versus a domestic environment from economic, political, cultural, and technological perspectives.

4. To explain the various factors affecting the business plans of entrepreneurs entering different markets.

5. To identify the major motivators for taking a business global or of conceiving a new business with a global focus.

6. To become familiar with the positive and negative aspects of each factor that contributes to the decision to take one's business global.

Introduction

Never before in the history of the world have there been such interesting and exciting international business opportunities. The movement of the once controlled economies of Eastern and Central Europe, the former U.S.S.R., and the People's Republic of China to more market-oriented ones and the advancement of the Pacific Rim provide a myriad of possibilities for entrepreneurs wanting to start a new enterprise in a foreign market as well as for existing entrepreneurial firms desiring to expand their businesses globally. The world is truly global.

As more and more countries become market-oriented and economically developed, the distinction between foreign and domestic markets is becoming less pronounced. What was once only produced domestically is now produced internationally. For example, Yamaha pianos are now manufactured in the United States, and Nestlé's chocolate, started in Europe, is made all over the world. Invacare's wheelchairs were once produced only in Ohio, but are now made in Germany and China in addition to the United States. This blurring of national identities will continue to accelerate as more products are introduced outside domestic boundaries earlier in the life of entrepreneurial firms.

Since the mid-1990s, organizations have been attempting to redefine themselves to be truly global. The pressure to internationalize is being felt in nearly every kind of organization: nonprofit and for-profit, public and private, large and small. This need to internationalize is accelerating because of the self-interest of these organizations as well as the effect of a variety of external events. Today more than seven-eighths of the markets of the world have some form of market economics. Even as late as August 1989, a few large trading blocs such as the European Union and NAFTA (the trade agreement between Canada, Mexico, and the United States) have emerged and are growing. Once developing countries, like China, are economic powers.

These changes are well recognized by organizations that are investing trillions of dollars in a world economy that includes emerging markets as some of the vehicles of future growth. About 85% of the world's population lives in developing countries, most of which are in need of major investment in infrastructure development. Just ask the potato farmers in the Chuvash Republic of Russia, who saw 26% of their crop rot because of inadequate distribution and warehousing, whether there is a need for this investment in infrastructure. Or, ask the economics professor in the Czech Republic, who had to leave the university to find other employment in order to live due to the low university wages, whether massive investment in education is needed. The professor, like many human resources in these developing countries, needs training and education to provide the manpower needed in the next century.

The need for physical and technological infrastructure is no more apparent than in one of the fastest growing markets in this decade—the Pacific Rim. This area offers economically viable locations for manufacturing and trade. Over half of the world's population lives in Asia, with China containing 20% of the world's population. India alone is twice the size of Latin America. And then there is Japan, with its world economy, ranking third in the world in exporting and importing, surpassed only by the United States and Germany. Japanese automobile companies voluntarily reduced their exports to the United States market because of their large market share, which had resulted from successfully competing with U.S. companies—Chrysler, Ford, and General Motors.

There are also the new market opportunities in Latin and South America, Africa, China, Vietnam, Iraq, and countries in transition throughout the world. These areas are becoming highly attractive to globally oriented companies that want to grow their business internationally and develop a strong market position as the economies of countries change through privatization and deregulation.

The globalization of entrepreneurship creates wealth and employment that benefits individuals and nations throughout the world. International entrepreneurship is exciting because it combines the many aspects of domestic entrepreneurship with other disciplines such as anthropology, economics, geography, history, jurisprudence, and language. In today's hypercompetitive world with rapidly changing technology, it is essential for an entrepreneur to at least consider entering the global market.

Many entrepreneurs find it difficult to manage and expand the venture they have created, especially into the global marketplace. To expand a venture, an entrepreneur needs to access his or her abilities in the management area to identify methods for domestic and international expansion. Some entrepreneurs tend to forget a basic axiom in business: The only constant is change. Entrepreneurs who understand this axiom will effectively manage change by continually adapting their organizational culture, structure, procedures, and strategic direction, as well as their products and services in both a domestic and an international orientation. Entrepreneurs in developed countries like the United States, Japan, the United Kingdom, and Germany must sell their products in a variety of new and different market areas as early as possible to further the growth of their firms.

Global markets offer entrepreneurial companies new market opportunities. Since 1950 the growth of international trade and investment has often been larger than the growth of the domestic economy even in the economies of the United States and China. A combination of domestic and international sales offers the entrepreneur an opportunity for expansion and growth that is not available solely in the domestic market.

THE NATURE OF INTERNATIONAL ENTREPRENEURSHIP

Simply stated, *international entrepreneurship* is "the process of an entrepreneur conducting business activities across national boundaries." It may consist of exporting, licensing, opening a sales office in another country, or something as simple as placing a classified advertisement in the Paris edition of the *International Herald Tribune*. The activities necessary for ascertaining and satisfying the needs and wants of target consumers often take place in more than one country. When an entrepreneur executes his or her business model in more than one country, international entrepreneurship is occurring.

The term *international entrepreneurship* was introduced around 1988 to describe the many untapped foreign markets that were open to new ventures reflecting a new technological and cultural environment (Morrow, 1988).

McDougall (1989, p. 387–399) defined international entrepreneurship as "the development of international new ventures or start-ups that, from their inception, engage in international business, thus viewing their operating domain as international from the initial stages of the firm's operation."

In 1997 McDougall and Oviatt introduced a broader definition of international entrepreneurship to include the study of established companies and the recognition of comparative (cross-national) analysis. They defined this field as "a combination of innovative, proactive, and risk-seeking behavior that crosses or is compared across national borders and is intended to create value in business organizations" (McDougall & Oviatt, 2000). This definition takes into account at the organizational level the notions of innovation, risk taking, and proactive behavior. It also focuses on the entrepreneurial behavior of these firms rather than only the characteristics and intentions of the individual entrepreneurs. The key dimensions of entrepreneurship—innovativeness, proactiveness, and risk propensity—can be found and developed at the organizational level.

A good definition and understanding was presented in the introduction to an issue devoted to the topic in *Entrepreneurship Theory and Practice* (Honig-Haftel, Hisrich, McDougall, & Oviatt, 1996). The authors broadly defined international entrepreneurship as any activity of an entrepreneur that crossed a national border. This understanding was further developed in a review article (Ruzzier, Antoncic, & Hisrich, 2006). Numerous research studies and definitions have emerged focusing on a wide variety of areas, such as the international sales of new ventures (McDougall, 1989), born-global ventures (McDougall & Oviatt, 2000), role of national culture (McGrath, McMillan, & Scheinberg, 1992), and the international-ization of small and medium enterprises (Lu & Beamish, 2001). It has also been applied in many geographic contexts, such as Eastern Europe (His-rich, 1994; Hisrich & O'Cinneide, 1991), Germany (Grichnik & Hisrich, 2004), Hungary (Hisrich & Fulop, 1993, 1995; Hisrich & Szirmai, 1993; Hisrich & Vecsenyi, 1994), Ireland (Hisrich & O'Cinneide, 1989), Israel (Lerner, Brush, & Hisrich, 1997), Northern Ireland (Hisrich, 1988), Slo-venia (Hisrich, Vahcic, Glas, & Bucar, 1998), Soviet Union (Hisrich, Ageev, & Gratchev, 1995; Hisrich & Gratchev, 1993, 1995), Ukraine (His-rich, Bowser, & Smarsh, 2006) and developing economies (Antoncic & Hisrich, 1999, 2000; Hisrich & Öztürk, 1999).

Finally, according to McDougall, Oviatt, and Shrader's definition (2003), international entrepreneurship is "a combination of innovative, proactive, and risk-seeking behavior that crosses national borders and is intended to create value in organizations."

With a commercial history of only 300 years, the United States is a rela-tive newcomer to the international business arena. As soon as settlements were established in the New World, American businesses began an active international trade with Europe. Foreign investors helped build much of the early industrial trade with Europe as well as much of the early indus-trial base of the United States. The future commercial strength of the United States, as well as the rest of the world, will depend on the ability of both entrepreneurs and established companies to be involved in markets outside their borders.

International Versus Domestic Entrepreneurship

Although international and domestic entrepreneurs alike are concerned with sales, costs, and profits, what differentiates domestic from interna-tional entrepreneurship is the variation in the relative importance of the factors affecting each decision. International entrepreneurial decisions are more complex due to such uncontrollable factors as economics, politics, culture, and technology (see Table 1.1).

ECONOMICS

In a domestic business strategy, a single country at a specified level of economic development is the focus of entrepreneurial efforts. The entire country is almost always organized under a single economic system and has the same currency. Creating a business strategy for a multicountry area means dealing with differences in levels of economic development; currency valuations; government regulations; and banking, venture capital, marketing, and distribution systems. These differences manifest themselves in each aspect of the entrepreneur's international business plan and methods of doing business.

One of the biggest problems entrepreneurs have is raising capital. The amount of private equity capital investments varies greatly by the area of the world and is significantly less than that available in the United States.

STAGE OF ECONOMIC DEVELOPMENT

The United States is an industrially developed nation with regional variances of relative income. While needing to adjust the business plan according to regional differences, an entrepreneur doing business only in the United States does not have to worry about a significant lack of such fundamental infrastructures as roads, electricity, communication systems, banking facilities and systems, adequate educational systems, a well-developed legal system, and established business ethics and norms. These

Table 1.1   Differences in Doing Global Versus Domestic Business

- Economics
- State in economic development
- Balance of payments, balance of trade
- Type of economic system
- Political-legal environment
- Cultural environment
- Technological environment
- Local foreign competition
- Subsidies offered by foreign competition

SOURCE: Adapted from Hisrich, R. D., Peters, M. A., & Shepherd, D. A. (2007). *Entrepreneurship* (7th ed.). Burr Ridge, IL: McGraw-Hill/Irwin, p. 90.

factors vary greatly in other countries, from those industrialized to those in the process of developing, and significantly affect the ability to successfully engage in international business.

BALANCE OF PAYMENTS

With the present system of flexible exchange rates, a country's *balance of payments* (the difference between the value of a country's imports and exports over time) affects the valuation of its currency. The valuation of one country's currency affects business transactions between countries. At one time, Italy's chronic balance of payments deficit led to a radical depreciation in the value of the lira, Italy's currency. Fiat Automobile SpA responded by offering significant rebates on cars sold in the United States. These rebates cost Fiat very little because fewer dollars purchased many more liras due to the decreased value of the lira. Similar exchange rate divergences have occurred for Japanese automobile manufacturers and many products produced by Chinese firms, including steel and steel alloys. The shrinking value of the U.S. dollar has helped U.S. firms export more due to lower prices of U.S. goods in foreign currencies as well as effected an increase in worldwide prices of oil and food.

TYPE OF ECONOMIC SYSTEM

Pepsi-Cola began considering the possibility of marketing in the former U.S.S.R. as early as 1959, following the visit of U.S. Vice President Richard Nixon. When Premier Nikita Khrushchev expressed his approval of Pepsi's taste, East-West trade really began moving, with Pepsi entering the former U.S.S.R. 13 years later. Instead of using its traditional type of franchise bottler in their entry strategy, Pepsi used a barter-type arrangement that satisfied both the socialized system of the former U.S.S.R. and the U.S. capitalist system. In return for receiving technology and syrup from Pepsi, the former U.S.S.R. provided the company with Soviet vodka and distribution rights in the United States. Many such *barter* or *third-party arrangements* have been used to increase the amount of business activity with the former U.S.S.R. and Eastern and Central European countries, as well as other countries in various stages of development and transition.

There are many difficulties in doing business in developing and transition economies. These problems reflect the lack of basic knowledge of the Western system regarding business plans, product promotion, marketing, and profits; widely variable rates of return; nonconvertible currency; differences in accounting systems; and communication problems.

POLITICAL-LEGAL ENVIRONMENT

The multiplicity of political and legal environments in the international market creates vastly different business problems, opening some market opportunities for entrepreneurs and eliminating others. For example, U.S. environmental standards have eliminated the possibility of entrepreneurs establishing ventures to import several models of European cars. Another significant event in the political-legal environment involves price fluctuations and significant increases in the last few years in oil and other energy products.

Each element of the business strategy of an international entrepreneur has the potential to be affected by the multiplicity of legal environments. Pricing decisions in a country that has a value-added tax are different from those decisions made by the same entrepreneur in a country with no value-added tax. Advertising strategy is affected by the variations in what can be said in the copy or in the support needed for advertising claims in different countries. Product decisions are affected by legal requirements with respect to labeling, ingredients, and packaging. Types of ownership and organizational forms vary widely throughout the world. The laws governing business arrangements also vary greatly with over 150 different legal systems and national laws.

CULTURAL ENVIRONMENT

The effect of culture on entrepreneurs and strategies is also significant. Entrepreneurs must make sure that each element in the business plan has some degree of congruence with the local culture. For example, in some countries, point-of-purchase displays are not allowed in retail stores as they are in the United States.

An increasingly important aspect of the cultural environment in some countries concerns bribes and corruption. How should an entrepreneur deal with these situations? What is the best course of action to take and still maintain the needed high ethical standards?

Sometimes one of the biggest problems is finding a translator. To avoid errors like these, entrepreneurs should take care to hire a translator whose native tongue is the target language and whose expertise matches that of the original creators.

TECHNOLOGICAL ENVIRONMENT

Technology, like culture, varies significantly across countries. The variations and availability of technology are often surprising, particularly to an entrepreneur from a developed country like the United States. While U.S. firms produce mostly standardized, relatively uniform products that can be sorted to meet industry standards, this is not the case in many countries, making it more difficult to achieve a consistent level of quality.

New products in a country are created based on the conditions and infrastructure operating in that country. For example, U.S. car designers can assume wider roads and less expensive gasoline than European designers. When these same designers work on transportation vehicles for other parts of the world, their assumptions need to be significantly altered.

LOCAL FOREIGN COMPETITION

When entering a foreign market, the international entrepreneur needs to be aware of the strength of local competitors who are already established in the market. These competitive companies can often be a formidable force against country entry as they are known companies with known products and services. This can be particularly difficult when there is a "buy national" attitude in the country. A sustained effort stressing the unique selling propositions of the entering product or service is necessary, including a guarantee to ensure customer satisfaction, in order to compete.

SUBSIDIES OFFERED BY FOREIGN GOVERNMENTS

Some governments offer subsidies to attract particular types of foreign companies and investments to help further the development of the country's economy. These subsidies can take different forms, such as cash or a tax holiday for a period of time, and usually focus on infrastructure development. This occurred for U.S. oil companies that built the oil fields and delivery system in the Middle East and for foreign banks that assisted in developing the banking system in China.

On the other hand, foreign governments can offer subsidies to local firms to help them compete against foreign products. This is often called an *infant industry protection policy.*

Motivations to Go Global

Unless you are born global, most entrepreneurs will only pursue international activities when stimulated to do so. A variety of proactive and reactive motivations can cause an entrepreneur to become involved in international business, as is indicated in Table 1.2. Profits are, of course,

Table 1.2   Motivations for Going Global

- Profits
- Competitive pressures
- Unique product(s) or service(s)
- Excess production capacity
- Declining home country sales
- Unique market opportunity
- Economies of scale
- Technological advantage
- Tax benefits

one of the most significant reasons for going global. Usually, the profitability expected from going global is not the actual profits obtained. The profitability is adversely affected by the costs of getting ready to go global, underestimating the costs involved, and some losses from mistakes. The difference between the planned and actual results may be particularly large in your first attempt to go global. Anything you think won't happen probably will, even to the extent of having significant shifts in foreign exchange rates.

The allure of profits is reflected in the motive to sell to other markets. For a U.S.-based entrepreneurial firm, the 95% of the world's population living outside the United States offers a very large market opportunity. These sales may even be necessary to cover any significant research and development and start-up manufacturing costs that were incurred in the domestic market. Without sales to these international markets, these excessive costs would have to be spread just over domestic sales, resulting in less sales and profits, which can be a problem particularly in price sensitive markets.

Sales to other markets may also reflect another reason for going global—the home domestic market is leveling or may even be declining in sales or sales potential. This is occurring in several markets in the United States with its aging demographics.

Sometimes an entrepreneur moves to international markets to avoid increased regulations or governmental or societal concerns about their products or services. Cigarette companies such as Philip Morris aggressively pursued sales outside the United States, particularly in developing economies, when confronted with increased government regulations and anti-smoking attitudes of consumers. Sometimes this took the form of purchasing existing companies in foreign markets, which is what occurred in Russia.

When the entrepreneur's technology becomes obsolete in the domestic market or the product or service is near the end of its life cycle, there may be sales opportunities in foreign markets. One entrepreneur found new sales life for the company's gas permeable hard contact lenses and solutions when the domestic market in the United States was negatively affected by highly competitive soft lenses. Volkswagen continued to sell its original VW Beetle in Latin and South America for years after stopping its sales in the United States.

Entrepreneurs often go global to take advantage of lower costs in foreign countries for labor, manufacturing overhead, and raw materials. The "Flip Watch," made by newly started HourPower, could never be marketed at its price point in Things Remembered and JC Penney stores without being produced in China. Waterford Crystal is manufacturing some products in Prague to help offset the higher labor costs in Ireland. This cost advantage may become obsolete as the Czech Republic develops as a member of the European Union. There are often some cost advantages by having at least a distribution and sales office in a foreign market. Graph Soft, a Hungarian software company, found its sales significantly increased in the United States when it opened a sales office in Los Angeles, California.

Several more esoteric motivations beyond the traditional ones of sales and profits also can motivate an entrepreneur to go global. One of the more predominant motivations is to establish and exploit a global presence. When an entrepreneur truly goes global, many company operations can be internationalized and leveraged. For example, when going global an entrepreneur will establish a global distribution system and an integrated manufacturing capability. Establishing these gives the company a competitive advantage because they not only facilitate the successful production and distribution of present products, but help keep out competitive products as well. By going global, an entrepreneur can offer a variety of different products at better price points.

Traits of an International Entrepreneur

Several characteristics and traits are identifiable in international entrepreneurs regardless of the country of origin. These include: embraces change, high desire to achieve, ability to establish a vision, high tolerance for ambiguity, high level of integrity, and knowing the importance of individuals.

EMBRACES CHANGE

A global entrepreneur likes and even embraces differences in people, as well as situations. He or she constantly seeks new and exciting things and likes to "break the mold" and challenge corporate orthodoxies. Living in and learning about different cultures and ways of doing things is an exciting way to live. New ways of doing things are encouraged. Employees are taught how to manage change.

DESIRE TO ACHIEVE

A global entrepreneur has good business savvy and a strong desire to achieve. To succeed an entrepreneur needs to have profit/loss experience and an ability to create value in a different culture. A possession of broad business knowledge, such as transfer pricing, foreign exchange, and international customs and laws, combined with a global mindset provides the basis for success.

ABILITY TO ESTABLISH A VISION

A global entrepreneur needs to establish a vision that employees and customers understand. Employees should feel that they are an important part of the global organization and essential to its success. A global entrepreneur is very optimistic, assuming that everything is possible, and establishes a limited number of short-term goals to obtain the vision. He or she focuses more on outcomes not processes, works long hours, has a high energy level, and does not fear failure.

HIGH TOLERANCE FOR AMBIGUITY

The passion for learning from a wide variety of sources and viewing uncertainty as an opportunity instead of a threat allows a global entrepreneur to develop mental maps that will lead to achieving the vision. Incrementally moving initiatives in a wide variety of areas without completing one regularly is not a problem for a global entrepreneur. This high tolerance for ambiguity makes utility a key virtue of any practice at the individual or company level.

HIGH LEVEL OF INTEGRITY

A global entrepreneur has an extremely high standard for individual and company honesty and integrity. These established standards are used inside and outside the company. The same high ethical standards are expected from all employees and activities of the venture.

INDIVIDUALS ARE IMPORTANT

A global entrepreneur focuses on the well-being of his or her employees and is a nurturing coach who helps them reach their potential. He or she focuses on building and inspiring people and works effectively with others in teams. Spending more time listening than talking, a global entrepreneur values people—employees as well as customers—and wants to build a sustainable enterprise in the particular culture and country.

The Importance of Global Business

Global business has become increasingly important to firms of all sizes, particularly today when every firm is part of a hypercompetitive global economy. There can be little doubt that today's entrepreneur must be able to move in the world of international business. The successful entrepreneur will be someone who fully understands how international business differs from purely domestic business and is able to respond accordingly. An entrepreneur entering the international market should address the following questions:

1. What are the options available for engaging in international business?

2. What are the strategic issues in successfully going global?

3. How is managing international business different from managing domestic business?

The many different aspects of international entrepreneurship include culture, political and legal environment, economy and economic integration, distribution channels, change, and communication. These important aspects of international entrepreneurship affect how an entrepreneurial firm can become truly global. Culture, political and legal environment, economy, and the available distribution channels vary significantly from country to country, and each needs to be taken into account when deciding to go global as discussed in the following summary. Change and communication are important aspects of operating in a global environment, as are market selection and entry.

Summary

At no other time in human history has the potential for great wealth and prosperity been accessible to so many. This first chapter introduces the reader to the concept of international entrepreneurship, the process of an entrepreneur conducting business activities across national boundaries. More businesses are deciding to go global early in their inception than ever before. Since over 85% of countries are developing, entrepreneurs have numerous opportunities from which to choose. The globalization of entrepreneurship helps these countries develop because it creates wealth and employment. The chapter also emphasizes how economics; state of economic development; balance of payments; economic system; and political-legal, cultural, and technological environments all play a large role in the establishment of an international versus domestic company. The motives for launching an international enterprise, including a large market opportunity and potential for profit, are also examined. Finally, the chapter discusses what questions an individual or company should consider before going global.

Questions for Discussion

1. What are some differences between domestic and international entrepreneurship?

2. What are the key characteristics to understand when moving a business from one country or region to another?

3. What potential problems might an entrepreneur encounter when entering a new country?

4. What does an entrepreneur need to be aware of before entering a foreign market?

Chapter Exercises

1. Define international entrepreneurship and describe an example of an international entrepreneur and his or her business.

2. Explain the aspects of international entrepreneurship. How would missing one or two of these variables affect a global venture?

3. What are the motivations for taking a business global? What factors influence this decision?

References

Antoncic, B., & Hisrich, R. D. (1999, May). The role of entrepreneurship in transition economies: Insights from a comparative study. *Proceedings of the 1999 Conference on Entrepreneurship, 214–215.*

Antoncic, B., & Hisrich, R. D. (2000, April). Intrapreneurship model in transition economies: A comparison of Slovenia and the United States. *Journal of Developmental Entrepreneurship, 5*(1), 21–40.

Grichnik, D., & Hisrich, R. D. (2004). Entrepreneurship education needs arising from entrepreneurial profiles in a unified Germany: An international comparison. In Miettinen, A., Landoli, L., & Raffa, M. (Eds.), *Internationalizing Entrepreneurship Education and Training Conference Proceedings,* 157–160. Napoli: Edizione Scientifiche Italiane.

Grichnik, D., & Hisrich, R. D. (2004, September) Entrepreneurship education needs arising from entrepreneurial profiles in a unified Germany: An international comparison. *Internationalizing Entrepreneurship Education and Training Conference Proceedings,* pp. 157–160.

Hisrich, R. D. (1988, July). The entrepreneur in northern Ireland: Characteristics, problems, and recommendations for the future. *Journal of Small Business Management, 26*(5) 32–39.

Hisrich, R. D. (1994). Developing technology joint ventures in central and eastern Europe. In Dana, L. (Ed.) *Advances in Global High-Technology Management: International Management of High Technology* (111–130). Greenwich, CT: JAI Press, Inc.

Hisrich, R. D., Ageev, A. I., & Gratchev, M. V. (1995). Entrepreneurship in the Soviet Union and post-socialist Russia. *Small Business Economics,* 7, 1–121.

Hisrich, R. D., Bowser, K., & Smarsh, L. S. (2006). Women entrepreneurs in the Ukraine. *International Journal of Entrepreneurship and Small Business.* 3(2), 207–221.

Hisrich, R. D., & Fulop, G. (1993, March). Women entrepreneurs in controlled economies: A Hungarian perspective. *Proceedings of the 1993 Conference on Entrepreneurship,* 590–592.

Hisrich, R. D., & Fulop, G. (1995, July). Hungarian entrepreneurs and their enterprises. *Journal of Small Business Management, 33*(3), 88–94.

Hisrich, R. D., & Grachev, M. V. (1993, November). The Russian entrepreneur. *Journal of Business Venturing,* 8, 487–497.

Hisrich, R. D., & Gratchev, M. V. (1995). The russian entrepreneur: Characteristics and prescriptions for success. *Journal of Managerial Psychology, 10*(2), 3–9.

Hisrich, R. D., & O'Cinneide, B. (1989, April). The entrepreneur and the angel: An exploratory cross cultural study. *Proceedings of the 1989 Conference on Entrepreneurship,* 530–531.

Hisrich, R. D., & O'Cinneide, B. (1991, May). Analysis of emergent entrepreneurship trends in eastern Europe: A public policy perspective. *Proceedings of the
1991 Conference on Entrepreneurship*, 594–596.

Hisrich, R. D., & Öztürk, S. A. (1999, Fall). Women entrepreneurs in a developing
economy. *Journal of Management Development, 18*(2), 114–124.

Hisrich, R. D., & Szirmai, P. (1993). Developing a market oriented economy: A
Hungarian perspective. *Entrepreneurship and Regional Development, 5*(1),
61–71.

Hisrich, R. D., Vahcic, A., Glas, M., & Bucar, B. (1998, May). Why Slovene public
policy should focus on high growth SME's. *Proceedings of the 1998 Conference
on Entrepreneurship*, 487–489.

Hisrich, R. D., & Vecsenyi, J. (1994). Graphisoft: The entry of a Hungarian software venture into the U.S. market. In Hisrich, R. D., McDougall, P. P., &
Oviatt, B. M. (Eds.), *Cases in International Entrepreneurship*, (1997), 80–96.

Honig-Haftel, S., Hisrich, R. D., McDougall, P. P., & Oviatt, B. M. (1996, Summer). International entrepreneurship: Past, present, and future. *Entrepreneurship Theory and Practice, 20*(4), 5–7.

Lerner, M., Brush, C., & Hisrich, R. D. (1997, July). Israeli women entrepreneurs:
An examination of factors affecting performance. *Journal of Business Venturing, 12*(4), 315–339.

Lu, J. W., & Beamish, P. W. (2001). The internationalization and performance of
SMEs. *Strategic Management Journal*, 22, 565–586.

McDougall, P. P. (1989). International versus domestic entrepreneurship: New
venture strategic behavior and industry structure. *Journal of Business Venturing*, 4, 387–399.

McDougall, P. P., & Oviatt, B. M. (1997). International entrepreneurship literature
in the 1990s and directions for future research. In Sexton, D. L., & Smilor,
R. W. (Eds.), *Entrepreneurship 2000*, (291–320). Chicago: Upstart Publishing.

McDougall, P. P., & Oviatt, B. M. (2000). International entrepreneurship: The
intersection of two research paths. *Academy of Management Journal, 43*,
902–908.

McDougall, P. P., Oviatt, B. M., & Shrader, R. C. (2003). A Comparison of international and domestic new ventures. *Journal of International Entrepreneurship, 1*, 59–82.

McGrath, R. G., MacMillan, I. C., & Scheinberg, S. (1992). Elitists, risk-takers,
and rugged individuals? An exploratory analysis of cultural differences
between entrepreneurs and non-entrepreneurs. *Journal of Business Venturing, 7*(2), 115–135.

Morrow, J. F. (1988). International entrepreneurship: A new growth opportunity.
New Management, 5(3), 59–60.

Ruzzier, M., Antoncic, B., & Hisrich, R. D. (2006). SME internationalization
research: Past, present, and future. *Journal of Small Business and Enterprise
Development, 13*(4), 476–497.

Suggested Readings

ARTICLES/BOOKS

Ajami, R. A., & Bear, M. M. (Editors). (2007). *The global enterprise: Entrepreneurship and value creation.* **New York: International Business Press.**

This book covers everything from the relationship between globalization and entrepreneurship, practical tools for entrepreneurs like economic cluster formation, market entry, and value creation. It also offers lessons on bringing products to the global market.

Gilmore, F., & Rumens, R. (2005, October). No logo, no future. *Brand Strategy,* **(196), 38–39.**

This article discusses how African producers and companies need to focus on brand strategy to successfully sell their products and help their local economies. In addition, it deals with how a product brand strategy can help an African company compete internationally. Finally, the article highlights the general need for local business formation and development in Africa to create a stronger regional economy and improve the continent's prosperity.

Javidan, M., Steers, R., & Hitt, M. (Editors). (2007). *The global mindset: Advances in international management.* **Greenwich, CT: JAI Press.**

Having a global mindset is fundamental to influencing people from a wide variety of cultures and heritages. Today's managers need to cultivate a global mindset to remain competitive themselves and make their businesses more competitive in an international context. The book's contributors show managers how to develop a global mindset. Being able to shape the thinking and actions of employees is a fundamental skill that any global manager needs to make the global company more integrated and responsive to different customer needs.

Koh, W. T. H. (2006, May). Singapore's transition to innovation-based economic growth: Infrastructure, institutions, and government's role. *R&D Management, 36*(2), 143–160.

This article addresses the need for technology and innovation to drive economic progress and growth as a country becomes more advanced. Using Singapore as an example, the author outlines specific actions taken by the Singaporean government to develop an innovation-based growth strategy that promotes entrepreneurship.

Kuratko, D. F. (2007). Entrepreneurial leadership in the 21st century. *Journal of Leadership & Organizational Studies, 13*(4), 1–11.

This article discusses how the Entrepreneurial Revolution that currently exists in the United States and around the world is not only about venture and job creation, but also about developing entrepreneurial skills within individuals. Risk taking, opportunity seeking, and tenacity are three characteristics that make any businessperson successful, whether he or she is creating a new venture or working within a large company. It explains the concept of entrepreneurial leadership and how it is a global necessity in business today.

Quelch, J. A. (Editor). (2007). *Business solutions for the global poor: Creating social and economic value.* **Hoboken, NJ: Wiley.**

This book tackles the question of how businesses can help alleviate poverty around the world by meeting the poor's basic needs. Using examples from 20 different countries, this book presents how businesses can effectively alter their value propositions and production systems to focus on the bottom of the pyramid (BOP) and also the challenges that companies face in this environment.

Rocha, H. O. (2004, December). Entrepreneurship and development: The role of clusters. *Small Business Economics, 23*(5), 363–400.

This article investigates whether or not clusters, that is, firms and business-related institutions in the same geographic area, have a positive effect on entrepreneurship and development. After examining the effects of clustered and nonclustered entrepreneurship, this article concludes that entrepreneurship overall has a positive correlation with economic growth. Because no firm conclusions can currently be drawn, the article gives the parameters that future research should follow.

Rugman, A. (2007). *Regional aspects of multinationality and performance. Research in global strategic management,* **(13). Greenwich, CT: JAI Press.**

This book presents a more accurate representation of the strategic performance of multinational enterprises. Following the Rugman and Verbeke thesis of regionalization, the author provides a method for examining the return of foreign assets (ROFA) and return on total assets (ROTA) by taking into account the relationship between multinationality (M) and performance (P).

Schramm, C. J. (2005, January). Closing the enterprise. *Vital Speeches of the Day, 71*(6), 174–178.

Carl J. Schramm, president and CEO of Ewing Marion Kauffman Foundation of Kansas City, Missouri, delivered this speech to the Enterprising Britain Policy Summit in London, England on November 15, 2004. In his speech he describes how a multifaceted system in the United States brings about high impact entrepreneurship, and then he suggests how the United Kingdom can adapt similar policies and tactics to promote entrepreneurship and develop an entrepreneurial environment.

Sood, H. (2004, June). Entrepreneurial performance of civil works contractors in Punjab, Haryana, and Chandigarh. *Finance India, 18*(2), 953–958.

Focusing on the construction industry in India, this study describes the role that technical entrepreneurs, such as civil work contractors, can play in development. The study evaluates how civil work contractors, motivation trainers, and policy formulators played a role in specific improvements within the construction industry. The researchers believe that technical entrepreneurs can impact economic development of a country better than the people coming straight out of an education system.

Todd, P. R., & Javalgi, R. G. (2007). Internationalization of SMEs in India: Fostering entrepreneurship by leveraging information technology. *International Journal of Emerging Markets, 2*(2), 166–180.

This article explores the factors influencing the internationalization of small- and medium-sized enterprises (SMEs) in India. After investigating and evaluating the Indian business environment, the paper then concentrates on how best entrepreneurship can prepare Indian SMEs for the international marketplace.

Williams, J. (2006, June 1). Small is beautiful. *Irish Independent.* **Retrieved August 14, 2008, from www.independent.ie/business/small-is-beautiful-90524.html**

This article emphasizes the importance of small businesses to the Irish economy with research and data taken from the Small Business Forum Report. The author also details the challenges that small businesses face, including the lack of employee development and training, burden of regulation, foreign competition, and the struggle to innovate.

WEB SITES

GEM 2005 Report on High-Expectation Entrepreneurship. *Gem Consortium.* **Retrieved August 14, 2008, from www.gemconsortium.org/document .aspx?id=445/**

High expectation entrepreneurs are at the center of job creation and innovation throughout the world. This global study focuses on entrepreneurs whose companies have 20 employees by their 5th year, meeting the definition of high expectation entrepreneurship. Its findings state that over three-fourths of the jobs created by new businesses come from ventures created by high expectation entrepreneurs, while they only account for 9.8% of the world's entrepreneurs.

Green Paper—Entrepreneurship in Europe. (2003). *Europa.* **Retrieved August 14, 2008, from http://europa.eu/scadplus/leg/en/lvb/n26023.htm**

The paper talks about the changes in the European Union business environment and why entrepreneurship contributes to job creation and growth. The commissioned paper shows that it is increasingly new and small firms, rather than large ones, that are the major providers of new jobs and countries exhibiting a greater increase in entrepreneurship rates tended to exhibit greater subsequent decreases in unemployment rates. Research suggests that entrepreneurship provides a positive contribution to economic growth, although gross domestic product (GDP) growth is influenced by many other factors.

Globalization and the International Environment

2

Profile: D. K. Matai

MI2G

D. K. Matai is an engineer turned entrepreneur and philanthropist with a keen interest in the well-being of global society. D. K. founded mi2g in 1995 in London, UK, while developing simulations for his PhD at Imperial College. His vision was to develop solutions for private and corporate banking while taking into account users' modern lifestyles. Imagine that you are in Beijing or Budapest and need secure access to a critical personal or business file. If there is a service that allows instant access to that file from anywhere in the world via a handheld device, an interactive digital television, or an Internet café PC in a safe way with guaranteed security, think how efficiently you could manage your life. This is where mi2g's product D2-Banking defines the next generation of personalized banking and modern wealth management enabled for well-known banks through in-house or outsourced software services.

> *Before the end of this decade every individual around the world will have the convenience and guaranteed security of one-stop D2-Banking, which will become second nature to its customers as they enjoy the ability to store and access data and finances from anywhere at any time without fear of being hacked or plagued by malicious software.* –D. K. Matai

D. K. Matai spoke at the 2006 Evian Group Plenary Meeting in Montreux, Switzerland, where he said there are 10 big global risks and opportunities that face the world today. These risks include climate chaos, radical poverty, organized crime, extremism, informatics, nanotechnology, robotics, genetics, artificial intelligence, and financial systems; all of which demand innovation and shared action at regional, national, and international levels.

The Big 10 global risks and opportunities of the 21st century depend on "Disruptive Innovation" to address and resolve some of these seemingly intractable yet interlinked confrontations. As those inherent confrontations accelerate and feed off each other's momentum, they possess the capability to damage and disrupt the delicate global dynamic equilibrium. Faced with this unpalatable prospect for humanity in the coming two decades or less, it is necessary to rethink strategically and come together in joint action. This is the main aim of the high-level global dialogue established by organizations such as The Evian Group, The Asymmetric Threats Contingency Alliance (ATCA), and The Philanthropia. D. K. believes we need to be moving toward a wisdom-based global economy, where longevity and sustainability are at the top of the agenda.

www.intentblog.com/archives/2006/11/the_grave_crisi.html

www.mi2g.com

Chapter Objectives

1. To understand the implications of taking a business or venture global.

2. To define the critical questions that each entrepreneur must answer before taking a company global.

3. To describe various organizations' aims at enhancing global ventures.

4. To identify and define strategic issues faced by entrepreneurs.

5. To determine methods for analyzing the environment in which a venture is operating.

6. To analyze the key components of planning and taking a venture global.

Introduction

To be a global entrepreneur, it is necessary to establish an international vision. Your level of international skills and knowledge, as well as that of any associates you may have in your company, will help determine the international strategy you implement. If you have not had any international experience, you may want to avoid a plan that needs significant overseas market involvement at the outset, such as a foreign sales office or an R&D alliance. Your success in global business will ultimately reflect how well you identify and leverage your core competencies and that of your venture.

Strategic Effects of Going Global

While going global presents a wide variety of new environments and new ways of doing business, it is also accompanied by an entire set of wide-ranging problems. Just the mechanisms of carrying out business internationally involve a variety of new documents, such as commercial invoices, bills of lading, inspection certificates, and shipper's export declarations as well as compliance with domestic and international regulations.

One major effect centers on the concept of proximity to the customers and ports. Physical and psychological closeness to the international market significantly affects some global entrepreneurs. Geographic closeness to the foreign market may not necessarily provide a perceived closeness to the foreign customer. Sometimes cultural variables, language, and legal factors make a foreign market that is geographically closer seem psychologically distant. For example, some U.S. entrepreneurs perceive Canada, Ireland, and the UK to be much closer psychologically due to some similarities in culture and language.

Three issues are involved in this psychological distance. First, the distance envisioned by the entrepreneur may be based more on perception than reality. Some Canadian and even Australian entrepreneurs focus too much on the similarities with the United States market, losing sight of the vast differences. Such differences are in every international market to some extent and need to be taken into account to avoid costly mistakes. Second, closer psychological proximity does make it easier for an entrepreneurial firm to enter a market. It may be advantageous for the entrepreneur to go global by first selecting a market that is closer psychologically to gain some experience before entering markets that are perceived differently. Finally, the entrepreneur should also keep in mind that there are more similarities than differences between individual entrepreneurs regardless of the country. Each has gone through the entrepreneurial process, taken on the risks, passionately loved the business idea, and struggled for success.

Additionally, choosing operations in countries that not only have a physical and psychological advantage, but also advantages such as trade agreements and current operations of other companies from the entrepreneur's home country, often makes entering and succeeding in a country more manageable. Today, close to 300 Regional Trade Agreements (RTAs) exist, while an additional 100 are proposed or under negotiation. Of these, 90% are free trade agreements making trade across borders much easier.

Some of the most popular include the European Union (EU), the European Free Trade Association (EFTA), the North American Free Trade Agreement (NAFTA), the Southern Common Market (Mercosur), the Association of Southeast Asian Nations (ASEAN), Free Trade Area (AFTA), and the Common Market of Eastern and Southern Africa (COMESA; World Trade Organization [WTO], n.d.). These RTAs do not include additional agreements made bilaterally between nations. I will discuss this later in the chapter.

With outsourcing becoming a reality for many entrepreneurs, understanding and becoming aware of the implications that free trade agreements can have on the business could potentially reduce costs and also duties on goods being imported, creating further opportunities. It is paramount to become aware of ongoing disputes affecting certain industries and regional trade blocs that perhaps prevent more than aid in the liberalization of trade, and to have an understanding for the trade environment in which the business will be entering. As an entrepreneur keeping these factors in mind when planning to go global is key to accomplishing an effective stratagem overseas.

Strategic Issues

Four strategic issues are of absolute importance to an entrepreneur going global: (1) the allocation of responsibility between the United States and foreign operations; (2) the nature of the planning, reporting, and control systems to be used throughout the international operations; (3) the appropriate organizational structure for conducting international operations; and (4) the potential degree of standardization. Each of these issues affects a firm's organizational structure through three primary stages.

- *Stage 1.* When making the first movements into international business, an entrepreneur typically follows a highly centralized decision-making process. Since the entrepreneur generally has access to a limited number of individuals with global experience, a centralized decision-making network is usually used.

- *Stage 2.* When the business is successful, the entrepreneur no longer finds it possible to use a completely centralized decision-making process. The multiplicity of environments becomes far too complex to handle from a central headquarters. In response, an entrepreneur often decentralizes the entire international operation. The philosophy at this point can be summed up as follows: There's no way I am ever going to be able to understand the differences between all of those markets. Let them make their own decisions.

- *Stage 3.* The process of decentralization carried out in Stage 2 becomes intolerable once further success is attained. Business operations in the different countries end up in conflict with each other. The U.S. headquarters is often the last to receive information about problems. When this occurs limited amounts of power, authority, and responsibility are pulled back to the U.S. base of operations. A balance is usually achieved with the U.S. headquarters having reasonably tight control over major strategic marketing decisions and the in-country operating unit having the responsibility for the tactical implementation of corporate strategy. Planning, reporting, and control systems become very important aspects of international success at this stage.

Opportunities and Barriers to International Trade

There are varying attitudes throughout the world concerning trade. Starting around 1947 with the development of trade agreements and the reduction of tariffs and other trade barriers through international organizations, there has been an overall positive atmosphere concerning trade between countries. Nonetheless, the global entrepreneur needs to be aware that risks and barriers also exist. Understanding each market and its specific environment will often determine success within those markets.

WORLD TRADE ORGANIZATION (WTO)

One of the longest-lasting agreements, and now the leading international organization on trade, is the World Trade Organization (WTO). Begun in 1947 under U.S. leadership as the General Agreement on Tariffs and Trade (GATT), the WTO was officially established in January 1995, under the Uruguay Round (1986–1994) as a multilateral agreement among nations with the objective of liberalizing trade by eliminating or reducing tariffs, subsidies, and import quotas. WTO membership includes over 150 nations that create policies in rounds. The WTO has had eight rounds of tariff reductions, and the ninth is currently in progress. Mutual tariff reductions are typically negotiated between member nations, although the current round, Doha (2001), has been in a stalemate due to disagreement on these same issues between developed and developing nations.

Monitored by the Dispute Settlement Board (DSB) of the WTO, established in 1995 along with the WTO, member countries are able to bring disputes to this mechanism if they feel that a violation has occurred. Often these cases are brought against more than one nation by more than one country, forming something similar to a bloc. If the investigation uncovers a violation, violating countries are asked to change their policy and conform to the agreed-upon tariffs and agreements, or barriers in other sectors can be levied by prosecuting countries to compensate for lost revenues. With over 370 cases (as of April 2008) already brought before the WTO DSB with successful trials, decisions, and according actions, many developing nations feel that a shift in power has occurred that gives them the power to bring justice against many of the major world powers (WTO, n.d.).

The case brought against the United States and its steel industry exemplifies the WTO DSB's role and its unilateral actions against dumping. The U.S. Congress used an anti-dumping fine to aid U.S. steel companies under the name of the Byrd Amendment. Creating an environment solely beneficial to the U.S. steel companies, the U.S. Congress had allowed this "fine" to be directed solely into the coffers of U.S. companies affected as a result of dumping. With a myriad of countries claiming unfair trade practices, Japan, the European Union, Mexico, South Korea, and a variety of others took the case to the DSB, and after appeal, the United States lost and the other countries were allowed to levy taxes against similar industries (*United States—Definitive Safeguard Measures on Imports of Certain Steel Products*). Under the ruling these nations could levy up to 72% of the money raised and distributed during the life of this amendment affecting other industries such as U.S. paper, farm goods, textiles, and machinery (WTO Rules in Favor of EU, 2004).

Important from an entrepreneurial aspect, these types of cases can affect industries and sectors in which the entrepreneur's new venture is operating. The importance of understanding the implications for each business venture is influential in deciding the direction and picking a strategy for each undertaking.

INCREASING PROTECTIONIST ATTITUDES

Although the support for the WTO varies and was relatively low in the 1970s, it increased in the 1980s due to the rise in protectionist pressures in many industrialized countries. The renewed support reflected three events. First, the world trading system was strained by the persistent trade deficit of the United States, the world's largest economy, a situation that caused adjustments in such industries as automobiles, semiconductors, steel, and textiles. Second, the economic success of a country perceived as not playing by the rules (e.g., Japan and then China) has also strained the world's trading system. Japan and China's successes as the world's largest traders and the perception that their internal markets are, in effect, closed to imports and foreign investment have caused problems. Finally, in response to these pressures, many countries have established bilateral voluntary export restraints to circumvent the WTO. China did this during the economic prosperity of the 1990s due to the pressures from the world, particularly the United States.

TRADE BLOCS AND FREE TRADE AREAS

Around the world groups of nations are banding together to increase trade and investment between nations in the group and exclude those nations outside the group. One little-known agreement between the United States and Israel, signed in 1985, establishes a Free Trade Agreement (FTA) between the two nations. All tariffs and quotas, except those on certain agricultural products, were phased out over a 10-year period. In 1989, an FTA went into effect between Canada and the United States that phased out tariffs and quotas between the two countries, which are each other's largest trading partners.

Many trading alliances have evolved in the Americas. In 1991 the United States signed a framework trade agreement with Argentina, Brazil, Paraguay, and Uruguay to support the development of more liberal trade relations. The United States has also signed bilateral trade agreements with Bolivia, Chile, Colombia, Costa Rica, Ecuador, El Salvador, Honduras, Peru, and Venezuela. The North American Free Trade Agreement (NAFTA) among the United States, Canada, and Mexico is a much publicized agreement to reduce trade barriers and quotas and encourage investment among the three countries. Similarly, the Americas, Argentina, Brazil, Paraguay, and Uruguay operate under the Treaty of Asunción, which created the Mercosur trade zone, a free-trade zone among the countries.

Another important trading bloc has been developed by the European Community (EC). Unlike NAFTA or a similar free trade agreement, the EC is founded on the principle of supranationality; member nations are not able to enter into trade agreements on their own that are inconsistent with EC regulations. As nations are added, the EC trading bloc becomes an increasingly important factor for entrepreneurs doing international business.

ENTREPRENEUR'S STRATEGY AND TRADE BARRIERS

Clearly trade barriers pose problems for the entrepreneur who wants to become involved in international business. First, trade barriers increase an entrepreneur's costs of exporting products or semi-finished products to a country. If the increased cost puts the entrepreneur at a competitive disadvantage with respect to indigenous competitive products, it may be more economical to establish production facilities in the country. Second, voluntary export restraints may limit an entrepreneur's ability to sell products in a country from production facilities outside the country, which may also warrant establishing production facilities in the country to compete. Finally, an entrepreneur may have to locate assembly or production facilities in a country to conform to the local product content regulations of the country.

Important Considerations

Regardless of industry or sector, an entrepreneur has further analysis to do before entering a new market. Coupled with the trade considerations from an outside perspective, the entrepreneur needs to also be clearly aware of the internal facets of a country that affect a business. This analysis includes political, economic, social, technological, and environmental factors, otherwise known as a PESTE analysis. Aiding the entrepreneur in scrutinizing the country in which the company will be entering, more in-depth consideration can save the entrepreneur from dealing with future concerns or difficulties. When Intel Corporation most recently expanded, it was not sure where to take its operations. Negotiating with Costa Rica, Brazil, Mexico, and Chile in Latin America, they finally decided on taking operations into Costa Rica based on the political stability during government transitions, the quality of the workforce and its labor unions, government incentives that wouldn't handcuff the company, and a variety of other reasons that crossed all facets of the PESTE.

No matter the size of the company, this analysis takes careful planning and study. As witnessed with Microsoft's entry of Windows into China in 1993, the lack of careful analysis and planning can have horrible results. Not only did Microsoft have minimal sales of Windows to Chinese consumers, but the company also found themselves blacklisted by the Chinese government in early 1994. On a personal visit to the Chinese President, Jiang Zemin, Bill Gates found that his espousal of the importance of adopting the U.S. dominated software fell on deaf ears. Instead, he was told that if he was going to sell to the Chinese customer, he needed to better understand their culture, among a variety of other things. Microsoft also faced piracy concerns, creating issues around having software that did not have full capabilities. Additionally, understanding that the majority of its business fell in the hands of the government required an economic and social concern that was not fully understood by the company before entry. After more than a decade, in 2006, both parties were able to reach positive closure while Gates and Microsoft finally found a solution and gained inclusion in one of the biggest markets in the world (Khanna, 2008).

To understand what is required for effective planning, reporting, and control in international operations, the entrepreneur should consider situational analysis, strategic planning, structure, operational planning, and controlling the program (see Table 2.1).

Table 2.1 Requirements for Effective Planning, Reporting, and Control in International Operations

---

Situational Analysis

1. What are the unique characteristics of each national market? What characteristics does each market have in common with other national markets?
2. Can any national markets be clustered together for operating and/or planning purposes? What dimensions of markets should be used to cluster markets?

Strategic Planning

3. Who should be involved in marketing decisions?
4. What are the major assumptions about target markets? Are these valid?
5. What needs are satisfied by the company's products in the target markets?
6. What customer benefits are provided by the product in the target markets?
7. What are the conditions under which the products are used in the target markets?
8. How great is the ability to buy our products in the target markets?
9. What are the company's major strengths and weaknesses relative to existing and potential competition in the target markets?
10. Should the company extend, adapt, or invent products, prices, advertising, and promotion programs for target markets?
11. What are the balance-of-payments and currency situations in the target markets? Will the company be able to remit earnings? Is the political climate acceptable?
12. What are the company's objectives, given the alternatives available and the assessment of opportunity, risk, and company capability?

Structure

13. How should the organization be structured to optimally achieve the established objectives, given the company's skills and resources? What is the responsibility of each organizational level?
14. Given the objectives, structure, and assessment of the market environment, how can an effective operational marketing plan be implemented? What products should be marketed, at what prices, through what channels, with what communications, and to which target markets?

Controlling the Program

15. How does the company measure and monitor the plan's performance? What steps should be taken to ensure that marketing objectives are met?

SOURCE: Adapted from Hisrich, R. D., Peters, M. A., & Shepherd, D. A. (2007). *Entrepreneurship* (7th ed.). Burr Ridge, IL: McGraw-Hill/Irwin, pp. 526–527.

SITUATIONAL ANALYSIS

As with the PESTE, it's important that the entrepreneur analyzes the situation in which he or she is entering based on many of the previously described. In addition, it's necessary to ask, what are the unique characteristics of each national market? What characteristics does each market have in common with other national markets? As with many regional markets, deciding between one market and another can mean the difference between gaining incentives to help build the business and grow for the future or face enormous competition from similar companies. When the computer company Dell entered into Latin America, the company was able to successfully leverage its knowledge of the national market in Brazil to its advantage by addressing these questions. In Brazil states are able to negotiate their own tax incentive packages to woo companies for investment. Realizing this, Dell pitted the states against each other to create the best package for the company itself. This understanding of the market was critical in Dell's success and entry into this market.

By beginning to cluster the markets, the entrepreneur increases his or her ability to understand how to operate within these environments. Can any national markets be clustered together for operating and/or planning purposes? What dimensions of markets should be used to cluster markets? These, too, are questions that should be answered as the market is chosen—the answers will only aid in the future success of the company or enterprise.

STRATEGIC PLANNING

After deciding on the market, the entrepreneur needs to strategically plan the direction and carefully consider implementation. Who should be involved in marketing decisions? What are the major assumptions about target markets? Are these valid?

Defining the target market is critical for proceeding with many strategic planning decisions including marketing, bringing the product to market, pricing against the competition, and a variety of other things. To do this a company must ask questions about the target market to better define and clearly delineate the basic wants of the customer. What needs are satisfied by the company's products in the target markets? What customer benefits does the product in the target markets provide? What are the conditions under which the products are used in the target markets? How great is the ability to buy our products in the target markets?

Analyzing the strengths and weaknesses of the company in this way makes it easier to judge where the enterprise stands in comparison to its competitors, if they exist, and how to better extend, adapt, or invent new products prices, advertising, and promotion programs to meet these needs.

STRUCTURE

After understanding the environment in which the entrepreneur is entering and strategically assessing how to take advantage of this, the next step is to determine the structure of the endeavor. How should the organization be structured to optimally achieve the established objectives, given the company's skills and resources? What is the responsibility of each organizational level? These questions should be clearly defined; doing so will add to the ability of the enterprise to function and grow in the global market.

OPERATIONAL PLANNING

Equally as important as the structure, the operational planning must be well thought out. Under a strong organizational structure, operations need to be determined to give the company better opportunities to market to its clientele. Given the objectives, structure, and assessment of the market environment, how can an effective operational marketing plan be implemented? What products should be marketed, at what prices, through what channels, with what communications, and to which target markets?

CONTROLLING THE PROGRAM

How does the company measure and monitor the plan's performance? What steps should be taken to ensure that marketing objectives are met? One key to successful strategic planning is an appreciation and excellent understanding of the market. While environmental analysis focuses on this dimension of the planning process, the first step in identifying markets and clustering countries is to analyze data on each country in the following six areas. First are the market characteristics, including size of market, rate of growth, stage of development, stage of product life cycle and saturation level, buyer behavior characteristics, social and cultural factors, and physical environment. The second area is the marketing institutions that take into account the distribution systems, communication media, and marketing services to reach the customer whether it's in advertising or research. The third is the industry conditions, focusing on competitive size and practices and technical development of the product as mentioned earlier. This can help the entrepreneur to adapt, extend, or invent new products or services. The legal environment is the fourth area, and this will be covered in depth in a later chapter. Resources are critical and make up the fifth area. This includes hiring personnel based on availability, skill, potential, and cost, along with considering the actual outlay of the venture itself and the impending costs of doing business in general.

The sixth and final consideration is the political environment. An understanding of the present and future outlook of the government, especially in emerging economies will stave off any impending disasters.

Summary

Chapter 2 presents the fundamental strategic questions that every entrepreneur must ask as he or she prepares to enter the global market. While an entrepreneur considers international expansion, he or she must prepare for and handle a myriad of problems that arise when dealing with multiple countries that have their own regulations, cultural tendencies, and economic considerations. Also, the entrepreneur must consider what effect the physical or psychological closeness to a foreign market has on the company's decision to enter that market. In particular, the entrepreneur must realize that psychological closeness is based on individual perception, which can help the company enter that market. This chapter also describes strategic issues that the global entrepreneur faces, including allocation of responsibility; nature of planning, reporting, and control systems; appropriate organizational structure; and potential degree of standardization. The evolution of the organization as it becomes international starts with highly centralized decision making; next it evolves into a decentralized structure; and finally, it reorganizes into a decentralized structure in which major decision making and controls come directly from headquarters. To best prepare to enter an international market, an entrepreneur must consider the business environment, strategic planning, organizational structure, operational planning, and marketing program.

Questions for Discussion

1. What are the most critical strategic factors to consider before entering a foreign market?

2. How does the control of foreign operations change as the enterprise grows?

Chapter Exercises

1. Describe each of the major issues and considerations an entrepreneur must address when launching his or her product or company in a new country.

2. Choose a country besides your home country and create a comparative table that describes the key environmental factors (economic, political, etc.) in that country versus your home country. What major differences exist and what is one major attribute that you must consider when doing business in the foreign country?

3. Suppose you are the CEO of a small firm that is taking its business into a new country. You are fortunate to have two gifted managers who have volunteered to handle the operational issues for this project, but you must choose just one to send to the new country. One of the managers has extensive work experience in all the operational aspects of running a business, and the other manager is from the new country and previously ran a business there. Which manager will you send and why?

References

Khanna, Tarun. (2008, March 28). Microsoft's China Foibles. Retrieved April 16, 2008, from www.forbes.com/books/2008/03/28/entrepreneurs-microsoft-china-oped-books-cx_tk_0328khanna.html

United States—Definitive Safeguard Measures on Imports of Certain Steel Products. World Trade Organization Dispute Settlement DS252. Retrieved May 5, 2008, from www.wto.org/english/tratop_e/dispu_e/cases_e/ds252_e.htm

World Trade Organization. (n.d.). *Chronological List of Disputes Cases.* Retrieved April 22, 2008, from www.wto.org/english/tratop_e/dispu_e/dispu_status_e.htm

World Trade Organization. (n.d.). *Regional Trade Agreements.* Retrieved April 24, 2008, from www.wto.org/english/tratop_e/region_e/region_e.htm

WTO Rules in Favor of EU in US Trade Row. (2004, August 31). *BBC News* [online]. Retrieved April, 20, 2008, from http://news.bbc.co.uk/1/hi/business/3615030.stm

Suggested Readings

Friedman, T. (2005, April 3). It's a flat world, after all. *The New York Times Magazine,* Section 6, p. 33.

Thomas L. Friedman is the author of *The World Is Flat: A Brief History of the Twenty-First Century,* in which he writes about how the world became flat through 10 flatteners, all which converged around the year 2000. The significance of the convergence is a global, Web-enabled playing field that allows for multiple forms of collaboration on research and work in real time, without regard to geography, distance, or language.

Held, D., McGrew, A. G., & Schott, G. (2007). *Globalization theory: Approaches and controversies* (1st ed.). Cambridge: Polity Press.

Globalization Theory is the fourth volume in the highly acclaimed Global Transformations series. It follows in the footsteps of *Global Transformations*, the *Global Transformations Reader*, and *Governing Globalization*. All these volumes have been widely adopted in courses on globalization and global governance across the world, and *Globalization Theory* will find a place alongside these texts. This book focuses on elucidating leading theoretical approaches to understanding and explaining globalization, both in its current form and potential future shapes. It is divided into two parts: the first examines competing explanatory theories of globalization in its contemporary form and the second looks at competing pre-scriptions for the future of globalization. The book's contributors are world renowned experts in their field, including G. John Ikenberry, Michael Doyle, Layna Mosley, Alex Callinicos, Anthony McGrew, Thomas Risse, Roland Robertson, John Tomlinson, Saskia Sassen, David Held, Thomas Pogge, Chris Brown, and Andrew Kuper. The book is designed as a textbook for courses on globalization and global governance at both the graduate and undergraduate levels. It will be of interest to students in politics, international relations, social geography, and sociology.

Kuivalainen, O., Sundqvist, S., & Servais, P. (2007). **Firms' degree of born-globalness, international entrepreneurial orientation and export performance.** *Journal of World Business, 42,* 253–267.

Despite the recent increase in "born-global" studies, there has been little research on how the scale and scope of being a born-global firm affects perfor-mance: most of the earlier research takes no account of either the number of or the distances between the countries on firm or export performance. This article begins with a review of the existing literature on born-globals, and subsequently explores the relationship between entrepreneurial orientation (EO) and two different born-global strategies, namely true born-global and apparently born-global (born-international), and the effectiveness of these two born-global path-ways. The results of an empirical study on 185 Finnish exporting firms show that those that qualified as true born-globals had better export performance. Further-more, depending on the degree of born-globalness, different dimensions of EO of importance.

The myth of China Inc. (2005). *Economist, 376*(8442), 63.

The article discusses concerns about the international expansion of Chinese industry. The scaremongers assert that the Chinese state is a single, and single-minded, entity with a master plan to reclaim China's rightful place at the center of the world. China's companies are thus mere tools of an expansionist policy propagated by Beijing's leadership. More subtle are the fears that, because it is impossible to untangle the ownership of most Chinese companies, foreigners can-not be sure to whom they are selling.

Ohmae, K. (2005). *Next global stage: The challenges and opportunities in our borderless world.* Philadelphia: Wharton School Publishing.

Globalization is a fact. You can't stop it; it has already happened; it is here to stay. And we are moving into a new global stage. A radically new world is taking shape from the ashes of yesterday's nation-based economic world. To succeed you must act on the global stage, leveraging radically new drivers of economic power and growth. Legendary business strategist Kenichi Ohmae, who in *The Borderless World*, published in 1990, predicted the rise and success of globalization, coining the very word, synthesizes today's emerging trends into the first coherent view of tomorrow's global economy, and its implications for politics, business, and personal success.

Szerb, L., Rappai, G., Makra, Z., & Terjesen, S. (2007). Informal investment in transition economies: Individual characteristics and clusters. Small Business *Economics, 28*(2–3), 257–271.

This paper investigates the factors driving informal investment in Croatia, Hungary, and Slovenia. Using Global Entrepreneurship Monitor (GEM) data, we find that the low rates of informal investment activity and the small amounts of investments in these countries are driven by entrepreneurial behaviors consistent with limited market economy experience. We extend prior studies by investigating the role of business ownership, and identify significant differences between individuals with and without business ownership experience in regards to having start-up skills, knowing an entrepreneur, and fearing failure. Cluster analysis identifies seven distinct groups of informal investors, and reveals the heterogeneity in terms of investors' age, gender, level of education, amount of investment, start-up skills, ownership status, income, opportunity perception, and country of residence.

Taber, G. M. (2005, September 22). Message in a bottle. *Wall Street Journal,* p. A16.

The article points out the globalization of wine and how the numbers have been steadily decreasing in France while consumers in the new world are benefiting from the large production of wines from California and Australia.

Tarun, K. & Krishna, G. P. (2006). Emerging giants. *Harvard Business Review, 84*(10), 60–69.

This article reports on companies from emerging markets that are gaining ground in the global marketplace. At first glance, Western, Japanese, and South Korean companies appear to hold near-insurmountable advantages over businesses in newly industrializing countries. Institutional voids, the absence of specialized intermediaries, regulatory systems, and contract-enforcing mechanisms have made corporations in emerging markets unable to access capital or talent as easily or as inexpensively as European and American corporations can. That often makes it tough for businesses in developing countries to invest in R&D or to build global brands.

Zeng, M., & Williamson, P. J. (2003). The hidden dragons. *Harvard Business Review, 81*(10), 92–99.

The article looks at how Chinese brands are beginning to become a force in world markets. The author reviews how China is the fastest-growing market on the planet. Statistics related to China's recent economic growth are reviewed. It is suggested that multinationals have been focused solely on setting up manufacturing facilities in China while ignoring the emergence of Chinese companies as powerful rivals. The author states that Chinese brands could soon become a global force in numerous industries. According to the author, the only Chinese organizations large enough to compete on a global scale are state-owned enterprises. Details related to the success of various Chinese companies are reviewed.

Zucchella, A., Palamara, G., & Denicolai, S. (2007) **The drivers of the early internationalization of the firm.** *Journal of World Business, 42,* 268–280.

Time in firm internationalization has different dimensions: it might refer to the early start of international activities, the speed of international growth, or to its pace and rhythm. This contribution considers the first dimension mentioned, and aims at understanding which variables determine an early international orientation. Building on a literature review, a theoretical framework is proposed to integrate a fragmented literature body. The framework is then tested through an analysis on a sample of 144 small- and medium-sized enterprises (SMEs). Among the drivers of early internationalization, the role of the previous experience of the entrepreneur, and especially of their international experience, frequently nurtured in internationally oriented family firms on one side or in multinational/foreign firms on the other one, was found significant. The positive association between precocity and niche positioning of the business enforces the relevance of entrepreneurship because focalization is a reflection of entrepreneurial orientation and strategic decisions.

Cultures and International Entrepreneurship 3

Profile: Jack Ma

ALIBABA

On a rainy weekend, 10,000 businessmen, hobby traders, and "net-heads" gathered in Hangzhou, a pretty Chinese city near Shanghai, to talk about e-commerce. Most went to meet and swap tips with other online traders. All came to the "Alifest" to sit at the feet of Jack Ma, a pixie-sized, boyish 42-year-old who is the founder of Alibaba, an e-commerce firm, and is regarded as the godfather of the Internet in China. In a country where businessmen are viewed with suspicion, his popularity is unusual. When he was invited recently to speak in Beijing's Great Hall of the People, Mr. Ma needed six bodyguards to escape a mob of online traders waiting outside to give him a hug.

Mr. Ma's rock star status reflects how he has enabled thousands of his countrymen to become their own bosses, build businesses, and make money—a dream ingrained in Chinese culture but repressed by decades of communist antipathy to private enterprise. Alibaba has become the world's largest online business-to-business (B2B) marketplace, Asia's most popular online auction site and, as a result of its acquisition of Yahoo! China, the 12th most popular Web site in the world. That combination makes Alibaba one of the few credible challengers to the global online elite of Google, eBay, Yahoo!, and Amazon.

Alibaba is far from being just a Chinese knockoff of these American giants. Indeed, they have borrowed ideas from him. "Jack is not just a Chinese visionary, but a global one. Western companies are taking pages from the Alibaba book," says Bob Peck, an analyst at Bear Stearns. At Alibaba's heart sit two B2B Web sites (www.alibaba.com and www.china.alibaba.com); one a marketplace for firms from across the world to trade in English, the other a domestic Chinese service. Rival e-commerce outfits, such as America's Ariba and Commerce One, sought to cut multinationals' procurement costs. In contrast, Alibaba's intention was to build markets for China's vast number of small- and medium-sized enterprises, which make everything from cufflinks to motorcycles, by allowing them to trade with each other and linking them to global supply chains. Today, traders in America buy from Alibaba and resell on eBay.

Mr. Ma has also led the charge into online communities and social networking, both now booming areas. In 2003 he added a consumer auction site, Taobao, that allowed instant messaging—a feature later added to his business sites. In contrast with eBay's relative anonymity, Taobao lets buyers and sellers get chummy through messaging and voicemail, and by posting photographs and personal details on the site. Turning e-commerce into a community of "friends" has been critical in a country beset by a lack of trust. And with 70% of China's Web users under age 30, Taobao's informal, blog-like format struck a chord—attracting more than 20 million users. Many have now gone professional, buying goods wholesale on Alibaba and reselling them on Taobao. The story goes that shortly after visiting Alibaba's offices and seeing Taobao, Meg Whitman, eBay's boss, bought Skype (an Internet-telephony start-up) for its instant messaging.

Alibaba has also outflanked the opposition in online payments. Aware that most Chinese do not have credit cards, Mr. Ma introduced AliPay, a system that keeps cash in escrow until goods arrive. That trick for getting around settlement risk was later adopted in China by eBay. China's powerful banking regulator has a hawkish eye on AliPay because it is, in effect, an online bank with thousands of credit histories (something mainland banks crave). Taobao's success has been startling. Its market share jumped from 8%–59% between 2003 and 2005, while eBay China's slid from 79%–36%. Mr. Ma trumpets that it is "game over" for eBay China. Many industry watchers expect eBay to retreat and sell out to a local outfit such as Tencent (a rising star in auctions) or Alibaba itself—as Yahoo! China did.

Mr. Ma is also at the forefront of the trend to integrate paid search with e-commerce. Alibaba's takeover of Yahoo! China gave the firm a search engine just as Google was demonstrating the huge potential of paid search, and the deal anticipated eBay's link-ups with portals (Yahoo! in the United States, and Google elsewhere). Baidu, China's main search engine, is a strong rival. But online advertising is surging in China and small firms are the biggest users of paid search, giving Alibaba an edge.

Mr. Ma seldom mentions technology. Whereas most Internet entrepreneurs are geeks (think of Yahoo! or Google's founders), Mr. Ma first touched a computer in 1995 on a trip to Seattle. "Someone as dumb as me should be able to use technology," he says. He insists on simplicity. A new feature is rejected if he cannot understand and use it. Mr. Ma's approach to running the company is similarly independent. He reads neither business books nor case studies, and ascribes Alibaba's survival and success to the fact that he "knew nothing about technology, we didn't have a plan and we didn't have any money." In truth, Mr. Ma had powerful backers early on, including Goldman Sachs and Softbank. Yahoo!'s Jerry Yang—who joined Mr. Ma at the Alifest—is also a longtime friend. In any case, he has money aplenty today: As part of its takeover by Alibaba, Yahoo! paid $1 billion for a 40% stake in the company.

Only one thing is missing: profits. As the boss of a private company in no rush to join the stock market, Mr. Ma is relaxed. Revenues should double to more than $200 million in 2009. But Alibaba has so far pursued market share rather than revenue. The global business site charges its users, but Taobao does not; an attempt to do so in 2008–2009 failed. Mr. Ma says it is too early: Only 30 million of China's 120 million online users have bought anything online. He wants to help the market grow—creating 1 million jobs in China in the next 3 years—not stifle it with charges. He will have to tackle profitability if he is really to call the tune.

www.alibaba.com

Chapter Objectives

1. To introduce the importance of culture in the feasibility and success of taking a company global.

2. To understand how language, verbal or nonverbal, can influence the marketing of a product or service and understanding of clients and consumers in an entrepreneurial venture.

3. To discuss how societal structure and religion affect decisions made by consumers, and how to best understand these influential sociocultural forces.

4. To discuss how economic and political philosophy sway the decisions of a culture and therefore the global entrepreneur.

5. To acknowledge the importance of the manners and customs of different cultures in successfully launching ventures.

6. To gain an understanding of culture within contexts.

7. To bring an understanding of various manners in analyzing cultures when preparing to enter new markets.

Introduction

The ever-increasing amount of global business, the opening of new markets, and hypercompetition have provided the opportunity for entrepreneurs to start or expand globally. The challenge for the global entrepreneur is to understand and take into account the culture of each country to be successful in his or her global efforts. This requires the entrepreneur to understand and tailor products and services to different attitudes, behaviors, and values when implementing strategic plans. Clothing, for example, is a cultural product. Suits that sell well in Italy may have little success in Japan. Styling and colors vary by culture. What sells well in the United States may have a limited market elsewhere. Additionally, for continued success, the global entrepreneur needs to meet and understand the cultural needs of suppliers and potential workforce to maintain and/or expand his or her business.

Nature of Culture

Probably the single most important aspect that must be considered in global entrepreneurship is crossing cultures. The word *culture* comes from the Latin word *cultura,* which means "cult or worship." Although culture has been defined in many different ways, the term generally refers to common ways of thinking and behaving that are passed on from parents to their children or transmitted by social organizations, are developed, and then reinforced through social pressure. Culture is learned behavior and the identity of an individual and society. Most would agree that culture is adaptive (humans have the capacity to change or adapt), learned (acquired by learning and experience, not inherited), shared (individuals as members of a group share their culture), structured (culture is integrated into a structure), symbolic (culture has symbols with meaning), and transgenerational (it is passed on from generation to generation; China's Pied Piper, 2006).

Culture encompasses a wide variety of elements including language, social structure, religion, political philosophy, economic philosophy, education, and manners and customs (see Figure 3.1). Each of these affects the cultural norms and values of a group.

Values are basic beliefs individuals have regarding good/evil, important/unimportant, and right/wrong. These are shared beliefs that are internalized by each individual in the group. The more entrenched the values and norms are in a group, the less the tendency for change. In industrialized countries, there is generally a positive attitude toward change. Any change is viewed negatively in tradition-bound systems,

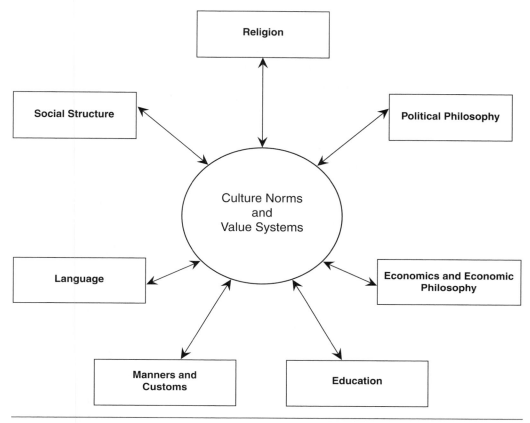

Figure 3.1   Cultural Determinants

particularly when it is introduced by a foreign entity. For example, although change is fairly well accepted in most sectors in the United States, this is far from the case in Japan, where there is strong resistance against change and foreigners.

At the same time, value similarities exist between cultures. Research has shown that managers from four different countries (Australia, India, Japan, and the United States) have similar personal values that relate to success (England & Lee, 1974). Not only was there a reasonably strong relationship between values and success across the four countries, but the value patterns could be used in selection and placement decisions.

While values, and of course culture, are relatively stable and do not change rapidly, change does occur over time. For example, the values of Japanese managers both inside and outside the country are changing. One study found that Japanese managers view the traditional attitudes or organizational values such as lifetime employment, formal authority, group orientation, paternalism, and seniority as being less important than previously (Reichel & Flynn, 1984). Similarly, there is evidence that individualism is increasing in Japan. Instead of denouncing individualism as a threat to society, many Japanese are starting to view individualism as a necessity for the country's economic well-being. This could be the start of an awakened entrepreneurial attitude and spirit in Japan.

Additionally, global entrepreneurs need to be aware of other cultural dimensions that will play significant roles in negotiations or the ability of the entrepreneur to succeed with local suppliers, customers, and workforce. Recent studies have analyzed the five cultural dimensions of power distance, individualism, masculinity, uncertainty avoidance, and long-term orientation. These dimensions give insight into the way the seven cultural determinants discussed next play a further role in how an entrepreneur approaches a new market (Hofstede, 2001). Additional studies have taken the five cultural dimensions one step further, focusing on the leadership of individuals within these cultural norms (Javidan, Dorman, de Luque, & House, 2005).

Seven Cultural Determinants

LANGUAGE

Language—sometimes thought of as the mirror of culture—is composed of verbal and nonverbal components. Messages and ideas are transmitted by the spoken words used, the voice tone, and the nonverbal actions such as body position, eye contact, or gestures. An entrepreneur or someone on his or her team must have command of the language in the country in which business is being done. Not only is it important for information gathering and evaluation, but also for communication with all involved and eventually in advertising campaigns. Even though English has generally become the accepted language of business, dealing with language almost always requires local assistance whether it is a local translation, a local market research firm, or a local advertising agency.

One U.S. entrepreneur was having a difficult time negotiating an agreement on importing a new high-tech microscope from a small entrepreneurial firm in St. Petersburg, Russia. The problems were resolved when the entrepreneur realized that the translations were not being done correctly and hired a new translator. Examples of some very problematic translation errors by major U.S. companies are shown in Table 3.1.

Equally important to verbal language is the nonverbal or hidden language of the culture. This can be thought of in terms of several components—directness, expressiveness, context, and formality. From a nonverbal standpoint, the directness and contextual uses of language can play a very large role in understanding a culture. Very low-context cultures use

Table 3.1   Potential Translation Problems

Lost in Translation		
Even the best-laid business plans can be botched by a careless translator. Here's how some of America's biggest companies have managed to mess things up.		
Kentucky Fried Chicken	English: "Finger lickin' good."	Chinese: "Eat your fingers off."
Adolpf Coors Co.	English: "Turn it loose."	Spanish: "Drink Coors and get diarrhea."
Otis Engineering Corp.	English: "Complete equipment."	Russian: "Equipment for orgasms."
Parker Pen Co.	English: "Avoid embarrassment."	Spanish: "Avoid pregnancy."
Perdue Farms Inc.	English: "It takes a tough man to make a tender chicken."	Spanish: "It takes a sexually excited man to make a chick affectionate."

SOURCE: Adapted from Speaking in Tongues, *Inc.*, June 2003, *25*(6) 50.

words and language to express themselves, and very high-context cultures use body language, facial expressions, and movements to convey their meaning. Consider four countries from different parts of the world. Argentina and China tend to be very high-context cultures, requiring an entrepreneur to understand that not everything is going to be expressed with words, but potentially more with actions. Closed doors to offices, carbon copying individuals on e-mails, preferring telephone use to talking face to face are examples of high-context clues that bring insight to certain cultures; in each case, the subtlety of the actions show the intentions or desires of the individuals. Germany and Denmark, however, are very low context, managing and negotiating very forthrightly. From a directness perspective, these cultures often explicitly express their wishes or desires when doing business, while others view this type of forwardness to be rude. Almost all Asian and Latin cultures tend to carry a more indirect approach to communication, preferring not to tackle issues in a confrontational manner (Training Management Corporation, 2008).

The expansion of the Bank of Nova Scotia in Canada into the Mexican market through obtaining an increased stake in the Mexican bank, Grupo Financiero Inverlat, is one example of the contextual and directness issues faced by cultures with opposite communication orientations. As the Canadian bank brought in Canadian managers, many key discussions were lost because meetings were conducted in English. Canadian managers, being more direct and low context, found their manner of communication and understanding, which was paramount to making decisions, was lost, while the Mexicans felt the same way. Instead of letting the Mexican managers discuss and carry on side conversations in meetings as was necessary for a very indirect and high-context culture, the frustration and more rigid style of the Canadians led to discontent among each party involved (Campbell, 1997).

Both verbal and nonverbal language affects business relationships. It is critical that the global entrepreneur understand this. For entrepreneurs, these types of communication styles must be considered and understood to better reach and understand the customers and workforce.

For example, in many countries it is far more important to understand a potential business partner on a personal level before any transactions occur or business is even discussed. One global entrepreneur in Australia met the president, the management team, and their families, each on a different social occasion, before any business between the two companies was discussed.

SOCIAL STRUCTURE

Social structure and institutions also affect the culture facing the global entrepreneur. While the family unit in the United States usually consists of parent(s) and children, in many cultures it is extended to include grandparents and other relatives. This, of course, radically affects lifestyles, living standards, and consumption patterns.

Social stratification can be very strong in some cultures, significantly affecting the way people in one social stratum behave and purchase. India, for example, is known for a relatively rigid, hierarchical social class system, which can offset the acceptance of new products/services..

Reference groups in any culture provide values and attitudes that influence behavior. Besides providing overall socialization, reference groups develop a person's concept of self and provide a baseline for compliance with group norms. As such, they significantly affect an individual's behavior and buying habits.

The global entrepreneur also needs to recognize that the social structure and institutions of a culture will affect the role of a manager and a subordinate and how the two relate. In some cultures, cooperation between managers and subordinates is elicited through equality, while in other cultures the two groups are separated explicitly and implicitly.

RELIGION

Religion in a culture defines the ideas for life that are reflected in the values and attitudes of individuals and the overall society. The affect of religion on entrepreneurship, consumption, and business in general will vary depending on the strength of the dominant religious tenets and these tenets' effect on the values and attitudes of the culture. Religion also provides the basis for some degree of transcultural similarity under shared beliefs and attitudes as seen in some of the dominant religions of the world—Christianity, Islam, Hinduism, Buddhism, and Judaism. Nonreligious or secularist societies, such as Marxism-Leninism as a state belief, are also powerful forces affecting behavior.

POLITICAL PHILOSOPHY

Political philosophy of an area also affects culture. Because this topic will be treated separately later in this chapter, suffice it to say here that the rules and regulations of the country significantly affect the global entrepreneur and the way he or she conducts business. For example, embargoes or trade sanctions, export controls, and other business regulations may preclude a global entrepreneur from doing business in a particular culture or at the very least will affect the attitudes and behaviors of people in that culture when business is done.

ECONOMICS AND ECONOMIC PHILOSOPHY

Economics and the economic philosophy affect the culture of a country and the global entrepreneur. Whether the country overall is for trade or trade restrictions, attitudes toward balance of payments and balance of trade, convertible or nonconvertible currency, and overall trading policy affect not only whether it is advantageous to do business in a certain market, but the types and efficiency of any transactions that occur. Some countries use import duties, tariffs, subsidization of exports, and restrictions on the importation of certain products to protect the country's own industry and maximize the gain of more exports than imports. Think how difficult it would be to do business in a country that restricts the exportation of the profits of an international company. Or how difficult it is to do business in a culture that is anti-materialism and more equalitarian.

EDUCATION

Both formal and informal education affects the culture and the way the culture is passed on. A global entrepreneur not only needs to be aware of the education level as indicated by the literacy rate of a culture, but also the degree of emphasis on particular skills or career paths. China, Japan, and India, for example, emphasize the sciences and engineering more than many Western cultures do.

The technology level of a company's products may be too sophisticated depending on the educational level of the culture. This also influences whether customers are able to use the good or service properly and understand the firm's advertising or other promotional messages.

MANNERS AND CUSTOMS

Manners and customs, the final aspect of culture, need to be carefully dealt with and monitored. Understanding names and customs is particularly important for the global entrepreneur when negotiating and giving gifts. In negotiations, unless care is taken, the global entrepreneur can come to an incorrect conclusion because the interpretations are based on his or her frame of reference instead of the frame of reference of the culture. The silence of the Chinese and Japanese has been used effectively in negotiating with American entrepreneurs if American entrepreneurs interpret this incorrectly as a negative sign. Agreements in these countries, as well as other countries in Asia and the Middle East, may take much longer because there is a desire to talk about unrelated issues. Aggressively demanding last minute changes is a mannerism used by Russian negotiators.

Probably the area which requires the most sensitivity is gift giving. Gifts can be an important part of developing relationships in a culture, but one must take great care to determine whether it is appropriate to give a gift, the type of gift, how the gift is wrapped, and the manner in which the gift is given. For example, in China a gift is given with two hands and is usually not opened at that time but rather in privacy by the recipient.

Cultural Dimensions and Leadership

HOFSTEDE'S FIVE CULTURAL DIMENSIONS

Having looked at the seven cultural determinants that can be the basis for understanding any culture, understanding the five cultural dimensions described by Geert Hofstede gives the entrepreneur further insight into how these determinants often play out in a business setting. Power distance, or the hierarchical gap between the least powerful (lowest level employee, lowest regarded individual in society) and the most powerful and the acceptance of this position, demonstrates to the entrepreneur the level of power and inequality that a society possesses. If an entrepreneur wanted to do business in South Korea, for example, it would be very important that decisions were made and discussed with only the top-level individuals, because power distance is high and these managers would be the only ones capable of rendering and carrying out decisions in general. Without this knowledge, the entrepreneur could be stuck negotiating for months with people of little to no importance, not furthering the enterprise in the least.

The second dimension, individualism, reflects how decisions are made, taking into account societies that include either a strong, integrated group mentality with typically unyielding loyalty and unquestioning authority, or a very individualistic mentality with the priority being the individual and the importance of regarding solely oneself and the immediate family. In collectivistic societies, such as those in Latin America and Asia, decision making is often based on what is best for the society, group, or company as a whole.

The third dimension, masculinity, can be an aspect of social structure because society determines the importance and role of genders. In many Middle Eastern countries, trying to negotiate with women can render the negotiations worthless because this would not be a typical role for women to play. In many Latin American countries, women have often been viewed as an important figurehead in the house, but their role in business was limited. These roles, however, are often in flux as evidenced in Latin America by the election of two women presidents, Michelle Bachelet in Chile and Cristina Fernandez de Kirchner of Argentina in 2006 and 2007, respectively, both residing in societies regarded as very high on the masculinity scale (Reel, 2007).

The fourth dimension is uncertainty avoidance. This measures the tolerance a society has to handle ambiguity and whether the members of society feel comfortable in situations that are not typical or structured in a manner in which the members are accustomed. In avoidance cultures, the people follow strict laws and rules and security measures where they do not openly accept opinions separate from their own. With opposite cultures, the rules are few and far between and people often have difficulty expressing their emotions. As an entrepreneur operating in this type of environment, rules are often very different from his or her own environment. For example, the importance of understanding that bribes are often considered not only acceptable, but necessary for transacting business is something that some entrepreneurs need to be aware of. Again, it would be useful to have local help to understand these types of orientations.

Finally, long-term orientation of a culture is based on the values of that specific society. In a culture with long-term orientation, thrift and perseverance are the two values that are most important, whereas a short-term oriented individual has a respect for tradition, social obligations, and the appearance of "face." In Japan, for instance, the name of the company for which one works is the basis for respect and gives "face" to the individual who works there, especially if he or she is someone of seniority. Table 3.2 indicates the positioning of many countries on each of these dimensions.

Table 3.2   Geert Hofstede Cultural Dimensions™

Country	Power Distance Index (PDI)	Individualist (IDV)	Masculinity (MAS)	Uncertainty Avoidance Index (UAI)	Long-Term Orientation (LTO)
Argentina	49	46	56	86	
Australia	36	90	61	51	31
Austria	11	55	79	70	
Bangladesh *	80	20	55	60	40
Belgium	65	75	54	94	
Brazil	69	38	49	76	65
Bulgaria *	70	30	40	85	
Canada	39	80	52	48	23
Chile	63	23	28	86	
China *	80	20	66	30	118
Czech Republic *	57	58	57	74	13
Denmark	18	74	16	23	
El Salvador	66	19	40	94	
Estonia *	40	60	30	60	
Finland	33	63	26	59	
France	68	71	43	86	
Germany	35	67	66	65	31
Greece	60	35	57	112	
Hong Kong	68	25	57	29	96
Hungary *	46	80	88	82	50
India	77	48	56	40	61
Indonesia	78	14	46	48	
Iran	58	41	43	59	
Ireland	28	70	68	35	
Israel	13	54	47	81	
Italy	50	76	70	75	
Japan	54	46	95	92	80

Country	Power Distance Index (PDI)	Individualist (IDV)	Masculinity (MAS)	Uncertainty Avoidance Index (UAI)	Long-Term Orientation (LTO)
Malaysia	104	26	50	36	
Malta *	56	59	47	96	
Mexico	81	30	69	82	
Morocco *	70	46	53	68	
Netherlands	38	80	14	53	44
New Zealand	22	79	58	49	30
Norway	31	69	8	50	20
Peru	64	16	42	87	
Philippines	94	32	64	44	19
Poland *	68	60	64	93	32
Portugal	63	27	31	104	
Romania *	90	30	42	90	
Russia *	93	39	36	95	
Singapore	74	20	48	8	48
South Africa	49	65	63	49	
South Korea	60	18	39	85	75
Spain	57	51	42	86	
Sweden	31	71	5	29	33
Switzerland	34	68	70	58	
Taiwan	58	17	45	69	87
Turkey	66	37	45	85	
United Kingdom	35	89	66	35	25
United States	40	91	62	46	29
Uruguay	61	36	38	100	
Venezuela	81	12	73	76	
Vietnam *	70	20	40	30	80

* Estimated values

SOURCE: Adapted from www.geert-hofstede.com/hofstede_dimensions.php

GLOBE AND LEADERSHIP

Building on Hofstede's Five Determinants, the GLOBE project focuses on how better understanding cultural dimensions can improve the leadership of the entrepreneur, creating success from the top down. This research also includes gender egalitarianism, power distance, and uncertainty avoidance, and the orientation to look toward the future (future orientation, similar to long-term orientation), but adds assertiveness, performance orientation, and human orientation as well. Building on the idea of the determinant of individualism or collectivism, the authors focus on institutional and in-group collectivism, separating to what degree individuals of society are rewarded for collective actions and to what degree individuals express pride in their organizations.

Assertive cultures determine those that enjoy competition in business such as the United States and Austria, whereas less assertive ones, such as Sweden and New Zealand, prefer harmony in relationships and emphasize loyalty and solidarity. Understanding this environment can help the entrepreneur from a marketing and competitive intelligence point of view, while giving additional techniques for better managing local suppliers, customers, and the workforce.

Performance orientation and human orientation give rise to how an enterprise operates based on the rewards offered to the individuals for excellence and additionally how the collective encourages and rewards their individuals for being fair, caring, and generous. From a performance perspective, Singapore and many Western nations score very high where training and development are emphasized; Russia and Greece are good examples of cultures where family and background are more important. As for human orientation, Egypt and Malaysia emphasize the collectivistic nature and reward individuals, whereas Germany and France are not so disposed in this way.

As an entrepreneur looking to benefit from these cultural studies, one can better understand how to take advantage of the market if one understands the culture. By having a better understanding, the entrepreneur can enter the market with less risk and a better guarantee of success knowing he or she can reach the target market, suppliers, workforce, and know how to manage them according to their dispositions.

This area is further elaborated upon in Chapter 10, which includes a table that shows countries in terms of global human resources.

Summary

A full understanding of the culture of the new market that a company plans to enter is vital to the venture's success. Chapter 3 outlines the important cultural considerations that each global entrepreneur must take into account as he or she decides to enter a new market or partner with individuals or companies from a different country. Culture generally refers to common ways of thinking and behaving that are passed on from parents to their children or transmitted by social organizations, developed, and then reinforced through social pressure. Every entrepreneur must keep in mind that by nature culture is adaptive, learned, shared, structured, symbolic, and transgenerational. This chapter also describes how social structure, language, religion/beliefs system, political philosophy, economic philosophy/system, customs, and manners can affect a country's culture. A few examples show how an entrepreneur needs to be aware of and adapt to cultural differences. An entrepreneur's understanding of a different culture can make or break a new venture.

Questions for Discussion

1. Why does an entrepreneur need to be aware of the culture of the country that he or she is entering into?

2. How should an entrepreneur act in a country with high power distance?

3. Why do you need to be culturally aware when you receive gifts in different countries?

Chapter Exercises

1. With a partner, discuss an instance of cultural misunderstanding that has personally happened to you. Could this misunderstanding have been avoided? If so, how?

2. Choose one of the cultural scenarios in the chapter. How would you have avoided the same cultural problems that the company faced?

3. Pick a foreign country where you would like to do business. Write a brief report explaining the cultural differences between your country and that country, and describe how you would handle them.

4. Find an article about a company that attributes its failure in a foreign country to misunderstanding the local culture. What could the company have done to prevent this failure?

References

Campbell, D. D. (1997, February 15). *Grupo Financiero Inverlat.* Version: (A), 9497L001. Ontario, Canada: Ivey Management Services.

China's Pied Piper. (2006, September 21). *The Economist. 380*(8496), 78.

England, G. W., & Lee, R. (1974, August). The relationship between managerial values and managerial success in the United States, Japan, India, and Australia. *Journal of Applied Psychology, 59*(4), 411–419.

Hofstede, G. (2001). *Culture's consequences: Comparing values, behaviors, institutions, and organizations across nations.* Thousand Oaks, CA: Sage.

Javidan, M., Dorman, P. W., de Luque, M. S., & House, R. J. (2005). In the eye of the beholder: Cross cultural lessons in leadership from project GLOBE. *Academy of Management Executive, 20*(1), 67–90.

Reel, M. (2007, October 31). South America ushers in the era of the presidenta. *The Washington Post,* A12.

Reichel, A., & Flynn, D. M. (1984). Values in transition: An empirical study of Japanese managers in the U.S. *Management International Review, 23*(4), 69–79.

Training Management Corporation. (2008). *The cultural navigator—Cultural orientation inventory.* Retrieved from www.culturalnavigator.com

Suggested Readings

Dana, L. P. (2007). *Asian models of entrepreneurship: From the Indian Union and the Kingdom of Nepal to the Japanese Archipelago: Context, policy, and practice.* Hackensack, NJ: World Scientific.

While entrepreneurship is a global phenomenon, its nature is affected by the unique characteristics of the different countries and regions in the world. This book provides vivid examples of the differences in entrepreneurship and entrepreneurial activity among and within countries in Asia, in particular Japan, China, Singapore, and South Korea.

Katsioloudes, M., & Hadjidakis, S. (2007). *International business: A global perspective.* Oxford, UK: Butterworth-Heinemann.

Using a purely multinational perspective instead of the traditional U.S. perspective, this text examines international business. Most important, it includes interviews with politicians and business executives from numerous countries, including the United States, Canada, Mexico, Brazil, Colombia, Argentina, India, Hong Kong, Taiwan, China, Japan, South Korea, Germany, Italy, and Russia, to give a better understanding of international business from not only the U.S. perspective but the "reverse" perspective as well.

Sebenius, J. K. (2002, March). The hidden challenge of cross-border negotiations. *Harvard Business Review, 80*(3), 76–85.

Crossborder negotiations are highly affected by cultural differences that go far deeper than surface behaviors and cultural characteristics. The author examines how the processes involved in negotiations and the ways people from different cultures reach agreements affect crossborder negotiations.

Theil, S., Fahmy, M., Ismail, G., & Krieger, Z. (2007, August 20). An Arab opening. *Newsweek International.*

This article highlights the growing spirit of entrepreneurship in Arab companies and how current high school and university students are being prepared to harness that spirit. Many Arab countries are reducing the obstacles to starting and running a business, and today's Arabic youth must be ready to take advantage of these changes.

Zhou, L. (2007). The effects of entrepreneurial proclivity and foreign market knowledge on early internationalization. *Journal of World Business, 42,* 281–293.

Foreign market knowledge can come either from the pursuit of entrepreneurial activities across national borders or the slower building of experience in foreign markets. The author examines the role of foreign market knowledge in early internationalization. This study furthers the theoretical development of international entrepreneurship.

4 Developing the Global Business Plan

The pair started by holding informal talks with people they had met to find out whether anyone shared their values. They then put together a business plan with revenue models and projections of how those models could support sustainable business growth. They made formal presentations to the people they had identified as having the most potential, and 90% came on board.

When it comes to financing start-ups, banks in Hong Kong are reluctant to lend money to entrepreneurs without a good track record. Apart from putting their own money into a venture, new business owners can consider borrowing money from family and friends, which is known as bootstrapping. They can also look for angel investors—successful businessmen willing to invest in a new enterprise. Venture capitalists—companies that fund new enterprises with considerable growth potential—are another option. "Venture capitalists are usually looking for something to invest in for 3 to 4 years," said Hanson Cheah, managing partner at AsiaTech Ventures. "Because of the risk they are taking they would expect a very large return. They would want their investment to grow four times in 4 years."

Many people approach venture capitalists with innovative ideas, but they need a viable business plan if they want to be taken seriously. In addition to having a competitive edge in a growing market, they should have a management team with the right potential. Most important, there needs to be significant room for growth and that is what Mr. Lin and Ms. Lin got right. "Venture capitalists wouldn't be interested in a restaurant, but they would be interested in a chain of restaurants," Mr. Cheah said. "Unless the business can grow at between 20% and 30% per year, most investors would not be interested and it is unlikely that a single outlet could sustain that kind of growth."

www.kosmoliving.com

Chapter Objectives

1. To know the internal and external purposes of a global business plan.

2. To be able to identify all the parts of the business plan and their purposes for each department or organizational function of the company.

3. To understand how each audience of stakeholders will use the plan and which section will be each stakeholder's key focus.

4. To be able to draft a global business plan from the outline and sample provided.

5. To be able to monitor and improve the business plan.

Introduction

In today's highly competitive business environment there is perhaps nothing more important than planning and, specifically, developing a business plan. In any organization there are many different types of plans—financial, human resource, marketing, production, and sales. These plans may be short term or long term, strategic or operational, and may vary greatly in scope. In spite of the differences in scope and coverage, each plan has a common purpose: to provide guidance and structure on a continuing basis for managing the organization in a rapidly changing hypercompetitive environment.

Purpose of a Global Business Plan

Given the hypercompetitive environment and the difficulties of doing business outside your home country, a global business plan is an integral part of strategically managing an organization. What is a global business plan? A global business plan is a written document prepared by the entrepreneur and the team that describes all the relevant external and internal elements in going global. By describing all the relevant external and internal elements involved in starting and managing a global organization, the business plan integrates the functional plans such as finance, marketing, and organizational plans, thereby providing a road map for the future of the organization.

Often a global business plan is read by a variety of stakeholders and can have several different purposes. It needs to be comprehensive enough to address the issues and concerns of advisors, bankers, consultants, customers, employees, investors, and venture capitalists. It can also have such purposes as to obtain financial resources, obtain other resources, develop strategic alliances, or provide direction and guidance for the organization. Although a global business plan can serve several purposes, its most frequent use is to obtain financial resources. Bankers, investors, and venture capitalists will not take an investment possibility seriously without a comprehensive global business plan. Some will not even meet with an organization without first reviewing the organization's business plan. A well-developed global business plan is important because it (1) provides guidance to the entrepreneur and managers in decision making and organizing the international direction of the company, (2) indicates the viability of an organization in the designated global market(s), and (3) serves as the vehicle for obtaining financing.

Opportunity Analysis Plan

Each and every innovative idea and opportunity should be carefully assessed by the global entrepreneur. One good way to do this is to develop an opportunity analysis plan. An opportunity analysis plan is *not* a business plan, as it focuses on the idea and the market (the opportunity) for the idea—not on the venture. It also is shorter than a business plan and does not contain any formal financial statement of the business venture. The opportunity analysis plan is developed to serve as the basis for the decision to either act on the opportunity or wait until another (hopefully better) opportunity comes along. A typical opportunity analysis plan has four sections: (1) a description of the idea and its competition, (2) an assessment of the domestic and international market for the idea, (3) an assessment of the entrepreneur and the team, and (4) a discussion of the steps needed to make the idea the basis for a viable business venture.

THE IDEA AND ITS COMPETITION

This section focuses on one of the major areas of the opportunity analysis plan: the idea itself and the competition. The product or service needs to be described in as much detail as possible. A prototype or schematic of the product is helpful in fully understanding all its aspects and features. All competitive products and competitive companies in the product (service) market space need to be identified and listed. The new product/service idea should be compared with at least three competitive products/services that are most similar in filling the identified market need. This analysis will result in a description of how the product/service is different and unique and will indicate its unique selling propositions. If the idea does not have at least three to five unique selling propositions versus competitive products/services on the market, the entrepreneur will need to even more carefully examine whether the idea is really unique enough to compete and be successful in the market.

THE MARKET AND THE OPPORTUNITY

The second section of the opportunity analysis plan addresses the size and the characteristics of the market. Market data should be collected for at least 3 years so that a trend is apparent for the overall industry, the overall market, the market segment, and the target market. This can be done through gathering as much secondary (published) data as possible. For example, if you had an idea for a motorized wheelchair for small children that was shaped like a car, you would get market statistics on the health care industry (overall industry), wheelchairs (overall market), motorized wheelchairs (market segment), and children needing wheelchairs (target market). This funnel approach indicates the overall industry market size as well as the size of the specific target market.

Not only should the size of these markets be determined, but also each of their characteristics. Is the market made up of a few large companies or many small ones? Does the market respond quickly or slowly to new entrants? How many (if any) new products are introduced each year in the market? How geographically dispersed is the market? What market need is being filled? What social conditions underlie this market? What other products might the company also introduce into this market? What is the nature and size of the international market? On the basis of this section of the opportunity analysis plan, the entrepreneur should be able to determine both the size and the characteristics of the market, and whether it is large enough and suitable enough to warrant the time and effort required to further develop a business plan and actually enter the market.

ENTREPRENEUR AND TEAM ASSESSMENT

Next, both the entrepreneur and the entrepreneurial team need to be assessed. At least one person on the team needs to have experience in the industry area of the new idea. This is one characteristic that correlates to the probability of success of the venture. Several questions need to be answered, such as: Why does this idea and opportunity excite you? Will this idea and opportunity sustain you once the initial excitement has worn off? How does the idea and opportunity fit your personal background and experience? How does it fit your entrepreneurial team? This section of the opportunity analysis plan is usually smaller than the previous two sections and allows the entrepreneur to determine if indeed he or she is really suited to successfully move the idea into the market.

THE NEXT STEPS

This final section of the opportunity analysis plan delineates the critical steps that need to be taken to make the idea a reality in the marketplace. The steps need to be identified and put in sequential order, and the time and the money needed for each step needs to be determined. If the idea cannot be self-financed, then sources of capital need to be identified. The entrepreneur should always keep in mind that most entrepreneurs tend to underestimate both the costs and the time it will take by about 30%.

Some questions to answer when developing an opportunity analysis plan are listed in Figure 4.1.

Description of the Product or Service Idea and Competition

1. What is the market need for the product or service?
2. What are the specific aspects of the product or service (include any copyright, patent, or trademark information)?
3. What competitive products are already available and filling this need?
4. What are the competitive companies in this product market space? Describe their competitive behavior.
5. What are the strengths and weaknesses of each of your competitors?
6. What are the NAIC and SIC codes for this product or service?
7. What are the unique selling propositions of this product or service?
8. What development work has been completed to date on the idea?
9. What patents might be available to fulfill this need?
10. What are total industry sales over the past 5 years?
11. What is anticipated growth in this industry?
12. How many new firms have entered this industry in the past 3 years?
13. What new products have been recently introduced in this industry?

An Assessment of the Market

1. What market need does the product/service fill?
2. What is the size and past trends over the last 3 years of this market?
3. What is the future growth and characteristics of this market?
4. What social conditions underlie this market need?
5. What market research data can be marshaled to describe this market need?
6. What does the international market look like?
7. What does the international competition look like?
8. What is the profile of your customers?

Entrepreneurial Self-Assessment and the Entrepreneurial Team

1. Why does this opportunity excite you?
2. What are your reasons for going into business?
3. Why will this opportunity sustain you once the initial excitement subsides?
4. How does this opportunity fit into your background and experience?
5. What experience will you need to successfully implement the business plan?
6. Who are the other members of your team?
7. What are their skills and experience?

Next Steps for Translating This Opportunity Into a Viable Venture

1. Examine each critical step.
2. Think about the sequence of activity and put these critical steps into some expected sequential order.
3. Determine the amount of time and the amount of money each step will require. If you cannot self-finance (provide this money), where would you get the needed capital?

Figure 4.1 Questions for the Development of the Opportunity Analysis Plan

Aspects of a Global Business Plan

Given the importance and purpose of a global business plan, it is imperative that it be comprehensive and covers all aspects of the organization. The plan will be read by a variety of individuals, each of whom is looking for a certain level of detail (Taylor, 2006). As is indicated in Figure 4.2, the global business plan can be divided into several areas, each of which has several sections.

EXECUTIVE SUMMARY

The first area, although the shortest, is perhaps the most significant, particularly when the purpose is to secure financing. This area consists of the title page, table of contents, and executive summary. The title page should contain the following information: (1) the name, address, telephone and fax numbers, and e-mail address of the organization; (2) the name and position of the principal individuals in the organization; (3) three to four sentences briefly describing the nature of the organization and the purpose of the business plan; and (4) a statement of confidentiality, such as "This is confidential business plan number 3, which cannot be reproduced without permission." This statement is important as each numbered business plan needs to be accounted for by recording the person and organization of the individual receiving it and the date of receipt. When trying to obtain financing, this is particularly essential as follow-up can be scheduled at the appropriate time, which is about 45 days from the receipt date, assuming the individual has not already initiated contact. As one venture capitalist commented, "One way I get a feel for the hunger and drive of the entrepreneur is by waiting to see if he or she initiates follow-up at the appropriate time."

The table of contents is perhaps the easiest part of the business plan to develop. It should follow the standard format with major sections and appendixes (exhibits) indicated along with the appropriate page numbers.

The final part of the first primary area of the global business plan—the *executive summary*—is the most important and most difficult to develop, particularly when the purpose of the plan is to secure financing or other resources. The executive summary should be no more than three pages. It is frequently used by upper-level investors, venture capitalists, and bankers to determine if the entire business plan is worth reading and analyzing. The executive summary becomes the screen or hurdle that determines if more detailed attention will be given to the plan. Imagine a typical venture capitalist who receives about eighty 200-page business plans per month. He or she needs to employ some mechanism for screening this large number down to perhaps 10 to 15 for more focused initial attention.

I. Title Page, Table of Contents, and Executive Summary	
Three-page description of the project.	

II. Introduction

The type of business proposed and an in-depth description of the major product/service involved. A description of the country proposed for market entry, the rationale for selecting the country, identification of existing trade barriers, and identification of sources of information.

III. Analysis of the International Business Opportunity

A. Economic, Political, and Legal Analysis of the Trading Country
  1. The trading country's economic system; economic information important to the proposed product/service; and the level of foreign investment in that country.
  2. The trading country's governmental structure and stability, and how the government regulates trade and private business.
  3. Laws and/or governmental agencies that affect the product/service such as labor laws and trade laws.
B. Trade Area and Cultural Analysis
  1. Geographic and demographic information; important customs and traditions; other pertinent cultural information; and competitive advantages and disadvantages of the proposed business opportunity.

IV. Operation of the Proposed Business

A. Organization
  Type of ownership and rationale; start-up steps to form the business; personnel (or functional) needs; proposed staffing to handle managerial, financial, marketing, legal, production functions; proposed organizational chart; and brief job descriptions.
B. Product/Service
  1. Product/service details include potential suppliers, manufacturing plans, and inventory policies.
  2. Transportation information: costs, benefits, risks of the transportation method, documents needed to transport the product.
C. Market Entry Strategy
D. Marketing Strategy Plan
  1. Pricing policies: what currency will be used, costs, markups, markdowns, relation to competition, factors that could affect the price of the product such as competition, political conditions, taxes, tariffs, and transportation costs.
  2. Promotional program: promotional activities, media availability, costs, and 1-year promotional plan outline.

V. Financials

A. Projected Income and Expenses
  1. Pro forma income statements for first 3 years operation.
  2. Pro forma cash flow statements for first 3 years of operation.
  3. Pro forma balance sheet for the end of the first year.
  4. A brief narrative description of the planned growth of the business, including financial resources, needs, and a 3-year pro forma income statement.
B. Sources and Uses of Funds Statement
  1. Country statistics
  2. Partner information
  3. Relevant laws

VI. Appendix (Exhibits)

Figure 4.2   Outline of an International Business Plan

Given its importance, the executive summary should be written last and be written and rewritten until it highlights the organization in a concise and convincing manner, covering the key points in the business plan. The executive summary should emphasize the three most critical areas for the success of the organization. In order of importance, these are the characteristics, capabilities, and experiences of the entrepreneur and management team; the nature and degree of innovativeness of the product or service and its market size and characteristics; and the expected results in terms of sales and profits over the next 3 years.

INTRODUCTION

The second section of the global business plan is the *introduction*, where the focus is on the new global initiative, the product/service to be offered, and the country to be entered. A detailed description of the global initiative provides important information on the size and scope of the opportunity. Besides discussing the mission and purpose of this initiative as well as the organizational structure, an in-depth discussion of the product/service to be offered should be delineated. The questions in Figure 4.3 will help the global entrepreneur prepare that aspect of this section.

The section also needs to discuss the proposed country, the selection process, existing trade barriers, and sources of information (see Figure

---

1. What is the mission of the new venture?

2. What are your reasons for going into business?

3. Why will you be successful in this venture?

4. What development work has been completed to date?

5. What is your product(s) and/or service(s)?

6. Describe the product(s) and/or service(s), including patent, copyright, or trademark status.

7. Where will the business be located?

8. Is the building leased or owned? (State the terms.)

9. What office equipment will be needed?

10. Will this equipment be purchased or leased?

Figure 4.3　　Describing the Venture

SOURCE: Adapted from Hisrich, R. D., Peters, M. A., & Shepherd, D. A. (2007). *Entrepreneurship* (7th ed.). Burr Ridge, IL: McGraw-Hill/Irwin.

4.2). Even though these terms are further developed in later sections of the global business plan, they should be summarized in this introduction section. Some key questions that should be considered by the global entrepreneur concerning the needed environmental and industry analysis in developing this section are provided in Figure 4.4.

ECONOMIC, POLITICAL, AND LEGAL ASPECTS OF THE INTERNATIONAL BUSINESS OPPORTUNITY

The third section of the global business plan addresses the *international business opportunity*. Since this important area has been addressed in Chapter 3 (Cultures and Global Entrepreneurship) and will be covered in Chapter 7 (Alternative Entry Strategies), only an overview will be presented here. Two focus areas should be addressed in this section—the target country's culture and the overall economic, political, and legal aspects

---

1. What are the major economic, technological, legal, and political trends on a national and an international level?

2. What are total industry sales over the past 3 years?

3. What is anticipated growth in this industry?

4. How many new firms have entered this industry in the past 3 years?

5. What new products have been recently introduced in this industry in the last 3 years?

6. Who are the competitive companies?

7. What are the competitive products or services?

8. Are the sales of each of your major competitors growing, declining, or steady?

9. What are the strengths and weaknesses of each of your competitors?

10. What trends are occurring in your specific market area?

11. What is the profile of your customers?

12. How does your customer profile differ from that of your competition?

Figure 4.4   Issues in Environmental and Industry Analysis

SOURCE: Adapted from Hisrich, R. D., Peters, M. A., & Shepherd, D. A. (2007). *Entrepreneurship* (7th ed.). Burr Ridge, IL: McGraw-Hill/Irwin.

of the country. It is important to understand the economic system operating in the country, including the various financial institutions and particularly the banking system. Frequently, especially in developing countries, it can be difficult to get funds transferred in and out of a country. In one country where one of the author's companies was doing business, currency needed to be hand carried into the country with transactions taking place in cash because the banking system operated very slowly at a very high cost per transaction, not allowing funds to be available in a timely manner. The government structure and its stability as well as the various laws affecting trade and businesses need to be examined. This is particularly important in deciding the best organizational structure, which is discussed in section four of the global business plan (see Figure 4.2). Also, trade and labor laws often affect a country entrance decision as well as the effect of doing business there. McDonald's, when entering Hungary in 1988, needed to get special dispensation from the labor law from the Hungarian government (then under control of the Soviet Union) to be able to fire workers who were not performing to its standards. Some countries have very high legally mandated severance costs, making it less desirable to do business there. As is indicated in Figure 4.5, while there are 0 weeks in pay in severance costs legally mandated in the United States, it is 8.6

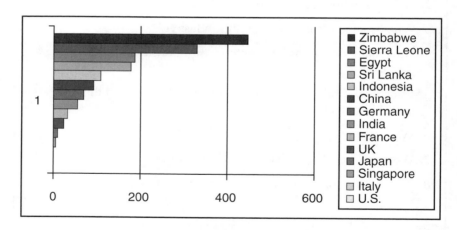

U.S.	0	Germany	69.3
Italy	1.7	China	91.0
Singapore	4.0	Indonesia	108.3
Japan	8.6	Sri Lanka	177.7
UK	22.1	Egypt	186.3
France	31.8	Sierra Leone	328.7
India	55.9	Zimbabwe	446.3

Figure 4.5   Legally Mandated Severance Costs in Select Countries (in Weeks of Pay)

weeks in Japan, 55.9 weeks in India, 91.0 weeks in China, 186.3 weeks in Egypt, and 446.3 weeks in Zimbabwe. Even though Indonesia should be well positioned to attract manufacturing because of the country's low wages and high productivity, its labor law requiring 108.3 weeks of pay in severance costs is a major deterrent to companies investing in manufacturing facilities there. One factory producing Lee Cooper brand jeans facing a cash-flow problem found it more economical to declare bankruptcy with all its workers losing their jobs rather than downsizing and laying off enough of the 1,500 employees to keep the business going at a lower level of output.

The second part of this section—cultural analysis—is equally important. The customs and traditions of the country need to be analyzed as well as any competitive products or services available. This will lead the global entrepreneur to identify the competitive advantages and disadvantages of the particular business opportunity.

The fourth section of the global business plan—the operation of the proposed business—is the most significant one. The organization, product/service, market entry strategy, and overall marketing strategy all need to be delineated.

ORGANIZATIONAL PLAN

The *organizational plan* is the part of the business plan that describes the venture's form of ownership—that is, proprietorship, partnership, or corporation. If the venture is a partnership, the terms of the partnership should be included. If the venture is a corporation, it is important to detail the shares of stock authorized and share options, as well as the names, addresses, and resumes of the directors and officers of the corporation. It is also helpful to provide an organizational chart indicating the line of authority and the responsibilities of the members of the organization. Some of the key questions the entrepreneur needs to answer in preparing this section of the business plan are:

- What is the form of ownership of the organization?

- If a partnership, who are the partners and what are the terms of agreement?

- If incorporated, who are the principal shareholders and how much stock do they own?

- How many shares of voting or nonvoting stock have been issued and what type?

- Who are the members of the board of directors? (Give names, addresses, and resumes.)

- Who has check-signing authority or control?

- Who are the members of the management team and what are their backgrounds?

- What are the roles and responsibilities of each member of the management team?

- What are the salaries, bonuses, or other forms of payment for each member of the management team?

This information provides the potential investor with a clear understanding of who controls the organization and how other members will interact when performing their management functions.

PRODUCT/SERVICE

The *product/service* to be produced and/or offered needs to be succinctly described. For technology-based products, this section should provide information on the nature of the technology, the unique differential advantage the technology has over rivals, and the degree that the technology is protectable by patents, copyrights, or trade secrets.

MARKET ENTRY STRATEGY

This section of the global business plan describes the *market entry strategy*, the focus of Chapter 7. Suffice it to say here that the various alternative entry strategies need to be carefully considered by the global entrepreneur and the one most appropriate for the country/product/market situation selected. The entry strategy needs to take into account potential suppliers, manufacturing plans, inventory policies, and an operations plan.

OPERATIONS PLAN

The *operations plan* goes beyond the manufacturing process (when the new venture involves manufacturing) and describes the flow of goods and services from production to the customer. It might include inventory or storage of manufactured products, shipping, inventory control procedures, and customer support services. A nonmanufacturer such as a retailer or service provider would also need this section in the business plan to explain the chronological steps in completing a business transaction. For example, an Internet retail sports clothing operation would need to describe how and where the products offered would be purchased, how they would be stored, how the inventory would be managed, how products would be shipped, and how a customer would log on and complete a transaction. In addition, this would be a convenient place for the entrepreneur to discuss the role of technology in the business transaction process. For any Internet retail operation, some explanation of the technology requirements needed to efficiently and profitably complete a successful business transaction should be included in this section.

It is important to note here that the major distinction between services and manufactured goods is that services involve intangible performances. This implies that they cannot be touched, seen, tasted, heard, or felt in the same manner as manufactured products. Airlines, hotels, car rental agencies, theaters, and hospitals, to name a few, rely on business delivery or quality of service. For these firms, performance often depends on location, facility layout, and personnel, which can in turn affect service quality (including such factors as reliability, responsiveness, and assurance). The process of delivering this quality of service is what distinguishes one new service venture from another and thus needs to be the focus of an operations plan. Some key questions or issues for both the manufacturing and nonmanufacturing new venture are as follows:

- Will you be responsible for all or part of the manufacturing operation?

- If some manufacturing is subcontracted, who will be the subcontractors? (Give names and addresses.)

- Why were these subcontractors selected?

- What are the costs of the subcontracted manufacturing? (Include copies of any written contracts.)

- What will be the layout of the production process? (Illustrate steps if possible.)

- What equipment will be needed immediately for manufacturing?

- What raw materials will be needed for manufacturing?

- Who are the suppliers of new materials and what are the appropriate costs?

- What are the costs of manufacturing the product?

- What are the future capital equipment needs of the venture?

MARKETING PLAN

The *marketing plan* is an important part of the business plan because it describes how the product(s) or service(s) will be distributed, priced, and promoted. Marketing research evidence to support any of the critical marketing decision strategies, as well as for forecasting sales, should be described in this section. Specific forecasts for a product(s) or service(s) are indicated to project the profitability of the venture. Budget and appropriate controls needed for marketing strategy decision are also needed. Potential investors regard the marketing plan as critical to the success of the new venture. Thus, the entrepreneur should make every effort to prepare as comprehensive and detailed a plan as possible so that investors can be clear as to what the goals of the venture are and what strategies are to be implemented to effectively achieve these goals. Marketing planning will be an annual requirement (with careful monitoring and changes made on a weekly or monthly basis) for the entrepreneur and should be regarded as the road map for short-term decision making.

FINANCIALS

The final area of the global business plan covers the financials. Like the other aspects of the global business plan, the *financials* are an important part of the plan. It determines the potential investment commitment needed for the new venture and indicates whether the business plan is economically feasible.

Generally, three financial areas are discussed in this section of the business plan. First, the entrepreneur should summarize the forecasted sales and the appropriate expenses for at least the first 3 years, with the first year's projections provided monthly. It includes the forecasted sales, cost of goods sold, and the general and administrative expenses. Net profit after taxes can then be projected by estimating income taxes.

The second major area of financial information needed is cash flow figures for 3 years, with the first year's projections provided monthly. Since bills have to be paid at different times of the year, it is important to determine the demands on cash on a monthly basis, especially in the first year. Remember that sales may be irregular and receipts from customers also may be spread out, thus necessitating the borrowing of short-term capital to meet fixed expenses, such as salaries and utilities.

The last financial item needed in this section of the business plan is the projected balance sheet. This shows the financial condition of the business at a specific time. It summarizes the assets of a business, its liabilities (what is owed), the investment of the entrepreneur and any partners, and retained earnings (or cumulative losses). Any assumptions considered for the balance sheet or any other item in the financial plan should be listed for the benefit of the potential investor.

APPENDIX (EXHIBITS)

The *appendix* of the business plan generally contains any backup material that is not necessary in the text of the document. Reference to any of the documents in the appendix should be made in the plan itself. Letters from customers, distributors, or subcontractors are examples of information that should be included in the appendix. Any documentation of information—that is, secondary data or primary research data used to support plan decisions—should also be included. Leases, contracts, or any other types of agreements that have been initiated also may be included in the appendix. Finally, price lists from suppliers and competitors may be added.

Dos and Don'ts of the Global Business Plan

The global business plan needs to carefully articulate all aspects of the global venture. Some of the dos and don'ts of preparing this important document are listed in Table 4.1. Two dos focus on the all important executive summary—write it last and make sure it is a powerful statement focused on the recipient and objectives of the global business plan. Also,

Table 4.1   Dos and Don'ts of a Global Business Plan

Do:	Don't:
• Write the executive summary last and revise it until it is a succinct and powerful statement of you, your company, and its goals. • Tailor the executive summary to each recipient of the business plan. • Include a dated and numbered statement of confidentiality to create a proper follow-up schedule. • Include information about the potential economic, legal, and political hurdles your company may face in a foreign market. • Clearly delineate the ownership of the company and its organizational structure. • Present multiple market entry strategies and assess each proposed strategy. • Describe in full the operations plan, including costs, from manufacturing or acquiring inventory to sales and shipment. • Strengthen your marketing plan by referring to in-depth market research. • Provide detailed sales and expense forecasts as well as projected cash flows and a balance sheet.	• Write the executive summary first and make minimal revisions. • Treat the business plan as a one-time report instead of a living document that should be constantly reviewed and updated. • Skip any of the sections of the business plan. • Use outdated data and figures when creating the operations plan and the financial projections. • Ignore market research when defining your market plan. • Limit your company to only one form of market entry strategy. • Hastily prepare the sales and expense forecasts and other financial data. • Be the only editor of the business plan.

the all important market entry strategy, marketing plan, and obtaining market research data are important.

Sample Global Business Plan

A sample global business plan created by a student, Joseph Naaman, for his company, Maktabi, can be found starting on page 471.

Summary

This chapter takes an entrepreneur through the important process of creating a business plan, which is integral in strategically managing an organization. Business plans are used by entrepreneurs to convince investors, such as venture capitalists, to support a company's launch or expansion into a new market or product line. They also examine the internal and external factors that affect a company's decision to go global. A well-developed global business plan provides guidance in decision making and organizing the international direction of the company; indicates the viability of an organization in the designated global market(s); and serves as the vehicle for obtaining financing. Each section of the business plan is described, including each section's necessary content. The primary sections of the business plan are the executive summary; introduction; political, legal, and economic aspects of the new opportunity; organizational plan; product/service; market entry strategy; operations plan; marketing plan; financials; and appendix.

Questions for Discussion

1. What role does a business plan play for a global entrepreneur?

2. What are the key sections of the plan?

3. What additional information is needed for a global plan than would be for a strictly domestic business?

Chapter Excercises

1. Create a table containing each section of the business plan, its primary audience, and its primary function and importance.

2. Explain the role of the financial section of the business plan, including where the information comes from, who the primary audience is, and what internal planning function this section serves.

3. Suppose you are an American donut company that has decided to launch a donut bakery and café in Shanghai, China. The company grosses US$25 million per year from donut and café sales, US$5 million of which is attributed to its bakery-cafés in Australia and New Zealand. Create an executive summary to convince a Chinese venture capitalist to invest in this project.

4. Consider your own business or business idea and outline a business plan for it. Identify which areas of the business plan will need more research, brainstorming, and calculations and what steps are needed to address these areas.

References

Taylor, M. (2006, May 27). Healthy living to be made out of wellness: Investors will only be interested if you have a business plan with significant room for growth. *South China Morning Post,* p. 8.

Suggested Readings

Choucri, N., Mistree, D., Haghseta, F., Mezher, T., Baker, W. R., & Ortiz, C. I. (2007). *Alliance for Global Sustainability Bookseries (1st ed.): Mapping sustainability: Knowledge e-networking and the value chain.* **New York: Springer.**

This book identifies and explains three interdependent barriers in knowledge and knowledge sharing in the move toward sustainability. It also shares potential ways to overcome these barriers using innovations in information technology and the calculation and representation of the related complexities. In addition, the book notes unexplored applications of new methodologies that further the understanding of sustainability issues.

Dick, H., & Merrett, D. (2007, May 7). The internationalization strategies of small-country firms: The Australian experience of globalization. *New Horizons in International Business Series.* **Cheltenham, UK and Northhampton, MA: Edward Elgar.**

This research project combines contemporary and historical analysis to trace the evolution of Australian multinationals. It provides unique insights into how firms from a small economy achieved global competitiveness in their niche markets, while examining the barriers that inhibited others. The evidence is presented in comparative, industry, and firm case studies, and tells the story of international business made in Australia.

Gruber, M. (2007, November). Uncovering the value of planning in new venture creation: A process and contingency perspective. *Journal of Business Venturing, 22(6), 782.*

This article describes how the different founding environments affect the planning process and regimes and new ventures. Select planning activities and swift planning should be used by entrepreneurs in highly dynamic environments, while a broader approach to planning is better in slower environments. The author's findings overall suggest entrepreneurs should use a flexible, toolkit approach to venture planning.

Wen, C., & Chen, Y. (2007). The innovation process of entrepreneurial teams in dynamic business plan competition: From sense-making perspective. *International Journal of Technology Management, 39(3/4), 346.*

Through the study of three venture teams at the third and fourth Technology Innovation Competition (TIC100) in Taiwan, the authors identified that sense making is a critical activity in the innovation and product development process. The sense-making process during this business plan competition helps students reach a consensus that reflects each team's collective wisdom and creativity.

Part 1

Cases

- Motrada Ltd.
- Parsek LLC
- Beijing Sammies
- Trimo

Motrada Ltd.

A European Entrepreneur Going Global

Paul M. Frentz, Guillaume Hébrard, and Katherine Macdonald

Introduction

Motrada Handels GmbH is a software/Internet services company that develops, sells, and provides a business-to-business (B2B) re-marketing service with an online Internet application. This application is specifically designed for the easy sale of used products. The application is able to generate a new platform, based on customer needs, in approximately 5 hours. The number of platforms that can be built upon the generic core application is unlimited. Currently, Motrada is concentrating on platforms for the used car market in Europe. In the future, the company's focus will expand to additional products and to global markets.

The Beginning

Guillaume Hébrard spent most of his professional career in car sales and knew the industry in Austria and its customers inside and out. For example, he knew that an elderly couple choosing between red and blue upholstery would be back in 4 days ordering green. When students began their search by looking for the least expensive version of the smallest car, Guillaume knew they would end up buying the car with the cool fender design (despite its cost). He would then throw in detailing extras, converting the student into a faithful customer. Guillaume was very successful at retaining his customers, selling multiple cars to the same clients over long periods of time.

One day in early 2005, Guillaume leaned back in his leather chair and folded his hands behind his neck. His eyes scanned the large showroom, and he attempted to guess how much rent his boss paid for this place. No doubt, it was expensive but there was still not enough room for all the cars the customers were interested in. All too often, he had to show his customers details in brochures or ask them for patience until a particular car was delivered to his location.

Guillaume was well versed in technology and very confident in the Internet. In fact, he was so confident in the Internet that he did most of his shopping online. This made him wonder, with such an adept resource at their fingertips, why did people still buy cars in showrooms? Internet technology was fast with the advent of broadband, many households and businesses had access, and eBay was just starting to be the next big thing. Suddenly it came to him—Guillaume decided to take car buying online.

Personal Background

Guillaume was born and raised in Southern France and moved to Vienna, Austria, in 1996. He moved to Austria as part of a program run by the French government. This program sent young men abroad (at the time he was 24) to work for French companies in place of military service. He did not speak much German, except for the remnants of an ERASMUS semester in Innsbruck, Austria, and with only a few friends from his school days, he had no network in the country. He went to Vienna without any expectations of either enjoying or prolonging his stay. He had no idea that he would base a significant portion of his professional career there.

Guillaume specialized in accounting at his business school in Rouen, France, leading to an initial appointment with Citroen in Austria. He spent his time at Citroen building a strong network of friends based on common interests (i.e., skiing and climbing) and fully immersed himself in the skills necessary to perform successfully in his industry. Rewarding his hard work, Citroen offered him a full-time position and asked him to support their sales team in a financial and controlling position. Citroen also gave him the responsibility of consulting for licensed Citroen dealers in Austria. After success in this position, Citroen promoted him to business and sales director of a subsidiary in Vienna. This made him responsible for the branch's new and used car sales, garage services, and spare parts sales. It was during this time that Guillaume became aware of the problems and inefficiencies within the used car market.

The B2B Used Car Market

In Austria, as in most of Europe, it is normal for major car companies and dealers to accept a used vehicle in exchange for part of the sale price of a new one. Fifty percent of these used vehicles are sold directly to private buyers. The other 50% are sold to dealers. The business-to-business (B2B) portion of the used car market caught Guillaume's attention primarily because the vehicles being sold in this market are usually damaged, sold before repair, and without warranty. Selling these cars presents many challenges. If a seller wants to get a used vehicle off their hands quickly, their chances of getting a good price for their vehicle are low for the following reasons:

- They have little time or desire to invest in an expert estimate of their vehicle's value.

- They cannot expect a good price if they sell a vehicle that is no longer under warranty.

- The purchasing dealer is averse to paying a high price for a vehicle that they will not be able to sell quickly or for a significant profit. The purchasing dealers are going to push the price down because they are aware that they have a stronger position.

- The purchasing dealers only purchase from companies they trust, which forces used car sellers to build a good reputation. Dealers generally purchase from networks of 10 to 15 trusted dealers that take a long time to build.

A black market is thriving because of the inability to establish a market price for used cars in the B2B marketplace. Salespersons sell a vehicle at a low price and charge an unofficial fee from the purchasing dealer. Accordingly, the purchasing company maintains low expectations for the vehicle's quality. The purchasing dealer usually enters into the deal with an end buyer in mind for the used car. Any money paid in the form of a "fee" to the salesperson is lost to the legitimate car sales or car leasing company since it represents how much the dealer would really be prepared to pay for the vehicle if going through official channels. Since there is no reliable data on these fees, it is impossible to size the actual demand of the B2B used car market.

A New Business Concept

Now in a leadership position, Guillaume was responsible for a sales team and had to choose between accepting the black market tendencies or maintaining his integrity. Maintaining his integrity would force him to attempt to change the way the market conducted its business. If he were successful in this transformation, he would be able to channel significant profits back into the company. Guillaume interviewed colleagues and peers in other companies and countries to gain their insight. He realized that the challenges he faced were the same all over the world and, in general, they were being ignored. This was unacceptable to Guillaume. He knew that transparency in the market was necessary to increase the selling price of the used cars to their real market value, and in turn, increase firm profits.

For Guillaume the solution to this problem was to auction the cars, creating a competitive situation where the sale would be awarded to the highest bidder. Guillaume was not the first to think of this model—for example, British Car Auctions (BCA) holds physical car auctions exclusively for registered car dealers. Auctions tend to widen the market, to push prices up, and to improve the security of deals. The drawbacks of auctions are that they require a lot of space, they cannot be held until there are enough cars to make it worthwhile, and the dealers have to go to the place of the auction and decide on the spot which vehicles interest them and which do not. Also, auctions would not inherently increase trust in the industry and did not account for the necessity of "awarding" sales for strategic reasons.

In an effort to mitigate these challenges, Guillaume decided that an Internet auction platform was a viable alternative to the live auctions. An Internet solution could widen the market to include more buyers and create better market dynamics. At the same time, it could allow for restriction possibilities—allowing the seller to offer their cars to a smaller circle of buyers. The platform could have standardized description facilities to alleviate trust issues. The platform would regulate descriptions to assure honesty from the seller and minimize the risk of nonpayment on behalf of the buyer. As the Austrian market was limited in both geography and inventory, Guillaume knew from the start that the platform would have to be international.

Market Data

Based on current trends, the European used car market will continue to grow significantly. This forecast is based on the following observations:

- worldwide overproduction of cars;

- product innovation—new cars turn into used cars faster and faster;

- better quality—cars are driven longer and can be traded more often;

- the Internet is making globalization and targeting foreign markets easier;

- e-trading is currently growing faster than any other distribution channel; and

- all players in the market are looking for more efficient distribution channels for used cars.

Based on this information, Guillaume decided to launch his online B2B sales platform with the used car market as his launch market. He chose this market for two reasons: first, because of its size and value, and second, because of its current lack of profitability and its inefficient organization.

THE EUROPEAN AUTOMOTIVE INDUSTRY AND MARKET SEGMENT GROWTH

The car industry can be divided into two main segments—the new car business and the used car business. Vehicles registered for the first time are classified as new, all others are used. These two segments are closely related because new cars are quickly converted to used cars. Based on European Automobile Manufacturers Association (ACEA) data, the 2006 European market was approximately 32 million used cars (see Table 1).

From the official figures of the new car market, the five largest European countries represent 60% of the total EU 25 market. The figures in Table 1 assume that they represent the same proportion of the used car market.

Approximately 45% of these 32 million cars are being traded in the business-to-consumer (B2C) sector (14.4 million). Based on a statistical survey by Citroen Europe, 35% of these 14.4 million used cars were traded on a B2B level before they were sold to the end customer, moving from one car dealer to another. As a result, in 2006, approximately 5.04 million vehicles represented the relevant market (see Figure 1 and Table 2).

Table 1   New and Used Car Sales in the European Union

Market (in 000s)	New Cars Total			Used Cars Total		
	2006	2003	2006/2003	2006	2003	2006/2003
EU 25	14,995	14,713	+1.9%	31,926	31,305	+2.0%
EU 5	9,596	9,175	+4.6%	19,345	18,527	+4.4%

SOURCE: ACEA, the European Automobile Manufacturers Association, Belgium (www.acea.be).

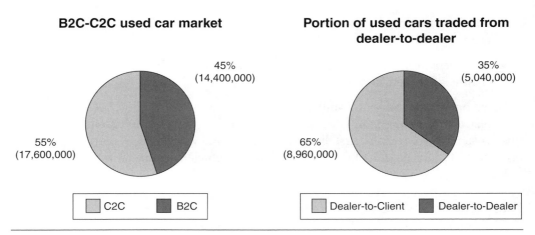

Figure 1   Used Car Market Trades

SOURCE: ACEA, the European Automobile Manufacturers Association, Belgium (www
.acea.be).

In the B2B sector, the Internet is currently used for exchanging information but not as a sales channel. Approximately only 1% of all cars sold are
sold via the Internet, which amounts to about 50,000 vehicles. The use of
the Internet in daily business and e-business is becoming more and more
common. The Internet will continue to gather momentum as a distribution channel and outgrow its role as solely an information provider. Forecasts for the development of this market segment are quite promising.

Table 2   Business-to-Business Market

	2006		2007		2008		2009	
	Volume	Market	Volume	Market	Volume	Market	Volume	Market
B2B market (in 000s) (1)	5,090		5,141		5,193		5,245	
B2B e-market (2)	76	1.5%	154	3%	260	5%	420	8%
Used car market share (3)	0.15	0.2%	3	2%	6.5	2.5%	12.5	3%

(1) Projection: annual growth of 1%.

(2) Projection: at the beginning of the development of the e-market.

(3) Target market (with reference to the B2B and e-market).

SOURCE: ACEA, the European Automobile Manufacturers Association, Belgium (www
.acea.be).

Table 3   Leasing Market

Markets 2006	Number of Leased Cars	Leasing Returns P.A. (2)
EU 25	4,090	1,227
EU 5 (1)	2,175	733

(1) Austria, France, Germany, Italy, and Spain.

(2) According to industry expectations, about 30% of the vehicles become leasing returns.

SOURCE: Leaseurope, European Federation of Leasing Company Associations (www.leaseurope.org).

THE LEASING MARKET SEGMENT

In the European car market there are approximately 890 leasing companies. In 2006 the number of cars financed by leasing contracts was about 4.09 million (see Table 3).

The number of cars financed via leasing rose from 1999 to 2006 with remarkable speed. According to national leasing associations, this development will continue. Table 4 shows an estimate for the number of potential clients.

Leasing companies are looking for efficient re-marketing tools.

- Annually, more than 1 million vehicles need to be re-marketed by leasing companies.

- Importers are using demonstration vehicles and short registrations in order to raise their market shares artificially. These vehicles also need professional re-marketing.

- Wholesalers are looking for an option for car sales without guarantee requirements (as opposed to B2C, warranties for used cars can be limited or excluded in the B2B market).

Table 4   Potential Market for Leased Cars

Market Players 2006	Car Leasing Companies	Car Importers	Licensed Car Dealers (2)	Licensed Car Dealers (3) (More Than 1,000 Vehicles Sold Yearly)
EU 25	887	585	118,000	5,900
EU 5 (1)	402	303	50,000	2,500

(1) Austria, France, Germany, Italy, and Spain

(2) CECRA, the European Council for Motor Trades and Repairs, Belgium (http://www.cecra.eu)

(3) Assumption that 5% of all car dealers are relevant customers

SOURCE: Leaseurope, European Federation of Leasing Company Associations (www.leaseurope.org).

Table 5   Market Share Statistics

Shares of the EU 5 Market	2006		2007		2008		2009	
	#	%	#	%	#	%	#
Leasing companies	3	3.7	15	10.0	40	14.9	60
Importers	1	1.7	5	6.6	20	10.0	30
Wholesale dealer	2	1.2	30	4.0	100	8.0	200

SOURCE: ACEA, the European Automobile Manufacturers Association, Belgium (www.acea.be).

Founding Motrada

When Guillaume launched Motrada, he was still working full-time for Citroen. It was a while before he took his own idea seriously and he spoke to very few people about it. He did not spend much time drawing up a financial plan, and instead focused on getting his project off the ground so that he could eventually leave Citroen. The main problems he confronted in the planning phase for the Motrada start-up included:

- The concept: Is it feasible? Is it good? Where should he begin? Will the market accept the idea?

- Where will he find the right business partners? The technical issues: Setting up an Internet platform is a big deal. The requirements and specifications would be enormous and need to be very specific.

- The people: Who? He realized quickly that it would be impossible to go it alone.

- The money: How was he going to manage financially? How long could he last without making a profit?

Guillaume knew that if he started worrying about money, he would not even take the first step. Therefore, he rounded up about EUR 70,000 from his "family, friends, and fools" and began his business.

PHASE 1—FIRST START, 2002

Guillaume was still working full-time for Citroen during his first attempt to launch Motrada. The team he pulled together consisted of two consultants and himself. The consultants were responsible for writing the business plan, finances, business structure, and programming. Guillaume stuck with his specialty—sales.

This first attempt failed for several reasons. All three members of the team had full-time jobs, and were unable to commit the necessary time to the venture. The team also did not have a good working relationship. Despite all this, Guillaume was committed to the success of his idea. He knew there was a market out there for his product.

PHASE 2—BETTER TEAM AND SECOND START, MARCH 2004

Guillaume built a friendship with Martin Putschek, who ran a mini-incubator. Martin, who worked with a financial partner and a private investor, focused on seed companies. He took an active part in Motrada's second launch attempt as he had the necessary contact network to find two professional programmers willing to take on the workload at an affordable price.

Once he started working with Guillaume, things started to move more quickly. The team recruited Ceus Media—the new programmers—in March 2004, before the specifications had been written. They wrote the specifications in 2 months and, unfortunately, the first version of the program, released in August, was far from Guillaume's original vision. It was a terrible disappointment.

Later, Guillaume described this disappointment:

> It is always a problem writing specifications that are precise enough. If you want everything to be exactly like the image you are seeing in your mind's eye you have to be extremely precise and that can take years: we took 2 months! No wonder I was disappointed at the result . . .

They had to pick up the pieces quickly—there was a deadline in sight. Motrada was invited to make an official presentation on January 10, 2005. Guillaume knew that this presentation was once in a lifetime and he instilled a strong sense of urgency in the team. While he could have lingered on what could go wrong, in Guillaume's mind, there was no other option than for his idea to succeed. At the end of April 2004, he finally quit Citroen to work on Motrada full time.

Between June and December, the team set up the operational side of the business: company name, registration, and creating an initial marketing concept. The product was launched on October 18, and to Guillaume's delight, he received positive feedback from a man he greatly respected, Wolfgang Sieber, who was an authority on the market. Sieber, the CEO of Denzel Group (the largest car importer in Austria), ordered the product on the spot. He was their first customer and he allowed them to use his company as a reference.

At the international level, Guillaume was still in close contact with people from the used car industry in France, Italy, Spain, and Germany. With their markets in mind, he built the application to be easily translated into different languages. Motrada's short-term goals for market development were

- achieving a market share of 3% of all European B2B sales in 2009;

- finding licensing partners in Spain and Italy by 2007, and in the UK and United States by 2008;

- finding a licensing partner for the Asia/Pacific region by 2009; and

- reaching approximately 45% ROS in 2009.

Motrada went live on February 28, 2005, and the launch was marked by a press conference in one of the trendiest Vienna hotels. Motrada earned good press coverage and started doing business with the Denzel Group. Cooperating with Denzel, Motrada sold four cars in the first week.

To get car dealers to go online and to trade on his platform, Guillaume used direct marketing methods including cold calling and mailings. He also put a publicity banner on another Web site. After the first quick surge of interest, the press coverage stopped and thorough marketing measures proved excessively expensive.

Table 6   Timing of Market Entrance by Country

	Time Frame						
	2006	**2007**		**2008**		**2009**	
Countries	**S2**	**S1**	**S2**	**S1**	**S2**	**S1**	**S2**
Austria	X	X	X	X			
Czech Republic—Slovakia	X	X	X	X			
France	X	X	X	X	X		
Germany		X	X	X	X		
Spain		X	X	X	X		
Italy			X	X	X	X	
Switzerland			X	X	X	X	
Belgium			X	X	X	X	
UK			X	X	X	X	
U.S.			X	X	X	X	
Asia				X	X	X	X

S1: January through June

S2: July through December

There were not enough cars on the platform or enough buyers registered and active. There were many passive registered dealers but the trust between buyers and sellers had not been established so all sales came gradually to a halt. Before running the whole business into the ground, Guillaume realized that the financial gap was growing too wide. He needed to do two things: modify the concept (it was not attracting enough dealers) and get more financing.

PHASE 3—HIGH LEVEL PROFESSIONAL SUPPORT FROM INiTS, DECEMBER 2005

Guillaume knew that adding to the team was essential for Motrada's future success so he sought out the support of a local high-tech business accelerator called INiTS. INiTS, based in Vienna, is the number one high-tech start-up incubator in Austria. Founded in 2002, INiTS has launched about 60 start-up projects since its founding (www.inits.at).

INiTS start-ups spend about 18 months in the incubator, and are subsidized with approximately EUR 35,000–55,000, depending on their project. About 30% of their start-ups are working in the field of life science/biotechnology, another 30% in IT. Through local and European networks, INiTS is able to provide entrepreneurs with access to a broad variety of strategic partners, fast market entry, and private equity. The incubator enables start-ups to finalize their business plan, develop a consistent IPR strategy, solve legal and patent issues, and build cross-functional start-up teams. INiTS also helps its start-ups found/incorporate their companies, establish a business network, produce prototypes and so forth, and supports pricing decisions and negotiations. When a start-up has been successful in these initial processes, INiTS helps it acquire the financial resources for the next stage of growth—for example, funding from venture capital firms, corporate investors, or public funds.

With intense INiTS support, Guillaume was finally able to complete the business plan he had put off since Motrada's founding. The incubator also enabled him to think about Motrada's strategy, pricing, timing, contracts, quality control, and financial planning. During this time he increased the sources of public financial support for his company while also maintaining the company's income from customers.

Guillaume developed the first major stable PAP (Private Auction Platform) version while at the incubator. His intentions were to sell the individual platform to the big car sales and car leasing companies so that they could use it to monitor their used vehicle resales. Based on customer and user response, the team started implementing countless minor adjustments and changes to the software on a daily basis. Guillaume kept searching and recruiting new team members; despite his budget restrictions, as quality was most important to him. He hired part-time employees from various nationalities in order to help with the market analysis in their respective countries, initial customer contacts, and implementation of the first negotiations. In addition, he set up co-operations with leading business schools in France and the United States in order to get access to fresh management talents.

Motrada's strategy was to introduce its product to leading customers in all the large European markets. However, after the experiences of its first attempts (prior to working with the incubator), Motrada knew that it had to decide whether it should grow as a "stand alone" beyond European borders, or if the company should sell to a software partner, platform provider, or to user or dealer organizations.

By this time the programmers were working for very little pay, so Guillaume began offering profit shares to boost team motivation. However, in October 2005, a breakthrough occurred. VolksBank Leasing ordered the first PAP. Despite the uncertainty of when the payment for the PAP would come, Guillaume continued to improve his product. His team finished the Czech, English, French, Spanish, and Italian translations. They focused on turning their European contacts into business opportunities. They developed a partnership system contacting influential players on foreign markets and used them to distribute the platforms in respective countries.

Once the VolksBank Leasing payments began to come in August 2006, Guillaume was in a position to gain further financing for re-investment. In order to gain this financing, Motrada had to prove that it was a useful tool to create a global market for individual sellers. The marketing approach to instill this image would be sales through licensing partners. Their target clients were mostly large established companies and to penetrate this market, Motrada needed to build brand recognition. The company achieved brand recognition by distributing Motrada products abroad via licensing partners that are already well known in their respective markets. For Motrada to work with them, a licensing partner must fulfill three requirements: experience in the industry, successful sales structures, and complete market coverage.

Guillaume was successful at finding good business partners in France and in Germany; in fact, Motrada has already made agreements with these partners. The results achieved by the first user companies have been much better than expected—making 150% more profit as compared to the prices gained through black market methods. Soon sales and technology finally began to run smoothly and normal processes replaced Motrada's earlier chaos. With this new stability, Guillaume had his business plan updated, translated, and handed over to U.S.-based networkers and investors. He also started to sketch out software version 2.0 and 3.0 to be finished by 2008 and 2009 respectively.

For a product demo of the PAP today, visit http://demo.motrada.com.

Appendix A

MOTRADA'S COMPETITIVE ADVANTAGE

Motrada has developed a multiclient capable and multilingual ASP application. With its application, Motrada can create thousands of adapted platforms, each in only 5 hours. These platforms offer a secure point of sale where authorized car dealers can buy from known sellers in a trustworthy environment.

Compared to other e-commerce platforms, Motrada is offering significant value-added benefits.

1. *Tailor made platform:* Motrada offers the only easily customized industry solution for the resale of leasing returns, company cars, and dealer cars. Platform customization options allow a customer to convey a professional tool with an individualized appearance. In addition, the customization costs are much lower than if the company were to order a personalized platform.

2. *Improved platform security:* By working only with individually chosen car dealers, the professionalism and confidence in the platform is high.

3. *Larger buyer pool:* The Internet significantly increases the number of potential buyers. With this platform, the selling dealer can use the "buyer group definition" option to enable transactions with other dealers they trust. This raises the probability of finalizing sales contracts and allows sellers to define the size of their buyer group.

4. *More profitable solutions:* Motrada's platform leads to higher profits through modern and efficient sales procedures. Its auction format allows for better prices for sellers and broader options for buyers.

5. *User friendly:* Motrada's platform provides fast and accurate information. Platform users do not need to monitor the system constantly, as they are informed of any new offers or any significant changes automatically.

6. *Less expensive:* The Motrada platform simply charges a monthly fee. This means that users do not have to bear high investment costs and may begin using their professional marketing tool immediately.

Appendix B

COMPANY HISTORY

10 Jan 2005	Motrada Handels GmbH founded by G. Hébrard and a financial partner in Vienna/Austria
Jan 2005	First presentation of Motrada at a trade fair (Auto-Zum-Fachmesse) in Salzburg/Austria: More than 120 dealers sign up with www.motrada.com
Feb 2005	Official launch of first platform version
March 2005	First online sale between two registered members
Aug 2005	First release and presentation of the Partner Auction Platform
Dec 2005	Motrada accepted for 18-month Incubation Program
May 2006	VolksBank Leasing signs client contract for an unlimited period with Motrada (first sales in July 2006)
June 2006	Motrada signs licensee agreement with Le Monde de l'Automobile SA—JTA in France. This important B2B player on the auto market will have exclusive sales rights for Motrada products in France.
July 2006	Client contract signed with PSA Finance Austria AG (first sales in August 2006)
Nov 2006	Client contract signed with PSA Finance Deutschland (first sales in February 2007)
Dec 2006	JTA sells first PAPs to two car wholesalers (operating on B2B level)
Jan 2007	Additional financing (AWS—ErsteBank) of EUR 110,000 and private equity of EUR 30,000
Mar 2007	New pilot customers in Spain and Italy

Case Questions

1. Name some crucial aspects of Guillaume's personality that were relevant for the development of his entrepreneurial spirit.

2. Do you think Guillaume represents the "one in a million" entrepreneur? How common is such a person in your own country? How much do you think you have in common with Guillaume at this point in Motrada's development?

3. Is there a market need for Guillaume's idea? Who would be willing to pay for a solution to the status quo?

4. Who would be the product's customers and users?

5. Why does the B2B market seem to be more promising than the B2C market?

6. Based on this situation—what are the crucial criteria for designing the business model and entering the market?

7. Describe opportunities and risks for this venture based on your knowledge of the market so far.

8. How innovative is this project: a "me too" project, a development and improvement upon existing technology, or a completely new idea?

9. How would you define the sequence of customer importance and of market entry in this scenario?

10. Are there more criteria for further segmenting this market?

11. Do you recognize a systematic structure in the short-term development of these data?

12. Do you regard these projections as "best case" or "worst case"?

13. For each of the three phases, please answer the following two questions:

    a. What are the three most important things—good and bad—one can learn from Guillaume's experience?

    b. What would you have done if you were in his position?

Parsek LLC

New Venture Creation Process and Early Internationalization

Mateja Drnovšek

Introduction

"Would you like to have another drink?" a flight attendant asked two partners from the Parsek Group during a flight from Frankfurt to San Francisco. It was November 2005 when the two Parsek Group co-founders, Andrej and Matej, flew to visit their third partner, Aljosa, who had recently matriculated in the full-time MBA program at the Haas School of Business at the University of California at Berkeley. During the flight the two co-founders reflected on the past 7 years, which they had spent managing their young company. The company performed phenomenally in its first 7 years; it went from a four-person operation to a multimillion dollar media giant. With all the divisions operating at different stages, however, the founders faced an interesting challenge: How should they harness their core competencies and strength to devise a strategy that would bring their company to a new height?

Emergence of an Entrepreneurial Team

The Parsek Group illustrates the full story of creating a technology venture from its early beginnings in a university environment to the company's internationalization to the markets of Southern and Eastern Europe.

The Parsek story began when a group of undergraduate students worked together on a student project—journal KOLAP$ in one of the faculty of economics' research labs at the University of Ljubljana. The lab at that time was headed by a professor of entrepreneurship who generously supported entrepreneurial aspirations of students working in his lab. He provided various electronic gadgets and unlimited access to the Internet and computer hardware and software. The atmosphere in the lab saw the coming together of creativity and entrepreneurial spirit through organization of interdisciplinary panel discussions and conferences to meet important people from business, the academic world, and politics.

Students working in the lab gained their first business experiences by professionalizing processes of the KOLAP$ journal. However, the first real market opportunity for the team came with the idea of publishing a Yearbook of Classmates of their school. This was a novel idea—none of the schools in the University of Ljubljana had their own yearbook. This was a huge undertaking that involved collecting data and making a profile of some 8,000 students. Although the team initially did not have any financial resources to implement the idea, they organized a sales force of 20 students who were paid variable commissions for (1) selling advertising space in the yearbook to larger Slovenian companies and banks, and (2) selling the yearbooks in advance at a discount rate. In so doing the students managed to start the production and conclude the project with a profit without having to invest any of their own money.

The team's initial project of identifying a new opportunity was accomplished by leveraging the automated database-driven application they had developed. They transformed this application into an online version of the yearbook called Studenet, with numerous community portal features students could use. While working on the project, the entrepreneurial roles were assigned to the members of the founding team. As a successful entrepreneurial test, the project and its profit were compelling enough to found a company and face the challenge of commercially harnessing the opportunities they identified.

As enterprising students were approaching the formal end of their studies, their need for self-realization and autonomy grew stronger. At a certain point, they all agreed they could never work as hired employees for a larger organization. Becoming independent entrepreneurs was their envisioned career choice. That is how they decided to jointly incorporate their activities in 1999 with a minimum start-up capital of EUR 9,000. The activities of the start-up firm focused on the three industries the team felt they had some experiences in: advertising, publishing, and Web development. At that stage, only the founders were working in the company, with specific roles based on their personal capabilities and competencies. Given that the initial yearbook project proved successful in their school, they looked for new markets. The yearbook concept was spread to five other colleges and high schools. Overall, the initial yearbook project was successful and the founders felt the need to consolidate their business and focus on the new, related opportunities forthcoming with the advent of the Internet.

The available financial funds they had accumulated were not sufficient to cover the rent for business premises and basic technical equipment. To secure the technical resources needed, they initiated a partnership with a major Slovenian information technology company. Its CEO was a very charismatic leader and, as an entrepreneur, he understood how it felt to see an opportunity to have the drive but not the resources to seize it. He wanted to help the young entrepreneurial team, but not for free. He challenged the team with a problem he had in his own company. To enter into a new market segment of Internet service provision he needed a new product to sell bandwidth Internet access to the household market.

Responding to the challenge, the Parsek team developed a packaged software solution that enabled users to set up Internet access autonomously without support from a call center. Such a solution was a clear market innovation at that time. The product solution performed beyond expectations and the founders got their first insights into the real business world. In so doing they also developed a very broad range of skills and discovered their potential for solving complex problems. During this project others joined the start-up company.

The goal the team clearly set for themselves in the very beginning was to secure cash flow liquidity. To do so they mostly focused on acquiring projects from larger, blue-chip companies only, despite an obvious lack of experience and track record. Back then they knew how to use the foot-in-the-door strategy of extending a one-time order into a long-term relationship and leveraging it to develop new opportunities with the client, which among others included the largest Slovenian port authority and logistics provider, Slovenian branch of car maker Renault, and several others.

Building the Initial Market

When the start-up entered the market in 1999, the Slovenian information technology (IT) marketplace was growing fast even though an increasing number of companies provided Internet solutions. The first wave of firms entered the IT industry at the beginning of the 1990s as resellers of computer hardware. A wide majority of firms then diversified to grow in the local market; only a few went international. After 1995 the IT industry consisted of several niche subindustries, such as outsourcing, accounting software, system integration, and enterprise resource planning. But with only 2 million inhabitants, Slovenia is a small and secluded business community. Being young university students with no prior experiences and no social capital at that time seemed to be the major obstacle and barrier to market entry faced by the entrepreneurial team.

Through a successful implementation of their projects for important Slovenian companies, the founding team was confident they were on the right track to fulfil the vision they initially set when starting their company: "world domination." Seeing immense entrepreneurial opportunities that emerged in the global market at that time, the team started to question how they could internationalize. Against their most optimistic expectations they were very soon, in early 2000, offered external financing by a UK-based venture fund. Given the start-up's prior revenues of some US$100,000, the expected investment would reasonably amount to some multiples of that figure. Yet, the founders insisted they would not do a deal for less than US$2 million. This was a very bold expectation from young entrepreneurs, whose average age at the time was 24 years, with an unproven business concept. The founders were well aware of drawbacks of having a strategic investor in the firm—they would lose control over the firm and each founder would remain with a less than 5% stake. That they would now have to work on another person's account was threatening, because they understood that with any further capitalization of the firm, they could easily be left without important stakes and control in the company.

On the other hand, they could not deny obvious trends of where the world Internet industry was developing. The external financing would enable them to develop a concept of an Internet advertising network similar to DoubleClick and 24/7 Media to take on a market segment that had recently yielded the highest returns in the global IT industry. In addition, they needed to find a strong international partner to gain a critical push for growth and internationalizing the business. They all agreed that a private placement would enable them to start working on large projects because they would have enough resources to employ talented designers and engineers. In addition, by leveraging an external investor's social networks, they would have easy access to new customers in Slovenia and abroad.

In May 2000 Parsek received US$1.5 million in return for 76% equity stake in the start-up company. Besides receiving financial support, Parsek gained business networks from the venture capital financing and—most important—a strong impetus to professionalize the organizational structure of the company to correspond to a tighter growth agenda. The business strategy was revised to specialize in development of Internet technologies that were organized around two different divisions with specific focuses: interactive and media. After receiving a financial injection, the company grew at a rate of 35% per annum to expand its businesses into the neighboring region of Croatia, Bosnia, and Serbia by 2004.

Because of major structural changes in the organizational structure of the venture capital fund that provided initial financing, an opportunity to buy back their original shares in the company was soon offered to Parsek's founders. By the middle of 2005, the founders completed the transaction by executing management buyout.

The Growth Agenda

The company's growth largely depended on trends in the Internet industry in the region and broader. The initial growth was secured in the local market of Slovenia. The roots of the Internet industry in Slovenia emerged from an intertwinement of information technology (IT) and advertising industries. The approximate size of the Slovenian IT market as of 2006 was estimated at EUR 260 million, with about 40% of revenues in software and about 60% in hardware development with the average per annum growth at approximately 11%. The major competitors in the industry were system integrators, mostly large companies that sold hardware, provided networking and security, and usually represented a major software vendor (such as IBM, Microsoft, and Oracle) whose technology they implemented in their solutions. Other business opportunities in that segment included support software, video games, Internet banking, and lately, enterprise resource planning software for medium-sized companies. Currently, the advertising budget in Slovenia totals approximately EUR 130 million, with most important market players being traditionally organized advertising agencies.

Given the industry specifics, human resource related competencies required to successfully compete in this market segment include Web-savvy designers, interactive technologists, and math-minded media planners. Companies who are new entrants to the industry build from agile market approach, flexibility in customer relations management, open-source technologies, and "perpetual beta mentality," which is related to the frequency of updates and new application features. Table 1 summarizes the industry dynamics.

The industry dynamics and new entrepreneurial opportunities that were spotted indeed drove the start-up's strategic development to organize into divisions by 2004: Interactive, Professional IT Services, SME Solutions, and Media Business, with each of them having different growth opportunities internationally. Having the four core groups of products organized, Parsek targeted different layers of the business-to-business (B2B) Internet services related market and leveraged specific strengths and competencies within the company.

Similarly to many businesses in the Internet industry, the *Interactive* division provides interactive communications services and Web engineering. Development of corporate Web sites, portals, intranets, extranets, and online advertising campaigns require skills in Web design, copywriting, service innovation, convergence strategies development, and customer

Table 1 Industry and Competition in the Parsek's Divisions (in EUR)

Interactive	Ownership	1999	2000	2001	2002	2003	2004	2005
Top 3 competitors								
Hal	Independent	158	288	446	472	372	440	487
Renderspace	AA (acquired)	29	78	373	573	749	1.016	1.206
Innovatif	AA (acquired)		42	104	158	151	97	539
Total market size (combined revenue of 20 largest firms)		662	1.102	2.246	3.210	3.981	5.535	7.032
Professional IT Services	**Ownership**	**1999**	**2000**	**2001**	**2002**	**2003**	**2004**	**2005**
Top 3 competitors								
BuyITC	Independent			81	157	239	303	326
Trivium	Major agency						17	728
Ice	Independent		280	623	1.301	1.205	1.202	1.819
Total market size (combined revenue of 10 relevant firms)		n.a.	n.a.	8.170	9.988	11.290	13.331	14.704
SMEs Solutions	**Ownership**	**1999**	**2000**	**2001**	**2002**	**2003**	**2004**	**2005**
Top 3 competitors								
Celtic	Independent				0	20	44	108
Enki Storitve	Independent				99	41	52	98
Digital Team	Independent				54	102	71	63
Total market size (combined revenue of 10 relevant firms)		n.a.	n.a.	n.a.	307	331	405	778
Media / Slovenia	**Ownership**	**1999**	**2000**	**2001**	**2002**	**2003**	**2004**	**2005**
Top 3 competitors								
Iprom	Independent			51	83	158	266	347
Najdi Search	Independent				400	500	800	1.255
Other media	Media groups					200	400	600
Total market size (est.)				313	767	1.198	1.937	2.952

NOTES: AA—Advertising agency
n.a.—not available

SOURCE: Interpretation of Parsek Group Annual Report and publicly available financial reports, 2005.

relations support. Parsek's Interactive division usually works with marketing departments to accommodate their initiatives. The company's brand in this market segment was positioned as prestigious and above-market. Competitive strengths spring from its track record of continuous innovation, professional account and project management, synergies with online advertising handled by the media division, and high number of multinational corporate clients in the industry that are present in the local market.

Parsek initiated *Professional IT Services* in 2004 to serve larger companies. Those have typically larger budgets per project that need comprehensive support of their online businesses embedded to their central information system. Typical engagements in this segment include e-commerce implementations, enterprise application integration, and custom application development. Implementation of such projects is vital for customers because the projects usually involve developing software support and back-office solutions for financial transactions that are embedded within the customers' core processes. The most important customers in this sector are IT departments of big corporations and governmental institutions. Budget per project averages in the range of EUR 50,000 with an additional fee for maintenance costs. Parsek was able to commoditize some of its originally developed technologies and package them as industry-specific solutions. Hence, this contributed to the more than 80% market share of the online insurance market, which involves four major insurance companies in the country, with the same percentage of mobile operators using Parsek's e-commerce platform. The division also developed and now operates the leading online payment gateway in the country. Strengths of the division spring from a combination of technology and business knowledge, in-company competences in development of proprietary technologies, and good client management that shows itself in the level of service offered and proactive attitude toward customers.

The third division of the group specialized in the development of *Internet Solutions for SMEs* (small- and medium-sized enterprises). The leading brand of the division is EasyWeb. The EasyWeb entails a subscription-based service for bringing a client on the Internet. Standardized process of customization makes the service cheap and affordable to the customers. Furthermore, by giving up exclusivity of Web design, the customers get a best practice solution with no up-front fees at low prices. They can pick among different design schemes, service packages, and subscription models. Other services includes server hosting, after-sales customer support, and upgrading possibilities that match the growth of clients' businesses. Examples of subscription services include e-presence, e-customer relationship management, and similar applications. Typical customers of the division are SMEs, such as service and manufacturing companies, sole-proprietorships, and crafts shops.

Parsek Group entered online *Media Business* by launching its subsidiary Httpool in 2000. The market at that time was underdeveloped; there were only a few relevant commercial online media with tiny advertising budgets and only a 12% user penetration. Httpool implemented world standard DoubleClick technology, replicated its Internet advertising network model, set standards, and educated marketers and advertising agencies. This was the foundation needed to internationalize company activities. After 5 years of market presence, Httpool became the major online advertising provider, representing 50 out of the top 100 online publishers, serving clients with media planning, media buying, ad distribution, optimization, and reporting. The most important customers include advertising agencies and media buyers representing thousands of small- and medium-sized firms that have slowly started to switch their budgets from mass media to more targeted forms of advertising.

Figure 1 depicts the business structure in the Parsek Group, and Table 2 overviews each division's revenues.

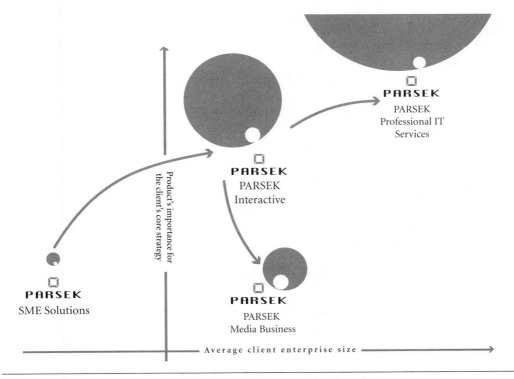

Figure 1   Synergies Among the Four Divisions of the Parsek Group

NOTE: White bubble: estimated market share of Parsek Group
         Gray bubble: total market

SOURCE: Parsek Group Annual Report, 2005

Table 2   Revenues per Division in the Parsek Group (in 000 EUR)

Parsek Group	Year of Start	1999	2000	2001	2002	2003	2004	2005	2006*
Interactive	1999	80	233	313	405	518	589	654	800
Professional IT Services	2004						218	212	320
Media Business	2001			262	284	518	741	1.251	1.865
Slovenia	2001			262	284	340	472	750	1.013
Croatia	2003					178	269	464	649
Bosnia	2005							30	68
Serbia	2005							3	80
Macedonia	2005							4	55
SME Solutions	2004						28	67	133
Total		80	233	575	689	1.036	1.576	2.184	3.118

NOTE: 2006*—projection

SOURCE: Parsek Group Annual Report, 2005

GROWTH THROUGH INTERNATIONALIZATION

Having the company organized into several divisions with varied growth potential driven by industry development, the company was set to embrace international challenges, with each division attacking different international markets and pursuing different growth-related goals.

Key elements of their internationalization strategy included

1. rigorous selection of local partners based on established market position;

2. building a strong client base by leveraging local networks and clients; and

3. purposeful development of capabilities, connections, and credibility to secure a long-term position.

The highest international growth potential that the company had was in the Internet media business market, locally and internationally. The growth of this market was largely dependent on the growth pace of the Slovenian online advertising market, which grew at 45% average annual rate, reaching EUR 2.5 million or 1.5% of total advertising expenditures of companies in 2005.

The expected growth is projected at EUR 10 million of online advertising budgets, or 5% of total advertising, by 2010. In the same period, online penetration has increased to over 50% of the Slovenian population, due to many new local online media and accessible broadband connections, positioning Internet as a "must be" media in the media mix. The competitive landscape is similar in the former Yugoslavian markets. The major differences are less competition, lower expected user penetration, and less developed advertising markets, with the exception of the Croatian market, which follows almost the same growth patterns that are identified in the Slovenian market. The perceived prospects of entering this market segment through Httpool activities (based on DoubleClick technology acquired through venture capital financing) were high.

Httpool as an independent business was incubated within the Interactive division. The opportunity for establishing this division emerged out of need, because Parsek Group was losing customers in the interactive Web development business, of which major competitors were advertising agencies. Those agencies perceived Parsek's media business as competitive, and as a remedy they directed their customers to other Web developing companies. Parsek realized the need to spin off the business with a separate and independent branding from the core business. Given that Httpool established its dominant position locally based on first mover advantage, investment in top-notch technology and know-how, those were competencies which could be easily replicated in new markets. Tactically speaking, new international markets were entered by a careful analysis of market conditions and key local players with an ambition of finding synergies among markets and the most appropriate partners for establishing joint ventures. Because of the key importance of social capital in those markets, the most viable market entry strategy for a smaller company was organic growth through partnering local firms. They provided strong local intertwinement and proven management teams and shared administrative, legal, and other support costs. Moreover, partnering with leading local Web developers provided strong mutual synergies, access to local clients from the very start, and strengthened both partners' positions in the market.

Speaking geographically, business was first expanded to the neighboring country of Croatia, followed by Httpool Bosnia and Httpool Serbia and Macedonia in 2005 (see Figure 2). All the subsidiaries were locally introduced successfully and gained leadership positions from the start. This was followed by a pan-European marketing initiative through partnerships with leading European Internet advertising networks to participate in activities and support client's promotional activities abroad.

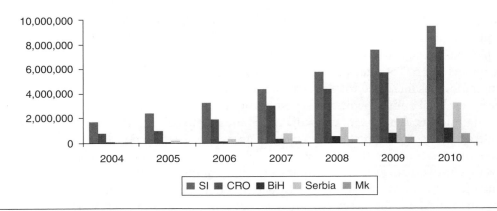

Figure 2   Expected Regional Market Growth in the Media Industry (in EUR)

SOURCE: www.gzs.si/katalogi/zacetna_stran_kataloga.asp?kat=037 and primary research

Other Parsek divisions had a less obvious growth potential through internationalization activities and relied more on diversifying in different local markets. By 2006 the Interactive division was meeting fierce competition in their market niche. Although the overall revenue in the industry was still increasing, one obvious sign of market maturity was reflected by strong trends of industry concentration in 2007. The most recent market trends have opened new opportunities for incumbents as well as newcomers because the necessary skill set required to compete successfully is now significantly different from the pure advertising business. The highest budgets are provided by regional branches of international corporations and large local corporations. This customer group's strongest motivations are financial and leverage.

The professional IT services market segment was entered because of technology reasons. The Web industry is currently being reinvented through the Web 2.0 paradigms, which signals maturity of the technology as an enterprise application platform. Companies are therefore evaluating hybrid Web frameworks as their new strategic environments require outside professional help to either implement next generation commercial technologies or to build proprietary open-source based solutions. Parsek identified opportunities for development of new products in new market segments by development of partially customized solutions (i.e., back-office solutions) for corporate customers. The company realized that the approach to the Internet should be built from a company-level perspective. Such new opportunities, which offer diversification possibilities, can be reacted upon because of a combination of technology and business knowledge, and in-company competences in development of proprietary technologies.

MARKET / BUSINESS	PRESENT	NEW
PRESENT	Interactive	Httpool SLO
NEW	SMEs Solutions Httpool	Professional IT Services

Figure 3   Ansoff Matrix of Business Development in the Parsek Group, 2000–2005

SOURCE: Author's interpretation

Finally, although the product group of *SME Solutions* emerged in response to a recognized need for online presence by SMEs, there was also a clear international potential through a development of a franchisee business in that product group. Similar global online services involve, for example, a Template Monster. The opportunity to develop EasyWeb business came with Parsek's brand recognition in the interactive industry, which was motivated by the demand from small- and medium-sized companies. Such an automated approach to Web development would also allow Parsek to disrupt the increasingly competitive lower segment of the market and could serve as a foot-in-the-door sales tactic for companies unwilling to pay premium prices. With general growth of the small-sized firm sector, the market opportunity is growing as well. This market segment also offered high possibilities of expansion to other emerging markets.

In summary, business development within the Parsek Group focused on the market as well as on new product development between 2000 and 2005, locally as well as internationally, which is illustrated in Figure 3. Because Parsek primarily targeted emerging markets, its growth strategies included substantial investments in building the market through their potential customers' awareness, which was raised through a personalized approach—aggressive sales with abundance of free service. The costs of new client acquisitions in such markets are initially high and decrease over time. In addition, an overall approach to acquiring new customers could be illustrated through the use of foot-in-the-door strategies to win important business contracts and dumping pricing policies in acquisition of public tenders. Another specific of entering Southern and Eastern European markets is that successful entry depends on breadth and strength of social networks rather than technological and market sophistication of the product.

Future Challenges

The future development of Parsek is based on strong product development activities as well as building social networks. In case of the latter, one of the founders identified this as an important asset and, with that purpose in mind, has recently started Young Executives Society network (YES). The organization became a highly prominent club for executives younger than 40 years old in building trust and facilitating business making among themselves. Pursuit of international growth strategy also included development of human resource competencies to provide operational support, which strongly affected the bottom line. The majority of new opportunities exploited were incubated within its existing operations. For example, professional IT services opportunities emerged within interactive engagements where there were frequent encounters with client's top management during sales activities. Founders were able to use such opportunities to present IT related initiatives and were able to win IT contracts from clients directly through top management, given their interest in final results rather than in the industry standards. Hence, the entrenched and conservative IT departments were bypassed. This was facilitated by a highly capable and motivated core development team. In parallel, the company developed a proprietary software platform whose product nature proved to be another strong sales point. Here there were even larger commitments to the quality of projects, so the clients were usually happy to find that the projects were delivered at fixed cost.

Given that the markets the Parsek Group is currently serving are heterogeneous and at different life cycle stages, the competitive strengths required are varied and technology changes are unpredictable. This opens numerous challenges for designing the company's future growth strategy.

What strategic alternatives are they confronting? Should they focus on the strategies of internal growth, such as organic growth in their interactive markets by market penetration through market consolidation and improved long-term agreements with existing and new clients? Should they diversify the interactive business to neighboring regions of the former Yugoslavia, Italy, and Austria? Or rather, why not develop agency businesses by entering into partnership with one of the leading new European search portals? Should they foster their international orientation by

People—"The law of crappy people" (the worst employee at any level becomes the de facto standard for that level)

Freedom—"That stimulates creativity and innovation"

Action—"To influence our dreams"

Beauty—"Taste is the enemy of creativeness" (Picasso)

Technology—"New is better"

Fun at work—"Improves the mojo, but not the bottom line"

Hard work—"Mandatory all-nighters"

Figure 4   Parsek's Value System

opening a spin-off company overseas to capitalize on the technology they developed, which needs to be marketed? Finally, there is opportunity to develop traditional advertising agency services as well. A viable external growth strategy may also result from consolidating their market position in the local market.

Like every entrepreneurial venture, the past, present, and future Parsek story will be greatly influenced by its people. The key human resource in the past was the founding team. Besides the founding team, several other individuals contributed to the development of the business. The company's value system (see Figure 4) is represented by people, the need for freedom, and the creative engagement of every individual, along with a passion for technology and beauty.

Case Questions

1. What factors contributed to the entrepreneurial event? What was the entrepreneurship opportunity?

2. What tangible and intangible assets did the founders invest in Parsek when starting their company? How did they meet their resource needs?

3. What were the risks the founders faced in the first year of operation? How did they control and overcome them?

4. Should the founding team have taken the money offered by the private investor? How should the company orient itself for future growth?

5. What differences exist in the marketing of high-tech products versus the marketing of other goods? Can you identify specific challenges in marketing high-tech products internationally?

6. Which marketing strategies has Parsek employed so far? Do you believe these strategies will be reasonable in the future, given the industry trends? What international marketing strategies would you suggest Parsek use in the future?

Beijing Sammies

This case was prepared by Christopher Ferrarone under the supervision of Boston College Professor Gregory L. Stoller as the basis for class discussion rather than to illustrate either effective or ineffective handling of an administrative situation.

When Sam Goodman opened a new Sammies cafe in Beijing's Motorola Building, he cut prices by 50% for the first 3 months to attract customers. The initial period was very successful, but when he returned prices to normal, sales dropped dramatically and fell short of targets. The local store manager, when presenting the figures, suggested that Goodman simply lower the sales targets. Goodman was frustrated; the manager had failed to address any of the issues that were keeping customers from returning. There were countless orders that went out with missing utensils, in the wrong bag, or [with items] simply left out. Delivery orders were being sent hours late or to the wrong location. This typified Goodman's early experience; the market was showing interest in Beijing Sammies' products, but he knew that without exceptional service, good food would not be enough. Goodman questioned whether he could find employees who were thinkers and problem solvers, and he wondered how to improve upon the business to turn Beijing Sammies into a sustainable and profitable enterprise.

According to Goodman, face and money were the two most important subjects. With experience as a student and businessman in China, he knew one must observe the cultural beliefs.

> Face is a huge issue here, and as the economy develops, so is money. If one is not relevant, the other is. Once you recognize this is crucial, it is not hard to learn. The difficult part is incorporating it into the business. We need to offer a superior experience in order for customers to justify paying more. This means providing a quality product with excellent service. It sounds easy, but in China the concept of service is not the same as in the West. I just can't seem to get my employees to understand that there is a way to serve the customer while also keeping the company's interest at heart. It is an "all for us" or "all for them" mentality here.

Throughout the company's initial years, Goodman sought to teach a service-oriented approach to his employees. In doing so, he ironically learned that face was as much of an important issue for Beijing Sammies' customers as it was for its employees.

Beijing Sammies

Canadian native Sam Goodman started Beijing Sammies in 1997. Aside from producing food for the everyday, walk-in customer, Sammies provided fare for company meetings, presentations, picnics, and gifts. Sammies was open for breakfast, lunch, and dinner and delivered all products to its customers. The menu included a selection of sandwiches, salads, bagels, brownies, cookies, coffee, soda, and tea (Figure 1).

Goodman started the company with personal savings and money borrowed from family. He opened his first cafe at the Beijing Language and Culture University with the goal of providing people with a place to hang out and enjoy homemade Western food.

By 2003 Beijing Sammies had five outlets composed of four deli-style cafes and one kiosk. The stores followed traditional layout and size for fast food restaurants. Two Sammies cafes were 1,200 square feet and the other two were roughly 800 square feet each. The kiosk was a stand-alone structure with open seating inside the lobby of a corporate building. All the cafe locations had enclosed seating that was maximized because there was no need for self-contained kitchens.

THE CENTRAL KITCHEN

Goodman found that revenues of the first cafe were driven as much by corporate delivery orders as they were by local walk-in customers. This motivated Goodman to open more cafes and a centralized kitchen in 1998. Located in Beijing's Chao Yang District, the kitchen ran from 10:00 p.m. to 5:30 a.m. each day, making the sandwiches and baked goods for all Sammies locations. Between 5:30 and 6:00 a.m., trucks delivered the goods from the kitchen to each Sammies outlet. No cooking was done at any of the Sammies locations. Every sandwich, cookie, and muffin was prepared, baked, and packaged centrally. Only coffee and smoothies were prepared onsite at individual retail cafes.

The central kitchen created a number of efficiencies for Beijing Sammies, but what Goodman liked even more was the quality control that it provided.

It is much easier for me to teach the kitchen staff how to make the food correctly than it is to teach all the employees at each location. At the kitchen

I can make sure that the product going out to all the stores is consistent. In the end that's what I am striving for: to offer a consistently great product with superior service. Only having one kitchen to manage makes this task much easier.

The central kitchen not only provided Beijing Sammies with efficient use of ingredients, machines, and manpower, but also allowed for larger customer capacity at each cafe location and enabled the employees to uniquely focus on customer service.

THE SAMMIE

The idea behind Beijing Sammies originated from Goodman. Moving to Hong Kong after college and subsequently moving to Beijing to attend Beijing Language and Culture University, Goodman yearned for a place to hang out and eat a traditional sandwich or "sammie" that reminded him of home. Three years later Beijing Sammies was named Beijing's #1 Western food delivery service by *City Weekend* magazine.

Modeled after Goodman's version of a New York deli, Beijing Sammies' staple is the sammie. Each sammie started with homemade bread made every night at Sammies' kitchen. Customers could order from a menu of standard sammies or could create their own. Goodman found the preset menu best for local customers, whereas many foreigners frequently customized their sandwich.

Having a menu of pre-crafted sandwiches is a necessity. Many Chinese customers simply do not know how to order. They do not understand the notion of selecting different types of deli meats and condiments for a sandwich. I didn't even think about this at first. Personally, I know exactly what goes with roast beef and what goes with turkey.

When we opened our first location many people came in and left without ordering. They didn't know how and did not want to look foolish ordering something inappropriate. Many times, and this still happens, people come in and just order whatever the person in front of them ordered. Putting complete sandwiches together allows the inexperienced customer to come in and feel more comfortable about ordering.

Creating pre-made selections of sandwiches worked so well for Sammies that Goodman put together an "Ordering Tips" section on the menu. The section not only suggested what types of products to order for breakfast and what products to buy for lunch, but also provided a guide for corporate clients to ensure correct portions and variety for meetings. In addition, Sammies trained sales clerks to act as customer service representatives who could assist both the walk-in client and a growing base of corporate delivery clients with their orders.

Exhibit 1

Ordering Information

Min Order:	PEAK HOURS: 100rmb	(Mon-Fri:10:30-13:30)
	OTHER HOURS: 50rmb	

Orders under 50 rmb: add 20 rmb service charge

Free delivery within Chao Yang CBD

Delivery takes 30-45 minutes during rush hours

For large orders or special time deliveries
please call 1 day in advance

Save Your Company Time & Money

Sammies Corporate Accounts

Convenience & Flexibility in
Payment, Ordering & Delivery

Sammies is a healthy alternative for your

Meetings o Seminars o Training Sessions

We provide menu suggestions.

For more information, special requests or
comments please call Customer Service:
English and Chinese service

6506 8838

www.beijingsammies.com

All prices subject to change.
Ingredients may change due to availability and freshness

Where East Eats West

CORPORATE DELIVERY

Monday - Friday:	8:00 a.m.-9:00 p.m.
Saturday - Sunday:	9:00 a.m.-7:00 p.m.

TEL: 6506 8838   FAX: 6503 2688

Online Ordering: www.beijingsammies.com

Breakfast & Lunch Meetings o Training Sessions

Where East Eats West

Exhibit 1

Baked Goods & Snacks

All baked goods are made with our original recipes and baked on
the premises, fresh everyday.

Bagels Plain, Sesame and Cinnamon Raisin	4
Cream Cheese (70g)	7
Strawberry Preserves (70g)	5
Freshly Baked Mini Muffins Apple Cinnamon Raisin, Banana Walnut, Banana Chocolate, Chocolate Chip, Plain, Whole Wheat Raisin,	3
Homemade Cookies Chocolate Chunk, Double Chocolate, Mom's Oatmeal Raisin Lg.	6
Chocolate Brownies	8
Biscotti Toasted Almond, Chocolate Chip	4
Cheese Cake 12 Pieces	180
Chocolate Cake 12 Pieces	180
(Please specify if you would like your dessert presliced or whole.)	
Potato Chips	10

Beverages

Apple Juice	Coke	
Orange Juice	Diet Coke	
Grape Juice 10	Sprite	
	Fanta	
	Mineral Water 8	

Breakfast or Brunch

Relax with a Sammies' breakfast brought to your door.

Bagels, Muffins, Cream Cheese, Butter, Strawberry Preserves,
Tuna Salad, Egg Salad, Chicken Salad, Pasta Salad, Garden Salad

Continental: Your choice of 2 Bagels, 2 Muffins and 2 Spreads	20
Executive: Your choice of 2 Bagels, 2 Muffins, 2 Spreads and 2 Salads	40
The Feast: Your choice of 3 Bagels, 2 Muffins, 2 Spreads, 3 Salads and a juice	60

Exhibit 1

Sammie Packs

When ease and efficiency are the names of the game, these packs hit the spot. No need to ask everyone what they want, variety will take care of that. Sammies are cut into 1/4's for convenience.

GOOD FOR 6~8 PERSONS, EACH PACK COMES WITH VEGGIES N' DIP.

Predator Pack
For meat lovers with healthy appetites! Dante's Inferno, Classic Grilled Chicken and Frankenstein. (2 of each) ·········· 160

Classic Favorites
Deliciously simple and filling! Classic Turkey, Ham n' Cheese and Poseidon's Pleasure. (2 of each) ·········· 160

The Conglomerate
An assortment to suit all! Classic Roast Beef, Funky Chicken, Turkey Shoot, Homestead, Poseidon's Pleasure, Garden Special ·········· 160

Vegetarian
Healthy and loaded with taste! Poseidon's Pleasure, Early Bird, and Veggies n' Cheese (2 of each) ·········· 150

Bakery Bundles

Sammies selection of freshly baked goods, great for any occasion; meetings, boosting staff morale, customer gifts, picnics or parties. Guaranteed to bring a smile to anyone's face.

Muffin Madness A satisfying breakfast or afternoon treat!
Includes all 6 varieties of Sammies' original recipe muffins. 18 small — 55

Cookie Monster Sammies' freshly baked, original recipe cookies!
Includes Chocolate Chunk, Double Chocolate and Oatmeal Raisin.
18 regular ·········· 55

The Bagel Bag Baked fresh everyday. Plain, Sesame & Cinnamon
Raisin (2 of each) whole or cut in half, served with cream cheese (140g),
strawberry preserves (70g) and butter ·········· 40

W.O.F.E (Warm Oven Fresh Eats) For meetings, after lunch, or anytime
of the day, this box suits all tastes! Includes 2 Brownies(cut into 1/4),
8 mini-muffins, 6 regular cookies and 2 Biscottis ·········· 65

Box Lunches

Great for meetings, bus tours, travelling, picnics and parties !

Classic Box ·········· 40	Health Box ·········· 40
Your choice of sammie	Your choice of sammie
Potato Chips	Veggies & Dip
Lg. Chocolate Chunk Cookie	Lg. Oatmeal Raisin Cookie

Exhibit 1

Sammies

The foundation of a perfect sammie is our homemade bread.
Choose White or Whole Wheat. All sammies are prepared
fresh throughout the day and can be made to suit your tastes.

Classic Sammies

Classic Roast Beef Edam cheese, lettuce, tomatoes, onions
w/ mustard and/or mayo ·········· 25

Classic Ham n' Cheese Edam cheese, lettuce, tomatoes, onions
w/ mustard and/or mayo ·········· 25

Classic Turkey Edam cheese, lettuce, tomatoes, onions
w/ mustard and/or mayo ·········· 25

Classic Grilled Chicken Edam cheese, lettuce, tomatoes, onions
w/ mustard and/or mayo ·········· 25

Poseidon's Pleasure Tuna, Cheddar cheese, lettuce, tomatoes,
onions, your choice of dressing ·········· 25

The Sunday Picnic Chicken salad, Edam cheese, lettuce,
tomatoes, onions, green peppers with Italian dressing ·········· 25

The Early Bird Cheddar cheese, egg salad, lettuce, tomatoes,
onions,with your choice of dressing ·········· 20

Veggies n'Cheese Cheddar cheese, tomatoes, onions, cucumbers,
green pepper, pickles, with your choice of dressing ·········· 20

Specialty Sammies

Dante's Inferno Seasoned roast beef, Cheddar cheese, lettuce,
onions, hot peppers, with spicy mustard and spicy tomato dressing ·········· 25

The Turkey Shoot Smoked turkey, Edam cheese, lettuce, tomatoes,
green peppers, pickles, with Sammies' spicy mustard and mayo ·········· 25

The Homestead Cooked ham, Edam cheese, lettuce, onions, cucumbers,
w/ Sammies' honey mustard ·········· 25

Deano Spambeano Grilled chicken breast, salami, pepperoni, Cheddar
cheese, onions, green peppers, black olives, with Creamy Italian ·········· 25

Frankenstein Smoked turkey, ham, roast beef, Cheddar cheese,
lettuce, tomatoes, onions, black olives, with mustard and mayo ·········· 25

The Funky Chicken Spicy grilled chicken, lettuce, tomatoes, onions,
w/ mustard and mayo ·········· 25

The Garden Special Grilled eggplant, zucchini, peppers, onions,
Cheddar cheese, lettuce, cucumbers, with your choice of dressing ·········· 20

Choose from our wide variety of dressings:

Mayonnaise	Mustard	Light Vinaigrette	1000 Island
Honey Mustard	Creamy Italian	Spicy Mustard	French Garlic

Salads

Our light, tasty salads are a healthy choice to help energize your day!
Includes Sammies' fresh bread and your choice of dressings.

Garden Salad
Fresh lettuce, cucumbers, zucchini,
tomatoes, carrots, and green
peppers ·········· 12

Add two scoops of your favorite
Chicken, Egg or Tuna ·········· 23

Pasta Salad
Spiral pasta, red and green peppers,
onions, celery and carrots ·········· 14

Add two scoops of your favorite
Chicken, Egg or Tuna ·········· 25

Veggies n' Dip
Carrot, celery and cucumber
sticks. A nice, healthy snack
with Italian Dressing ·········· 10

Figure 1   Beijing Sammies Menu

CORPORATE CLIENTS AND SAMMIES REWARDS

As Beijing Sammies realized a growing corporate delivery base, Goodman adapted the model to provide the business client with as much flexibility and customization as possible. Sammies set up corporate accounts, online ordering, flexible payment options, and a rewards program.

Corporate customers who registered with Beijing Sammies could choose weekly or monthly payment terms whereby Beijing Sammies would send out itemized statements and invoices. Clients could choose to set up a debit account as well. Under the debit account, clients prepaid a certain amount (usually a minimum of RMB1000[1]) that was credited to an account and deducted each time an order was placed.

Along with flexible payment options, corporate customers could become enrolled in the Bonus Points program, which offered credits based on the frequency and size of orders. Customers who spent between RMB500 and 750 received an RMB50 credit; orders between RMB750 and 1000, an RMB75 credit; and orders over RMB1000 were given an RMB100 credit. Furthermore, each time a client cumulatively spent over RMB5000 they were rewarded with an RMB500 credit. All of this could be done over the Beijing Sammies Web site, www.beijingsammies.com, where customers could log in and manage their account (Figure 2).

The Bonus Points program was offered to walk-in customer as well. Customers who registered with Beijing Sammies online could become enrolled in the program. Every registered customer received a point for each RMB they spent. Every 10 points could be redeemed for RMB1 off the next order. Extra points could be received for filling out surveys, referring new customers, or attending selected special events. The point system was well received by Beijing Sammies' customers and contributed to a solid base of returning foreign clients (Figure 3).

CHARITY SPONSORSHIP

Beijing Sammies served large numbers of foreigners, and consequently, Goodman felt a strong responsibility to sponsor charity, youth, and community events focused around the expatriate community in Beijing.

The Canadian community in Beijing and around China in general is pretty strong. As a foreign student here I really appreciated the sense of kinship that I felt even though I was far away from home. In addition, the foreign businesses and tourists have been very supportive of Beijing Sammies, so I really enjoy and feel compelled to participate in the community's events.

---

1. Conversion rate is RMB8.3 = US$1.

Exhibit 2
Beijing Sammies Introductory Email

```
OUR NEW SILK ALLEY SAMMIES CAFE IS
ALSO OPEN! Drop on by to enjoy
some of your Sammies favorite...and
more!

**Enjoy our wider breakfast selection

**Choose from cafe beverages and goodies

**Select from smoothies, espresso, cappuccinos,
and our selection of baked goods

**Warm, inviting cafe atmosphere - whether
you're networking, on a date, getting a meal-to-go
or getting social, Sammies Xiu Shui Jie cafe is the
place to be!

Located at the Silk Alley / Xiu Shui Jie south
entrance on Chang An Jie, in the Chaoyang District;
open every day from 07:30 to 24:00.


**WHERE EAST EATS WEST**


====================
**THANKS FOR REGISTERING! NOW YOU CAN
ORDER ALL YOUR SAMMIES FAVORITES
THROUGH THE WEB! Browse online and order
our delicious Sammies sandwiches, salads,
baked goods including muffins, cookies, brownies,
biscotti, and bagels. Great for business meetings,
social events, breakfast, lunch, or dinner!
Registration allows you to enjoy the following:


***SAVE TIME***
One-time registration of delivery information -
no need to re-explain your contact info at
every order.

Just login, order, and then submit for successful
delivery every time you come to the Web site.
```

Figure 2   Beijing Sammies Introductory E-mail   (*Continued*)

```
***SAVE MONEY***
Bonus points for future discounts -
sign up and receive bonus points based
on every RMB you order, which you can
redeem for future discounts and
Sammies products.



***IMPROVED EFFICIENCY***
Online ordering and delivery- Order directly
from our Web site menu and we'll deliver
to you!

***CUSTOM-MADE ORDERS***
Customize your Sammies, and track your
orders with our new menu and online ordering
interface.



***RE-ORDER YOUR FAVORITES***
Quick ordering of your favorite Sammies items -
registered users can re-order from a recorded
list of past favorite orders.



***ORDER 24 HOURS A DAY***
Order hours or days in advance.
====================


Questions? Please email our helpful customer service
staff at beijingsammies@yahoo.com. Tell a friend to
visit us at www.beijingsammies.com!
```

Figure 2   (Continued)

Along with providing snacks and food, Beijing Sammies helped certain organizations by allowing promotional and ticket sale efforts to be staged from Sammies' locations. Sammies' sponsorship events included.

- Special Olympics
- Canadian Day and Independence Day

- Nokia China Investment
- U.S.A. Embassy
- Canada Embassy
- Intel PRC, Corp.
- Boeing
- AEA SOS
- American Chamber of Commerce
- Agilent
- Andersen Consulting
- Australia Embassy
- APCO Associates Inc.
- Benz
- Ford Foundation
- Henkel
- Hewlett Packard
- IBM China Co., Ltd.
- Motorola China Electronics, Ltd.
- Western Academy of Beijing
- Reuters

Figure 3   Corporate Clients

- Sporting and school events held by the Western Academy of Beijing and The International School of Beijing
- Annual Terry Fox Run for Cancer
- ACBC baseball events

Sammies' Evolution

Starting out with $25,000 borrowed from friends and family back in Canada, Goodman opened Beijing's first sandwich shop. To more easily get past the bureaucracy involved with opening the cafe, Goodman located a Chinese partner. After an initial 4 months of business, Beijing Sammies was a hit. The store was so successful that the new partner attempted to strong-arm Goodman out of the company by locking him out. In response, Goodman rallied some friends and broke into the shop one night and removed the appliances and supplies. The partner agreed to be bought out.

Soon after Goodman regained control, his landlord disappeared. The government demanded the tenants cover his back taxes. When they could not, it demolished the whole row and left the tenants with the bricks. Goodman was able to sell them for $25.

Goodman responded by opening a cafe at the Beijing Language and Culture University. Again, Sammies opened to a steady stream of customers, particularly foreign students and local corporations. In 1998, after realizing success with the first cafe in its newfound location, Goodman found another business partner. Together they planned to invest another US$350,000 into Beijing Sammies. The next step was to build a centralized kitchen and add more cafe locations. Soon after construction started, however, the funds supposedly coming from the newfound business partner quickly dried up and Goodman was left financing the new kitchen on his own.

At the end of 1998, Sammies had a central kitchen with great capacity but no new store locations to deliver to. Goodman was able to generate yet another round of financing. With some western investment and all the profits from his previous 2 years in business, Goodman was able to put US$150,000 together and open three new cafes.

In addition to the first cafe located at Beijing Language and Culture University, Sammies cafes were opened between 1998 and 2001 at the Silk Alley Market, 1/F Exchange Beijing, and The Motorola Building. A Sammies kiosk was also opened at the China Resource Building (Figure 4). The expansion allowed Goodman to more adequately serve the Beijing area while also firmly establishing Beijing Sammies in an increasingly competitive environment.

> Overall, I see the expansion into multiple cafes as a success. Two of the cafes are doing well while the two others have not met sales targets yet. The kiosk, because of less rent, is doing moderately well but is still not as busy as I'd like it to be. 2002 looks to be our best year to date with a revenue increase of 54%, and an operating profit of $20,000. However, due to the fact that the central kitchen is its own cost center, we will record a $24,000 loss (including depreciation). 2003 should show our first profits.

By the end of 2001, Beijing Sammies was recording monthly revenues over RMB500,000 and by 2003 the company had recorded positive net income in certain months (Figure 5).

Exhibit 4

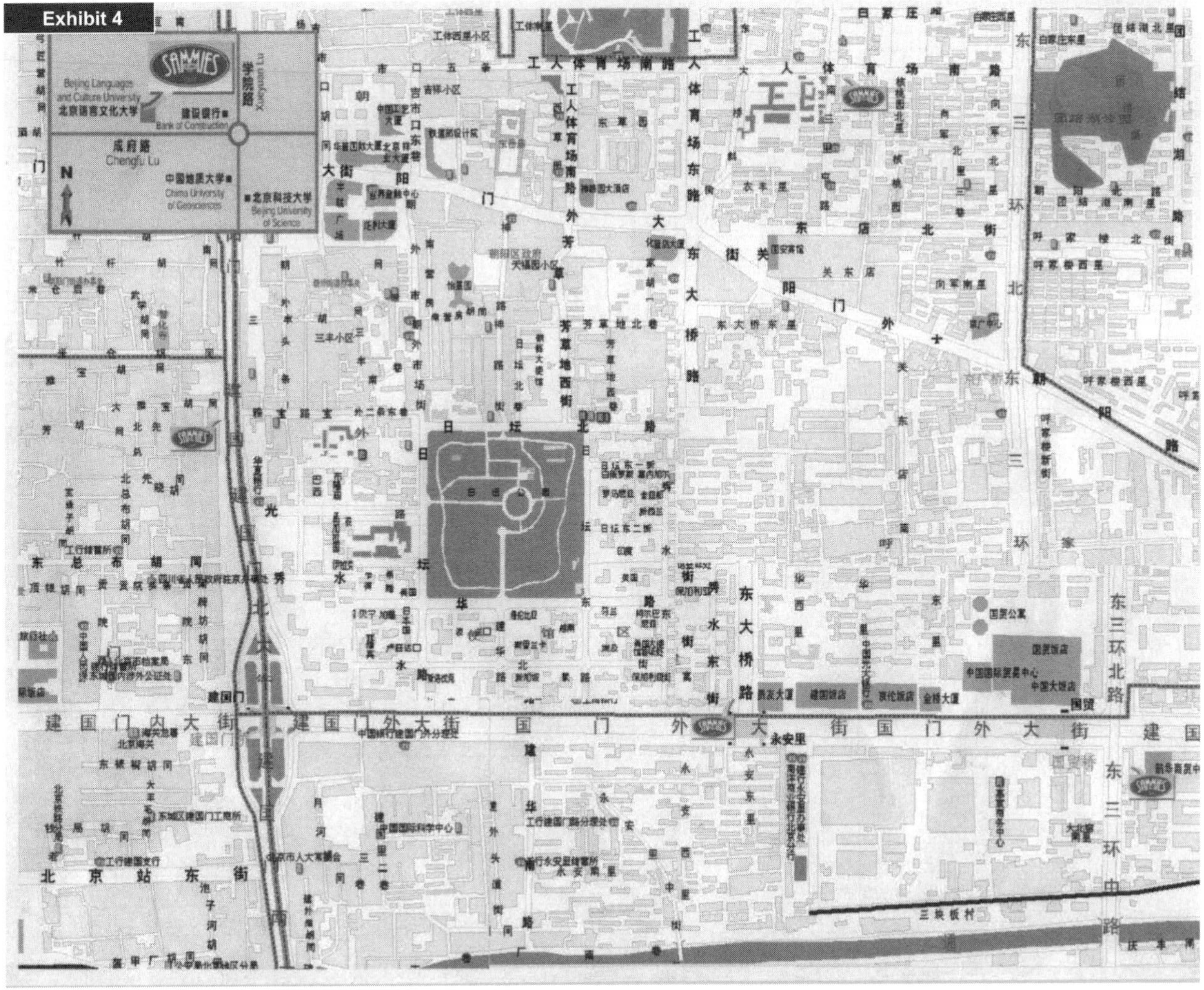

Figure 4 Beijing Sammies Locations

Exhibit 5: Income Statement

Beijing Sammies	Kitchen Office	Kitchen Production	Kitchen Delivery	Kitchen Café	BY Café	SA Café	CR Café	EB Café	2002YTD	
									RMB	US$
										0.120479942 conversion factor
Revenues			2,007,921.19		1,562,707.90	2,413,590.26	253,667.83	308,161.39	6,546,048.56	788,667.55
Cost of goods sold	17,886.73		641,106.51		458,643.00	660,387.10	85,284.58	116,182.07	1,979,489.98	238,488.84
Gross profit	-17,886.73		1,366,814.68		1,104,064.90	1,753,203.15	168,383.25	191,979.32	4,566,558.58	550,178.71
Gross margin			68.07%		70.65%	72.64%	66.38%	62.30%	69.76%	69.76%
Taxes	8,983.00		99,884.24		26,129.18	126,258.34	8,716.06	15,408.20	285,379.02	34,382.45
Salary	583,260.12	308,911.56	267,225.53		295,125.60	280,945.80	43,670.25	90,302.94	1,869,441.80	225,230.24
Insurance	57,067.01	24,131.97			12,160.29	6,641.12	2,151.96		102,152.34	12,307.31
Rent related	185,246.10	102,917.10	82,331.60	41,165.80	104,000.00	585,000.00	28,199.80	85,322.84	1,214,183.23	146,284.73
Utilities	38,075.39	41,237.04	22,891.23	2,531.10	45,492.79	7,103.90	7,587.91	6,598.31	171,517.66	20,664.44
Office expenses	131,989.31	445.38	5,750.55		4,298.84	14,296.32	3,451.76	17,737.90	177,970.07	21,441.82
Marketing/advertising	29,687.74		25,129.00		18,306.60	41,151.07	17,203.88	43,155.50	174,633.78	21,039.87
Transportation	37,798.57	256.75	20,545.85		4,286.23	743.60		237.90	63,868.90	7,694.92
Maintenance	68,965.65	6,357.00	1,560.00		12,139.01	21,128.90	1,843.40	1,625.00	113,618.96	13,688.81
Entertainment	16,660.54	1,033.50	2,388.10		6,477.25	1,123.20		789.10	28,471.69	3,430.27
Law and other expenses	47,623.29								47,623.29	5,737.65
Bank charges	-91.60					-103.48	7.15	39.00	-148.93	-17.94
Other	1,238.08	5,987.22	10,414.69		6,236.88	4,112.19	250.76	43.63	28,283.44	3,407.59
Hr	8,580.00								8,580.00	1,033.72
Legal/gov't charge	33,566.00					533.00			34,099.00	4,108.25
Low cost and short-lived articles	14,581.58	21,594.56	4,869.28		5,411.90	2,859.58		13,277.94	62,594.84	7,541.42
Ck service fee	-327,302.43		100,396.06		78,135.40	120,679.51	12,683.40	15,408.07		
Total expenses	935,928.34	512,872.07	643,386.13	43,696.90	618,199.96	1,212,473.04	125,766.30	289,946.32	4,382,269.07	527,975.52
Gross income	-953,815.07	-512,872.07	723,428.55	-43,696.90	485,864.94	540,730.11	42,616.95	-97,967.00	184,289.51	22,203.19
Amortization pre-operating costs	154,663.52							15,468.34	154,683.36	18,636.24
Amortization renovations	71,500.00							16,300.87	92,852.02	11,186.81
Depreciation expense	49,392.72	144,283.10	2,296.71		16,088.84	10,502.70	11,881.35	24,125.41	241,254.13	29,066.28
Total	275,576.24	144,283.10	2,296.71		16,088.84	10,502.70	11,881.35	55,894.62	488,789.51	58,889.33
Net income	-1,229,391.31	-657,155.17	721,131.84	-43,696.90	469,776.10	530,227.41	30,735.60	-153,861.62	-304,500.00	-36,686.14

120

Exhibit 5: Income Statement

Beijing Sammies	Jan 02	Feb 02	Mar 02	Apr 02	May 02	Jun 02	Jul 02	Aug 02	Sep 02	Oct 02	2002YTD RMB	2002YTD US$ 0.120479942 conversion factor
Revenues	474,490.19	340,345.07	633,584.38	636,305.41	714,801.13	768,954.55	819,787.15	743,912.26	659,126.31	754,742.12	6,546,048.56	788,667.55
Cost of goods sold	116,310.43	112,891.03	209,662.56	221,218.57	185,420.17	221,374.62	271,224.40	216,298.58	210,682.54	214,407.10	1,979,489.98	238,488.84
Gross profit	358,179.76	227,454.05	423,921.82	415,086.84	529,380.96	547,579.93	548,562.76	527,613.68	448,443.78	540,335.02	4,566,558.58	550,178.71
Gross margin	75.49%	66.83%	66.91%	65.23%	74.06%	71.21%	66.92%	70.92%	68.04%	71.59%	69.76%	69.76%
Taxes	21,449.26	15,003.20	21,514.52	21,744.06	31,754.91	24,373.65	42,118.17	32,275.32	25,169.18	49,976.76	285,379.02	34,382.45
Salary	195,127.49	200,044.95	179,709.69	197,527.25	172,055.86	208,886.93	151,037.11	172,597.30	181,573.80	210,881.44	1,869,441.80	225,230.24
Insurance	9,027.64	8,697.01	10,910.74	10,991.92	7,642.39	10,484.72	12,577.94	10,606.44	10,606.44	10,607.09	102,152.34	12,307.31
Rent related	118,045.59	118,045.53	118,045.66	118,045.92	118,046.11	112,665.80	99,665.80	124,581.20	142,870.82	144,170.82	1,214,183.23	146,284.73
Utilities	14,993.68	20,974.36	13,872.64	13,989.55	14,436.11	18,413.58	16,504.80	14,210.99	19,398.47	24,723.49	171,517.66	20,664.44
Office expenses	7,002.19	9,775.81	10,184.63	15,715.78	23,112.66	15,346.73	21,650.58	29,671.43	33,736.55	11,773.71	177,970.07	21,441.82
Marketing/advertising	2,080.00	8,476.00	5,473.00	7,670.00	17,500.60	24,986.00	23,403.09	33,382.75	24,166.45	27,495.88	174,633.78	21,039.87
Transportation	3,458.00	1,738.10	4,951.70	3,695.64	4,497.74	11,303.50	5,270.98	18,112.15	5,557.37	5,283.72	63,868.90	7,694.92
Maintenance	7,800.00	5,281.25	309.40	4,564.30	6,630.00	38,958.40	26,887.90	9,034.61	7,272.20	6,880.90	113,618.96	13,688.81
Entertainment	3,216.20	6,073.60	3,313.70	2,471.30	852.80	4,378.14	546.00	461.50	4,406.35	2,752.10	28,471.69	3,430.27
Law and other expenses	1,798.33	1,798.33	6,998.33	1,798.33	14,798.33	1,798.33	8,038.33	6,998.33	1,798.33	1,798.33	47,623.29	5,737.65
Bank charges	104.00	78.00	-379.54	-13.17	163.15	-425.63	176.80	117.00	9.36	21.10	-148.93	-17.94
Other	845.00	234.00	7,179.64	4,312.10		3,208.14	3,867.12	3,606.10	1,757.47	3,273.87	28,283.44	3,407.59
Hr	650.00	975.00	4,615.00		975.00					1,365.00	8,580.00	1,033.72
Legal/gov't charge	1,950.00	1,950.00	16,016.00	1,950.00	1,950.00	2,483.00	1,950.00	1,950.00	1,950.00	1,950.00	34,099.00	4,108.25
Low cost and short-lived articles	2,171.00	1,295.84	3,055.00	10,031.27	10,522.07	5,995.31	3,622.32	20,954.62	3,919.89	1,027.00	62,594.32	7,541.36
Total expenses	389,718.38	400,440.96	405,770.11	414,494.24	424,937.72	482,856.60	417,316.94	478,559.73	464,192.68	503,981.21	4,382,268.55	527,975.46
Gross income	-31,538.62	-172,986.92	18,151.72	592.60	104,443.24	64,723.33	131,245.82	49,053.95	-15,748.90	36,353.81	184,290.03	22,203.25
Amortization pre-operating costs	15,468.34	15,468.34	15,468.34	15,468.34	15,468.34	15,468.34	15,468.34	15,468.34	15,468.34	15,468.34	154,683.36	18,636.24
Amortization renovations	7,150.00	7,150.00	7,150.00	7,150.00	7,150.00	7,150.00	7,150.00	16,300.87	13,250.58	13,250.58	92,852.02	11,186.81
Depreciation expense	24,125.41	24,125.41	24,125.41	24,125.41	24,125.41	24,125.41	24,125.41	24,125.41	24,125.41	24,125.41	241,254.13	29,066.28
Total	46,743.75	46,743.75	46,743.75	46,743.75	46,743.75	46,743.75	46,743.75	55,894.62	52,844.32	52,844.32	488,789.51	58,889.33
Net income	-78,282.37	-219,730.67	-28,592.03	-46,151.14	57,699.49	17,979.58	84,502.07	-6,840.67	-68,593.23	-16,490.51	-304,499.48	-36,686.08
Cumulative net income	-78,282.37	-298,013.04	-326,605.07	-372,756.22	-315,056.73	-297,077.14	-212,575.08	-219,415.74	-288,008.97	-304,499.48		

Figure 5   Income Statement

121

2001–2002 COMPARISON

Beijing Sammies

	Jan	Feb	Mar	Apr	May	Jun	Jul	Aug	Sep	Oct	Nov	Dec	Total	Average	%	Total US$	Average US$
																0.12048 conversion factor	
Revenues-Total																	
2002	474,490	340,345	633,584	636,305	714,801	768,955	819,787	743,912	659,126	754,742	0	0	6,546,049	654,605	32.94%	788,668	78,867
2001	195,360	221,729	273,194	322,826	360,585	487,627	485,567	479,232	495,706	501,579	565,923	534,743	4,924,071	410,339		593,252	49,438
Revenues-CD																	
2002	125,663	101,290	209,557	173,213	226,170	269,890	360,783	338,797	92,303	110,257	0	0	2,007,923	200,792	12.52%	241,914	24,191
2001	118,331	167,267	157,382	190,320	164,654	161,971	153,994	142,709	138,926	111,007	146,241	131,628	1,784,429	148,702		214,988	17,916
Revenues-BY																	
2002	150,800	55,375	173,870	202,190	213,181	245,040	86,393	20,944	191,542	223,374	0	0	1,562,708	156,271	1.18%	188,275	18,827
2001	77,029	54,462	115,812	132,506	122,457	161,166	130,244	112,095	136,210	155,964	173,991	172,487	1,544,423	128,702		186,072	15,506
Revenues-SA																	
2002	171,306	166,733	221,391	231,774	255,840	229,739	286,696	260,326	273,640	316,147	0	0	2,413,592	241,359	66.65%	290,789	29,079
2001	0	0	0	0	73,473	164,492	172,101	197,597	197,532	216,702	221,035	205,347	1,448,279	193,104		174,489	23,265
Revenues-CR																	
2002	26,722	16,949	28,768	29,128	19,612	24,287	28,860	26,354	27,414	25,579	0	0	253,672	25,367	72.63%	30,562	3,056
2001	0	0	0	0	0	0	29,229	26,832	23,036	17,908	24,656	25,284	146,944	24,491		17,704	2,951
Gross Profit																	
2002	358,180	227,454	423,922	415,087	529,381	547,580	548,563	527,614	448,444	540,335	0	0	4,566,559	456,656	33.45%	550,179	55,018
2001	136,161	155,046	181,279	216,507	243,420	334,135	340,288	353,393	340,074	360,762	406,459	354,387	3,421,909	285,159		412,271	34,356
Total Expenses																	
2002	389,718	400,442	405,770	414,495	424,938	482,856	415,874	478,560	439,563	503,981	0	0	4,356,196	435,620	25.44%	524,834	52,483
2001	199,170	212,702	203,262	204,741	292,468	293,136	271,625	318,711	367,199	358,769	367,961	383,097	3,472,840	289,403		418,408	34,867
Salary																	
2002	195,127	200,045	179,710	197,527	172,056	208,887	151,037	172,597	181,574	210,881	0	0	1,869,442	186,944	5.67%	225,230	22,523
2001	130,803	135,100	123,547	123,572	136,526	141,993	143,111	165,208	161,795	163,081	169,485	174,984	1,769,204	147,434		213,154	17,763

	Jan	Feb	Mar	Apr	May	Jun	Jul	Aug	Sep	Oct	Nov	Dec	Total	Average	%	Total US$	Average US$
															0.12048 conversion factor		
Rent Related																	
2002	118,046	118,046	118,046	118,046	118,046	112,666	99,666	124,581	142,871	144,171	0	0	1,214,183	121,418	28.69%	146,285	14,628
2001	36,833	36,833	36,833	36,833	93,180	93,180	71,500	71,500	112,666	118,045	118,048	118,047	943,497	78,625		113,672	9,473
Insurance																	
2002	9,028	8,697	10,911	10,992	7,642	10,485	12,578	10,606	10,606	10,607	0	0	102,152	10,215	174.55%	12,307	1,231
2001	0	0	0	260	0	3,894	5,203	6,003	4,694	6,516	5,049	5,589	37,207	3,101		4,483	374
Utilities																	
2002	14,994	20,974	13,873	13,990	14,436	18,414	16,505	14,211	19,398	24,723	0	0	171,518	17,152	-0.10%	20,664	2,066
2001	11,239	13,459	7,232	8,932	11,063	11,041	13,607	16,717	24,505	18,764	17,195	17,936	171,690	14,307		20,685	1,724
Office Expenses																	
2002	7,002	9,776	10,185	15,716	23,113	15,347	21,651	29,671	33,737	11,774	0	0	177,970	17,797	63.35%	21,442	2,144
2001	5,437	4,486	5,652	7,899	9,877	9,994	8,281	12,463	9,611	10,245	10,773	14,229	108,948	9,079		13,126	1,094
Marketing/Advertising																	
2002	2,080	8,476	5,473	7,670	17,501	24,986	23,403	33,383	24,166	27,496	0	0	174,634	17,463	42.87%	21,040	2,104
2001	1,950	7,150	2,842	3,900	19,682	17,508	6,838	14,598	9,460	9,494	17,076	11,736	122,234	10,186		14,727	1,227
Transportation																	
2002	3,458	1,738	4,952	3,696	4,498	11,304	5,271	18,112	5,557	5,284	0	0	63,869	6,387	149.15%	7,695	769
2001	1,158	1,131	2,298	2,662	2,989	1,219	2,428	2,522	2,510	2,626	1,651	2,439	25,635	2,136		3,088	257
Maintenance																	
2002	7,800	5,281	309	4,564	6,630	38,958	26,888	9,035	7,272	6,881	0	0	113,619	11,362	588.67%	13,689	1,369
2001	735	371	3,788	1,707	98	1,110	1,365	1,754	1,252	1,273	681	2,366	16,498	1,375		1,988	166
Entertainment																	
2002	3,216	6,074	3,314	2,471	853	4,378	546	462	4,406	2,752	0	0	28,472	2,847	-13.33%	3,430	343
2001	0	520	4,976	5,881	2,896	0	1,123	255	12,332	372	759	3,738	32,852	2,738		3,958	330
Law and Other Expenses																	
2002	3,748	3,748	23,014	3,748	16,748	4,281	9,988	8,948	3,748	3,748	0	0	81,718	8,172	123.09%	9,845	985
2001	3,613	6,500	6,500	2,665	3,848	0	867	4,767	6,136	867	867	0	36,630	3,053		4,413	368
Taxes																	
2002	21,384	15,003	21,515	21,744	31,755	24,374	42,119	32,275	25,169	49,977	0	0	285,315	28,531	83.43%	34,375	3,437
2001	6,871	5,950	8,639	8,813	6,360	6,163	13,657	15,219	16,592	25,346	16,892	25,046	155,546	12,962		18,740	1,562

Figure 6 Income Statement Comparisons

123

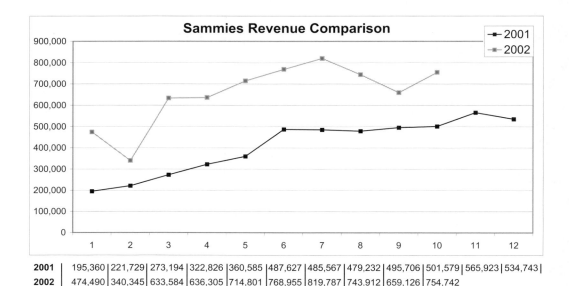

2001	195,360	221,729	273,194	322,826	360,585	487,627	485,567	479,232	495,706	501,579	565,923	534,743
2002	474,490	340,345	633,584	636,305	714,801	768,955	819,787	743,912	659,126	754,742		

Figure 7   Income Statement

Competition

The economic expansion of the late 1990s dramatically changed dining in Beijing. Private establishments that catered to China's emerging middle class replaced old state-run restaurants. Most traditional meals were under US$5 per person. Peking duck and other local specialties were the most popular, but new restaurants opened that offered regional tastes from all around Asia. Additionally, the number of Western-style restaurants targeting tourists, expatriates, and younger, trendy Chinese customers increased.

Sam Goodman viewed all restaurants physically close to Sammies as competitors.

> As far as I'm concerned, everyone in Beijing who orders lunch is a potential customer and every restaurant serving it is a competitor. There are those who stick to the traditional Chinese meal, but who is to say that they will never try Sammies?
>
> I do not want to restrict Sammies to serving just Western businesses or students. We are delivering not only to Western businesses but to traditional Chinese companies as well. While we rely on Western students for our walk-in business, we do have Chinese customers who come to Sammies every day. There are others who only come once in a while. These people go to the Chinese restaurants when they don't come here. So I must think broadly in terms of who my customers are and who my competition is. Of course, Western restaurants like McDonald's, Subway, Schlotzskys, and Starbucks

are the most obvious competitors. Competition in this business is day-to-day as people rarely eat lunch at the same location each afternoon.

Like most major cities, Beijing has an array of restaurant choices ranging from traditional Chinese to Mexican, German, Scandinavian, Italian, Swiss, and English Continental.

The Great Wall of China

As Beijing Sammies adapted to the competitive environment, Goodman increasingly turned to the delivery business for revenue. But the model did not work as planned, due to the lack of experience Goodman had in delivery logistics. Corporate clients were more demanding and lunch delivery complicated. Goodman states:

> We started out delivering from a central source. At first, things did not go as planned. Quite frankly, I was an inexperienced manager and made quite a few mistakes. The delivery model here in China is very different from the West. Clients have no understanding of what goes on behind the scenes, and they do not understand that it is nearly impossible for us to take a large delivery order for a corporate luncheon and bring it to them 10 minutes later. I didn't plan for all of the possible problems that a different culture would bring. I should have put more effort and time into educating the customer about the product. This definitely had a negative impact on the business at first.

In addition to overcoming the existing perceptions and expectations of the customer, Goodman learned about the prevailing attitude of the employees. One of his biggest challenges was not securing the hard-to-come-by ingredients, dealing with the local government, or raising capital, but rather teaching his employees the concept of service. For many of Beijing Sammies' employees, service was little more than opening the store in the morning and closing it at night. To Goodman, service was much more. It was what he believed would differentiate Beijing Sammies from the other Western food establishments, and what would cause the traditional Chinese consumer to pay more money for lunch. Service was not only delivering the product on time, with the correct number of forks and knives, but was also helping the customer to understand the product.

According to Goodman:

> For most of my employees it doesn't matter "how" you get things done—it just matters that you get the end result. The concept of face for them manifests itself with the feeling that appearance is much more important

than the service or quality of the product. While for the customer, the service provided by us is part of the final product.

Just as the client base did not understand the wait for a delivery, the employees did not understand the product that Beijing Sammies was trying to sell.

The staff does not understand the urgency needed in running a service-oriented business. The whole concept of service is new in China. The business traditions are very strong here. I don't know if it's because of the issue of face and pride, the political history, or something else, but our employees have a very difficult time understanding how we need to deliver service as much as we need to deliver a sandwich.

For Sam Goodman the initial years of operation proved that Beijing Sammies could hold a niche. While he was pleased to see Beijing Sammies growing toward profitability, he was concerned about whether it could ever become cash-flow positive, and if so, whether he could sustain it. In addition, Goodman was no closer to finding the type of employee who would adopt his concept of service than he was when he started, and wondered if the answer lay in increased automation, training, or somewhere else.

Case Questions

1. Describe the nature of the industry in terms of size and characteristics.

2. What are the critical factors for success in this industry?

3. To date, how is Beijing Sammies doing?

4. Discuss the skills and attributes of Sam Goodman. Discuss the skills that he needs. Why do you think he is having a difficult time hiring employees that can perform to his expectations?

5. Discuss the aspects of doing business in China that may be different than doing business in the European Union or the United States. Discuss the value propositions of Beijing Sammies. What are the company's unique selling propositions?

6. Analyze the financial performance and results of all aspects of the company. Where can significant improvements be made?

7. Determine the value of the company today.

8. What are Goodman's next steps for building and funding his business?

TRIMO

Brane Semolic, PhD[1]
Director of INOVA Consulting
Professor of Project, Technology Management and Entrepreneurship
Head of Project & Technology Management Institute
Faculty of Logistics, University of Maribor, Slovenia

TRIMO History

TRIMO was founded in 1961, when *Kovinsko Podjetje Trebnje[1] (Trebnje Metal Company)* was established. The company was completely restructured and rebranded as TRIMO. TRIMO became a publicly owned company after the privatization process in 1994. The TRIMO transition came about during the extensive national privatization program that occurred in Slovenia during the mid-1990s. Slovenia was a part of former socialist Yugoslavia until 1990, when the country disintegrated into several independent nations. Slovenia is now a democratic, multiparty society.

A SUMMARY OF TRIMO'S PRODUCT HISTORY

In 1974 TRIMO began manufacturing thermally insulated plates with polyurethane filling. They then began manufacturing construction plates filled with mineral wool in 1987. In 1989 they began manufacturing containers. The company's first antinoise fences were manufactured in 1995 and the TPO—Dom roof was first presented in 1996. The following year a new technology was applied for continuous manufacture of fire-resistant panels. In 2002 the TRIMOFORM roof represented an innovative approach to the TRIMO roofing systems by being marketed to individual customers. The next year, a new line of TRIMOTERM fire-resistant façade panels was launched. As of 2001 a comprehensive approach has been applied to the development of TRIMO's new products, technologies, and

---

1. Sources: General Manager, answers from questionnaire, and the TRIMO Web site.

systems, which has led to a range of new products in roofing, façades, pre-fabricated steel constructions, and decorative elements entering the market. With the start-up of a new development-innovation center in 2006, TRIMO Institute, the company introduced its next development phase.

LEADERSHIP

One of the most important drivers within the company is Tatjana Fink (picture below). She joined the company immediately after graduating university in 1980. She began in the controlling department; later, she was promoted to director of finance, sales, design, and commercial department. In 1992 she was promoted to general manager of TRIMO.

Figure 1   General Manager, Tatjana Fink

Under her leadership TRIMO flourished and became one of the most successful manufacturing and construction companies in the region. Tatjana Fink has received numerous awards from national and international professional associations. She was chosen as the most powerful and influential female manager in Slovenia in 2006. In 2007 she was selected as the most respected manager in Slovenia. Throughout her time as director, TRIMO also received much recognition in its different fields of activities.

TRIMO QUALITY

In 1993 the company acquired the ISO 9001 Quality Certificate, and in 2000 the ISO 14001 Environmental Certificate. The Slovene Committee on Business Excellence granted TRIMO an award on behalf of the Republic of Slovenia for business excellence. This award is the highest state honor given to recognize the maintenance of high standards of the quality of products, services, and operations due to the development of knowledge and innovation. TRIMO also placed high importance on the health and safety of its employees. In 2003 the company was awarded the OHSAS 18001 Certificate in recognition of their hard work to ensure safety on the job. The next step on the road to business excellence was taken in 2004, when the European Foundation for Quality Management (EFQM) recognized TRIMO for excellence in their industry. In 2007 TRIMO was selected as a finalist for the EFQM award.

TRIMO Business Network and Its Dynamics

The first foreign subsidiary of TRIMO was established in 1990. By the end of 2006, TRIMO had 14 subsidiaries, 7 representative offices, and 8 agents in relevant markets. TRIMO's story of development, which was primarily Europe-oriented, began in 1992 with the motto, "Satisfied customers make the largest profit." Every year this motto was updated to support and modernize the foundation of TRIMO's operations. The 2007 motto, "Innovation for sustainable growth and development," exhibits TRIMO's new development leap. TRIMO is now an international company employing over 1,000 people, selling in more than 50 world markets, and manufacturing in Slovenia and abroad.

Comprehensive customer relationship management (CRM) and the establishment of long-term partnerships with all target public groups is a key strategy for TRIMO. The company has established strategic partnerships with customers, investors, suppliers, architects, designers, specialists, and other partners by segmenting their public groups, offering relationships adjusted to their requirements, and organizing work procedures tailored to customer needs. TRIMO assesses each of its target groups' satisfaction levels to gain feedback to improve future products, services, and processes.

TRIMO'S Key Competencies and Strategic Orientations

TRIMO strives to ensure complete solutions in the field of prefabricated steel buildings, roofs, façades, steel constructions, and containers. The company's customers are offered efficient and integrated solutions from the very first concept to the final construction thanks to TRIMO's knowledge, research and development, design, advanced technology, and top quality building materials.

Figure 2   EUROPARK Shopping Mall in Slovenia

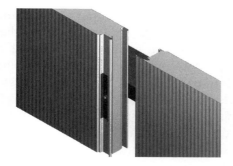

Figure 3   TRIMOTERM® Panel

TRIMO's main advantages are its clear vision and strategy, capital strength, ambitious and innovative employees, and its extensive marketing and sales network. TRIMO's key competencies are represented by their advanced construction technologies, solutions to complex client problems, quality products and services, and their profound individual and organizational competencies.

At TRIMO special consideration is given to the individual competencies of employees. Employees are encouraged to develop their communication skills, innovation capabilities, teamwork, and self-management. This is how new technical, specific, process, and company knowledge is developed through the entire organization. Throughout the learning process, motivation, creativity, responsibility, and ethics are of utmost importance. Continuous development of competencies by TRIMO employees results in added value for all TRIMO customers.

Balanced company growth and development are ensured by the adherence to its development plan, the introduction of new products, and pursuing the company's marketing objectives. These objectives include maintaining existing markets as well as entering new strategic markets. For TRIMO an important factor in developing new products is cooperation with independent experts from companies, institutes, and universities, which contributes to TRIMO's knowledge and innovation center.

Construction Industry

OVERVIEW

TRIMO operates and generates sales from its products and solutions in the construction sector. The construction market is divided into three segments: residential buildings, nonresidential buildings, and infrastructure construction. For TRIMO the most important segment is the development of nonresidential buildings in Europe. In 2005 the size of the nonresidential building market was estimated at EUR 400 billion. Its largest subsegment was the construction of industrial facilities, followed by commercial and business facilities. Construction of storage facilities is currently on the rise, especially in Eastern Europe and Russia. The nonresidential buildings market in Eastern Europe is increasing by 6% a year, on average, and due to substantial investments in these markets, this growth rate can also be projected into the future.

According to the microsegmentation of the construction sector, TRIMO is a competitor in the global market for insulation sandwich panels. This is part of the construction mezzo-market of roofs and façades. Insulation sandwich panels are a modern alternative to the classical construction of roofs and façades using concrete, wood, and other materials. Insulation panels differ according to the type of filling. The insulation panels with the largest market share in Europe are filled with polyurethane; however, the use of panels made of mineral wool and extruded polystyrene (EPS) is on the rise due to tough safety legislation.

The entire European panel market is estimated at 140 million square meters, of which 15%–20% is mineral wool panels. TRIMO is the leading European manufacturer of this product. The predominant European manufacturers of PU-panels, and TRIMO's other major competitors, come from Italy, Great Britain, Germany, and France. The strongest markets for insulation panels in Europe are France, Great Britain, Germany, and Spain. Italy is the largest exporter of insulation panels to the European markets.

By providing comprehensive solutions in the field of prefabricated steel buildings, TRIMO creates its competitive edge in relation to its competitors. In the European construction market, the top five construction companies are Vinci, Skanska, Bouygues, Hochtief, and Ferrovial. These major market players are not direct competitors with TRIMO because TRIMO also serves as their supplier for many projects. With this in mind, TRIMO considers the following companies its main competitors: Rukki, Kingspan, Paroc, and Metecno.

TRENDS IN THE CONSTRUCTION INDUSTRY

Growth in the construction sector is largely dependent on economic trends and investments in the private and public sectors. In the Western European market, the growth of the construction sector is expected to continue at a relatively slow rate. According to projections, this rate will ultimately decrease as interest rates are expected to grow and thus negatively influence credit and loan operations. The interest rate increase will decrease consumer spending, leading to less investment in construction projects. In the Western European construction market, the fastest growth is expected in the field of building renovation.

Compared to Western Europe, the booming markets of Central and Southeastern Europe represent a great business opportunity. All development prospects and expectations are oriented toward these markets, which are predicted to generate the largest profits in the European construction business through 2010. Market development is focused toward the following regions:

1. The markets of new European Union (EU) member states (i.e., the Czech Republic, Poland, Hungary, and the Baltic states), which together attained a mere 4.5% of the European construction market share in 2004. Growth rates in these markets were much faster than in Western Europe (5%–6% a year on the average). Growth leveled off in this region in 2007.

2. The markets of Southeastern Europe (i.e., Bulgaria, Romania, Croatia, Bosnia-Herzegovina, Serbia, Montenegro, and Macedonia) together attain a mere 1.3% of the European construction market. They maintain a fast growth rate that is strongly supported by programs to move toward EU membership. A two-figure number will mark their growth in the construction market.

3. The Russian states attained only 3.5% of the European market share in construction. However, this market is currently in a building boom, substantially contributed to by the Russian prosperity derived from oil and gas. Because of its natural resources, Russia has recently become a magnet for foreign investors. The construction growth rate in Russia is expected to go beyond 20% a year. Apart from Russia, Belarus and Ukraine are also considered very attractive markets.

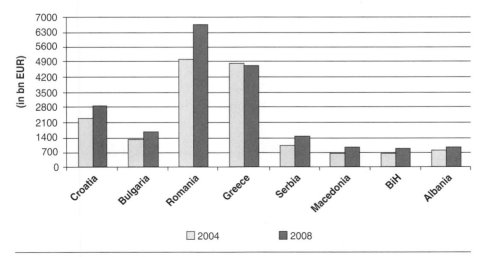

Figure 4   Value of Construction Output in Southeastern Europe

SOURCE: Croatian Government Statistics

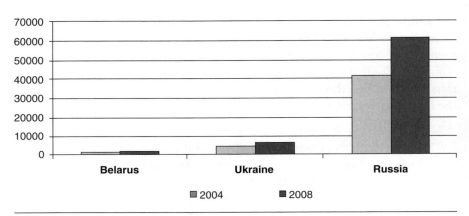

Figure 5   Value of Construction Output in (Ex) Russian Countries

SOURCE: Croatian Government Statistics

The graphs in Figure 4 and Figure 5 compare the size of the construction sector in 2004 and 2008 in Southeastern Europe and the former Russian nations. The fastest growth is predicted for the Russian market, followed by Romania, Croatia, Serbia, and Ukraine.

KEY FACTORS OF SUCCESS OF AN INDUSTRY BRANCH

The success of an industry branch strongly depends on the overall economic situation in a particular market. The following are key factors of success in an industry branch:

- Fast economic growth

- Substantial foreign direct investment

- Development programs supported by the EU, European Bank of Reconstruction (EBRD), European Industrial Bank (EIB), and the World Bank

- Ability to ensure comprehensive solutions in the field of construction

- Strong research and development (R&D) and technical support

- Launching of new products (new construction materials, new types of construction, speed and ease of assembly, etc.)

- Systematic implementation of CRM in particular target segments (architects, investors, etc.)

TRIMO's Marketing Strategy in Southeastern Europe

TRIMO's marketing strategy in Southeastern Europe strives for the company to become the leading European provider of comprehensive prefabricated steel building solutions. They are successfully gaining recognition in the Southeastern European market by providing innovative and high-quality comprehensive solutions for fireproof roofs, façades, and nonresidential construction. The company is jointly engaged in assuring quality solutions, fulfilling the needs of its clients, completing its projects in a timely fashion, and constantly improving its customer support.

TRIMO's strategy for entering into the Southeastern European markets is divided into three main parts:

1. Marketing
   - Approach clients
   - Acquire new clients
   - Follow strategic clients
   - Follow foreign investors
   - Set trends in the field of façades
   - Expand their market network
   - Enter new markets
   - Increase market share
   - Increase regional sale distribution channels

2. Research and Development
   - Increase innovation
   - Joint development with suppliers and clients
   - Transfer technology and technological knowledge
   - Develop products that are catered to the market and target groups
   - Market new products with a higher added value

3. Production and Purchase
   - Market comprehensive solutions
   - Use local sources for purchase of raw materials
   - Acquire a less costly workforce
   - Lower transportation costs
   - Find local manufacturers

TRIMO's marketing strategy is pursued through the effective use of different tools and steps in marketing communication. Their strategy is oriented toward producing effective business plans for each region

TRIMO enters and by raising the company's reputation and recognition within the target markets. TRIMO's business plans are oriented toward long-term two-way relationships, strengthening the TRIMO brand, supporting sales, and ensuring access for new products and services in new markets. TRIMO supports their efforts by giving presentations at specialized trade fairs, presentations for target groups such as architects and investors, advertising in trade magazines, as well as promotional articles and television advertising.

Because of the size of the Southeastern European market, the expansion and development of the TRIMO sales network is carried out by establishing local sales companies and sales representatives. By doing so, the marketing of products and services is country/region specific and more effective execution of marketing communication is ensured.

TRIMO on the Croatian Market

TRIMO'S MARKETING STRATEGY FOR THE CROATIAN MARKET

The TRIMO network is based on a unified organizational culture and the high standards it holds for its projects in all markets. The business model for the Croatian market is based on overall corporate strategy, but is targeted specifically to the local market situation, local buyer characteristics, and the development of the local branch.

Figure 6   GETRO Shopping Mall (construction in progress) Croatia

Figure 7   MANI Zagreb Croatia

In 2001 TRIMO established TRIMO Gradenje[2] Ltd. in Croatia. TRIMO Gradenje's headquarters were located in Croatia's capital, Zagreb, which continues to grow annually and is characterized by highly qualified personnel. In 2006 the Croatian branch had 14 employees working in sales, project planning, assembly, and imports. TRIMO Gradenje works closely with the mother company TRIMO.

The Croatian company has successfully established its position in the market. TRIMO Gradenje organized presentations for architects and investors in Croatia's larger cities (Zadar, Osijek, Rijeka, and Zagreb) to continue its networking efforts and increase its brand recognition. They also participated in a Split[3] construction fair, where they acquired many new and important contacts, extending their network to all regions of Croatia. Some examples are shown in Figures 6 and 7.

TRIMO Gradenje informs their market about innovations through advertising in specialized magazines. They also increase their recognition and innovation opportunities through cooperation with local universities and their faculties of civil engineering in Zagreb and Split. For example, the company holds competitions for students in these local universities. They also hold organized visits to their construction sites and the TRIMO Inc. headquarters in Trebnje, Slovenia, for fourth-year students from the faculty of civil engineering. The company's results for 2003 through 2006 are indicated in Table 1.

THE MARKETING SITUATION, MARKET STRUCTURE, TARGET CLIENTS, RISKS, AND OPPORTUNITIES

Construction is one of the most important industry sectors in Croatia. It alone represents approximately 15% of the annual Croatian gross domestic product (GDP). This fast growth in the construction sector was spurred by the increasing flow of net foreign investments. The growth is also aided by the large concentration of construction companies present in the market—the top ten companies (according to income) exceed 30% of the entire Croatian construction market. The main foreign and international companies on the Croatian construction market are Bechtel, Strabag, and Bouygues (through a joint venture with Bina Istra).

Residential construction holds the largest share and represents approximately 40% of all construction activities on the Croatian market. Nonresidential construction and infrastructure construction are gaining value in the construction business. At first the growth of nonresidential construction increased because of the restoration of old tourist attractions, but today the number of new buildings in this sector is growing. The construction of shopping centers and logistic centers and investment in business premises is becoming increasingly essential to the Croatian economy. Croatia's pending accession into the EU is also providing a significant impetus for the construction and upgrade of nationwide infrastructure.

Croatia is one of the biggest markets in Southeastern Europe and one of five essential markets for the TRIMO Company. As mentioned previously, the road to TRIMO's success is paved by strong relationships with their clients built on satisfying their clients' needs efficiently and effectively. TRIMO Građenje successfully cooperates with their existing strategic partners and continues to acquire new clients and potential strategic partners in the Croatian market. Their target clients and respective partners include investors, architects, project planners, engineering companies, construction companies, assembly companies, licensed partners, tradesmen, and agents.

TRIMO Građenje's key advantages in the Croatian market lie in its complete solutions, which are praised by clients, architects, and project planners alike. TRIMO's roof assemblies and façades are highly regarded because clients have recognized the quality proven by the many acquired certificates. TRIMO Građenje's additional advantage on the market is its ability to offer engineering services, which include project planning, assembly, transportation, and construction work. There is strong competition in the Croatian market coming from Italy, Austria, the Czech Republic, and other countries, and the local competition has an increasingly strong position. Nevertheless, TRIMO is confident that it will be able to sustain its market share.

Table 1   TRIMO Građenje—Key Financial Performance Data (in EUR)

	2003	2004	2005	2006
Net Sales Revenue	6.272.774	10.466.736	13.171.008	16.729.997
Net Profit	93.172	72.635	217.940	249.335
Assets	2.740.716	4.085.951	5.112.387	9.411.116
Financial Liabilities	0	0	0	0
Average Number of Employees	8	7	11	14

The risks for TRIMO in the Croatian market are increased local and foreign competition, unsolved economic and political issues, and the unpredictable environment as a whole. There are numerous opportunities in the Croatian market that the company recognizes and builds into its strategic and annual activity plans. It is very clear to TRIMO that the need for flexibility and ensuring individual solutions is increasing. Their clients are becoming more demanding, the competition is stronger, and it is vital that they are able to react in time to reap the benefits of the changing market conditions.

TRIMO Građenje—Into the Future

By ensuring the employment of personnel with the knowledge and leadership capabilities essential for success, TRIMO Građenje is becoming an increasingly stronger local competitor. To achieve continued growth and development, it is vital that the employees constantly develop their skills and that they continue to pursue additional education and qualifications.

Notes

1. Trebnje—town on the South of Slovenia (EU)

2. Građenje—Croatian word for "construction"

3. Split—the biggest town in the Dalmatia region on the Adriatic coast

Case Questions

1. Describe the nature of the European panel industry in terms of size and characteristics.

2. Explain the trends in the European construction industry.

3. What are the critical factors for success in this industry?

4. Why is a business network so important for TRIMO?

5. How does TRIMO develop and maintain its competitive advantage?

6. What are the main characteristics of the TRIMO marketing strategy in Southeastern Europe?

7. Describe the TRIMO marketing strategy for the Croatian market.

8. Why did TRIMO establish TRIMO Građenje in Croatia?

9. What is the role of TRIMO Građenje in the TRIMO corporation?

Part 2

Entering the Global Market

Selecting International Business Opportunities $\quad$ 5

Profile: Karan Bilimoria

COBRA BEER

Karan Bilimoria, founder and chief executive of Cobra Beer, has two missions: to brew the finest Indian beer ever and to make it a global brand. One of the fastest growing beer companies in the UK, Cobra Beer is well on its way to achieving both goals.

Cobra Beer tries to set itself apart from the competition by emphasizing that its product is smooth and less gassy. Bilimoria explains, "I saw that the market was dominated by harsh, gassy 'Eurofizz' beers, all poor partners to food. I wanted to produce a premium, high-quality lager that would complement rather than fight against food." The aim is to appeal to both ale and lager drinkers and to people eating Indian food. "We built the business in the UK on the Indian restaurant niche sector," says Dynshaw Italia, the company's finance director and chief operating officer.

Lord Bilimoria's (he became Lord Bilimoria of Chelsea in June 2006) unrelenting entrepreneurial spirit and pursuit of excellence sets the company apart. A Cambridge law graduate and qualified chartered accountant, he founded the company in 1989 at the age of 27 with GBP20,000 of student debt.

Change of Location

In 1990 Bilimoria began brewing Cobra Beer in Bangalore, India, and shipped the brand from there to the UK, the world's most competitive beer market. Although demand surged, the brewer increasingly produced a beer of uneven quality and was late with consignments. Consequently, in 1997 he moved its production to the UK, where he established a license with Charles Wells, a well-known brewer.

The company later hired Palm Breweries in Belgium and its subsidiary, Browar Belgia in Poland, as breweries to guarantee several suppliers to meet the demands for Cobra in the European and worldwide market. Browar Belgia is one of Europe's leading and most modern breweries as well as Poland's fourth largest brewer. "When we decided to look at various options and countries, a major criterion was matching the taste of the beer," says Mr. Italia. Browar Belgia was able to match the taste of the beer within two or three tries.

Success Story

In 2007 Cobra Beer was so successful that it enjoyed a retail value turnover of GBP125m, up from GBP80m reported in 2006. In 10 years its compound annual growth rate has been more than 42%. Sold mainly in draft form, the beer is found in nearly 6,000 UK Indian restaurants and 6,000 bars, pubs, and clubs. "We're starting to expand to the supermarkets, as well as to the off-trade and on-trade markets," reports Mr. Italia. Cobra Beer is exported to almost 50 countries and maintains subsidiaries in India, South Africa, and the United States, but the UK remains its largest market.

The company positioned itself to enter the big leagues of the beverage industry. "To go to that next stage requires a giant leap," says Mr. Italia. Since 2006 Cobra Beer has undergone major changes that included increasing its staff from 10 to 113. A well-known managing director and a marketing director from major beverage and spirit companies were hired. Next, Cobra plans to extend its brand in the UK to different occasion categories and expand its position overseas. "At the moment people associate the beer with Indian food," says Mr. Italia. "But people are starting to drink it on different occasions."

Indian Market

Cobra is also stepping up its presence in India. Tariffs there are so high that importing beer makes it difficult to compete against the local brands. Consequently, Cobra Beer has partnered with Mount Shivalik Group, India's largest independent brewing company, to brew Cobra under license for India's rapidly growing domestic market. Most significant, Mount Shivalik Group was capable of matching the taste of the Cobra Beer brewed in the UK, which resulted in Cobra Beer being awarded a gold medal at the Monde Selection in Brussels.

Since 1999 the beer has won a string of awards, including one grand gold medal and eleven gold medals at the 2006 Monde Selection; two grand gold medals and nine gold medals in 2005; two grand gold medals and four gold medals in 2004; and gold for three successive years at the 2003, 2002, and 2001 awards. Monde Selection also presented Cobra with the International High Quality Trophy in 2006 for its achievements.

To maintain quality control, Cobra Beer retains its own staff in the outsourced breweries. Consequently, within a year it has already captured 1.5% of India's beer market. The upshot is huge, especially given that the beer market has been growing by 7%–8% a year in the previous 5 to 6 years and has risen by 27% this last year alone. "What's really fascinating is that regulations regarding licensing laws are starting to show signs of becoming more lenient," says Mr. Italia. Given the potential that the Indian market provides, Cobra Beer's executives see India as an opportunity that the company cannot miss.

Supporting Demand

Exporting remains an important function, although not the company's primary focus. "We are taking a more reactive than proactive approach there by supporting demand in South Africa and the United States without overinvesting in those markets," says Mr. Italia.

Although South Africa is a limited market, sales are doing well. The company has a small office in the United States, where the beer is sold under the name Krait because American brewing giant Anheuser-Busch produces a malt liquor called King Cobra. Brand recognition has been the company's biggest obstacle in the United States.

An underlying philosophy of Cobra Beer is to do things differently and to do them better. For example, while other beer companies sold beer in small bottles, in 2003 Cobra introduced its award-winning embossed bottle. To penetrate the supermarket sector, it introduced a full range of packaging formats, including cans and multipacks. Product development has also created significant sales opportunities. In 2005 the company launched Cobra 0.0%, an alcohol-free beer; Cobra Lower Cal, with half the calories of a regular Cobra; and King Cobra, the world's first double-fermented strong lager sold in champagne-style bottles. "Now we have launched fruit flavored beers," Mr. Italia says. The drink is brewed as a beer first and then fruit extract is added.

In March 2006 Cobra launched The Cobra Foundation, its own independently run charitable trust, and in April held the inaugural CobraVision Awards, which were attended by British film and television stars.

Financing Initiatives

Innovative financing from government-backed small loan guarantees to invoice finance and factoring have played an important role in moving the company ahead. "We are one of the first companies in the UK to use what is called a payment-in-kind instrument," says Mr. Italia. Adopted first in the United States, the instrument operates like an unsecured loan with no cash payments and no dilution of equity to shareholders, only an increase in interest. "At the time you exit the company or in 5 or 10 years, you pay back the debt plus the interest that has added up," he explains. It is a risky loan, but executives at Cobra Beer believe that the value they are building with the company far outweighs the debt. "When you are a small company competing with the giants, you have to do things differently," says Mr. Italia. "This is how you change the entire marketplace." Cobra Beer is so successful that it enjoys a retail value turnover of GBP125m, up from GBP80m reported last year (Thuermer, 2007).

www.cobrabeer.com

Chapter Objectives

1. To develop an understanding of how to best select the most appropriate foreign market for each venture.

2. To determine the best indicators for entry into a foreign country or market.

3. To identify primary and secondary sources for information on specific foreign market industries or sectors.

4. To recognize how to collect country market data.

5. To demonstrate the importance of positioning the venture correctly and how to pursue competitive intelligence to enhance this strategy.

6. To learn how to assess competitive strengths and weaknesses in foreign markets and determine a strategy to combat them.

Introduction

With so many potential markets and prospective countries available, critical issues for the global entrepreneur are foreign market selection and entry strategy (the focus of Chapter 7). Should the global entrepreneur enter the top prospective country or should he or she employ a more regional focus? Should he or she choose the largest market possible or one that is easier to understand and navigate? Is a more developed foreign market preferable to one that is developing?

These are just some of the questions confronting the global entrepreneur when deciding which market to enter. The market selection decision should be based on past sales and competitive positioning, as well as assessment of each foreign market alternative. Data needs to be systematically collected on both a regional and a country basis. A region can be a collection of countries, such as the European Union, or an area within a country, such as the southeastern part of China.

A systematic process is needed to establish a ranking of the foreign markets being considered. Why is ranking markets so important? Ranking helps avoid the problem of so many entrepreneurs—doing a poor job of establishing a rigorous market selection process and relying too much on assumptions and gut feelings. As discussed in Chapter 1, there are significant differences between doing global and domestic business. These differences and the entire global decision process require that the market selection process be a series of steps in which informed decisions are made at each step based on as much information as possible. The data collected for each item should contain information for at least 3 years so that a trend is evident. The global entrepreneur must always remember that a single data point does not make a trend, so any less than three periods of data needs to be interpreted cautiously. The same data collected and analyzed for market selection will also be used to develop the appropriate entry strategy and marketing plan.

Foreign Market Selection Model

Although there are several market selection models available, one good method employs a five step approach: (1) develop appropriate indicators, (2) collect data and convert into comparable indicators, (3) establish an appropriate weight for each indicator, (4) analyze the data, and (5) select the appropriate market from the market rankings.

In step one, appropriate indicators need to be developed based on past sales, competitive research, experience, and discussions with other global entrepreneurs. Specific indicators for the company need to be developed in three general areas: overall market indicators, market growth indicators, and product indicators. Market size indicators generally center on population, per capita income, market for the specific product for consumer products and for types of companies and their sales, and profits of particular industrial products. In terms of market growth, the overall country growth (gross domestic product, or GDP) should be determined as well as the growth rate for the particular market of the venture. Finally, appropriate product indicators, such as export of the specific product category to the market and the number of sales leads and interest, should be established.

Step two is collecting data for each of these indicators and converting the data so that comparisons can be made. Both primary data (original information collected for the particular requirement) and secondary data (published data already existing) needs to be collected. Typically, secondary data is gathered first to establish what information still needs to be collected through primary research. When collecting international secondary data, there are several problems that vary to some extent based on the stage of economic development of the country. These problems include (1) comparability (the data for one country will not be the same as data for another); (2) availability (some countries have much more country data than others, usually reflecting the stage of economic development); (3) accuracy (sometimes the data has not been collected using vigorous standards or is even biased due to the interests of the government of the country; the latter is particularly a problem in nonmarket-oriented economies); and (4) cost. (The United States has the Freedom of Information Act, which makes all government-collected data that does not pertain to security or defense available to all. This does not exist in all countries.) For example, one global entrepreneur was interested in opening the first western health club in Moscow. He was going to charge two rates: a higher hard currency rate to foreigners and a lower ruble rate to Russians and other citizens of countries in the former Soviet Union. In determining the best location, he was interested in finding areas of the city where most foreigners lived. After significant searching to no avail and a high degree of frustration, he finally was able to buy the data needed from the former KGB (Soviet Union security branch).

When researching foreign markets, you will usually want economic and demographic data such as population, GDP, per capita income, inflation, literacy rate, unemployment, and education levels. There are many sources for this and other foreign information at government agencies, Web sites, and embassies. One important source of data is STAT-USA and its National Trade Data Bank (NTDB), which is managed by the U.S. Department of Commerce. The STAT-USA database has good information, due in part to the large number of government agencies contributing information. This results in a large number of international reports such as Country Reports, Country Analysis Briefs (CABS), Country Commercial Guides (CCG), Food Market Reports, International Reports and Reviews, Department of State Background Notes, and Import/Export Reports.

Another good source of data is trade associations and U.S. and foreign embassies. Although trade associations are a good source of domestic and international data, sometimes more specific information can be obtained by contacting the U.S. Department of Commerce industry desk officer or the economic attaché in the appropriate U.S. or foreign embassy.

The collected data then needs to be converted to a point score for each selected indicator so that each indicator of each country can be numerically ranked against each other. Various methods can be used to achieve this, each of which involves some judgment by the global entrepreneur. Another method is to compare country data for each indicator against global standards.

The third step establishes appropriate weights for the indicators that reflect the importance of each in predicting foreign market potential. For one company manufacturing hospital beds, the number and types of hospitals, the age of the hospitals and its beds, and the government expenditure on health care and its socialized system were the best country indicators in selecting a foreign market. This procedure results in each indicator receiving a weight that reflects its relative importance. The assignment of points and weights, as well as the selection of indicators, varies greatly from one global entrepreneur to another and indeed are somewhat arbitrary. Regardless, this requires intensive thinking and internal discussion, which results in better market selection decisions.

Step four involves analyzing the results. When looking at the data, the global entrepreneur should carefully scrutinize and question the results. Look for errors because mistakes can be easily made. Also, a "what if" analysis should be conducted by changing some of the weights and seeing how the results vary.

The fifth and final step is selection of a market to enter and follow-up markets so that an appropriate entry strategy can be selected and a market plan developed. China, India, Ireland, and Germany are countries ICU Global, a videoconferencing provider, is targeting, according to founder and chief executive Stephen McKenzie. The company employed six people in the UK and had a turnover of approximately £3 million pounds in 2007. But McKenzie says it's easy to expand into other countries even when you're a small business as long as you can provide "the same quality assurance to end users." He adds, "Technology allows you to provide full-support, virtual operations in other countries." The countries in question have been selected because they offer the greatest opportunities for ICU Global. "It's good to have a base in Germany because you can easily access the rest of Europe," McKenzie offers. "Meanwhile, Ireland has a large number of companies from continental Europe and the United States investing in it, so there is good opportunity in the context of new technology. Then, there's a thriving technology center in India" (Woods, 2008).

Developing Foreign Market Indicators

While some global entrepreneurs, especially those who have had success in their domestic markets, have an idea of the best foreign markets to enter based on sales or past experience, most do not. Especially for this latter group, it is important to identify some indicators of potential success in foreign markets to assist in the selection process.

INTERNAL COMPANY INDICATORS

Several internal company indicators can be used to develop foreign market indicators, including competitive information, information from fellow global entrepreneurs, previous leads and sales, and trade show information. Indicators of foreign markets with good potential are ones that a company's competitors are entering. Because this assumes that the competitive company has done its homework in selection, care must be taken in using this approach.

Another good internal way to establish foreign market indicators is to discuss the various markets with noncompeting global entrepreneurs. Since globalization is a topic entrepreneurs like to discuss and assist in, these individuals can provide significant information on their experience in specific foreign markets and advice on the potential of your company's product success in those markets. The time and experience of the global entrepreneur in these countries can supply exceptional inside knowledge. Perhaps you can even establish a mentoring relationship with a more experienced global entrepreneur.

A third source for developing marketing indicators is your own company's past sales and leads. Leads and actual sales, while doing business domestically, from out-of-country markets are by far the best indicators of foreign market potential. Care needs to be taken to ensure that potential leads really are meaningful and not just distributors trying to establish product lines for their country without much, if any, analysis of the market potential. A sale to a foreign country is another matter because this signifies that at least for one customer your product can compete.

The final sources for developing foreign market indicators are leads from domestic and foreign trade shows. These are usually the most important gatherings for firms and buyers in a particular product area and as such provide a great opportunity to gather market information to determine market potential in various countries. They also provide an opportunity for you to gather competitive information on both domestic and foreign products.

Primary Versus Secondary Foreign Market Data

One of the most important foundations of any market selection decision is market and demographic information on the foreign country. This can be secondary data (data that is already published) or primary data (original data gathered specifically for the particular decision). Although primary data is generally more accurate, it is also more costly and time consuming to collect versus data that already exists and has been collected by third parties. It is usually best for the global entrepreneur to start the data gathering process by first identifying the secondary data available about the foreign country.

SECONDARY DATA

The first step in obtaining secondary data is to identify the classification codes associated with the company's product/service. These include the Standard Industrial Classification (SIC), the North American Industry Classification System (NAICS), the Standard International Trade Classification (SITC), and the Harmonized Commodity Description and Coding System (Harmonized System); each of which will be discussed in turn.

The SIC code is appropriate for an initial appraisal of the extent and nature of the need in a foreign market, particularly for industrial products. Standard industrial classifications, which are the means by which the federal government classifies manufacturing industries, are based on the product produced or operation performed. Each industry is assigned a two-digit, three-digit, or, where needed for further breakdown, four-digit code. There are 82 two-digit industry groupings, such as 01 Agricultural Production Crops; 23 Apparel and Other Textile Products; 50 Wholesale Trade Durable Goods; 57 Furniture and Home Furnishing Stores; 62 Security, Commodity Brokers and Services; 70 Amusement and Recreation Services; and 94 Administration of Human Resources. Each two-digit group is further broken down into three- and four-digit groups, depending on the industry. For example, the three-digit groups for 72 Personal Services are as follows: 721 Laundry, Cleaning, and Garment Services; 722 Photographic Studios, Portrait; 723 Beauty Shops; 724 Barber Shops; 725 Shoe Repair and Hat Cleaning Shops; 726 Funeral Services and Crematories; and 729 Miscellaneous Personal Services. Where needed, each three-digit group is further refined. The 721 Laundry, Cleaning, and Garment Services includes such categories as 7211 Power Laundries, Family and Commercial; 7214 Diaper Service; 7215 Coin-Operated Laundries and Cleaning; and 7217 Carpet and Upholstery Cleaning.

To determine the primary market demand using the SIC method, it is necessary to first determine all potential customers that have a need for the product or service being considered. Once the groups have been selected, the appropriate basis for demand determination is established and the published material on the industry groups obtained from the *Census of Manufacturers*. Then the primary demand can be determined from the relationship established. The Web site for using the SIC code is www.osha.gov/oshstats/sicser.html.

The North American Industry Classification System (NAICS) is a newer system designed to replace the SIC system. This newer system is based on a six-digit code versus the four-digit code of the SIC system and has new industries, particularly in the service and technology sectors that were not included in the SIC system. The NAICS system is used in the United States, Canada, and Mexico, allowing for greater country comparisons than previously available. The Web site for the NAICS system is www.census.gov/epcd/www/naics.html.

Once the global entrepreneur has obtained the SIC and NAICS codes for his or her product/service, these can be converted to the code system used in the European Union. Each NAICS Rev. 1.1 code is shown with its corresponding ISIC Rev. 3.1 code on an easily accessible Web site (http://unstats.un.org/unsd/cr/registry/regso.asp?Ci=26&Lg=1).

The final two systems are more useful for international data. The Standard International Trade Classification (SITC), developed by the United Nations in 1950, is used to report international trade statistics. It classifies products and services based on a five-digit code, but frequently data is available at only the two- or three-digit code level. Approximately 140 countries report their import and export trade statistics each year to the United Nations. The data are compiled and printed in the United Nations' *International Trade Statistics Yearbook.* The data are also available at http://unstats.un.org/unsd.

The final and perhaps best system for obtaining international data is the Harmonized Commodity Description and Coding System, better known as the International Harmonized Codes. Each product or service is identified by a 10-digit number that is broken down by chapter (first 2 digits), heading (first 4 digits), subheading (first 6 digits), and the commodity code (all 10 digits). Some example international harmonized codes are:

Name	Harmonized Code
peanut butter	2008.11.1000
grand pianos	9201.20.0000
farmed Atlantic salmon	0302.12.0003

Care must be taken when using the Harmonized Commodity codes because they may be different between countries, as well as vary within a country depending on whether they are used for exporting or importing products. This is the case in the United States, where the purpose of the commodity codes is different for importing and exporting. For importing the code is used to determine the import duty (if any); for exporting the primary use of the code is for statistical reporting. This results in two sets of commodity codes in the United States: one set for importing and one set for exporting. The exporting system of classification is labeled Schedule B, and the importing system of classification is called the Harmonized

Tariff Schedule (HTS), maintained by the Office of Tariff Affairs and Trade Agreements.

PROBLEMS IN COLLECTING SECONDARY DATA

There are several problems in collecting international secondary data. The first, and perhaps the most troublesome one, is *accuracy*. Often the data collected in a country is not done in a rigorous fashion, resulting in data that does not reflect the true situation in the country. Or, particularly in more controlled countries, the data is collected for a political agenda instead of for statistical reliability.

The second problem is *comparability*—the data available in one country may not be comparable to the data collected in another country. This may be due to the different methodologies used, errors in the data collection, or differences in applying the commodity coding system.

Lack of current data in a country is a third problem. In many countries, especially those with developing economies, the frequency of data collection can be much less than in more developed countries—perhaps as long as 5-year intervals. In dynamically changing economies, 4- to 5-year-old data is obsolete and not very valuable in decision making.

The final problem in secondary data is the *cost*. In many countries the data may only be available at a fairly high price.

Sources of Country Market Data

Finding useful, accurate data for your country selection decision can sometimes be challenging. Even the global entrepreneur has had experience collecting data in the United States, the process of collecting data in other countries is much more difficult and usually more expensive. There are several sources for both country market and industry data discussed in the following sections.

COUNTRY INDUSTRY MARKET DATA

Economic and country data on such things as age, population, gross domestic product, inflation, literacy, and per capita income is often available from a variety of sources depending on the country. The *CIA World Factbook* provides data on various aspects of a country such as demographics of population, economic indicators, geography, military, politics, and resources available. This is collected by the CIA from numerous sources and agencies and made available in a yearly report. The Country Commercial Guides (CCG) are produced for most countries on a yearly basis. Each guide contains the following information on a country: executive summary, economic trends and outlook, political environment, marketing U.S. products and services, leading sectors for U.S. exports and investments, trade regulations and standards, investment climate, trade and project financing, and business travel. It also has numerous appendices in such areas as country data, domestic economy, trade, investment statistics, U.S. and country contacts, market research, and trade event schedule. These are invaluable to the global entrepreneur in understanding the numbers and trade possibilities in a country. Even though this data is mainly U.S. focused, the reports contain valuable information for global entrepreneurs regardless of country. The National Trade Data Bank (NTDB), maintained by the U.S. Department of Commerce, is also an important database available to the global entrepreneur at virtually no cost. The NTDB database is comprised of international reports, trade statistics, research, and leads on trading opportunities.

Another source of country market data is STAT-USA. This international data source, managed by an agency of the U.S. Department of Commerce, is enormous and includes the NTDB previously discussed, GLOBUS (Global Business Opportunities), and the State of the Nation database. Contributed to by many governmental agencies, STAT-USA contains a multitude of international and national reports available including:

- African Development Bank Business Opportunities

- Asia Commerce Overview

- Bureau of Export Administration (BXA) Annual Report

- Computer Markets

- Country Analysis Briefs (CABS)

- Directory of Feasibility Studies and Projects

- Fish and Fishery Product Imports and Exports

- Food Market Reports

- Foreign Labor Trends

- International Automotive Industry

- Latin American/Caribbean Business Bulletin

- Minerals Yearbook

- Steel Monitoring Report

- Telecommunications Information and Reports

- Trade Associations and Publications

- U.S. Foreign Trade Reports

- U.S. International Trade in Goods and Services

- World Agricultural Production Reports

- World Bank International Business Opportunities

Because this is just a small sampling of the reports and data available, it is important that every global entrepreneur look into STAT-USA when collecting the needed international data.

One of the best sources of information is from the World Bank, which ranks every country with various criteria on the ease of doing business in that particular country. The index ranks countries (economies) from 1 to 178 and is calculated by averaging the percentile rankings on each of the ten topics covered in *Doing Business 2008*. The criteria being ranked include: ease of doing business, ease of starting a business, dealing with licenses, employing workers, registering property, getting credit, protecting investors, paying taxes, trading across borders, and closing a business. The rankings for selected countries are shown in Table 5.1. Singapore, New Zealand, and the United States were ranked 1, 2, and 3 respectively on the ease of doing business. Australia, Canada, and New Zealand were ranked 1, 2, and 3 respectively on the ease of starting a business.

TRADE ASSOCIATIONS

Trade associations in the United States and throughout the world are also a good source for industry data about a particular country. Some trade associations do market surveys of their members' international activities and are strategically involved in international standards issues for their particular industry.

TRADE PUBLICATIONS AND PERIODICALS

There are numerous domestic and international publications specific to a particular industry that are also good sources of information. The editorial content of these journals can provide interesting information and insights on trends, companies, and trade shows by giving a more local perspective on the particular market and market conditions. Sometimes trade journals are the best, and often the only, source of information on competition and growth rates in a particular country.

Table 5.1 Rankings of Countries on Various Business Criteria

Economy	Ease of Doing Business Rank	Starting a Business	Dealing With Licenses	Employing Workers	Registering Property	Getting Credit	Protecting Investors	Paying Taxes	Trading Across Borders	Enforcing Contracts	Closing a Business
Singapore	1	9	5	1	13	7	2	2	1	4	2
New Zealand	2	3	2	13	1	3	1	9	16	13	16
United States	3	4	24	1	10	7	5	76	15	8	18
Hong Kong, China	4	13	60	23	58	2	3	3	3	1	15
Denmark	5	18	6	10	39	13	19	13	2	30	7
United Kingdom	6	6	54	21	19	1	9	12	27	24	10
Canada	7	2	26	19	28	7	5	25	39	43	4
Ireland	8	5	20	37	79	7	5	6	20	39	6
Australia	9	1	52	8	27	3	51	41	34	11	14
Iceland	10	14	23	42	8	13	64	27	11	4	12
Norway	11	28	55	94	6	36	15	16	4	9	3
Japan	12	44	32	17	48	13	12	105	18	21	1
Finland	13	16	39	127	17	26	51	83	5	7	5
Sweden	14	22	17	107	7	36	51	42	6	53	19
Thailand	15	36	12	49	20	36	33	89	50	26	44
Switzerland	16	35	29	20	12	26	158	15	37	25	33
Estonia	17	20	14	156	21	48	33	31	7	29	50
Germany	20	71	16	137	47	3	83	67	10	15	29
Chile	33	39	58	68	34	48	33	34	43	64	98
South Africa	35	53	45	91	76	26	9	61	134	85	68
Mexico	44	75	21	134	71	48	33	135	76	83	23
Hungary	45	67	87	81	96	26	107	127	45	12	53
Turkey	57	43	128	136	31	68	64	54	56	34	112
China	83	135	175	86	29	84	83	168	42	20	57
Nicaragua	93	70	127	59	130	68	83	156	87	69	63
India	120	111	134	85	112	36	33	165	79	177	137
Brazil	122	122	107	119	110	84	64	137	93	106	131
Indonesia	123	168	99	153	121	68	51	110	41	141	136
Ukraine	139	109	174	102	138	68	141	177	120	46	140

SOURCE: World Bank Doing Business Rankings 2008: Retrieved August 27, 2008, from www.doingbusiness.org/economyrankings/

Competitive Positioning

One similar cause of success in both international and domestic markets is competitive positioning—knowing the competition very well and being able to position your company and product in that product/market space. In positioning your company internationally, it is even more important to identify the strategy of each competitive company. The strategy will significantly affect the manner and commitment of a company in an international market, which in turn affects the nature and degree of its competitive behavior in that market. A competitive company's international strategy may not be the same as yours. If the global entrepreneur emphasizes the competitive analysis too much without taking into account the competitive company's strategy, then he or she can create a reactive strategy that can be totally ineffective and inappropriate for his or her company. This is particularly important in developing economies where some companies use a "hit or miss" strategy, realizing that many of the markets will lose money and will not be viable over a long period of time.

The global entrepreneur should begin competitive positioning by first documenting the current strategy of each primary competitor. This can be organized by using the method indicated in Table 5.2. Information on competitors can be gathered initially by using as much public information as possible and then complementing this with a marketing research project. Newspaper articles, Web sites, catalogs, promotions, interviews with distributors and customers, and any other marketing or company information available should be reviewed. Articles that have been written on the competitors can be found by using a computer search in any university or local library. These articles should be scanned for information on competitor strategies and should identify the names of individuals who were interviewed, referenced, or even mentioned in the articles. Any of these individuals, as well as the author of the article, can then be contacted to obtain further information. All the information can then be summarized in the model provided in Table 5.2. Once the competitors' strategies have been summarized, the global entrepreneur should begin to identify the strengths and weaknesses of each competitor, as shown in the table.

All the information included in Table 5.2 can then be used to formulate the market positioning strategy of the new venture. Will the new venture imitate a particular competitor or will it try to satisfy needs in the market that are not being filled by any other company? This analysis will enlighten the global entrepreneur and provide a solid basis for developing the market entry plan for the international market.

One method for analyzing a market opportunity in light of competition is shown in Table 5.3. Using this evaluation process, various elements of the opportunity are evaluated, such as (1) the creation and length of the opportunity, (2) its real and perceived value(s), (3) its risks and returns,

Table 5.2   An Assessment of Competitor Market Strategies
                and Strengths and Weaknesses

	Competitor A	**Competitor B**	**Competitor C**
Product or service strategies			
Pricing strategies			
Distribution strategies			
Promotion strategies			
Strengths and weaknesses			

SOURCE: Hisrich, R. D., Peters, M. P., & Shepherd, D. A. (2007). *Entrepreneurship: Starting, developing, and managing a new enterprise* (7th ed.). New York: McGraw-Hill.

(4) its competitive environment, (5) its industry, and (6) its fit with the personal skills and goals of the entrepreneur.

It is important for the entrepreneur to understand the nature and root cause of the opportunity. Is it technological change, market shift, government regulation, or competition? These factors and the resulting opportunity have a different market size and time dimension. The market size and the length of the window of international opportunity form the primary basis for determining the risks and rewards involved. The risks reflect the market, competition, technology, and amount of capital involved. The amount of capital forms the basis for the return and rewards.

In this evaluation the competition and potential competition are carefully appraised. Features and potential price for the product/service should be evaluated along with those of competitive products presently in the product/market space in the country. If any major problems and competitive disadvantages are identified, modifications can be made or a new market investigated.

The relative advantages of the product/service versus competitive products can be determined through the following questions: How does the new idea compare with competitive products in terms of quality and reliability? Is the idea superior or deficient compared with products currently available in the market? Is this a good market opportunity? One method for evaluating the idea against competing products or services is the conversational interview. Here, selected individuals are asked to compare the idea against products presently filling that need. By comparing the

Table 5.3 Determining the Company's Competitive Position

Factor	Aspects	Competitive Capabilities	Company's Idea/ Capability	Differential Advantage	Unique Selling Proposition
Type of Need Continuing need Declining need Emerging need Future need					
Timing of Need Duration of need Frequency of need Demand cycle Position in life cycle					
Competing Ways to Satisfy Need Doing without Using present way Modifying present way					
Perceived Benefits/Risks Utility to customer Appealing characteristics Customer tastes and preferences Buying motives Consumption habits					
Price Versus Performance Features Price-quantity relationship Demand elasticity Stability of price Stability of market					
Market Size Potential Market growth Market trends Market development requirements Threats to market					
Availability to Customer Funds General economic conditions Economic trends Customer income Financing opportunities					

SOURCE: Adapted from Hisrich, R. D. (2004). *How to fix and prevent the 13 biggest problems that derail business.* New York: McGraw-Hill.

characteristics and attributes of the new idea, some uniqueness of the idea can be forthcoming.

An initial competitive analysis should determine if there is really a need for, as well as the value of, the idea in the international market in light of competition. To accurately determine the need, it is helpful to define the potential needs of the market in terms of timing, satisfaction, alternatives, benefits and risks, future expectations, price-versus-product performance features, market structure and size, and economic conditions (see Table 5.3). The factors indicated in Table 5.3 should be evaluated not only in terms of the characteristics of the idea, but also in terms of the idea's competitive strength relative to each factor. This comparison with competitive products will indicate the strengths and weaknesses of the idea.

The need determination should focus on the type of need, its timing, the users involved with trying it, the importance of controllable marketing variables, the overall market structure, and the characteristics of the international market. Each of these factors should be evaluated in terms of characteristics of the product/service being considered and the aspects and capabilities of present methods for satisfying the particular need. This analysis will indicate the extent of the international market opportunity available.

In determining the value of the product/service in the international market, financial scheduling—such as cash outflow, cash inflow, contribution to profit, and return on investment—needs to be evaluated in terms of other ideas. Using the form in Table 5.4, the dollar amount of each of the considerations important to the new idea should be determined as accurately as possible so that a quantitative evaluation can be performed. These figures can be revised later as better information becomes available.

Finally, the product/service/international market must fit the personal skills and goals of the global entrepreneur. It is particularly important that the entrepreneur be able to put forth the necessary time and effort required to make the venture succeed. Although many global entrepreneurs feel that the desire can be developed along with the venture, typically this does not materialize and therefore dooms the venture to fail. A global entrepreneur must believe in his or her idea so much that he or she will make the necessary sacrifices to develop the idea into a sound business model that will be the basis for a successful new venture in the international market.

International Competitive Information

There are many good international sources for competitive information, including both secondary and primary data. These include company information, databases, journals, newspapers, trade associations, and personal interviews.

Table 5.4   Determining the Value of the Product/Service in the International Market

Value Consideration	Cost (in $)
Cash Outflow R&D costs Marketing costs Capital equipment costs Other costs	
Cash Inflow Sales of new product Effect on additional sales Salvageable value	
Net Cash Flow Maximum exposure Time to maximum exposure Duration of exposure Total investment Maximum net cash in a single year	
Profit Profit from new product Profit affecting additional sales of existing products Fraction of total company profit	
Relative Return Return on shareholders' equity (ROE) Return on investment (ROI) Cost of capital Present value (PV) Discounted cash flow (DCF) Return on assets employed (ROA) Return on sales	
Comparisons Compared to other investments Compared to other product opportunities Compared to other investment opportunities	

SOURCE: Hisrich, R. D. (2004). *How to fix and prevent the 13 biggest problems that derail business*. New York: McGraw-Hill.

COMPANY INFORMATION

Particularly for publicly traded companies, the company itself provides a significant amount of data useful to the global entrepreneur. This is often the best and easiest source of competitive information and is usually very accurate (particularly for companies in developed economies) because the information comes directly from the company itself. All company literature and information regarding their international activities should be collected. Sometimes this is very easily obtained at international trade shows, where more detailed information is available from the individuals manning the company's booth. Of course, the Web site of the company should be thoroughly explored, as well as the Web sites of overseas customers and distributors. Companies are increasingly putting more and more important information on their Web sites, knowing that it is available for everyone.

The international advertising of each competitive company should also be examined. This will be very helpful in developing the market entry strategy and marketing campaign. This is also particularly helpful in providing much-needed pricing information. Whenever possible, be sure to determine if the advertisement was placed by the company or the distributor in the international market. If the advertisement mentions only one distributor as the contact and provides no details on how to reach the company or if there are products featured from more than one manufacturer, the advertisement was probably placed by the distributor. This is important because the manufacturer's direct involvement in the placement of the advertisement would suggest a strong possibility that the particular market is a priority. Direct placement of advertisements in a market indicates a huge level of commitment and involvement in the particular market. The advertisements also provide insight into how the competitive company is competing in the particular market; a company's competitive strategies may vary from one international market to the next.

INTERNATIONAL DATABASES

There are four primary databases that provide good sources of international competitive information. These include Directory of United States Exporters, Port Import Export Report Service (PIERS), United Nations International Trade Statistics Yearbook, and United States Exports by Commodity. Each will be discussed here in turn.

The Directory of United States Exporters, published each year by the *Journal of Commerce*, is a combination of some information from PIERS and company responses to a questionnaire. The data for each company includes

- Address

- Telephone and fax numbers

- Number of employees

- Year established

- Bank SIC code

- Modes of transportation used

- Contact names and titles

- Commodity code and description of products exported

- Destination countries

- Annual twenty-foot equivalent units of containers (TEUs)

- Annual number of shipments

- Company PIERS identification numbers

Sometimes one of the most important pieces of information—destination country—is not reported directly but simply indicates worldwide. The Directory of United States Exporters is available in both print and CD-ROM versions directly from the *Journal of Commerce* and can often be used at the state trade assistance center.

The second useful database is the Port Import Export Report Service (PIERS). The information in this database comes from the manifests of vessels loading international cargo outbound from the United States, as well as the manifests of all inbound shipments (imports). Although not every item is available in every situation, the information in the PIERS database includes

- Product description

- PIERS product code

- Harmonized tariff code and description

- U.S. and overseas port name

- Container size, quantity, TEU count, and cubic feet

- Steamship line and vessel name

- Manifest number

- Cargo quantity and unit of measure

- Cargo weight

- Voyage number

- Estimated cargo value

- Payment type

- Bank name

- Shipment direction

- U.S. and overseas origins and destinations

- Marks and numbers

- Name and address of U.S. importer (imports only)

- Bill of lading number

- Name and address of U.S. exporter

- Container number

- Name and address of foreign shipper (imports only)

- Customs clearing district (imports only)

- Name and address of notify party

- Arrival and departure dates in U.S. ports

The PIERS database has been expanded to include the shipping activities of most ports of Latin American countries and Mexico.

Although the data from PIERS is very good, there are several downsides to using this database. First, it is very expensive to use the ongoing monthly service as well as to buy individual reports. Second, it is based only on waterborne shipments and does not include other shipments into a country such as by land or air. Usually, however, the data is worth the cost as it provides detailed competitive information, including such details as the frequency and timing of shipments.

JOURNALS, NEWSPAPERS, AND TRADE ASSOCIATIONS

Journals, newspapers, and trade associations provide another very valuable source of information on competition. Most trade journals are very industry specific and often focus on international activities in that industry. There are also industry trade journals in foreign markets. From these, competitive product and other competitive information, distribution lists, advertisements, and other industry data can be easily obtained at little or no cost through the various search and retrieval options available. Many are available on the Internet. The *Financial Times* regularly features information on markets and competition (see Figure 5.1).

While not usually as valuable, newspapers can also provide competitive information, particularly the local newspaper in the city where the competitive company is headquartered. The local newspaper often provides information not found anywhere else in its coverage of the company and interviews with company managers.

Finally, trade associations in the industry often have summary data on sales and pricing in the industry. Most trade associations track international

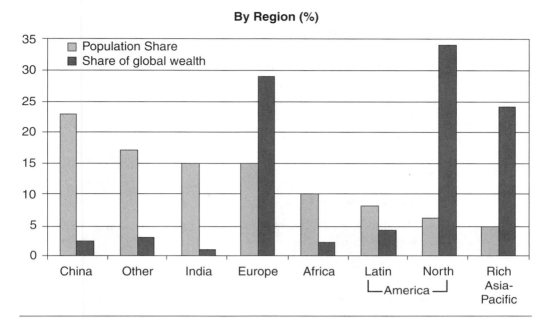

Figure 5.1   Population and Wealth Shares by Region

SOURCE: United Nations. (2006, December 9–10). Giles, Chris. Chinese to soar up the super-rich ranks. *Financial Times, London, UK,* p. 6.

trends and data. Even just a list of association members provides information about the companies interested in a particular industry.

PERSONAL INTERVIEWS

Probably the best and most comprehensive source of competitive information comes from personal interviews with individuals who really know the competitor company. By interviewing staff writers of journals and newspapers, the global entrepreneur can obtain up-to-date information and speculation. Even though they are not company specific, government contacts in a particular country can provide information about competitive trends and challenges. Industry experts can provide detailed information on the industry and usually on companies in that industry. And, best of all, foreign customers and distributors can provide detailed information about the local market and the activities of competitors. These are all an excellent source of specific, detailed, and timely competitive information.

While you need to analyze foreign markets and the competition, and adapt your product or service to meet local market needs to expand internationally, you will also need a person to run the operation. No one knows this better than Bruce McGaw, president of Bruce McGaw Graphics, a West Nyack, New York, fine-arts poster publisher. "As smart as I am about the American market, my knowledge doesn't necessarily apply abroad," admits McGaw. Rather than sending one of his U.S. employees to establish a London distributorship, he decided to search for a local manager to run his United Kingdom operation. Because he didn't want to "run over there every other week," he began searching for "someone talented, who would take the ball and run with it." The individual needed the following:

- Significant industry experience and real marketplace intelligence

- An understanding that customer service was central to the company's success

- The ability to take charge and run the business as if it were "his own little business"

McGaw found the right individual—a customer whose business was struggling. McGaw Graphics bought the company and the individual became the UK manager. Five years later European sales accounted for $3.5 million of the company's total $15 million in revenue; the UK operation was considered a market leader. McGaw used a similar strategy in France when he acquired a business run by an American. "Where you set up your business is not as important as finding the right person to run it," says McGaw. Although his strategic plan includes expansion into Germany, Italy, and Spain, McGaw will not move until he finds the right managers (Fenn, 1995).

Summary

This chapter deals with how global entrepreneurs should research and select the best foreign markets to launch their company or to expand their business. Finding the best market for one's product or service is only possible with thorough research using multiple resources, including information from potential competitors. The chapter describes an effective five-step foreign market selection process that a global entrepreneur should use: (1) develop appropriate indicators, (2) collect data and convert into comparable indicators, (3) establish an appropriate weight for each indicator, (4) analyze the data, and (5) select the appropriate market from the market rankings. A global entrepreneur must determine the best indicators for whether or not his or her company will do well in the foreign market and then collect information based on those indicators from federal and international commerce and trade institutions, as well as from competitors and other global entrepreneurs that are working in the same market. At least 3 years of detailed information must be collected and analyzed. The information will be either from primary sources, which is a more costly and time-consuming process, or secondary sources, which is normally much easier to access but not as specific. The main problems that a global entrepreneur will find with secondary data are its lack of accuracy, comparability between countries/regions, lack of current data, and potentially high costs. Analyzing the strengths and weaknesses of competitors' strategies can give the global entrepreneur guidelines for developing his or her own strategy and for determining if the right market exists for his or her product or service.

Questions for Discussion

1. What types of information should entrepreneurs seek out before deciding which foreign market to enter?

2. What are the different types and sources of information that are available?

3. What are some potential problems with data collected in another country?

4. Jean-Marie is considering expanding her bakery business from France into Croatia. What information would help her determine a good location to start her business there?

Chapter Exercises

1. Pick a business and create the key indicators that you will use to analyze the new market.

2. Using the same business you chose for Exercise 1, outline the information that you will need to collect about the new market.

3. For the same business you used in the previous exercises, create a list of competitors in the new market and identify primary sources to interview about these competitors.

References

Fenn, D. (1995, June). Opening up an overseas operation. *Inc., 17*(8), p. 89.

Thuermer, K. E. (2007, August). Cobra Beer—From small beer. *Foreign Direct Investment London,* p. 1.

Woods, C. (2008, April 8). *ICU Global grabs international opportunities*, www.realbusiness.co.uk/news/international-business/5213436/icu-global -grabs-international-opportunities.thtml

Suggested Readings

Berry, H. (2006, December). Shareholder valuation of foreign investment and expansion. *Strategic Management Journal, 27*(12), 1123–1140.

In this article, Berry argues that shareholders may not value a firm's investment in a developing country if the firm does not have previous experience with international investment or the management of risk and uncertainty. After analyzing the foreign investments of 191 U.S. manufacturing firms over a 20-year period, the author reaffirms her argument that prior international expansion, firm capabilities and experience, and industry knowledge affect the valuation of firm investments by shareholders.

Blankson, C., & Kalafatis, S. P. (2007). Positioning strategies of international and multicultural-oriented service brands. *Journal of Services Marketing, 21*(6), 435–450.

To further the operationalization of positioning, this article examines the positioning strategies of service brands that are international or multicultural. It also measures whether a target group's perception of a firm's positioning strategy fits with both the management's presumed positioning strategy and the firm's actual positioning practices.

Lynch, R. (2006). International acquisition and other growth strategies: Some lessons from the food and drink industry. *Thunderbird International Business Review, 48*(5), 605–622.

This article explores acquisition versus organic international growth in developing a profitable international growth strategy when markets are mature. Through a two-stage study of companies in the food and drink industry, the author identified acquisitions focused on the company's current product portfolio as the most popular form of international growth. It also suggests that organic growth strategy is less risky and problematic than the more desirable international acquisition strategy.

Waheeduzzaman, A. N. M., & Pradeep, A. R. (2006). Market potential and foreign direct investment: Exploring the relationship in emerging markets. *Advances in Competitiveness Research, 14*(1), 44–60.

Using the Market Potential Indicator (MPI) of Michigan State University (MSU), this study shows that the MPI's individual indicators of market size, market growth rate, market intensity, market consumption capacity, commercial infrastructure, economic freedom, market receptivity, and country risk do not create a full explanation of foreign direct investment in emerging markets. Using factor analysis and then regressing those findings on foreign direct investment, the dimensions of power of the market, openness and growth, and capacity and infrastructure provide a better understanding of market potential and foreign direct investment. These preliminary findings need to be examined again using more data to better understand what influences foreign direct investment.

World Bank. (2007). *World development indicators*. Herndon, VA: World Bank Publications.

World Development Indicators (WDI) is an annual publication of data about development from the World Bank. Over 900 indicators in more than 80 tables are included in the 2007 WDI, covering world view, people, environment, economy, states and markets, and global links.

6 International Legal Concerns

Profile: Dr. Fred Moll

INTUITIVE SURGICAL

In June 2000 the United States Patent and Trademark Office issued the broad-based Patent No. 6.063.095, offering Computer Motion Inc., a principal leader in medical robotics, the patent on hand tremor elimination with a robotic surgical system during minimally invasive surgery. In the meantime Computer Motion filed suit in the United States, alleging infringement by Intuitive Surgical of seven U.S. patents, equally relating to robotic surgery. Patent No. 6.063.095 will bring this number to eight.

Computer Motion believes their invention is used by Intuitive Surgical Inc. in their *da Vinci*® Surgical System product. Intuitive Surgical designs and manufactures the *da Vinci*® Surgical System, a computer-enhanced surgical platform enabling surgeons to realize the benefits of open surgery, such as intuitive instrument control, natural range of motion, fine tissue manipulation capability, and 3D visualization, while operating through the small puncture incisions of minimally invasive surgery (MIS).

According to Intuitive Surgical, the original prototype for the *da Vinci*® System was developed in the late 1980s at the former Stanford Research Institute under contract to the U.S. Army. Although initial work was funded in the interest of developing a system for performing battlefield surgery remotely, possible commercial applications were even more compelling: It was clear to those involved that this technology could accelerate the application of a minimally invasive surgical approach to a broader range of procedures.

In 1995 Dr. Fred Moll co-founded Intuitive Surgical to test this theory. In January 1999 Intuitive launched the *da Vinci*® Surgical System, and in

2000 it became the first robotic surgical system cleared by the FDA for general laparoscopic surgery. In the following years, the FDA cleared the *da Vinci*® Surgical System for thoracoscopic (chest) surgery, for cardiac procedures performed with adjunctive incisions, and urologic and gynecologic procedures.

The company is headquartered in Sunnyvale, California, and today has more than 500 employees in offices worldwide. Sales for the 2005 fiscal year totaled $227.3 million, up 64% from $138.3 million in 2004. Recurring revenue totaled $102.7 million, or 71% of total revenue in 2005, compared to $60 million in 2004.

www.intuitivesurgical.com

Chapter Objectives

1. To determine the best method for operating in countries based on the legal and political concerns faced.

2. To understand how political activities can affect an entrepreneurial venture and how to analyze those activities.

3. To explain the implications of morals and ethics on the global business.

4. To define the growing concerns about various types of political risk in developed or developing nations.

5. To illustrate the various types of legal and regulatory systems faced by an entrepreneur in a global venture and how to navigate these various arenas.

6. To understand the difference between collectivism and individualism, as well as democracy and totalitarianism, and how these ideas form a country's political system.

7. To assess the level of corruption and bribery in a foreign country and how it affects the business environment in that country.

8. To learn the elements of political risk and what factors to consider when entering a new market.

9. To know the different legal traditions and how they affect (1) property rights, (2) contract law, (3) product safety, and (4) product liability.

Introduction

The legal and political systems confronting the global entrepreneur vary significantly around the world. Overall, the political system (the government system of a country or other economic unit) needs to be analyzed according to its degree of collectivism versus individualism and the degree of democracy versus totalitarianism. Although related (e.g., a system emphasizing collectivism tends to be totalitarian), there is a gray area because some democratic societies emphasize a mixture of collectivism and individualism.

In collectivism, a system stressing the primacy of communal goals, the needs of a society as a whole are more important than individual freedom. Therefore, an individual may not have the right to do something if it is counter to the good of society. Socialism and Marxism are two examples of collectivism. Individualism, the opposite of collectivism, is a system where the individual has the freedom to pursue his or her own economic and political activities. In this case, the interests of the individual usually take precedence over the interests of society (state). Similarly, democracy and totalitarianism are opposites on the political spectrum. While democracy is a political system in which government is by the people, either exercised directly or through elected representatives, totalitarianism is a system of government where one person or political party exercises absolute control over everything and no opposing political parties are allowed.

Although most global entrepreneurs prefer to do business in stable and freely governed countries, good business opportunities often exist in different conditions. It is important to assess each country's policies as well as its stability. This assessment is referred to as *political risk analysis.* There is some political risk in every country, but the degree of risk from country to country varies significantly; and even in a country with a history of stability and consistency, these conditions could change. There are three major types of political risks that might be present: operating risk (risk of interference with the operations of the venture), transfer risk (risk in attempting to shift assets or other funds out of the country), and the biggest risk of all—ownership risk (risk where the country takes over the property and employees). Of course, conflicts and changes in the solvency of the country are major risks to a global entrepreneur in particular countries. This can take such forms as guerilla warfare, civil disturbances, and even terrorism, where the global entrepreneur's company and employees are the target. As evidenced by the 9/11 attacks on the World Trade Center and Pentagon, international terrorists can target U.S. interests both in and out of the country.

The legal system of a country also affects the global entrepreneur. The legal system is the rules and laws that regulate behavior as well as the process by which the laws are enforced. A country's laws regulate the business practices in a country, the manner in which business transactions are executed, and the rights and obligations of the parties involved in any business transaction.

Political Activity

There are two primary areas of political activity that can affect the global entrepreneur: trade sanctions and export controls, and regulations of global business behavior.

TRADE SANCTIONS AND EXPORT CONTROLS

The term *trade sanction* refers to a government action against the free flow of goods and services, or even ideas, for political purposes. Sanctions can be used to influence the type and amount of trade in a particular category and can be extended to prohibit all trade in that category—a *trade embargo*. The United States, for example, placed a trade embargo on Cuba prohibiting any trade except humanitarian aide and even embargoed travel of U.S. citizens between the United States and Cuba.

Trade sanctions and embargoes have been used by countries as a foreign policy tool for centuries. The purposes of such actions have ranged from upholding human rights to stopping nuclear proliferation and terrorism to forcing countries to open their home markets. The intent generally is to change the policies of a country or, in some cases, change the country's government.

Export controls are used to restrict the flow of specified goods and services to a country. The United States and other industrialized nations have established strong export controls to deny or at least limit the acquisition of strategically important goods, particularly nuclear in nature, to certain countries deemed adversarial. In the United States, these controls are based on the Export Administration Act and the Munitions Control Act. A list of commodities needing approval in the form of an export license has been established by the Department of Commerce working with such government agencies as the Departments of Defense, Energy, and State.

Given the increase in availability of products of all types, the rapid dissemination of information and innovation on a global basis, and the speed of change and new technology advancement, the denial of any product has become much more difficult to enforce. Export controls based on capacity criteria, which occurred in computer technology, are mostly irrelevant because the technology changes so quickly, obsolescing previous capacity constraints. About 75% of sales in the data processing industry each year are from new products and services introduced in the last 2 years. Given the rapidly changing technology and worldwide information dissemination via the Web, export controls are becoming less and less enforceable.

Political Risk

Given these conflicts and differences in the political environments in countries, the global entrepreneur must manage as well as possible the *political risks* involved. Generally, political risk tends to be lower in countries that have a history of stability and consistency. Political risk has three major components: ownership risk, operating risk, and transfer risk.

Ownership risk is the possibility of loss of property and life, which can happen when conflict breaks out or international terrorism occurs. International terrorists frequently target U.S. business facilities, operations, and personnel.

Operating risk refers to the interference of ongoing operations in a foreign country. Countries can impose new controls in prices and production or restrict access to resources or labor markets. These can disrupt or even close down the foreign operations of the global entrepreneur.

The final aspect of political risk—*transfer risk*—affects the movement of funds within a country or between countries. Transfer risk can result in currency and remittance restrictions that are not beneficial to the foreign entrepreneurial venture (this is elaborated on in Chapter 8).

The global entrepreneur must manage these risks to the extent possible. One way to reduce the risk of government intervention is to demonstrate a concern for the society of the host country and a desire to be a good global citizen. This attitude is reflected in such actions as good pay, good working conditions, good hiring and training practices, contributing to the economic development of the region, and having a joint venture with local national partners who will share in the sales and profits of the venture. The global entrepreneur should also carefully monitor any and all political developments. Potential problems and negative future regulations should be discovered as soon as possible so appropriate action can be taken.

Finally, the global entrepreneur should consider purchasing insurance that covers at least some possible losses due to political risk. In the United State, the Overseas Private Investment Corporation (OPIC) provides three types of risk insurance for currency inconvertibility, expropriation of resources, and political violence at a cost that is not particularly prohibitive. Of course, the best risk management is good country selection as discussed in Chapter 5.

Legal Considerations

One of the main difficulties in being a successful global entrepreneur is the challenges resulting from the many different legal and regulatory environments. Even though there are a variety of legal and regulatory systems apparent, each is based on one of four foundations: common law, civil law, Islamic law, and socialist law.

The common law system, stemming from English law, is the foundation of the legal system in such countries as Australia, Canada, the United Kingdom, and the United States. The civil law system, stemming from Roman law, is the basis of law in such countries as France and some countries in Latin America. Derived from the Quran and the teachings of the Prophet Mohammed, Islamic law is in most Islamic countries. Finally, socialist law is derived from the Marxist socialist system and influences, to some degree, the law and regulations in China, Cuba, North Korea, Russia and the former Soviet republics, and Vietnam.

These foundations lead to a variety of dissimilar laws and regulations of business, which are compounded by the treaties and conventions in each country. To handle this facet of going international, the global entrepreneur needs to have an overall sense of the legal system of a country and must have legal counsel to handle specifics. Ideally this legal counsel would have its headquarters in the United States with an office in the host country. Several areas are critical to some extent for every global entrepreneur: (1) property rights, (2) contract law, (3) product safety, and (4) product liability.

Countries vary significantly in the degree their legal system protects the property rights of the individual and business. The property rights of a business are the resources owned, the use of those resources, and the income earned from their use. Besides buildings, equipment, and land, the protection of intellectual property is a very grave concern, particularly for technology global entrepreneurs. Intellectual property such as a book, computer software code, a score of music, a video, a formula for a new chemical or drug, or other unique ideas are very important to a firm and need to be protected when going outside the United States. The three major ways of protecting intellectual property in the United States are patents, copyrights, and trademarks. Few countries have laws and court procedures protecting intellectual property like the United States. You have probably heard how videos can be purchased in China at 10% of the cost in the United States, sometimes even before being officially released. Even the *Entrepreneurship* book, which the author coauthored, has legal editions in several languages including Arabic, Chinese, Hungarian, Indonesian, Portuguese, Russian, Slovenian, and Spanish, and has an illegal edition in the Iranian language because Iran does not recognize world corporate copyright laws. Before entering a country, the global entrepreneur needs to assess the country's protection of the intellectual property of his or her venture and the costs if copied illegally.

Another area of concern is the contract law of the country *and* how it is enforced. A contract specifies the conditions for an exchange and the rights and duties of the parties involved in this exchange. Contract law varies significantly from country to country, in part reflecting two types of legal tradition—common law and civil law—previously discussed. Common law tends to be relatively nonspecific, so contracts under this law are longer and more detailed with all the contingencies spelled out. Because civil law is much more detailed, contracts under it are much shorter.

In addition to the law itself, the global entrepreneur needs to understand how contract law might be enforced and the judicial system securing this enforcement. If the legal system of the country does not have a good track record of enforcement, the contract can contain an agreement that any contract disputes will be heard in the courts of another country. Because each entrepreneur might have some advantage in his or her home country, another country is usually selected. This aspect is very important for global entrepreneurs operating in developing economies with little or even a bad history of enforcement and other anti-business countries. One company exporting Hungarian wine into Russia made sure any disputes in all its Russian contracts were heard in the Finnish court system instead of the Russian one.

The final overall area of concern is the laws of the country regarding product safety and liability. Again, the laws have significant variances between countries from very high liability and damage awards in the United States to very low levels in Russia. These laws also raise an ethical issue for the global entrepreneur, particularly one from the United States. When doing business in a country where the liability and product safety laws are much lower than one's home country, should you follow the more relaxed local standards or adhere to the stricter standards of your home country and risk not being competitive and losing the business? Each global entrepreneur must answer this question when doing business in a particular country.

Intellectual Property

Intellectual property, which includes patents, trademarks, copyrights, and trade secrets, represents important assets to the global entrepreneur. Often global entrepreneurs, because of their lack of understanding of intellectual property, ignore important steps needed to protect these assets.

Because all business is regulated by the laws of the country the global business is located in, the global entrepreneur needs to be aware of any regulations that may affect his or her new venture. At different stages of the start-up, the entrepreneur will need legal advice, which will vary based on such factors as whether the new venture is a franchise, an independent start-up, or a buy-out; whether it produces a consumer versus an industrial product; whetherit is nonprofit or for-profit; and whether it involves exporting or importing.

The infringement on the global entrepreneur and his or her venture, particularly in the case of intellectual property, reflects the disparity in laws of various countries, particularly emerging ones. For example, China, since entering the World Trade Organization (WTO) in 2001, has strengthened the rights of the owners of intellectual property and is continuing to do so. Even though China's intellectual property laws and the laws of other industrialized nations are not fully harmonized, a global entrepreneur can still receive and enforce intellectual property rights in China.

The form of organization as well as the type of franchise agreement offer many options an entrepreneur can choose from. The global entrepreneur should understand the advantages and disadvantages of each type regarding such issues as liability, taxes, continuity, transferability of interest, costs of setting up, and attractiveness for raising capital in the particular country.

Patents

A *patent* is a contract between the government of a country and the global entrepreneur. In exchange for disclosure of the invention, the government grants the inventor exclusivity regarding the invention in the country for a specified amount of time. At the end of this time, the invention becomes part of the public domain.

The patent gives the global entrepreneur a negative right because it prevents anyone else from making, using, or selling the defined invention. Even if the global entrepreneur has been granted a patent, he or she may find during the process of producing or marketing the invention that it infringes on the patent rights of others. There are several types of patents

- *Utility patents.* A utility patent basically grants the global entrepreneur protection from anyone else making, using, and/or selling the identified invention; it usually protects new, useful, and unobvious processes such as film developing; machines such as photocopiers; compositions of matter such as chemical compounds or mixtures of ingredients; and articles of manufacture such as the toothpaste pump. A utility patent in the United States has a term of 20 years, beginning on the date of filing with the Patent and Trademark Office (PTO). The time period and filing process varies by country.

- *Design patents.* These patents cover new, original, ornamental, and unobvious designs for articles of manufacture. A design patent reflects the appearance of an object and is granted for a 14-year term in the United States. Again, this time period varies by country. Like the utility patent, the design patent provides the global entrepreneur with a negative right, excluding others from making, using, or selling an article having the ornamental appearance given in the drawings included in the patent. Companies such as Reebok and Nike are very interested in obtaining design patents as a means of protecting their original designs. These types of patents are valuable for global ventures that need to protect molded plastic parts, extrusions, and product and container configurations.

- *Plant patents.* These are issued under the same provisions as utility patents and are for new varieties of plants. Few of these types of patents are issued in the United States.

Patents in the United States are issued by the PTO. In addition to patents, this office administers other programs, such as the Disclosure Document Program, whereby the inventor files disclosure of the invention, giving recognition that he or she was the first to develop or invent the idea. In most cases the inventor will eventually patent the idea. A second program is the Defensive Publication Program. This gives the inventor the opportunity to protect an idea for which he or she does not wish to obtain a patent. It prevents anyone else from patenting this idea, but gives the public access to the invention.

INTERNATIONAL PATENTS

With international trade increasing each year, there is a need for an international patent law to protect firms from imitations by providing some protection in global markets. In response, the Patent Cooperation Treaty (PCT), with over 100 participants, was established to facilitate patent filings in multiple countries in one office rather than filing in each separate country. Administered by the World Intellectual Property Organization (WIPO) in Geneva, Switzerland, it provides a preliminary search that assesses whether the filing firm will face any possible infringements in any country. The company can then decide whether to proceed with the required filing of the patent in each country. There is a 20-month time frame to file for these in-country patents. Even though the PCT allows for simultaneous filing of a patent in all member countries, there may be significant differences in patent laws in each of these countries. For example, patent laws in the United States allow computer software to receive both patent and copyright protection. In the European Union, patent protection is not extended to software (Pike, 2005).

In China, for example, patent applications are filed with the State Intellectual Property Office (SIPO) in Beijing. The enforcement varies throughout the country because the local SIPO offices are responsible. Since China is a signatory of the Patent Cooperation Treaty, the country can be designated when a patent is filed in the United States or any time within 12 months after this filing. Unlike the United States and the European Union, where each patent application is examined based on its merits, Chinese patent applications are examined only if the applicant makes a request for examination. Otherwise, if no request is made, the application will be abandoned.

The use of business method patents has emerged with the growth of Internet use and software development. Amazon.com owns a business method patent for the single clicking feature used by a buyer on its Web site to order products. Priceline.com claims a patent regarding its service whereby a buyer can submit a price bid for a particular service. Expedia was forced to pay royalties to Priceline.com after being sued for patent infringement. Many firms that hold these types of patents have used them to competitively position themselves as well as providing a steady stream of income from royalties or licensing fees. Whether these types of patents will hold up over a long period of time is still not clear (Scheinfield & Sullivan, 2002).

Trademarks

A *trademark* is a word, symbol, design, slogan, or even a particular sound that identifies the source or sponsorship of certain goods or services. Unlike the patent, a trademark can last indefinitely, as long as the mark continues to be used in its indicated function. For all registrations, the trademark is given an initial 10-year registration with 10-year renewable terms in the United States. In the 5th year, the global entrepreneur needs to file an affidavit with the PTO indicating that the mark is currently in commercial use. If no affidavit is filed, the registration is canceled. Between the 9th and 10th year after registration, and every 10 years thereafter, the global entrepreneur must file an application for renewal of the trademark.

If this does not occur, the registration is canceled. Trademark law in the United States allows the filing of a trademark solely on the intent to use the trademark in interstate or foreign commerce. The filing date then becomes the first date of use. This varies by country.

Generally, throughout the world, there are four categories of trademarks: (1) coined marks denote no relationship between the mark and the goods or services (e.g., Mercedes, Kodak) and offer the possibility of expansion to a wide range of products; (2) an arbitrary mark is one that has another meaning in the language of the United States (e.g., Apple) and is applied to a product or service; (3) a suggestive mark is used to suggest certain features, qualities, ingredients, or characteristics of a product or service (e.g., Halo shampoo) and suggests some describable attribute of the product or service; and (4) a descriptive mark must have become distinctive over a significant period of time and gained consumer recognition before it can be registered. Registering a trademark can offer significant advantages or benefits to the global entrepreneur in each country.

In China trademark applications are filed with the China Trademark Office. Registered trademarks have more protection in China than unregistered ones similar to the United States. Unlike the United States, China has a "first to file" trademark system which does not require evidence of prior use or ownership of the trademark. Early filing and a good Chinese translation of the trademark is essential based on input from a native Chinese speaker familiar with the goods or services. Without this accurate translation, often unintelligible trademarks result in the Chinese language.

Copyright

A *copyright* protects original works of authorship. The protection in a copyright does not protect the idea itself, and thus it allows someone else to use the idea or concept in a different manner. Copyright law has become especially relevant because of the tremendous growth in the use of the Internet, especially in downloading music, literary work, pictures, videos, and software.

Copyrights in the United States are registered with the Library of Congress and usually do not require an attorney. To register a work, the global entrepreneur sends a completed application (available online at www.copyright.gov), two copies of the work, and the required filing fees (the initial filing fee). The term of the copyright is the life of the global entrepreneur plus 70 years in the United States. This time period also varies by country.

Besides computer software, copyrights are desirable for books, scripts, articles, poems, songs, sculptures, models, maps, blueprints, printed material on board games, data, and music. In some instances, several forms of protection may be available.

Chinese copyrights are registered at the National Copyright Administration (NCA) in Beijing. Even though China recognizes protection for original works of authorship from countries belonging to the international copyright conventions without the works being specifically registered in China, to adequately enforce the copyright, the global entrepreneur should register the copyright with the NCA. Two of the author's books in the Chinese language are registered with the NCA, protecting these well-selling Chinese editions.

Trade Secrets

The global entrepreneur may prefer to maintain an idea or process as confidential and to keep it as a *trade secret*. The trade secret will have a life as long as the idea or process remains a secret.

A trade secret is not covered by any laws, but is recognized under a governing body of common laws in some countries. Employees involved in working with an idea or process may be asked to first sign a confidential information agreement that will protect the global entrepreneur against the employee giving out the trade secret either while an employee or after leaving the global venture. A simple example of a trade secret nondisclosure agreement is illustrated in Figure 6.1.

The amount of information to give employees is a difficult decision and is often determined by the global entrepreneur's judgment. Usually global entrepreneurs tend to protect sensitive or confidential company information from anyone else by simply not making the information available.

Most global entrepreneurs who have limited resources can choose not to protect their ideas, products, or services. This can become a serious problem because obtaining competitive information legally is easy to accomplish unless the global entrepreneur takes the proper precautions. It is usually easy to learn competitive information through such means as trade shows, transient employees, media interviews or announcements, and even Web sites.

Under China's Unfair Competition Law (UCL), protection is available for trade secrets as well as unregistered trademarks and packaging. The law is enforced by the Fair Trade Bureau of the State Administration for Industry and Commerce (SAIC) in Beijing. The enforcement of this law by the Chinese courts and administrative agencies varies greatly from province to province.

WHEREAS, New Venture Corporation (NVC), Anywhere Street, Anyplace, U.S.A., is the Owner of information relating to; and

WHEREAS, NVC is desirous of disclosing said information to the undersigned (hereinafter referred to as "Recipient") for the purposes of using, evaluating, or entering into further agreements using such trade secrets as an employee, consultant, or agent of NVC; and

WHEREAS, NVC wishes to maintain in confidence said information as trade secrets; and

WHEREAS, the undersigned Recipient recognizes the necessity of maintaining the strictest confidence with respect to any trade secrets of NVC,

Recipient hereby agrees as follows:

1. Recipient shall observe the strictest secrecy with respect to all information presented by NVC and Recipient's evaluation thereof and shall disclose such information only to persons authorized to receive same by NVC. Recipient shall be responsible for any damage resulting from any breach of this Agreement by Recipient.

2. Recipient shall neither make use of nor disclose to any third party during the period of this Agreement and thereafter any such trade secrets or evaluation thereof unless prior consent in writing is given by NVC.

3. Restriction on disclosure does not apply to information previously known to Recipient or otherwise in the public domain. Any prior knowledge of trade secrets by the Recipient shall be disclosed in writing within (30) days.

4. At the completion of the services performed by the Recipient, Recipient shall, within (30) days return all original materials provided by NVC and any copies, notes, or other documents that are in the Recipient's possession pertaining thereto.

5. Any trade secrets made public through publication or product announcements are excluded from this Agreement.

6. This Agreement is executed and delivered with the State of _____ and it shall be construed, interpreted, and applied in accordance with the laws of that State.

7. This Agreement, including the provision hereof, shall not be modified or changed in any manner except only in writing signed by all parties hereto.

Effective this _____ day of _____ 20 _____

RECIPIENT: _____

NEW VENTURE CORPORATION:

By: _____

Title: _____

Date: _____

Figure 6.1   A Simple Nondisclosure Agreement

SOURCE: Hisrich, R. D., & Peters, M. P. (1989). *Entrepreneurship: Starting, developing, and managing a new enterprise.* Homewood, IL: B.P.I./Irwin.

Licensing

Licensing is an arrangement between two parties, where one party has proprietary rights over some information, process, or technology protected by a patent, trademark, or copyright. This arrangement, specified in a contract (discussed later in this chapter), requires the licensee to pay a royalty or some other specified sum to the holder of the proprietary rights (licensor) in return for permission to copy the patent, trademark, or copyright. Licensing has significant value as a marketing strategy to holders of patents, trademarks, or copyrights to grow their business in new markets when resources or experience in those markets are lacking. It is also an important marketing strategy for global entrepreneurs who want to start a new venture but need permission to incorporate the patent, trademark, or copyright with their ideas.

Although licensing opportunities are often plentiful, they must be carefully considered as part of the global entrepreneur's business model. Licensing is an excellent option for the entrepreneur to increase revenue in a global market without the risk and costly start-up investment. To be able to license requires the global entrepreneur to have something to license, which is why it is so important to seek protection for any new product, information, or name with a patent, trademark, or copyright.

Contracts

When starting a new venture, the global entrepreneur will be involved in a number of negotiations and *contracts* with vendors, landlords, and clients. A contract is a legally enforceable agreement between two or more parties as long as certain conditions are met. It is very important for the global entrepreneur to understand the fundamental issues regarding contracts.

Often business deals are concluded with a handshake. Ordering supplies, lining up financing, or reaching an agreement with a partner are common situations in which a handshake consummates the deal. When things are operating smoothly, this procedure is sufficient; if disagreements occur, the global entrepreneur may find that because there is no written contract he or she is liable for something never intended. The global entrepreneur should never rely on a handshake if the deal cannot be completed within 1 year.

Nearly 5 years after bringing its popular ice cream to Russia, Ben & Jerry's Homemade Inc. is pulling out. Legal, tax, and management problems, which plague many Western investors in Russia, forced the South Burlington, Vermont, ice cream maker to rethink a production and sales joint venture that started in 1992 in the spirit of a "social mission" with the northern province of Karelia, said Bram Kleppner, Ben & Jerry's manager of Russian operations.

Mr. Kleppner said the company's financial loss on Russian operations had been minimal, under $500,000, but the real drain had been executive time spent trying to resolve, among other problems, a court case with one of its partners. Operations were also partly financed through an $850,000 grant from the U.S. Agency for International Development. "We simply don't have the people and resources to run a business in Russia," Mr. Kleppner said by telephone from Vermont. "We're a small company. You tie up two or three senior managers and you end up having a measurable effect on the company's performance."

Ben & Jerry's started the joint venture, Iceverk, mainly as a goodwill gesture, to prove that high-quality ice cream could be made by Russian employees using mostly local ingredients. The ice cream, including the company's signature flavors like Chunky Monkey and Cherry Garcia, quickly became a local hit. Three "scoop shops" in the Karelia region, next to Finland, were among the busiest in Ben & Jerry's entire chain. Employing 100 local employees, the joint venture also distributed ice cream to Moscow and St. Petersburg, had five franchisees, and posted sales of $1 million a year.

But the venture never turned a profit, according to Mr. Kleppner. Expansion led to quality-control problems, with shipments of ice cream often arriving melted and refrozen. An unexpected change in the tax status for joint ventures sent tax liabilities soaring, with the venture unable to meet the increased tax burden. And like scores of other joint ventures in Russia, this one went bad when a local financial institution, PetroBank, successfully sued Ben & Jerry's for the return of a 20% stake the U.S. partner insisted it had legally bought back.

Ben & Jerry's has turned over its 70% equity stake in the venture to a third partner, Karelia's capital city of Petrozavodsk. It has also donated installed equipment and written off debts of about $150,000 owed by the joint venture. The venture now will make and sell ice cream under a new trademark, said Alexander Mukhin, head of the Petrozavodsk municipal-property committee (McKay, 1997).

Business Ethics in a Global Setting

A global entrepreneur must consider how to conduct business in an ethical manner throughout all parts of his or her firm's operations. By operating ethically, a global venture will be better able to secure repeat business and make a profit, while also adding value to the consumer. Consumers want to have a clear conscience about the type of company that their purchases support, and knowing that a company has high ethical standards guarantees this peace of mind.

Ethics are the principles that guide an entrepreneur's decision making and should be based on three basic values: integrity, transparency, and accountability. Integrity requires the entrepreneur to conduct all operations and transactions with honesty and respect for the law, including refraining from bribery and other forms of corruption. Transparency demands that the entrepreneur undertakes internal and external functions in an open manner and does not try to hide or disguise the firm's actions. Finally, accountability requires the firm to accurately record all transactions and take responsibility for its decisions and actions. Conducting business in foreign markets should not change or alter the ethical principles that the entrepreneur follows. In short, while the entrepreneur must continue to grow the firm's bottom line, he or she must also make sure that these decisions are made with integrity, transparency, and accountability.

Countries often establish laws and regulations to ensure that the business activities of foreign firms are within moral and ethical boundaries that are considered appropriate. Of course, what is considered morally and ethically appropriate ranges considerably from one country to the next, resulting in a wide range of laws and regulations as well as enforcement activities. A global entrepreneur must consider a country's laws and regulations while conducting business activities in an ethical manner. Sometimes this causes the global entrepreneur to choose between paying substantial fines or losing business.

One particular regulatory activity that affects global entrepreneurship is antitrust laws. These laws empower government agencies to closely oversee and regulate joint ventures with a foreign firm, acquisition of a domestic firm by a foreign entity, or any other foreign business activity that can restrain competition or negatively affect domestic companies and their business activities. Some countries use these laws to protect their "infant industries" as they attempt to establish themselves and grow.

Global entrepreneurs are also strongly affected by laws against bribery and corruption. In many countries, payments or favors are expected in return for doing business or gaining a foreign contract. To establish a foreign operation, obtain a license, or even access electricity and water, global entrepreneurs are often asked to pay bribes to government officials at all levels. Due to the increased incidences of this, the United States passed the Foreign Corrupt Practices Act in 1977, making it a crime for U.S. executives of publicly traded companies to bribe a foreign official to obtain business. Although this act has been very controversial and its enforcement varies, the global entrepreneur must carefully distinguish between a reasonable way of doing business in a particular country and illegal bribery and corruption. The work of the nonprofit Transparency International provides a good resource for judging the level of corruption, real and perceived, in a foreign country. Table 6.1 provides the rankings for the level of perceived public sector corruption for a selection of countries based on Transparency International's yearly survey. While New Zealand, Denmark, and Finland are ranked 1, Ukraine is ranked

Table 6.1   Public Sector Corruption Perceptions Index

Economy/Country	Ranking	Score
New Zealand	1	9.4
Denmark	1	9.4
Finland	1	9.4
Singapore	4	9.3
Sweden	4	9.3
Iceland	6	9.2
Switzerland	7	9.0
Canada	9	8.7
Norway	9	8.7
Australia	11	8.6
United Kingdom	12	8.4
Hong Kong, China	14	8.3
Germany	16	7.8
Ireland	17	7.5
Japan	17	7.5
United States	20	7.2
Chile	22	7.0
Estonia	28	6.5
Hungary	39	5.3
South Africa	43	5.1
Turkey	64	4.1
Mexico	72	3.5
China	72	3.5
India	72	3.5
Brazil	72	3.5
Thailand	84	3.3
Ukraine	118	2.7
Nicaragua	123	2.6
Indonesia	143	2.3

NOTE: The rankings listed above come from the *2007 Transparency International Corruption Perceptions Index*. This index measures the perceived levels of public sector corruption in a given country from the opinions of both businesspeople from that country as well as country analysts from various international and local institutions. The scores are on a scale of 0–10 for each country, with 10 implying a highly clean public sector and 0 implying a highly corrupt public sector. This data is useful for global entrepreneurs as they choose new markets to enter and assess the costs, risks, and ethical issues that they might face in doing business in a foreign market. Transparency International produces this index annually and publishes the results on its Web site at www.transparency.org.

SOURCE: 2007 Transparency International Corruption Perceptions Index.

118, Nicaragua 123, and Indonesia 143. While the United States is ranked 20, China is ranked 72.

Finally, the global entrepreneur is confronted with the general standards of behavior and ethics. Is it all right to cut down the rain forest and employ people at above national wages? Can you manufacture a product under different working conditions than those that occur in the United States yet pay wage levels far higher than average in the country? Can you fire employees in a country? Some countries severely restrict this even though the individual has not been working hard or, even worse, stealing from the company. These are just some of the issues confronting the global entrepreneur as he or she does business in certain foreign countries. Hopefully, global entrepreneurs will assert leadership in establishing standards that help promote a quality of life throughout the world.

Ethics and expectations of ethics do vary by country, depending in part on whether the country is based on the philosophies of Aristotle and Plato or Confucius, for example. In developing countries without a codified system of business laws that have been in place and enforced for a period of time, there is a great temptation to use bribes (facilitation payments) to expedite the business deal. Warner Osborne, Chairman and CEO of Seastone LC, in working with thousands of companies during his 20 plus years' experience in China and other countries advises, "We make sure all partners we work with know we won't tolerate that [facilitation payments—bribes]." He says when dealing with foreign firms, "We begin by establishing the ground rules—including the ethical rules that are critical to us—one-on-one verbally." (Dutton, 2008) These rules, of course, need to be fully understood by each employee.

Summary

A thorough understanding of a country's political and legal system is vital to the success of a new venture in a foreign country. Chapter 6 provides an overview of the major political and legal considerations that a global entrepreneur must analyze and prepare for before entering a new market. A political system, which governs a country, must be analyzed according to its degree of collectivism versus individualism and the degree of democracy versus totalitarianism. A country will use certain political tools, such as trade sanctions and export controls and regulations, to control who is doing business in that country. Also, different political systems allow (and expect) different levels of corruption and bribery. A savvy global entrepreneur must learn how to navigate these political questions while also maintaining standards of behavior and ethics. Conducting political risk analysis assesses threats to the ownership, operation, and finances of an entrepreneur's organization from a country's political system and stability. A country's legal system and, in particular, its protection of both intangible and tangible property rights must also be understood by the global entrepreneur. Four different traditions of law influence the legal systems around the world: common law, civic law, Islamic law, and socialist law. Legal counsel can be particularly useful to the global entrepreneur in interpreting and enforcing contracts, property rights, liability, and product safety.

Questions for Discussion

1. How can an entrepreneur mitigate potential political and legal risks prior to them happening?

2. What are the four different types of legal systems, and which countries follow each of these systems?

3. How should a contract be structured differently in a country with common law compared to one with civil law?

Chapter Exercises

1. Pick one of the BRIC countries (Brazil, Russia, India, China) and analyze its political structure (collective vs. individual and democratic vs. totalitarian) compared with your home country. What is the greatest difference that exists? What is your assessment of the political risk to a business entering that country?

2. Research and explain the difference between outright bribery and corruption versus a "facilitation payment."

3. Find an article describing a legal dispute that a multinational corporation has had outside its home country. What is the legal tradition of the foreign company? What is the major legal issue of the dispute and is there a different understanding of that issue in the home country versus the foreign country?

References

Dutton, G. (2008, May). Do the right thing. *Entrepreneur, 36*(5), p. 92.

McKay, B. (1997, February 7). Ben & Jerry's post-cold war venture ends in Russia with ice cream melting. *Wall Street Journal,* (Eastern Edition), p. A, 14:2.

Pike, G. H. (2005, May). Global technology and local patents. *Information Today, 22*(5), 41–46.

Scheinfield, R. C., & Sullivan, J. D. (2002, December 10). Lawyers and technology Internet-related patents: Are they paying off? *New York Law Journal*, 5.

Suggested Readings

ARTICLES/BOOKS

Acs, Z., & Szerb, L. (2007). Entrepreneurship, economic growth, and public policy. *Small Business Economics, 28*(2–3), 109–122.

As an introduction to the second Global Entrepreneurship Research Conference, the papers in this volume provide several entrepreneurship-focused policy recommendations, including the early creation of enterprise development policies in middle-income countries and the reduction of regulations in developed economies.

Blaas, W., & Becker, J. (2007). *Strategic arena switching in international trade negotiations*. Hampshire, UK: Ashgate.

This book analyzes rule making in international trade across multilevel and multiarena perspectives to explain the arena preferences of both state and non-state actors. It also shows how the rules of different arenas relate to one another and why certain institutional designs can serve one group better than the other.

Drahos, P. (2005, October). An alternative framework for the global regulation of intellectual property rights. (CGKD Working paper). [Electronic version]. *Austrian Journal of Development Studies*. Retrieved November 20, 2008, from, http://cgkd .anu.edu.au/menus/workingpapers.php

This article first examines the conflict between the international regime of intellectual property protection and the need for developing countries to set their own efficient standards of protection. Then it puts forth a new framework for intellectual property protection in the form of a treaty on access to knowledge.

Hsu, P. S. P. (2002, April). *Intellectual property: The knowledge society and global trade*. Paper presented at the Evian VII Plenary Meeting, Montreux, Switzerland.

The Trade Related Intellectual Property Agreements (TRIPs) of the World Trade Organization (WTO) has the potential to create a uniform and global intellectual property (IP) protection regulatory environment. The author posits that the WTO could help stimulate technology transfer and commercialization.

Kim, J., Chong, J. C., & Chen, S. (2006). Innovation management and intellectual property in knowledge-oriented economies. *International Journal of Technology Management, 36*(4), 295–304.

This article attempts to analyze the interface between and among *innovation,* technology, knowledge, and *intellectual property* in today's global Internet society.

The purpose of this paper is twofold: to analyze the role of measurement and intangibility in the standard-making process of *intellectual property,* especially differences in *intellectual property* across regions of the world, and to emphasize the importance of measurement costs and the intangibility of value in technology management knowledge in organizations, institutions, and society in the 21st century.

Li, S. (2007, February). *The legal environment and risks for foreign investment in China* **(1st ed.). Berlin: Springer.**

The author points out the attractiveness of the market in China, but also the risks involved in doing business there due in part to the overall legal environment and the changing scene for direct foreign investment. The book provides some insights into both of these while covering two investment options: greenfield, and mergers and acquisitions. However, the book does not provide great insight concerning managing some of the legal risks or how the main dispute resolution channels operate in the country.

Nasheri, H. (2004, November). *Addressing global scope of intellectual property law.* **U.S Department of Justice, Document Number 208384, NCJ 208384.**

This study examined the current state of law and enforcement efforts in terms of the protection of intellectual property rights (IRPs). Intellectual property describes the "ideas, inventions, technologies, artworks, music, and literature that are intangible when they are first created, but become valuable and tangible as they become products." IRPs are becoming a growing concern for both criminal and civil justice systems worldwide, given the ease with which many types of products are quickly and inexpensively reproduced. The current study sought to assess the current laws and enforcement efforts, in a global context, aimed at the protection of IRPs, as well as to examine weaknesses in current law and enforcement efforts.

Siddique, M. A. B. (Editor). (2007). *Regionalism, trade and economic development in the Asia-Pacific region.* **Cheltenham, UK: Edward Elgar.**

This book examines the effect that Regional Trade Agreements (RTAs) in the Asia-Pacific have on the peoples of this region. In addition it shows how the costs and benefits associated with RTAs change country by country and how these agreements work in relation to foreign exchange rates, the WTO, and agriculture.

Thursby, J., & Thursby, M. (2006). Here or there? A survey of factors in multi-national R&D location. [Electronic version.] Retrieved November 20, 2008, from www.kauffman.org/items.cfm?itemID=678

This article focuses on what attracts companies to locate their research and development activities outside their home country. The results of the study of 200 multinational companies, mostly U.S. and Western Europe based, identified intellectual capital and university collaboration as the primary motivators. These findings debunk the myth that costs are a primary motivator. Countries such as China and India, where access to scientists and engineers and potential collaborative partnerships, should be major beneficiaries of this global relocation.

Hearing on intellectual property rights issues and dangers of counterfeited goods imported into the United States **(testimony of T. Trainer before the U.S.-China Economic and Security Review Commission, June 8, 2006).**

Counterfeiters exist all over the world, whether you are in Los Angeles, Dubai, or Malta. The author argues that stronger measures are needed from trading partners to enforce intellectual property protection and reduce the strain on governments and corporate resources.

World Trade Organization. (2007). *Dispute settlement reports 2005.* **Cambridge, UK: Cambridge University Press.**

The Dispute Settlement Reports of the World Trade Organization (WTO) include Panel and Appellate Body reports, as well as arbitration awards, in disputes concerning the rights and obligations of WTO members under the provisions of the Marrakesh Agreement Establishing the World Trade Organization. It is an essential addition to the library of all practicing and academic trade lawyers, and needed by students worldwide taking courses in international economic or trade law.

World Trade Organization, Legal Affairs Division. (2007). WTO analytical index (2 volume set): Guide to WTO law and practice (2nd ed.). Cambridge, UK: Cambridge University Press.

This book will assist in the identification of existing jurisprudence and relevant decisions in any WTO agreement. As such, the book can assist anyone working in countries abiding by WTO law and can be reviewed as a legal guide to legal interpretations of WTO-based agreements.

WEB SITES

www.stopfakes.gov/smallbusiness has been created by the U.S. Patent and Trademark Office (USPTO) to help small businesses consider the benefits of strong intellectual property (IP) protection, both in the United States and overseas. Although every IP-based business is vulnerable to piracy and counterfeiting, small businesses can be at a particular disadvantage because they lack the resources and expertise available to larger corporations. Small businesses may also often lack the familiarity with the process of protecting intellectual property: research conducted in the spring of 2005 by the USPTO indicates that only 15% of small businesses that do business overseas know a U.S. patent or trademark provides protection only in the United States.

7 Alternative Entry Strategies

Profile: Tetsuhiro Shikiyama

NIPPURA

What do over 120 big aquariums across the world, from New York and Barcelona to Shanghai and Riyadh, have in common? They all use use acrylic glass made by Nippura, a Japanese firm with only 60 employees, which has won around three-quarters of the global market for these panels. Nippura made the world's biggest acrylic glass panel for the Okinawa Chura-umi Aquarium, which opened November 2002. The panel, 8.2 m (27 feet) tall and 22.5 m (74 feet) wide, provides a stunning view into a tank that holds 7,500 cubic meters of water (1.9 million gallons) and houses such creatures as a manta ray and a whale shark.

Tetsuhiro Shikiyama founded Nippura, based in Kagawa on the island of Shikoku, in southern Japan, in 1969. Its handful of workers made acrylic boards for store signs, design cases, and lamps. Now it is a rare Japanese example of a successful small firm that, despite prods from banks and even the government, has stubbornly chosen to stay small and, so far, unlisted.

Unlike many small firms, it has prospered despite Japan's miserable economy. According to Teikoku Databank, a research company, Nippura's net profits rose from ¥3 million (US$28,000) in 1996 to ¥117 million (US$6.3 million) in 2007, while sales increased by 50%.

Nippura's chance came in 1970 with a request from a local aquarium in Yashima that wanted large windows instead of small portholes for a better view of the fish in its tank. When Japan's top glass makers rejected the request, saying it was too difficult, Mr. Shikiyama rose to the challenge. He had to overcome two problems: how to make large acrylic glass panels thick enough to bear the weight of hundreds of gallons of water, and how to keep them clear. Mr. Shikiyama's secret weapon was glue. After years of studying and refining the materials necessary to make design cases and acrylic lamp shades, he created a powerful adhesive that made layers of acrylic glass transparent once it was poured between them.

Yet he soon came up against a typical Japanese business barrier. Seeing his success, big acrylic-fiber suppliers, such as Mitsubishi Rayon, the leader, entered the fray. Nippura struggled against their brand names, financial clout, and connections. Like other start-ups shunned in Japan that later became global leaders (such as Rohm, a specialist manufacturer of custom-made integrated circuits, and Nidec, the world's biggest producer of precision motors for hard-disk drives), Nippura decided that to survive it had to go abroad and develop fresh, unbiased markets. In 1982 it bid on work at the Monterey Bay Aquarium. Monterey, impressed by the quality of Nippura's work, accepted its bid. Only then did Mr. Shikiyama learn that the United States levied a 36% import tax on acrylic-resin board. His pleas for help to Japan's then Ministry of International Trade and Industry met with indifference. In despair he went to the U.S. embassy in Tokyo, and then to the U.S. Commerce Department. He flew to Washington, D.C., where he was advised to import the acrylic glass as a product (which he named AquaWall) not as a material, because the tax would drop to 2%, saving Monterey Bay Aquarium almost $1 million. He was praised fulsomely at the aquarium's opening ceremony, paving the way for fresh contracts.

A keen inventor and an enthusiast for diversification, Mr. Shikiyama has found other ways to combine glue and plastic. His latest product is a 24.93438 feet seamless acrylic display screen, the first of its kind. Projectors behind the screen (which can be used for home theaters) send images that are captured in the glue and then diffused onto the screen. With one of America's top projector makers already interested, Nippura started large-scale production in November 2003, which continues today. Other applications include bullet-proof plastic masks for the police. Layers of glue, specially designed to stick to bullets (which heat up as they drill through plastic), slow bullets enough to prevent them from penetrating the mask.

Now the 70-year-old Mr. Shikiyama faces a problem common among many aging, successful entrepreneurs in Japan: finding a successor. "This company has survived because it is constantly developing new technologies. But I look around, and it is worrying. Even if I promote someone to president, at this rate I'm still going to have to stick around to develop new products" (Joy of Fish, 2003).

www.nippura.com

Chapter Objectives

1. To determine the best overall strategy for bringing a venture to market through relevant factors.

2. To understand how to best enter the market based on timing and scale of a venture.

3. To understand how each different market entry strategy works and which one applies best to your business.

4. To select the best timing to enter a new market, and whether a first or second mover position is better.

5. To explain the various market entry methods and their advantages and disadvantages.

6. To determine the most appropriate type of entry mode and the best way to engage this market.

7. To understand the benefits of entrepreneurial partnering with home country entrepreneurs and how to select a partner in a foreign market.

Introduction

Once the business and market opportunity has been selected in light of any international political and legal concerns (the focus of the previous two chapters), it is important that the global entrepreneur develop a strategy for his or her company to go international. This global strategy outlines the actions the entrepreneur and his or her management team will take to obtain the international goals established and successfully enter the international market(s) selected. To be profitable (making sure that total revenues [price × units sold] are greater than total costs), the global entrepreneur must be competitive and offer something that has value to customers at a price that they are willing to pay. This requires that the global entrepreneur be very attentive to the value of what is being offered for sale to create an opportunity for premium pricing, as well as reducing the costs of the offering.

Formulating the Global Strategy

To develop a sound global strategy, a global entrepreneur frequently undertakes the following steps: (1) scan the external environment, (2) determine the strengths and weaknesses of the entrepreneur and the company, and (3) develop the goals and strategy. Each of these will be discussed in turn.

SCAN THE EXTERNAL ENVIRONMENT

Environmental scanning is a way to provide the global entrepreneur with a good sense of the geographic area being considered for global business. Two main features of this were the focus of Chapters 5 and 6: selecting the international business opportunity and understanding international legal concerns. Other areas of interest where forecasts are also done include competition, consumer data, the overall economy, and political stability. A typical environmental scanning will forecast the following:

- Markets for the products/services
- Per capita income of the population
- Labor and raw material availability
- Exchange rates, exchange controls, and tariffs
- Inflation rate
- Competitive products/services available
- Positioning
- Political risk

The resulting forecasts and assessments provide the global entrepreneur with a risk profile and profit potential of several geographic areas. This is the basis for a more accurate decision about which global market(s) to enter.

DETERMINE THE STRENGTHS AND WEAKNESSES OF THE ENTREPRENEUR AND THE COMPANY

Along with environmental scanning, it is important for the global entrepreneur to assess the strengths and weaknesses of the company and his or her self. This assessment provides an understanding of the venture's financial, managerial, marketing, and technical capabilities, as well as the critical factors for success that affect how well the venture will perform. The goal of this analysis is for the global entrepreneur to match as closely as possible the external opportunities identified through the scanning of the environment with the internal strengths of the entrepreneur and the venture. When the people and resources are present to develop and maintain the critical factors for success, the correct market entry strategy can be defined and implemented.

DEVELOP THE GOALS AND STRATEGY

Although a global entrepreneur already has some general goals that initiated the environmental scanning, it is now time to establish more specific goals based on the results obtained from both the external and internal analysis. Goals are usually established in the areas of finance, human resources, marketing, and profitability.

Profitability is a very important goal in going global; in general a venture should achieve higher profitability from its international business than its domestic activities to compensate for the additional effort and risk. For those ventures having significant success in their domestic markets, achieving additional market share is often very costly and difficult. Global markets offer an ideal alternative for increasing growth and profitability. Profitability is so important that it warrants sound strategic goals and careful monitoring of those goals and related activities. Based on the established strategic goals, the global entrepreneur will need to develop specific operational goals and controls. Specific parameters and guidelines need to be established to ensure that the overseas group operates in a way that supports the strategic goals in the plan.

Timing of Market Entry

Once the market(s) has been selected and the global strategy formulated, it is important to determine the best timing of the market entry. One consideration is whether to enter a market before other foreign firms—first mover advantage—or after other foreign businesses have been established in the market—second mover advantage. First mover advantages associated with early market entry include (1) preempting competitive firms and capturing sales by establishing a strong brand name, (2) creating switching costs tying customers to your company's products or services, and (3) building sales volume that provides an experience curve and cost advantages over later market entrants.

The global entrepreneur also has some disadvantages, often referred to as pioneering costs, in being the first entrant into a foreign market. Pioneering costs can often be avoided or minimized by late entrants into the foreign market. Because these costs can be particularly problematic and high when the business system in the foreign market is very different from the firm's home market, considerable effort, expense, and time are needed to learn the new market situation. The highest cost is, of course, business failure due to a lack of understanding of doing business in the foreign market. Other pioneering costs include the cost of educating the foreign market customer about the product through promotion and advertising. In developing economies where the rules and regulations governing businesses are still evolving, the first mover may have extra costs of reformulating the company's strategy to take into account any changes that occur. Sometimes the entire business model used in market entrance is invalidated.

The second mover has the advantage of observing and learning from the entrance and mistakes made by early entrants. The later entrant can use a business model that takes these mistakes into account, as well as any changes in the business laws and regulations of the foreign market. The reduction in liability and costs and the increase in learning raises the probability of success for global entrepreneurs entering a foreign market after several other foreign firms have already entered.

Scale of Entry

A final issue that a global entrepreneur needs to address before selecting an entry mode into a foreign market is the scale of entry. Entering a market on a large scale involves a significant amount of time and resources and significantly increases risk. This requires a strategic commitment to the market that has long-term effects on the global entrepreneur and is a decision that is very difficult to reverse.

It also signals to the competition the firm's commitment and significantly influences the nature and reaction of incumbent firms. This strategic commitment to a foreign market will make it easier to attract customers and establish a base of sales, and may also make other companies deciding to enter the market at least reconsider because they will have to compete with the first firm in the market in addition to national companies. On the negative side, a full-scale commitment will alert incumbent firms of the competition and could elicit a rigorous competitive response.

The strategic commitment to enter a foreign market on a large scale decreases the flexibility of the global entrepreneur. Committing heavily to one market leaves fewer resources available to support entrance and expansion in other markets. Few firms have the resources needed to have many (if any) large-scale market entries.

Although large-scale market entries are neither always good nor always bad, it is important for the global entrepreneur to carefully think through the implications of this decision because it will definitely change the competitive landscape. It is important to identify the nature of the competitive reactions, realizing that large-scale entry will increase sales substantially and provide economies of scales and some barriers to entry in terms of presence and switching costs.

A small-scale market entry allows the global entrepreneur to learn more about a foreign market with limited exposure. Information can be obtained about the foreign market before significant resources are committed. This increases the venture's flexibility and reduces the risk. The potential long-term rewards are likely to be lower because it will be more difficult and time consuming to build market share and capture all the first mover advantages.

Foreign Market Entry Modes

There are various ways a global entrepreneur can market products internationally. The method of entry into a market and the mode of operating overseas are dependent on the goals of the entrepreneur and the company's strengths and weaknesses. The modes of entering or engaging in international business can be divided into three categories: exporting, nonequity arrangements, and direct foreign investment (see Table 7.1).

EXPORTING

Usually an entrepreneur starts doing international business through exporting. *Exporting* normally involves the sale and shipment of products manufactured in one country to a customer located in another country. There are two general classifications of exporting: direct and indirect.

Indirect Exporting

Indirect exporting involves having a foreign purchaser in the local market or using an export management firm. For certain commodities and manufactured goods, foreign buyers actively seek out sources of supply and have purchasing offices in markets throughout the world. An entrepreneur wanting to sell into one of these overseas markets can deal with one of these buyers. In this case, the entire transaction is handled as though it were a domestic transaction, even though the goods will be shipped out of the country. This method of exporting involves the least amount of knowledge and risk for the entrepreneur.

Export management firms, another avenue of indirect exporting, are located in most commercial centers. These firms provide representation in foreign markets for a fee. Typically, they represent a group of noncompeting manufacturers from the same country that have no interest in becoming directly involved in exporting. The export management firm handles all the selling, marketing, and delivery, in addition to any technical problems, in the export process.

One method for indirect exporting is through the use of the Internet. This is exemplified in Green & Black's decision to open an online shop to

Table 7.1   Various Entry Modes

Entry Mode	Advantage	Disadvantage
Exporting	Ability to realize location and experience curve economies	High transport costs Trade barriers Problems with local marketing agents
Turn-key contracts	Ability to earn returns from process technology skills in countries where FDI is restricted	Creating efficient competitors Lack of long-term market presence
Licensing	Low development costs and risks	Lack of control over technology Inability to realize location and experience curve economies Inability to engage in global strategic coordination
Franchising	Low development costs and risks	Lack of control over quality Inability to engage in global strategic coordination
Joint ventures	Access to local partner's knowledge Sharing development costs and risks Politically acceptable	Lack of control over technology Inability to engage in global strategic coordination Inability to realize location and experience economies
Wholly-owned subsidiaries	Protection of technology Ability to engage in global strategic coordination Ability to realize location and experience economies	High costs and risks

SOURCE: Hisrich, R. D., Peters, M. P., & Shepherd, D. A. (2006). *Entrepreneurship* (7th ed.). Homewood, IL: McGraw-Hill/Irwin.

expand its operations internationally. The organic chocolatier's retail site went live on November 15, 2006, enabling both U.S. and UK consumers to buy its products online for the first time. Products available include gift items ranging from dinner party to birthday selections, as well as Green & Black's flagship bar products. Customers tailor their gift by picking their own assortment of bars, which is presented in a ribbon-wrapped gift box. The products are also tailored for occasions such as Christmas and Mother's Day.

Green & Black's senior brand manager, Katie Selman, indicated that the launch of the online shop was the first time the company had offered a gifting service to customers. "The online shop allows customers to create tailor-made gifts, which show they put that little bit more thought into them." The brand is entering a competitive arena. Hotel Chocolat, which launched more than 10 years ago, originally as a catalog retailer, has been selling products online for the last 5 years (Gemma, 2006).

Another form of indirect exports for the global entrepreneur, particularly in the United States, is through home shopping networks. TV shopping on networks such as QVC and Home Shopping Network (HSN) has resulted in products getting instant brand recognition as well as selling thousands of units. QVC and HSN reach nearly 200 million homes in the United States with the following viewer demographics: 75% women between the ages of 25 and 54 with an average household income of $60,000. These home shopping networks conveniently provide quality at an affordable price and have evolved into more stylish backdrops for televising and even featuring celebrities.

Home shopping networks are particularly open to global entrepreneurs with innovative new products and a background and story that are interesting to their viewers. Both QVC and HSN attend relevant trade shows to find new product opportunities; they both also accept online submissions at www.qvcproductsearch.com and www.hsn.com/corp/vendor/default. aspx. Both networks look for very unique products that are usually recognizable and have broad appeal. One small inventor of a cleaning compound for outdoor furniture was amazed when 100,000 18-oz. bottles of his cleaning compound sold in one session on QVC. Laurie Feltliner, founder of Hot in Hollywood, in California, a company specializing in trendy clothes and accessories modeled on Hollywood fashions, recently called HSN's CEO. She soon had a personal meeting to present her concept to the network. Now supplying HSN alone is a multimillion dollar business. According to Feltliner, who appears on HSN six to eight times each year, "At this point, I am really happy with my business at HSN. It is growing, it's keeping me busy and interested, and I don't see any reason to complicate my life any further" (Wilson, 2008).

Direct Exporting

If the entrepreneur wants more involvement without any financial commitment, *direct exporting* through independent distributors or the company's own overseas sales office is a way to get involved in international business. Independent foreign distributors usually handle products for firms seeking relatively rapid entry into a large number of foreign markets. This independent distributor directly contacts foreign customers and potential customers, and takes care of all the technicalities of arranging for export documentation, financing, and delivery for an established rate of commission.

Entrepreneurs can also open their own overseas sales offices and hire their own salespeople to provide market representation. When starting out the entrepreneur may send a domestic salesperson to be a representative in the foreign market. As more business is done in the overseas sales office, warehouses are usually opened, followed by a local assembly process when sales reach a level high enough to warrant the investment. The assembly operation can eventually evolve into the establishment of manufacturing operations in the foreign market. Entrepreneurs can then export the output from these manufacturing operations to other international markets.

Dieter Kondek, a German-born entrepreneur, was talking with friends at a dinner party, expressing his distaste for the lighting designs of the hotel and resort developments opening around his home in Cape Coral, Florida. A German company, Moonlight, that manufactures glowing orbs that can light a room, illuminate a path, or float in a pool was mentioned by a friend.

"They create light like the moon," says Kondek. "This is what was fascinating to us." He researched the company and found that the polyethylene globes can withstand temperatures from -40° to 170° Fahrenheit, range in size from 13 to 30 inches in diameter, and are powered with rechargeable batteries or hardwired into an outlet. Kondek also found out that Moonlight's products were decorating wealthy homes in Europe, Asia, and the Middle East, but were not in the United States. So, after 30 years in the high-tech field, Kondek, along with his wife and two friends, launched Moonlight U.S.A. and became the exclusive U.S. distributor. Worldwide, Moonlight has sold more than 10,000 balls, which cost from $325 to $1,000, and Kondek believes that the United States can make up half the company's sales (Centers, 2008).

NONEQUITY ARRANGEMENTS

When market and financial conditions warrant the change, an entrepreneur can enter into international business by one of three types of *nonequity arrangements:* licensing, turn-key projects, and management contracts. Each of these arrangements allows the entrepreneur to enter a market and obtain sales and profits without direct equity investment in the foreign market.

Licensing

Licensing involves an entrepreneur who is a manufacturer (licensor) giving a foreign manufacturer (licensee) the right to use a patent, trademark, technology, production process, or product in return for the payment of a royalty. The licensing arrangement is most appropriate when the entrepreneur has no intention of entering a particular market through exporting or direct investment. Since the process is low risk, yet provides a way to generate incremental income, a licensing agreement can be a good method for the entrepreneur to engage in international business. Unfortunately, some entrepreneurs have entered into these arrangements without careful analysis and later found that they have licensed their largest competitor into business or that they are investing large sums of time and money to help the licensee adopt the technology or know-how being licensed.

Wolverine World Wide, Inc. opened a Hush Puppies store in Sofia, Bulgaria, through a licensing agreement with Pikin, a local country combine. Similar arrangements were made a year later in the former U.S.S.R. with Kirov, a shoe combine. Stores in both countries are doing well.

Turn-Key Projects

Another method by which the entrepreneur can do international business without much risk is through *turn-key projects.* The underdeveloped or lesser-developed countries of the world have recognized their need for manufacturing technology and infrastructure and yet do not want to turn over substantial portions of their economy to foreign ownership. One solution to this dilemma has been to have a foreign entrepreneur build a factory or other facility, train the workers, train the management, and then turn it over to local owners once the business is operational, hence the name turn-key operation.

Entrepreneurs have found turn-key projects an attractive alternative. Initial profits can be made from this method, and follow-up export sales can also result. Financing is provided by the local company or the government, with periodic payments being made over the life of the project.

Management Contracts

The final nonequity method the entrepreneur can use in international business is the *management contract.* Several entrepreneurs have successfully entered international business by contracting their management techniques and skills. The management contract allows the purchasing country to gain foreign expertise without giving ownership of its resources to a foreigner. For the entrepreneur, the management contract is another way of entering a foreign market without a large equity investment.

DIRECT FOREIGN INVESTMENT

The wholly owned foreign subsidiary has been a preferred mode of ownership for entrepreneurs using *direct foreign investment* for doing business in international markets. Joint ventures and minority and majority equity positions are also methods for making direct foreign investments. The percentage of ownership obtained in the foreign venture by the entrepreneur is related to the amount of money invested, the nature of the industry, and the rules of the host government.

Minority Interests

Japanese companies have been frequent users of the minority equity position in direct foreign investment. A *minority interest* can provide a firm with a source of raw materials or a relatively captive market for its products. Entrepreneurs have used minority positions to gain a foothold or acquire experience in a market before making a major commitment. When the minority shareholder has something of strong value, the ability to influence the decision-making process is often far in excess of the amount of ownership.

Joint Ventures

Another direct foreign investment method used by entrepreneurs to enter foreign markets is the *joint venture*. Although a joint venture can take many forms, in its most traditional form two firms (for example, one U.S. firm and one German firm) get together and form a third company in which they share the equity.

Joint ventures have been used by entrepreneurs most often in two situations: (1) when the entrepreneur wants to purchase local knowledge as well as an already established marketing or manufacturing facility, and (2) when rapid entry into a market is needed. Sometimes joint ventures are dissolved and the entrepreneur takes 100% ownership.

Even though using a joint venture to enter a foreign market is a key strategic decision, the keys to its success have not been well understood. The reasons for forming a joint venture today are also different from those of the past. Previously, joint ventures were viewed as partnerships and often involved firms whose stock was owned by several other firms. Joint ventures in the United States were first used by mining concerns and railroads as early as 1850. The use of joint ventures, mostly vertical joint ventures, started increasing significantly during the 1950s. Through the vertical joint venture, two firms could absorb the large volume of output when neither could afford the diseconomies associated with a smaller plant.

What has caused this significant increase in the use of joint ventures, particularly when many have not worked? The studies of success and failure of joint ventures have found many different reasons for their formation. One of the most frequent reasons an entrepreneur forms a joint venture is to share the costs and risks of a project. Projects where costly technology is involved frequently require resource sharing. This can be particularly important when an entrepreneur does not have the financial resources necessary to engage in capital intensive activities. Another reason for forming a joint venture is to obtain a competitive advantage. A joint venture can preempt competitors, allowing an entrepreneur to access new customers and expand the market base. Joint ventures are frequently used by entrepreneurs to enter markets and economies that pose entrance difficulties or to compensate for a company's lack of foreign experience. This has been the case for the transition economies of Eastern and Central Europe and the former U.S.S.R. It is not surprising that it is easier to establish a joint venture in Hungary because of fewer registration requirements than it is to start your own company there.

Majority Interests

Another equity method for the entrepreneur to enter international markets is to purchase a majority interest in a foreign business. In a technical sense, anything over 50% of the equity in a firm is *majority interest*. The majority interest allows the entrepreneur to obtain managerial control while maintaining the acquired firm's local identity. When entering a volatile international market, some entrepreneurs take a smaller position, which they increase up to 100% as sales and profits increase.

Mergers

An entrepreneur can obtain 100% ownership to ensure complete control. Many U.S. entrepreneurs desire complete ownership and control in cases of foreign investments. If the entrepreneur has the capital, technology, and marketing skills required for successful entry into a market, there may be no reason to share ownership.

Mergers and acquisitions have been used significantly to engage in international business, as well as within the United States. During periods of intense merger activity, entrepreneurs may spend significant time searching for a firm to acquire and then finalizing the transaction. Any merger should reflect basic principles of any capital investment decision and make a net contribution to shareholders' wealth, but the merits of a particular merger are often difficult to assess. Not only do the benefits and cost of a merger need to be determined, but special accounting, legal, and tax issues must be addressed. The entrepreneur, therefore, must have a general understanding of the benefits and problems of mergers as a strategic option, as well as an understanding of the complexity of integrating an entire company into present operations.

There are five basic types of mergers: horizontal, vertical, product extension, market extension, and diversified activity. A *horizontal merger* is the combination of two firms that produce one or more of the same or closely related products in the same geographic area. They are motivated by economies of scale in marketing, production, or sales. An example is the acquisition of convenience food store chain Southland Stores by 7-Eleven Convenience Stores.

A *vertical merger* is the combination of two or more firms in successive stages of production that often involve a buyer-seller relationship. This form of merger stabilizes supply and production and offers more control of these critical areas. Examples are McDonald's acquiring its store franchises and Phillips Petroleum acquiring its gas station franchises. In each case, these outlets became company-owned stores.

A *product extension merger* occurs when acquiring and acquired companies have related production and/or distribution activities but do not have products that compete directly with each other. Examples are the acquisitions of Miller Brewing (beer) by Philip Morris (cigarettes), and Western Publishing (children's books) by Mattel (toys).

A *market extension merger* is a combination of two firms producing the same products but selling them in different geographic markets. The motivation is that the acquiring firm can economically combine its management skills, production, and marketing with that of the acquired firm. An example of this type of merger is the acquisition of Diamond Chain (a West Coast retailer) by Dayton Hudson (a Minneapolis retailer).

The final type of merger is a *diversified activity merger*. This is a conglomerate merger involving the consolidation of two essentially unrelated firms. Usually, the acquiring firm is not interested in either using its cash resources to expand shareholder wealth or actively running and managing the acquired company. An example of a diversified activity merger is Hillenbrand Industries (a caskets and hospital furniture manufacturer) acquiring American Tourister (a luggage manufacturer).

Mergers are a sound strategic option for an entrepreneur when synergy is present. Synergy is the qualitative effect on the acquiring firm brought about by complementary factors inherent in the firm being acquired. Synergy in the form of people, customers, inventory, plant, or equipment provides leverage for the joint venture. The degree of the synergy determines how beneficial the joint venture will be for the companies involved. Several factors cause synergy to occur and make two firms worth more together than apart.

The first factor, economies of scale, is probably the most prevalent reason for mergers. Economies of scale can occur in production, coordination, and administration; sharing central services such as office management and accounting; financial control; and upper-level management. Economies of scale increase operating, financial, and management efficiency, thereby resulting in better earnings.

The second factor is taxation or, more specifically, unused tax credits. Sometimes a firm has had a loss in previous years but not enough profits to take tax advantage of the loss. Corporate income tax regulations allow the net operating losses of one company to reduce the taxable income of another when they are combined. By combining a firm with a loss with a firm with a profit, the tax-loss carryover can be used.

The final important factor for mergers is the benefits received in combining complementary resources. Many entrepreneurs will merge with other firms to ensure a source of supply for key ingredients, to obtain a new technology, or to keep the other firm's product from being a competitive threat. It is often quicker and easier for a firm to merge with another that already has a new technology developed—combining the technological innovation with the acquiring firm's engineering and sales talent—than to develop the technology from scratch.

Entrepreneurial Partnering

One of the best methods for an entrepreneur to enter an international market is to partner with an entrepreneur in that country. These foreign entrepreneurs know the country and culture and therefore can facilitate business transactions while keeping the entrepreneur current on business, economic, and political conditions. This partnering is facilitated by understanding the nature of entrepreneurship in the country.

There are several characteristics of a good partner. A good partner can help the entrepreneur achieve his or her goals, such as market access, cost sharing, or core competency obtainment. A good partner also shares the entrepreneur's vision and is unlikely to try to opportunistically exploit the partnership for his or her own benefit.

How do you select a good partner? First, you need to collect as much information as possible on the industry and potential partners in the country. This information needs to be collected from embassy officials, members of the country's chamber of commerce, firms doing business in that country, and customers of the potential partner. The entrepreneur will need to attend any appropriate trade shows. References for each potential partner should be checked and each reference asked for other references. Finally, it is most important that the entrepreneur meet several times with a potential partner to get to know the individual and the company as well as possible before any commitment is made.

Summary

Chapter 7 discusses developing a market entry strategy, choosing the right time for market entry, defining the scale of entry, and finally establishing the best mode of entry. To develop a sound entry strategy, a global entrepreneur must (1) scan the external environment, (2) determine the strengths and weaknesses of the entrepreneur and the company, and

(3) develop the goals and strategy. The global entrepreneur must always keep in mind that the international business should be more profitable than the domestic business to compensate for the higher risk involved. The timing for market entry centers on whether the global entrepreneur is the first to enter the foreign market or if he or she enters after other competitors have already established their businesses. The primary advantages for "first movers" are preempting competitors and gaining market share; creating switching costs that tie the customer to the entrepreneur's product/services; and building sales volume to maintain profitability after competitors enter the market. A later entry into a foreign market allows a global entrepreneur to learn from the mistakes of the first entrant while also reducing some of the pioneering costs. The global entrepreneur must then weigh the advantages and disadvantages of entering a market on a large scale, so that he or she can command the market, or on a small scale, so that he or she can make sure the foreign market is right for the product or service. Finally, the best mode for entering the market must be defined. Market entry falls into three categories: exporting (indirect or direct), nonequity arrangements (licensing, turn-key projects, and management contracts), and direct foreign investment (wholly-owned foreign subsidiaries, joint ventures, majority and minority equity positions, and mergers). The chapter concludes by discussing one more option for entry into a foreign market—partnering with an entrepreneur from that country.

Questions for Discussion

1. What are the different ways to enter a foreign market? What are the advantages and disadvantages of each?

2. What factors should an entrepreneur consider when deciding on an entry strategy?

3. Anastasia is considering introducing her new line of high-end food products into Mexico. She has heard through a friend that one of her competitors is planning to do the same. Give the arguments as to why it can be better to be the first mover into the market and why it might be better to be the second.

Chapter Exercises

1. Using your own company or business idea, choose a new market for your product or service. Define the external environment, your own and your company's strengths and weaknesses, and a basic strategy to enter that market.

2. What are the advantages of a first mover strategy? What are the best market conditions in which to use this strategy?

3. Imagine that you are the inventor of unique, robotic dolls that have been very successful and popular in your home country. You see a great opportunity in bringing this product to Germany. Conduct a basic analysis of the German market and suggest the best entry mode (exporting, nonequity, or direct foreign investment) for your product.

References

Centers, J. (2008, April 1). Great balls of light. *Fortune Small Business, 18*(3), 25.

Gemma, C. (2006, October 18). Green & Black's in Web shop. *Marketing*, p. 12.

The joy of fish: Not every Japanese firm fears going under water. (2003, August 28). *Economist*, 55

Wilson, S. (2008, May). Big break. *Entrepreneur, 36*(5), 102–108.

Suggested Readings

ARTICLES

Chun, B. G. (2007, August). Firm's choice of ownership structure: An empirical test with Korean multinationals. Korea: The Bank of Korea, Institute for Monetary and Economic Research.

This paper shows that the choice of equity ownership by multinational firms (MNFs) based in a newly developed country like South Korea varies depending on the home country's characteristics. The authors discovered a preference among MNFs for sharing control rights with a local partner when there is a large black market, vast sociocultural differences between the home and host country, and the affiliate is in the resources-based sector.

Ellis, P. D. (2007). Paths to foreign markets: Does distance to market affect firm internationalization? *International Business Review,* **16, 573–593.**

This paper examines whether distance to a market affects firm internationalization, especially when viewed as geographic, cultural, or psychic distance. Using the location of markets, the sequence of market entry, the rate of international expansion, and the relationship between sequentially linked markets, this paper gives a comprehensive assessment of whether distance does impact internationalization.

Glückler, J. (2006). A relational assessment of international market entry in management consulting. *Journal of Economic Geography, 6*(3), 369–293.

The author of this article believes that social networks have a huge effect on international market entry and the form that it takes. Firm-specific sources alone cannot fully account for the internationalization of business services according to the results of qualitative exploration and logistic regression analysis of fieldwork and survey data. The article also explores the need for analysis of internationalization using interfirm relationships.

Kovac, P. (2007). Building successful vendor partnerships and customer strategies. *AgriMarketing, 1,* 52.

The author states that Process + Partnership = Success is at the core of successful customer relationship marketing (CRM), direct marketing campaigns, and the selection of the best vendor partners. A smart, well-defined process will not only help identify the most important market place facts, but also establish a single, strategic game plan.

Larimo, J. (Ed.). (2007). *Market entry and operational decision making in East-West business relationships.* **Binghamton, NY: International Business Press.**

The individual contributors of this volume explore the East-West business relationship in connection with business and operational decisions as well as regionalization and internationalization. The exploratory nature of the articles should inspire conversation and deeper research into these topics.

Lu, J. W. (2006). Partnering strategies and performance of SMEs international joint ventures. *Journal of Business Venturing, 21*(4), 461–486.

When looking for growth, many small- and medium-sized enterprises (SMEs) seek international joint ventures (IJVs). SMEs must carefully consider the partnering strategies for an IJV since it can have a significant effect on performance. In particular, an SME should consider its partner's host country knowledge and size-based resources.

Quer, D., Claver, E., & Andreu, R. (2007, June). Foreign market entry mode in the hotel industry: The impact of country- and firm-specific factors. *International Business Review, 16*(3), 362–376.

Many different factors influence the choice of entry mode by hotel firms in the internationalization process. According to this study, cultural distance decreases the need for equity entry modes. In addition, a greater commitment to the international expansion process is expected due to firm profitability and internal financial funds availability.

Walker, B. (2006). Tomorrow the world. *Caterer & Hotelkeeper. 196*(4446), 76.

Focusing on restaurant chains in Great Britain, this article discusses their operations and international expansions, including choosing between a wholly owned subsidiary, a joint venture, or a franchise agreement.

What's behind the overseas forays of U.S. online giants? (2004, July 28). *Knowledge@Wharton.* Retrieved September 22, 2008, from http://knowledge .wharton.upenn.edu/article.cfm?articleid=1013
Although one might expect Internet-based companies to have an easy time entering international markets, success with Internet-based and other ventures in international markets is not guaranteed. A company must examine whether or not its architecture fits in another setting.

WEB SITES

World Franchising **Web site.** (2005). Retrieved September 22, 2008, from www .worldfranchising.com
This Web site provides a comprehensive directory of global franchise information and opportunities.

Part 2

Cases

- Fitz-Ritter Wine Estate
- *Mamma Mia!*
- Federal Express
- UniMed and EduMed

Fitz-Ritter Wine Estate

220 Years of Tradition and Entrepreneurship

Lambert T. Koch, Marco Biele, and Sean Patrick Sassmannshausen
IGIF—Institute for Entrepreneurship and Innovation Research
University of Wuppertal, Germany

The Fitz-Ritter Wine Estate was founded in 1785. In 1837 the estate broadened to include champagne production facilities. Today the young owner, Johann Fitz, is the managing director of both companies, the ninth generation of his family to lead the business. German wine producers have been facing global challenges for several years. This case shows how an entrepreneurial spirit through generations of leadership has contributed to the survival of a vineyard. It also shows how a medium-sized business can cope with global challenges if it commits itself to take advantage of international opportunities. In this complex environment, Johann Fitz has to make decisions concerning strategic positioning, customer relations, distribution channels, new business segments, investments, and how to manage the international business.

Introduction

Johann Fitz opens the door to his office on a Monday morning, holding the first bottle of a brand new product in his hands. The combination of premium sparkling wine and passion fruit will be the new FitzSecco Passion fruit, a variant for the younger generation of wine drinkers. Johann is excited and rushes to the phone to call Alice, his mother, who has been responsible for the estate's marketing and exports for the last 2 decades. Impatiently he dials her number. While he is waiting, he looks at his watch. He wonders why his mother does not answer the phone; it is only her voicemail. Johann opens his e-mail, searching for a correspondence from his mother: "August 25—New York wine exhibition; August 27—Chicago; August 29—Detroit." New York City is 7 hours behind; no wonder she is not answering the phone. He peruses the attached spreadsheet with the latest figures of Fitz-Ritter's exports. Johann

is calculating some key figures, unsure how to continue with the export busi-
ness. Should he, as the new head of the company, expand foreign businesses
or should he concentrate on domestic projects? Things are changing more
rapidly on the domestic market, while the export market requires great atten-
tion and expenses, but achieves relatively smaller sales volumes. The doorbell
rings. Johann switches off his laptop. With a number of construction plans
stacked under his arm, he prepares to meet two men from the local monument
protection office, guiding them into the historical cross-vault cow barn. "I will
call her later," he is thinking, "now it is time for my next project."

Fitz-Ritter Estates

Johann Fitz is part of the ninth generation of his family at Fitz-Ritter Wine
Estates, succeeding his father, Konrad Fitz, who ran the family business for
37 years. The young vintner inherited his passion for wine from his parents. At first this passion remained unknown to him; his interests lay in
other areas. Only weeks ago, however, he took over the lead of the Fitz-
Ritter Wine Estate, right after completion of his studies in economics at
the University of California at Berkeley. The wine estate, founded in 1785,
is located on the fringes of Bad Durkheim, a wine-growing spa town at the
edge of the Rhine Plain in southwestern Germany. Famous for its high-
quality white wine, it is one of the largest wine estates in the area. Its 22
hectares (approximately 52 acres) are situated in the largest German wine-
growing region, the "Pfalz" (Palatinate).

Johann is a new type of vintner, combining respect for the traditional
family business with an entrepreneurial spirit. In the last 20 years, the German wine market has changed immensely. Globalization had a tremendous effect on the European wine industry. Conservative strategies and
antiquated structures prevented German wine estates from achieving
global competitive positions. A few years ago, however, a young generation of vintners entered leading positions at an increasing number of wine
estates, determined not to be smothered with so-called protective state
intervention, but to face competition and react successfully to market
forces. "Being a young German vintner is not just an occupation, it is a
movement. These days, it is not just about age, it needs a certain entrepreneurial mind-set to be a young German vintner," claims Johann Fitz.

In the summer of 2006, Johann inherited a renowned family business,
well-known for producing more than just quality wine. Growing the first
Chardonnay ever in Germany and launching a small museum and boutique wine store, Alice and Konrad Fitz were always ahead of their local
competitors in terms of innovative thinking and entrepreneurial spirit.
"The production of premium wine and champagne needs passion," says
Konrad Fitz. "Unfortunately, some German vintners lost track some

Antique Engraving of the Estate (Photo provided by Johann Fitz)

decades ago, trying to compete with New World wine estates in mass production. Thereby, the decreasing quality of some German wines, combined with high production costs, almost ruined the international standing of German wine and many wine estates."

The Fitz-Ritter Company— Family Business Since 1785

The Fitz-Ritter Estate was founded in 1785 by Mr. Fitz, a merchant who decided to make a change and start something new. The vineyard is located at the famous "Deutsche Weinstraße" (German Wine Street), which crosses an area known for its warm, sunny climate and ideal grape growing conditions. The origins of The Champagne Company, the family's sparkling wine production facility, in some ways reflect the entrepreneurial spirit that would continue throughout the family and its winery. In 1832 Johann Fitz (called "The Red Fitz") spearheaded the German vintners' protestations for the elimination of customs duties on wine.

The Red Fitz (Photo provided by Johann Fitz)

Because of his involvement at the Hambacher Fest (a peaceful demonstration calling for more liberty), he was persecuted by the police of the Bavarian King. The Red Fitz took refuge in France, hiding in the Champagne region where he studied the production of champagne. Later he returned home, accompanied by a cellar master, and together with some members of his family, co-founded one of the first German champagne productions, the Durkheimer Champagne Factory. It is now the oldest sparkling wine producer in the area and the third oldest in Germany.

In 1842, despite the fact The Red Fitz was still wanted by political police, the Durkheimer Champagne Factory became the supplier to the royal Bavarian court. As time and tastes changed, it became clear that the king would rather maintain his supply of champagne than imprison a political antagonist, a sign that The Red Fitz was making some quality wines. Thus, traditional wine and champagne production can be traced back more than 220 years. Now Johann Fitz, several generations removed from The Red Fitz, has taken over from his father, Konrad Fitz, and is attempting to lead the company into a new and different age.

The family's entrepreneurial spirit is shown in its vision and willingness to explore new opportunities to expand its business. On the ground floor of the Ritz-Fitter Estate, the family business operates the Bacchus Boutique, a gift shop founded by Alice Fitz, who has been responsible for marketing and export for many years. After Alice married Konrad Fitz, she became familiar with the wine business. "First I fell in love with Konrad, but soon, I fell in love with the wine business too," she said. Her attempts at contributing something to the business were supported by her earlier studies in business and economics. One of the first actions she took was to launch the Bacchus Boutique, which at the time was a new idea among traditional wine makers and disregarded as foolish by many of them. But later, when it proved to be a success, it was imitated by almost all of them. In line with the boutique gift shop, Alice organizes charity events and classical concerts on the estate site. The company sponsors art galleries and wine festivals. Alice recalls:

> Even Johann cannot imagine the shape this estate was in when we took it over. In 1970 no one here had ever heard the word marketing. To German vintners, it was absolutely unknown to build a brand by cultural or social endorsement and event marketing. Now, this concept is broadly accepted, but most wine estates are too small to follow our strategy. Nevertheless, most of the bigger estates and cooperatives have created their own brand strategy nowadays, but we still have some first mover advantages because our events had been well established at the time competitors entered.

Along with the boutique and the Fitz-Ritter branding, international expansion was an area in which the winery was leading its German counterparts. Alice began the effort with a focus on the U.S. market because she was American and more familiar with it. According to VDP (Verband Deutscher Praedikats-und Qualitaetsweingueter, the Association of German Praedikat Wine Estates), today's export average is about 20% of the total wine production, with a trend toward increasing growth (VDP, n.d.).

The Fitz Family: Alice, Konrad, and Johann (Photo provided by Johann Fitz)

Fitz-Ritter started the export business in the late 1970s. It all happened more or less coincidentally. While Alice's American mother was on vacation in Germany, they began thinking about how to deliver wine into the United States, not for business, but for their own needs. Soon came the idea of expanding, and the export business into the United States was born. A few years later, when Konrad and Alice went to wine exhibitions, importers from Japan, Great Britain, and the Netherlands became interested in Fitz-Ritter wines and started to order. "But everything started more or less with the export into the United States," Alice emphasizes.

The wine is shipped to the United States and unloaded and cleared by an importer, who needs an alcohol license. Moreover, the importer is also responsible for the distribution of the wine. Although Alice travels across the United States to promote the wine at trade fairs, often meeting directly with consumers, she is not allowed to sell directly to them, but rather sells to distributors through the importer due to restrictive import laws in the United States. This system poses great challenges to smaller establishments like Fitz-Ritter that are trying to enter the market.

The importers and distributors intermediary positions are very important for the export business as a whole. "You rely on the effort and contacts of your importer and your distributors," Konrad Fitz says. Alice adds:

It has a lot to do with trust, and loyalty is hard to find. It took us years to identify trustworthy importers and distributors in the United States and other markets. It is a time and money consuming trial-and-error process. Trust is an emotion in the beginning, and proof only occurs when time passes by. Even if you have found a trustworthy, talented, and ambitious distributor, you still need to do a lot of sales promotion all by yourself. And if you are not present to offer the new vintage, the importer and distributors will forget you very soon. While Fitz-Ritter was obliged to give exclusive rights to one importer, this importer has many German wines in his portfolio. Exclusiveness is part of an adhesion contract: None of the licensed importers will negotiate exclusive contracts, so a family business like Fitz-Ritter only makes up a small portion of the importer's portfolio and thus, only relatively small efforts will be spent on sales promotion. Moreover, in a family business selling products made by good craftsmanship, customers want to know the entrepreneurial family behind the product, so they can judge the product and the reliability of delivery by the people representing the company. Furthermore, the financial stability of the importer you choose is, of course, vital. In the United Kingdom, we trusted one import agent and were absolutely gutted. For this reason we are not present in the UK market anymore, and we are still looking for a trustworthy importer to take on this market.

Alice has traveled all across the United States to promote her German wines, speaking with distributors and presenting at national and international exhibitions. The Fitz-Ritter Gewurztraminer was especially embraced by Americans because of its semiarid or smooth taste, and the fact that it is full of herbs and flavor with a low amount of alcohol. "While most German exporters focused on the Riesling, soon the Gewurztraminer became our hot seller within the United States, where we positioned ourselves within a niche market," explains Alice. "But our Riesling is demanded, too," Konrad adds. Business in the United States today, however, is getting harder and harder due to factors such as the strengthening of the euro as compared to the U.S. dollar, the presence of more competitive wineries on the export scene, and difficult relationships with intermediaries who want to own their share of the profits, making it difficult to sell premium wine. Fitz-Ritter is present in many states, though sales are concentrated in some New England states, New York City, Michigan, and California. Massachusetts has proven to be one of the toughest U.S. markets to enter. It is costly to penetrate all states with personal sales promotion; one promotional tour costs an average of EUR 5,000, and up to five tours are necessary each year. Thus, Alice tries to build personal relationship and loyalty with distributors, who consequently can focus more on increasing volume.

"The business has changed a lot," says Konrad Fitz. Today the winery has to sell its wine at exhibitions and through more innovative distribution channels. Several decades ago the winery sold exclusively to commission agents without any direct sales. Commission agents actually traveled from door to door, offering their product portfolio. To their potential customers, usually stay-at-home mothers and wives, they offered the opportunity to taste the wine and learn more about each product before buying any bottles. Thus, the wine distribution business was slow, but it was reliable, and good traders knew their business very well, knowing the high purchasing customers in their area, their customers' tastes and price range, resulting in reasonable sales levels.

Now the door-to-door business model is antiquated. As the population became more urban and mobile, and high crime rates introduced hesitation to opening doors to strangers, door-to-door salesmen were increasingly treated with mistrust and uncertainty. A new distribution model was needed, and Johann Fitz saw this early on: "When I entered the business I instinctively knew we desperately needed new distribution channels. This is why I started an online shop. There was the risk that retailers would ban us because we decided to introduce direct customer services via the Internet, but thus far all is fine. We notice that online trade is an additional business with a certain set of customers and thus does not harm other distribution channels." (The online shop can be accessed at www.shop .fitz-ritter.de.)

The choice of grape varietals is also something that Johann must seriously focus on. It requires long-term planning and a willingness to accept a level of risk. As Johann describes it, "If we decided to produce different types of grapes on some acres, this would mean that on these acres over a period of at least 3 years, no grapes will be harvested at all. Planting vines is a long-range strategic decision; change needs 3 years at least and bears some risks, and the amortization of the plants takes many years. If your

Fitz-Ritter Wine Cellar (Photo provided by Johann Fitz)

decision is led by trend and fashion, you better make sure that the kind of grape won't be out of fashion again soon."

Vines have a productive life of 60 to 70 years; it takes 3 to 4 years after planting for them to produce their first harvest, 5 to 7 years to achieve full productive capacity, and up to 35 years to produce the best quality grapes needed for wine. There is a correlation between age of vines and quality. In addition, the vintner can take many actions to increase quality. Most activities are labor intensive and therefore costly. For Fitz-Ritter premium

Wine Acreage in Bad Durkheim (Picture provided by Johann Fitz)

Table 1   Product Portfolio*

Nr.	Wine	Price € B2B	Price € E to C***	Nr.	Wine	Price € B2B	Price € E to C***
619	2005 Durkheimer Rittergarten Riesling	2.80	5.60	613	2006 Durkheimer Blanc de Noir	3.95	7.10
621	2006 Durkheimer Abtsfronhof Riesling	3.20	6.40	616	2006 Durkheimer Spielberg Chardonnay	5.15	9.30
624	2006 Riesling classic	3.20	6.40	425	2004 Durkheimer Abtsfronhof Gewurztram.	6.20	10.90
335	2003 Ungsteiner Herrenberg Riesling	7.70	13.50	627	2006 Durkheimer Abtsfronhof Gewurztram.	4.60	8.40
536	2005 Michelsberg Durkheim Riesling GG**	11.45	19.00	339	2003 Durkheimer Hochbenn Riesling "Ice wine"	62.00	93.00
533	2005 Kanzel Ungstein Riesling GG**	12.05	20.00	938	1999 Durkheimer Abtsfronhof Riesling Selection	46.00	70.00
511	2005 Durkheimer Dornfelder red wine	3.30	6.60	645	2006 Cuvée "Red Fitz"	4.10	7.40
612	2006 Pinot Noir	4.30	7.90	415	2004 Cuvée "Revoluzzer"	8.10	14.20
218	2004 Durkheimer Cabernet Dorsa	9.00	14.90	314	2003 Durkheimer Pinot Noir	9.90	16.50
416	2004 Durkheimer Spielberg Chardonay	9.95	16.50	001	Rittergold "dry" (0.75 litres) sparkling wine	2.85	5.70
A	FitzSecco Blanc	2.60	5.20	003	Riesling "dry" (0.2 litres) sparkling wine	0.90	1.85
B	FitzSecco Rosé	2.60	5.20	003	Riesling Extra Brut (0.75 litres) sparkling wine	4.50	8.10
C	FitzSecco Passion Fruit (0.75 litres)	2.85	5.70	E4	2006 Fitz-Ritter Riesling (1 litre)	2.45	4.90
D	FitzSecco Passion Fruit (0.2 litres)	0.90	1.80	F3	2006 Fitz-Ritter red wine (1 litre)	1.85	4.70

*Figures taken from Fitz-Ritter price list (modified); business-to-business prices (B2B) modified for classroom calculations only

**GG = "Gross Gewaechse" Great Growth

***E to C: Prices for direct sale from the estate to private customers.

wines for instance, workers cut off 50% of each bunch of grapes in spring, allowing the energy and sugar of the vine to concentrate in the remaining grapes, resulting in much more intense flavor.

Two-thirds of Fitz-Ritter's acreage is planted with Riesling grapes. The best spots are the rolling hillsides named Herrenberg, Spielberg, Abtsfron-hof, and Michelsberg. Due to their geographic situation and special soil, these hills offer the foundation for premium wine, especially the number one premium class, Grosse Gewaechse (Great Growth), the label for the highest premium wines of The Association of German Prädikat Estates (VDP). Each vine is officially documented by the VDP with the aim to guarantee the highest quality. Quantities are limited and growing and harvesting of grapes, as well as wine production, has to be carried out tra-ditionally by hand, combined with the most modern innovations in sustainable enology for a gentle treatment of grapes and wine during the process. Thus, production remains a craft, not an industrial process, and as a result is more expensive. A wine with its own personal character representing richness and complexity in taste is the reward for vintners, cellar masters, and consumers. Table 1 shows an excerpt of the compre-hensive product portfolio of wines that the Fitz-Ritter wine estate is pro-ducing today.

The German Wine Industry and the Global Wine Market

"The Riesling Renaissance" (Lynam, 2001) and "Following hard times, German Rieslings rise again" (Wolkoff, 2006) are current headlines Ger-man winemakers are pleased to read. Such headlines restore their pride. After years of difficulty, the German wine industry is hoping that its for-tunes are in fact changing, though it must continue to adapt to a shifting competitive environment. Domestic competition is getting tougher, the economic strength of the German people has increased, and foreign wines are now well-known entities with a good cost-to-quality ratio. These fac-tors combine to keep Germany as the number one importer of wine in the world. And though this growing demand should bode well for domestic producers, many things have occurred that make it less than certain that they will be able to capitalize on the opportunity.

German wines, Riesling for example, have a reputation of excellence, but the last 50 years put a "variety of demons" on them (Wolkoff, 2006). In the first two decades after World War II, Germans were drinking Ger-man wines, except for a small market segment at the higher end of the price scale, which was occupied by famous French red wines. The giant overseas wine estates were not yet founded or at least not yet recognized.

Transportation costs were high, creating a natural barrier to market entry, at least for non-European producers. But over the years, the situation changed. Wine consumption increased, and foreign wine became more and more fashionable; at first Italian wines, then wines from Spain and other European origins. During this time the so-called New World wine producers (Australia, Chile, New Zealand, South Africa, and the United States) began to learn the skills and grow the grapes necessary to compete in the global market. Decreasing transportation and production costs, combined with an increase in quality, made it possible to enter and aggressively compete in the European market. The market entry coincided with fierce price competition among German discounters and supermarket chains, such as ALDI, LIDL, Metro Group, and Tengelmann Group.

To succeed, discounters search for a cheap supply of a good and stable-quality wine. Therefore, the ideal wine for these retailers is a generic, medium-quality one that can be produced in a quantity high enough to satisfy growing demand. New World wine producers have been able to match these criteria. Moreover, they are able to differentiate themselves by marketing the exotic origins of their wines, places like South Australia, Napa Valley, Chile, New Zealand, and South Africa—regions that have become as fashionable as Italy, France, or Spain.

For a long time the European producers, particularly the French, Spanish, and German vintners, held to their traditions and downplayed the overseas producers and their products. Consequently, the Old World winemakers were shocked when they finally realized the changing demand of wine consumers and retailers, as well as the increasing quality of their competitors' products. This realization came as they saw the rising market share of the New World producers (for more detail, see Bartlett, 2003). New methods of winegrowing, new production systems, and technical innovations resulted in competitive advantages for the New World vintners. They were able to produce comparable wine with lower costs and flood Europe with it. The response of European vintners was to call for state intervention and protection to keep these wines out. Soon numerous regulations were issued in relation to grape varieties, controlled cultivated land, and sugar content. Price guarantees were given by the European Union (EU) and national agricultural subsidies in France and Spain that were meant to support vintners by converting the overproduction of low-quality wines into cash. Prices were stabilized by state intervention; wine that could not be sold on the market was simply purchased by the EU or national state authorities.

Attempts to respond to the entrance of the New World wine producers resulted in a disaster for German winemakers. The Germans tried to copy the successful strategy from overseas producers by mass producing white wine. The production was increased at the expense of quality. One major obstacle was the New World producers' ability to increase cultivable land by buying additional unimproved land very cheap, whereas in Europe that

Table 2   Viticulture Companies in Germany*

Company Size From . . . to . . EGE**	Number of Companies		
	1999	2003	+/-
<8	12,233	10,688	12.6
8 – <16	4,123	3,696	-10.4
16 – <40	4,716	4,210	-10.7
40 – <100	3,656	3,561	-2.6
100 – <250	648	1,193	84.1
>250	55	97	76.4
	25,431	**23,445**	**-7.8**

*Only companies with a contribution margin from above 75% from wine production

**EGE—EUROPEAN unit, 1 EGE = 1,200 € contribution margin

SOURCE: Adapted from Bundesministerium für Ernährung, Landwirtschaft und Verbraucherschutz "Ertrgslage Garten-und Weinbau 2007; Daten-Analyse;" p. 120

strategy was impossible. The German wine producers faced geographical and regulatory limits that prevented them from increasing their cultivable land because all viticulture areas were already allocated (see Table 2). Therefore, increasing the production meant increasing the output of a given vineyard by trying to get more wine out of each grape. This in turn lowered the quality significantly. Decreasing quality resulted in decreasing reputation. In addition, productivity increased slowly in comparison with overseas wine industries because the landscape of many German vineyards does not allow the use of heavy machinery and robots. Vineyards are typically located on very steep hillsides alongside river valleys such as Rhine, Moselle, and Main. Another setback for German vintners was suffered from changes in international consumer demand in the 1990s, when there was a dramatic shift in consumption from light white wines toward red wines. The conclusion after one generation of investment in mass production was that due to the small size of many estates, limited acreage and steep hillsides of many vineyards, domestic production cannot ever be expected to cover domestic demand. For importers, this gap makes it much easier to enter the German market.

Germany is the largest importer of wine in the world, with demand continuing to grow. Unfortunately for German producers, this increasing demand is mostly being satisfied by imports from outside the country. There are a variety of reasons for this development. Wine drinking habits have changed in the last few decades; in many parts of society, drinking wine is subject to changes in fashion and lifestyle. This is not only true for the upper classes, but also for students, skilled labor, middle classes, and pensioners. These changing habits in the consumption and perception of wine were first surveyed in the world's largest nonproducing wine market,

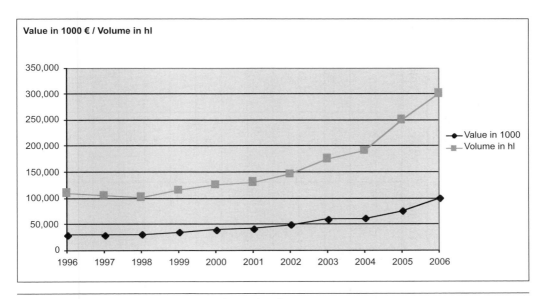

Figure 1   German Exports Into the United States

SOURCE: Verband Deutscher Weinexporteure e.V. (VDW; Association of German Wine Exporters), www.vdw-weinexport.de; referring to Statistisches Bundesamt der Bundesrepublik Deutschland.

England. The marketing departments for New World producers identified Great Britain as an ideal target market because its growing demand offered opportunities for new entrants, allowing them to win the so-called "Battle of Britain" (Bartlett, 2003, p. 8) in the wine industry. Success on the English market is regarded as an indicator for international competitiveness: "If you make it there, you'll make it everywhere," as wine marketing managers say.

Since advertisement presents drinking wine as the common upper-class lifestyle, copying this style makes members of the middle classes feel part of the upper class. This opens new and growing market segments around the world. The largest market for German wine is located in the United States. As shown in Figure 1, German wine exports are still increasing to the United States. The growth coincided with the first of the new generation of young German vintners who successfully started discovering their abilities to produce first-class white wines, especially Riesling. Accordingly, German export of wine sales are increasing, particularly outside the European market (Table 3). The most important export markets for German wine, especially white wine, are the United States, Japan, Canada, and Russia; whereas in Europe the largest markets for German wines are Great Britain, the Netherlands, Sweden, Norway, France, and Belgium. Table 3 underlines the changing export trend among German wine estates, which seem to have withdrawn from highly competitive markets like Great Britain and France. They are focusing more on growing markets like the United States, the Scandinavian

Table 3   The Global Wine Market

Rank	Countries	2006 Value 1.000 EUR	2006 Volume hl	2006 Volume EUR/hl	Annual Percentage Change (05/05) Value	Annual Percentage Change (05/05) Volume	Percentage Share 2006 Value	Percentage Share 2006 Volume
1	EEC 25	354,661	2,185,513	162	9.7	2.5	63.2	75.2
2	Others	206,573	720,822	287	36.6	40.6	36.8	24.8
3	Great Britain	128,342	825,122	156	1.2	-8.1	22.9	28.4
4	USA	100,350	301,649	333	29	21.2	17.9	10.4
5	Netherlands	69,104	476,526	145	17.7	17	12.3	16.4
6	Norway	25,602	85,529	299	53.1	17.2	4.6	2.9
7	Sweden	23,687	176,100	135	5.8	-2.1	4.2	6.1
8	Russia	22,765	169,132	135	113.9	172.6	4.1	5.8
9	Japan	22,759	62,394	365	1.6	0.9	4.1	2.1
10	France	18,542	104,334	178	-3.9	-4.4	3.3	3.6
11	Canada	15,308	57,211	268	49.4	40.7	2.7	2
12	Swiss	13,804	24,569	640	68,6	22.9	2.5	0.7
13	SUMMARY	561,234	2,906,335	193	18.2	9.9	100	100

SOURCE: Verband Deutscher Weinexporteure e.V. (VDW; Association of German Wine Exporters), www.vdw-weinexport.de

Table 4   Development of the Institutional Setting
in the Global and Domestic Wine Market

Past	Present
Germany	Germany
German Wine Law 1971; WeinG 1994 Strict regulations of viticulture methods; rejection of non-European viticulture methods; strict rules for labeling; classification into four categories (quality wine with "prädikat," quality wine of certain regions, land wine, table wine)	German Wine Law 1971; WeinG 1994; modification of wine law planned Critisism of top wine producers (e.g., VDP); additional classification without legal protection. Goal: better differentiation of quality vineyards, common international labeling standards
EEC	EEC
Each country has its own wine law; strong regulations; rejection of non-European viticulture methods	Treaty between EEC and United States (2006); mutual acceptance of viticulture method
United States	United States
Bureau of Alcohol, Tobacco, and Firearms (ATF) Approved Viticulture Areas (AVA); percentage of grapes used from AVA area is important for classification	Treaty between EEC and United States guarantees protection of semi-generic names
World	World
Conglomerate of bilateral treaties; Old World vs. New World, state protection; protectionism against new viticulture methods especially in EEC	Conglomerate of bilateral treaties; tendency toward more liberalization; downsizing protectionism

countries, and especially Russia. There are also opportunities in Asia (e.g., India and China) that have yet to be sought.

The 2006 trade agreement between the European Union and the United States marked a turning point in the liberalization of the global wine market. The ultimate achievement of this treaty is the mutual acceptation of wine growing methods and the protection of semi-generic names, for example Burgundy, Port, or Champagne. The agreement's goal to open the market contrasts to previous attempts by Old World producers to shield themselves from the pressure of the New World winemakers (Table 4). However, globalization, lower transportation costs, and a growing desire for overseas products resulted in increasing pressures to liberalize the world market for wine.

But the market is far from being truly open. The EU is still paying huge amounts of state subsidies to wine producers to support the domestic wine industry. Old-fashioned thinking relies on the faith that state

Wine Testing (Photo provided by Johann Fitz)

subsidies and import quotas can manage increasing demand for foreign wine, a notion that is proving to be far from accurate. In the face of these market pressures, wine producers have to rely on innovation to retain their market position, something Johann Fitz recognized early on.

Johann Fitz and the New Entrepreneurial Spirit in the German Wine Industry

Johann Fitz is one of the young German vintners who realized he had to change his business model to compete. In addition to the online shop and the new product, FitzSecco passion fruit, one of his first projects as successor to Konrad Fitz was the refurbishment of the historical cross-vault cow barn. It was converted into a ball and dining room with winter garden, where dignified events can take place. Johann's idea of a modern wine estate is as simple as his mission statement: Deliver high quality wine in combination with features to retain customers. For example, he hosts weddings in the room and uses various techniques to build brand awareness: "If you celebrate your wedding here, you will receive a lifetime discount and a tailored label for your special day. This is the perfect way to win over customers for our vineyard." The difficulty for vintners in such a highly competitive market is customer retention; Johann believes this is a way to achieve that.

The Refurbishment of the Historical Cross-Vault Cow Barn (Photo provided by Johann Fitz)

To Johann, the transformation of the historical cross-vault cow barn into a ballroom is a symbol of the new spirit he brought into the company. Even though he was unsure about taking over the family business, he now is searching for opportunities and change. "It required a little convincing, but soon I knew that I wanted to run the company and implement new ideas," emphasizes Johann. "My parents were leading the vineyard with an entrepreneurial mindset, and I want to continue this track. And continuation means change. Like many human beings, my attention and power is limited. I need to concentrate on just a few projects at a time. Consequently, I have to develop the estate step by step. I need a priority list, showing which projects or opportunities are crucial for success and then concentrate investments on first things first." This is why he is still unsure about building the export business with its inherent risks.

"Export is an affair of my mother's heart," Johann explains. "She put so much effort in it, but the weak dollar is wearing the profits down." A small company like Fitz-Ritter has to pass through 100% of all currency changes. "Our INCO terms (International Commercial Terms) usually refer to CIF (Cost, Insurance and Freight, which applies especially when carried on ships) and CIP (Carriage and Insurance Paid, which applies in case of airfreight). In the international wine business, it is commercial custom that prices are negotiated in foreign currencies on the day of order. Payment is due after delivery. Hence, we carry the risk of exchange rates, and I can tell you, we have not been lucky with the euro to U.S. dollar ratios during the past few years. Just to increase the price in U.S. dollars is not the answer, because we soon would bust market prices and our wine would become unsellable."

But Johann is optimistic: "I will find a solution and make a decision, one way or the other." He is someone who likes to tackle a problem. "I am a person who likes to put my hand on it," he adds. Recounting a story from his years of study at the University of California at Berkeley, he says, "During the summer I took part in a management program and there was a competition where students had to run a very small company. I was the manager of a painting company. It was exciting. I did all the planning and administrative processes myself, but I employed a few people for operational work. I did very well and finally won the competition. It was a great experience. But then after winning, I was supposed to explain and teach my strategies and ideas to other students, but there I failed badly," he says with a smile on his face. "I am a person who just does things, but I am not one to talk about it. I am not a coach or a teacher."

Although the idea proved a promising opportunity to build a connection between customers and the brand, Johann had to be careful not to stray too far from the core business.

> We have returns on investment from wine production, but the surplus reserve cannot cover the entire project. It can only contribute a little equity to the amount of cash needed. So I faced the task of financing the project. First, I limited the need for capital by having a clear focus on our core competence. The project is intended to foster our sales of wine, during the event and for future delivery. It is not designed to run a restaurant. This would mean the need to employ a chef, cooks, waiters, and so on. Therefore I decided to outsource the catering. Guests are free to choose any caterer they like, and thus all the diverse demands for cuisine that may occur can be easily fulfilled. The only product I put restrictions on is wine and champagne. It has to be purchased from the Fitz-Ritter Wine Estate or the Sekt-kellerei Fitz KG (the official name of the sparkling wine business). Aside from that, the outsourcing of catering is to our advantage because the expense is detached from our variable costs. Consequently, the need for capital is equated with the costs of transforming the site. The break-even point will be reached almost with the first bottle sold after the interests on the invested capital are paid.

Table 5 shows the investment costs and the source of funds.[1]

---

1. To protect the company's interests, all financial data and sources of funds have been subject to modification. Nevertheless, the data given is realistic and the source of financing is the most important for entrepreneurial start-ups and business successors in Germany. It was chosen to give the case an universal validity for entrepreneurial finance in Germany.

Table 5   Entrepreneurial Finance for a SME in Germany—An Example

Total Investment	500,000€					
Sources of capital						
Equity from surplus reserve	75,000€					
Mezzanine Capital from KfW-Mittelstandsbank (Capital for Entrepreneurship Program)	125,000€					
Investment loan from "KfW-Mittelstandsbank" (Entrepreneurship Loan)	300,000€					
Interest rates and amortizations (Year 1 starts on January 1, 2008)						
Mezzanine Capital						
Year	1	2	3	4	Years 5–6	Years 7–15
Interest %*	0.0	3.0	4.0	5.0	6.50	6.50
Amortization**	0.0	0.0	0.0	0.0	0.0	13.888.89€ p.a.
Investment Loan						
Year	1	2	3	Years 3–20		
Interest %*	Max. 4.45–7.30 (depending on rating), Fitz-Ritter is rated A (4.45)					
Amortization**	0.0	0.0	0.0	17,674.06€ p.a.		

*Interest rates are subject to change (for actual rates, see www.kfw-mittelstandsbank.de).
**If required by the entrepreneurial enterprise, amortization can be expedited.

In the financial plan, KfW-Mittelstandsbank plays a decisive role. This public financial institution was created to help Germany recover from World War II and to distribute aid from George C. Marshall's European Recovery Program (ERP). Most European countries used the money from the program for immediate development, but the German government chose a different model: They founded the KfW Bank as a fund holder. The KfW did not spend the money on subventions, but invested it by offering loans to innovative small- and medium-sized enterprises (SMEs). Hence, the aid, once given by the United States, still accumulates interest and remains available to the German economy. The market for informal equity is not well developed. For this reason, the KfW-Mittelstandsbank offers not only investment loans but also mezzanine capital. On condition that the entrepreneur will get involved with 15% equity, up to an additional 25% of total investment can be financed by the mezzanine capital program. The remaining 60% of investment can be covered by an investment loan.

The new project looks promising. Although it has only just been started, 15 couples have already booked the room and the garden for their wedding parties at a rate of EUR 2,100 per day. In addition to the rent, Johann plans to sell around 100 bottles per event at retail prices (see Table 1). At least 40 to 45 events per year could be scheduled throughout the season. "Aside from the cash that we put into the project, we used our Estate's garden and the cross-vault next to it, both representing assets that have been idle for many years but soon will contribute to our business." Market analysts state that the average German couple spends EUR 14,000 on their wedding. In addition, many companies, clubs, associations, and private persons are looking for unique locations to make their function a special event. Thanks to word of mouth, Internet advertisements, and a "Google strategy,"[2] the business plan expects the number of events to increase to 60 or even 70 per year until the fourth year. Operation of the facility began in May 2008.

Confident in his future plans, Johann is taking the necessary steps to achieve his strategy to become the best wine company in the region. "We work very hard on increasing the quality of our wines," he emphasizes. From the first seeding to the harvest, the vintner's family and its employees are controlling most aspects of the business. Even filling the wine bottles, labeling, marketing, and selling will be done by the small group of people at the Fitz-Ritter winery. "Today, this is special," says Konrad Fitz, "We do everything on our own. It is demanding but we believe that you can taste it. High-quality wine is our passion, and we control the total process."

Johann's next plan is to increase the quality of wine by investing in human resources and industry know-how. "You can always increase the quality of wine. We have achieved a lot but still have some space left to climb up the ladder to the top German vineyards," says Johann. The shift in methods of achieving quality has been drastic during the last 15 years, along with the way that that quality is measured and communicated. The Internet and other types of easily accessible mass media create more transparency; consumers and reviewers can quickly share their wine experiences with others. Recommendations and ratings are popular. Some of the so-called experts have a lot of power; they influence consumer behavior and thus give incentives for higher quality. Today, markets reward quality much more than they did years or decades ago.

One struggle for Johann is finding a good supply of grapes to meet growing demand. Increasing acreage is not an option because of the high

---

2. Searching for a wedding reception location within 100 miles of Bad Durkheim at www.google.de, one would find the "historical cross-vault cow barn" among the first hits. The city of Frankfurt, financial capital of German economy, is located within this area.

cost of land in Germany. "Purchasing good wine from another vintner is another possibility, especially in the cuvée and sparkling wine production," the young vintner adds. This strategy is feasible and can help to bypass bottlenecks in delivery, especially with his latest innovation, FitzSecco passion fruit, as Johann explains:

> It is a product for young people who like to enjoy good quality wine with the flavor of passion fruit. It is a stylish product, which is brand new and already the "in-drink" here in our region. Demand is higher than we thought, so for production, quality wine has to be bought in addition to our own volume. With this new flavored sparkling wine, Fitz-Ritter is targeting young people, especially young women. It has a great potential to become the next hot-seller for our vineyard.

In addition, FitzSecco passion fruit will soon be available in smaller piccolo bottles (0.2 liters), with the latest trend in bottling, the "twist and plop" cap. Due to its low alcohol content and fruity, refreshing taste, it is a good alternative to the alco-pops sold at pubs and clubs. "Changing our product portfolio, I can imagine dedicating our entire acreage to the production of premium wines of the highest quality and rounding out the portfolio with quality wine bought from other vintners," Johann adds. "The additional wine would be placed in the medium price range and in the production of cuvées for Champagnes, sparkling wines, and FitzSecco."

Perspectives and Discussions

The Fitz-Ritter company is facing a crucial period in its history where several decisions will have to be made that depend massively on the strategy Johann wishes to pursue. The wine industry has changed and continues to evolve. In Germany and elsewhere in Europe, smaller wine estates already had to react to the challenges of a global wine industry. In Germany the consolidation process has started but has yet reached its inflection point. Rumors persist that some of the largest German vineyards have received takeover offers from overseas. The passage of leadership from Konrad to Johann is just beginning, and the company must react to this change. Steps have been taken by Fitz-Ritter to make this transition as smooth as possible; Johann received an education in enology, economics, and entrepreneurship. Konrad Fitz has retired, but is still on the estate to help with his rich experience. Alice is willing to promote exports for several more years. The company is 100% family owned. Nevertheless, future plans have to be made—it is just not enough to rest on what has been achieved so far.

The new projects Johann Fitz has executed thus far are all in line with the overall strategy of the company: the development of a premium wine estate that combines tradition and innovation. Projects have included:

- The introduction of new products such as the FitzSecco passion fruit sparkling wine

- A reorganization of product portfolio, stressing those products with the highest quality and prices

- The reorganization of distribution channels in the domestic market, including the establishment of an Internet shop

- The historical cross-vault cow barn project to increase direct sales onsite, which also has the potential to increase customer loyalty

- New labels and elegant designs for bottles containing the most expensive wines

- Investments in human resources; for example, hiring of a famous first-class enologist and employing a cellar master of excellent craftsmanship

Yet still more decisions lie ahead for Johann. Because every project mentioned above bears the risk of failure, it is necessary to have alternative plans. At this point many questions remain and many options are available.

Why not concentrate on the domestic market and leave the cost-intensive and difficult job of export to the competition? Even though she has decades of experience, Alice admits, "Export business is a perplexing and troublesome job, with markets not easy to understand." Domestic demand is sufficient, especially if the historical cross-vault cow barn project turns out fine. So why should Johann Fitz continue with the export business? Should the 25% of given production capacity that is used for international business be dedicated to the domestic market in the near future?

What about distribution and product portfolio? Do changes in climate offer any new opportunities for differentiation of the product portfolio? Are there any growth strategies Fitz-Ritter should take advantage of? In which areas of the Fitz-Ritter business can one recognize such opportunities for growth? Are exhibitions and Internet appearance enough to survive? How can the company use its latest innovation, the FitzSecco passion fruit? What could the marketing plan for FitzSecco passion fruit look like? How can Johann gain and retain more young customers?

These difficult questions are on Johann's mind when he returns from the cow barn refurbishment site. The monument protection officials felt comfortable with how the ancient renaissance character of the building has been preserved. After taking leave from the officials, Johann enters his office. The phone is ringing. It is Alice calling, with excitement in her voice: "Johann, our premium wine is positively reviewed by today's New York Times *and to boot, the* Wine Spectator *ranked the Michelsberg and the Kanzel Ungestein*

Riesling above 90 points. So to speak, we have just entered the international champions' league at a top rank."

"What news, and the day has just started," Johann says. "Our strategy seems to be turning out fine, and tonight we shall definitely open one of the best bottles of champagne from our cellar." But before this, Johann makes good use of the day, considering the rewards of the challenging export business from a new perspective, rethinking his opportunities, and reweighing his options.

Appendix A

Table 1   Fitz-Ritter Wine Estate: Growing Areas

Growing Area	Acerage	%*	Wine	Use in Production	Potential Quality*
Durkheimer Abtsfronhof	3.2 ha (7.9 acre)	35	Riesling	A++, A+++, and A+S	C–A+++ and A+S
		30	Gewurztraminer	A++, A+++	C–A+++ and A+S
		20	Chardonay	SWP**	C–A+++
		15	Sauvignon Blanc	SWP	C–A+++
Durkheimer Fronhof	0.8 ha (1.98 acre)	100	Riesling	B, A, SWP	C–A++
Durkheimer Fuchsmantel	0.56 ha (1.38 acre)	100	Riesling	B, A, SWP	C–A++
Ungsteiner Herrenberg/ Kanzel	1.44 ha (3.46 acre)	100	Riesling	A+++	C–A+++ and A+S
Durkheimer Hochbenn	4 ha (9.88 acre)	100	Riesling	B, A, SWP, A+S	C–A+++ and A+S
Wachenheimer Mandelgarten	2 ha (4.94 acre)	50	Pinot Gris	B, A,SWP	C–A+
		50	Pinto Blanc	B, A, SWP	C–A+
Michelsberg	0.7 ha (1.73 acre)	100	Riesling	A+++	C–A+++ and A+S
Rittengarten	1.86 ha (4.6 acre)	40	Riesling	A	C–A+++
		25	Dornfelder	A, A+, A++	C–A+++
		20	Cabernet Sauvignon	A++, A+++	C–A+++
		15	Cabernet Dorsa	A++	C–A+++
Drukheimer Spielberg	0.7 ha (1.73 acre)	100	Chardonay	A++	C–A+++
Others	5,74 ha (14.1 acre)	100	Diverse	A+, A++, A+++	C–A+++

NOTE: Figures adapted and modified from the authors for calculations only

**SWP = usage for sparkling wine production

Table 2   Purchasing Prices for Wine (Cuvée Production)

Wine	C	A	B	A+–A+++ and A+S
Average White	0.75	0.8	0.90	No Purchasing Possible
Average Red	0.80	0.85	0.95	No Purchasing Possible
	In percent of wholesale price.			

NOTE: Figures for classroom calculations only

Table 3   Wine Segments Based on Quality Assessment

Per Bottle	Table Wine	Average	Quality	Premium	Top	Top Special	Specailty
Price range wholesale	<1.25	1.00–2.00	2.50–3.50	3.50–5.50	6.00–10.00	10.00–18.00	>20.00
Average margins for retailers	100%	>100%	100%	>80%	>75%	>66%	>50%
Price range estate to consumer	<2.50	2.50–4.99	5.00–7.00	7.01–9.99	10.00–14.99	15.00–30.00	>30.00
Average profit (€) in wholesale	0.05	0.10	0.20	0.30	0.50	1.00	2.00
Code	C	B	A	A+	A++	A+++	A+S
Average litres per ha	140,000	100,000	65,000	50,000	30,0000	20,000	5,000

NOTE: Figures adapted and modified by the authors for classroom calculations only, VDP wines will be classified "A" at least

Table 4   Development of Exchange Rates

Currency	19.10.2007	29.12.2006	30.12.2005	21.12.2004	31.12.2003	31.12.2002	28.12.2001
Euro / U.S. Dollar	1.425 USD	1.317 USD	1.180 USD	1.362 USD	1.263 USD	1.049 USD	0.881 USD
Euro / British Pound	0.698 GBP	0.672 GBP	0.685 GBP	0.705 GBP	0.705 GBP	0.651 GBP	0.609 GBP
Euro / Yen	165.51 JPY	156.93 JPY	138.90 JPY	139.65 JPY	135.05 JPY	124.39 JPY	115.33 JPY

SOURCE: Unmodified data: www.bankenverband.de

Figure 2   New Products and New Designs for Bottles and Labels

Case Questions

1. Do you agree with the owner that there is a fit regarding the company's strategy and resources?

2. What is Fitz-Ritter's competitive advantage? How did the company manage to survive in a highly competitive wine business?

3. Regarding the company's strategy, what do you think is the most important thing the new owner has to do? And why?

4. Concerning Fitz-Ritter's export business, how should the owner reorganize the export business? Does he need a new strategy for it? If he does, what would be your suggestion to the owner? Why would you continue with the export business? And why not?

5. Why is the Association of German Prädikat Wine Estates so important for the company? How do you think Fitz-Ritter could improve its network? If you do not think it is important, why not? Where do you see arguments for and against the partnership?

6. Johann Fitz wants to strengthen the firm's position in the market and he is thinking about how to grow—do you see any potential areas for growth? How could he use the new FitzSecco?

7. Fitz-Ritter's product portfolio embraces about 40 different products. Where are the strengths and weaknesses in its product portfolio?

8. Imagine you are the new owner. What are the next steps and why? Where do you see areas to improve?

References

Bartlett, C. A. (2003). *Global wine wars: New World challenges Old.* Boston: Harvard Business School Publishing.

Lynam, R. (2001, March). The Riesling Renaissance. *Hong Kong Business, 18*(225), 98.

Wolkoff, I. (2006, June 2). Following hard times, German Rieslings rise again. *Medical Post, 42*(20), 39.

Verband Deutscher Praedikats-und Qualitaetsweingueter (VDP). (n.d.) Web site. Retrieved September 29, 2008, from www.vdp.de/verband/daten-zahlen-fakten/

Mamma Mia![1]

The Little Show That Could!

Christopher Ferrarone[2]

I n the spring of 1988, Björn Ulvaeus, Benny Andersson, and Judy Craymer agreed that poor Broadway reviews marked the beginning of the
end for *Chess*. As the executive producer of the musical, Judy Craymer
reflected on the recent failure and wondered what factors, other than the
reviews, had contributed to *Chess's* Broadway failure. More immediate,
however, was the question of how she was going to resurrect her career. As
she left the project behind in search of new work, Craymer was convinced
that there was a musical to be created out of ABBA's songs.

Almost a decade later, and after numerous attempts, Craymer finally
received the approval of ABBA's Ulvaeus and Andersson to plan a musical
based around their songs. By 2001 Craymer had flourishing productions
of *Mamma Mia!* running in London, Toronto, and on tour across the
United States. But even with this success, both Craymer and Ulvaeus were
anxious about the show's fate once they decided to bring *Mamma Mia!* to
Broadway in the fall of 2001. After all, bad reviews in New York 13 years
earlier had caused their production of *Chess* to close after only 68 shows.
Moreover, ABBA's music was more than 20 years old and consumer tastes
in theater had undoubtedly changed in the new millennium. Another
Broadway flop would likely wipe out the momentum behind the productions in Canada and on the road, while also bringing 15 years of Craymer's
hard work to an end. Was the idea of a show surrounded and hyped by

---

1. The phrase "The Little Show That Could" was coined by a member of the Las
Vegas touring company.

2. This case was prepared by Christopher Ferrarone under the supervision of
Boston College Professor Gregory L. Stoller as the basis for class discussion rather
than to illustrate either effective or ineffective handling of an administrative situation. This case was prepared entirely from existing, publicly available sources.

already existing songs a solid business proposition? Would theatergoing audiences find merit in such a creation? Was risking the success of the other *Mamma Mia!* productions a sound decision?

The initial fears quickly subsided when *Mamma Mia!* tallied over US$27 million in advance ticket sales before the October 18 opening, the second highest advance sale ever on Broadway (Tustin, n.d.). But even as ticket sales continued to break records, Craymer and Ulvaeus could not help but wonder why *Mamma Mia!* was having such great success while *Chess* had done so poorly. Moreover, as Craymer began to win awards and achieve recognition for the production, she wondered to what extent it mattered that she had not created anything "new." She questioned whether it was ABBA or she who deserved the accolades and whether the production would ever be considered on the same level as more traditional works such as *Les Miserables* or *Cats,* the show that *Mamma Mia!* had just replaced at the Winter Garden Theater (Tustin, n.d.).

ABBA

The ABBA history began in 1966 when Björn Ulvaeus and Benny Andersson first met. The two were singers in different bands; Björn in a musical group named the Hootenanny Singers and Benny in a group called the Hepstars. After the two became acquainted with one another they began co-writing songs. As the decade progressed, they increased their collaborative efforts.

Three years later, in the spring of 1969, Björn and Benny met Agnetha Faltskog and Anni-Frid Lyngstad. At the time both women were mildly successful solo singers in Sweden. Eventually, Benny would marry Faltskog and Björn would marry Lyngstad and the quartet would become ABBA, an acronym of their first names.

In the early 1970s, the group performed together as a cabaret act called Festfolk. Mostly, the four covered a combination of existing music and humorous acts. It was quickly evident that audiences did not particularly enjoy the covered material; however, they did react positively to one of the group's original songs, "Hej gamle man." The team quickly put their efforts into creating a routine made up of their own material. In the spring of 1972 they recorded a song called "People Need Love," which was regarded as a moderate hit.

In 1974 the group changed their name to ABBA and entered the Eurovision Song Contest with their song "Waterloo." They won the contest, and "Waterloo" consequently reached number one on the music charts across Europe and attained a spot on the U.S. Top Ten.

Soon thereafter the group released the album titled *Waterloo,* which became a huge hit in Sweden. From there, they continued to work on their music, releasing numerous albums. But it took nearly a year and a half before they obtained another worldwide hit. It was the song "SOS," from their third album, titled *ABBA*. After "SOS" the group produced many hit singles throughout the 1970s.

Waterloo	No. 1 in April 1974
Ring Ring	No. 32 in July 1974
I Do I Do I Do I Do I Do	No. 38 in July 1975
SOS	No. 6 in September 1975
Mama Mia	No. 1 in December 1975
Fernando	No. 1 in March 1976
Dancing Queen	No. 1 in August 1976
Money Money Money	No. 3 in November 1976
Knowing Me Knowing You	No. 1 in February 1977
The Name of the Game	No. 1 in October 1977
Take a Chance on Me	No. 1 in February 1978
Summer Night City	No. 5 in September 1978
Chiquita	No. 2 in February 1979
Does Your Mother Know	No. 4 in May 1979
Angel Eyes/Voulez-Vous	No. 3 in July 1979
Gimme Gimme Gimme	No. 3 in October 1979
I Have a Dream	No. 2 in December 1979
The Winner Takes It All	No. 1 in August 1980
Super Trouper	No. 1 in November 1980

"Mamma Mia,"[3] also from the album *ABBA,* gave the group a number one spot on the British hit list, a feat that they were able to accomplish nine times between 1974 and 1980 (behind only The Beatles and Elvis). "Mamma Mia" was also a number one hit in Australia in 1975. Australia increasingly became one of ABBA's most successful regions, where the group managed to release a total of six number one songs. An ABBA television show even ran in Australia, drawing more viewers than the first moon landing.

As ABBA continued to rack up hit songs, they released compilation albums filled with their most popular music. In 1976 ABBA released *Greatest Hits* and *The Best of ABBA*. These two albums contributed to the group's worldwide fame and helped them to achieve a number one rating in the United States with "Dancing Queen" in 1977 (which would be their only song ever reaching a number one place on the U.S. charts). At one time during the late 1970s, only the automaker Volvo surpassed ABBA as Sweden's top export.

---

3. "Mamma Mia" the song is separate from the musical *Mamma Mia!*

In late 1976 ABBA released its fourth album, *Arrival*. This was followed by concert tours in Europe the following year. The tour completely sold out and was consequently brought to Australia, where the group decided to begin working on a film titled *ABBA: The Movie*. In 1978 the group came to the United States on a promotional tour that preceded the release of their sixth album, *Voulez-Vous*. Earlier in the year, however, Björn and Agnetha had announced their divorce. While the group remained determined to continue their work as ABBA, the news started rumors of the group's breakup. In late 1979 the group released a second compilation album, *Greatest Hits Vol. 2*, that coincided with a major tour of Canada, the United States, and Europe. In March 1980 ABBA took their tour to Japan for what turned out to be one of their last live concerts. For the rest of the year, the group recorded the album *Super Trouper*. In February 1981 Benny and Frida also announced their divorce. Many fans considered this the breakup of the group. Yet the event did not stop the foursome from working together. At the end of the year, ABBA released their eighth album, *The Visitors* (ABBA, n.d.).

Chess

At the end of 1982, the group decided to take a break. Benny and Björn had tired of ABBA and were looking to branch out into musical theater. At the same time, Tim Rice was looking for someone to write the score for his musical *Chess*. Working as a lyricist and producer, Rice reached fame by collaborating with producer Andrew Lloyd Webber in *Joseph and the Amazing Technicolor Dreamcoat* and *Jesus Christ Superstar*, and was considered to be a musical pioneer in theater. As Rice pointed out:

> Doing shows on record first and without a book may have been things that Andrew [Lloyd Webber] and I pioneered, but we really did it by mistake. The only reason we recorded *Jesus Christ Superstar* first was because we couldn't get a theater deal. It had no book because we didn't know anyone who could write one. Geography had a lot to do with our success. Had we been in America, we would have been subject to the Broadway tradition. But because we were so far away we felt there was no need to follow any rules. After the Beatles, anybody with ambitions to write songs went into records and performing. But since we weren't performers and since Andrew loved theater so much, we took all our favorite rock things and used them in our scores. As with the Beatles, it finally wasn't brilliant thinking so much as luck that made us so successful. We happened to be in the right place at the right time. (Holden, 1998)

Rice's reputation and the work that he was doing (he has since been a major part of productions such as *Evita, Aladdin, Beauty and the Beast,*

The Lion King, and *Aida*) turned out to be an instant draw for Benny and Björn. They immediately signed on to the project.

Using the world of international chess as a metaphor, Tim Rice wrote a musical about how the Cold War affected the lives of all those it touched. The story follows an international chess match from Bangkok to Budapest. The plot revolves around Florence, a Hungarian-born woman who works as an assistant for the upstart American challenger, Freddie. Freddie is jointly modeled after Bobby Fischer and the tennis star John McEnroe. In the middle of the match with the Russian champion, Anatoly, Freddie precipitates a dispute. As the match seems about to fall apart, Florence, attempting to intercede, meets and falls in love with the Russian, who promptly decides to defect to the West. When the Russians pressure Anatoly to change his mind, he becomes the focus of an international tug of war.

Rice originally approached Andrew Lloyd Webber to write the score, but his former partner was already committed to other projects. Then, in 1981, producer Richard Vos introduced Rice to Benny Andersson and Björn Ulvaeus. The team immediately set about creating a concept album. Two numbers did well on the charts. "One Night in Bangkok" first appeared on the U.K. charts on November 10, 1984, and stayed there for 13 weeks, at one point reaching number 12. In the United States, it jumped to number nine in April of 1985 and topped the charts in France, Australia, Belgium, Austria, South Africa, Denmark, Israel, West Germany, Switzerland, Holland, and Sweden. Another single, "I Know Him So Well," followed, eventually reaching number one on the U.K. charts during its 16-week run. With *Chess* already a worldwide phenomenon before it had even opened, expectations were high. The London production team of Tim Rice, Judy Craymer, Andersson, and Ulvaeus brought the show to the West End[4] on May 14, 1986, where it ran for 3 years. However, the high-tech spectacle never garnered a lot of interest from London's theatergoers and failed to generate enough revenue to cover its initial investment. The production team, still believing in the project, decided to bring the show to Broadway.

The show was drastically altered before moving to Broadway. Instead of having the performance completely sung-through[5] as it had been in London, director Trevor Nunn chose to bring in playwright Richard Nelson to write a book. Rice also added several new songs including "Someone Else's Story."

The Broadway production opened at the Imperial Theater on April 28, 1988, with an entirely new cast. With a poor review from *The New York Times* leading to a series of unfavorable criticisms, the show proved even less of a commercial success than its predecessor, losing US$6 million and closing after only 68 performances. A later concert, however, that featured

4. London's version of Broadway.

5. All dialogue and character lines in musical verse.

the Broadway cast at Carnegie Hall, was a huge hit (ABBA, n.d.). The concert was a bittersweet end to the *Chess* story for Björn Ulvaeus:

> We weren't surprised in one sense that *Chess* failed because the bad review in *The New York Times* came right after our run in the West End and we were already losing steam. The songs were hits 4 years earlier and their popularity was not recent enough to carry us through [the bad review]. But we were very proud of it—the music and lyrics and everything. (Proctor, 2003)

Where the *Chess* episode did succeed, however, was in bringing Ulvaeus and Andersson into the world of theater, offering the duo a unique platform for continuing their love of composing while also offering a fresh start.

London Theater

London theater falls into three broad and sometimes overlapping categories: West End, National Repertory Companies, and Off-West End/Fringe, terms analogous to Broadway, Regional Theater, and Off-Broadway in the United States.

Geographically, the West End encompasses a two square mile section of London in the vicinity of Leicester Square, Piccadilly, and Covent Garden, where more than 40 picture frame theaters, most dating from the Victorian and Edwardian eras, are clustered. These are commercial theaters in which producers present shows with the expectation of making a profit.

The most prestigious groups of British theater are the two national repertory companies that enjoy the support of government subsidies through the Arts Council, as well as through their huge ticket sales. The Royal National Theater, located in a three-stage complex on the South Bank, and the Royal Shakespeare Company (RSC), with stages in London at the Barbican Center and in Stratford-upon-Avon, are large companies of actors, directors, and technicians who produce a formidable number of plays in repertory throughout the year. On these stages audiences see performances of the highest quality, made possible by conditions not often met in commercial theater: longer rehearsal periods, freedom to commit to new work and innovative approaches, support from expert voice coaches, the security of a firmly scheduled run, and, most significantly, the devotion of seasoned British actors who return to these companies throughout their careers. In these venues, as well, audiences discover emerging actors, directors, and designers who are about to become the leading figures of British theater, film, and television.

At any one time, there are around 70 small Fringe theaters operating in pubs, warehouses, and a few purpose-built theaters in and around

London. They constitute the breeding ground from which the rising generation of British actors, directors, playwrights, and designers emerge and to which seasoned theater artists occasionally return to be able to see and do cutting-edge work.

Cross-fertilization from the subsidized companies and the varied Off-West End and Fringe theaters to the commercial West End accounts for the high productivity of the entire British theater. Major productions from the Royal National Theater and the RSC are sometimes picked up by a commercial producer for long runs in the West End. The repertory company benefits from extended royalties, sometimes many years' worth, as in the case of the RSC's *Les Miserables*. That show opened at the Barbican Theater in 1985 and soon transferred under commercial sponsorship to the Palace, where it continued to run through May 2003. The West End producer benefits from getting a production that has already demonstrated it has legs and will go on attracting audiences when its limited repertory run is over.

The work of the Off-West End and Fringe sector is an important aspect of British theater. These companies cultivate audiences for a wide range of new work and new talent. As a result, in London a high number of very young directors and writers get significant career opportunities. Productions from these theaters sometimes transfer to the commercial West End, as in the case of the 1992 production *Medea,* which went on to a long run in the West End and then played on Broadway.

JUDY CRAYMER

With a pedigree in London theater including working for the likes of Tim Rice, Cameron Mackintosh, and Andrew Lloyd Webber on productions of *Cats, Les Miserables, Phantom of the Opera,* and *Miss Saigon,* Judy Craymer was well known throughout the theater production world. This reputation suffered with her work on *Chess* but ultimately allowed her to continue on her quest to produce an ABBA musical.

From the time *Chess* closed down in 1988, Craymer worked to make her idea of an all-ABBA musical a reality. She was convinced that there was a theatrical performance behind the songs of ABBA and would toil for 10 years on the project, selling her house and eventually squatting in her office to keep the project alive (Moore, 2002). It was her determination and passion that persuaded ABBA's Benny Andersson and Björn Ulvaeus to take a chance and let her hire writer Catherine Johnson and director Phyllida Lloyd to create *Mamma Mia!* Johnson remarked:

> Benny and Björn didn't think it was such a great idea at first, because they had really moved away from ABBA, but Judy pursued this concept with them for 10 years. Finally Björn told Judy that if she found a writer who

could come up with a story everyone is keen on, then she could go ahead with the project. (Moore, 2002, p. A-F01)

CATHERINE JOHNSON

In 1997, after finally getting the go-ahead from Benny and Björn to create a story, Craymer found Catherine Johnson, a single, nearly broke mother of two. The two women worked on a script from opposite ends of England, each taking the train half way to save money in order to conduct meetings with each other. There was a lot of collaboration and work on the book because it was the key to getting ABBA's consent on the whole project. Johnson noted:

> Judy Craymer conceived the original idea in 1988 when she was working on *Chess* with Björn and Benny, but it took her ever so long to come up with a writer. I came on board when she was working with a director that I once worked with. She told him about the project and he suggested me. It was very fortunate because I hadn't heard of it and it certainly wouldn't have been something I would have thought of doing. (Moore, 2002, p. A-F01)

For Ulvaeus and Andersson, the story was what would either make or break the project. They had told Craymer that they wanted the plot to be the first and foremost priority, with the music coming in afterward to help the narrative. As Ulvaeus pointed out:

> I said to Catherine, "We have a catalog of 95 to 100 ABBA songs, and you can choose whatever you like, not just the hits." I told her, "The story is more important than the songs." I saw this as a challenge and an experiment, and was ready to call it off at any point. In the end what I saw was a seamless story, not something that would make you say, "They've shoehorned the songs in." (Proctor, 2003, p. H-1)

Johnson's story follows 20-year-old Sophie on the eve of her wedding. Sophie has been raised by her mother, Donna, on a Greek island without ever knowing her father. Eager to have him walk her down the aisle, Sophie tracks down the three probable candidates based on her mother's youthful indiscretions and secretly invites each of them to the wedding. She confronts her potential dads, but none of them seem to be the right one. As the plot moves along, complications arise among the characters, most notably with her mother, who is forced to confront her past. There are many other secondary characters that add to the stereotypes and humorous situations that come about. All the action is carried along and highlighted by 22 ABBA songs mixed throughout the performance.

PHYLLIDA LLOYD

Once the story was completed, Craymer and Ulvaeus brought director Phyllida Lloyd onto the project. Renowned for her work at England's Royal National Theater and on international opera productions, Lloyd helped the project gather further momentum. She was behind the assembly of the creative team of Mark Thompson (design), Howard Harrison (lighting), Andrew Bruce and Bobby Aitken (sound), Martin Koch (musical supervisor), and Anthony Van Last (choreography), who were credited with making the show as successful as it was. Lloyd told the actors at an early workshop: "*Mamma Mia!* is the musical Benny and Björn wrote years ago. They just decided to release the songs first."(www.playbill.com, n.d.)

The Road Show

Traditionally, Broadway had been the proving ground for most large-scale theatrical productions, known as equity productions—*equity* referring to the large amounts of money needed to produce fancy, glamorous shows. These performances are a large draw for audiences.

During the 1998–1999 season, more than 11.6 million people attended a show on Broadway. This amounted to over US$588 million in gross ticket sales. Of those shows, the ones that realized success then sent touring companies on the road. During the same season, these touring companies brought shows to over 100 U.S. cities and sold tickets to 14.6 million people, yielding US$707 million in gross road receipts (Winn, 2000). That represents nearly 55% of the industry's combined US$1.3 billion take in New York and on the road.

As such, road shows today are big business and have a rather involved process. Every road show starts with the producer who then hires a booking agent, whose job it is to contact presenters at theaters across the country and book the production into their theaters for specific weeks during the season. Presenters range from entrepreneurs who rent theaters, to performing arts organizations and municipalities who own and operate their own locales and venues.

In many cases production companies search for shows that they are interested in booking. For the popular musicals it is not uncommon for bidding wars to take place among production companies looking to take the show on the road. Sometimes the original Broadway producers even take their own shows on the road.

Once the decision to take a performance on the road has been made, the booking agent, in conjunction with the producer or production company, decides where to take it and how long to stay at certain locations. For the large productions, surveys and marketing data are collected and analyzed to aid in this process of determining the best travel destinations. In some cases, the size of the venue or city determines how long a run the show will have (Lazarus, n.d.).

From there, producers negotiate guarantees[6] with presenters. This amount, coupled with the show's capitalization and weekly expenditure requirements, ultimately determines how many weeks the production must be on the road for. Of course, the producers always also get a percentage of the box office receipts above and beyond the guarantee.[7]

Originally, road shows were nonequity or bus-and-truck[8] versions of the Broadway originals and were dramatically scaled down productions with fewer, less known actors and simpler sets. This trend changed in the late 1970s. Some credit English producer Cameron Mackintosh with these changes. Mackintosh produced *Miss Saigon, Cats, Les Miserables,* and *Phantom of the Opera.* When he started, the road was primarily made up of the bus-and-truck variety; however, Mackintosh did not want to do that with *Les Miserables:*

> When I first put *Les Miz* out I was not going to cut corners in any way. I wanted to give audiences the same show that they would see on Broadway. And the combination of my four big shows completely changed the standards of the road. (Looking Out, 2002)

These productions sent box office receipts soaring and resulted in theaters upgrading their facilities and cities even building state-of-the-art performing arts centers to take advantage of the blockbusters. To be profitable, these productions required multiweek stays at a minimum. But in the absence of blockbuster productions, and proportionally scaled down ticket prices, few patrons actually filled the seats (Looking Out, 2002). As such, the manner in which road shows are produced has tended to change as the popularity of theater has cycled.

Taking *Mamma Mia!* on the Road

In total Craymer was able to fund the first production of *Mamma Mia!* with US$4.8 million (Tustin, n.d.). In 1999 *Mamma Mia!* debuted in London's Prince Edward Theater and was met by rave reviews from fans.

---

6. A "guarantee" is the weekly figure the presenter promises to pay the producer no matter what the box office intake happens to be.

7. This percentage is typically around 40%.

8. The term *bus-and-truck* comes from the way in which sets, actors, musicians, etc., were carted around the country. Typically, these shows have runs at theaters for no more than a week or two.

Once the show opened, it took fewer than 27 weeks for Craymer to make back the initial investment. The show continued to have advance ticket sales of more than US$6.5 million through 2003.

Very little advertising was done as Craymer relied on word-of-mouth advertising for nearly 2 years. As the show proved capable of delivering a return for investors, the decision for Craymer was not whether to take the act to North America, but rather how. The costs for a large-scale production were immense, particularly if the group was going to tour through Canada and the United States. However, a scaled down production could result in poor ticket sales and reviews, and could stop a tour before it was able to gain any momentum. Craymer was able to put this decision off, at least for a few months.

In May of 2000, the group brought the show to Toronto's Princess of Wales Theater, where it planned a 6-month stay before going on the road across the United States. A full-scale production, Craymer believed, would draw audiences and positive reviews while the extended stay would serve as insurance if the production failed to live up to expectations. In short, future road shows in the United States could be cancelled without incurring the large upfront costs of a full-scale tour. While Craymer believed the strategy was sound, she ultimately altered the plans to take advantage of the situation:

> Our strategy was to see if it worked in London, and it did. Then we had the opportunity to go to Toronto for 6 months, and the bookings were so positive that they suggested we stay in Toronto and create a new touring company in the United States. (Moore, 2002, p. A-F01)

In fact, two touring companies were created, and *Mamma Mia!* brought productions to Buffalo, Atlanta, Cincinnati, Columbus, Charlotte, Louisville, Norfolk, Pittsburgh, Providence, Memphis, Miami, Nashville, Rochester, and Tampa (Buckhan, 2003).

As the touring companies performed across the United States and the Toronto and London productions continued to sell out, Craymer and the production team slowly edged closer to bringing the show to Broadway. Hype for the musical was built slowly by word of mouth and the producers continued to use little advertising. Craymer explained:

> After the first London preview, the audience came out of the theater, got on their cell phones and called their friends, saying, "You've just got to come see this." That's the effect we wanted to create before we came to Broadway. (Rizzo, 2003)

Mamma Mia! proved popular enough to sustain multiweek runs on the road without the usual publicity of a successful Broadway run. In its first 18 months, *Mamma Mia!* had proved a hit at every major theatrical level except Broadway.

With the four *Mamma Mia!* productions performing at once, three of which were in North America, Benny, Björn, and Craymer decided to finally take the plunge and return ABBA to the world of Broadway.

Broadway

As soon as Ulvaeus and Andersson gave her the go-ahead, Judy Craymer began planning for the *Mamma Mia!* Broadway debut. It proved to be a long, hard-fought battle. Craymer recalls:

> The whole thing started 12 years before we would bring the show to New York. I used to go home and listen to ABBA records, dreaming of songs as part of a Broadway musical. When we finally got the show together there was no way that Benny and Björn would let it go straight to Broadway because of *Chess*. (Souccar, 2001, p. 3)

Because of Benny and Björn's stance, Craymer began devising alternative ways to bring the show to the United States:

> London and Europe were never going to be problems; everyone knew ABBA. It was getting the show to the States that I worried about. We couldn't bring it right to Broadway and when I came up with the strategy of building interest through a tour, people told me that it would never be successful unless it was a Broadway-branded production. Either way, the stakes were quite high; I just kind of followed my heart and instincts. (Souccar, 2001, p. 3)

As skeptics quickly discovered, the tour was a huge success and the word-of-mouth strategy had proven successful as each new tour location routinely sold out before opening night. The financial returns were further magnified by the reduced need for advertising. Moreover, to the delight of Craymer and Ulvaeus, as *Mamma Mia!* got closer and closer to Broadway, advance sales began racking up. Officially, *Mamma Mia!* sold over US$27 million worth of tickets before opening night. The production team could not have been happier; they had achieved all their goals and had the momentum to roll over any poor review.

This momentum, however, came to a violent stop a little over a month before opening night, when the World Trade Center was attacked. At first there was little thought about her own problem as Craymer worried for the actors who were rehearsing in studios close to ground zero. As a few days passed, and when it was determined that everyone involved was safe, Ulvaeus and Craymer asked themselves, "Can we really go on with this?" (Maslin, 2001). They questioned whether or not it would be appropriate to stage such an exuberant show amid the intense mourning of an entire city. Very quickly they made the decision to carry on. Ulvaeus pointed out:

> At first I did not know what to do. I did not know if our feel-good music and text would strike the right chord. But then what was said by many people and by Mayor Giuliani especially made sense to me: [New Yorkers] needed to see people coming here from the outside and doing things, moving ahead. This is how you fight back; this is how you don't give in. I thought: Maybe we're meant to be here to do this show for people, now of all times.(Maslin, 2001)

Judy Craymer agreed:

> Many of the cast had seen it happen, because the rehearsal rooms are downtown. I was just off to the dentist when I saw it on television. But to have withdrawn would have been a huge psychological blow to New York. Having seen a preview performance, I think the show had come at exactly the right time. The audience was on its feet dancing at the end. (Maslin, 2001)

The recession and loss of tourists resulting from 9/11 cost most shows millions of dollars, closed a myriad of productions, and threatened a number more. *Mamma Mia!*, however, proved to be somewhat immune. The Broadway version cost US$10 million to produce and was able to recoup its entire investment in just 6 months. The show played to near sell-outs for the first 2 years, breaking all kinds of box office records along the way. The show not only gave a boost to Broadway but also to the community, and in addition raised nearly US$500,000 for the attack victims' families.

Mamma Mia! the Corporation

The success on Broadway helped the production company expand its reach around the world. Before Broadway there were productions of *Mamma Mia!* running in London, Toronto, and touring the United States. A second U.S. tour opened in Providence, Rhode Island, in February of 2001, playing shorter runs in many cities. A third production was opened in Melbourne, Australia.

With six productions of the show performing concurrently worldwide, Craymer began licensing the show to production companies in other countries, where it was translated into different languages. The first foreign show was a German version in Hamburg in November 2002. A second production in Japanese began in December 2002. A third and fourth opened shortly thereafter in Moscow and Madrid. According to Craymer, "*Mamma Mia!* had become a corporation in a sense; it had turned into a sizable organization running shows all over the world (*Mamma Mia!* 2002).

By the end of 2002, the global phenomenon had grossed more than US$400 million with a one-day box office record in London of US$831,000 in ticket sales. While the numbers suggest a well thought-out business plan combined with experienced market savvy, Craymer called the success "a sheer fluke," and Ulvaeus agreed:

> I thought when we split up in 1981, that it was the end of it. I thought I would hardly hear ABBA again. I have no idea why all this is happening and why the music is so much [more present now]. (www.playbill.com, n.d.)

While Craymer's realization of an ABBA inspired musical had exceeded her dreams, she and Ulvaeus were still not certain as to why the results of *Chess* and *Mamma Mia!* had differed to such a great extent. Unlike *Chess*, *Mamma Mia!* had started with a loose concept and became a worldwide sensation. Along the way it had overcome skeptics, poor reviews that had similarly sunk *Mamma Mia's* predecessor, and even 9/11. They wondered how their original, simple business plan had morphed into a nine-production sensation employing over 700 people.

The Business of *Mamma Mia!*

Critics from both inside and outside performing arts circles have heavily debated the run of *Mamma Mia!* While a great deal of criticism subsided when the show became an unabashed success, some still continue to question whether the production team's accolades are warranted, since nothing new has really been created with the exception of a story line around some old hit songs.

The question ultimately centers on how theater, and its broader category of the performing arts, is classified by business analysts and the world around them. Are plays, musicals, and productions merely another avenue through which to make money? Or are other metrics, such as creative expression, the true return on investment? Are these types of ventures managed like traditional businesses with a projected profit motive, or is performance quality emphasized above all else? Perhaps it's a combination of the two approaches that matters to producers, directors, and choreographers alike.

Additionally, where does *Mamma Mia!* stand when compared to Broadway classics like *Les Miserables, Miss Saigon,* and *Cats?* Can those who come up with something new in theater be considered entrepreneurs? What about people like Craymer, who simply bring existing material into a new arena? Is she an entrepreneur? Is the success of *Mamma Mia!* attributable to skill and business acumen, or was it a fluke?

In the end does it really matter to Craymer, her critics, and the many fans?

Case Questions

1. Can the performing arts be considered an industry?

2. From an entrepreneurship perspective, highlight the issues that must be considered when dealing with creations in the performing arts that have cultural or classical roots.

3. Are there special conditions or conflicts of interest that apply in the quasi-public sector of the performing arts to businesses such as *Mamma Mia!*?

4. What do you think of the *Mamma Mia!* show? Is it entrepreneurship?

References

ABBA Web site. (n.d.) Retrieved September 26, 2008, from http://abbasite.com/people/bio.php?id=395&page=5

Buckhan, T. (2003, January 18). *Mamma Mia!* proves a record crowd pleaser. *Buffalo News,* p. 81.

Holden, S. (1998, April 24). *Chess* seeks to shed its checkered past. *The New York Times,* Section 2, p. 5.

Lazarus, B. (n.d.) Getting your act together and taking it on the road. *Producer's Corner.* Retrieved July 2003.

Mamma Mia! (2002, October 28). *Associated Press.* Newswires 1:52 PM.

Maslin, J. (2001, October 14). Trying to make ABBA's oldies young again. *The New York Times,* Section 2, p. 1.

Moore, J. (2002, November 24). Viva ABBA! Three women's dream changes face of theater. *Denver Post,* p. A, F-01.

Proctor, R. (2003, February 9). ABBA Cadabra It's *Mamma Mia! Richmond Times Dispatch,* p. H-1.

Rizzo, F. (2002, October 27). Looking out on a different Broadway, *Hartford Courant,* p. G6.

Rizzo, F. (2002, November 3). *Mamma Mia! Hartford Courant,* p. G1.

Souccar, M. (2001, December 17). Dancing queen *Mamma Mia!* charms in Broadway slump. *Crain's NY Business,* p. 3.

Tustin, M. (n.d.) Retrieved September 26, 2008, from www.abbamail.com/mamma_bwy_variety.htm

Winn, S. (2000, January 23). Paying big bucks and getting shortchanged. *San Francisco Chronicle,* p. 30.

Federal Express

Leo Dana

Federal Express, or FedEx, came to China in 1984, and since then it has become a major hub in the company's growing international operations. Its strategy in China is simple—have a vibrant business in Asia's largest economy. The company's first direct flight from southern China to North America with next-day service launched in 2003, and in 2005 it launched flights to Europe from China. Over the past 24 years, FedEx has expanded service to cover more than 200 cities across the country, with plans to add 100 additional cities over the next few years. Today, China is growing exponentially and one of FedEx's greatest challenges will be to maintain the capacity to keep up with this growth.

Industry Background[1]

Before the U.S. airfreight industry developed, all that existed was the U.S. airmail system. All air transport of packages occurred by means of the U.S. Postal Service. Time sensitive shipments were not possible because airfreight was not transported on its own planes; rather, package delivery and transport depended on the scheduled service of passenger airlines.

In 1977 the U.S. government deregulated the airfreight industry and the industry changed dramatically. Airfreight companies were able to acquire their own aircraft to create a privatized industry for the express air delivery service. Large-scale overnight deliveries soon became the heart of the

---

1. Information for this section was compiled from Allbusiness.com, www.allbusiness .com/transportation-by-air/air-transportation-scheduled/3779842-3.html.

airfreight industry. This system, commonly called the hub-and-spoke system, is characterized by all packages being shipped to a central distribution center then resorted and distributed to their destinations across the country. This system was started by FedEx and is still the method used by most airfreight firms today.

Many overnight airfreight companies joined the industry throughout the 1980s. But by 1999 only five companies dominated the industry: the U.S. Postal Service, Federal Express, UPS, DHL, and Airborne Express. An interesting observation on the part of analysts is that the status of the airfreight industry is representative of the U.S. economy overall. When the economy is in a downturn or stagnant, consumers cut back on their express shipping costs in preference for the lower cost 2-day delivery option. During an economic upturn, overnight delivery services take an upward turn as well.

The success of the express airfreight industry accounts for most of the growth in the airfreight industry as a whole. Air express deliveries accounted for 60% of air shipments in 1998, with overnight letters and envelopes claiming 27% of both shipments and revenues for the industry.

As the airfreight industry has matured, companies have begun to integrate their services and refine their offerings. They now guarantee morning and afternoon deliveries, have higher weight limits, expanded tracking, and automated billing services. According to the Colography Group, an Atlanta-based research firm specializing in the airfreight and air express industries, there were 2.8 billion domestic air shipments made in 1998. The U.S. Postal Service (USPS) moved 1.3 billion Express and Priority Mail parcels and represented 45% of the domestic market. In late 1999 USPS announced an affiliation with DHL Worldwide Inc. for expedited global service to 65 countries.

The Growth of an Entrepreneur

Frederick W. Smith, a Memphis native whose father made his fortune by founding a bus company, conceived of the idea to begin an air cargo company while studying at Yale University during the 1960s. He authored a paper describing the concept of a freight-only airline that would fly all packages to one central point, where they would then be distributed and flown out again to their respective destinations. His proposed operations would occur overnight when airports were less crowded, and with the proper logistics, the packages would reach their destination by the next day. Whether it was the novelty of his idea, that his professor was a

staunch supporter of the current system of airfreight, or that it was written
in one night and turned in late, the first presentation of Smith's grand idea
earned him a solid C.

Smith's idea was about more than a creative term paper, however. He
had seen how the technological base of the country was changing. More
companies were becoming involved in the production of mass produced
technology, such as computers, and Smith was convinced that his air
cargo plan would help control their inventory costs. Overnight delivery
from a single distribution center to anywhere in the United States could
satisfy customers' needs without a company needing to duplicate investment in inventory to be stored in regional warehouses. Smith even considered the Federal Reserve Banks a potential customer, with the vast
quantities of checks that had to be shipped to all parts of the country
every day.

The key to Fred Smith's company would be its ability to service a large
segment of the business community from the very beginning, and the key
to the required level of service was cash. Smith went to Chicago and New
York, confident that he would be returning with the funds necessary to
start his venture. Progress turned out to be slower than he anticipated, but
he was relentless and through his technical knowledge of the airfreight
industry he was finally able to find an enthusiastic backer in New Court
Securities. This Manhattan-based, Rothschild-backed, venture-capital
investment bank contributed around US$5 million in capital to his start-
up. New Court's support encouraged others to jump on Fred Smith's
bandwagon. Five other institutions, including General Dynamics and Citi-
corp Venture Capital, Ltd., decided to commit funds. Smith eventually
returned to Memphis with US$72 million. This was the largest venture-
capital start-up deal in American business history.

FedEx's Capabilities

FedEx began its operations in April 1973, at which time it introduced a
fully integrated door-to-door overnight delivery, small package express
service. The firm introduced the hub-and-spoke system of route structures, which was later adopted by passenger airlines. Federal Express carried computer components and later documents and packages. Until 1977
Federal Express used a fleet of Falcon 20 twinjets. Then, the Cargo Reform
Act allowed the firm to purchase larger jets.

During the 1980s Smith decided to take his company global and Federal
Express expanded to Europe. In 1988 financier Saul Steinberg (who owned
16.5% of Tiger International) approached Federal Express and offered to
sell Tiger International's Flying Tigers cargo airlines. At the time Federal

Express served only five airports outside the United States: Brussels, London, Montreal, Tokyo, and Toronto.

In 1989 Smith's Federal Express paid US$895 million for Tiger International. The acquisition of Flying Tigers led to increased advertising by Federal Express. The acquisition was trumpeted as a purchase of both capital and international knowledge and global experience:

> By joining forces with Flying Tigers, we not only acquired 40 years' worth of international shipping experience, we also created the world's largest full-service cargo airline, Federal Express—The Best Way to Ship It Over There. (Federal Express advertisement, 1990)

The Federal Express Corporation subsequently acquired other firms in Australia, Canada, France, and Mexico. Smith defined the business as time-definite transportation and distribution throughout the world.

In 1992 Federal Express received publicity when Cessna ran an ad about Federal Express's use of big, tough, and reliable aircraft—the Cessna Grand Caravan. This type of airplane can haul 340 cubic feet of cargo up to 1,000 nautical miles at speeds of up to 180 knots. With an optional cargo pool, the Caravan's capacity is increased to 451 cubic feet (Cessna Aircraft Company, n.d.). Federal Express reportedly had over 200 Cessna Grand Caravans. Yet that same year Federal Express reported its first loss of US$147 million. Experts suggested that this was a result of growing too fast. Nevertheless, in 1993 Federal Express expanded operations to 180 countries, up from 127 in 1992. A new corporate image was established in 1994 with an abbreviated company name—FedEx. The carrier continued to grow as an industry leader, but international competition was significant.

- *DHL Worldwide Express (DHL):* Unlike other U.S.-based express firms, DHL started with a very international outlook. During the 1970s DHL worked with maritime shippers along the Pacific Rim. DHL expanded by chartering flights and subcontracting to other firms. In addition, it developed its own route network with a hub in Cincinnati.

- *Emery Worldwide:* In contrast to other firms that focused on documents or the small package market, Emery's primary target market was identified as the business-to-business commercial shipper. In 1989 Emery Worldwide was acquired by Consolidated Freightways (CF), and its operations merged with those of CF AirFreight. In 1991 Emery president W. Roger Curry oversaw a major restructuring. The firm opted to move away from envelope services, and this enabled it to downsize its personnel by 2,000 employees and to reduce its ground fleet by 1,800 vehicles.

- *TNT Express Worldwide (TNT)*: The Australian firm TNT is a provider of worldwide door-to-door express service, with world headquarters in Amsterdam. TNT also has a U.S. head office, led by David Siegfried in Miami Lakes, Florida. TNT operates direct, all-cargo flights between Europe and the United States as well as between the United States and the Pacific Rim, including Australia and Southeast Asia. The firm specializes in same-day service. Its fleet includes Boeing 727 trijets and four-engine BAe 146 jets.

- *United Parcel Service of America, Inc. (UPS):* Based in Louisville, Kentucky, UPS owns and operates the world's largest privately-owned package distribution and courier system. The firm launched its air service in 1953. Yet for its first couple of decades it owned no aircraft. Instead, it leased space in commercial aircraft. In 1981 it bought its first airplanes, a fleet of seven Boeing 727s, operated by a contractor. In 1990 UPS revenues reached US$13.6 billion. This was more than the entire express industry earned in 1987. By 1992 UPS had ordered 162 aircraft. In addition, it used 259 on a charter basis. Today, more than 335,000 employees operate 2,400 UPS facilities, over 132,000 vehicles, and over 500 dedicated aircraft. The firm's 1,500 daily flights serve over 600 airports in about 200 countries. UPS has an US$800 million aircraft hub and package sorting facility at Louisville International Airport. It is designed to service 100 airplanes and sort 300,000 packages per hour. UPS created the following worldwide services: (1) UPS SonicAir, a fast service available 24 hours daily; (2) UPS Worldwide Expedited, a low cost door-to-door service taking up to 5 days, and (3) UPS Worldwide Express, guaranteed rush service for urgent deliveries, often overnight. Yet modest quarterly earnings were offset by the growth of international business operations. With a regional office in Singapore, UPS has Asian gateway operations at several airports, including Hong Kong, Taipei, Tokyo, Singapore, and Seoul. UPS provides a daily average of 50 regional flights, serving all the major countries in Asia.

Federal Express obtained permission to work in China in 1995 through an acquisition from Evergreen International Airlines. Under this authority, Federal Express is the sole U.S.-based, all-cargo carrier with aviation rights to the world's most heavily populated nation. Today FedEx has the world's largest airfreight fleet, including McDonnell-Douglass MD-11s, and Airbus A-300s and A-310s. The planes have a total daily lift capacity of more than 26.5 million pounds. In a 24-hour period, the fleet travels nearly 500,000 miles while its couriers log 2.5 million miles a day—the equivalent of 100 trips around the earth. Today, FedEx delivers to more than 210 countries (FedEx, n.d.).

China Market Information

In 2004 the European Union (EU) became China's top trading partner. China's exports during this same year to the EU grew at a faster rate than China's overall export growth. China's trade with the United States continues to be strong, and the United States is the number one single nation trading partner with Asia's largest economy. In 2006 they traded US$262.7 billion with the United States, up 24.2% from 2005. China's trade with its other top ten trading partners also increased significantly during those years. Japan–China trade increased 12.5%, Hong Kong–greater China trade increased 21.6%, and South Korea–China trade grew 20%. In Europe, Germany's trade with China grew by 23.6%, putting it in the fifth position of China's top trade partners for 2006 (U.S. China Business Council, 2008).

Toward the Future

FedEx is the world's largest express transportation company. It established its express operations in China in 1984; in 2005 it established freight operations. FedEx China's headquarters are in Shanghai, and from here the company serves more than 220 countries and territories. Within China FedEx delivers to more than 200 cities and employs over 6,000 people. The company has hubs in three airports: Capital Airport in Beijing, Pudong Airport in Shanghai, and Bao'an Airport in Shenzhen. MD-11 and A-310 aircraft make 26 flights a week to and from Beijing, Shanghai, and Shenzen. Despite covering more than 200 cities within China, FedEx had only 100 drop-off locations domestically as of 2008 (FedEx, n.d.).

FedEx has built its business on the basis of moving fast with new technology and providing impeccable service. In March 2007 it completed a US$400 million acquisition of its Chinese partner firm and now has full authority over the brand's actions in the country (Commercial Appeal, 2007). As FedEx continues to extend its corporate strategy to include the relatively new focal point China, how can it expand its operations? How should it monitor and plan its growth in China, a country with a centrally controlled economy? Can FedEx maintain the capacity to keep up with China's growth?

Case Questions

1. In April 2008 Delta Airlines announced its intention to merge with and absorb Northwest Airlines, formerly known as Northwest Orient. Delta Airlines had already grown through the acquisition

of Northeast in 1972 and Western Airlines in 1986. Northwest was also a large airline, having absorbed Republic Airlines, itself a merger of North Central Airlines, Southern, and later Hughes Airwest. Republic had an important hub in Memphis, as did Federal Express. The result would be a global airline with hubs in Asia and Europe as well as across the United States. Will an enlarged Delta Airlines be a threat for FedEx?

2. How can FedEx maintain the capacity to keep up with China's growth?

3. What risk does FedEx encounter when subcontracting?

4. In 2008 crude oil cost more than US$100 per barrel and this was reflected by the price of jet fuel at the pump. Why might this be of concern to FedEx?

5. How might a devalued American dollar hurt FedEx?

References

Cessna Aircraft Company. (n.d.). Wichita, KS: Author. Retrieved September 28, 2008, from www.cessna.com

Commercial Appeal. (2007, March 2). *FedEx takes full control in fast-growing China.* Retrieved September 28, 2008, from www.commercialappeal.com/mca/business/article/0,1426,MCA_440_5428448,00.html

FedEx China's Web site. (n.d.). Retrieved September 28, 2008, from http://fedex.com/us/about/overview/worldwide/china/quickfacts.html?link=2

FedEx Corporate Web Site. (n.d.). Retrieved September 28, 2008, from http://fedex.com/us/about/today/history/

Federal Express advertisement. (1990, May). *Air Cargo World, 5,* 14–15.

U.S. China Business Council. (2008). *Table 7: China's Top Trade Partners 2006.* Retrieved September 28, 2008, from www.uschina.org/statistics/tradetable.html

UniMed and EduMed

Omar M. Zaki

I n April 2004 Dr. Michael Zachary and his son, Oscar Zachary, were faced with a critical go or no-go decision. The no-go decision would close an almost 3-year chapter on a vested effort between them to create a world-class global telemedicine network, which by that point seemed to be unfeasible based on their efforts and capabilities alone. The go decision, however, could potentially create a new business prospect that would help them recapture their investment.

They sat and discussed the new opportunity that was brought to them: teaming up with new business partners who would help facilitate the creation of a new business entity through securing tangible projects in continuous medical education with major multinational pharmaceutical companies.

DR. ZACHARY: What do you think Oscar? This is finally an opportunity for us to make our investment into UniMed back and at least break-even after all this effort and money spent.

OSCAR: But it's a completely different business concept, model, and market strategy than what we've been focused on for the last 3 years. Plus, I'm not sure if I'm comfortable with the idea of partnering with these folks just yet; do you trust them?

DR. ZACHARY: Well, I've worked with Ahmed on a separate project before, and the guy is pretty knowledgeable about this market and how to take advantage of its growth opportunities. Plus, he doesn't give me a bad feeling when we discuss ideas, and in fact seems to be a real trustworthy guy. I don't know the other guys very well, but my feeling is they're OK since they came through Ahmed.

OSCAR: I don't know, we would be putting all of our relationships and expertise on the line, and who knows what we might lose if something goes sour. I'm almost ready to just say let's pack up for now what we've got, get back to the drawing board, and seek out some stronger financial backing to get the Web portal going. That's the real goal here, isn't it? This educational conference stuff just doesn't seem to be what we were trying to do.

DR. ZACHARY: I agree with you, but look at it this way: it's a way for us to put to use all the research and relationships we've built thus far and at least see how it works. Although it won't be patient related services, we will still be providing some benefit to the medical community through these education projects, and we can build some credibility at the same time. Who knows, maybe it's what leads us to making UniMed a reality instead of a dream down the road.

The Telemedicine Industry

HISTORY OF TELEMEDICINE

Telemedicine is the practice of rendering medical diagnoses, advice, opinions, education, and even participating in surgery over long distances through current technology and telecommunication applications, without the physical presence of a doctor or patient being required. The idea of performing medical examinations and evaluations through the use of telecommunications is not new. Shortly after the invention of the telephone, attempts were made to transmit heart and lung sounds to a trained expert who could assess the state of the organs; however, poor transmission systems made the attempts a failure. Although it may seem that recent interest in telemedicine can be attributed to advances in the Internet and telecommunications, the truth is that telemedicine has been around since the 1960s, when astronauts first went into space. In fact, NASA built telemedicine technology into early spacecraft and spacesuits to monitor astronauts' physiological parameters. Other milestones mark telemedicine's journey to where it is today.

- 1906: ECG Transmission—Einthoven, the father of electrocardiography, first investigated on ECG transmission over telephone lines in 1906.

- 1920s: Help for Ships—Radios were used to link physicians standing watch at shore stations to assist ships at sea that had medical emergencies.

- 1955: Telepsychiatry—The Nebraska Psychiatric Institute was one of the first facilities in the country to have closed-circuit television in 1955. In 1971 the Nebraska Medical Center was linked with the

Omaha Veterans Administration (VA) Hospital and VA facilities in two other towns.

- 1967: Massachusetts General Hospital—Telemedicine was established in 1967 to provide occupational health services to airport employees and to deliver emergency care and medical attention to travelers.

EVOLUTION OF TELEMEDICINE—A GLOBAL PERSPECTIVE

In the past access to quality medical care has been restricted both within and between countries by geographic limitations, the inconsistent distribution of physician specialists, and limitations of existing technology. Although telemedicine has been successfully deployed in several countries and in numerous large-scale projects already, recent advances in telecommunications and technology have shown promising opportunities for explosive growth and the ability to provide the highest quality health care throughout the world.

Limitations to the widespread implementation of telemedicine technologies were imposed by bandwidth, because the transmission of images and interactive video imaging demanded robust communications support. Those barriers have been steadily falling away, however, allowing telemedicine to become a realistic, cost-effective, and timely solution to the problems caused by inconsistent access to health care specialists. Telemedicine has successfully expanded the remote delivery of health care expertise from a broader range of medical specialties and applications, although the various specialty areas are at differing levels of sophistication and acceptance. Examples of those that have been successfully deployed include teleradiology, telecardiology, teledermatology, telepathology, and continuous medical education for health care professionals.

THE BENEFITS OF TELEMEDICINE

Telemedicine has allowed for real-time consultations across great distances—whether between physicians, between facilities, or between patients and physicians. High-quality medical care is not delayed by the time required for travel. Not only is the quality of care improved in its timeliness, but the patient is not subjected to the additional stress of long hours of travel and being away from the support of home, family, and friends. With current advances in technology and the growth of telemedicine equipment, software, and service providers, new lines of telemedicine have emerged, such as home care, mobile medical units, and connected rural health centers, which are making medical expertise more readily accessible and simultaneously cutting down on a myriad of health care costs.

Beyond the technology, however, there are many lessons learned from previous telemedicine programs and efforts. Without an adequate investment in infrastructure development, quality programs, careful vendor selection, contracting and management, the potential benefits to be gained from the use of technology fall short of expectations. Although physicians have become enamored with the concept of telemedicine, there are different demands in the provision of services to a wide geographic area, and the benefit of an experienced support team becomes critical to the success of a telemedicine project, both in terms of the quality of services offered and maintaining financial viability.

Telemedicine is a reality today and represents the future of how quality health care services can be provided on a global scale. The advantage rests with those countries possessing the adequate communications infrastructure, funding, and innovation. To that degree, therefore, health care access will still be unequally distributed worldwide.

Health Care in the Middle East

HISTORY

The Middle East health care market is a very complex one because it is comprised of several individual nations each with their own laws, policies, regulative bodies, economies, infrastructure, demographics, and history. Countries such as Egypt, Syria, Jordan, and Saudi Arabia have traditionally been considered major medical markets in the region due to their historical medical academic systems, extensive medical infrastructures, and large market sizes. Thought leaders tend to come out of these markets, making them medical service destinations for many other nations in the region that are close by and have a similar native tongue. Other nations such as Lebanon, Tunisia, Libya, and the Gulf states (Qatar, Bahrain, Kuwait, United Arab Emirates) are still considered either primitive or very young with regard to their capacity for medical services and expertise.

With expanding populations and the emergence of new policies for health care restructuring, nations such as the United Arab Emirates, Qatar, Saudi Arabia, Kuwait, and Bahrain are investing a great deal of money, time, and effort to build and expand their health care infrastructures and capacity to serve their people better, in addition to promoting health care tourism in the region. The reality though is that Western medical care is still far more superior in its quality and outcomes, and remains the most trusted destination for those who have the capacity and ability to travel.

THE 9/11 EFFECT

One of the most devastating events to ever occur on U.S. soil was the terrible attacks on New York City, Pennsylvania, and Washington, D.C., that occurred on September 11, 2001. This set of unfortunate events had a definite negative effect on the international patient care market. Before 9/11, many large medical institutions in the United States relied heavily on international patients; for many, 20%–40% of their profits came directly from international patients. Patients would come to the United States to take advantage of the great medical services available, get check-ups, diagnoses, and additional treatments or services that they required.

This was a great source of income for the U.S. health care and general economy for two main reasons. First, the shear volume of patients continually coming to the United States to receive treatment provided a steady base of tourism and spending in the country. Second, the reason international patients are so valuable is that they are generally dollar-for-dollar, cash-basis patients, unlike domestic Medicaid/Medicare patients who pay around $0.40 to the dollar. In other words, institutions receive full payment for services provided to international patients instead of government or insurance subsidized payments. The events of 9/11 changed everything for these facilities.

After 9/11 the inflow of international visitors decreased dramatically. Visas were harder to come by. Fears lead many potential patients to consider other options before coming to the United States to receive medical treatment and diagnosis. Travel declined and was sometimes made too difficult. This opened the floodgates for telemedicine.

TELEMEDICINE—A NATURAL FIT

Telemedicine solved problems for both the patient who wanted superior medical service and the domestic medical institutions that had lost so much revenue post-9/11. By allowing international patients and medical practitioners to send x-rays, digitized records, and other medical tools across the world in real time, telemedicine instantly connected patients to the great medical institutions in the United States. This process cut costs and time, and it gave both sides the opportunity to overcome the aftermath of 9/11. Through telemedicine, medical institutions would be able to change their business processes slightly and still gain revenue from these international patients who were no longer making the long trip to the United States. Telemedicine had become a natural fit and solution for everyone involved. All that was needed was a company to connect the patients and doctors in the Middle East with the medical prowess of the U.S. medical system. UniMed saw telemedicine's natural fit and sought to capitalize on the opportunity through having a first-mover advantage in the region.

Building a Network

THE UNIMED CONCEPT

International patients have been coming to the United States and Europe for diagnosis and treatment for many years. In the last decade, increasing numbers of U.S. medical institutions have created programs specifically to serve the needs of international clientele. UniMed's mission was to dramatically improve medical services for patients residing in the Middle East by making Western medicine readily accessible. The concept was spawned through Dr. Zachary's experience managing international patient divisions at leading hospitals in the Washington, D.C., area and the effect he personally witnessed on the international patient business shortly after 9/11.

UniMed's business opportunity was to combine telemedicine capabilities with a world-class network of medical institutions and physicians to create an efficient, market-leading medical service portal for Middle East patients seeking Western medical services. By providing access to an extensive network of medical institutions through telemedicine technology, UniMed sought to offer second opinions, e-consulting, and patient referral management services for the patients who choose to travel overseas for medical diagnosis and treatment (Figure 1). Patients' medical files and images would be digitally sent to consulting physicians for review and diagnosis (see Figure 2). Additionally, by having an extensive network of health care constituents, UniMed would be able to offer targeted marketing services for hospitals and physicians who want ready access to these high-margin, high-dollar medical patients.

THE VALUE PROPOSITION

UniMed's first guiding principle was that a well-informed patient can and should make their own decisions regarding their health care. UniMed thus took responsibility for helping patients become informed, get access, and develop reasonable expectations of the process they are going to experience to fully understand the capabilities of participating institutions and physicians, and the associated costs. UniMed's second guiding principle was to ensure a positive experience for the patient. Medical problems are

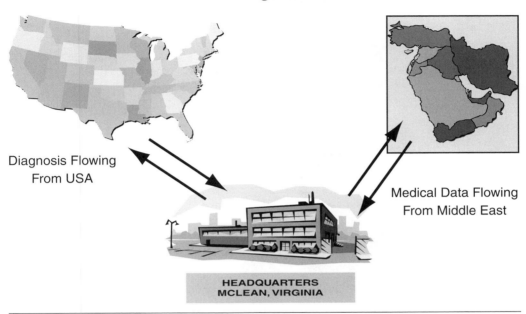

Figure 1   Patient Information and Service Flow

traumatic and the uncertainty of dealing with the unknown makes it more so. The UniMed team was committed to working quickly and effectively on the patient's behalf while being a good and empathetic listener. This was considered a global solution-selling concept for the health care industry, because it was a highly customized service for patients and providers alike. UniMed planned to offer the following services: e-consultation, second opinions, and referral management services.

E-Consultations

Patients or their physicians submit questions to Western physicians via e-mail at the satellite UniMed office. The requests are processed, forwarded, and tracked as indicated in Figure 3.

Responses are received, the patient is notified, and the response is then delivered. Assistance is available in understanding and interpreting the response. A fee of US$50 is charged for electronic consultations.

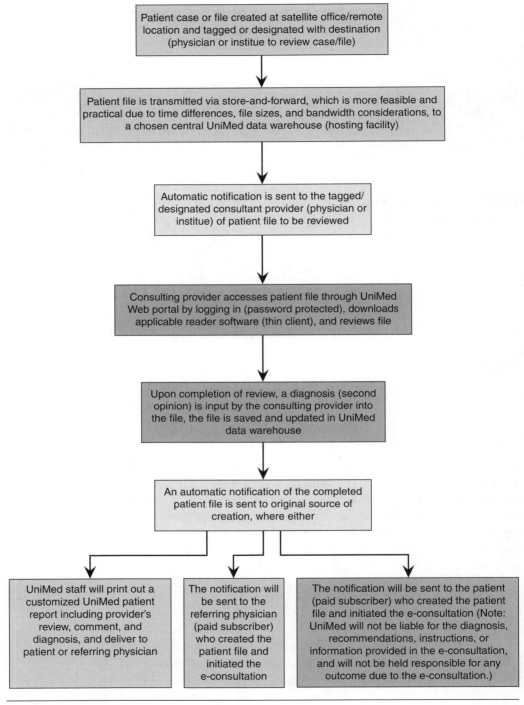

Figure 2   Transactional Flow of Patient Files

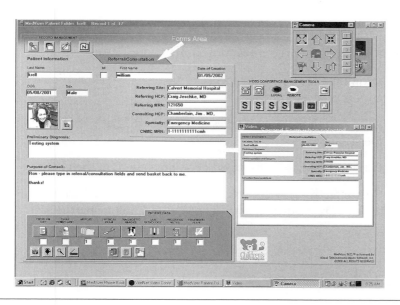

Figure 3   Sample Telemedicine Interface Used by UniMed Personnel

Second Opinions

Patients or their physicians submit medical records for second opinions from Western physicians via the telemedicine workstation at the satellite UniMed office. This typically requires scanning and digitizing the patient's medical records unless the digitized files are brought or e-mailed to the satellite office. Second opinions generate an average of US$400 in fees.

Referral Management Services

Patients who choose to travel outside the Middle East to obtain second opinions or surgery begin their process with an examination of their options at the UniMed office. The staff provides all the options that fall within the patient's parameters so that they can make the best decision. Once the patient makes an informed decision, UniMed processes the referral to the participating institution and provides whatever level of support the patient desires on an a la carte basis. Management fees are a flat rate of US$150, in addition to a percent-based brokerage fee to the institution or physician where the patient is referred.

The benefits of telemedicine as practiced by UniMed include

- Access to advanced medical resources

- Avoiding the time and expense of travel when telemedicine is an appropriate alternative

- Accelerating the time it takes to connect the patient with a Western physician

- Patients make well-informed decisions based on their own criteria

- Cost-effective services due to UniMed's negotiated arrangements with PPOs, medical institutions, and technology partners

The Early Stages of a Start-Up

UniMed, LLC, was founded by Dr. Zachary and his son Oscar in early 2002, and headquartered in Washington, D.C. The company was based on a functional structure that would maximize the skills and talents of individual consultants and advisors in the early development of the company. The initial strategy was to establish two satellite offices in the Middle East, one in Egypt and one in the United Arab Emirates, as wholly owned subsidiaries owned by the parent UniMed, LLC, and then open additional satellite offices as the company grew. This strategy was based on studies done by both Dr. Zachary and Oscar on establishing a business in those two countries. The offices were to function as patient centers that would process medical documents and records for second opinions and e-consultations. Those two locations were chosen initially as the starting point for UniMed because of their market attractiveness, such as available resources (e.g., staffing, infrastructure); relatively low mobilization costs, especially in Egypt; and market factors, such as demand and growth, and even government tax incentives in Egypt that were available to companies marketing Internet-based services to help promote Information and Communications Technology (ICT) sector growth.

RELATIONSHIPS ARE EVERYTHING

UniMed was positioning itself as an innovative service that would hopefully lead to high-margin business. Building relationships was vital to the success of UniMed. Being a start-up company spawned many challenges for UniMed, many of which would prove extremely difficult to overcome. Because UniMed was a new entity in a new industry, the dynamics of building the necessary relationships was different from that of other companies. There were many barriers to entry that UniMed would have to overcome if it was to be successful.

Building the company required intense dedication and a keen feel for the needs and wants of both the customers and the doctors. One of the most difficult obstacles would be raising capital. Without money the company had no chance of getting off the ground. Gaining access to resources and information were also big barriers to entry for UniMed. There was no existing network set up for this type of service, and there were no tried and tested structures to model the company after. The concept was new within a relatively young industry in itself that still had not formalized standards and protocols. The software and equipment providers had not been prepared for this type of service model and much customization and creativity was needed to develop the ideal application service provider (ASP) solution.

The telemedicine industry was not like any other industry. The Internet industry, for example, had an established structure and form, making it possible to follow standards and protocols that had already been set. To gain the necessary support and create a solid network, the founders of UniMed had one choice: to build a network from the ground up bit-by-bit, ensuring each brick in the foundation of the network was sturdy and meshed well with the overall corporate objective. To build a global network of providers and customers, many key relationships and strategic alliances had to be formed; and because the concept was new, the founders of UniMed had to sell the idea.

Much of UniMed's success would come as a direct function of how well it could provide credibility to the service, industry, and business it represented. It had to attract some of the greatest medical institutions and doctors in the entire world to buy into the idea and therefore help create the credibility it so greatly needed. Names such as Partner's Healthcare, Johns Hopkins, and Cleveland Clinic were industry leaders and sought after medical destinations for the potential customer base UniMed was targeting. Institutional partners like these would help UniMed get off the ground by leveraging their reputations and experience.

To start the process of building a network, Oscar decided to join the American Telemedicine Association and attended its annual conference in 2002 in Los Angeles. The conference exposed him to the major players in the industry, both companies and individuals, and provided him with tremendous knowledge on the latest things happening in the industry. Through the conference Oscar was able to gain valuable insight and direction from leaders in the telemedicine world and to embark on building the initial relationships that would prove to be vital to UniMed's success.

One such relationship was made with a pioneer in the industry named Dr. Saunders. Dr. Saunders was an accomplished physician and was considered the Godfather of Telemedicine because of his long-standing involvement, contributions, and impact on the industry. Oscar attended Dr. Saunders' lecture during the conference and was amazed at how he painted such a simple yet compelling picture of the value and benefits of telemedicine. Immediately after Dr. Saunders' presentation, Oscar approached him and discussed with him the idea for UniMed, which Dr. Saunders thought was excellent. They both realized that their offices were very close to each other in Washington, D.C., and scheduled a meeting to discuss the possible business opportunities, paths to follow, and resources required for implementation. Dr. Saunders had extensive relationships and clout in the industry, so without hesitation Oscar retained his services as a chief advisor to UniMed. Immediately, Dr. Saunders began to facilitate introductions that Oscar pursued and tried to nurture relationships out of.

These initial relationships were very good starting points for UniMed. They opened the doors to forming key partnerships with leading medical institutions like Partner's Healthcare and Johns Hopkins, in addition to technology vendors that could help develop Web-based solutions for the company. Through these medical institutions, UniMed would be able to cover every major medical specialty and gain the prestigious credibility that would be needed for the start-up of the company.

THE CHICKEN OR THE EGG?

Client Buy-In or Provider Buy-In?

UniMed's next task was to gain support and buy-in from prospective patients and physicians who would like to use this type of service. Because much of the Middle East used public sponsored health care services through government and military coverage, the first logical path to pursue was getting the buy-in of the decision makers, and therefore financers, of all the patients traveling abroad for health care services. By the beginning of 2003, UniMed had built several solid industry relationships and had access to many of the resources required to set up a solution. The military in Egypt and the United Arab Emirates were the first two pieces of the puzzle for linking the Middle East with U.S. medical doctors and facilities.

The challenge at this point, however, was that UniMed still did not own its own solution yet. Because it was still only a start-up with limited financial resources, it lacked the significant capital necessary to put the middle part of the solution, the software and hardware, into play. Additionally, it was still only Oscar and Dr. Zachary who were running the show, wearing all hats. Eventually they would need to build a competent team of managerial, technical, and administrative staff both in the United States and the Middle East for the service model to be operational.

To initiate the process, the plan was to set up a project with the military in either country and have them pay for the consulting and building of the first system. The prospects all thought it was a great, innovative, and desirable solution for the region; but no one wanted to be the first to take a leap of faith with this new idea, and the bureaucracy was astounding. Furthermore, Oscar and Dr. Zachary began to experience the politics and corruption inherent in doing business in the region. For instance, because no legitimate business was yet established with a potential patient base in the region, exclusive contracts still could not be set up between UniMed and the medical institutions in the United States, which then led to some prospective customers in the Middle East wanting to bypass UniMed and go directly to the medical institutions and technology vendors themselves.

Pilot Project

After a little over 2 years of marketing and trying to build a project base that would warrant investing into a system and organizational structure UniMed would require to deliver the service, an opportunity and idea came about to test the concept. The founders obtained the medical records of 20 real patients through Dr. Zachary's extensive relationships with the medical industry in Egypt and sought to use them for a pilot project. They developed a relationship with an independent doctor/computer programmer who claimed to have an open-source electronic patient record (EPR) solution and virtual data center, and had expressed interest in being a part of UniMed's growth. He offered to build a model for the entire company, based on an initial retainer fee to keep the pilot project going, and upon user and provider acceptance, gain equity into the company as it developed its project base.

Oscar and Dr. Zachary wanted to test the concept they had worked so hard on for over 2 years. Piloting the concept by sending real medical records to 5 independent doctors they had strong relationships with was the only way for them to make sure it worked. If they could gain the end-user (physicians and patients) acceptance of the system and business model, they were sure to capture real business and patient transaction flow. The unfortunate outcome, however, was that UniMed was again faced with another example of corruption and deceit with the doctor/computer programmer, who conned the founders by taking his retainer and providing UniMed with a useless, nonfunctioning software solution. UniMed was back to square one again.

TAKING A SIDE-STEP

Half a million dollars and 2½ years after the birth of a company and concept, there were still no tangible projects or visible success stories. There were continuous costs to maintain the offices in the United States and Egypt, consultants and advisors, and other expenses, which were becoming too much. Oscar began feeling the frustration of carrying the company's weight all on his shoulders, and started to think he could not continue doing everything on his own anymore. Both he and Dr. Zachary were becoming disappointed with the progress of the company.

END OF THE ROPE

After all the trials and troubles, corruption, and deceitfulness UniMed faced, Oscar decided to return to the United States and take a step back from the entire project. With money running out and relationships quickly fading, he felt there was no real way to continue. He started his own job search and agreed with Dr. Zachary to continue attempts to build UniMed on a part-time basis, scaling back all the activities to save on costs. After a couple of months searching for new work, Oscar was about to accept one of two job offers he had received.

OPPORTUNITY KNOCKS

Just as Oscar was considering new employment, he received an interesting call from his father. Dr. Zachary had just met with a gentleman in Abu Dhabi, Dr. Ahmed, who had previously worked with him on a medical education project sponsored by a large pharmaceutical entity in collaboration with the hospital Dr. Zachary managed at the time. When Dr. Ahmed heard about what UniMed was attempting to do, he thought it was an amazing concept and had an epiphany. He knew he could use this type of technology in the pharmaceutical industry to train and educate medical doctors in the Middle East, which was a requirement now with recent ethical guidelines in the industry, but was exceedingly difficult to do with quality content after the reality of 9/11. After 9/11 it had become challenging to train and educate doctors because many U.S. and European doctors that had previously come to the Middle East to speak were reluctant to do so now because of fears and anxiety over the geopolitical situation in the region. Additionally, the Middle Eastern physicians who used to travel to the United States for training had more difficulty doing so after 9/11 because of problems with visas and rising travel costs. This ultimately caused major problems for the pharmaceutical industry, making it difficult to maintain fruitful relationships with health care professionals and ensure loyal use of their products.

Simultaneously, health care in the Middle East was undergoing major restructuring and process and quality improvements, including the implementation of educational requirements for physicians to maintain their licensing in an effort to help raise the standards of care. Pharmaceutical companies were under pressure to keep doctors happy and provide educational opportunities for the doctors through their extensive marketing budgets. Video and Web-based communications from the United States, which UniMed specialized in for medical purposes, would help to reunite doctors and the medical sector in the Middle East to those of the Western world for an exchange of best practices and information.

EduMed Is Born

Faced now with a new opportunity to leverage their knowledge and relationships, Dr. Zachary and Oscar considered taking on this new possibility to develop a business slightly different in its objective from UniMed, but nonetheless viable in itself. Dr. Ahmed proposed involving two other associates of his, who he considered influential in the pharmaceutical industry, and proceeded to facilitate a meeting in April of 2004, bringing together his associates, Dr. Zachary, and Oscar to discuss the idea and potential for the market. Dr. Zachary, Dr. Ahmed, and his associates discussed starting a new business entity based in Dubai, named EduMed, which would develop, market, and execute continuous medical education (CME) projects (Figure 4) using the same technical and academic resources UniMed had developed relationships with. They sought to create a successful profit generating business by securing tangible projects that could be facilitated through the industry relationships of Dr. Ahmed and his associates. Meanwhile, Oscar sat and observed during the meeting without much involvement, listening to the new potential business partners' suggestions and ideas, with a bit of skepticism based on his previous experiences.

Oscar knew there would be many similar potential pitfalls to what UniMed faced, but the majority of them would be new due to a shift in the market focus and strategy for acquiring business EduMed would pursue. There was no way to know if EduMed could have a better fate than UniMed, and there was still a sense of attachment and almost parental protection that was felt by both Dr. Zachary and Oscar with regards to letting UniMed's inner core be exposed to these new business partners. The fact remained, however, that UniMed was still not generating any revenue on its own, and for the sake of recapturing the vast investments

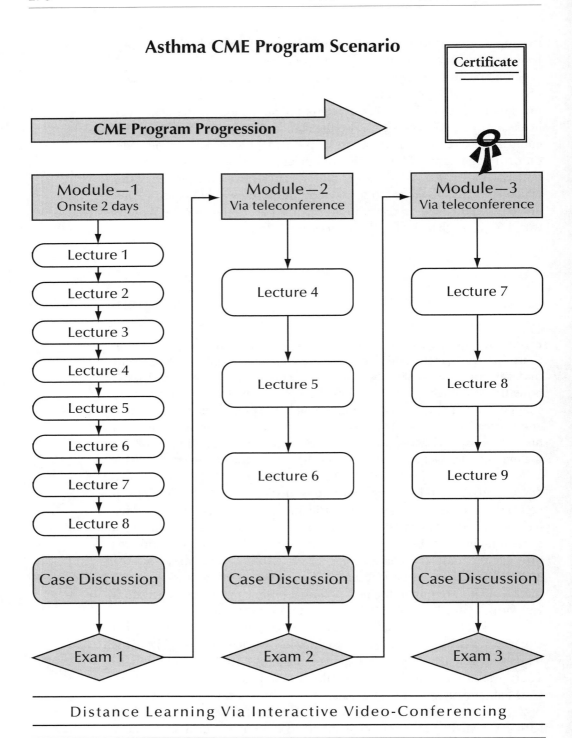

Figure 4 Typical EduMed CME Project Structure

made into the company, Dr. Zachary and Oscar both realized that Edu-Med was a necessary endeavor. By 2005 EduMed had secured 12 CME projects throughout the Middle East with many multinational pharmaceutical companies as clients, and the founders had finally recouped their investment in UniMed.

Case Questions

1. What are the key market factors that drove UniMed's business model?

2. What were some of the core elements in creating the UniMed business?

3. What was UniMed's value proposition?

4. What were some of the challenges UniMed faced?

5. What was the dilemma with EduMed?

6. What were the opportunities with EduMed?

7. For EduMed to be a success, what seemed to be required?

Part 3

Managing the Global Entrepreneurial Enterprise

The Global Monetary System 8

Profile: Charles Lewis Tiffany

TIFFANY & CO.

Noriko Nakano, 20, a part-time waitress in suburban Tokyo, has loved Tiffany & Co. since she was a girl. "I always wanted Tiffany," she says, gazing at the elegant facade of the new store the retailer opened in Tokyo's swanky Ginza area in May 1972. "Every time I go to Hawaii, I visit Tiffany's," she says, pointing to her gold necklace.

Not that she ever had to go that far. Since 1972 Tiffany has been building slowly in Japan, where the market is as valuable as the legendary Tiffany Diamond sparkling in the Ginza store. But now, with profits in the region soaring, Tiffany is opening a host of glitzy new Asian shops to make it even easier for free-spenders like Nakano to pick up their baubles.

For years Tiffany's Japanese retail operations were run by the posh department store chain Mitsukoshi Ltd., which has 29 Tiffany boutiques in its stores. As sales exploded in the late 1980s, however, the New York-based jeweler realized it was missing out. Although Tiffany had a decent wholesale business, Mitsukoshi got the juicy margins at retail. And while demand grew even as Japan's economy slowed, a struggling Mitsukoshi couldn't invest in expansion. So in 1993 Tiffany paid US$115 million for its Japanese operations and inventory.

The costly buyout handed Tiffany a US$10 million loss in 1993, but the shift has paid off. While Tiffany has kept its boutiques at Mitsukoshi and at rival department store Daimaru Inc., it now pays them an operating fee based on sales and keeps the rest. Tiffany leases 7,700 square feet in Ginza, Japan's priciest district, for its company-owned store—three times the size of a Mitsukoshi boutique. That lets Tiffany display more and offer something for every wallet. The result: Yen-denominated sales in stores open a year or

281

more grew 13% in 1995—and Japan is now the brightest jewel in Tiffany's tiara. With sales of US$226 million, Japan made up 28% of Tiffany's revenues in 1994, up from 19% in fiscal year 1993. Better yet, higher prices helped Japan bring in 53% of Tiffany's operating profits (before corporate expenditures) that same year. At US$68 million, that's more than double its 1993 profits. "Other businesses have suffered (from the recession)," says Thomas J. O'Neill, senior vice president of international sales, "but we haven't."

That's partly because of people like Yumiko Murayama and fiancé Shinjiro Yokoyama, one of several couples crowding a wedding band display. "It isn't so very expensive," Yumiko giggles, glancing coyly at her betrothed. Wedding related items bring in more than 35% of sales, and it's not just rings. At Japanese weddings, guests bring money and the newlyweds give them gifts called hikidemono. One hot item is a US$72 Imperial cup and saucer set. With families buying in bulk, hikidemono means big sales at retail prices. "We're going after the bridal market in a big way," O'Neill says.

Ginza is just the start of Tiffany's push into Asia. O'Neill says he's looking for an Osaka site. Since June 1991, Tiffany has opened stores in Singapore, Hong Kong, and Korea, with plans for up to 10 more by 2001. Yet if Tiffany becomes too accessible, it may dilute its appeal among shoppers who like traveling long distances for their status symbols. "The designs are better overseas—and cheaper too," sniffs Nakano. But if young waitresses can be so discriminating, Tiffany will do just fine (Updike, 1996).

www.tiffany.com

Chapter Objectives

1. To analyze various types of financial management tools in managing exchange rate variations for global businesses.

2. To understand the financial implications of doing business globally.

3. To illustrate what the foreign exchange market is and how it affects global businesses in daily operations and the risks involved.

4. To understand the aspects of the foreign exchange market that could aid in relevant business transactions.

5. To describe the global capital market and the role it plays in helping entrepreneurs invest.

6. To explain balance of payment concerns and the roles international organizations play in setting policies that potentially affect ventures within certain nations.

7. To learn how to protect a business from the financial exposure in international financial transactions.

Introduction

Probably the most difficult aspect of doing international business for most global entrepreneurs is understanding the global monetary system and foreign exchange rates. The purpose of this chapter is to explain the nature of foreign exchange, foreign exchange transactions, and the manner in which foreign exchange rates are established and fluctuate. Following the discussion of the international monetary system and international capital markets, the chapter concludes by discussing the role of the International Monetary Fund (IMF) and the World Bank.

Functions and Nature of Foreign Exchange

What is the foreign exchange market and its accompanying rates? The foreign exchange market is the open market for converting the currency of one country to the currency of another country at the rate of convertibility determined by the market at the time of the transaction (the foreign exchange rate). The main function of the foreign exchange market is to convert the prices of the goods and services in one country's currency into the currency of another. Each country (or group of countries) has its own currency: Australia (Australian dollars); Canada (Canadian dollars); China (Renminbi); France (euro); Germany (euro); Japan (yen); United Kingdom (British pound); and the United States (U.S. dollars). Each currency is converted into another at the exchange rate operating on the date that the exchange occurs. Some example exchange rates are listed in Table 8.1.

These exchange rates operate for foreign tourists exchanging currency in a country, but more important, they are used in the currency transactions in international trade. A company converts the money it receives from sales of its exports, income from licensing agreements, and income from its foreign investments into home country currency or the currency of another country where payments need to be made. Companies also convert home country currency into that of a country where they are interested in investing in or buying goods and services from. Some companies purchase foreign currencies on speculation that there will be a change in the exchange rate that will benefit them. The benefit of using futures is that there is no cost to the company as opposed to options that require an initial capital outlay.

Table 8.1 Foreign Exchange Rates

Country	Currency	Dollar	Euro	Pound	Country	Currency	Dollar	Euro	Pound
Argentina	(Peso)	3.1063	4.0181	6.0819	New Zealand	(NZ$)	1.4350	1.8563	2.8097
Australia	(A$)	1.2954	1.6757	2.5364	Nigeria	(Naira)	128.075	165.671	250.765
Bahrain	(Dinar)	0.3771	0.4878	0.7383	Norway	(NKr)	6.3105	8.1629	12.3556
Bolivia	(Boliviano)	7.9950	10.3420	15.6538	Pakistan	(Rupee)	60.7300	78.5573	118.906
Brazil	(R$)	2.1374	2.7649	4.1850	Peru	(New Sol)	3.1980	4.1368	6.2616
Canada	(C$)	1.1828	1.5300	2.3159	Philippines	(Peso)	49.1350	63.5586	96.2039
Chile	(Peso)	544.650	704.532	1066.40	Poland	(Zloty)	3.0440	3.9375	5.9599
China	(Yuan)	7.7745	10.0567	15.2221	Romania	(New Leu)	2.6343	3.4075	5.1577
Colombia	(Peso)	2262.20	2926.27	4429.27	Russia	(Ruble)	26.5591	34.3555	52.0014
Costa Rica	(Colon)	518.375	670.544	1014.95	Saudi Arabia	(SR)	3.7508	4.8518	7.3438
Czech Rep.	(Koruna)	21.8198	28.2250	42.7221	Singapore	(S$)	1.5398	1.9918	3.0148
Denmark	(DKr)	5.7627	7.4544	11.2831	Slovakia	(Koruna)	27.2506	35.2500	53.3553
Egypt	(Egypt £)	5.7063	7.3814	11.1726	South Africa	(R)	7.3163	9.4640	14.3249
Estonia	(Kroon)	12.0958	15.6465	23.6830	South Korea	(Won)	940.450	1216.52	1841.35

Country	Currency	Dollar	Euro	Pound	Country	Currency	Dollar	Euro	Pound
Euro(0.7730)	(EUR)	1.2936	—	1.5137	Sweden	(Skr)	7.0070	9.0639	13.7194
1 Month		1.2953	—	1.5116	Switzerland	(SFr)	1.2546	1.6229	2.4564
3 Month		1.2985	—	1.5073	Taiwan	(T$)	32.9720	42.6509	64.5576
1 Year		1.3102	—	1.4889	Thailand	(Bt)	34.2750	44.3365	67.1088
Hong Kong	(HK$)	7.8112	10.1041	15.2939	Tunisia	(Dinar)	1.3156	1.7018	2.5759
Hungary	(Forint)	198.724	257.060	389.093	Turkey	(Lira)	1.4275	1.8465	2.7950
India	(Rs)	44.2050	57.1814	86.5512	UAE	(Dirham)	3.6729	4.7511	7.1913
Indonesia	(Rupiah)	9122.50	11800.40	1786.40	UK	(£)	1.9580	0.6607	—
Iran	(Rial)	9231.00	11940.80	18073.80	1 Month		1.9579	0.6615	—
Israel	(Shk)	4.2540	5.5028	8.3292	3 Month		1.9573	0.6634	—
Japan	(Y)	121.905	157.690	238.684	1 Year		1.9507	0.06716	—
1 Month		121.442	157.298	237.773	Uruguay	(Peso)	24.2750	31.4010	47.5293
3 Month		120.511	156.486	235.870	United States	($)	—	1.2936	1.9580
1 Year		116.341	152.427	226.947	1 Month		—	1.2953	1.9579
Kenya	(Shilling)	70.5000	91.1953	138.036	3 Month		—	1.2985	1.9573
Kuwait	(Dinar)	0.2893	0.3742	0.5664	1 Year		—	1.3102	1.9507
Malaysia	(M$)	3.5025	4.5307	6.8577	Venezuela	(Bolivar)	4389.25	5677.72	8593.93
Mexico	(New Peso)	11.0824	14.3357	21.6988	Vietnam	(Dong)	16050.00	20761.50	31425.10

Exchange Rate Fluctuations

The foreign exchange market can be used to provide some protection for the global entrepreneur against wide fluctuations in exchange rates. This is accomplished through three basic mechanisms: currency swaps, forward exchange rates, and spot exchange rates.

Currency swaps are used to protect against fluctuations and foreign exchange risk when there is a need to move in and out of a currency for a limited period of time. For example, many companies do business in Europe, buying and selling from member countries. Let us say, for example, Alcoa buys and sells finished goods and parts with its wholly owned plant in Hungary and wants to ensure that the US$1 million that it will need to pay some bills in Hungary at EUR .76/US$1 is available at a known exchange rate. It also will collect EUR 20 million in 75 days when some accounts are due. If today's spot exchange rate is US$1 = EUR .76 and the forward foreign exchange is US$1 = EUR .90, Alcoa can enter into a 75-day forward exchange currency swap for converting EUR 20 million into U.S. dollars (US$). Since the euro is at a premium on the 75-day market, the company will receive US$22.2 million (EUR 20 million /.90 = US$22.2 million). Of course, this could be reversed if the euro was trading at less than EUR .76/US$1 in 75 days.

When the global entrepreneur and another company agree to execute a transaction and exchange currency immediately, the transaction is called a spot exchange. In this type of transaction, this spot exchange rate is the rate that the currency of one country is converted into the currency of another country on a particular day. This rate also applies when someone is traveling to London and wants to convert euros into British pounds at a London bank. The spot exchange rate may not be the most favorable exchange rate because the value of the currency is determined by the interaction of demand and supply of each country's currency with respect to the currency of other countries on that particular day.

A final form of protection for the global entrepreneur against widely fluctuating currencies is the forward exchange rate. Forward exchange can be used by two parties to exchange currency and execute a deal at some specific date in the future. The exchange rate used in this type of transaction is called the forward exchange rate and is usually quoted 30, 90, or 180 days into the future, as indicated in Table 8.1. Let us assume a U.S. company and a Swiss company are doing a US$5 million transaction in 90 days, where the Swiss company is purchasing US$5 million of computer software and equipment. Both companies want to enter into a 90-day forward exchange contract. Today the Swiss franc is trading at SF .806/US$1. Since the two companies feel that in 30 days forward it will be SF .808/US$1, 90 days forward it will be SF .812/US$1, and 180 days forward it will be SF .818 /US$1, they enter into a 90-day forward contract guaranteeing that the Swiss company would not pay more than US$6.16 million (US$6.16 million = US$5 million ÷ SF .812/US$1) for the software and equipment. The higher foreign exchange rate in 90 days reflects the expectation that the U.S. dollar would appreciate against the Swiss franc over the next 90 days.

For most global entrepreneurs, foreign exchange should not be a profit driver for their venture. Companies that spend too much time trying to predict or speculate on changes in foreign exchange rates usually end up losing focus on their core product or service and will lose out in the marketplace. Through the use of the tools previously discussed, global entrepreneurs can improve the predictability of their business and reduce one of the potential risks inherent in international business.

Aspects of the Foreign Exchange Market

As is indicated in the previous examples, the foreign exchange market plays an important role in making global transactions possible. Because a global network of banks, brokers, and foreign exchange dealers connect electronically, the market provides easy access to a company in any country, usually through a bank in the local economy. Even though it is a worldwide network, there are three primary trading centers: London, New York, and Tokyo. There are also several major secondary centers: Frankfurt, Hong Kong, Paris, San Francisco, Singapore, and Sydney. Of these, due to historical and geographic reasons, London is the most important trading center.

There are several interesting features of the market that are important to the global entrepreneur. First, the U.S. dollar plays a very important role because most transactions involve dollars. A manufacturer with Japanese yen wanting to buy Swiss francs will often purchase U.S. dollars to buy the needed Swiss francs. Dollars are easy to use in any transaction. Besides the U.S. dollar, other important currencies are the European euro, the Japanese yen, and the British pound.

Second, the foreign exchange market is always open. Even during the few hours that all three primary trading centers (London, New York, and Tokyo) are closed, trading continues in secondary markets, particularly San Francisco and Sydney.

Finally, all the markets, and particularly the primary and secondary trading centers, are so closely integrated and connected electronically that the foreign exchange market acts as a single market. This means there are no significant differences in exchange rates quoted in any trading center, even those outside the primary and secondary ones. Since there are so many companies involved, any exchange rate discrepancies are small and corrected immediately as dealers attempt to make a profit through arbitrage, or buying a currency low and selling it at a higher price.

The Global Capital Market

A global capital market benefits both borrowers and investors because it brings together those from around the world who want to invest money and those who want to borrow money better than any single domestic market. For the borrowers the global capital market increases the funds available for borrowing and lowers the cost of capital. In a domestic market, the pool of investors is limited to those who live in the particular country, so there is an upper limit on the supply of funds available. A global capital market increases the number of investors and supply of funds available from the larger pool.

Also, the broader pool obtained in a global market eliminates the limited liquidity found in a domestic capital market and lowers the cost of capital. This means that the dividend yield and expected capital gains on equity investments, as well as the interest rate on loans (debt), are lower. This lower price of obtaining capital is very important to companies all over the world. This is particularly beneficial in less developed countries, where the pool of investors tends to be smaller than in more developed economies.

From the investor's perspective, the global capital market provides a wider range of investment opportunities than is available in any domestic market. This allows investors to reduce their risk by diversifying their portfolios over a wide range of industries geographically dispersed. As the number of investments increases in an investor's portfolio, generally the risk in the portfolio declines, at first rapidly and then approaches the systematic risk of the market. Systematic risk is the risk associated with the value in a portfolio attributable to macroeconomic forces affecting all firms in an economy and not a specific individual firm. Because the movement of stock and interest rates are country specific and are not perfectly correlated across countries, the investor's risk is reduced by investing in various countries. By doing this, the losses incurred when an investment(s) in one country goes down are offset by gains in investment(s) in another country. This low correlation of value and interest rates among countries reflects the different macroeconomic policies and different economic conditions on a country-by-country basis. It also reflects the capital controls in place in countries that restrict to some extent crossborder capital flows.

Balance of Payments

Almost every global entrepreneur has heard about the concern over disparities in the balance of payments between countries. The balance of payments measures all the international economic transactions between two countries. There are, of course, hundreds of thousands of international transactions such as imports, exports, repatriation of profits, grants, and investments that occur each year, all of which are recorded and classified.

By definition, the balance of payments must balance or there is an error in counting. While there can be an imbalance in currency or trade between two countries, the entire balance of payment of each and every country is always balanced. In recording all international transactions over a period of time, the balance of payments is tracking the flow of purchases and payments between every country. Two types of business transactions dominate the balance of payments: real assets (the exchange of goods and services for other goods and services, either through barter or, more commonly, money) and financial assets (the exchange of financial claims such as stocks, bonds, loans, purchases, or sales for other financial claims or money). The balance of payments consists of two primary subaccounts—the current account and the capital and financial account—and two minor subaccounts—the official reserve account and the net errors and omissions account. Each of these will be briefly discussed in turn.

The current account includes all international economic transactions with income or payment within the year. It includes goods trade, services trade, income, and current transfers. Goods trade consists of the export and import of goods, the oldest form of international economic activity. Many countries attempt to keep a balance or, even better, a surplus of exports over imports. Services trade deals with the export and import of services. Significant activity in services trade involves construction services, financial services provided by banks, and travel services of airlines. Income is mostly current income from investments made in previous periods. Any wages or salaries paid to nonresident workers of subsidiaries of out-of-country companies are also considered income. Finally, current transfers are composed of any financial settlements in change of ownership of real assets or financial items as well as a one-way transfer, gift, or grant from one country to another.

While every country has some trade, most of the trade involves merchandise (goods trade). The balance of trade, which is widely discussed in the business press, refers to the balance of imports and exports of goods trade only. This, for large industrialized countries like Japan, the United States, and the United Kingdom, is misleading because it does not include the other three areas of the current account, particularly services trade, which can also be very large and significant.

The capital and financial account of the balance of payments measures all international transactions of financial assets and has two major subaccounts—the capital account and the financial account. The capital account is composed of all the transfers of financial assets and the acquisition of nonproduced and nonfinancial assets. This is a very small part of the total combined account. The financial account is by far the largest component of this dual account and consists of three parts: direct investment, portfolios investment, and other long-term and short-term capital transfers.

Each of the financial assets is classified by the degree of control over the particular asset the claim represents. In a portfolio investment the investor has no control, but in a direct investment the investor exerts some degree of control over the asset.

One of the minor subaccounts of the balance of payments—the official reserve account—is composed of the total currency and metallic reserves held by the official monetary authority of the government of each country. Most of these revenues are in the major currencies of the world used in international trade and financial transactions.

The final minor subaccount of the balance of payments is the net errors and omissions account. This very small account, as the name implies, makes sure that the balance of payments is always in balance.

Role of the International Monetary Fund and World Bank

In addition to the balance of payments, another area important for the global entrepreneur to understand before engaging in international business is the role of the International Monetary Fund (IMF) and the World Bank. Both the IMF and the World Bank were established in 1944 when representatives from 44 countries met at Bretton Woods, New Hampshire (USA), to design a new international monetary system. The overall goal of the meeting was to design an economic order that would endure and facilitate the economic growth of the world following the end of World War II. While the IMF was established to maintain order in the international monetary system, the World Bank was established to promote general economic development. Each will be discussed in turn in terms of its importance for the global entrepreneur.

INTERNATIONAL MONETARY FUND (IMF)

Due to the worldwide financial collapse after World War II, competitive currency devaluations, high unemployment, and hyperinflation occurring particularly in Germany in 1944, the IMF was established to avoid a repetition of these events through discipline and flexibility. The discipline part of the equation was achieved through the establishment of a fixed exchange rate, thereby helping to control inflation and improving economic discipline in countries. This fixed exchange rate lasted until 1976 when a floating exchange rate was formalized and established.

To help minimize the rigidity of the fixed exchange rate, limited flexibility was built into the system in the form of the IMF lending facilities and adjustable parities. Each member of the IMF made available gold and currencies to the IMF to lend to member countries to cover short-term periods of balance-of-payment deficits to avoid domestic unemployment in that country due to a tightening monetary or fiscal policy. The IMF funds could be lent to countries to bring down inflation rates and reduce the country's balance-of-payment deficits. Because a persistent balance-of-payment deficit would deplete a country's reserves of foreign currency, a loan to reduce this deficit would help a country avoid devaluing its currency. When extensive loans from the IMF fund are given to a country, that country must submit to increasingly stringent supervision of the IMF of its macroeconomic policies.

The system of adjustable parities established by the IMF allows for the devaluation of a country's currency by more than 10% if the IMF feels that this will help achieve a balance-of-payment equilibrium in the country. The IMF felt that in these circumstances, without devaluation the member country would experience high unemployment and a persistent trade deficit.

THE WORLD BANK

The World Bank, officially named the International Bank for Reconstruction and Development (IBRD), was established initially to help finance the rebuilding of Europe following World War II. Because this was successfully accomplished by the Marshall Plan of the United States, the World Bank focused on development in the form of lending money to third world countries. The general focus was power stations and transportation in the 1950s and the support of agriculture, education, population control, and economic development in the 1960s.

The World Bank makes loans for projects in developing economies through two schemes. The first one, the IBRD scheme, raises money for the project through the sale of bonds in the international capital market. The second scheme involves International Development Association (IDA) loans from money supplied by wealthier member nations. A global entrepreneur may have the opportunity to be involved in one of these funded projects.

Trade Financing

One of the keys to successful global expansion is having funds available. One alternative to acquiring these funds, and often the only option available to the global entrepreneur, is *bootstrap financing*. This approach is particularly important at start-up and in the early years of the venture when capital from debt financing (i.e., in terms of higher interest rates) or from equity financing (i.e., in terms of loss of ownership) is very expensive.

In addition to the monetary costs, outside capital has other costs as well. First, it usually takes between 3 and 6 months to raise outside equity capital or to find out that there is no outside capital available. During this time of raising equity capital, the global entrepreneur may not focus enough on the important areas of marketing, sales, product development, and operating costs. A business usually needs capital when it can least afford the time to raise it. One company's CEO spent so much time raising capital for global expansion that sales and marketing were neglected to such an extent that the forecasted sales and profit figures on the pro forma income statements were not met for the first 3 years after the capital infusion. This led to investor concern that, in turn, required more of the CEO's time.

Second, outside equity capital can decrease a firm's drive for sales and profits. One successful global entrepreneur would never hire a person as one of his commissioned salespeople if he or she "looked too prosperous." He felt that if a person was not hungry enough, he or she would not push hard to sell. The same concept could apply to outside funded companies that may have the tendency to substitute outside capital for income from successful operations.

Third, the availability of capital increases the global entrepreneur's impulse to spend. It can cause a company to hire more staff before they are needed and to move into more costly facilities. A company can easily forget the basic axiom of venture creation: staying lean and mean.

Fourth, outside capital can decrease the company's flexibility. This can hamper the direction, drive, and creativity of the global entrepreneur. Unsophisticated investors are particularly a problem because they often object to a company's moving away from the focus and direction outlined in the business plan that attracted their investment; this often occurs in taking the venture into international markets. This attitude can encumber a company to such an extent that the needed change cannot be implemented or else is implemented very slowly after a great deal of time and effort has been spent in consensus building. This can substantially demoralize the global entrepreneur who likes the freedom of not working for someone else.

Finally, outside capital may cause disruption and problems in the venture. Capital is not provided without the expectation of a return. Sometimes equity investors pressure the entrepreneur to continuously grow the company so that an exit (payback) such as an initial public offering can occur as soon as possible. This emphasis on short-term performance can be at the expense of the long-term success of the company.

In spite of these potential problems, an entrepreneur at times needs some capital to finance international growth, which can be slow or nonexistent if internal sources of funds are used. Outside capital should be sought only after all possible internal sources of funds have been explored. And, when outside funds are needed and obtained, the entrepreneur should not forget to stay focused on the basics of the business. Two good sources of external funds for expanding the business are from family and friends and commercial banks.

FAMILY AND FRIENDS

Family and friends are a common source of capital to go international, particularly if their origins are from the country to be entered. These individuals are most likely to invest due to their past knowledge and relationship with the entrepreneur as well as knowledge of the country. Family and friends usually provide a small amount of equity funding for the global venture. Although it is often easy to obtain money from family and friends, like all sources of capital, there are positive and negative consequences. Although the amount of money provided may be small, if it is in the form of equity financing, then the family members or friends have an ownership position in the venture and may feel they have direct input into the operations of the venture. This may have a negative effect on employees, facilities, or on sales and profits when concentration is needed on the international market. Usually, family and friends are more patient in desiring a return on their investment.

To avoid problems in the future, the entrepreneur should present the possible positive and negative consequences and the nature of the risks of the investment opportunity in the international market. The business arrangements are strictly business. Any loans or investments from family or friends should be treated in the same businesslike manner as if the financing were from an impersonal investor. Any loan should specify the rate of interest and the proposed repayment schedule of interest and principal. If the family or friend is treated the same as an investor, future conflicts can be avoided. Everything should be in writing. It is amazing how short memories become when money is involved.

The global entrepreneur should carefully consider the effect of the investment on the family member or friend before it is accepted. Particular concern should be paid to any hardships that might result should the international market not be successful. Each family member or friend should feel that the international opportunity is a good investment, not because they feel obligated.

COMMERCIAL BANKS

Commercial banks are one of the best sources of funds for global expansion when collateral is available. The funds are in the form of debt financing and, as such, require some tangible guaranty or collateral—some asset with value. This collateral can be in the form of business assets (land, equipment, or the building of the venture), personal assets (the entrepreneur's house, car, land, stocks, or bonds), the assets of the cosigner of the note, or the assets of doing business (accounts receivable, inventory). There are several types of bank loans available to the global entrepreneur. To ensure repayment, these loans are based on the assets or the cash flow of the venture, such as accounts receivable, inventory, or equipment.

Accounts receivable provide a good basis for a loan to do international business, particularly if the customer base is well known and creditworthy. For creditworthy customers, a bank may finance up to 80% of the value of their accounts receivable. When the customer is a foreign government, a global entrepreneur can develop a factoring arrangement whereby the factor (the bank) actually "buys" the accounts receivable at a value below the face value of the sale and collects the money directly from the foreign purchaser. In this case, if any of the receivables is not collectible, the factor (the bank) sustains the loss, not the global entrepreneur. The cost of factoring the accounts receivable is of course higher than the cost of securing a loan against the accounts receivable, because the bank has more risk when factoring. The cost of factoring involves the interest charge on the amount of money advanced until the time the accounts receivable are collected, the commission covering the actual collection, and protection against any possible uncollectible amount.

Inventory is another of a firm's assets that is often a basis for an international loan, particularly when the inventory is more liquid and can be easily sold. Usually, the finished goods inventory can be financed for up to 50% of its value.

Equipment can be used to secure long-term financing, usually on a 3 to 10 year basis. Equipment financing can fall into any of several categories: financing the purchase of new equipment, financing used equipment already owned by the company, sale-leaseback financing, or lease financing. When new equipment is being purchased or presently owned equipment is used as collateral, usually 50%–80% of the value of the equipment can be financed depending on its salability. Given the entrepreneur's tendency to rent rather than own, sale-leaseback or lease financing of equipment is widely used. In the sale-leaseback arrangement, the global entrepreneur "sells" the equipment to a lender and then leases it back for the life of the equipment to ensure its continued use.

The other type of debt financing frequently provided by commercial banks and other financial institutions is cash flow financing. These conventional bank loans include lines of credit, installment loans, straight commercial loans, long-term loans, and character loans. Lines of credit financing is perhaps the form of cash flow financing most frequently used by global entrepreneurs. In arranging for a line of credit to be used as needed, the company pays a commitment fee to ensure that the commercial bank will make the loan when requested and then pays interest on any outstanding funds borrowed from the bank. Frequently, the loan must be repaid or reduced to a certain agreed-upon level on a periodic basis.

One problem for the global entrepreneur is determining how to successfully secure an international loan from a bank. Banks are generally cautious in lending money, particularly to new ventures and ventures doing business in global markets. Regardless of geographic location, commercial loan decisions are made only after the loan officer and loan committee carefully review the borrower and the financial track record of the business.

These decisions are based on both quantifiable information and subjective judgments. The bank's lending decisions are made according to the five Cs of lending: character, capacity, capital, collateral, and conditions. Past financial statements (balance sheets and income statements) are reviewed for key profitability and credit ratios, inventory turnover, aging of accounts receivable, the entrepreneur's capital invested, and commitment to the business. Future projections on the international market size, sales, and profitability are also evaluated to determine the ability to repay the loan. Several questions are usually raised regarding this ability: Does the entrepreneur expect to have the loan for an extended period of time? If problems occur, is the entrepreneur committed enough to spend the effort necessary to make the business a success? Does the business have a unique differential advantage in a growth market? What are the downside risks? Is there protection (such as life insurance on key personnel and insurance on the plant and equipment) against disasters? The intuitive factors, particularly the first two Cs, character and capacity, are also taken into account. This part of the loan decision—the gut feeling—is the most difficult part to assess. The global entrepreneur must present his or her capabilities and the prospects for the company in a way that elicits a positive response from the lender. This intuitive part of the loan decision becomes even more important when there is little or no track record, limited experience in financial management, a nonproprietary product or service (one not protected by a patent or license), or few assets available.

Some of the concerns of the loan officer and the loan committee can be reduced by providing a good loan application. Although the specific loan application format of each bank differs to some extent, generally the application format is a mini business plan that consists of an executive summary, business description, owner/manager profiles, international business projections, financial statements, amount and use of the loan, and repayment schedule. This information provides the loan officer and loan committee with insight into the creditworthiness of the individual and the venture, as well as the ability of the venture to make enough sales and profit to repay the loan and the interest. The global entrepreneur should evaluate several alternative banks, select the one that has had positive loan experience in the particular business area, call for an appointment, and then carefully present the case for the loan to the loan officer. Presenting a positive business image and following the established protocol are necessary to obtain a loan from a commercial bank. The global entrepreneur needs to establish a good relationship with a globally oriented bank.

LETTERS OF CREDIT

The use of letters of credit in international trade has significantly increased in the past few years, particularly in the United States where global entrepreneurs were not as familiar with their use as global entrepreneurs in other countries. A letter of credit is simply a letter from one bank to another bank requesting that the second bank do something (usually pay money to someone) once certain conditions are fulfilled, such as the receiving or shipping of merchandise. Banks issue letters of credit for a fee, and some banks take the money from the customer's account or freeze that money in the account until needing to release the money to another bank when the terms and conditions are met, which can be 3 to 4 months later.

Suppose a German manufacturer wants to buy some component parts from a supplier in China. How could the transaction take place? The German company could send a check along with the order or wire transfer the money to the bank of the Chinese company. In this transaction, the German manufacturer could not be guaranteed that the component parts will be received. Instead, the Chinese company could ship the component parts to the German manufacturer along with an invoice for the amount due. When doing this, the Chinese company could not be assured that payment will be received. This is where a letter of credit plays an important role. The two companies need to reach an agreement on when the seller (the Chinese company in this case) gets paid and provide that information to the bank of each company.

This is very important when the bank issuing the letter of credit (the bank of the German company) does not take control of the amount of money of the letter of credit when it is issued. In this case the buying company (the German company) may have 60 to 90 days before the actual money is withdrawn. If the payment is specified at a certain time and condition, the selling company (the Chinese company) can usually get most of the amount of the letter of credit by drawing a draft for this amount at its receiving bank. The receiving bank will discount the draft at the prevailing discount rate. If the discount rate is 8% and the payment period is 90 days, then the discount will be 2% (90/360 on a quarter of 8%). This can be a very inexpensive way of getting money now instead of later. Some banks, often in the United States, take the money from the issuer's account (the German company) once the letter of credit is issued.

Banks vary on their application form for obtaining a letter of credit. All forms contain such information as the demographic information on the buying and selling company, the exact items being purchased, and the specific requirements of the transaction including how payment is to be made. The agreement between the buyer and seller may specify that payment is to be made after the items have been inspected or upon shipment or the presentation of the appropriate documents. Also included may be the latest shipping date acceptable to the buyer and who is responsible for freight.

The exact cost of a letter of credit varies greatly by bank and by country. There is always a bank charge for writing the letter of credit, and it can vary from $100 to $400. There is also a percentage charge for the amount of money involved. This ranges from .5%–2.5%. Even at the highest fee and percentage, letters of credit enable the global entrepreneur to more easily buy and sell internationally.

Summary

The creation, use, and effects of the global monetary system are discussed in Chapter 8. Since there are numerous currencies being used all over the world, a global entrepreneur must understand how the foreign exchange rates and foreign exchange market function. When a product or service is sold in a foreign country, this market converts the prices of goods and services in one country into the currency of another on the date of the exchange. The global entrepreneur will use the foreign exchange market whenever he or she is making a sale, receiving income from foreign agreements and investments, receiving payments from foreign countries, investing in a foreign country, purchasing goods or services from a foreign country, or taking part in currency speculation. Exchange rate fluctuations can deeply affect the costs and profits of a global enterprise. There are three mechanisms to reduce the risk of currency fluctuations to a global entrepreneur: currency swaps, forward exchange rates, and spot exchange rates. The U.S. dollar is the primary currency used in international transactions along with the European euro, the Japanese yen, and the British pound. The global capital market is very useful to global entrepreneurs because it pools funds from investors all over the world from which the entrepreneur can borrow. The chapter concludes with an overview of two major international financial institutions, the International Monetary Fund (IMF) and the World Bank, both of which could partner with a global entrepreneur on certain ventures.

For a small company, a bank is often the best resource for assistance in managing financial transactions. Banks can provide letters of credit that show the creditworthiness of a company to its potential customers in foreign markets. Letters of credit shift the credit responsibility from the individual or company to an established bank. This can prove necessary when both buying and selling in the international market because there is often less knowledge of buyers and sellers in different markets.

Questions for Discussion

1. What are the potential effects of a change in the € / NZ$ exchange rate for an Italian entrepreneur who frequently does business in New Zealand?

2. How would a weak Swiss franc benefit a Swiss entrepreneur who exports much of his product?

3. Explain the different roles of the International Monetary Fund and the World Bank.

4. Mike just signed a US$1 million contract to sell small engines to a Slovenian manufacturer. Delivery will take place in 1 month, but he does not expect to receive his payment in euros for 3 months. What are the potential risks? What are some of the ways to mitigate these risks?

Chapter Exercises

1. Choose a foreign currency and visit the Web site www.Xe.com to familiarize yourself with how the exchange rate between your home currency and that foreign currency functions.

2. Pick a country that has recently dealt with severe currency devaluation and research how that devaluation has affected foreign investment and holdings in that country.

3. Select a country besides your own and see how the balance of payments works between your country and that foreign country.

4. Go to the International Monetary Fund and World Bank Web sites, www.imf.org and www.worldbank.org, to familiarize yourself with their roles in the global economic system. How do these roles differ?

References

Updike, E. H. (1996, August 26). And when you need an imperial cup and saucer. *BusinessWeek*, (3490), 68.

Suggested Readings

ARTICLES

Berg, A. (2006, October). Global monetary systems: Then and now. *Futures* **35(13), 62–64.**

This article focuses on the most significant change since the end of the Bretton Woods System in 1999 with the introduction of the euro. The introduction of the euro also presented an interesting case of a partial reversal of the floating rate system. In addition, this article reviews how conflicts in the 20th century have generally been the cause of the collapse of various monetary systems.

Coffey, P., & Riley, J. P. (2006). *Reform of the international institutions: The IMF, World Bank and the WTO.* **London: Edward Elgar.**

The authors provide original, independent assessments of the International Monetary Fund (IMF), World Bank, and World Trade Organization (WTO) from both American and European perspectives. In addition, they offer proposals for reform and improvement to shape the future of the international monetary and trading systems.

Fuchita, Y. (2007). *New financial instruments and institutions: Opportunities and policy challenges.* **Washington, DC: Brookings Institution Press.**

This book covers recent innovations in the financial industry, primarily in the United States and Japan, to meet the ever-changing needs of fund users and suppliers. It explains new financial instruments and institutions and how they are affecting the financial sectors.

International Monetary Fund. (2007). *Balance of payments statistics 2006: Yearbook.* **Washington, DC: Author.**

The Balance of Payments Statistics (BOPS) Yearbook, usually published in December, contains balance of payments statistics for most of the world, compiled in accordance with the International Monetary Fund's (IMF's) Balance of Payments Manual.

Malliaris, A. (2002). Global monetary instability: The role of the IMF, the EU and NAFTA. *North American Journal of Economics & Finance,* **13(1), 72.**

The author believes that since the collapse of the Bretton Woods Regime of the International Monetary Fund in 1971, the global monetary system has exhibited significant instability. The paper gives an account of regional monetary arrangements, the three building blocks toward a more stable global monetary and financial system, and the role of the U.S. dollar as the world's central currency.

Titus, D. (2006, September). Tax incentives for special economic zones. *Asialaw,* **1.**

In February 2006, the Government of India put into place a special economic zone (SEZ) policy to increase the interest in India as an export hub for both

Indian and foreign companies. As part of the government's economic liberalization program, these special zones have liberal tax incentives that make India very attractive to global entrepreneurs.

World Bank. (2007). *A guide to the World Bank* **(2nd ed.). Washington, D.C.: World Bank Publications.**

As a basic reference guide to the World Bank, International Finance Corporation, Multilateral Investment Guarantee Agency, and International Centre for Resolution of Investment Disputes, this book explains how the Bank Group is organized and operates. In addition, it covers the role of countries and regions as a focus for its work and the major topics in development in which the Bank Group is active. Appendices provide worldwide contacts, historical information, and additional data on the organization.

WEB SITES

www.imf.org

The IMF is an international organization of 185 member countries that promotes international monetary cooperation, exchange stability, and orderly exchange arrangements; fosters economic growth and high levels of employment; and provides temporary financial assistance to countries to help ease balance of payments adjustment.

Global Marketing and R&D 9

Profile: Derek and Geoffrey Handley

THE HYPERFACTORY

Co-founder Derek Handley describes The Hyperfactory as an "Asia Pacific leader in mobile marketing. It connects people who use mobile phones with brands and media companies." In other words, The Hyperfactory is one of those companies that sends out advertising and promotions by way of mobile phones.

Derek (age 27) and his brother Geoffrey (age 30) realized that mobile phones were going to be big. They extrapolated that potential, took a look at the international landscape, and figured out that there weren't too many companies gearing up to use phones for advertising. How could they not become a fast growing company? Look how quickly mobile phones have moved from text-only messages to pictures to video.

The Hyperfactory campaigns reach mobile phone users who opt-in after seeing a promotion on a package or a billboard. The users then text a response over their phones in regard to a specific campaign. What better audience for your campaign than one that asks for it? Mobile phones are good for advertising for other reasons too: people always carry them and ads are in real time.

Other key success factors for The Hyperfactory include:

1. Early identification of a niche in a growing market.

2. They didn't have or need a lot of money at the beginning, but had lots of determination and a belief in their business model.

3. They stay innovative—it's key, says Derek, to keep fresh and not get stale, especially in a space that moves so fast.

4. They benchmark internationally. Derek says they don't compare themselves with other New Zealand companies, but with ones in London or New York.

5. Being co-founders and brothers works well. The two bring very different and complementary skill sets. (Sykes, 2005)

www.thehyperfactory.com

Chapter Objectives

1. To understand how telecommunications technology will affect the global entrepreneur through marketing products and services.

2. To understand the role of innovation for a global entrepreneur.

3. To describe innovation and how often this determines the future of organizations and ventures.

4. To learn how to adapt a product to the market it is entering.

5. To determine how to best introduce products to the market while maintaining top quality.

6. To define the product life cycle and how to plan and develop this process.

7. To show how to evaluate new products for suitability to enter a market.

8. To understand the global marketing mix and its key components.

Introduction

The four major problems facing the global entrepreneur when entering or expanding in an international market(s) are: (1) the technological environment; (2) product policy and the total quality issue; (3) adopting the best research and development strategy; and (4) developing and implementing the best marketing strategy. Each of these problems has accelerated due to the effect of rapidly changing technologies, shorter and shorter product life cycles, changing consumer tastes, and changing economies, particularly the significant increase in developing economies. In the next decade, these causal conditions will continue if not accelerate further. Depending on the nature of the global market, there can be significant problems in each of the four areas, particularly in the short run. When General Electric (GE) pur-

chased a controlling interest in Tungstrum, the Hungarian light bulb manufacturing company, it expected to turn the company around, solve the
total quality issue, and sell light bulbs to the countries in the European
Union in a much shorter period of time than actually occurred. The GE
manager in charge of the Tungstrum operation was continually heard saying, "In 6 months we will have light bulbs for Europe." Six months turned
into three years before the product was sufficient to sell in Europe. Yet, in
2005 GE announced that it was going to move all of its research and development in light bulbs to Tungstrum in Hungary.

Technological Environment

The technological environment varies greatly from country to country,
and worldwide it is changing at lightning speed. There are several ways in
which technology will affect the global entrepreneur in the next decade.
First, and perhaps foremost, is the Internet and its usage. The Internet
allows individuals from around the world to obtain information from millions of sources. In the United States, for example, about 50% of people 12
years of age and older go online every day. Second, soon automatic translation telephones will be available, allowing people to communicate in
their own language with anyone who has a telephone. Third, satellites will
play an increasing role in communication and learning, enabling people
in even very remote areas to read and receive voice and data through
handheld telephones. Fourth, the increasing use of nanotechnology to create products at such a small scale will change the world. Fifth, advances in
biotechnology will transform agriculture and medicine. And, sixth, more
and more power computers will use faster and faster silicon chips. The
resulting issues that will radically affect the global entrepreneur the
most—telecommunication and e-business—are discussed in more detail
in the following sections.

TELECOMMUNICATIONS

Previously, one of the biggest obstacles in global business, particularly
in less developed and transition economies, was telecommunications;
but that is rapidly changing. Because it is no longer necessary to hard-
wire, economies are leapfrogging from phones being unavailable to cellular phones being available everywhere, even in the remotest parts of
China and Africa. Because of the quick and relatively inexpensive instal-
lation of this new infrastructure and the merging technology of the
computer and telephone, a growing number of people, even in rural

areas of Asia, are accessing the Web through cell phones, allowing business transactions to take place in the remotest of areas. During the next decade, the further merger of wireless technology and the Internet will radically change the way people communicate and will open even more markets in less developed countries and rural areas. Cellular phones are also making an impact in developed countries, like Finland, Norway, and Sweden, where over half of each country's population are cellular subscribers.

With telecommunication services providing an efficient communication system, many governments believe this is the key to their economic development and the attraction of foreign direct investment. Some telecommunication operations are state run, such as in the Asia-Pacific region, but an increasing number are private sector companies. Some former state-owned companies that have been privatized, often with the help of foreign companies, include Korea Telecom, Philippines Global Telecom, and Thailand's Telecom Asia. Most of the investment needed to privatize and expand the telecommunication systems in developed and developing countries will come from outside those countries.

E-BUSINESS

As the number of individuals and companies having access to the Internet continues to expand, the role of e-business in international commerce will similarly have an increasing affect on the global entrepreneur. This includes both business-to-consumer and the more frequent usage in business-to-business arenas. Two areas of e-business will have a significant effect on global consumers: retailing and financial services. Eventually, there will be a convergence of business transactions, money, and personal computers making electronic cash available. The forerunner of this is in existence already: prepaid smart cards. When the convergence occurs, 24-hour buying and selling throughout global worldwide markets will be a regular event.

This worldwide e-commerce system (both business-to-business and business-to-consumer) has significantly affected the role of financial institutions. Companies do not have to wait as long for their money after a sales transaction occurs, substantially reducing the amount of bad debts.

This speed in cash obtainment will in turn affect the foreign currency markets. Today, if a company in China buys goods in the United States and wants to pay in Chinese Renminbi (RMB), a system is needed for converting RMBs to U.S. dollars. This is now handled by regulated foreign exchange markets as discussed in Chapter 8. To speed up the process, this system's move to a single common exchange market using the prevailing exchange rates will eventually be seamless.

Product Policy and Total Quality

Goods or services are the core of a global entrepreneur's international operations, so his or her success is dependent on how well the goods or services offered satisfy the wants and needs of the market, and how they are different (their unique selling proposition) from competitive products and services available. This important issue will be discussed in terms of product adaptation and total quality.

PRODUCT ADAPTATION

There are two major factors that affect the degree to which a domestic product needs to be changed for a global market: the domestic product itself and characteristics of the international market on both a country and local basis. The needed changes range from minor, such as translating the label, to major, such as physical product changes. These changes generally affect brand names, instructions on usage labels, logos, measurement units, packaging, and product features and design.

Aspects of the Domestic Product

The type and characteristics of the domestic product significantly affect the degree to which it can be taken directly into an international market. A global entrepreneur must ensure that his or her product does not contain ingredients that violate the legal requirements or religious or social customs of a country. For example, in Islamic countries vegetable shortening needs to be used versus animal fats. In Japan, it is illegal to have any formaldehyde in hair and skin products. In India, mutton needs to be used instead of beef. In many countries the product may not be operable in the global market due to the major differences in electric power systems.

A major difficulty confronting the global entrepreneur is having the required parts, repairs, or servicing for a product. If the product breaks down and repairs and service are not up to standard, the product and company image suffer and future sales become difficult. Sometimes a product designed for use in one way in the domestic market will be used for entirely different purposes in the global market. It is important that the global entrepreneur provides good training for the individuals providing the repairs and service. This is usually most easily accomplished through outsourcing to a local firm.

Brand names and aesthetics provide another challenge. Since the brand name conveys the image of the product or service, it is important to standardize it as much as possible across global markets. Standardizing the name is particularly difficult for the global entrepreneur with a variety of products in many different countries. Sometimes, the global entrepreneur must standardize other elements such as colors, packaging, and symbols versus the brand name itself.

Packaging is an area where the global entrepreneur generally makes some modifications to enter the global market. This in part reflects the longer time that the product remains in the distribution system and the differences in the channel members of the distribution itself. Usually the international package uses more expensive materials. Additionally, more expensive transportation modes are also required, such as air tight, reclosable containers used in the global distribution of food products.

The labeling of the packaging almost always needs modification. Sometimes this means conforming to the legal requirement that everything is bilingual, such as French and English in Canada, and Finnish and Swedish in Finland. Global government regulations often require more informative labeling about the content and percent of ingredients on food products, for example. This provides for better consumer education and protection. Not conforming to the content, language, or description laws of the country will often cause a product to be held up in customs, such as when a global entrepreneur tried to import wine from Hungary that did not have the alcohol content of the wine correctly provided on the label.

Characteristics of the Global Market

Typically the characteristics of the global market(s) mandate many product modifications. These often result from government regulations, some of which may be protecting domestic industry or responding to political controversies among nations. Not only must the global entrepreneur be aware of present regulations but he or she must also be aware of exceptions and possible future changes. Products entering some global markets, such as the European Union, must comply with the product standards established by the European Union as well as adopt the overall system approved by the International Standards Organization.

Tariff and nontariff barriers also affect product adaptations. If tariffs are so high that the domestic product is not price competitive, then a less costly version may have to be developed. Nontariff barriers, such as bureaucratic red tape, product standards, required testing or approval procedures, or domestic product subsidies, can also affect product adaptation. Because some nontariff barriers may be intended to protect domestic products and industries, they may be the most difficult obstacle for the global entrepreneur.

Competitive products and features often affect product adaptation. Already established in their domestic market, these competitive products must be carefully analyzed to determine any product changes needed for competitive positioning. Ideally the changes made will not only establish a strong competitive market position, but will be hard to duplicate by domestic product manufacturers.

The stage of economic development of the foreign market and the economic status of potential users can also affect the product. As the economy of a country becomes stronger, buyers are usually better able to afford and demand better product alternatives. Sometimes the economic stage of a country requires that the product be significantly simplified or downgraded due to the lack of purchasing power or usage conditions.

Purchase decisions are also affected by the attitudes, behavior, beliefs, and traditions of the purchaser in the global market. The global entrepreneur must be very aware which of these cultural aspects affect the changes needed in the product to gain customer approval and result in sales. Such cultural aspects particularly affect the product's positioning in the market—the perception of the consumers of the global product with respect to competitive products. For instance, Coke entered the Japanese and European Union markets using the name Coke Light instead of Diet Coke so as not to confront consumers with the idea of weight loss. The promotional theme behind Coke Light was not weight loss but rather figure maintenance.

TRAINING THE GLOBAL MANAGERS

Training global managers for overseas assignments is very important. Proper training can help global managers understand the culture, customers, and work habits of the specific market situation. The most common topics covered in this cultural training include business etiquette, customs, economics, history, politics, and social etiquette of the country.

The type of training also reflects the global entrepreneur's overall philosophy of international management. Some global entrepreneurs prefer to send their own people to fill an overseas position, but others prefer to use host-country locals. The management philosophy of global entrepreneurs tends to be one of the following three: (1) ethnocentric philosophy (putting home-country people in key international positions); (2) geocentric philosophy (integrating diverse regions of the world through a global approach to decision making); or (3) polycentric philosophy (using local host-country nationals in key international positions). The venture with the ethnocentric philosophy will do the training at the headquarters in the home country while the polycentric philosophy will have the local key managers do the training in the host country.

LEADERSHIP IN AN INTERNATIONAL CONTEXT

The behavior of global entrepreneurial leaders tends to be in one of three styles: (1) authoritarian leader (focuses on work-centered behavior to ensure task accomplishment); (2) paternalistic leader (uses work-centered behavior along with a protective employee-centered concern); or (3) participative leadership (uses both a work-centered and a people-centered approach). These three styles take on different approaches in various parts of the world. Both similarities and differences have been found in leadership in China, Europe, Japan, and the United States.

Of course, an outstanding global leader is a transformational one—a visionary leader with a sense of mission who is able to motivate his or her employees to accept the vision, new goals, and new ways of doing things. These global leaders have several things in common regardless of the culture of operation. First, the transformational global leader is charismatic and has the admiration of his or her employees. He or she increases confidence, loyalty, and pride at all levels of the organization. Second, a global transformational leader can get his or her employees to question old paradigms and accept new ways of doing things, effectively articulating the vision and mission. Finally, a transformational global leader can determine the needs of employees and further develop these individuals so they are more effective and efficient.

The leadership in a particular country needs to reflect the culture of the country. This has been studied in the GLOBE project, which evaluated cultural dimensions such as performance orientation, assertiveness, future orientation, humane orientation, institutional collectivism, in-group collectivism, gender egalitarianism, power distance, and uncertainty avoidance across many countries. As shown in Table 9.1, countries vary on each of these dimensions. While the United States and Russia scored high on performance improvement, Singapore and Sweden, collectivistic countries, scored high on institutional collectivism. In terms of power distance (the degree to which members of an organization should expect power to be distributed equally), entrepreneurial companies in high power distance countries such as Brazil, France, and Thailand tend to have more hierarchal decision-making processes with limited participation and communication. A good global entrepreneurial leader takes into account these country dimensions in his or her leadership style in the particular country he or she is doing business in.

Table 9.1   Cultural Clusters Classified on Societal Culture Practices

Cultural Dimension	High-Score Clusters	Mid-Score Clusters	Low-Score Clusters
Performance Orientation	Confucian Asia Germanic Europe Anglo	Southern Asia Sub-Saharan Africa Latin Europe Nordic Europe Middle East	Latin America Eastern Europe
Assertiveness	Germanic Europe Eastern Europe	Sub-Saharan Africa Latin America Anglo Middle East Confucian Asia Latin Europe Southern Asia	
Future Orientation	Germanic Europe Nordic Europe	Confucian Asia Anglo Southern Asia Sub-Saharan Africa Latin Europe	Middle East Latin America Eastern Europe
Humane	Southern Asia Sub-Saharan	Middle East Anglo Nordic Europe Latin America Confucian Asia Eastern Europe	Latin Europe Germanic Europe
Institutional Collectivism	Nordic Europe Confucian Asia	Anglo Southern Asia Sub-Saharan Africa Middle East Eastern Europe	Latin Europe Latin America
In-Group Collectivism	Southern Asia Middle East Eastern Europe Latin America Confucian Asia	Sub-Saharan Africa Latin Europe	Anglo Germanic Europe Nordic Europe
Gender Egalitarianism	Eastern Europe Nordic Europe	Latin America Anglo Latin Europe Sub-Saharan Africa Southern Asia Confucian Asia Germanic Europe	Middle East

(Continued)

Table 9.1   (Continued)

Cultural Dimension	High-Score Clusters	Mid-Score Clusters	Low-Score Clusters
Power Distance		Southern Asia Latin America Eastern Europe Sub-Saharan Africa Middle East Latin Europe Confucian Asia Anglo Germanic Europe	Nordic Europe
Uncertainty Avoidance	Nordic Europe Germanic Europe	Confucian Asia Anglo Sub-Saharan Africa Latin Europe Southern Asia	Middle East Latin America Eastern Europe

SOURCE: Javidan, M., Dorfman, P., de Luque, M. S., & House, R. J. (2006, February). In the eye of the beholder: Cross cultural lessons in leadership from project GLOBE. *Academy of Management Executive, 20*(1), 67.

TOTAL QUALITY ISSUES

One major issue for the global entrepreneur is total quality; international customers want their expectations met or exceeded regardless of the provider. This is true even in developing economies where some products and services provided in the past have not been high quality. To accomplish this the global entrepreneur must focus on quality, cost, and innovation.

China, India, Ireland, and Germany are all countries ICU Global, a videoconferencing provider, is targeting, according to founder and chief executive Stephen McKenzie. The company currently employs six people in the United Kingdom and is anticipating turnover of £3m. McKenzie says it's easy to expand into other countries even when you're a small business so long as you can provide "the same quality assurance to end users." He adds, "Technology allows you to provide full-support, virtual operations in other countries" (Woods, 2008).

The countries for expansion have been selected because they offer the greatest opportunities for ICU Global. "It's good to have a base in Germany because you can easily access the rest of Europe," McKenzie offers. "Then, there's a thriving technology center in India." McKenzie also has personal ties to Germany, having been born there, and has been able to take advantage of the possibilities in India because a former employee returned home to the subcontinent. "Therefore there was an opportunity to move into the main cities in India," he says.

ICU Global's dealings with China are at an early stage. The company is doing research and development work with a Chinese counterpart, and McKenzie notes, "It's a situation that will only grow" (Woods, 2008).

Some global entrepreneurs falsely believe that by increasing the quality of their product or service to a very high level, costs would also increase, resulting in a need to raise the price too high. However, companies measuring quality in terms of defective parts per million have found that as the error rate (expressed in terms of sigma) fell (the level of sigma increased) so did the cost of producing the product. In other words, quality and cost are inversely related. A global entrepreneur can produce quality at a lower cost per unit when producing with low error rates than when producing with higher error rates.

Historically, a similar false belief surrounded high technology. Many global entrepreneurs falsely felt that any new technology should be best exploited by getting to an international market first and charging premium prices. Now they realize that often the best way to exploit the advantage of a new high technology is to lower the price in an international market. This allows the company to grow its market share as quickly as possible, driving less efficient competition from the market while increasing overall revenues and profits. Paradoxically, high-tech global entrepreneurs can thrive at the same time their prices are falling the fastest. Because this can result in significantly reduced margins and lower return on investment (ROI), these global entrepreneurs are compensating by generating more revenue for the technology by using it in a wide variety of products or services. This means it is imperative to be at the cutting edge of the technology.

All this requires global entrepreneurs to outsource more and more of their manufacturing and focus on developing new technologies. They also understand the need to continually add features that increase the value to keep their product from becoming generic or sold almost strictly on price. This requires the effective use of benchmarking—identifying what leading-edge competitors are doing and using this to produce improved products or services. Whenever possible, a global entrepreneur should employ mass customizations—tailor-making mass production products to meet the expectations of the customer. Indeed, offering quality goods and services always pays off.

International Research and Development

A good international research and development process covers three areas: (1) defining what innovation is to the company, (2) performing opportunity analysis, and (3) understanding the product life cycle.

INNOVATION

Innovation is the key to the future of any company. As technologies change, old products decrease in sales and old industries dwindle. Inventions and innovations are the building blocks of the future of any international organization. Thomas Edison reportedly said, "Innovative genius is 1% inspiration and 99% perspiration."

There is a wide variety of views regarding what constitutes innovation. To some, it is a new technological breakthrough. For others, it is a new invention or way of doing things. Still for others, innovation is a new design or new business model. For some, it is managing chaos or turbulence. The only commonality among these many views is "new." Indeed, while innovation requires something new and involves creativity and invention, true innovation requires one more thing—delivering customer value. Until the innovation is on the market delivering some new value to customers, it is not really innovation. In the marketplace, innovation can take a wide variety of forms, such as a new design, a new delivery system, a new package, a new production process, a new invention, or a radical new technological breakthrough.

Types of Innovation

There are various levels of innovation based on the uniqueness of the idea. As indicated in Figure 9.1, there are three major types of innovation, in decreasing order of uniqueness: breakthrough innovation, technological innovation, and ordinary innovation. As you would expect, the rarest innovations are of the breakthrough type. These extremely unique innovations often establish the platform on which future innovations in an area are developed. Given that they are often the basis for further innovation in an area, these innovations should be protected as much as possible by strong patents, trade secrets, or copyrights. Breakthrough innovations include such ideas as penicillin, the steam engine, the computer, the airplane, the automobile, the Internet, and nanotechnology.

The next type of innovation—technological innovation—occurs more frequently than breakthrough innovation and in general is not at the same level of scientific discovery and advancement. Nonetheless, these are very meaningful innovations, because they do offer advancements in the product/market arena. As such, they usually need to be protected. Such innovations as the personal computer, the flip watch for containing pictures, voice and text messaging, and the jet airplane are examples of technological innovations.

The final type of innovation—ordinary innovation—is the one that occurs most frequently. These more numerous innovations usually extend a technological innovation into a better product or service or one that has

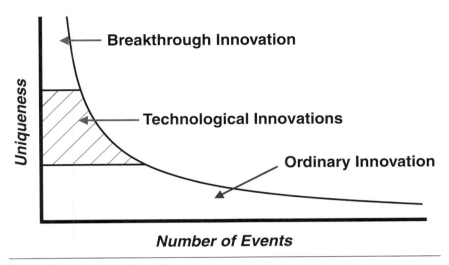

Figure 9.1   Innovation Chart

a different—usually better—market appeal. These innovations often come from market analysis and pull, not technology push. In other words, the market has a stronger effect on the innovation (market pull) than the technology (technology push). One ordinary innovation was developed by Sara Blakely, who wanted to get rid of unsightly panty lines while also being able to wear open-toed shoes and sandals. To do this, she cut off the feet of her control-top pantyhose to produce a footless pantyhose. Investing her total money available (US$5,000), Sara Blakely started Spanx, an Atlanta-based company, which in 5 years had annual earnings of US$20 million.

Defining a New Innovation (Product or Service)

One of the dilemmas faced by global entrepreneurs is defining a "new" product or identifying what is actually new or unique in an idea. Fashion jeans became very popular even though the concept of blue jeans was not new. What was new was the use of names such as Sassoon, Vanderbilt, and Chic on the jeans. Sony made the Walkman one of the most popular new products of the 1980s, although the concept of cassette players had been in existence for many years.

In these examples the newness was in the consumer concept. Other types of products, not necessarily new in concept, have also been defined as new. When coffee companies introduced naturally decaffeinated coffee, which was the only change in the product, the initial promotional campaigns made definite use of the word *new* in the copy.

Other old products have simply been marketed in new packages or containers, but have been identified as new products by the manufacturer.

When soft drink manufacturers introduced the can, some consumers viewed the product as new, even though the only difference from past products was the container. The invention of the aerosol can is another example of a change in the package or container that added an element of newness to old, established products, such as whipped cream, deodorant, and hair spray. Flip-top cans, plastic bottles, aseptic packaging, and the pump have also contributed to a perceived image of newness in old products. Some firms, such as detergent manufacturers, have merely changed the colors of their packages and then added the word *new* to the package and their promotional copy. Pantyhose are another product that has undergone significant marketing strategy changes. L'eggs (a division of Hanes Corporation) was the first to take advantage of supermarket merchandising, packaging, lower prices, and a new display.

In the industrial market, firms may call their products "new" when only slight changes or modifications have been made in the appearance of the product. For example, improvements in metallurgical techniques have modified the precision and strength of many raw materials that are used in industrial products, such as machinery. These improved characteristics have led firms to market products containing the improved metals as "new."

In the process of expanding their sales volume, many companies add products to their product line that are already marketed by other companies. For example, when a drug company added a cold tablet to its product line and a longtime manufacturer of soap pads entered the dishwasher detergent market, both advertised their products as new. In both cases the product was new to the manufacturer but not new to the consumer. With the increased emphasis on diversification in the world economy, this type of situation is quite common today. Firms are constantly looking for new markets to exploit in order to increase profits and make more effective use of their resources. Other firms are simply changing one or more of the marketing mix elements to give old products a new image.

CLASSIFICATION OF NEW PRODUCTS

New products may be classified from the viewpoint of either the consumer or the firm. Both points of view should be analyzed by the global entrepreneur, because both the ability to establish and attain product objectives and consumer perception of these objectives can determine the success or failure of any new product.

From a Consumer's Viewpoint

There is a broad interpretation of what may be labeled a new product from the consumer's viewpoint. One attempt to identify new products classifies the degree of newness according to how much behavioral change or

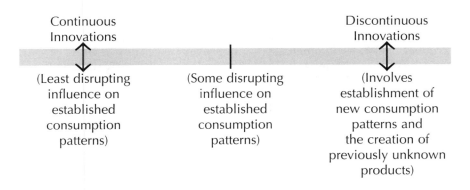

Continuous Innovations		Discontinuous Innovations
(Least disrupting influence on established consumption patterns)	(Some disrupting influence on established consumption patterns)	(Involves establishment of new consumption patterns and the creation of previously unknown products)

Figure 9.2   Continuum for Classifying New Products

SOURCE: Adapted from Robertson, T. (1967, January). The process of innovation and the diffusion of innovation. *Journal of Marketing,* 14–19.

new learning is required by the consumer to use the product. This technique looks at newness in terms of its effect on the consumer rather than whether the product is new to a company, is packaged differently, has changed physical form, or is an improved version of an old or existing product.

The continuum proposed by Thomas Robertson (shown in Figure 9.2) contains three categories based on the disrupting influence that product innovation has on established consumption patterns. Most new products tend to fall at the continuous innovations end of the continuum. Examples are annual automobile style changes, fashion style changes, package changes, or product size or color changes. Products such as compact discs, Sony Walkmans, and the iPod tend toward the dynamically continuous portion of the continuum. Truly new products, called discontinuous innovations, are rare and require a great deal of new learning by the consumer because these products perform either a previously unfulfilled function or an existing function in a new way. The Internet is one example of a discontinuous innovation that has radically altered our society's lifestyle. The basis for identifying new products according to their effect on consumer consumption patterns is consistent with the marketing philosophy that satisfaction of consumer needs is fundamental to a venture's existence.

From a Firm's Viewpoint

The innovative entrepreneurial firm, in addition to recognizing the consumer's perception of newness, may also find it necessary to classify its new products on some similar dimensions. One way to classify the objectives of new products is shown in Figure 9.3. In this figure, an important distinction is made between new products and new markets (i.e., market development). New products are defined in terms of the amount of

Technology Newness ⟶

Market Newness	Product Objectives	No Technological Change	Improved Technology	New Technology
No market change			Reformation Change in formula or physical product to optimize costs and quality	Replacement Replace existing product with new one based on improved technology
Strengthened market	Remerchandising Increase sales to existing customers	Improved product Improve product's utility to customers	Product life extension Add new similar products to line; serve more customers based on new technology
New market	New use Add new segments that can use present products	Market extension Add new segments modifying present products	Diversification Add new markets with new products developed from new technology

Figure 9.3   New Product Classification System

SOURCE: Hisrich, R. D., Peters, M. P., & Shepherd, D. A. (2007). *Entrepreneurship* (7th ed.). Chicago: McGraw-Hill/Irwin.

improved technology, whereas market development is based on the degree of new segmentation.

The situation in which there is new technology *and* a new market is the most complicated and difficult—and it has the highest degree of risk. Since the new product involves new technology and customers that are not currently being served, the firm will need a new and carefully planned marketing strategy. Replacements, extensions, product improvements, reformulations, and remerchandising involve product and market development strategies that range in difficulty depending on whether the firm has had prior experience with a similar product or with the same target market.

OPPORTUNITY RECOGNITION

Some entrepreneurs have the ability to recognize a business opportunity—a skill that is fundamental to the entrepreneurial process as well as growing a business. A business opportunity represents a possibility for the entrepreneur to successfully fill a large enough unsatisfied need that enough sales and profits result. Significant research has yielded several models of the opportunity recognition process.

Recognizing an opportunity often results from the knowledge and experience of the individual entrepreneur and, when appropriate, the entrepreneurial business. This prior knowledge results from a combination of education and experience; the relevant experience could be work-related or could result from a variety of personal experiences or events. The global entrepreneur needs to be aware of this knowledge and experience and have the desire to understand and make use of it. The other important factors in this process are entrepreneurial alertness and entrepreneurial networks. The interaction between entrepreneurial alertness and the entrepreneur's prior knowledge of markets and customer problems has a tremendous effect on success. Those entrepreneurs who have the ability to recognize meaningful business opportunities are in a strategic position to successfully complete the product planning and development process and launch new ventures.

OPPORTUNITY ANALYSIS PLAN

Each and every innovative idea and opportunity should be carefully assessed by the global entrepreneur. One good way to do this is to develop an opportunity analysis plan, as discussed in Chapter 4. An opportunity analysis plan is *not* the business plan; it focuses on the idea and the market (the opportunity) for the idea—not on the venture. It also is shorter than a business plan and does not contain any formal financial statements of the business venture. The opportunity analysis plan is developed to serve as the basis for the decision to either act on the opportunity or wait until another (hopefully better) opportunity comes along. A typical opportunity analysis plan has four sections: (1) a description of the idea and its competition; (2) an assessment of the domestic and international market for the idea; (3) an assessment of the entrepreneur and the team; and (4) a discussion of the steps needed to make the idea the basis for a viable business venture (see Chapter 4).

PRODUCT PLANNING AND DEVELOPMENT PROCESS

Once ideas emerge from idea sources or creative problem solving, they need further development and refinement. This refining process—the product planning and development process—is divided into five major stages: idea stage, concept stage, product development stage, test marketing stage, and commercialization. It results in the start of the product life cycle (see Figure 9.4).

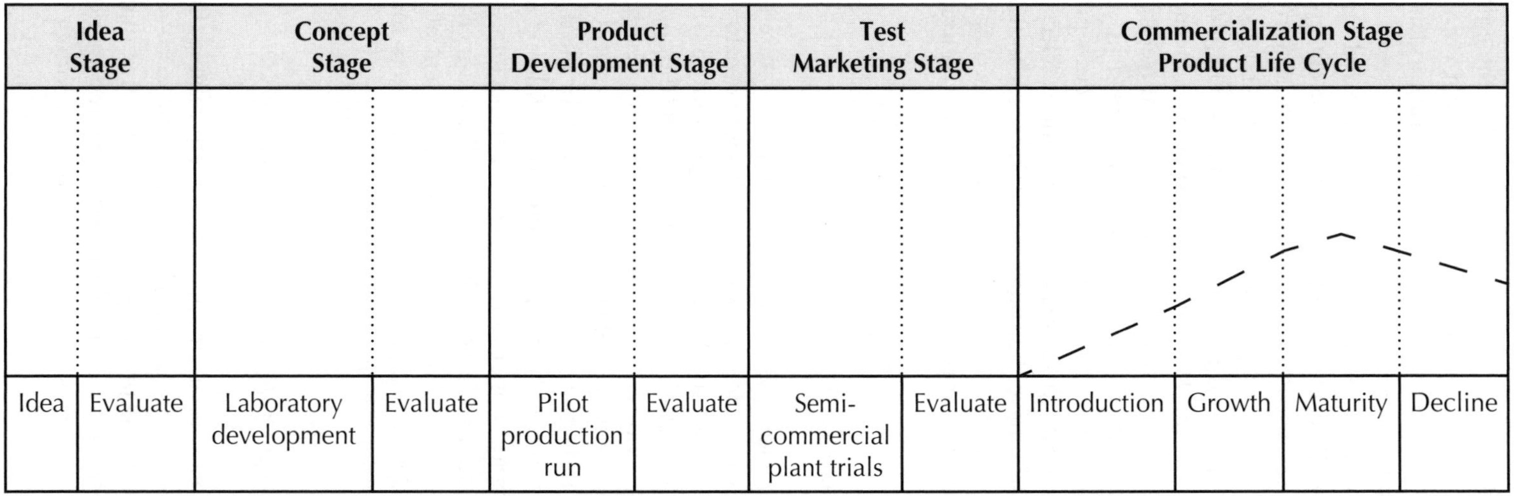

Idea Stage		Concept Stage		Product Development Stage		Test Marketing Stage		Commercialization Stage Product Life Cycle			
Idea	Evaluate	Laboratory development	Evaluate	Pilot production run	Evaluate	Semi-commercial plant trials	Evaluate	Introduction	Growth	Maturity	Decline

Figure 9.4 The Product Planning and Development Process

SOURCE: From Hisrich, R. D., & Peters, M. P. (1991). *Marketing decisions for new and mature products* (2nd. ed.). Reprinted with permission of Pearson Education, Inc., Upper Saddle River, NJ.

Establishing Evaluation Criteria

At each stage of the product planning and development process, criteria for evaluation need to be established. These criteria should be all-inclusive and quantitative enough to screen the product carefully in the particular stage of development. Criteria should be established to evaluate the new idea in terms of market opportunity, competition, the marketing system, financial factors, and production factors.

A market opportunity in the form of a new or current need for the product idea must exist. The determination of market demand is by far the most important criterion of a proposed new product idea. Assessment of the market opportunity and size needs to consider the characteristics and attitudes of consumers or industries that may buy the product, the size of this potential market in dollars and units, the nature of the market with respect to its stage in the life cycle (growing or declining), and the share of the market the product could reasonably capture.

Current competing producers, prices, and marketing efforts should also be evaluated, particularly in terms of their effect on the market share of the proposed idea. The new idea should be able to compete successfully with products and services already on the market by having features that will meet or overcome current and anticipated competition. The new idea should have some unique differential advantage based on an evaluation of all competitive products and services filling the same consumer needs.

The new idea should have synergy with existing management capabilities and marketing strategies. The firm should be able to use its marketing experience and other expertise in this new product effort. For example, General Electric would have a far less difficult time adding a new lighting device to its line than Procter & Gamble. Several factors should be considered in evaluating the degree of fit: the degree to which the ability and time of the present sales force can be transferred to the new product; the ability to sell the new product through the company's established channels of distribution; and the ability to piggyback the advertising and promotion required to introduce the new product.

The proposed product or service should be supported by and contribute to the company's financial well-being. The manufacturing cost per unit, the marketing expense, and the amount of capital need to be determined along with the break-even point and the long-term profit outlook for the product.

The compatibility of the new product's production requirements with existing plant, machinery, and personnel should also be evaluated. If the new product idea cannot be integrated into existing manufacturing processes, additional plant and equipment costs will need to be taken into account. All required materials for production need to be available and accessible in sufficient quantity.

Global entrepreneurs need to formally evaluate an idea throughout its evolution. They must be sure that the product can be the basis for a new venture. This can be done through careful evaluation that results in a go or no-go decision at each of the stages of the product planning and development process: the idea stage, the concept stage, the product development stage, and the test marketing stage.

Idea Stage

Promising new product and service ideas should be identified and impractical ones eliminated at the *idea stage*, allowing maximum use of the company's resources. One evaluation method successfully used at this stage is the systematic market evaluation checklist, where each new idea is expressed in terms of its chief values, merits, and benefits. Consumers are presented with clusters of new product or service values to determine which, if any, new product or service alternatives should be pursued and which should be discarded. A company can test many new alternatives with this evaluation method; promising ideas can be further developed and resources will not be wasted on ideas that are incompatible with the market's values.

It is important to determine the need for the new idea as well as its value to the company. If there is no need for the suggested product, its development should not be continued. Similarly, the new product or service idea should not be developed if it does not have any benefit or value to the firm. To accurately determine the need for a new idea, it is helpful to define the potential needs of the market in terms of timing, satisfaction, alternatives, benefits and risks, future expectations, price-versus-product performance features, market structure and size, and economic conditions. A form for helping in this need determination process is shown in Table 9.2. The factors in this table should be evaluated not only in terms of the characteristics of the potential new product/service but also in terms of the new product/service's competitive strength relative to each factor. This comparison with competitive products/services will indicate the proposed idea's strengths and weaknesses.

The need determination should focus on the type of need, its timing, the users involved with trying the product/service, the importance of controllable marketing variables, the overall market structure, and the characteristics of the market. Each of these factors should be evaluated in terms of the characteristics of the new idea being considered and the aspects and capabilities of present methods for satisfying the particular need. This analysis will indicate the extent of the opportunity available.

In determination of the value of the new product/service to the firm, financial scheduling—such as cash outflow, cash inflow, contribution to profit, and return on investment—needs to be evaluated in terms of other product/service ideas as well as investment alternatives. With the use of the form shown in Table 9.3, the dollar amount of each of the considerations

Table 9.2   Determining the Need for a New Product or Service Idea

Factor	Aspects	Competitive Capabilities	New Product Idea Capability
Type of Need Continuing need Declining need Emerging need Future need			
Timing of Need Duration of need Frequency of need Demand cycle Position in life cycle			
Competing Ways to Satisfy Need Doing without Using present way Modifying present way			
Perceived Benefits/Risks Utility to customer Appeal characteristics Customer tastes and preferences Buying motives Consumption habits			
Price Versus Performance Features Price-quantity relationship Demand elasticity Stability of price Stability of market			
Market Size and Potential Market growth Market trends Market development requirements Threats to market			
Availability of Customer Funds General economic conditions Economic trends Customer income Financing opportunities			

Table 9.3 Determining the Value for a New Product or Service Idea

Factor	Cost (in $)
Cash Outflow R&D costs Marketing costs Capital equipment costs Other costs	
Cash Inflow Sales of new product Effect on additional sales of existing products Salvageable value	
Net Cash Flow Maximum exposure Time to maximum exposure Duration of exposure Total investment Maximum net cash in a single year	
Profit Profit from new product Profit affecting additional sales of existing products Fraction of total company profit	
Relative Return Return on shareholders' equity (ROE)	
Return on investment (ROI) Cost of capital Present value (PV) Discounted cash flow (DCF) Return on assets employed (ROA) Return on sales	
Compared to Other Investments Compared to other product opportunities Compared to other investment opportunities	

important to the new idea should be determined as accurately as possible so that a quantitative evaluation can be made. These figures can then be revised as better information becomes available and the product/service continues to be developed.

Concept Stage

After a new product or service idea has passed evaluation at the idea stage, it should be further developed and refined through interaction with customers. In the *concept stage*, the refined idea is tested to determine consumer acceptance. Initial reactions to the concept are obtained from potential customers or members of the distribution channel when appropriate. One method of measuring consumer acceptance is the conversational interview in which selected respondents are exposed to statements that reflect the physical characteristics and attributes of the product or service. Where competing products (or services) exist, these statements can also compare their primary features. Both favorable and unfavorable product features can be discovered by analyzing consumers' responses. Favorable features can then be incorporated into the new product or service.

Features, price, and promotion should be evaluated for both the concept being studied and any major competing products by asking the following questions:

- How does the new concept compare with competitive products or services in terms of quality and reliability?

- Is the concept superior or deficient compared with products and services currently available on the market?

- Is this a good market opportunity for the firm?

Similar evaluations should be done for all aspects of the marketing strategy.

Product Development Stage

In the *product development stage*, consumer reaction to the physical product or service is determined. One tool frequently used at this stage is the consumer panel, in which a group of potential consumers are given product samples. Participants keep a record of their use of the product and comment on its virtues and deficiencies. This technique is more applicable for product ideas and works for only some service ideas.

The panel of potential customers might also be given a sample of the product and one or more competitive products simultaneously. Then one of several methods—such as multiple brand comparisons, risk analysis, level of repeat purchases, or intensity of preference analysis—can be used to determine consumer preference.

Test Marketing Stage

Although the results of the product development stage provide the basis of the final marketing plan, a market test can increase the certainty of successful commercialization. This last step in the evaluation process, the *test marketing stage*, provides actual sales results, which indicate the acceptance level of consumers. Positive test results indicate the degree of probability of a successful product launch and company formation.

Developing the Global Marketing Mix

Once an international market is selected, the global entrepreneur needs to develop the appropriate marketing mix—product, price, distribution, and promotion. A first step is to determine the extent to which these elements should be standardized.

STANDARDIZATION

This critical decision about how much to standardize will affect the global entrepreneur when entering international markets. Should he or she adopt a crossnational strategy rather than a fully localized strategy or a fully standard one? Some factors that favor standardization include a shrinking world marketplace; the increasing use of English as the language of business; economies of scale in production; and economies in research, development, and marketing. Other factors favor a more localized (market-specific) strategy, such as different buyer behavior patterns; different uses; government regulations; and severe local market differences and distinctiveness. Generally the global entrepreneur should adopt a flexible marketing strategy that is not at either extreme and in reality thinks globally but acts locally. This approach incorporates differences into the global marketing strategy that can be implemented locally.

PRICING DECISIONS

Pricing decisions are much more complicated in international versus domestic markets due in part to currency and cost differences and government regulations and policies. Two critical issues involved in pricing decisions are foreign market pricing and transfer (intracompany) pricing.

Foreign Market Pricing

The factors affecting the price in a particular market (costs, competitive prices, customer price sensitivity and behavior, market structure and conditions, and objectives of the company) vary from market to market, requiring pricing decisions to vary as well. The global entrepreneur should avoid the ease of having a uniform pricing policy and use price as a competitive factor in the overall marketing policy. Although individual prices should reflect the specific conditions of a market, prices should also be coordinated on a worldwide basis, particularly when economic integration is occurring across markets. One way to do this is to set maximum and minimum prices within which the local countries' price needs to be established. This approach allows flexibility in pricing to reflect local market conditions, but does not allow so much price deviation that a price-quality relationship cannot be established or crossborder shopping encouraged.

Almost every global entrepreneur must confront the issue of export pricing. Export pricing generally uses a standard worldwide price, different prices for domestic and export products, or market-differentiated pricing. When the global entrepreneur uses standard worldwide pricing, domestic and export products are priced the same based on average unit costs of fixed, variable, and export cost. When using dual pricing that differentiates between domestic and export prices, the global entrepreneur can use either cost plus pricing or marginal cost pricing. Cost plus pricing means that a margin is put on top of the full allocation of domestic and foreign costs. While this ensures that a margin or return occurs, the result can be a price too high for the market. The marginal cost method for pricing exports uses the direct costs for producing and selling for export as the floor of the pricing decision. Any research and development costs and domestic production and marketing costs are not used. A margin is then added to this floor cost.

The aforementioned export pricing methods focus on costs, not demand. One demand-oriented pricing method—market-differentiated pricing—focuses on competitive prices in a market to establish an export price. Unique export costs, such as any cost for modifying the product, costs of the export operation, and any costs for entering the foreign market, are taken into consideration.

Transfer Pricing

Transfer pricing is pricing items for sale to other members of the company. It is often referred to as intracompany pricing. The pricing of intracorporate sales can have a significant effect on the price of the product in the international market and therefore global sales and profits. Various factors affect both the method and the level of transfer pricing, such as import duties, taxes, tariffs, government regulations, and rules concerning repatriation of profits. A low transfer price on goods shipped to a subsidiary and a high transfer price on goods imported from it results in a maximum tax liability for the subsidiary, which is beneficial if the tax in the subsidiary country is substantially lower than the tax in the home country of the company.

Generally a global entrepreneur will use one of four methods for transfer pricing: (1) transfer at the price that unrelated parties would have reached on the transaction, or arm's length pricing; (2) transfer at the price of direct cost; (3) transfer at the price of direct cost plus any additional expenses; and (4) transfer at a price derived from the end-market price. Oftentimes a company can have its price challenged by either the home country tax authority who thinks that the price is too low or the tax authority in the foreign country who thinks the price is too high. These challenges result in favor of the company about 50% of the time. Given this incident rate, it is far safer for the global entrepreneur to use the arm's length pricing method when establishing the company's transfer price. This also helps the company's image as a good global citizen.

DISTRIBUTION DECISIONS

One of the most difficult aspects of international business is understanding and using the channel of distribution in the international market, because each country varies particularly in this aspect. Distribution decisions can be the hardest to change, and they require the global entrepreneur to give up some degree of control over the product being sold.

Establishing the Channel

The selection of the best channel members is very important to being successful in international business. This process is called determining the channel design—the length and width of the channel. The best channel design is influenced by a number of factors, the most important ones being the culture of the market, the type of product, the competition, and the customer.

The global entrepreneur needs to carefully examine the overall culture of the market and the culture of the existing distribution system. Of any of the marketing activities, the distribution systems have the most variance from one culture to another. Part of this is due to the country's legislation, which directly affects the distributors and agents operating there. In some countries, only a few selected distributors are permitted to distribute for foreign companies. In other countries, only distributors 100% locally owned can do this distribution. In others, no dealers are allowed.

The type of product or service to be distributed and its price point is the second factor affecting channel design. A short channel is usually best for bulky, expensive, perishable, or specialized products, as well as those that require after-sale service and services themselves. Staple items can have a longer channel. The positioning and price point also affect channel choice, because the channel itself helps create an image for the product or service being offered. The channel member also absorbs some of the risk for the customer who is dealing with a known home-court entity, not a foreign company.

Of course, competition affects the channel design decision. The global entrepreneur should carefully evaluate the channel used by competitors. These channels may be the best or even the only ones accepted by both the trade and customers alike. When this occurs, these same channels should be used, but more effectively and efficiently. Whenever possible, a totally unique distribution approach is better because it will become a unique selling proposition of the company that is difficult to replicate.

The final and most important factor in the channel design is the customer. The demographic composition of the target market should be the basis for the channel design because it is the essential link between the foreign company and the customers in the target market. The buying process of the customer and the many aspects of the buying decision affect how the product or service should be made available for purchase. Sometimes two or more different channels of distribution are needed to effectively reach the customers with different characteristics.

Selecting and Managing the Channel

Once the channel design has been determined, it is important for the global entrepreneur to carefully select the channel members that will represent his or her company. This selection process is as important as hiring and recruiting within the company. An ineffective or bad distribution decision can set the company back for years, or even permanently, in a foreign market. Trade directories such as Dun & Bradstreet, telephone directories, and the U.S. Department of Commerce can be used to identify possible company representatives that might be suitable.

Each identified prospect should be carefully screened on his or her performance and professionalism; as much information as possible should be collected on each prospect. Once the channel members are in place and the channel is operating, it needs to be carefully managed. A good cooperative channel relationship will establish the best possible link between the foreign company and the local customer.

PROMOTION DECISIONS

The final decision the global entrepreneur needs to make in conjunction with pricing and distribution decisions is the promotion mix decision—selecting and implementing the right combination of advertising, publicity, personal selling, and sales promotion that will expedite sales in the selected target market.

Started in 1994, Blue Tomato is a snowboard company based in Austria and founded by a former champion in the sport. From the beginning the company used its roots in the sport to keep close to its customers and followed its young customer profile onto the Internet in 1999. Success followed rapidly and within 7 years Internet sales accounted for 90% of total revenues.

The adoption of an online sales presence immediately provided the company with almost every international market. One barrier to this can be language. Blue Tomato's biggest market is Germany, so the company's first Web site presence was in the firm's native German. The Internet also led to certain other developments for Blue Tomato that affected its international growth. It enabled the company to increase the sales mix by keeping more products available and reducing its dependence on seasonal markets. The Internet also enabled the company to vary and refine its service offerings through different languages and pricing strategies.

Blue Tomato again used many ways open to it in the networked world to access international markets with an effective multichannel strategy:

- a snowboard catalog distributed to customers and stockists in two languages, in addition to a regular newsletter;

- direct contact to customers by e-mail and telephone, with customer service lines staffed by experienced snowboarders;

- promotions at various snowboarding events;

- partnerships with other related Web sites;

- sponsorship of top snowboarding professionals; and

- sponsorship of snowboard facilities.

Internally, communications and structure seem to work well. The company makes the most of the casual snowboarding lifestyle and work ethic, while it splits the operations of the retail and training centers. Although many sports companies that are created by people intimately involved in the sport have done well initially, only to fall by the wayside as the initial surge of interest in product offerings wane, Blue Tomato is still achieving 100% growth with 80% of sales in international markets (Foscht, Swoboda, & Morshett, 2006).

Advertising

The key issues in establishing a good advertising campaign for the foreign market are the advertising budget, the media strategy, and the message. The global entrepreneur needs to first establish an overall promotion budget for all four areas of the promotion mix (advertising, publicity, personal selling, and sales promotion) and then determine the amount that should be allocated to advertising. This budgeted amount for advertising should be enough to accomplish the sales objectives of the firm. Often a percentage of the sales objective (somewhere around 3%–7% depending on the industry) is used to establish the first year's budget.

The type of media to use is very dependent on the market being entered. For example, if entering Peru or Mexico, a higher percentage of the advertising budget will be allocated to television as 84% of the media spending in Peru and 73% of the media spending in Mexico is spent on television advertising. If entering Bolivia, outdoor advertising would be used often, as 48% of the media budget there is spent in this area. If entering Kuwait or Norway, concentration would be in print media, with 91% and 77% of media spending in print advertising for each country respectively.

Probably the most errors are made in the third issue of advertising, the message—particularly by U.S. global entrepreneurs. Careful consideration needs to be given to culture, language, economic development, and lifestyles when creating the best message for a specific global market. Although it is nice if a single world brand can be established throughout the foreign markets of the venture, many global entrepreneurs abandon identical campaigns for more localized ones, making sure that the advertising message is customized to the particular local global market.

Publicity

Strong publicity can be helpful in entering a foreign market by portraying the foreign company as a good global citizen interested in the well-being of a particular culture or country. The global entrepreneur should consider partnering with a nongovernmental organization (NGO) in the country to work on issues in the country such as diversity, energy, or healthcare. Any way that a solid company image can be established greatly benefits sales in a foreign market.

Personal Selling

In the early stages of market entry, most global entrepreneurs rely heavily on personal contacts. Personal selling is particularly important in high-priced industrial goods. Usually a local country salesperson, when properly trained, can be more effective than someone from outside the country, especially in those countries with high levels of nationalism.

Sales promotion activities such as trade shows, coupons, samples, premiums, point-of-purchase materials, and give-aways can be especially effective when tailored to the specific product or service being offered and to the culture of the company. To be effective, the sales promotion campaign must be accepted and used by the channel members. When carefully crafted and implemented, a well designed sales promotion effort can be very cost effective when entering and developing a foreign market.

Summary

Chapter 9 discusses how effective international research and development and marketing can help the global entrepreneur handle the challenges of rapidly changing technology, shorter product life cycles, changing consumer tastes, and changing economies. Advances in telecommunications, such as cellular technology and e-business, are allowing a greater connectivity between producers and consumers, which is rapidly moving toward constant 24-hour buying and selling. A product's ability to satisfy consumer needs and wants and its uniqueness must be sensitive to and adapt to changing consumer tastes and preferences. Products also must be customized to the local culture, for example the packaging and labeling, to be successful. The global entrepreneur needs to use a good international research and development process, including defining what innovation is to the company, performing opportunity analysis, and understanding the product life cycle. When entering a new market or launching a new product, every entrepreneur must deal with (1) the technological environment; (2) product policy and the total quality issue; (3) adopting the best research and development strategy; and (4) developing and implementing the best marketing strategy. The product planning and development process is divided into five major stages: idea stage, concept stage, product development stage, test marketing stage, and finally commercialization, which results in the start of the product life cycle. Global entrepreneurs must formally evaluate any idea at each of these stages. Once the product has reached the commercialization stage, the entrepreneur must establish the best marketing mix, including pricing, distribution, and promotion. Identifying the best distribution channel, as well as selecting the best in-country representatives in the foreign market, are highly important decisions for the global entrepreneur to make. Finally, the promotion of the product consists of identifying the right mix of advertising, publicity, personal selling, and sales promotion within a predetermined budget. The global entrepreneur must also identify the best types of media to use in the foreign market—whether radio spots, in-store promotions, or magazine advertisements—and also take care to craft an advertising message that resonates with the local culture.

Questions for Discussion

1. What are the three types of innovation? Give an example of each.

2. What is the purpose of creating an opportunity analysis plan? How does it differ from a business plan?

3. What factors should be considered when an entrepreneur sets his or her price for a product or service in a foreign market?

Chapter Exercises

1. Pick a foreign market and a product. Research the alterations that are necessary for the product to be allowed in that market (e.g., package design, labeling).

2. Using that same product, find research that indicates the product will be successful in the country that you are choosing to enter.

3. Take one of your product ideas and outline how that product will be carried through from the idea stage to commercialization.

4. You are a paper clip holder manufacturer launching your product in a new market. Identify how you will have to alter your product, pricing, distribution, and communication. What is the best distribution channel for this product? How will you develop the channel distribution?

References

Sykes, C. (2005, September 14). Fast50 Profile: The Hyperfactory. *Unlimited.* Retrieved September 24, 2008, from http://unlimited.co.nz/unlimited.nsf/fast50/06D22A81B18552CACC25707B00814A97

Woods, C. (2008, April 18). ICU Global grabs international opportunities. Retrieved September 24, 2008, from www.realbusiness.co.uk/news/international-business/5213436/icu-global-grabs-international-opportunities.thtml

Foscht, T., Swoboda, B., & Morschett, D. (2006). Electronic commerce-based internationalization of small, niche-oriented retailing companies: The case of Blue Tomato and the snowboard industry. *International Journal of Retail & Distribution Management, 34*(7), 556–572.

Suggested Readings

ARTICLES

Khurana, A. (2006). Strategies for global R&D. *Research Technology Management,* **49**(2), 10.

Lower costs and strategic advantages are encouraging senior executives in every large or mid-size company in the United States and Europe to conduct part of their R&D overseas. Low-cost locations, like India, China, Israel, and Hungary, are becoming more and more popular R&D destinations with the improved availability of digital connectivity, scientific and technical talent, intellectual property protection, substantial cost differentials, and the potential of large markets. Using case studies in six industries, this paper addresses five key roles that R&D in low-cost locations can play and how to effectively manage each R&D location.

Larimo, J. (Ed.). (2007). *Contemporary Euromarketing: Entry and operational decision making.* Binghamton, NY: International Business Press.

With contributions from academics and researchers in Finland, Spain, Denmark, Italy, France, Portugal, and the Czech Republic, this book examines the international sales strategies of small- and medium-sized firms in Europe, particularly international new ventures (INV) and born globals (BG). The contributors' analyses cover both outward and inward types of operations, foreign sourcing, foreign partner selection, the impact of culture on advertising-related issues, and international counterfeiting.

Lim, L. K. S., Acito, F., & Rusetski, A. (2006). Development of archetypes of international marketing strategy. *Journal of International Business Studies,* **37**(4), 499–524.

This article takes international marketing strategy beyond its traditional, linear characterizations of standardization-adaptation, concentration-dispersion, and integration-independence to the need for a new, integrative classification scheme. Taking into consideration the gestalt combinatorial patterns, the authors suggest that strategies should be created around multidimensional archetypes.

Quelch, J. (2003, August). The return of the global brand. *Harvard Business Review,* **81**(8), 22–23.

This article describes the resentment of American brands and U.S. brand hegemony around the globe and how it affects consumer willingness to participate in the global marketplace. Quelch argues that not only is supranational positioning necessary to counteract U.S. brand hegemony but is also critical in the rise of a brand power like China.

Paliwoda, S., & Marinova, S. (Eds.). (2007). The marketing challenges within the enlarged single European market. *European Journal of Marketing, 41*(3/4), 233–244.

This article addresses the changing nature of marketing in the largest integrated market, the European Union (EU). As EU membership has increased and companies have expanded into the new member states, marketing now plays the role of protecting diversity. The article highlights the challenges and opportunities that marketers face as a result of EU expansion.

Young, R. B., & Javalgi, R. G. (2007). International marketing research: A global project management perspective. *Business Horizons, 50,* 113–122.

This article provides internal client-side marketing research managers with a proper framework for conducting international market research projects. The piece also addresses the factors and challenges that conducting research across national borders present, including constructing questionnaires and the finer points of primary data collection.

WEB SITES

Grassroots Marketing. (n.d.). *Inc.com* **[online] Retrieved September 24, 2008, from www.inc.com/guides/marketing/24074.html**

Grassroots Marketing, a practical guide from *Inc.* magazine, highlights businesses that have found cost-effective ways to promote their business and retain customers.

10 Global Human Resource Management

Profile: Ho Kwon Ping (KP Ho)

BANYAN TREE

The Times calls him the Branson of the East, but the title doesn't fit.

True, there are some commonalities. Ho Kwon Ping (better known as KP Ho) is as expert a marketer as the high-flying founder of the airline Virgin Group. Both the Chinese Singaporean and the Englishman can teach experts a trick or two about global branding. Both are pioneers when it comes to redefining old businesses. While Richard Branson recreated the romance of flying, KP Ho put romance back into luxury holidays. But the similarities end there.

Everything that KP Ho (born in 1952) does stems from his roots as a development economist, a former journalist, and a committed environmentalist. One example: spending US$400,000 on desalination plants to turn seawater into freshwater so as to avoid damaging the fragile ecosystems near the Banyan Tree projects.

At the same time, he is a shrewd, smart manager. He joined the family business (the Wah Chang Group) in 1981, but over the past decade, converted the lackluster construction-to-commodity trading business into one of the fastest growing luxury hotel chains in the world, using the organic diversification route.

The Banyan Tree group is a family affair for KP. The first hotel started as a "fun" project with his brother Kwon Cjan (now head architect of all Banyan Tree projects) and wife Claire Chiang (a former Nominated Member of Parliament [NMP] and executive director of the Banyan Tree Gallery that promotes local arts and handicrafts).

The first Banyan Tree resort opened in Phuket, Thailand, in 1995 with just seven staff members. KP had to wait 13 years to own the next one, the Banyan Tree in Bangkok. Since then there has been no looking back. Currently the group owns 18 hotels and resorts, 46 spas, and 2 golf courses; it employs 4,380 staff from 32 different nationalities.

What or who is the force behind the tremendous achievements of Banyan Tree? Apurv Bagri, a member of *The Smart Manager* advisory board and a longtime friend of the stylish hotel tycoon, tries to unveil the man behind the success in this open-ended interview.

Q: *You once said, 'Everything in my past has contributed to my today.'*
Can you elaborate?

KP: I said that because when I talk to young people, I feel there is too little awareness on their part that everything they are or will be is a slow accumulation of their everyday experiences.

Also, I made that remark because of my pretty checkered career: many people ask me how journalism, my childhood, and other events have contributed toward my present business and to what I am today. Upon reflection, I now recognize that everything that I have done in my life built the person who is now able to do what I am doing.

For example, the Banyan Tree is not a national brand and people of many nationalities work in our organization. This comes from the fact that I never grew up in one single country: I grew up in Singapore and Thailand. And when I was younger, I had a great passion not only for backpacking, but also for the romance of travel in a very inexpensive manner.

The Banyan Tree culture is built out of my experiences. When I think back, I realize that the total accumulation of all my experiences has had a big influence on what I am today in a nonapparent sort of way. It's probably true for everybody.

We do use traditional training programs. But one of the big issues we face (and this is one of the contradictions of luxury tourism) is the great disparity in income between the workers of tourism and the consumers of tourism. If this is not handled in a positive manner, it can end in what I call the Caribbean situation, where people working in the hospitality industry actually resent the guests.

Q: *Another area where you have been a pioneer is in training programs*
for your workforce. I understand the Banyan Tree employs about
4,000 people from 32 nationalities. What did you try that was different
and why?

KP: In our training programs we conduct all the skills-based training as others do, such as how to set a table, how to answer the telephone, and so forth. Where we try to go beyond is attempting to create an emotional nexus between the service people and the consumer so that they realize the customer truly adds to the livelihood of our staff.

One of the ways we do this is to ask our staff to stay in a luxury villa so that they experience and know what it is like to stay there. An overwhelming majority of employees would be minorities in a developed country, yet the setting is very U.S.-centric. In the international luxury hotel business, you do have a situation where whites dominate other nationalities, so we try to create a culture of internationalism. We prepare training programs that are not just skill based but are oriented toward building a Banyan Tree culture. (Bagri, 2005)

www.banyantree.com

Chapter Objectives

1. To determine the importance of motivating employees and various methods to accomplish this across cultures.

2. To define types of human capital and the use of each as a venture progresses over time.

3. To explain hiring concerns and how to best define them.

4. To illustrate the importance of hiring global-minded employees for the success of a venture and training these same employees to succeed.

5. To demonstrate the leadership necessary to inspire and recruit personnel for future accomplishment.

6. To understand the critical role of proper human resource management in a successful global enterprise.

7. To identify the major sources of personnel and when to potentially use them.

8. To show means of identifying and training a resource for a global assignment.

Introduction

The importance of having good global managers and a quality international workforce cannot be over emphasized throughout the globalization process of an entrepreneurial firm. Although the focus of the venture does change, the importance and need does not.

In the early stages of going global, the focus is on understanding cultural differences, the political risks, and the best way to enter the international market. Typically, this first stage can involve the marketing or sales manager or the global entrepreneur being responsible for selecting a market and beginning some export activities. Usually, an export manager and small staff are hired externally next, due to the need for international experience. This staff handles the paperwork and facilitates the international transaction and documentation to make sure that sales and profits are not lost. As the level of global business progresses to more direct involvement, the global human resource focuses on assessing existing personnel and their abilities to handle the needed global markets and functions. Plans are then developed and implemented for the recruitment, selection, and training of employees for the needed positions.

The global entrepreneur must make sure that clear career paths for managers assigned overseas are established and a clear system of human resource management is operant. This defines promotion criteria and eliminates many of the perceived problems in motivating managers to want foreign assignments. The global venture can also more easily determine which individuals in the company are able and willing to accept overseas assignments. This important area of global human resource management is addressed by looking at motivation across cultures; sources and types of human capital; selection criteria and procedures; the global mindset; compensation policies; the hiring process; the training of international managers; and leadership in global business.

Motivation Across Cultures

Motivation is a psychological process by which unsatisfied needs lead to drives that seek to achieve goals or incentives that at least partially satisfy these needs. As such, the process has three elements: needs, drives, and goal attainment. Although the process is universal in nature, the specific content needs and goals that are pursued are significantly influenced by the local culture. For example, in the United States personal achievement is an important need and individual success through promotion and money is an important goal. In China, on the other hand, group affiliation is an important need and harmony a desired goal. While a key incentive for individuals in the United States is money, it is respect and power for individuals in Japan, and respect, family considerations, and a good personal life in Latin America.

The effect of culture on motivations changes over time, particularly with any significant changes in the economic or political environment of the country. As more countries move toward market economies, the ways in which individuals in these countries are motivated continually changes as well.

Culture also significantly affects the view of quality of life in a country, which directly affects the view of work and the type of work. In Sweden, there is a fairly high degree of individualism, which is reflected in the emphasis on individual decision making on the job. Conversely, in Japan there is a high degree of uncertainty avoidance, which is reflected in the structured tasks of most jobs in which individuals can have security and know what is to be done and how it is to be done.

The importance of work in an individual's life (work centrality) also varies by culture. Japan has the highest level of work centrality, followed by Israel with a moderately high level. There are average levels of work centrality in Belgium and the United States and moderately low levels in Germany and the Netherlands. This means, depending on the country, other areas of interest such as church, family, or leisure are more important to differing extents.

Sources and Types of Human Capital

The location and nationality of the candidates for a particular job are big issues for global human resources. This usually changes as the global venture moves through the stages of internationalization. In the start-up stage outside expertise is usually hired; as the venture expands and gains more foreign operations, it starts to develop more of its own personnel for international operations. As this staff continues to expand and grow, the venture will rely less on home-country personnel and have more host-country nationals in management positions.

There are four basic sources of personnel: home-country nationals (expatriates), host-country nationals, third-country nationals, and inpatriates.

HOME-COUNTRY NATIONALS (EXPATRIATES)

Home-country nationals, often called expatriates or expats, are citizens of the country where the venture of the global entrepreneur is headquartered. These individuals are willing to work for the global venture in a foreign country for a period of time. The major advantages of using expats in a foreign country are that they know the products and culture of the venture; relate easily and efficiently to corporate headquarters; have the particular technical or business skills needed; put the venture ahead of the country and will therefore promote the interests of the venture; and are less likely to take the venture's knowledge and set up a competing business.

The major disadvantages of using expats are evident in the trend away from using them. Even the Japanese, who had the highest percentage of expat employment, are now less inclined to use them. There are many disadvantages to using expats. Firms often have reintegration and retention problems because a high percentage of expats leave the venture after an overseas experience. The costs of relocation, housing, education, and overseas living allowance are usually high. Some expats return early before completion of the assignment, and it can be difficult to find good managers willing to move overseas in the first place. Finally, there are longer start-up and wind down times and a shortsighted focus.

HOST-COUNTRY NATIONALS

Host-country nationals, or local managers hired by the global entrepreneur, are a particularly good source of middle and lower level managers. Some foreign governments, and even customers, expect and can even stipulate that a firm hire host-country nationals to further the country's employment and training. Most global ventures use home-country managers to start the operation in a country and turn this position over to a host-country manager as soon as he or she is trained and ready to assume the position. The decision to use host-country nationals depends on such factors as the nature of the industry, the complexity and life cycle of the product, the functional areas that need staffing, and the availability of a country's resources. The service sector typically uses the largest number of host-country nationals.

THIRD-COUNTRY NATIONALS

A third source of managers is third-country nationals. These managers are citizens of a country that is neither the home country of the venture nor the host country of operation. These managers are typically used in the later stages of the internationalization process of the venture or when there are no host-country nationals with the needed expertise. Often third-country managers have technical expertise or are from cultures quite similar to the culture of the host country.

Third-country managers tend to build a career with the company in the host country and are often lured away by competitive companies needing management talent in that particular market. These third-country national managers, particularly if they have been with the venture in a different country, are often able to achieve corporate objectives much quicker and more effectively than either expats or host-country nationals. They also bring a broader perspective to the management position.

INPATRIATES

In recent years a new type of manager has emerged—an inpatriate. This is an individual from the host country or a third-country national who works in the home country. These new managers are a new breed who can truly manage across borders and are thus truly global managers. They are very good at developing the global core competency of the venture.

Selection Criteria

Making an effective selection decision for an overseas assignment can be a major problem for the global entrepreneur. Traits that are used in this process range from the ideal to the real. Over time, a venture establishes more defined, accurate international selection criteria based on the experience it obtains. Normally the selection criteria include technical knowledge; experience; knowledge of the area and language; interest in and appreciation of overseas work and the specific culture; adaptability of the family; and demographics, such as age, education, sex, and health.

Technical competence in the functional area needs to be at a superior level, because an overseas manager usually has far more responsibility and less support than a domestic manager. The individual selected needs to be self-sufficient in making decisions and running the business. This technical competence is almost always reflected in outstanding past performance and solid, diverse experience in the company and industry. Experienced corporate managers going overseas also ensure the continuation of the company culture in the overseas location.

Although knowledge of the area, culture, and language are important, their roles are debatable. The ability to speak and understand the language of the host country is by far the most important. A manager who does not know the language of the country may get by with the help of associates and translators, but he or she will never fully understand or be a part of the situation. This is still the case even though English is widespread and, in most cases, the language of international businesses regardless of country.

Another factor in the selection is the manager's interest in an international assignment and his or her appreciation of the culture of the specific country. This desire, knowledge, and adaptability to change are important for success in the overseas assignment. Some managers go through an "exhilaration curve"—they are very excited at the beginning of the overseas assignment, but after a time frustration and confusion with the new environment set in like a delayed culture shock. An appreciation and knowledge of the particular culture allows the overseas manager to become more easily a part of the new culture and operation. This allows for total integration and a much more successful experience in the new position.

This ability to integrate into the culture also depends on the manager's family situation, because living overseas usually puts more strain on other family members than on the manager. If a family is not happy, the manager often performs poorly and is frequently terminated or leaves the company. The characteristics of the family as a whole are important. Is the marriage stable? Does the family work together? Are there any behavioral problems with the children? Most firms today are interviewing both the spouse and the manager before deciding on an overseas assignment. A family that has successfully lived abroad previously is usually a less risky choice.

Finally, demographic characteristics are important selection criteria in an overseas assignment. Reflecting a minimum age and experience requirement, many overseas assignments are filled by managers in their mid-30s or older. Although the number of women in overseas assignments is increasing, it is significantly lower than the number of men. To a certain extent, this reflects the view of women in some cultures. Any overseas manager must also be in good physical and emotional health. Many host countries have radically different environmental conditions than the home country that could aggravate existing health problems or cause new ones to occur. An overseas manager needs to be dependent and self-reliant. He or she must be able to make decisions and work at various levels in the organization without the support staff usually available in the home country.

The Global Mindset

The globalization of the business world has brought individuals and organizations from many different parts of the world together as customers, suppliers, partners, or creditors. The success of global corporations is increasingly dependent on their ability to bridge cultural gaps and to work effectively under different environments from their home country.

To succeed in their roles, global entrepreneurs need to influence individuals and groups inside and outside their organization from different parts of the world to help achieve organizational goals. Global mindset is a set of individual attributes that facilitate the influence process. Global entrepreneurs who have a global mindset are better able to influence individuals, organizations, and systems that are different from their own. They are better able to understand and interpret global issues and more effectively understand the viewpoints of people from other parts of the world.

What are the components of global mindset? Global mindset consists of three major groups of individual attributes: intellectual capital, psychological capital, and social capital. Intellectual capital consists of:

- knowledge of the global business and industry
- knowledge of the global political and economic systems
- ability to build and manage global value networks
- ability to build and manage global teams
- ability to understand and manage the tension between corporate requirements and local needs and challenges
- understanding of other cultures and histories
- understanding cultural similarities and differences
- knowledge of other languages
- ability to adapt, learn, and cope with complex cross-cultural and global issues

Psychological capital consists of the following attributes:

- self-confidence and self-efficacy
- resiliency
- curiosity
- fearlessness and risk-taking propensities
- quest for adventure
- desire and passion for learning about and being in other cultures
- openness and ability to suspend judgment
- passion for cultural diversity
- adaptability
- ability to connect to people from other parts of the world

- collaborativeness

- ability to generate positive energy in people from other parts of the world and to excite them

Social capital is the ability to work with people from other parts of the world, the ability to generate positive energy in people from other parts of the world, and most important, the ability to build trusting relationships with people from other cultural backgrounds. Trust is the most critical factor in building long-term relationships with others, whether they are employees, colleagues, supervisors, customers, or partners. Building trust in a cross-cultural setting is more complex because even the definition of trust is culture specific. The outcome of trust is universal.

The combination of intellectual, psychological, and social capital composes the global mindset, which enables global entrepreneurs to be successful. It helps them develop behavioral tools to influence those from different sociocultural systems to contribute to the achievement of organizational goals. Professor Mansour Javidan of the Thunderbird School of Global Management has developed a measuring instrument that allows an organization to determine the extent of the global mindset of any of its employees.

Selection Procedures

In addition to establishing the appropriate selection criteria, the global entrepreneur also needs to establish the best selection procedure. The selection procedure can employ interviewing, testing procedures, or both.

Most global firms use interviews to screen and select managers for overseas assignments. Usually both the manager and the spouse are interviewed. Often the interview is conducted by several people in the venture to ensure that the responses are heard correctly and all the needed information is obtained. Developing and using standard interview questions and a format assists in the process.

There are many different tests available. One test determines the nature and extent of the global mindset. Just a few of the over 2,000 employment tests are listed in Table 10.1. These tests are either cognitive tests or personality tests generally used by many global companies. Care must be taken to use the right test, because using the wrong test can result in the selection of the wrong person or can even dismiss some very qualified individuals. The results of the test used and the performance of the individual should be recorded and compared so that a good testing instrument is developed.

Table 10.1 Testing Procedures for International Managers

Global Personality Inventory
This 300-question test is used to test executives, mid- to senior-level managers, and senior salespeople. The cost is around US$40 to $50 per individual tested.
Hogan Personality Inventory
This test, using true or false responses to attitude and biographical questions, measures individuals on personality areas such as ambition and prudence, and occupational scales such as clerical potential or service orientation. The cost per individual tested is US$25 to $175 depending on the amount of detail in the report.
Multidimensional Aptitude Battery II
This 303-question test measures the ability to reason, plan, and solve problems of technical, managerial, and professional individuals. The cost is US$190 for a 25-test kit.
Occupational Personality Questionnaire
This test asks candidates to choose the statement that is most and least like them from a set of 104. The test can measure general profile or specific leadership or sales potential traits. The cost is US$30 and higher depending on the measurement desired.
NEO Personality Inventory
This test measures executive or managers on five scales: agreeableness, conscientiousness, extroversion, neuroticism, and openness to experiences. The test costs US$245 for a 25-test kit.
Personality Research Form
This 352-question test is appropriate for any level of employee. It measures 22 job-relevant personality traits. The cost is US$80 for a 5-test kit.
Watson-Glaser Critical Thinking Appraisal
This test of 40 rather difficult questions appraises such things as creativity and problem-solving skills of all levels of executives and managers. The test costs between US$10 and $20 per individual.
Wesmann Personnel Classification
This test uses a combination of verbal and numerical questions to predict on-the-job performance and the ability to learn of managers at all levels. The cost is US$7 to $15 per individual tested.
16PF
This test of 185 questions measures 16 personality factors of managers in leadership positions. The cost is US$8 to $20 per individual tested.

Compensation Issues

The global venture's compensation program needs to provide an incentive to leave the home country and take the foreign assignment, maintain an established standard of living in that country including family needs, and facilitate return to the home country. Salaries and costs of global managers can be three to five times higher than their home-country counterparts. While the overall compensation package will vary from country to country as well as from company to company, the compensation of most managers overseas includes base salary, salary-related allowances, nonsalary-related allowances, and taxes.

The base salary of the manager, of course, is dependent on the responsibilities and duties of the position. The foreign position salary should have equity and comparability with the domestic position, reflecting the normal salary received in the home country. For example, a manager in a German venture would receive a base salary for working in Spain that reflects the salary structure of the venture in Germany.

In addition to the base salary, there is usually a foreign service premium, valued at 10%–25% of the base salary. Sometimes the percentage decreases each year the manager is abroad, such as 20% for year one and 15% for year two. Sometimes the percentage slides in salary increments such as 25% of the first US$50,000 base salary; 20% for the second US$50,000; and 10% for any base salary over US$100,000. Sometimes a ceiling is set for the total amount of foreign service premium received.

There are several nonsalary allowances paid such as benefits, cost-of-living allowances, housing allowances, and hardship allowances. The benefit packages are usually 25%–30% of the base salary for health care and insurance and need to be carefully evaluated in the international setting. The cost-of-living allowance makes sure that the global manager can maintain as closely as possible the same standard of living as he or she would have in the home country. This is usually calculated by selecting a percentage of base salary that would be spent at the foreign location. Almost all firms provide a housing allowance that is commensurate with the global manager's salary level and position. Because this is usually the largest cost, most firms establish a range within which the global manager must find housing. Most ventures pay for utilities in the housing unit outright. Finally, in some instances, there are hardship allowances to account for working and living in a very difficult environment; the percentage paid varies by the degree of difficulty.

Nonsalary-related allowances typically include: (1) allowances related to housing, such as a home sale, rental protection, shipment and storage of household goods, or household furnishings in the host-country location; (2) automobile coverage, including selling a car in the home country and purchasing a car in the host country; (3) travel expenses to host country and one or two trips each year for the manager and his family to return to the home country, called home leave; (4) temporary living expenses; and (5) a relocation allowance to pay for any additional expenses of the move.

The final aspect of the compensation package is taxes. A global manager may have two tax bills—one for the host country and one from the home country. It is usually good to have in place a tax-equalization plan in which the global venture pays the difference if the tax rate in the host country is higher than what would be paid in the home country or keeps the difference if the tax rate is lower. The plan would take into account differences (higher or lower) if taxes are paid in both the home and host country.

Basic economic and noneconomic compensation options are indicated in Figures 10.1 and 10.2.

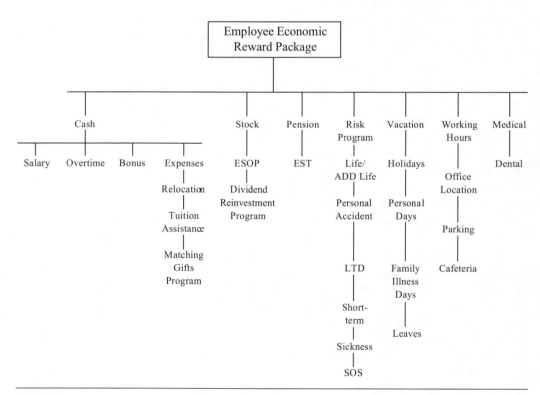

Figure 10.1   Compensation Options: Employee Economic Reward Package

SOURCE: Hisrich, R. D. (2004). *Small business solutions: How to prevent and fix the 13 biggest problems that derail business.* New York: McGraw-Hill.

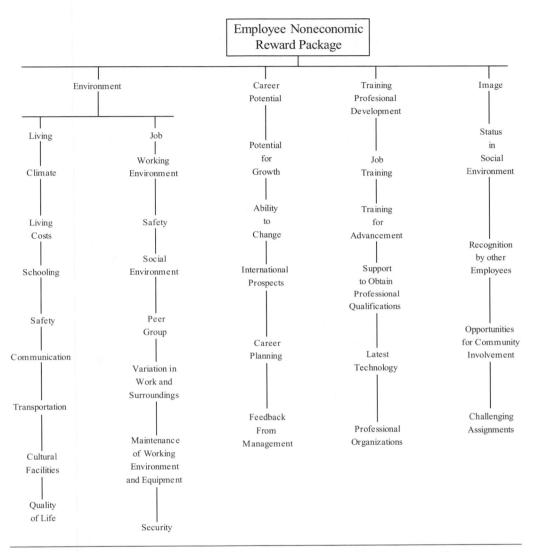

Figure 10.2   Compensation Options: Employee Noneconomic Reward Package

SOURCE: Adapted from material of Girard Torma, Director of Compensation and International Human Resources, Nordson Corporation. Hisrich, R. D. (2004). *Small business solutions: How to prevent and fix the 13 biggest problems that derail business.* New York: McGraw-Hill.

The Hiring Process

The global entrepreneur needs to establish a standardized hiring process that can be used throughout the global operation of the venture. This includes having an established system for selecting and hiring that will be used again and again. Some entrepreneurs do not feel hiring can be reduced to a series of processes and instead rely more on feeling and judgment. In hiring for global positions, a more established systematic approach will provide a fuller, more balanced view of the candidates and the opportunity to hire the best individual.

The systematic approach includes developing a standardized interview format and testing procedures. Because a traditional interview results in a subjective, narrow view of a candidate in which most interviewers prefer candidates similar to themselves, a more structured behavioral interview should be established. A behavioral interview involves several interviewers defining qualities needed, asking the same questions to each candidate to give past examples of how they demonstrated those qualities, and taking copious notes. How the candidate has responded on a past job is indicative of how he or she will respond in a future job—a principle of historicity. Eventually, a standard template for what is needed for a global manager is established that can be modified for various managerial levels.

These behavioral interviews should be combined with some tests, which can often be administered online. It is usually better to use both a cognitive test measuring cognitive abilities and a personality test that measures personality traits. Table 10.1 contains examples of each type of test. Cognitive tests generally have a slightly closer correlation with job success than personality tests.

Summary

Chapter 10 focuses on how to identify and recruit the right people for the global entrepreneur's venture. In selecting the right people, the global entrepreneur must be attuned to implications of cultures on motivation. What motivates individuals in one country, whether wealth, status, or group membership, varies greatly from other countries. The global entrepreneur could decide to staff his or her overseas venture with individuals from the home country (expatriates), individuals from the host country (local or host-country managers), individuals from neither the host or home countries (third-party nationals), or individuals from host or third-party countries in the home country (inpatriates). The choice of manager or employee is based on what the firm emphasizes to be successful—for example, a deep understanding of the firm's culture and vision (expatriate), or the ability to motivate individuals from different cultures (third-party nationals), or thorough knowledge of the local country and culture (home-country nationals).

For the sake of consistency and easing the hiring process, a global entrepreneur ideally will establish specific hiring criteria and processes, which will normally involve a mixture of interviews and tests to better understand both the cognitive abilities and personality of prospective managers. The principle of historicity states that how a candidate has responded on a past job is indicative of how he or she will respond in a future job. The manager in the overseas venture must also be able to handle varying amounts of support staff, compared to his or her home-country counterparts. Also, because the overseas ventures normally contain a mix of expatriate and third-party national managers, a global entrepreneur must keep in mind the need to interview both spouses when determining if the overseas position fits with the candidate. As the global entrepreneur builds his or her overseas workforce, particular attention needs to be paid to compensation of the international manager, including maintaining the same base pay between the home-country managers and host-country managers while also covering relocation costs and perhaps offering a foreign service premium. Once the best managers have been selected by the global entrepreneur, providing the proper training is fundamental to the manager's success in the overseas venture. Finally, the global entrepreneur must provide the visionary leadership to inspire, teach, and guide his or her managers and make the company a success.

Questions for Discussion

1. Why would an expatriate manager be better in one situation but a host-country manager better in another?

2. What traits in a manager make him or her a good candidate for a foreign assignment?

3. What components, besides salary, are important parts of a compensation package for an expatriate assignment?

4. How can you train and prepare a manager for a role in a different country?

Chapter Exercises

1. Imagine that you are leading a small company and need to find someone to handle your operations in the new market that you are entering. What characteristics are the most desirable for this employee to have? Why?

2. What are the advantages and disadvantages of relying on an expatriate, a third-country national, an inpatriate, or a home-country national to oversee your operations in a new market?

3. Choose one of the management styles and analyze how that style works well for a multicountry operation.

References

Bagri, A. (2005, May 26). Published with permission of *The Smart Manager* at Rediff.com. Retrieved October 6, 2008, from www.rediff.com/cms/print.jsp?docpath=//money/2005/may/26spec2.htm

Suggested Readings

ARTICLES

Engardio, P. (2007, August 20). A guide for multinationals: One of the great challenges for a multinational is learning how to build a productive global team. *BusinessWeek*, (4047), 48.
This article discusses the need for multinational corporations to provide better coordination and collaboration across their globally dispersed workforces. With the ultimate goal of creating superfast, efficient organizations, multinationals must essentially undergo a management revolution that recognizes the move away from hierarchical, single outfits to fluid organizations with shifting networks of suppliers and workers.

Larson, M. (2006). U.S. employers' international expansion raising demand for overseas background checks. *Workforce Management, 85*(11), 43–44.
After 9/11, the need for candidate screening has dramatically increased. Companies are using background checks on foreign applicants for domestic and international jobs to reduce the potential for security, legal, and financial risk. Background checking services are growing in countries and markets targeted by U.S. companies.

Mendenhall, M. E. (2006). The elusive, yet critical challenge of developing global leaders. *European Management Journal, 24*(6), 422–429.
This article describes the necessary competencies that are vital to developing global leaders. Addressing the need of senior executives to have effective global leadership training programs, the article also provides senior executives with tools to measure the competencies needed and then create a training program.

Smilansky, J. (2007). *Developing executive talent: Best practices from global leaders.* **San Francisco: Jossey-Bass.**

Identifying, developing, and effectively utilizing executive talent is a key activity and concern of many large businesses in the United States and Europe. No single company has a perfect talent management process, and each company will develop its own approach based on its stage of development, environment, and level of commitment. *Developing Executive Talent* helps companies identify their own approaches to talent management compared to other business while also offering alternatives processes for identifying and developing tomorrow's leaders.

Stidham, R., Jr. (2006, July). Selecting the "right" path to global development. *Franchising World, 38*(7), 67–70.

International expansion strategies, including international corporate expansion and international master franchising, face numerous problems and issues as they are developed and executed. The success of a company's international expansion relies on its ability to hire and retain key international staff who will support the mission.

(2007). Training for success in emerging markets: Innovative HR a key to unlocking Far East success. *Strategic Direction, 23*(9), **36–38.** Retrieved from www.emeraldinsight.com/Insight/viewContentItem.do?contentType= Article&contentId=1621659

Ensuring performance in emerging markets is a challenge to many western companies that have not been able to reach their operational and revenue goals even in countries like China and India. Key business areas, as explained in the "Innovation in Emerging Markets" report from Deloitte's Global Manufacturing Industry Group, must be addressed: risk management, organizational structure, and talent and HR management strategy in each market. In particular, the talent and HR strategy must place more emphasis on nonmonetary rewards and recognition, career advancement, and training instead of just relying on compensation.

WEB SITES

Society for Human Resource Management Web site. Retrieved October 6, 2008, from www.shrm.org/global/

The Society for Human Resource Management (SHRM) is comprised of over 205,000 individual members with 550 affiliated chapters in more than 100 countries. Founded in 1948, the association provides comprehensive resources to HR professionals and advances the human resource profession and its vital role in creating and implementing organizational strategy.

11 Implementing and Managing a Global Entrepreneurial Strategy

---

Profile: Reinhold Wurth

Reinhold Wurth likes setting targets. For more than 5 decades, one of Germany's best-known entrepreneurs has driven growth at Wurth—the world's largest seller of screws, nuts, bolts, and other fasteners—by setting daunting 10-year goals for workers.

Wurth made DM 1.4 billion in revenues and came up with a bold prediction: by 2000 the German group would make DM 10 billion. "Workers looked at me like I was mad," he says. But when the accounts closed in early 2000, Wurth had hit the number.

Mr. Wurth, 72, has sustained an entrepreneurial spirit in the company despite it being based in one of the most basic industries in the world: selling fasteners and other products to workshops around the world. His formula has been a simple business model, the early pursuit of internationalization, and a focus on innovation to repel the threat of low-cost competitors.

Wurth has enjoyed a compound annual growth rate of 25% since he took over from his father in 1954. In 2008 it is on target to make EUR 9.4 billion (US$14.3 billion)."When you think we don't sell anything high-tech—just screws, dowel pins, and machine tools—it is a little astounding," says Mr. Wurth, who still owns the company but has stepped back from day-to-day management.

Mr. Wurth's business story began at the age of 14, when he left school to start an apprenticeship at the company his father had just founded. Five years later, on his father's death, he found himself in charge of two other workers. In his first full year the business grew by 20% and has never looked back. The company now employs 63,000 people worldwide. Mr. Wurth, meanwhile, became a professor of entrepreneurship at the University of Karlsruhe and a prominent business figure in Germany, with a penchant for Harley-Davidsons and collecting modern art.

Wurth's innovative business model was based on outsourcing before the word was coined. Instead of making its own products, the company would get suppliers to do it instead and then market them under the Wurth brand. The key, Mr. Wurth says, is a focus on being the best. "Quality beats price is our motto," states Mr. Wurth in an office adorned with modern art at the company's headquarters in the rural southern German town of Kunzelsau. "We never went into low-cost, as our customers would never have understood it. His earliest obstacle was simply finding the products. Germany was in its post-World War II boom and it was difficult to keep up with demand. "It was sometimes harder to buy the products than to sell them," he says.

Mr. Wurth relied from the beginning on an army of salesmen—now with more than 30,000, the largest full-time employed salesforce in the world—to create relationships with professional customers such as mechanics and small workshops. To this day the average sale at Wurth is for just five items with a value of about EUR 200, but there are 20,000 such orders daily.

Mr. Wurth spotted an opportunity to expand the business abroad and opened a subsidiary in the Netherlands in 1962. Today Wurth has 400 subsidiaries in 86 countries from Costa Rica to Indonesia. "We went international before the word 'globalization' even existed," he says. Wurth operates in what he calls a "polypoly" (in contrast to an oligopoly) in that his main competitors are the hundreds of thousands of local companies supplying workshops with material. "In this scenario it is not so difficult to win market share. We don't need any market studies from McKinsey or the like to help us," he says.

Wurth's market share is 5% in Germany and less abroad; Mr. Wurth believes it can always be improved and woe betide any manager who disputes his targets: "In a recession demand on screws goes down by maybe 2%, but we can gain market share. Nobody in this company is allowed to talk about the economy or recession as excuses."

In his view, low-cost competitors, such as those in China, cannot compete with Wurth because they fail to provide the quality small workshops need. Even if they could, he adds, they would not enjoy the close relationship a Wurth salesperson cultivates with his or her customers. And the Internet has yet to damage the model; mechanics still prefer to see a human face than to order their products over the Web.

Mr. Wurth says he learned his entrepreneurial skills on the job—"my university was life"—but confesses he devoured management and economics books from an early age. One of his favorites is von Clausewitz's *On War*: "Von Clausewitz writes that if you have to defend a fortress of the empire and you are surrounded by enemies you should send out a minor part of your troops to engage the enemy as far away as possible to enable the rest of your troops time to prepare."

Mr. Wurth put this into practice to defend his business of selling to professional customers—a highly profitable market. He started by selling bulk industry products to large manufacturers, a lower margin business and one he didn't care much about. "But it kept our competitors very busy so that they didn't even entertain the idea of going to our main customers," he recounts with glee.

Not everything has been smooth sailing. In the early 1970s he had to close Wurth Bau, the construction subsidiary he had built, with a loss of DM 10 million and 250 workers. Despite not being directly involved, he went to see the workers himself and afterward found new jobs for nearly all of them. "Even though I wasn't involved I took political responsibility for it. People know that when Mr. Wurth says he has to close (a plant), he has looked at all other options," he says.

Mr. Wurth espouses a broader belief that innovation and efficiency can only thrive when employees are given the freedom to make decisions. Divisions at Wurth operate with an unusual degree of latitude, a decision he says has paid off: "The more successful the worker is, the more freedom he or she receives. It is one of the strengths of this company that we can run it in a decentralized manner, but if something goes wrong we switch to centralized mode immediately—be it helping an individual or a country." When trouble looms, task forces are sent out straightaway to assess the problem. This happened recently when dozens of employees in Canada left the company for no apparent reason.

Mr. Wurth's long-term aim is a desire to give all workers a vision they can share. But it comes with strings attached, in this case an eye-watering target of EUR 22.5 billion in revenues by 2017. "If the management doesn't think that a company can grow by 15%–20%, then it won't happen," he says. "The balance sheet is just a mirror of how management thinks. I happen to believe any company that doesn't grow by 10% annually is sick."

Cash bonuses, flights, and art galleries keep workers inspired. Worker motivation is a pet topic of Reinhold Wurth. He says that when there are rumors of workers being unmotivated, in 95% of cases it is because they have nothing to do. He adds, "It is like children in a sandbox. They are angry because they have nothing to do until you bring along a Lego box and then they are happy. It is the same for people of 30, 40, or 50. People need to have challenges."

He believes in rewarding managers when they have worked hard. This ranges from the commonplace—every worker at Wurth's logistics centre in Kunzelsau received a EUR 65 bonus in January as revenues in Germany rose by 8% to EUR 94 million—to the extravagant—every 2 years the top workers and their spouses are flown to a different location for conferences and sightseeing (the next is in South Africa).

Motivational initiatives extend beyond work to art galleries in various national headquarters filled with work bought by Mr. Wurth, who has amassed one of the largest modern art collections in Germany with 11,000 works (Milne, 2008).

www.wurth.com/

Chapter Objectives

1. To analyze the various organizational structures that best meet the needs of the enterprise.

2. To determine what some decision-making structures are and understand how they can affect various businesses.

3. To determine the need for performance evaluation and benchmarking as relevant techniques for controlling a venture.

4. To recognize the balance between local and global control of operations for an entrepreneurial enterprise.

5. To understand global organizational structures and the benefits and drawbacks of each.

6. To learn how to control the global venture and the measurements and evaluations needed to do this.

Introduction

The recent changes in the world marketplace have been rapid and significant. National leaders are becoming increasingly irrelevant as most countries move toward market-oriented economics. Competition is at a very high level with companies needing to remain competitive by matching or preempting competitive moves. There is a growing scale and mobility in the world's capital markets. Given these opportunities and challenges in the global marketplace, it is imperative that the global entrepreneur establish a strategic planning process to match the products of the venture with less available markets and maximize the employment of company resources to strengthen the long-term competitive advantage of the venture.

Global Strategic Planning

The global strategic planning process has basically the following three stages, which do not have to be done sequentially: (1) developing the core global strategy; (2) developing the global program; and (3) implementing and controlling the global effort.

DEVELOPING THE CORE GLOBAL STRATEGY

The global strategic plan starts with a clear definition of the business model and the core strategy of the venture. An assessment of the realities of the global market and its economics usually produces a modification of both of these. Because establishing a global strategy on a country-by-country basis does not produce a clear strategy and optimal results, the global entrepreneur should start this process by first identifying the underlying forces that affect his or her business success in the global marketplace. Planning across a broad range of markets balances the risks and resource requirements and develops a long-term position for profitability. To develop this type of plan one must understand the common features of consumer requirements and buying processes as well as competition.

The resources of the venture must also be taken into account to determine the capacity for creating and sustaining a competitive position in the global marketplace. Although deep pockets are not a necessity, a realistic view of the costs and a long-term time frame of at least 5 years are important. Often the needed human resources also must be addressed.

Key decisions need to be made about the nature of the competitive strategy for market entrance and about which market(s) to enter. Two basic strategies are available: cost leadership and differentiation. When employing a cost leadership strategy, the global entrepreneur plans to offer a very similar product or service at a lower cost than competitors. This strategy does not imply that his or her product is a commodity, but rather that the venture has some efficiencies that allows the product to be offered at a lower price. A differentiation strategy focuses on some unique aspect of the product or service (its unique selling proposition) that clearly separates it from competitive products presently on the market. One hybrid strategy for global market entrance and expansion is to combine a strong differentiation strategy with cost containment. This can be facilitated through economies of scale of both production and marketing activities.

The country market choice, previously discussed in Chapter 5, is also important because it serves as a vehicle for market entrance and expansion. This decision takes into account internal strengths of the venture as measured by resources available, market share, product fit, contribution margin, and country attractiveness as measured by market size and growth rate, degree of competition, and the economic and political environment of the country. Combining the original country market choice and the internal strengths of the company as well as possible synergies for expansion and future market entries provides a solid strategy for the global venture. Care must be taken to insure that there are sufficient company resources for the expansion, which was not the case for GU Sports.

GU Sports (Sports Street Marketing) was founded in Berkeley, California, in the early 1990s by Dr. William Vaughan. The mission from day one was to provide athletes the best exercise-specific nutrition products available.

After formulating the world's first energy bar, Dr. Vaughan was disappointed that the bar, due to its high level of fat, fiber, and protein, did not work for athletes while they were training and racing. "How can we call it an energy bar for athletes when all it does is shut down the system for 45 minutes or so while the body digests all those useless-to-athletes ingredients?" asked a frustrated Dr. Vaughan. So in the late 1980s, he began experimenting with carbohydrates in gel form. Because gels did not require any ingredients for solidity (fat, fiber, and protein) they could transport energy to working muscles within minutes without any stomach distress. The perfect food for athletes during workouts, training, and racing was invented. After extensive testing and trial use by all types of athletes, GU Energy Gel was perfected in 1991 (www.gusports.com). The 1- or 1½-ounce foil packets of gel offer carbohydrates combined with electrolytes, sodium, and amino acids that quickly dissolve into the bloodstream.

Sold primarily through specialty shops or online to top high-endurance competitors, GU needs to enter the mainstream consumer market to reach other athletes preparing for triathlons, marathons, and other adventure sports. Malik (2006) reports that in the increasingly competitive landscape of energy-gel sales, GU Sports finds itself in an entrepreneurial predicament: It needs bigger sports-nutrition rivals to grow the market, while still keeping its dominance in the niche.

GU is not able to launch a campaign to bring the gels into the mass market and educate consumers about its product due to limited financial resources. Ideally, bigger rivals with greater financial resources would expand the market without taking GU's market share. "With US$15 million in U.S. gel sales expected, GU currently has a strong hold on the market with a 50% share, followed by PowerBar® (acquired by food giant Nestlé SA in 2000) with 35%, and Clif Bar Inc., also based in Berkeley, with 15%, according to Matt Powell, analyst at industry data source SportsOneSource" (Malik, 2006).

Nestlé has increased distribution and marketing campaigns for PowerBar Gels, which GU's Will Garratt, Jr. feels will "definitely help create a better awareness" to the general public (Malik, 2006). However, this type of market expansion has both potential and risks for a small company such as GU.

GU is taking many steps to remain competitive with the larger companies, including developing new products with different tastes. With 25 employees, it manufactures its own product in a 6-hour process that produces 18,000 units selling for US$1.25 each. Approximately 90% of its sales are in the United States, but other countries where its product is gaining popularity include South America, South Africa, Australia, and New Zealand. According to Garratt, the company's gel sales have increased about 20% in each of the past 5 years along with the gel market, but with increased competition, it has had to fight a lot more for the same growth by increasing spending on advertising and sponsorships (Malik, 2006).

DEVELOPING THE GLOBAL PROGRAM

Once the core global strategy is established, the overall global program needs to be developed and implemented. Actually, this piece of the process occurs in parallel with the strategy formulation. Although the core product or technology used to produce the product may be standardized, the product or service itself needs to reflect local market conditions to the extent possible. Localization is particularly needed in the marketing program. The overall marketing plan and position needs to be global, but the tactical elements of the plan should be market-specific—very localized. Production, customer service activities, and warehousing should be concentrated as much as possible to obtain any cost savings rather than being present in each country. Frequently, the resources in one global market are used to fight competitive advances in other global markets to maintain the venture's competitive advantage.

IMPLEMENTING AND CONTROLLING THE GLOBAL EFFORT

Successful global entrepreneurs understand the need to balance local and global concerns. Local differences need to be taken into account when standardizing programs and policies by the headquarters. As much autonomy as possible should be given to the local country organization. Overstandardization and inflexibility in planning and implementation are probably the two biggest problems in executing the global program. Good local market research will ensure that the product launch in a specific country reflects the characteristics of the market conditions in that country. Without this, the launch could fail. On the other hand, too much local customization can cause the venture to lose its overall global position. A successful global entrepreneur carefully balances local needs and overall global strategy. This means that neither headquarters nor local country managers are entirely in charge. Without the local managers and their commitment, no global program can be successful.

This success in part depends on the free flow of information between each country and headquarters as well as among country organizations themselves. In this way, ideas are exchanged and the overall venture and its values are strengthened. This can also be accomplished through periodic meetings of the global managers or worldwide conferences.

Any personnel interchange facilitates this. The more experience each manager has in working with others from different nationalities, the better the integration and working relationships become. Managers become familiar with different markets and people. This is particularly important for managers at headquarters, who will then become more sensitive in developing and implementing global policies. Once a global strategy or program has been developed, it is usually better to permit local managers to develop and implement their own specific local programs within specified parameters and subject to approval. This develops a spirit of cooperation and trust that does not occur when local managers are forced to strictly adhere to the global strategy.

This also prevents the not-invented-here syndrome from occurring that can accompany local resistance and imitation. The global entrepreneur can take some proactive actions as well to help minimize the occurrence of this syndrome. One good way is to make sure that local managers participate in the development of the venture's global strategies and programs. Another way is to give local managers a discretionary budget that they can use to respond to local competition and customer needs. A final way is to encourage local managers to submit ideas for consideration at the corporate level. Establishing this balance between headquarters and local country managers along with the right organizational structure, the topic of the next section, allows the global entrepreneur to establish a truly global culture that favors no specific country and has managers with a global mindset.

SUSTAINABILITY

One key issue that needs to be addressed in the global venture is sustainability. Al Gore's book, *An Inconvenient Truth*, and Hurricane Katrina stimulated consumer interest in the sustainability movement, making it a significant global concern for organizations all over the world that are attempting to integrate it into their strategic visions.

The level of concern about sustainability and the greening of the environment vary by country. In countries like Germany, where the population density is much higher than the United States, consumers have become concerned about environmental concepts much faster than the United States in part because of government mandates. Even though there are these degrees of concern, the number of unconcerned people is getting smaller and smaller in every country in the world.

Endorsing green movements as well as the issues of sustainability makes a global venture more profitable, often even in the short run. Sustainability can be about making money. Dial Corporation is producing concentrated detergents to reduce packaging wastes. Intel Corporation is developing microchips that cut the amount of energy wasted in home electronics. Arizona Public Service encourages employees to shut down energy wasting computer monitors when they are not in use. Wal-Mart is examining hybrid-diesel trucks for its massive fleet.

Global Organizational Structure

As a venture moves from a totally domestic orientation to a global one, its organizational structure must change to reflect the new orientation. The organizational structure will vary depending on the stage of internationalization of the venture. The type of organization that is appropriate is one that facilitates the development of worldwide strategies while maintaining flexibility in implementing at the local market level. This concept is captured in the phrase "organize to think and plan globally but act locally."

Overall Organizational Structure

Important factors in choosing and implementing a specific organizational structure are the focus of decision making (where decision-making authority within the organization will occur), the roles of the different entities in the organization, the needed coordination and communication, and the needed controls. These factors are the basis for the global entrepreneur's decision to use one of the following three organizational approaches: (1) little emphasis on the international activities of the venture; (2) recognizing the ever-growing importance of the international activities occurring; and (3) being a truly global organization with no domestic/international split.

In the early stage of international activity, these actions are usually coordinated by domestic operations. Because they tend to be of such a small size, they really have no effect on the organizational structure of the venture. Often the transactions are actually facilitated through the use of entities outside the organization, such as an export management company or a freight forwarder as discussed in Chapter 7. As international sales increase and become more important to the venture, these are often separated from domestic sales in a separate entity such as an export department in the overall organizational structure. This is the first step toward internationalizing the venture. At this stage any international licensing activity takes place in the research and development and legal areas. The faster the growth in international sales, the more quickly the export department becomes obsolete. The amount of coordination and control needed necessitates the need for a more formal international organizational structure, which often results in the establishment of an international division.

The international division centralizes all the non-home country activities of the venture to better serve the global customers. While this division focuses on international activities by overseeing and having authority over the sales and information about the market and other market opportunities, manufacturing and other functional activities remain in the domestic division. To avoid conflict, coordination between the divisions is necessary. This coordination is often achieved through a joint staff that interacts regularly to discuss problems and develop the strategic plans for the venture.

As the international sales grow in size, diversity, and complexity, the international division tends to also become obsolete, requiring a new organizational structure to be implemented. There are several structural forms available as discussed in the following section.

TYPES OF ORGANIZATIONAL STRUCTURES

There are several types of global organizational structures available for implementation by the global entrepreneur. These include area structure, customer structure, product structure, mixed structure, or the matrix structure. The *global area structure* is a widely used approach that uses geographical areas as its basis. For example, one U.S. entrepreneurial company organizes its activities into four areas: Asia-Pacific, Europe, North America, and South America. No preference is given to the headquarters in the United States, as staff for each of the areas support and monitor the activities and develop the companywide global strategy. The increased use of the global area structure has been caused by regionalization activities, such as NAFTA and the European Union. The area approach aligns itself well with the marketing concept because each area has similar characteristics and can be given concentrated marketing attention. It works particularly well for those entrepreneurial ventures that have narrow product lines with similar end users and uses. When there are many diverse product lines or diverse end users and uses, the global area approach may not be the best one to employ. The areas can be designated on the basis of cultural similarity, such as Asia, or historical connections between the countries such as the Balkans.

The *global customer structure* is used when the customer groups served are dramatically different. This is often called verticals. Customer groups include consumer, government, and industrial. Another more specific group would be along the lines of industry such as the automobile industry, the printing industry, and the mining industry. Even though the products to each customer group may be similar or even the same, the buying process is so different that a specific marketing and service approach is needed. Some groups may require industry specialists.

The *global product structure* is the organizational form most often used by global entrepreneurs. This approach places the responsibility for global activities in each product area. This approach allows improved cost efficiency through the centralization of manufacturing. It is used almost always by consumer-product firms where the world market share of a product helps determine its competitive position. The global product structure balances functional input to the product with the ability to quickly respond to any specific product problems. This allows for each product to be adapted to the extent needed for each foreign market. Coordination between the product groups in each market is essential as well as hiring managers who have adequate country market experience. Otherwise, duplication can occur and confusion arises among the customers, particularly when a customer buys multiple products from the venture.

The *mixed global structure*, as the name implies, uses two or more of the above mentioned global structures, providing significant attention to the area, customer, and/or product. It is often used in a transition period following a merger or acquisition or before implementing the final global organizational structure—the global matrix structure.

The *global matrix structure* is a complex structure adopted mainly by large entrepreneurial corporations for planning and controlling many independent businesses, resources, and geographic areas. A worldwide business unit may be practical for information systems or automotive aftermarket products. The matrices developed vary in the number of dimensions and allow for better cooperation between business managers, product managers, and area managers. Because most managers report to at least two people, problems can easily develop and numerous conflicts occur. Often even minor problems have to be solved through committee discussion, which seriously reduces the reaction time of a venture. This is particularly a problem in today's hypercompetitive environment, which requires a quick response time. Some companies using a matrix organization have changed to one of the other four global organizational structures: area, customer, product, or mixed.

Authority and Global Decisions

Although the organizational structure is important, it does not necessarily indicate where the authority for decision making and control resides. This is a critical decision for the global entrepreneur and can be referred to as the degree of centralization of the venture. Many global entrepreneurs prefer a high degree of centralization in which all the strategic decisions are made at headquarters (often by them) and the controls are tight. Sometimes this high degree of centralization occurs in some functions such as finance, human resources, and research and development, while in other functions, such as marketing, it does not. The more autonomy each global structural unit is given and the lighter the controls, the more decentralized the venture becomes. Here the information flow between the structural units is financial because each is considered a profit center.

The more a venture is decentralized, the better able its global units can market effectively and react quickly at the local level. This encourages a high level of participation at the local level and usually results in a much higher corporate morale.

Because a high degree of decentralization seriously modifies the control aspect of headquarters, some companies are now using coordinated decentralization. In this hybrid model, the overall company strategy is developed at headquarters and each global structural unit is allowed to adjust and implement this strategy within agreed upon parameters.

Controlling the Global Venture

In today's hypercompetitive environment, it is imperative that the global venture establish a system for evaluating the performance and controlling the venture. Part of this system would be internal and external benchmarking. External benchmarking, when the data is available, allows the global entrepreneur to evaluate his or her performance against competitors of similar size in the same industry. The problem is that frequently the data is not available to do this.

Every venture, however, can regularly do internal benchmarking. This provides needed information for control purposes and for sharing best practices throughout the company. This knowledge transfer is most important for growing a truly global organization.

The control of both the outputs of the international activities (sales, production, profits, growth) and behavior (culture, employee behavior, management capabilities) can be accomplished through either bureaucratic, formalized control or cultural control.

FORMALIZED VERSUS CULTURAL CONTROL

While formalized control relies on rules and regulations that indicate the needed level of output, cultural controls rely on shared beliefs and expectations of personnel in the venture. A formalized control system relies on a standardized budget, reporting system, and policy manuals. The budget and reporting system is the major control mechanism for a local country operation and establishes the nature of the relationship between these local entities and headquarters. As much uniformity as possible should occur without sacrificing the ability of local country units to grow and respond in a timely manner. Establishing the appropriate manuals for each major function facilitates uniformity and reduces report preparation time.

When emphasizing the values and culture of the venture, or cultural control, evaluations are based on the extent to which there is a fit between the individual or entity and the norms. This requires extensive informal personal interaction and training on the corporate culture and the way things are done. Sound cultural control requires that good selection and training programs are established in the venture. Regardless of the positioning on the formalized, cultural continuum, it is important for the global entrepreneur to understand and use some control techniques as discussed in the next section.

CONTROL TECHNIQUES

There are several useful performance measures: financial performance, personnel performance, and quality performance. Financial performance of a local country operation is based on sales, profit, and return on investment (ROI). Profit is affected by management capabilities as well as external, uncontrollable factors, such as currency value and exchange rates. If a local country's currency value decreases (devaluation), sales will increase because the price of the products will be lower for foreign buyers. The opposite occurs when the currency increases.

Control using personnel performance as a measure needs to be done periodically. This appraisal of each manager's output and behavior is done differently in different cultural settings. Turnover among global managers should be minimized, but no turnover may indicate that evaluations are too infrequent or standards and expectations are too low. The last control technique, based on quality performance, makes sure the goods and services and the operation of the local country unit and headquarters are at the highest possible level of quality. This can occur through the use of total quality management techniques, quality circles, and employee reward and recognition systems. A well run global venture will employ performance measures in each of these three areas to ensure that a proper control system is operational.

About 5 years ago, Stef Wertheimer came across Gamila Hiar, a Druze woman with no formal education who had learned the ancient art of making soap from wild herbs and olive oil as a child. She was supplementing her family's income by producing about 500 soap bars a week from a corner room underneath her house in Pqi'in, a village in the Galilee region of northern Israel. Wertheimer was impressed. "We found that she was an entrepreneur," says Wertheimer. "She just needed more space to dry her soaps. I asked her if she wanted to come to one of my industrial parks."

Hiar, now 68, ended up at Tefen Industrial Park, a bold philanthropic enterprise located about 8 miles from the Lebanese border. Wertheimer, the founder of Iscar Metalworking, established Tefen in 1985 to encourage entrepreneurship in one of Israel's most undeveloped and low-income regions with a population split largely between Arabs and Jews. According to Wertheimer, "There are no unemployed, only people who are unlucky to find a job."

The Tefen model is based on a business and social incubator concept. In a country with few natural resources and a tiny domestic market, its purpose is to help develop businesses that manufacture for export. Start-ups are given space to rent and a number of business and administrative services. Although many of the companies are small, the park's structure allows each firm to operate and export on a much larger scale than it could were it operating independently.

Gamila Secret occupies a 12,916 square-foot facility within Tefen's 30-acre campus and produces some 15,000 bars of soap a day. The company employs about 20 workers, all of whom come from Gamila's home village of Pqi'in. The company, managed by Gamila's two sons, Fuad and Imad, generates roughly US$8.4 million in sales in 20 countries including Japan, Germany, and Great Britain. Fuad expects sales to triple by 2009 and is looking to begin distribution in the United States (Perman, 2008).

Managing Chaos

Chaos and change are two dimensions of every global entrepreneurial venture. Change is an opportunity as well as a challenge for global entrepreneurs who can live with chaos. The scale and complexity of change and chaos are even greater for global entrepreneurs than their domestic counterparts, particularly in today's hypercompetitive business environment. To understand change and be better able to manage chaos, it is important for the entrepreneur to understand the dynamics that occur according to Prigogine's concept of far-from-equilibrium dynamics, Heisenberg's Uncertainty Principle, and Zadeh's fuzzy logic.

Ilya Prigogine's concept of far-from-equilibrium dynamics reflects his comprehensive and judicious understanding of the history of science (Prigogine & Stengers, 1984). He felt that the paradigm of Newton, particularly its treatment of change and chaos, does not apply to many important phenomena. According to Prigogine, while the state of a system stabilizes around its equilibrium, fluctuations disturb this equilibrium, making its behavior unpredictable before the system returns to equilibrium and becomes predictable again. While this is true for some systems, many common and important systems are so far-from-equilibrium that they can be destructive. Still some order forms at the edge of chaos. In those conditions the process of self-organization can form and proliferate, not by imposing order into the chaos, but by negotiating it and creating a new complex form of order.

Heisenberg's Uncertainty Principle proposes that it is not possible to measure with equal precision the position and the momentum of a quantum element (Heisenberg, 1950). Although mainly applicable to the quantum world, it also applies to the macroworld of organizations when the position and movement are interdependent and change rapidly and unpredictably, sometimes resulting in things becoming the opposite when at the extreme. The new resulting position and momentum cannot be predicted from the previous states of each, making uncertainty more the norm in most systems.

Zadeh views this dynamic through fuzzy logic in which categories are opposites and multivalent (Zadeh & Yager, 1987). Both Z and not Z can coexist to some degree according to Zadeh, particularly as the complexity of the system increases. In these cases, managers do not have the ability to make precise and relevant statements and predictions until a threshold is reached. "It is then that fuzzy statements are the only bearers of meaning and relevance." Fuzzy logic provides an understanding to change for managers when they do not attempt to achieve absolute precision.

These three principles, as well as the art of managing chaos, are illustrated particularly well in the cases of Google and Enron. Larry Page and Sergey Brin, Google's founders, introduced the concept on Stanford's internal Web site in 1996, and Google was a commercial enterprise by 1998. With more than 50% of the world's Internet users using Google as their search engine, no wonder the company is worth more than US$35 billion and handles more transactions every day than the combination of the New York, London, Frankfurt, and Paris stock exchanges. Google embraces chaos, and profits from it with a work environment employees call the "Google way of working," where mistakes are viewed as tools for learning and employees are encouraged to come up with outrageous ideas. The informal environment—there is no dress code or rules for behavior—recognizes that the most valuable resource of the company is the mind and thought processes of its employees. Google indeed thrives by managing this chaos.

Enron provides another classic example, in another perspective, of managing chaos (McLean & Elkind, 2003). At Enron, change was continuous, sometimes going as intended but more often than not producing paradoxical outcomes. The company was a constantly changing entity on an exponential growth curve that was accelerating over time. The change blurred boundaries, with the potential for great success and catastrophic losses coexisting for many years. Enron can be viewed from each one of the theoretical perspectives of managing chaos. It became a company driven by steeper and steeper growth curves and expectations and having to hit quarterly targets expected by Wall Street despite having a far-from-equilibrium world of distortions. This unmanaged chaos eventually led to illegal accounting practices and the company's bankruptcy.

Summary

This chapter focuses on the need for a global entrepreneur to define and execute a strategic plan, establish the best organizational structure, and use proper benchmarking and control techniques to realize the full potential of his or her company. The strategic plan is rarely established before the business is launched and is often a continuous work in progress in which the global entrepreneur uses numerous indicators to adjust and refine the strategy. The basis for the strategic plan lies in defining the core strategy of the venture through the careful examination of the underlying forces that affect the business' success in the global marketplace and the business' resources. Two basic strategies that can be employed are differentiation or cost leadership. Once the strategy has been chosen, the global entrepreneur institutes a global program in which he or she takes the standardized product and adapts it to the local market(s), taking into consideration the culture and mores of the particular locality. When developing the strategy and program, the global entrepreneur must beware of overstandardization and inflexibility. As the global venture grows, the entrepreneur normally will have to reorganize and adapt the organization to handle the greater demands of more markets or products. First the entrepreneur must address (1) how much to emphasize the international activities of the venture; (2) how much recognition the ever-growing importance of the international activities demand; and (3) what being a truly global organization with no domestic/international split entails. The answer to these questions will help the entrepreneur decide which type of organizational structures to use, such as global area structure, global customer structure, global product structure, global mixed structure, and global matrix structure. Finally, the global entrepreneur must establish whether a centralized or decentralized decision-making and control structure is best for the firm. The global entrepreneur must also evaluate financial performance, personnel performance, and quality performance to create benchmarks to measure the success of the firm. In addition to the output-focused measurements, the global entrepreneur must examine the effectiveness of company culture and employee behavior in reaching strategic goals.

Questions for Discussion

1. To what situations is a cost leadership strategy better suited? When might a differentiation strategy be better?

2. Describe the different organizational structures and at what stage in the venture they might be best for an entrepreneurial enterprise.

3. How does organizational control change as a venture achieves more success in a foreign market?

Chapter Exercises

1. Find articles about a company that attributes its success to meeting the goals set forth in its strategic plan. What is the company's core strategy? Identify its indicators of success beyond profitability.

2. Suppose you are the owner of a successful electric-powered, environment-friendly scooter company and plan to launch your product in India. Pick either the cost leadership or differentiation strategy and explain how you bring the scooter to India. Will you have to alter the design at all? What difficulties could the Indian market pose, and how will your strategic plan deal with them?

3. Create a table listing the common organizational structures for a global firm and find examples of multinational companies that use each type of structure.

4. Discuss with a partner the best way to lead a global firm. Which method is better—formalized or cultural leadership? Why?

References

Emerald Group Publishing Limited. (2007, June 26). Googling out of control: Can Google's chaos management style ensure continuing success? *Strategic Decision, 23*(8), 25–27. Retrieved October 29, 2008, from www.emeraldinsight .com/Insight/viewContentItem.do?contentType=Article&contentId=1611071

Heisenberg, W. (1950). *The physical principles of the Quantum Theory.* New York: Dover.

Malik, N. S. (2006, November 13). Risky business: GU Sports could benefit from Nestle Energy Gels, but competition stiffens. Reprinted from *The Wall Street Journal: Monday Extra.* Retrieved October 29, 2008, from http:// wsjclassroomedition.com/monday/mx_06nov13.pdf

McLean, B., & Elkind, P. (2003). *The smartest guys in the room: The amazing rise and scandalous fall of Enron.* New York: Portfolio.

Milne, R. (2008, March 4). The nuts and bolts of growth. *Financial Times,* 1.

Perman, S. (2008, March 14). An entrepreneurial path to peace. Retrieved October 6, 2008, from www.businessweek.com/smallbiz/content/mar2008/ sb20080313_861884.htm

Prigogine, I., & Stengers, I. (1984). *Order out of chaos: Man's new dialogue with nature.* New York, NY: Bantam.

Zadeh, L. A., & Yager, R. R. (1987). *Fuzzy sets and applications: Selected papers.* New York: Wiley.

Suggested Readings

ARTICLES

Le Mesurier, K. (2006, February 16). Global ambition. *BRW, 28*(6), 58–59.

Having a global expansion plan at the beginning of a business process gives small enterprises distinct advantages. Executives from a digital arts industry-focused publishing house used this global expansion strategy when they created an online Web site for the Computer Graphics Society. Instead of using traditional exporting channels such as retailers, the Web site allowed them to sell directly to customers worldwide.

Porter, M. E. (2006). What is strategy? *Harvard Business Review,* Nov./Dec. 2006, *74*(6), 61–78.

Michael E. Porter's article, "What is Strategy?" carefully explains the differences between enhanced operational effectiveness and a viable, adaptable strategy, which is the true basis of sustained profitability and competitive advantage. Operational effectiveness is a company's ability to perform a particular, single activity better than its rivals. Strategic positioning and strategy, on the other hand, focuses on how to perform different activities than your rivals or how to carry out the same activities in a different way. The author also emphasizes how operational improvements through total quality management, benchmarking, partnering, and so forth will not necessarily create sustainable profitability, unless superior leadership is guiding the process.

Porter, M. E. (1990, March/April). The competitive advantage of nations. *Harvard Business Review, 68*(2), 73.

Using a 4-year, ten-nation study of the patterns of competitive success in leading trading countries, this article discusses how companies achieve success in international markets with innovation; how innovation is manifested; and the role of information in sustaining competitive advantage. It argues that contrary to the assumption that the role of the nation-state has declined with the rise of globalization, instead it plays a vital economic role today in making its companies competitive in the international market. It then describes the national diamond technique for evaluating national or regional strength within an industry using four forces: factor conditions; demand conditions; related and supporting industries; and company structure, strategy, and rivalry. The article also provides an example of the correct approach to globalization and whether government policies serve as catalysts or hindrances to business.

12 Global Family Business[1]

Ernesto J. Poza

Profile: María Luisa Ferré, Grupo Ferré Rangel

María Luisa Ferré, fourth-generation president of the Grupo Ferré Rangel, explains:

> Our success with continuity in this generation comes from learning from the failure of the second- and third-generation transitions. My father set out to do it differently, and he approached it very conscientiously with a lot of discipline, having learned in his generation that a group of entrepreneurially prone individuals without a coherent structure can get into a lot of trouble. (Personal conversation with the author, October 2005)

The Grupo Ferré Rangel is a media group operating in Puerto Rico and the U.S. mainland. In its fourth generation now, the company has 1,600 employees and US$300 million in annual revenues. *El Nuevo Día*, the flagship newspaper, enjoys 50% market share in the Puerto Rico public relations market and commands 80% of the newsprint advertising.

The first-generation business was a foundry. As the business grew, it added paper and cement to the mix. Over the generations, the company expanded to Florida, Panama, Cuba, and then lost some of those businesses—in some cases for political and economic reasons, in others because the businesses were mismanaged. In the 1960s the third-generation leader, Luis A. Ferré, entered politics and became the governor of Puerto Rico. Soon thereafter, the

---

1. From POZA. *Family Business*, 2E. ©2007 South-Western, a part of Cengage Learning, Inc. Reproduced by permission. www.cengage.com/permissions

company confronted a financial crisis that led to restructuring. When the company was split, some of the businesses, then owned by individual third-generation family branches, survived; others did not.

One of Luis A. Ferré's sons, Antonio L. Ferré, became the CEO of the Ferré family-controlled but NYSE-listed Puerto Rican Cement. For US$400,000 he also bought a little daily newspaper in Ponce, the southern-most city in Puerto Rico, from his father. The purchase of *El Día*, as it was named then, took place at a time when the northern and most populous city, San Juan, was controlled by two other newspapers, *El Mundo* and *El Imparcial*. *El Nuevo Día* took 80% market share in the most important market on the island, all in one generation! Antonio L. Ferré was clearly a third-generation leader with a mission.

Antonio, in collaboration with fourth-generation members of the family, continued to grow the company by launching a new newspaper in 1997. The paper, *Primera Hora*, is a *USA Today*-style newspaper. These two major papers plus a couple of smaller city newspapers, a Hispanic newspaper in Orlando, Florida, a printing company, an Internet company, a direct marketing company, and a recycling company now make up the Grupo Ferré Rangel.

To what does the next generation attribute the success that this family has had in preserving the company across four generations? The fourth generation, composed of three daughters and two sons, is entrepreneurial. With that recognition, fourth-generation siblings have dedicated themselves to building a coherent structure that will not stifle entrepreneurship but that will effectively govern the relationships between them. María Luisa also credits her father and her mother, Luisa Rangel, with promoting strong family unity coupled with unusual support for individual differences in this fourth generation. Perhaps because of the journalistic culture that runs in the family, the opinions of the individual children, however different, were constantly sought and appreciated as they grew up.

María Luisa continues, "as a fourth generation, we also fundamentally bought into the idea that we have to grow, experiment, create new business plans or we would end up becoming our own worst enemies." Zero-sum dynamics, the fourth generation recognizes, represent a powerful social field, particularly among naturally entrepreneurial and competitive siblings. And when the zero-sum dynamic gets played across family branches, gender, generations, and those active and inactive in management, continuity is threatened. Zero-sum dynamics refers to a win–lose outcome between two or more parties that nets out to a zero gain. In no-growth contexts the initial win–lose outcome degenerates into self-reinforcing cycles of lose–lose outcomes. When a union and management fight over contract issues to the point at which both employment and firm survival are put at risk, as we saw happen in both the steel and automotive industry in the United States in the 1980s, you can argue that a zero-sum dynamic has taken hold. The same can happen between branches of an extended family, between heirs of different genders, or between family members who are and are not employed in the family business.

María Luisa Ferré adds: "Our success in continuing the entrepreneurial spirit is a result of five professionals who know they complement, they need each other, to be successful. We respect each other and our differences. The siblings have selected me to lead them. So the major distinction between us and the previous generation is the sense of confidence that comes from knowing that we now have a coherent structure to govern the relation between people who are naturally entrepreneurial in nature."

Chapter Objectives

1. To gain an appreciation for the immense challenge that family business continually represents.

2. To promote understanding of the uniqueness of family business.

3. To explore the fundamental role of strategy and family communication in business continuity.

Introduction

Entrepreneurial companies often become family-owned businesses. While founder spouses may have done work on behalf of the new venture in the early stages, the real transition from an entrepreneurial to a family business typically happens when the sons and/or daughters of the company founder join the business as employees. The business may very well continue to be an entrepreneurial company and prefer to be known that way, concerned with the perception of nepotism and lack of professionalism often ascribed to family businesses. But once next generation members join the ranks of employees and/or shareholders, the nature of the firm changes, as do its challenges and unique competitive profile.

Family businesses are ubiquitous. Family-owned and family-controlled firms account for approximately 90% of all incorporated businesses in the United States, where approximately 17 million family firms (including sole proprietorships) operate (Astrachan & Carey, 1994). A full one-third of all *Fortune 500* companies are family-controlled, and about 60% of all publicly traded firms remain under family influence. Many family businesses are small, but there are approximately 138 billion-dollar family firms in the United States alone, with 19 such firms operating in France, 15 in Germany, 9 each in Italy and Spain, and 5 each in Canada and Japan

(Rottenberg, 2002). In the United States, family firms account for 64% of the gross domestic product or approximately US$6 trillion, 85% of private-sector employment, and about 86% of all jobs created in the past decade. One study also found that contrary to the prevalent stereotype of family businesses as nepotistic and conflict-ridden underperformers, family firms perform better than nonfamily firms. In fact, the study notes, 35% of the S&P 500 firms are family-controlled (with the families owning nearly 18% of their firms' outstanding equity). And these family-controlled firms out-performed management-controlled firms by 6.65% in return on assets during the past decade. Similar results were found regarding return on equity. Family firms were also responsible for creating an additional 10% in market value between 1992 and 2002, as compared with the 65% of the S&P firms that are management-controlled (Anderson & Reeb, 2003).

In another study, conducted in 2003 and involving a sample of 700 listed family businesses in Germany and France, firms in which families had significant influence and there was considerable overlap between ownership and management roles enjoyed appreciably improved financial performance. But when the family's representation in management far exceeded the cash flow rights emerging from their ownership stake, their performance suffered (Jaskiewicz, 2003).

In Spain, the performance of 8,000 large- and medium-sized family and nonfamily firms was compared based on 2002 data. Spanish family firms performed better in terms of return on equity than their nonfamily counterparts of the same size and in the same industry (Menéndez-Requejo, 2005).

A European study of six stock exchanges from London's FTSE to Spain's IBEX done by Thomson Financial and reported in *Newsweek* consistently found that family firms outperformed their counterparts in Europe (Miller, 2004).

In Latin America, a study of 175 firms traded in the Bolsa de Comercio de Santiago (Chile's principal stock exchange) compared the performance of 100 family firms with that of 75 nonfamily firms during the 10 years between 1994 and 2003 and found that family firms outperformed their counterparts in return on assets and return on equity. They also performed better in Tobin's Q, a proxy measure of market value creation during that period. In Chile a majority of the publicly traded firms (57%) were family-controlled (Martinez & Stohr, 2005).

Arguably, family businesses are the primary engine of economic growth and vitality in free economies all over the world. The contributions of family businesses to the global economy are summarized in Table 12.1.

On the downside, approximately 85% of all new businesses in the United States fail within their first 5 years of operation according to the National Federation of Independent Businesses. Among those that survive, only 30% are successfully transferred to the second generation of the

Table 12.1   Family Business: The Statistical Story

- Family businesses constitute 80%–98% of all businesses in the world's free economies.
- Family businesses generate 64% of the gross domestic product (GDP) in the United States.
- Family businesses generate more than 75% of the GDP in most other countries.
- Family businesses employ 80% of the U.S. workforce.
- Family businesses employ more than 85% of the working population around the world.
- Family businesses create 85% of all new jobs in the United States.
- A total of 37% of *Fortune 500* companies are family-controlled.
- Family business outperformance of nonfamily businesses: 6.65% in return on assets (ROA) and 10% in market value

SOURCES: Anderson, R. C., & Reeb, D. M. (2003). Founding family ownership and firm performance: Evidence from the S&P 500. *The Journal of Finance, 58*(3), 1301–1328.

Astrachan, J., & Carey, M. (1994). Family businesses in the United States economy. Paper presented to the Center for the Study of Taxation, Washington, D.C.

Beehr, T., Drexler, J., & Faulkner, S. (1997, May). Working in small family businesses: Empirical comparisons to nonfamily businesses. *Journal of Organizational Behavior, 18*(3), 297.

Daily, C., & Dollinger, M. (1992, June). An empirical examination of ownership structure in family and professionally managed firms. *Family Business Review, 5*(2), 117–136.

Dreux, D. (1990). Financing family business: Alternatives to selling out or going public. *Family Business Review, 3*(3), 225–243.

Gomez-Mejía, L., Larraza-Kintana, M., & Makri, M. (2003, April). The determinants of executive compensation in family-controlled public corporations. *Academy of Management Journal, 46*(2), 226–237.

Oster, S. (1999). *Modern competitive analysis*. New York: Oxford University Press.

founding-family owners. Not all family businesses that are not passed down to the next generation go on to close their doors, but many do. This high failure rate on continuity within the founding family amounts to the squandering of a significant opportunity for job and wealth creation in many communities.

And the odds get worse in the transition between the second and third generations, and the third and fourth generations, when only 12% and 4% of such businesses, respectively, remain in the same family (Ward, 1987). This seems to prove true the old adage "from shirtsleeves to shirtsleeves in three generations."

Yet, in the presence of widespread global hypercompetition, niche-focused family businesses providing high quality and great customer service are thriving. You might be surprised to learn that Smucker's, Perdue Farms, Gap, Levi Strauss, Hermés, Ferragamo, L.L. Bean, Mars, Femsa Carta Blanca, Bacardí, Hallmark, Fidelity Investments, Timken, LG Electronics, Samsung, Marriott, American Greetings, Ford Motor, BMW, Kohler, Roca, Carrefour, Nordstrom, Metro AG, SC Johnson, Bigelow Tea, *The New York Times*, *The Washington Post*, *El País*, and Wal-Mart are all family-owned or family-controlled. There are thousands of smaller and less well known, but just as successful, family-owned businesses—companies that build homes and office buildings, manufacture unique products, and provide custom services. These businesses are the backbone of most supply chains and distribution channels, and also are the retailers for much of what consumers buy.

What Constitutes a Family Business?

What do we mean by the term *family business*? Because of the variety of firm profiles, the definition has proven more elusive than you might think. Family businesses come in many forms: sole proprietorships, partnerships, limited liability companies, regular corporations, holding companies, and even publicly traded, albeit family-controlled, companies. That is why estimates of the number of family businesses operating in the U.S. economy range between 17 and 22 million. In the free economies of the world, estimates of the share of all enterprises considered to be family businesses range between 80%–98%.

Family businesses constitute the whole gamut of enterprises in which an entrepreneur or next-generation CEO and one or more family members significantly influence the firm via their participation, their ownership control, their strategic preferences, and the culture and values they impart to the enterprise.

Participation refers to the nature of the involvement of family members in the enterprise, whether as part of the management team, as board members, as shareholders, or as supportive members of the family foundation. *Control* refers to the rights and responsibilities family members derive from significant voting ownership and the governance of the agency relationship. *Strategic preferences* refers to the direction family members set for the enterprise through their participation in top management, consulting, the board of directors, shareholder meetings, or even family councils. *Culture* is the collection of values, defined by behaviors that become embedded in an enterprise, as a result of the leadership provided by family members, past and present. Family unity and the nature of the relationship between the family and the business also define this culture.

Ownership structure aside, what differentiates family businesses from management-controlled businesses are often the intentions, values, and strategy-influencing interactions of owners who are members of the same family or partnering families. The result is a unique blending of family, management, and ownership subsystems that form an entire family business system. This family–management–ownership interaction can produce significant adaptive capacity and competitive advantage. Or it can be the source of significant vulnerability in the face of generational or competitive change.

Thus, we arrive at a working definition of a family business. A family business is a unique synthesis of the following:

1. Ownership control (15% or higher in the case of a publicly-traded, family-controlled business or 50.1% in the case of a privately-held firm) by two or more members of a family or a partnership of families

2. Strategic influence by family members on the management of the firm, whether by being active in management, by continuing to shape the organization's culture, by serving as advisors or board members, or by being active shareholders

3. Concern for family relationships

4. The dream (or possibility) of family-business continuity across generations

Succession and Continuity in Family Companies

Family firms are unique in the extent to which succession planning assumes a key and very strategic role in the life of the ongoing concern. Because competitive success, family harmony, and ownership rents are all at stake at the same time in the one firm, carefully orchestrating the multiyear process represented by succession across generations of owner-managers is a priority. There are hundreds of reasons why organizations fail, but in family-owned and family-controlled companies, the most prevalent reason relates to a failure in succession planning. Whether the causal reason is incompetent or unprepared successors, unclear succession plans, a tired strategy that is unable to contain competitors, or family rivalries and bids for power, a successfully crafted succession process is the key to the family business' survival.

Without vision and leadership from members of two generations and the use of select family, management, and governance practices, the future is bleak for family-controlled enterprises. The blurring of boundaries among family membership, family management, and family ownership subjects family businesses to the potential for confusion, slow decision making, or even corporate paralysis. An inability to adapt to changes in the competitive marketplace or powerlessness to govern the relationship between the family and the business will ultimately undermine the enterprise. As a result, a family business that lacks multigenerational leadership and vision can hardly be positioned to retain the competitive advantages that made it successful in a previous, often more entrepreneurial, generation.

LESSONS IN ADAPTABILITY AND CONTINUITY FROM CENTENNIAL FAMILY COMPANIES

Global economic activity has accelerated to record speeds in the past decade. Similarly, the speed at which fundamental changes have stormed through the global economy, whether the catalyst was technology, the financial and capital markets, customers, global competition, or a combination of these, is unparalleled in human history. Perhaps then, it should not be a surprise to find that the life cycle of the corporation is shortening too. Worldwide, corporate sustainability and continuity are much more challenging objectives today because of hypercompetition; because of China, South Korea, and Eastern Europe; because of increasing commoditization; because of Wal-Mart, Metro AG, Carrefour, and Reliance Industries' new grocery store concept in India; because of rapidly changing technology and supply chains; because of declining profit margins; and because of shorter product life cycles. This means that more companies are requiring new products, services, and growth opportunities more often to stay alive.

In 2001 I began an inquiry into the resiliency and continuity of family-owned and family-controlled corporations by interviewing fourth-, fifth-, and sixth-generation leaders of companies that were at least 100 years old. All chairpersons, presidents, and CEOs interviewed are members of the founding family. In a world where entrepreneurship is becoming more important and corporations seem unable to last, what are these long-lasting family businesses, these centennial family companies, doing to survive and even thrive? Are they promoting a continuing spirit of entrepreneurship, are they relying on serial entrepreneurship (a continuing series of entrepreneurial ventures), or do they have elements in their cultures that enable them to reinvent themselves with every generation? The conclusions are preliminary because the sample is limited to 16 companies to date. Their annual revenues range from US$18 million to US$5 billion, and they operate in a variety of industries: newspapers, textbook distribution, brick and tiles, food and beverage, wine, steel and bearings, insurance, bakery and baked goods retailing, farm equipment distribution, auto retailing, and leather accessories. The companies are headquartered in the United States, Latin America, and Europe. I was particularly interested in developing an understanding of the nature of the change efforts to promote continuity these fourth-, fifth-, and sixth-generation leaders had engaged in and in discerning the level of appreciation they had for what their predecessors had done while in leadership positions. Related investigations have been carried out in Spain and England (Gallo & Amat, 2003). Because the family-firm leaders I interviewed came from successful centennial companies, we cannot say with certainty that some of these same practices will not be found in companies that have not lasted a century or have been unsuccessful in their continuity efforts. Still, the research provides valuable insights into the actions that leaders of successful centennial family companies consider most critical to their ability to build great companies that last. What follows in this chapter is organized around the major themes discovered, followed by some of the evidence from the interviews supporting that theme. I also sought additional information from company Web sites, business cases, public records, books, electronic databases, and trade publications. I hope that drawing a preliminary sketch of successful long-run companies, rooted in the real-life experiences of next-generation CEOs, will assist readers in creating their own visions or dreams of continuity—that is, that the long-range aspirations for your entrepreneurial business become clearer as a result of reading this chapter.

FAMILY CULTURE, ORGANIZATIONAL CULTURE, AND CULTURAL BLUR IN FAMILY FIRMS

Edgar Schein (1992) defines *organizational culture* as a set of values, beliefs, and assumptions that influence the practices and behaviors of organization members. An organization's culture largely reflects what has proven successful over time to an organization. This proven way of thinking becomes the organization's culture. It becomes so matter of fact that Schein argues that the culture and its values and beliefs drop out of awareness—that is, until the culture is found wanting or there are new challenges to the established culture. At that moment, a reexamination process may make the existing culture more explicit. The culture's set of values, beliefs, assumptions, practices, and behaviors may then be targeted for change in the interest of adaptation. The literature on organizational culture remains rather pessimistic about the capacity to change organizational cultures. Even when it concedes the possibility of doing so through great effort, the literature remains rather skeptical on the ability to do so with speed and a sense of urgency (Kotter, 1996).

The concept of culture is particularly useful in the context of family firms because these tend to exhibit strong cultures (Dyer, 1986) and a form of cultural blur—that is, there is little differentiation between assumptions that go into decision making depending on whether the issue is a family, ownership, or business-management issue. And family values and rules often influence decision making and behavior in the business—as when family members are not held accountable because they are dearly loved relatives. Or just as easily, business values and rules may influence behavior in the context of the family—as when members of the family that have been terminated from employment in the firm appear exiled from the family circle.

Cultural blur may, on the other hand, endow a business with invisible crossovers, or what the strategic planning literature calls "intangible assets," that can be converted into unique competitive advantages. Love in the family may be the source of a strong commitment to quality and customer service in the organization. Strong ownership commitment may also lead to the "patient capital effect" ascribed to family firms that have a longer time horizon on their expectations about return on capital. This form of owner commitment is also credited in the social-capital and the resource-based-view literature with the transfer of knowledge advantage (Cabrera-Suarez, De Saa-Perez, & Garcia Almeida, 2001) that is so evident in the sports world by the success of young athletes like Tiger Woods, Serena and Venus Williams, and Dale Earnhart, Jr. These young successful people were all mentored and coached by their respective parents.

A family value of independence may be translated into a risk-management principle in the corporation. A low debt/equity ratio, for instance, may become a corporate goal, as it has for the Timken Company, discussed later in this chapter. A strong work ethic, an individual value of a founder or successor, may become part of the corporate culture and be evident as a companywide commitment to high productivity. And creativity, which some of the CEOs interviewed acknowledged as a contributing quality of their predecessors, is evidenced in the context of continuing entrepreneurship and innovation at the corporate level (Schein, 1995).

Cultural blurring, then, can be the source of competitive advantage and sustainability in a family business. Fisk Johnson, President of SC Johnson, quotes his father and fourth-generation CEO as saying, "We call our values 'Family values . . . World class results.' They are not radically different from the values you hear from major Fortune 500 companies, but I think we are better able to practice those values as a family-owned business. People care about making quality products, really care about the family, each other, and the success of the company. I believe this caring attitude translates into the success of the company." Fisk proceeds to elaborate on the advantage that this cultural feature represents for SC Johnson, "When we do a new product launch or a change in our line, we don't have to do all the motivation, resistance-to-change training, and public relations campaigns to convince the employees of the wisdom of bringing about this change." Then he added, "When we decided to take CFC propellants out of our entire product line, we did it in 5 working days and 8 years before the government required us to do so. It was an incredible advantage vis-à-vis our competition. We were able to do it because our employees understood that customers made a connection between high-quality products and environmentally friendly products." (F. Johnson, personal conversation with author, June 1996.) Because SC Johnson products often occupy that high relative quality position in the marketplace, protecting the brand's position and doing the right thing for the environment represented a compelling win-win situation.

LONG-TERM CONTINUITY THROUGH PRODUCTS AND VALUES

The Timken Company of Canton, Ohio, was founded in 1899. Timken is a publicly traded S&P 500 company that operates in 29 countries, has US$5 billion in annual revenues (in 2006), and 26,000 employees (see www.timken.com). The Timken family retains a controlling share in the company. A member of the Timken family has been active in top management in every generation. Tim Timken, a member of the fifth generation, is currently chairman of the board of directors. He comments on the reasons for Timken's outstanding record of continuity:

> First of all, we make the best products in the world. We are the leader in bearings. We are the leader in alloy steel. We also recently made a significant acquisition that broadens our product line consistent with the core of the business. So from a product point of view and a service point of view, we believe we are the best at what we do.
>
> Behind the product, there are consistent values. The Timken Company has always believed that our four values—ethics and integrity, quality, innovation, and independence—are central. We have been consistent with them for over 105 years. These values go back to our founder, my great-great grandfather, who believed passionately in them, and to this day we hold those in everything that we do. So those are the two primary drivers of our continuity. In addition, we've also always believed in having professional management. We spend an awful lot of time recruiting qualified people early in their careers, straight out of college.
>
> I think, finally, that the company was formed on innovation. My great-great grandfather invented the tapered roller bearing as a solution to friction problems in carriages at the time. So going back 105 years, the company has been dedicated to creating value for our customers through innovation. That is still true today, whether it is in our automotive business, our industrial business, or our steel business. Unless we can find a way to create value through innovation, we are just a commodity player and that's not a position we feel we can win with.

He adds, "Today, as an example of our commitment to innovation, we spend US$50 to 60 million dollars a year on research and development.

We've got dedicated facilities all around the world—one here in Ohio, one in Romania, one in France, and one in India—and we run a global network for research and development. If you look at the products that we make today, the core concepts are the same but they look very, very different, and that is the result of the investment that we have made in innovation." (For additional historical data on the Timken Company and Timken's commitment to quality and innovation, see Pruitt, 1998.)

Timken continues:

> And regarding our value of independence—our belief is that as a company, we need to control our own destiny. That influences the type of alliances and relationships we enter into; whether it's joint ventures, investments around the world, or labor policy, we believe we are better suited to run our business than anyone else, and as a result we keep our debt to equity capital ratio low. We don't want bankers running our business. Over the years we have enjoyed the flexibility to make significant investments when we need to. (T. Timken, personal communication, August, 2004)

Tim Timken's developmental track has included operations and sales assignments in field locations across Latin America, Europe, and the United States; an MBA (after years of managerial experience); a corporate assignment as director of strategic planning; and president of the steel division.

A PROUD BRAND AND A PROFESSIONALLY MANAGED CORPORATION

J.M. Smucker is the number one U.S. producer of jams, jellies, and preserves. Smucker's also makes dessert toppings, juices, and specialty fruit spreads. The J.M. Smucker Company was established in 1897. At the time, Richard Smucker's great-grandfather sold apple butter out of the back of a wagon. Richard Smucker is fourth-generation president and co-CEO with his brother, Tim, of the Orville, Ohio, company that employs 3,000, operates in 45 countries, and had revenues of over US$2 billion in fiscal year 2006. When I asked him about the drivers of continuity for the 108-year-old company, he confidently said, "A family with the same religious values, a board of directors with independent outsiders, and a deep appreciation that the consumer is king so we have to continue to improve and innovate." He also highlighted the exemplary role that his father and CEO (Paul Smucker) played by not hanging-on, but instead becoming a statesman for the company in 1981 when Tim and Richard succeeded him; and the tremendous influence of his mother, a strong matriarch (R. Smucker, personal communication, March 2006).

Just as significant though, Richard Smucker points out that the last two generations have made very different contributions to the competitive advantage of the J.M. Smucker Company. In the third generation, Paul turned away from making private label products for supermarket chains that continually insisted on cost reductions and were responsible for margin erosion. Paul Smucker took the significant risk of abandoning a large portion of total company sales to turn Smucker's into a branded products only company, and in doing so committed the family to creating one of the truly great brands in America.

Fourth-generation members Tim and Richard, both Wharton School graduates, have taken the company to the next level by professionalizing management and modernizing the management of the firm. They brought with them strategic planning processes, the latest financial concepts and methods, and a cadre of key nonfamily management that was every bit their peer in age and managerial education. That renewed managerial competency is evidenced by the strategy deployed by the firm in the last decade, including the recent acquisition of other powerful brands that are now part of Smucker's: Jif peanut butter, Crisco cooking oil, and Pillsbury baking products. And, in its consistent recognition, since the 1998 inception of *Fortune* magazine's annual survey of the 100 Best Companies to Work For, as one of the top 25 companies to work for in the United States.

With five members of the fifth generation already working in the company, Richard Smucker appears quite confident that the J.M Smucker Company would be strategically adapted again by this next generation in the process of providing for continuity across generations of owner-managers.

GENERATIONAL CONFLICT AND CULTURE CHANGE

Research on organizational culture postulates that strong cultures are a business asset and that strong cultures that fit the strategy are even better. But because of the constant changes in the competitive environment, the culture must also be flexible and agile (think new age composite, as opposed to steel), or the organization could get into trouble by failing to adapt appropriately (Kotter, 1996).

From this perspective, and moving beyond conflict, two generations can add value in surprising ways. In fact, I would argue (on the evidence of the research [Kellermans & Eddleston, 2004; Poza, 2004] and my 25 years of experience as an advisor to family businesses) that the conflict that is inherent across generations is actually one of the keys to the survival of the family business. Other businesses, which cannot count on the emotional component of passionate disagreements about strategic direction, may not get the kind of wake-up call that they need to reinvent themselves as conditions change.

With regard to continuity, then, the proposition is that the business is well served by a disagreement between the generations of owner-managers on the strategy of the entrepreneurial or family-controlled company. The business is well served when the older generation actively represents what has worked well in the past and brings to bear the confidence and wisdom distilled from that success. The new generation, on the other hand, serves the family business well by challenging that wisdom because its time horizon, which is different from that of the previous generations, naturally alerts next-generation members to the fact that there are new opportunities and new challenges surfacing within that longer time horizon.

THE NOTION OF REQUIRED CULTURAL REVOLUTIONS

Because of the rather strong organizational cultures observed in many family companies (Dyer, 1986), I interviewed these CEOs with the premise that revolutions and revolutionaries may sometimes be needed to provide these firms and their owning families with the requisite variety necessary to adapt and be future-ready across generations of owners. Ignacio Osborne, sixth-generation CEO of Osborne, a Spanish wine company founded in 1772, disagreed with the premise. According to Ignacio:

> It was not a revolution. Even though my family has been in the south of Spain for more than 230 years, the British calm is still in the veins of most of the family. It was not easy—it was complicated—but there were no big conflicts or disagreements with the fundamental change process that my generation was leading. There were many meetings, many sessions. I had only been with the company for 3 years. It was hard, we listened to the disagreements and comments, but there was no conflict or revolution. (I. Osborne, personal communication, August, 2004)

Ignacio joined the company in 1993, helping the managing director during a 2½-year transition period. His father and uncle had led Osborne in the fifth generation. Now as the sixth generation took over (Tomas, Ignacio's cousin, is the chairman of the company), competitive conditions had changed. Casa Osborne may not have needed a revolution, but it certainly needed to change its culture and its strategy to respond to its increasingly successful competitors.

The wake-up call for the change was quite intimate for the family. As Ignacio Osborne reveals:

> Up until the fifth generation, at least some of the Osborne family members could live from the dividends generated by the company. In the sixth generation, none of us could live from the dividends. I know this is not very romantic or very family-business oriented, but in practical terms, this was very important. What we did to create the needed fundamental change was to present very early in our leadership of the company a series of alternatives

to the board and described eloquently what the challenging situation of the company was. The contrast between our vision and the current situation set the task out for the board and the company. We also described to the board how our generation thought the company had to be managed in order for it to have a future." (I. Osborne, personal communication, August, 2004)

The inability of a family company to generate sufficient dividend income to maintain the living standards of a family that generally grows with each generation had issued a wake-up call for other families in business. The McIlhenny family, of Tabasco sauce fame in the United States, for example, did not gun the engines of growth through new products as a result of a grand strategic planning exercise led by McKinsey and Bain Management or the Boston Consulting Group. Instead it adopted a new strategy and promoted growth opportunities as a result of its CEO putting a fundamental choice to family shareholders during a family retreat on Avery Island. The choice simply was to either invest in growth so as to expand the profit-generating capacity of the firm or invest in social worker and psychologist fees through a family assistance program aimed at helping family members adjust to their new, less affluent reality. The family wisely chose to place the challenge with the higher system level, the organization, to find resolutions to their quandary, and supported reinvestment in growth. The creation of new products and product line extensions resulted in successful company growth from which the shareholders benefited.

THE EROSION OF THE ENTREPRENEURIAL CULTURE

Multigenerational businesses that are in later stages of development really may be experiencing the interaction between family and business as a cost rather than as a resource. The entrepreneurial stage is widely recognized as one that endows the organization with the capacity to be nimble, largely because at that formative stage, owners know that the essence of being successful is getting the customers' dollars to move from their bank accounts to the entrepreneur's. In other words, making the sale is the basis of success.

But it does not seem to take long anymore for companies to be asked by their customers to be ISO 9001 certified, to be asked by their lenders to apply standard accounting principles that promote greater transparency (and paperwork), and to have to meet a growing list of industry and government-initiated requirements. So increased regulation and the growing needs for coordination create the necessity for meetings and more meetings and memos and more e-mailed memos that make the business naturally become more bureaucratic. Collectively, these multiplying requirements may contribute to the business experiencing time delays it never experienced during its entrepreneurial phase.

More important to this discussion is the possibility that the family itself will become an important source of inward-focused time-wasters, in which case the family begins to represent an important cost to the firm rather than the resource that the combined owner-manager role of a family member represented during the entrepreneurial stage (Zahra, Hayton, & Salvato, 2004). Speed is one of the competitive advantages often inherent in entrepreneurial firms, resulting from the invisible crossovers between ownership and management. But in later generations, the family-business interaction, which in earlier periods represented an intangible asset that could be converted into the strategic advantage called speed and agility, can become a cost, that is the loss of agility in the face of change. A family that is paralyzed because of conflicting views across generations or across branches of the extended family can become inward-looking and become fertile ground for turf wars and feelings of entitlement. In the process, it can forget its most basic comparative advantage in relation to often larger, more bureaucratic corporations—its nimbleness. And, more important, by focusing inside, it can lose the ability to keep an eye on new competitive dynamics and the ever-changing marketplace.

Ignacio Osborne, reflecting on this very development, comments:

> The biggest source of resistance to any change may have been that the family name is on every product label. So we had to try to explain to family members who have been managing the company that in business today you have to focus on the customer and you have to forget a little bit about the vineyards, the countryside, and the craftsmanship in production and look more into the market and what is going on in the world. I think that was the biggest resistance. After all, the company has been very successful with the original business model for many years, so why change? (I. Osborne, personal communication, August 2004)

FAMILY UNITY AND A POSITIVE FAMILY–BUSINESS INTERACTION

Competitive advantages that are more likely available to the family firm are highlighted by the resource-based view of organizations (Cabrera-Suarez et al., 2001). From this theoretical perspective, the firm has specific, but often complex and intangible, resources that are unique to it. These resources, often referred to as organizational competencies, include internal processes (e.g., lean processes that result in speed of execution), human resources (e.g., knowledge and skills that result in higher-quality service and support), or other intangible assets (e.g., brand and reputation).

The unique resources are credited to a combination of family unity and career opportunities created by the family firm and can provide the firm with a competitive advantage in certain circumstances (Poza, Hanlon, & Kishida, 2004). One of these resources in a family firm would be the overlapping owner and manager (agent) relationship, which could lead to advantages from powerful monitoring mechanisms of the owners on the operators. The advantages could include reduced overall costs, such as reduced financial reporting, regulatory compliance, and administrative costs. Faster decision making and longer time horizons for increased efficiency in investment activity could represent another advantage. Another resource unique to some family firms is creating value for the customer through an organizational culture that is rooted in close interpersonal relationships with customers and suppliers. This resource is converted by some family firms into a competitive advantage through high quality and high customer service strategies. Marriott and its Ritz-Carlton brand are good examples of capitalizing on this resource.

Similarly, the details and nuances that make execution an important element of any strategy can be transferred from one generation to the next in ways that are simply not available to nonfamily management. This transfer of knowledge and networks of relationships can represent a significant advantage. The advantage resulting from this transfer of knowledge and of a social network of influential contacts is evident in family-controlled media companies. Donald Graham, Chairman and CEO of The Washington Post Companies, has been eloquent on this gift, part of the legacy built by his mother and previous CEO, Katherine Graham.

A CUSTOMER-CENTRIC PARADIGM

Family firms are particularly prone to becoming inward-focused and losing sight of the customer and relevant competitive shifts as generations transition, and wealth and the number of family branches increase. The significant power that the family's emotional life wields on the ownership group often makes the business lose the obsessive customer orientation that defined it during its early entrepreneurial stage.

For Tim Timken, chairman of the board of directors of the Timken Company and fifth-generation leader, keeping the customer first is a very important function to play to promote continuing adaptation. His perspective mirrored that of Ignacio Osborne, of Osborne Wines in Spain, as to the healthy effect of a customer orientation on a successful family ownership group, one that by nature of its success is vulnerable to hubris. "At the end of the day it all starts with the customer," Timken explains. "We as a company believe that unless we have a firm grasp on what the customers need, we're not going to be able to provide value for them. So I spend about

50% of my time in the field working with my customers, understanding the directions they are headed in, and understanding how we apply our core competencies to create value for them. That's the start of it all. Then, we need to step back occasionally and ask, OK, how we are doing against that standard? Are there other things that we should be doing to create that kind of value?" (T. Timken, personal communication, August 2004)

Because of this overriding customer-centric paradigm (von Hippel, Thomke, & Sonnack, 1999), "the overall vision for the company has evolved over time. We started as the world's best maker of tapered roller bearings, period. And back in 1917, we got into the steel business to support that vision. In recent times, we've expanded it though. We began to push the envelope and say there's a service package that you can wrap around this product. That core product, which used to be a single roller-bearing now becomes a package or assembly for the wheel end of a light truck or SUV. It's that kind of constant evolution versus revolution that we've pursued over time. It has worked out very well for us."

At Casa Osborne, Ignacio Osborne observes, "It used to be that the taste of Osborne family members, sophisticated as it was, determined the taste of our products and defined what quality in wines meant. Not anymore. Now we conduct market research, do focus groups, pay attention to trends and changing consumer tastes." He adds:

> One of the successes we had is we moved very quickly. A new business plan for the company was drafted, then discussed by the board until we reached some consensus for the future of the company. It was just business and company (not family) and then we managed the communication with the rest of the shareholders to let them know what we were trying to do and why. (I. Osborne, personal communication, August 2004)

So, a clearer understanding of the drivers of longevity, continuity, and profitability arises from what these third-, fourth-, and fifth-generation family business leaders have stated. A new shared vision emerges as a response to customers' needs through product, service, and innovation. This reenergized vision drives the strategic regeneration process. Family management and family shareholders are both a part of that process. Family shareholders are kept in the information loop even if they do not work in the company or regularly attend family meetings. Extensive acknowledgment of family interest in the family council or family meetings are linked to the family's board agenda through at-large representation of the family on the board. This means that current-generation CEOs have to address the issue of corporate control and shareholder liquidity, because, as Jim Collins says in *Good to Great* (2001), who is on the bus is ultimately very important. Ray Koenig, CEO of the third- to fourth-generation, 105-year-old Deere farm equipment distributor with US$88 million in annual revenues, for example, suggests that a recent change in the corporation's code of regulations was an attempt to provide for both a nice retirement for members of the third generation and an orderly transfer of control to next-generation members active in the business.

In family businesses, *who* is on the shareholder bus is extremely important to the long-run commitment and the patient capital required. Unless company leaders provide exit opportunities, the bus ride may become quite unpleasant, its trajectory quite unpredictable, and its destination truly regrettable. But the family need not do this work alone. The board, as Ignacio Osborne tells us next, "ends up doing a lot of the lead work in this process of adapting the corporation to its new competitive reality."

THE ROLE OF THE BOARD, FAMILY COUNCIL, SHAREHOLDERS, AND NONFAMILY MANAGEMENT

The role of the board is prominent in the governance of the relationship between a family and its business when the family–business interaction is preserved as a positive-sum dynamic. Because of the board's importance, these next-generation leaders frequently undertake a critical review and restructuring effort involving their board. They all come back to the idea that a lot of communication and education needs to take place beyond what is deemed traditional board work and strategic planning processes because of the family's legacy on the board. The family's identity remains attached to the company's, so if the company is going to change to adapt and grow, the board composition has to change. Ignacio Osborne confessed that "in the span of 2 years, I took 12 years out of the average age of our board."

The textbook distributor in the study sample (the company and the family prefer to remain anonymous) received its wake-up call from fifth-generation members of the family. Very concerned (much more so than the older top management team) and feeling a sense of urgency about the implications that e-commerce had for the more traditional textbook distribution and retail model, the fifth generation spearheaded approval of a multimillion-dollar unbudgeted capital expense. The fifth-generation member chairman of the board aimed at the sudden and accelerated onslaught of Internet-based booksellers with investments in new technology. The company successfully repelled the incursions from new entrants and protected its business model by expanding its brick-and-mortar retail channels to include business-to-business, business-to-education, and business-to-consumer electronic commerce. Wake-up calls are often needed when a strong record of success conspires against the minimum level of dissatisfaction with the status quo that is generally essential to being receptive to change. Koenig Equipment's CEO considers the need to create a sense of urgency in the midst of the success that the family has enjoyed in the business to be his biggest challenge as leader of the transition to the next generation. After all, since 1999 the company has grown from four to six locations, more than doubled its sales to US$88 million, entered a metropolitan area market with Deere lawn care equipment, and taken on an additional brand in another market. For a family steeped in values of humility and frugality, that is accelerated growth and significant success.

NEXT GENERATION LEADERSHIP

When asked about his own trajectory at The Timken Company, Tim Timken replied:

> I'm having a ball. I walked into my first steel mill probably when I was 9 or 10, and for anybody who has ever been in a steel-making facility, it gets under your skin. So there are mornings when it's a little tough to get out of bed, but I'll tell you I wouldn't want to do anything else. We are believers in the future of U.S. manufacturing and in the process we're able to create shareholder value; we're able to maintain employment of 26,000 people around the world; and that's what we do and I believe that we do it well. So to be a part of that, boy I'll tell you, I am having fun. (T. Timken, personal communication, August 2004)

Ignacio Osborne also thrives in his role as fifth-generation CEO. But he adds, "An important part of our success comes from having quickly set the new goals and having quickly shown shareholders positive results against those goals. You cannot come to every board or shareholder meeting and announce what you are going to be achieving next year. You have to show them what you achieved this year or people start not trusting you" (I. Osborne, personal communication, August 2004).

Successful next-generation leaders in family firms that are successful in the long term are very aware that their motto is partnership (see Table 12.2). They are cognizant of the fact that they serve the company and the family and may provide the spark for a renewed but collective effort on behalf of the business and the family. Tim Timken, for example, served as director of strategic planning for the Timken Company, "so that I provided the spark for some important conversations about strategy, yes, but the vision is customer driven—it wasn't about me, it was about the customer. And to make it successful I have to share leadership with or create a partnership with other family members through the family council, family meetings, and shareholder meetings. And build a partnership with key nonfamily management, through the top management team, the operating committee, the board of directors" (T. Timken, personal communication, August 2004).

Table 12.2   Next-Generation Leadership

The next generation:

- Provides the customer-driven vision that promotes innovation and regenerates the company
- Creates a partnership with:
  - Other family members through the family council, family meetings, shareholder meetings, and hundreds of informal conversations that inform and educate
  - Key nonfamily management through top management team, operating committees, etc.
  - Boards of directors
  - New members of the ever-changing supply chain
- Engages in a lifelong journey of preparation for leadership rather than rushing to the presidency, and then act as stewards of the family and its wealth. They serve the company and family members through the successes they work hard to achieve.

INCUMBENT GENERATION LEADERSHIP

The current generation, on the other hand, builds institutions that will effectively govern the relationship between family, management, and ownership through a strong board, family meetings, the appointment of professional nonfamily employees in top management, equity structures that facilitate control, and buy–sell agreements. Incumbent CEOs in effect clean house for the next generation before transferring power. (See Table 12.3 for incumbent-generation CEO leadership initiatives.)

This then allows the next generation to focus on the future, not on the past. Here is an eloquent statement from Ignacio Osborne on the important role of the preceding generation:

> Something that is very important, and perhaps I had not mentioned it earlier because we were lucky enough to have it, is a previous generation that always worked for the transition. So once I got the responsibility for the company, I only had to think of the business and of the next generation. They anticipated a lot of problems. When the next generation gets into the company and for the first 2 or 3 years of their term all they are doing is trying to repair conflicts and problems that they have inherited from the previous generation, then a lot of time is wasted. When we started working, we worked on the present and the future; the past had all been settled. (I. Osborne, personal communication, August 2004)

Table 12.3 Incumbent-Generation CEO Leadership

- Builds the institutions that will effectively govern the family–business interaction: strong board, family meetings, key nonfamily employees in top management, buy–sell agreements, and equity structure that facilitates control
- In effect cleans house for the next generation and only then transfers power (with customers, suppliers, employees) while in full command of the corporation

When this responsibility is not carried out by the incumbent generation, the next generation has to perform it before being able to dedicate itself to building the future. Viena Capellanes, a premium bakery and baked goods chain based in Madrid, Spain, was founded in 1873. It relied on a family council formed by four cousin members of the fourth generation to bring the company back from near catastrophe. The incumbent CEO died unexpectedly, without so much as having considered succession. The four cousins, concerned about the state of the company and the widespread dispersion of the estate, pruned the family tree and set about turning the company around. All that was left was a very strong reputation and tremendous brand equity for its products. That great reputation for premium baked goods coupled with hard work and a future orientation by the four highly committed cousins has brought life back to Viena Capellanes, which currently serves customers through a much larger retail chain of bakeries and cafés. The cousins unanimously declared that they would have rather had the incumbent CEO resolve family issues left over from the past and create a blueprint for governance.

Lessons From the Journey So Far

There are a number of things to be learned about the continuity of family businesses from the evidence gathered thus far.

1. Being a family does not guarantee unity or good relations, but disagreements may be the creative spark needed for adaptation and continuity.

2. If the family is not doing well, the business is hurt. Family unity is the ultimate resource.

3. Planning by the current generation for the benefit of the next is of the essence.

4. Without a new vision by the next generation that pulls the company into the future, there is no commitment to continuity.

5. World-class key nonfamily managers are essential to the process.

6. External assistance by consultants and board members may also be essential.

7. The incumbent generation needs to build the governance infrastructure for a positive family–business interaction. It also has to be generous in the transfer of power.

8. The next generation is well served by being appreciative of the previous generation's efforts and struggles in the process. At the same time, it should advocate a renewed and revitalized strategic vision for the enterprise that is rooted in innovation.

Summary

The first part of the longevity story is all about competitiveness, adaptation, and innovation. In fact, it may not be much of an overstatement to suggest that the only disagreement worth having in a family business is a disagreement about strategy. When the disagreements are about pay, perks, and the presidency, the path of least resistance often leads to win–lose situations and zero-sum dynamics. And families cannot support zero-sum dynamics because the losers will eventually get their chance at harming the winners, even if it means the destruction of the company and the family.

Keeping the business growing through a customer-centric paradigm and providing career opportunities for family and nonfamily employees is at the heart of that positive-sum dynamic and the capacity to have that virtuous cycle working for the owning family.

The second part of the lesson from centennial family companies' stories is about commitment by shareholders to govern their relationships for a higher purpose on behalf of continued ownership and control. Communication, information, and engagement that promote family unity are as important to the success of these centennial companies as managing strategically to remain competitive. The primary asset in creating competitive advantage is embedded in the family through the invisible crossovers from the family's culture: the intangible assets, the patient capital, the thrift principle, a strong work ethic, the commitment to excellent quality, the commitment to the long term, and the commitment to financial independence.

Centennial family companies have also learned to govern the family–business interaction and mitigate shareholder disunity through more formal structures and processes such as:

- hiring and retaining professional nonfamily employees in top management;

- influential, independent boards;

- business planning and strategic planning processes;

- extensive communication using family councils and frequent family meetings; and

- an equity structure appropriate to continued control by family members.

Finally, centennial family companies have learned to change to continue to realize, across generations, the value of their traditional or new and very idiosyncratic competitive advantages. These are advantages that are often rooted in the unique family and family-business culture. Next-generation family-business leaders are cognizant that their cultural foundation is not easy to change, notwithstanding what may be the urgent need to do so in response to significant changes in their competitive environment. In partnership, the incumbent and next generations assume the responsibility for leading the change effort. In the best of cases, the incumbent generation focuses its efforts on pruning from the family business unnecessary legacy effects (e.g., highly compensated family members who are no longer adding value to the business and old agreements and policies that no longer make sense) so that the next generation can focus on the present and the future.

Questions for Discussion

1. What are your take-aways on the contributors to family business continuity based on the review of centennial family company lessons?

2. What are the unique roles of the incumbent and next generations in fostering continuity, or what should family business leaders do to ensure longevity based on the evidence presented in this chapter?

3. Specifically, what management and governance best practices were identified by the leaders of centennial family companies?

Chapter Exercises

1. Consider your current entrepreneurial plans. What role do your family members currently play? What role could they play?

2. Research a prominent family business (not described in depth in this chapter) that has recently gone through a leadership change. Who took over the leadership position—a family member or an outsider? Why? Did this change contribute to legacy effects at all?

References

Anderson, R., & Reeb, D. (2003). Founding family ownership and firm performance: Evidence from the S&P 500. *The Journal of Finance, 58*(3), 1301–1328.

Astrachan, J., & Carey, M. (1994). Family businesses in the United States economy. Paper presented to the Center for the Study of Taxation, Washington, DC.

Cabrera-Suarez, K., De Saa-Perez, P., & Garcia Almeida, D. (2001). The succession process from a resource and knowledge-based view of the firm. *Family Business Review, 14*(1), 37–47.

Collins, J. (2001). *Good to great: Why some companies make the leap . . . and others don't.* New York: HarperBusiness.

Dyer, W. G. (1986). *Cultural change in family firms: Anticipating and managing business and family transitions.* San Francisco: Jossey-Bass.

Gallo, M., & Amat, J. (2003). *Los secretos de las empresas familiares centenarias.* Barcelona: Deusto.

Jaskiewicz, P. (2003). Family influence and performance: An empirical study for Germany and France. Unpublished paper presented at a meeting of the International Family Enterprise Research Association, European Business School, International University Schloß Reichartshausen, Germany.

Kellermans, F., & Eddleston, K. (2004, Spring). Feuding families: When conflict does a family firm good. *Entrepreneurship Theory and Practice, 28*(3), 209–227.

Kotter, J. (1996). *Leading change.* Boston: Harvard Business School Press.

Martinez, J., & Stohr, B. (2005). Family ownership and firm performance: Evidence from public companies in Chile. Unpublished paper presented at a meeting of the International Family Enterprise Research Association, University of Oviedo, Spain.

Menéndez-Requejo, S. (2005). Ownership structure and firm performance: Evidence from Spanish family firms. Unpublished paper presented at a meeting of the International Family Enterprise Research Association, University of Oviedo, Spain.

Miller, K. (2004, April 12). Best of the Best—A *Newsweek* study shows family firms are outrunning their rivals on all six of the leading stock indexes in

Europe, and ranks the top 10 companies. Family Firms. *Newsweek International,* Atlantic Edition, 42.

Poza, E. (2009). *Family Business,* (3rd ed.). Mason, OH: Cengage South-Western.

Poza, E., Hanlon, S., & Kishida R. (2004). Does the family business interaction factor represent a resource or a cost? *Family Business Review, 17*(2), 99–118.

Pruitt, B. (1998). *Timken: From Missouri to Mars—A century of leadership in manufacturing.* Boston: Harvard Business School Press.

Rottenberg, D. (Ed.). (2002, Winter). The oldest family businesses. *Family Business Magazine, 13*(1), 44.

Schein, E. (1992). *Organizational culture and leadership* (2nd ed.). San Francisco: Jossey-Bass.

Schein, E. (1995). The role of the founder in creating organizational culture. *Family Business Review, 8*(3), 221–238.

von Hippel, E., Thomke, S., & Sonnack, M. (1999). Creating breakthroughs at 3M. *Harvard Business Review, 77*(5), 47–55.

Ward, J. (1987). *Keeping the family business healthy: How to plan for continued growth, profitability, and family leadership.* San Francisco: Jossey-Bass.

Zahra, S., Hayton, J., & Salvato, C. (2004, Summer). Entrepreneurship in family vs. non-family firms: A resource-based analysis of the effect of organizational culture. *Entrepreneurship Theory and Practice, 28*(4), 363–381.

Suggested Readings

ARTICLES

Anderson, R., & Reeb, D. (2003). Founding family ownership and firm performance: Evidence from the S&P 500. *The Journal of Finance, 58(3),* 1301–1328.

This article presents the findings from the first long-term comparison of the financial performance of family enterprises and management-controlled enterprises. It led the way for a dozen other studies worldwide that have consistently shown family firms outperforming other businesses by anywhere from 6%–16% annually in return on equity.

Poza, E. J. (2007). *Family Business* (2nd ed.). Mason, OH: Thomson.

This textbook and workbook is a comprehensive interdisciplinary resource on global family business. Identifying what makes family enterprises different and how they can leverage their unique strengths while governing their distinct vulnerabilities is the fundamental contribution of this book. Topics addressed include: succession and continuity planning, family communication and family unity, boards of directors and advisory boards, family councils, estate planning, business valuation and strategic planning by the next generation. Challenging concepts are presented in a clear, understandable, and actionable manner. Exhibits and 18 cases from family enterprises all over the world increase its take-away value.

Part 3

Cases

- Logisys
- Sedo.com
- Fasteners for Retail
- The Vega Food Company
- Reliance Industries

Logisys

A Small Company With International Potential

Dominika Salwa[1], PhD Student at Cracow University of Economics, Chair of International Management

Logisys is a small company that was established by young engineers from Cracow, Poland. Due to the strong synergy between the qualifications and abilities of the founding partners, the company is thriving and making a mark in its industry. After receiving the prestigious European Auto ID Award 2006 and the gold medal at the Poznan International Fair (PIF; the third largest fair organizer in Central and Eastern Europe) within its first year of existence, the core business idea of Logisys seems promising.

Let us take a look at how the idea for a product was born and how a plan of action was gradually carried out in this start-up company.

A New Start-Up Company

The idea of introducing a new product and creating a new start-up company was born at the beginning of 2005 in one of the Cracow's small IT companies. This was where the three future co-founders of Logisys, Bart, Luke, and Martin, met. Each of these young entrepreneurs shared the passion and ambition to make a start-up venture viable. From the beginning, though, it was Bart and Luke who were to play the main roles in Logisys. Martin, due to previous obligations, joined the team at a later date but had to move on to other things after a few months. From that point forward, Bart and Luke formed an inseparable and complementary business team.

1. The author would like to thank the entrepreneurs from Logisys, Bartosz Jacyna and Lukasz Musialski, for their sincere discussions and helpful materials in writing this case study.

Bart was the development manager at their former company, and is a determined, analytical, open-minded, attentive observer. Already a student of economic faculty, he was recognized as a person who could easily combine common efforts to organize several valuable projects, many of which are still successfully implemented at Jagiellon University in Cracow. As he admits, he likes bringing his visions to reality.

Luke was the product manager at the previous company, and is intelligent, creative, rhetorical, and naturally happy. In discussions both as a schoolboy and later as a physics student, Luke often sided with the weaker arguments, just to exercise his oratorical skills. He is inquiring and a fierce competitor. "Luke can accumulate and process information in an amazing way. He sees details that I arrange generally," says Bart.

In this team one couldn't exist without the other, and both are crucial to Logisys' potential.

As with most start-ups, the beginning was the critical period of the development phase. Logisys was created as a limited liability company for legal purposes. This type of legal incorporation gives the company more opportunities to revise its status and organization in the future.

Everything needed to be arranged and thought through, from operational matters to strategic ones: people, technology, strategy, goals, marketing, financing, and sales. The business first started in the kitchen and living room of one co-founder's flat, similar to Hewlett-Packard starting out in a garage. They moved from there after a couple months and, due to various circumstances, have moved four more times since.

Despite the tenuous start, Logisys' main technology and core business didn't change. Bart and Luke's vision still remains a star on the horizon.

The Conception of a Product

The idea behind Logisys is based on a product conceived by Luke. The proposed business solution was connectivity software, or middleware, that provided a linking component for the integration of automatic identification devices (auto-ID). In other words the product was intended to be the part of efficient logistics processes between auto-ID equipment and sophisticated over-systems, like enterprise and manufacturing resource planning (ERP/MRP II).

There was a gap in the market for a tool that could integrate all the devices and applications with the main system in a cohesive, fluid manner. This was exactly the gap that Logisys filled, with its new integration platform Agilero. A brief illustration of the processes before and after the Logisys solution is shown in Figure 1.

Before the implementation of Agilero, integration of processes in hardware takes place throughout individual programs needed to operate a process. The lack of two-way information flow is characteristic.

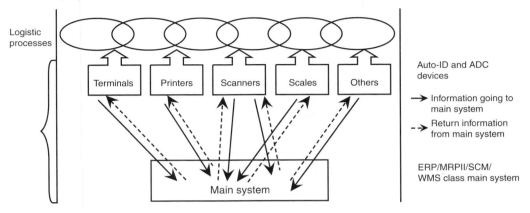

After Agilero implementation there is integration of processes and information flow in real time between hardward—auto-ID and ADC devices and main systems.

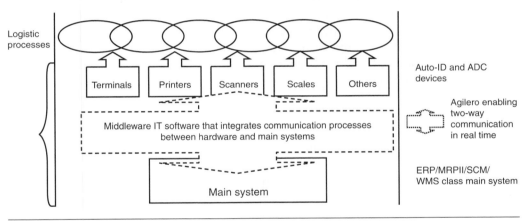

Figure 1   Schema of Logistics Processes Operation Before and After Inventing Agilero

SOURCE: Dominika Salwa and Bartosz Jacyna

The conception of this product was an innovation, but that didn't mean there was an easy way to implement it into a business reality. Logisys still needed to fight for its niche. In this case the market difficulties were not a result of competition, because Logisys had no competitors, but from its own structure and the place of its proposed product in the market. An important market discovery was the identification of who most often decides to implement such a middleware solution. Typically, customers, as final users, follow the suggestion of system integrators and device suppliers, and are not aware of how necessary and useful a middleware class software application is. This lack of customer knowledge about what the Agilero platform could do influenced the way Logisys took action and perceived the market.

The Idea for Business

Understanding where the Agilero platform fit into the logistics processes market led the company to think of a strategy that would allow Logisys to win the struggle for this market.

Luke and Bart thought: "This component [middleware] is often skipped. Everybody thinks that somehow it'll go in or someone will cover it. Time passes, and it turns out that no one covers it and no one even feels like doing it, because there's a cost. Even though the missing component—middleware—is logical, logic isn't an argument good enough to make a thing exist. Integrators and auto-ID companies are aware of the necessity of middleware, but in Poland they usually use makeshift and single solutions that enable single integration and are potentially costly in the long term. The market we are in is uneducated. To survive we have to educate it! Our mission is to teach the market what it should look like. We claim that enlarging the cake—blue ocean strategy—is worth fighting for."

From those thoughts an idea for their business was conceived. Logisys now had to do two things: (1) market education, from which the basis for further focus on consulting emerged, and (2) creation of the Agilero platform and its technology. During its first two years of existence, Logisys developed those two business models.

Market education was realized directly and indirectly: directly through partners and indirectly through specialized media such as press conferences, industrial trade fairs, and collaboration with scientific institutions. Logisys had been working with five well-known Polish logistic solutions magazines, writing opinions and articles; participating in research at three main scientific institutions; and actively presenting their solutions at selected industrial fairs.

They also began to contact other companies to look for potential partners in the market and to sell Agilero. Many different avenues were pursued to create partnerships: private contacts, official meetings, and short educational presentations. Logisys' main partners to date are Hogart, Datalogic, Logifact, Aspekt, Datascan, Sato, Ewa-bis, Symbol, Koncept-L, Softex-Data, and Anixandra. Hogart and Datalogic seem the most important, while the rest provide differing levels of benefits.

As education progressed, Logisys was developing the Agilero platform, which was not finished and needed more research. This part of the
company's activity was very costly. With up to four employees working
on Agilero, Bart and Luke were sure the initial finances would be
depleted and the product would have to pay for itself within a short
period of time.

Initial Marketing Issues

Logisys' first steps in the business world seemed well thought out—the
ideas about the business, the conception of its product, and even the marketing issues—and Bart felt they fit very well with Drucker's expression
that "only innovation and marketing counts." The company's name was
seriously considered. It had to directly address the company's need to
explain its function, be unregistered, explicitly readable in a few main languages, and have an available free Internet domain. The name Logisys
seemed perfect.

There were more discussions regarding 'Agilero,' but they ultimately
decided it was perfect. Agilero comes from *agile*, which largely describes
the character of the product, and *ro*, which was to signal the harmonious
spirit of the southern European countries. In the end people remembered the software name, even associating it with the singer Christina
Aguilera.

The company's brand (logos and colors) was designed by Media
United. The Logisys and Agilero logos are different, but nevertheless are
unintentionally complementary of each other (Figure 2). Keeping in mind
that both might operate as separate entities in the future, this was a clever
business trick.

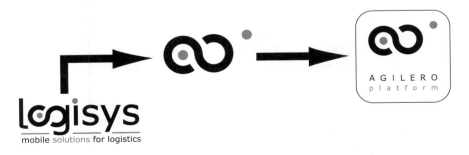

Figure 2   The Logos of Logisys and Agilero

SOURCE: Logisys materials

Another issue that was even more important was Logisys' marketing strategy. After inventing the technology, Bart and his engineers had difficulty explaining to others what their product did. LAP Development helped Logisys design a business marketing strategy. LAP first figured out what Logisys did, and then told them how to communicate it to others.

The result of Logisys' relationship with LAP was an understanding of the whole process from the client point of view, as well as attractive marketing materials and Web pages with a clear description of the company's core business, values, and identity.

Logisys' values and identity came directly from its founders, who stated, "Logisys competes through quality and range." They would not consider reducing prices at the cost of quality. This was a basic requirement to ensure the highest quality of products and services.

External quality can only come from homogenous internal quality and organizational culture. Bart knew this to be true, and took care of employees' quality of work. He created documents to explain the company's internal operations, its structure, and each employee's responsibility. Those moves were the seeds of the company's future internal marketing.

Market Opportunities, Appreciated Efforts, and Struggles

Logisys had built a good foundation by 2006, and the company felt rapid growth in 2007 could be achieved. The development plans were optimistic: more employees, the leading position in its market, international commitments and cooperation, and operational and financial stability including liability payment.

Within its first year, Logisys received two awards: the Euro ID Messe in Germany (European Auto-ID Award 2006) and a gold medal at the Poznan International Fair in Poland. The two awards confirmed the need for Logisys' Agilero platform technology.

Shortly after the fair in Germany, Logisys received an invitation to join the RFID Konsortium. This newly formed entity was comprised of about 10 small German companies who needed a solution for the implementation of RFID tagging in the supply chains of retail giants METRO and REWE. Each company in the Konsortium was supposed to cover a certain range of knowledge in the IT and RFID markets. That was seen as a great opportunity for the small Polish start-up, and Logisys' expectations were high. This chance could open the door to potential internationalization, which had been in the minds of the young entrepreneurs from the very beginning.

For nearly two years, Bart and Luke drove back and forth to Germany for RFID Konsortium meetings. However, the group had not been able to effectively cooperate and increase their cultural homogeneity, and many conflicts emerged between companies. Logisys wanted to withdraw from this inefficient collaboration, but the overall cost of its commitment would weaken the company's financial situation.

In Poland sales were developing more slowly than expected. Logisys received less orders for Agilero implementation as well as consultancy. However, good company references were being established.

Meanwhile, more potential partners and customers implemented Logisys' solutions, including Wix Filtron, a Hogart customer and producer and distributor of filters for the automotive industry (having a 43% share in the Polish filter market); Merlin, the biggest online bookstore in Poland (after Logisys implementation the company became twice as efficient in packaging and sending its product without increasing the costs); Dako, the wrapping-paper print house; and Wyborowa SA, one of the biggest Polish companies marketing alcoholic beverages (realized through Hogart). In 2008 Logisys acquired another important consultancy project from the M&M Company.

Unfortunately, in addition to the successful projects there were also some that cost Logisys time and resources but didn't bring the anticipated incomes. Those were always hard for the company's finances, but this was a way of learning how to manage risk in their business.

Sales and Internal Employee Rotations

The main task of any business is to sell its product, whatever it is. For nearly 4 months in the beginning, the Logisys team worked on the Agilero platform. Later they started to think about selling it and arranging the distribution channel. It seemed harder than the entrepreneurs expected. They thought that having a good technology was enough, but it wasn't. While looking for partners, Logisys had to develop crucial selling skills. Bart was responsible for operational and strategic management in the company, Luke for Agilero and technology. Neither of them knew exactly how to develop the selling infrastructure.

The issue of hiring the right people became almost critical. It wasn't easy, especially in the Polish economy, which had been good for the past couple of years. The market was flourishing with opportunities that included high earnings and attractive work environments for good tradesmen and computer specialists. Logisys couldn't offer much: typical salary, creative freedom, independence and the opportunity to use one's intellect. This was a weakness that reduced the potential of the company. In the middle of 2007, an employed tradesman didn't prove himself. After a year of his work, Bart and Luke discovered his incompetence and low motivation. He was dismissed, but his impact on the company's abilities was negative. Logisys had to reorganize and start-up again, and needed to find someone to sell. At that point, after 3 years of activity, the entrepreneurs made an important decision: They needed to learn how to properly sell what they had to offer. This was a critical point for the company.

Similar problems appeared later with the computer specialists. The job was attractive for students, but not for qualified software engineers. Even the main Agilero engineer couldn't endure the daily tension and became confrontational. He had to be replaced. As Bart stated, "For a small company, ineffective teamwork and deteriorated mood are very critical issues." Although the engineer's replacement by another specialist was critical, he didn't work out and soon resigned. The final solution was an agreement for support with a former employee, an engineer who had worked on Agilero's concept at the beginning. However, this move meant a slow down in the technology's development.

Finances

The main problem for the majority of entrepreneurs is to get financing for their business idea. Some ideas require less money, while others need more. Agilero platform needed a lot of financial support. Employees, including three engineers who worked on the product development, had to be paid.

As Logisys was a limited liability company, there was a legal requirement for them to have their own contributions. Bart and Luke contributed 50,000PLN (1PLN = about US$2.60) at the beginning, plus additional contributions of 150PLN.

This was insufficient for company expenses and product development, and they needed more financial support. The entrepreneurs luckily received a long-term, low-interest loan of 600 000PLN from Doris, Bart's wife. This financial preservation let the company operate for a period of time while earnings were very irregular (see Tables 1 and 2).

Having had a sense of Agilero technology's future financial requirements, Bart looked for additional sources of capital. Analysis of the ventures he found drove him to conclude that in Polish realities, the market and the company were not stable enough for a potential venture investor.

After 2.5 years of activity, 2008 was the first year Logisys was able to make a living. Unfortunately, the irregularity of income, loss due to participation in RFID Konsortium, and other nonprofitable projects resulted in no profits thus far. Due to these circumstances, Doris' loan may not be repaid and by the end of 2008 it will be converted into shares belonging to her.

Even if Logisys' financial situation seems normal for a start-up, Bart and Luke are still working for a low salary. This means they finance the company with their own work. Such a situation intensifies tension in both families, which require more stability in their lives.

Strategic Reorganization and Reorientation

Three years of Logisys existence, with many ups and downs, have put the company in a difficult situation. On the one hand, there is hope; but on the other, the hard daily life has forced Bart and Luke (the only ones who remain from the initial team of five people) to make difficult decisions about Logisys future.

First, the business model needed verification in two areas (Agilero platform development and consulting), especially in the face of high financial inputs in technology that still didn't pay for itself. Second, the Polish logistics processes market is still not stable. This brings into question the presumed "blue ocean strategy," which works better in well-developed economies rather than in still developing ones. Additionally, too much trust in the customers and carelessness in customer selection has led Logisys to unnecessary problems.

The internal situation, including the office moving several times and personnel turnover, was an additional point of uncertainty. In 2005 Logisys started with four employees plus Bart and Luke, having a maximum of nine people by the middle of 2007. However, they were forced to reduce their operational costs. By the middle of 2008, Logisys had retained four employees and revised its personnel policy. The general policy of Logisys had to change and strategic reorientation had to take place.

Bart and Luke decided to concentrate on logistic consulting in the area of its core business and move toward networking cooperation (with partners employed for certain projects instead of full-time job agreements). "Once you are engaged in a company as a consultant, you mold its consciousness. You become a part of the company's know how, and you gain its confidence. The product usually has secondary meaning. The most important thing is to solve the client's problems," both Bart and Luke

(Text continues on page 414)

Table 1   Logisys' Balance Sheet for 2005 and 2006

ASSETS

+/-	Pos.	Position name			01/01/2005–12/31/2005	01/01/2006–12/31/2006
-	A	Fixed assets			5,419.68	17,855.74
-	I	Intangible assets			0.00	0.00
			1	Costs of finished development works	0.00	0.00
			2	Company's value	0.00	0.00
			3	Other intangible assets	0.00	0.00
-	II	Tangible fixed assets			3,319.68	15,755.74
	-		1	Property, plant, and equipment	3,319.68	15,755.74
			2	Engaged fixed assets	0.00	0.00
			3	Downpayments for fixed assets	0.00	0.00
-	III	Long-term debtors			0.00	0.00
			1	From subsidiary and associated companies	0.00	0.00
			2	From other companies	0.00	0.00
-	IV	Long-term investments			2,100.00	2,100.00
			1	Properties	0.00	0.00
			2	Intangible assets	2,100.00	2,100.00
	-		3	Long-term financial assets	0.00	0.00
			4	Other long-term investments	0.00	0.00

+/-	Pos.	Position name		01/01/2005–12/31/2005	01/01/2006–12/31/2006
-	-	V	Long-term deferred expenses	0.00	0.00
		1	Deferred income tax	0.00	0.00
		2	Other deferred expenses	0.00	0.00
-	B		Current assets	53,632.77	164,664.57
	-	I	Stocks	0.00	0.00
		1	Materials	0.00	0.00
		2	Half-finished and underway products	0.00	0.00
		3	Ready products	0.00	0.00
		4	Goods	0.00	0.00
		5	Advance payment for supply	0.00	0.00
	-	II	Current receivables	12,515.20	151,162.15
		1	From subsidiary and associated companies	0.00	0.00
		2	From other companies	12,515.20	151,162.15
	-	III	Short-term investments	40,699.08	12,270.29
		1	Short-term financial assets	40,699.08	12,270.29
		2	Other short-term investments	0.00	0.00
		IV	Short-term deferred expenses	418.49	1,232.13
			Total assets	59,052.45	182,520.31

(Continued)

Table 1   (Continued)

LIABILITIES

+/-	Pos.	Position name	01/01/2005– 12/31/2005	01/01/2006– 12/31/2006
-	A	Shareholders' equity	50,295.10	-249,037.59
	I	Share capital	50,000.00	50,000.00
	II	Due payments on share capital (negative quantity)	0.00	0.00
	III	Own shares (negative quantity)	0.00	0.00
	IV	Reserve capital	150,000.00	150,000.00
	V	Revaluation capital	0.00	0.00
	VI	Other reserve capitals	0.00	0.00
	VII	Prior years' profit (loss)	0.00	-149,704.90
	VIII	Net profit (loss)	-149,704.90	-299,332.69
	IX	The deduction from net profit in working year (negative quantity)	0.00	0.00
-	B	Liabilities and reserves for liabilities	8,757.35	431,557.90
	-	I	Reserves for liabilities	0.00	0.00

+/-	Pos.	Position name		01/01/2005–12/31/2005	01/01/2006–12/31/2006
		1	Reserve for deferred income tax	0.00	0.00
		2	Provisions for pension and similar benefits	0.00	0.00
		3	Other provisions	0.00	0.00
-	II		Long-term liabilities	0.00	384,546.40
	-	1	To subsidiary and associated companies	0.00	384,546.40
	-	2	To other companies	0.00	0.00
-	III		Current liabilities	8,757.35	47,011.50
	-	1	To subsidiary and associated companies	0.00	0.00
	-	2	To other companies	8,757.35	47,011.50
		3	Special funds	0.00	0.00
-	IV		Accrued expenses and deferred income	0.00	0.00
		1	Negative company value	0.00	0.00
	-	2	Other accrued expenses and deferred income	0.00	0.00
			Total shareholders' equity and liabilities	59,052.45	182,520.31

SOURCE: Logisys' materials

Table 2 Consolidated Profit and Loss Account 2005–2006

+/-	Pos.	Position name	01/01/2005–12/31/2005	01/01/2006–12/31/2006
-	A	Net income from sales and leveled with them, including:	33,930.52	226,766.67
	-	From subsidiary and associated companies	0.00	0.00
	I	Net income from sales of products	33,930.52	224,016.67
	II	Products' state change (increasing-positive quantity, decreasing)	0.00	0.00
	III	Cost of products for unit's own needs	0.00	0.00
	IV	Net income from sales of goods and materials	0.00	2,759.00
	B	Operating activity costs	183,525.33	517,513.48
	I	Depreciation	24,554.87	4,019.48
	II	Materials and energy consumption	3,030.18	11,655.06
	III	Foreign services	7,972.42	108,673.59
	IV	Taxes and charges, including:	2,378.40	4,145.10
	-(1)	Excise duty	0.00	0.00
	V	Renumerations	95,847.64	215,275.38
	VI	Tax, subsidy, duty, social and health insurance and others	21,177.13	47,482.11
	VII	Remaining generic costs	28,564.69	123,998.76
	VIII	Worth of sold goods and materials	0.00	2,265.00
-	C	Profit from sale (A-B) (loss)	-149,594.81	-290,746.81
-	D	Other operating income	2.43	1,342.31
	I	Profit from selling nonfinancial fixed assets	0.00	1,338.91
	II	Revaluation of fixed assets	0.00	0.00
	III	Other operating costs	2.43	3.40
	E	Other operating costs	5.66	2.41
	I	Loss on selling nonfinancial fixed assets	0.00	0.00
	II	Revaluation of nonfinancial assets	0.00	0.00

+/-	Pos.	Position name	01/01/2005–12/31/2005	01/01/2006–12/31/2006
	III	Other operating costs	5.66	2.41
	F	Profit (loss) on operating activities	-149,598.04	-289,406.91
-	G	Finance revenue	23.91	23.51
-	I	Dividend and share in profits, including:	0.00	0.00
	-(1)	from associated units	0.00	0.00
-	II	Interest, including:	23.91	23.51
		-(1) from associated units	0.00	0.00
	III	Profit on selling invetsments	0.00	0.00
	IV	Revaluation of investments	0.00	0.00
	V	Other operating costs	0.00	0.00
-	H	Financial costs	130.77	9,949.29
	I	Interest, including:	0.00	9,546.40
		-(1) for associated units	0.00	0.00
	II	Loss on selling investments	0.00	0.00
	III	Revaluation of investments	0.00	0.00
	IV	Other	130.77	402.89
	I	Profit (loss) on business (F+G-H)	-149,704.90	-299,332.69
-	J	Results of extraordinary events (J.I.-J.II.)	0.00	0.00
	I	Extraordinary profits	0.00	0.00
	II	Extraordinary losses	0.00	0.00
	K	Gross profit (loss) (I-/+J)	-149,704.90	-299,332.69
	L	Income tax	0.00	0.00
	M	Other obligatory profit reductions (loss increases)	0.00	0.00
	N	Net profit (loss) (K-L-M)	-149,704.90	-299,332.69

SOURCE: Logisys' materials

admit. Consulting is less cost demanding than technology development, and success in this domain could possibly finance other activities.

This decision caused legal changes, and Bart and Luke have a civil company for consulting services only. This is much more favorable from the tax policy point of view. The limited liability status company will remain for Agilero platform and Logisys technology.

The second half of 2008 will hold decisive moments for Logisys' future and even its existence at all, Bart and Luke have decided. They do not want to spend another couple of years struggling for food in the battle for their business.

Glossary of Terms

ADC (Automatic Data Capture) is a key to the success in the information strategy of companies. Accurate and honest data download on a proper level permits the optimization of company processes. The growing importance of ADC is visible everywhere, especially in logistics and transport.

Automatic identification is a technology that identifies the units of a logistic process. Bar code and radio tag technology are most often used in automatic identification. Image recognition technology also exists, but is less popular and is used in very specific conditions. ***Auto-ID devices*** identify these logistic units. Among them are bar code readers (also called scanners), mobile terminals, and bar code printers, radio terminals, automatic scales, radio frequency identification (RFID) printers and readers.

EDI (Electronic Data Interchange) is a set of standards for streamlining electronic information interchange outside and inside the enterprise.

Main systems of enterprises are IT systems used to streamline enterprise management. These systems enable optimization of resources and processes. Among main management systems there are ***ERP*** (Enterprise Resource Planning), ***MRP II*** (Manufacturing Resource Planning), and ***SCM*** (Supply Chain Management). Among the types of main systems we can find SAP, Axapta, JDEdwards, Navision, and others.

RFID (Radio Frequency Identification) is identification technology that uses properly modulated radio waves to carry the data. ***RFID tagging technology*** introduces a new quality of optimization of logistic processes. An ***RFID tagging label*** contains a chip with an antenna that enables data gathering and transmission outside by radio. Appropriate logistic information is not placed on documents (it is natural that they are unreliable), but on logical units themselves, thanks to RFID labels.

Case Questions

1. Describe threats and opportunities in the market that Logisys has entered (from both the local and international perspective).

2. Analyze the Logisys situation over the past 3 years of its existence (its strengths and weaknesses, its behavior and strategy).

3. Try to estimate the chances for Logisys success in the future.

References

Drucker, P. F. (1985) *Innovation and entrepreneurship.* New York: Harper Business.

Sedo.com

The Founder's Dilemma: When Is the Right Time for Exiting?

This case study has been prepared by Christian Koropp under the supervision of Professor Dietmar Grichnik. It is based on publicly available data and on a personal interview with Tim Schumacher, CEO and co-founder of Sedo, in May 2007.

> *When starting a company, it is probably the right thing not to think about an exit at all and instead simply focus on growing the company, but it's at least a valid question to ask yourself once a year.*
>
> Tim Schumacher, CEO of Sedo

On a lukewarm spring evening in 2006, Tim Schumacher, Ulrich Priesner, Ulrich Essmann, and Marius Wuerzner, the founders of Sedo, GmbH[1], sat together at a Boston restaurant to discuss the future of their organization, Sedo. Sedo, a German company with offices in both Germany and the United States, experienced enormous growth in its 7 years since it was founded and is now the world's leading online marketplace for domain names. Despite this success the company's founders were faced with a challenging decision. They had invested all their private wealth into the company and were now contemplating the benefit of diversifying their personal risk by partially divesting from Sedo.

Background

Sedo—an acronym for Search Engine for Domain Offers—was born from a youthful endeavor of Tim Schumacher, Ulrich Priesner, and Marius Wuerzner. These three men knew each other from their school days when they developed a soccer management simulation called *Offensiv*. They sold this game over the Internet and bought the domain name offensiv.de to support it.

---

1. A GmbH is a legal form in Germany that equals an LLC in the United States.

After graduation the three young men attended university in different parts of Germany. Tim Schumacher studied business administration in Cologne. Ulrich Priesner studied computer engineering in Mannheim. Marius Wuerzner studied history and philosophy in Freiburg. The time commitment needed for their studies ended the *Offensiv* project. Despite concluding the project, the three friends still owned the domain offensiv .de. It was at this time that they asked themselves: What can we do with this unused domain name? The idea to develop a marketplace for used domain names was born, and they spent hour after hour outside of their studies to bring their idea to fruition.

In September 1999 the three students created an official partnership to formalize their endeavor and launched their first Web site to garner feedback from the Internet community. The industry's first offer/counteroffer system enabling domain name buyers and sellers to negotiate directly with each other was now a reality. Despite a lack of marketing, it did not take long until the users began to register their used domain names.

At the beginning of 2000, the young entrepreneurs decided to invest more of their time and money into the business. They booked banner advertisements on Web sites and created positive relationships with the press. This occurred at the height of the Internet hype, leading to an overwhelming response from the media and the Internet community. The contacts they gained during this time were invaluable: potential business partners, investors, and future competitors.

One of these competitors was Ulrich Essmann, a medical student working on a project similar to Sedo. He had already acquired the sizable customer base that Sedo lacked. After assessing Sedo's potential, Essman decided to join the Sedo venture. The Sedo founders, now including Essman, quickly began negotiations with potential investors.

Negotiations were arduous, as the dot-com crisis was now in full effect. The men persevered and, by February 2001, they succeeded in finding a major investor. United Internet AG[2] (together with their subsidiary 1&1 Internet AG), at that time Germany's largest registrar for domain names, took a minority stake in the newly founded Sedo, GmbH. With a strong and experienced investor backing them, Sedo began offering services in all areas of domain name trading, still not yet foreseeing the tremendous growth ahead of them.

Sedo's Ownership Structure

Significant changes in Sedo's ownership have occurred during the organization's short history. The first major change was a conversion from the

---

2. The acronym AG refers to companies being a corporation.

original founded partnership to a limited partnership, Sedo, GmbH. The second major change occurred when United Internet AG bought 41% of Sedo, GmbH for nearly EUR 400,000 while also providing a shareholder's loan. The remaining 59% of shares was still owned by the four founders. This was preserved as a strategic move by both parties.

At the beginning of 2004, United Internet implemented their call option that was agreed upon in their 2001 investment package. As previously arranged in the call option, United Internet bought an additional 10% of Sedo's shares for EUR 575,000 (United Internet, 2004). This deal made the company's four founders minority shareholders of their own business. Despite the restructuring, the purchase did not change the everyday functioning of the business. With the new investment, Tim Schumacher, Ulrich Priesner, Ulrich Essmann, and Marius Wuerzner, were even more motivated to realize Sedo's global potential.

Only 15 months later, in April 2005, United Internet restructured its own company portfolio. The 51% stake of United Internet and another 1% from one of the founders' holdings were sold to AdLink Internet Media AG, a public but majority-owned subsidiary of United Internet[3], for EUR 14.3 million (AdLink Internet Media, 2005). This sale caused some major changes for Sedo's management team. AdLink's company was much smaller than United Internet's, which increased the attention on Sedo and its growth. AdLink provided Sedo with more support but also insisted on greater management intervention. Nevertheless, the entrepreneurial spirit of the founders remained unscathed. Innovations to guarantee Sedo's future success would continue to occur.

The Domain Market

Every company and product that seeks to succeed needs a reasonable and memorable brand name. In the age of e-business and the Internet, companies also need memorable domain names. The market for domain names (domain market) is divided into a primary market and an aftermarket, or secondary market.

The primary domain market is the market where new domain names are registered for the first time using the first-come-first-serve principle. Market partners are the users who want to register a domain name (registrants) and the accredited domain issuers (registrars). The price for a new domain is a standard registration fee, usually only a few dollars.

Because most of the promising domain names are already registered, there is a need for a market to buy and sell used domain names. This is the

---

3. AdLink Internet Media is—like United Internet—publicly traded on the Frankfurt Stock Exchange (ticket symbol ISIN DE0005490155), but United Internet owns 82% of the shares, with a small 18% remaining.

domain aftermarket. Transactions in this market are much more complex than primary market transactions. Many changes in the aftermarket regarding transaction procedure, market structure, and market growth have emerged in the last 10 years due to the development of domain name marketplaces like GreatDomains, Afternic, and Sedo. These marketplaces have simplified the domain selling process by reducing relevant transaction costs. For example, search and information costs are reduced by the marketplace's metasearch engine and domain name databases.

Domain aftermarket development has been rapid and unstable. The annual growth rates of the market were tremendous until the beginning of 2000. Then, because of the dot-com crisis, the prices for domain names decreased rapidly along with the total volume on the domain aftermarket. This slump leveled out in mid-2003 and the domain aftermarket enjoyed a strong rebound—the market volume increased by double-digit growth rates. By the end of 2006, the total amount of aftermarket transactions increased to US $96.9 million (Sedo, 2007).

The structure of the domain aftermarket has changed significantly since Sedo entered the market. In 2000 the market was dominated by only two companies: Afternic and GreatDomains. The dot-com crisis detrimentally affected these organizations and wiped out the market. Once the crisis ended, the market's growth attracted many smaller competitors leading today's highly competitive market (see Table 1). Despite this increased competition, Sedo has been the world's leading domain aftermarket since 2004, with a market share of nearly 40%. Predictions of the domain aftermarket's future

Table 1   Market Share for Domain Sales Above US$2,000

Marketplace	2004	2006
Sedo	41%	39.9%
Pool	18%	1.1%
Afternic	10%	4.6%
GreatDomains	8%	–
Moniker DS	8%	5.4%
Snapnames	7%	18.9%
Enom's Club Drop	6%	0.9%
Namewinner	1%	–
Moniker TRAFFIC	–	7.9%
Private Sale	–	14.3%
Buy Domains	–	4.1%
Forums	–	0.2%
Other	1%	2.7%

SOURCE: Sedo (2005, 2007)

are highly uncertain, and it is likely that today's leaders will not be industry leaders 5 years from now.

Nevertheless, the aftermarket's growth is predicted to be positive. There are greatly underserved markets throughout the world, namely in emerging countries throughout Asia and Eastern Europe. Millions of people will gain Internet access during the next 10 years. This increase in users will inevitably increase the demand for new and used domain names.

Valuing a Domain Name

The most important issue for domain name vendees and vendors is the determination of the domain name price. As long as a domain name is unregistered, its intrinsic value is equal to the registration fee. But, once that domain name is registered, the resale value is determined by various factors:

- General domain name demand

- Market power distribution

- General economic conditions

- Existence of similar domain names

- Political, regulatory, and sociocultural forces

- Brand name eligibility

- Traffic[4] generating potential (largely dependent on the consumers ability to remember and recognize the domain name, but also includes the name's descriptive power, length, use of common misspelling or mistyping, and its top-level domain [TLD][5])

- Pricing mechanism (usually auction system, offer/counteroffer system, or a combination of both)

In 2004 a new method for determining domain value arose in the industry. This method, called domain parking, connects idle domains with banner advertisements related to the domain's name. Every time a Web user accidentally visits the idle domain, the Web site generates

---

4. Within this context, traffic means the frequency of visits to a Web site measured by the amount of page impressions or unique visitors.

5. Top-level domains are the domain extensions indicating the class of organization behind the Web site (e.g., *.com* for commercial organization or *.edu* for educational organizations) or the country where the Web site owner is located (e.g., *.de* for Germany or *.cn* for China).

Table 2   Top Sale Prices in the Domain Name Aftermarket (in US$)

Domain Name	Year	Price
sex.com	2005	$12,000,000
porn.com	2007	$9,500,000
business.com	1999	$7,500,000
diamond.com	2006	$7,500,000
casino.com	2003	$5,500,000
asseenontv.com	n/a	$5,000,000
altavista.com	1997	$3,250,000
loans.com	2000	$3,000,000
wines.com	2000	$3,000,000
vodka.com	2006	$3,000,000
creditcheck.com	2007	$3,000,000
creditcards.com	2004	$2,750,000
tom.com	2000	$2,500,000
autos.com	1999	$2,200,000
express.com	2000	$2,000,000

advertisement revenues through pay-per-click fees, generating up to six-figure dollar revenues each month. Aside from the revenue generation potential, this tool establishes a solid track record of revenues and traffic potential for the idle site that simplifies its future appraisal.

Today, domain names are increasingly viewed as assets. Professional domain investors who create domain portfolios own most of the domain names. The prices paid for domain names increased as the aftermarket became more successful. The majority of domain name sales are below $2,000; however, select domain name sales reach seven or eight figures (see Table 2). Sedo's most profitable deal was the brokerage of *Vodka.com* for US$3 million.[6] Sedo brokered the deal between a private U.S. domain holder and the buyer, Russian Standard Vodka Company. Once purchased, Russian Standard used the domain to successfully enter the international vodka market.

---

6. It is mentionable that prices are often not published due to nondisclosure agreements.

Sedo's Business Model

The founders created Sedo to replace the highly fragmented domain name aftermarket. The heart of Sedo's services is a specially developed search engine and database that by mid-2007 contained more than 8 million domain names. In addition to its searchable online marketplace, Sedo introduced an escrow service to prevent clients from fraud within domain name transfers. This was an important service addition because fraud was prevalent in other marketplaces.

To facilitate domain name pricing, Sedo additionally launched a domain name appraisal service based on scientific valuation.[7] Sedo also established a domain brokerage that provides expert negotiation services for domain name buyers or sellers. To generate alternative sources of revenue, the company developed a domain-name parking program, earning revenues from advertisements on idle domains.

Sedo began by operating on the small local domain name aftermarket in Germany; but the four founders had international aspirations. Since its founding, internationalization has been a cornerstone of Sedo's business strategy. The 20 nationalities represented by Sedo's staff display the organization's commitment to diversity. Their network of localized Web sites includes Sedo.com, Sedo.us, Sedo.co.uk, Sedo.de, Sedo.fr, Sedo.dk, Sedo.it, Sedo.nl, Sedo.se, Sedo.at, Sedo.ch, Sedo.jp, and Sedo.kr. In addition to the local Web sites, Sedo offers content in four languages: English, French, Spanish, and German.

In 2004 Sedo opened a second office in Boston, Massachusetts. This was the most significant step toward globalizing the brand and allowed Sedo to grab a firm hold on the U.S. domain market. With an office in Boston, Sedo was able to satisfy U.S. customer demands by facilitating faster bank transfers and more efficient customer service.

Despite their internal innovation efforts (product diversification and internationalization), Sedo also used external strategies such as horizontal integration to foster their first priority: growth. Sedo acquired Great-Domains, a former competitor that specialized in premium domain name auctions. In addition, Sedo built partnerships with major companies along the entire domain name value chain: top registrars in Europe, the United States, and Asia; domain financiers like Domain Capital; and advertising agencies, such as Google AdWords.

Sedo's revenue model is based on three major columns:

- Domain trading: For every sold domain Sedo charges 10% of the selling price, or at least EUR 50 (for most TLDs); the additional use of the brokerage service is charged with a EUR 69 handling fee.

---

7. The approach was drawn from Tim Schumacher's master's degree thesis "Price Formation in the Trade of Internet Domain Names."

- Domain parking: Sedo earns up to 50% of the parked domain name's advertising revenues, depending on the size and negotiating power of the domain name owner.

- Domain appraisal: Sedo charges EUR 29 for a standard appraisal and EUR 49 for a premium domain name appraisal. While an important service, its contribution to total revenue is negligible.

THE BUSINESS MODEL'S CHALLENGES

Despite Sedo's success, there are several challenges that jeopardize the organization's growth. Product and service innovations in the area of Internet applications are rarely protected by law and this lack of legal protection allows the competition to benefit from Sedo's advancements. A consequence of this void is that most domain name trading marketplaces offer virtually the same services. Furthermore, marketplace designs are often similar. For example, compare the layouts of sedo.com and afternic .com. The opportunities to stay unique and ahead of the market are fast fading, and it is exceedingly difficult for consumers to differentiate between the available marketplaces and their level of quality.

In the last 2 years, competition in the domain name aftermarket has grown rapidly due to the low barriers to entry. Many small companies have taken advantage of the opportunity to enter the market and hope to capitalize on the success of Sedo and its competitors. The existing earnings-before-interest-and-taxes (EBIT) margins of the domain name aftermarket are endangered and will presumably decrease in the near future.

Sedo's revenue model and the key numbers presented in Table 3 reveal another challenge. Sedo's revenues, and the majority of its profits, are generated by one product: their domain parking service. This single-product dependency is likely to cause challenges for Sedo if competition in this market niche increases and EBIT margins decline.

SEDO'S ADVANTAGES

Throughout its development, Sedo's greatest advantage has been its customer-centric service offerings. In the early 2000s, the uncertainty of the existing auction systems and the prevalence of fraud in the established marketplaces was noticeably dissatisfying domain name customers. These imperfections led Sedo to introduce a pricing system on an offer/counter-offer basis that allowed buyers and sellers to negotiate directly. In addition, Sedo eliminated the danger of fraud by developing a domain escrow service.

Table 3   Key Numbers of Sedo's Success Story

	2000	2001	2002	2003	2004	2005	2006	2007[1]	2008[1]
Revenue	€100,000	€500,000	€635,000	€2,000,000	€7,570,000	€20,780,000	€41,000,000	€62,100,000	€80,400,000
Direct Gross Profit	n/a	n/a	n/a	n/a	n/a	€8,000,000	€19 600 000	€27,900,000	€35,800,000
Employees	3	8	15	22	50	80	120	150	180
Transferred Domains	n/a	n/a	n/a	1,927	5,417	10,989	17,850	30,000	50,000
Average price	n/a	n/a	n/a	€1,416	€1,402	€1,661	€1,720	€1,700	€1,700
Domain Sales Volume	n/a	n/a	n/a	€2,728,632	€7,594,634	€18,252,729	€30,702,000	€51,000,000	€85,000,000
Domains in Database	n/a	100 000	400,000	800,000	1,600,000	3,000,000	6,000,000	10,000,000	15,000,000
Parked Domains	no service	no service	50,000	400,000	500,000	1,000,000	2,000,000	3,500,000	5,000,000

[1]Estimated

SOURCE: All figures are delivered exclusively for this case study by Tim Schumacher, CEO of Sedo.

Even today, Sedo is the only player in the aftermarket to have offices located in Europe and the United States. This physical presence has proven important for gaining positive press, potential partners, and an increasing customer base. Sedo is the only truly multilingual and IDN[8]-ready marketplace.

The Sedo team's technical background is another major asset to their success. The technical heart of Sedo's service is the world's largest domain name database, containing 8 million domain names listed for sale, and their metasearch engine. The research and development department is constantly innovating current and future service offerings. Recently, Sedo became the first marketplace to offer financing programs for high value domains.

November 2006

On that lukewarm spring evening, the four founders sat together late into the night and discussed the prospect of selling a portion of their shares. By the end of the evening, they came to a unanimous decision—they would each sell half of their shares, equaling 24% of all company shares. The more difficult decision was deciding to whom they would sell the shares.

AdLink, already a major investor, was an eager prospect. But the founders also considered other investors, particularly private equity companies who were attracted by Sedo's fast growth and future potential. The decision-making process was not as easy as it had been in 2001 when United Internet acquired 41% of Sedo's shares. It took the founders 6 months to reach a decision and, ultimately, it was their intuition and past experiences that allowed them to come to a consensus. Tim Schumacher, Ulrich Priesner, Ulrich Essmann, and Marius Wuerzner decided to sell their shares to their present investor, despite higher offers from other bidders.

AdLink increased its stake in Sedo to 76% for nearly EUR 35 million in cash. Today, the four founders still work at Sedo in top management positions. They all hope to remain with the company as it realizes its potential and continues to grow.

Case Questions

1. How did Sedo's market value develop from 2000 to 2006?

2. To what extent was the 2006 exit strategic for the founders and the investor AdLink?

---

8. An IDN, or Internationalized Domain Name, is a domain name that can contain non-ASCII characters such as Arabic or Chinese characters.

3. Was the 2006 exit a bargain, fair valued, or overpriced? Take into account that Sedo's estimated EBIT was EUR 16 million and average EBIT multiples range between 5.5 and 8.1 for companies in the information technology industry.

4. How can Sedo's management team sustain the company's current market position in the future?

References

AdLink Internet Media. (2005). *Annual report 2005*. Montabaur: Author.

Sedo. (2005). *2004 record year for internet domain trader*. Electronic Press Release. Retrieved March 14, 2008, from www.sedo.de/presse/presse_190105.php4?tracked=&partnerid=&language=d

Sedo. (2007). *Sedo domain market survey 2006*. Electronic Press Release. Retrieved March 14, 2008, from www.sedo.de/presse/presse_260307.php4?tracked=&partnerid=&language=d.

United Internet. (2004). *Annual report 2004*. Montabaur: Author.

Fasteners for Retail

A Question of Succession

Research associate Tracey Eira Messer prepared this case under the supervision of Professor Ernesto J. Poza as the basis for class discussion rather than to illustrate the effective or ineffective handling of an administrative situation. For permission to publish this case, grateful acknowledgment is made to Gerald Conway, chairman emeritus of Fasteners for Retail.

In December 1999 Gerry Conway faced the toughest decision of his 37 years as an entrepreneur. Something had to be done about the long-term future of Fasteners for Retail (FFr), the business he had founded in 1962. The company had been extremely successful, with sales doubling every 5 years since the 1980s and the market for the company's point-of-purchase display products still growing. Within the last 2 years, the company had begun to expand from an enormously successful catalogue company into a full-service provider to global retail chains.

With no dominant players in FFr's niche, Conway saw nothing but opportunity ahead. Still, he was concerned. The company had been debt-free from the start, but feeding its continuing growth would require an infusion of cash. At 69, Conway felt that this was more risk than he wanted to assume. Of even more pressing concern was his son and heir apparent's recent announcement that he did not want to become FFr's next president and instead planned to leave the company. None of his other children were interested in becoming part of the leadership team. Conway mused:

> I am a good entrepreneur, but I am not managerial in nature and I don't like that part of the business. I have a good manager here in Don Kimmel [the nonfamily company president]. It is time to move on. Until a year ago, I couldn't decide what to do because I was ambivalent, but now I have reached a point where I want to make a transition.

This decision would affect the future of his family, his business, and its 95 employees. Should he sell the company, appoint a nonfamily CEO, or persuade another family member to come into the business?

The Founder

Gerry Conway was the classic American entrepreneur—visionary, charismatic, driven, impatient, and independent. Born in Cleveland in 1931, Conway was the ninth of thirteen children. His love of the retail environment, his strong independence, and his deep appreciation of people stemmed from his childhood experiences:

> With a little exaggeration, I can say that I've been in retail for 60 years. My dad managed approximately 200 food stores, and my first jobs were as a stock boy and butcher's assistant. At home we'd talk about business over the dinner table. With 11 sons and 2 daughters in the family, it was a lively conversation. I already had the entrepreneurial itch, and, from the grocery experience and from having a newspaper delivery route, I learned how to get along with people.

After college Conway and his wife, Marty, returned to Cleveland. He began working for an industrial firm and quickly learned that while sales attracted him, working in a large corporation did not. Conway's next job was with a smaller firm:

> I started selling display lithography for a small printer. When that company went belly up, I founded Gerald A. Conway & Associates and became a display-printing broker. I was 31 years old, had $600 in the bank and a wife and six kids counting on me. For the first 5 years, I had one goal—survival. Even after we were established, the company was a central part of my life.

Conway was an extremely personable man. He made friends and networked with ease. One day a colleague suggested that he sell the plastic parts that retailers use to display signs (called display and merchandising accessories) as part of his printing broker business. The advantage of selling accessories was that he could sell the same product to many companies simultaneously, which wasn't possible in display printing, where each printing job was customized. An early product idea was the Arrowhead® fastener, which was designed to hold coupons and signs on store shelves (see Figure 1). It was a best seller from the start. For the next decade, Gerald A. Conway & Associates was a printing broker and a supplier of display accessories.

During this time Conway struggled with alcohol: "In 1970 alcohol was becoming a problem, but through a self-help program I chose sobriety and regained focus in my life. The following year, my first year sober, my income shot up by about 35%—a direct correlation. So, anyway, that was a significant event in the business and for my family."

110

our very first fastener for retail

Here's where it all started. Our very first product: the AF-101 Arrowhead® Fastener. Still in widespread use today, holding coupons or signage from shelf channels and a myriad of other flat display surfaces.

sign holders
Arrowhead®

AF-101 Arrowhead® Fastener

A cost-effective way to securely hold pads of coupons or single signs in the centered flush position.
▶ Fits most standard 1 ¼" shelf channels
▶ 530 78951 02 has permanent adhesive for use on most flat surfaces
▶ Stem ½" L
▶ Natural Polypropylene

530 78951 01

Part No.	Style	1-999	1,000	2,500	5,000
530 78951 01	w/o adh	52.00/M	39.00/M	29.00/M	24.00/M
530 78951 02	w/ adh	72.00/M	59.00/M	49.00/M	44.00/M

Custom colors available. (minimum order required)

AF-101F Arrowhead® Fastener

Designed for even easier insertion in shelf channels.
▶ Easy flex design
▶ Holds coupon pads or single signs
▶ Fits most standard 1 ¼" shelf channels
▶ Stem ½" L
▶ Natural Polyethylene

530 78951 04

Part No.	Size	1-999	1,000	2,500	5,000
530 78951 04	½" L	52.00/M	39.00/M	29.00/M	24.00/M

Custom colors available. (minimum order required)

AF-102 Arrowhead® Fastener

Securely pin coupon pads or single signs to shelf fronts.
▶ Fits most standard 1 ¼" shelf channels
▶ 530 77348 02 has permanent adhesive for use on most flat surfaces
▶ Stem ⅞" L
▶ Natural Polypropylene

530 77348 01

Part No.	Size	1-999	1,000	2,500	5,000
530 77348 01	w/o adh	79.00/M	60.00/M	49.00/M	45.00/M
530 77348 02	w/ adh	104.00/M	85.00/M	74.00/M	70.00/M

Custom colors available. (minimum order required)

800.422.CLIP (2547)

Figure 1   Arrowhead Fasteners

The Point-of-Purchase (POP) Industry

In the mid-1970s, Gerald Conway & Associates was renamed Fasteners for Retail (FFr) to acknowledge its exclusive focus on display accessories and fasteners within the point-of-purchase (POP) industry.

Point-of-purchase products include the signs, displays, devices, and structures that are used to merchandise services or products in retail stores. The POP industry was estimated to be a US$13.1 billion sector, based on 1997 industry figures (see Figure 2). FFr's segment was estimated to be approximately US$600 million. Although the broader POP market was expected to grow at 4% annually, FFr and its competitors experienced much higher growth rates. FFr, for example, had grown 19.6% annually since 1984.

The accessory hardware segment (FFr's niche) was highly fragmented. No single supplier had more than 10% of the subsupplier market, and many competed in only a few product categories. FFr was the largest company in this niche, with a market share of approximately 7.5%. The company's major

---

POP TRENDS

POP is defined as displays signs, structures and devices that are used to identify advertise, and /or merchandise an outlet, service, or product and which serve as aids to retailing.

POP IS A RAPIDLY GROWING INDUSTRY

2002 (Projected)	$16.0 billion
1997	$13.1 billion
1996	$12.7 billion
1995	$12.0 billion
1994	$11.1 billion

Almost three-quarters of customer purchase decisions are made in-store, at the point of purchase.

Product Proliferation is on the rise.

Supermarket Assortments:
        1992 13,067 SKUs
        2001 30,580 SKUs

SOURCES: Point of Purchase Advertising Institute; POPAI Consumer Buying Habits Study; and Food Marketing Institute.

Figure 2   POP TRENDS

product offerings included shelf and nonshelf channel sign holders, display hooks, display construction, and custom products. FFr also offered shelf systems, ceiling display systems, product strips, hang tabs, literature holders, and other accessories. Several key contractors manufactured these products for FFr, but no single manufacturer had unique or proprietary capabilities.

Value Added From the Start

FFr distinguished itself from its competitors in several important ways. The company offered a broad and innovative product line, free samples, quick turnaround on orders, and a liberal return policy.

PRODUCTS

The willingness to emphasize new products became a defining characteristic of the business. While the company's early expansion began with imported Swedish design accessories, the product line grew because of Conway's creativity and dissatisfaction with the status quo.

Successful design accessories are functional, fit a specific space, and are inexpensive. New products were developed from scratch, acquired, or adapted from other industries. Conway excelled in all aspects of product development—imagining how new products could meet customer needs and seeing how existing products could be used in or improved for the POP market. Two products in particular, the Shipflat® literature holder (see Figure 3) and SuperGrip® sign holders (see Figure 4), were critical to FFr's success in the early 1980s. (The complete FFr online catalogue can be found at www.ffr.com.)

Shipflat Literature Holder

At a trade show, Citibank challenged FFr to make a better literature holder. At the time literature holders were made from rigid plastic. Only four holders could be shipped per box, and they frequently broke in transit. After a year of effort, FFr successfully designed attractive and durable literature holders that were unique in that they shipped flat and were set up at the point of use, eliminating breakage and reducing inventory space and shipping cost. Citibank had exclusive rights to the Shipflat for several years, and it placed the Shipflat at the core of its credit card program. Working with Citibank enhanced FFr's credibility and raised its visibility in the market; Citibank recognized the company as an "Outstanding Merchant" for its product and customer service. The Shipflat became

194

Shipflat Literature Holders

Shipflat® literature holders ship flat, eliminating breakage and reducing your inventory space and shipping costs by up to 50%! A few simple folds turn your Shipflat® into a rigid information holder. The clear material helps present literature in the best possible light, whether freestanding or wall-mounted.

IS Shipflat® Literature Holder

These literature holders ship flat and feature both pop-out and easel mounting holes.

- Simple, snap-together design
- Wide range of sizes
- Also available in custom colors
- Color imprinting available (below)
- Clear K-Resin

IS-91 (920 76692 01)
- Holds literature up to 3 7/8" W
- 3 7/8" W x 7" H x 1 5/8" D
- Imprint field 3 5/16" W x 1 9/16" H

IS-2 (920 19821 01)
- Holds literature up to 3 7/8" wide
- 3 7/8" W x 10" H x 1 5/8" D
- Imprint field 3 3/8" W x 1 9/16" H at base plus additional imprint area on header

IS-4 (920 80594 01)
- Holds literature up to 4 1/8" wide
- 4 1/8" W x 7" H x 1 5/8" D
- Imprint field 3 5/8" W x 1 1/2" H

IS-4H (920 16546 01)
- Holds literature up to 4 1/8" wide
- 4 1/8" W x 7" H x 1 5/8" D
- Imprint field 3 5/8" W x 2 1/2" H

IS-6 (920 77745 01)
- Holds literature up to 6 1/8" wide
- 6 1/8" W x 7" H x 1 5/8" D
- Imprint field 5 1/2" W x 1 9/16" H

IS-8 (920 18977 01)
- Holds literature up to 8 1/2" wide
- 8 1/2" W x 10" H x 1 3/4" D
- Imprint field 8" W x 2 1/2" H

new lower prices!

Part No.	Width	1-9	10	25	100	200	500	1000
920 76692 01	3 7/8"	2.88 ea	2.16 ea	1.80 ea	1.44 ea	1.31 ea	1.19 ea	1.05 ea
920 19821 01	3 7/8"	3.24 ea	2.48 ea	1.94 ea	1.71 ea	1.55 ea	1.45 ea	1.30 ea
920 80594 01	4 1/8"	2.25 ea	1.95 ea	1.75 ea	1.55 ea	1.40 ea	1.25 ea	1.08 ea
920 16546 01	4 1/8"	3.19 ea	2.43 ea	1.89 ea	1.66 ea	1.52 ea	1.42 ea	1.28 ea
920 77745 01	6 1/8"	3.60 ea	2.88 ea	2.34 ea	1.98 ea	1.85 ea	1.75 ea	1.58 ea
920 18977 01	8 1/2"	5.24 ea	3.24 ea	2.84 ea	2.34 ea	2.24 ea	2.04 ea	1.94 ea

Patented

920 76692 01

920 16546 01

Shipflat® Imprinting

One-color imprinting is available on the front face of all Shipflat® Literature Holders.*

- Actual-size camera-ready art required
- 2- and 3-color imprinting available with prior art approval (call for details)
- Die Charge: $125.00 per color
- Minimum order: 100 pieces

*IS-2 model (920 19821 01) can also be imprinted on the header (above)

Part No.	100	200	500	1,000	2,500
IS-IMPRINT	.60 ea	.35 ea	.20 ea	.15 ea	.12 ea

800.422.CLIP (2547)

Figure 3   Shipflat Literature Holders

FFr's first proprietary product in the literature holder category and was well received by auto clubs, insurance companies, and pharmaceutical firms, among others. Within 2 years, the Shipflat became FFr's top seller.

SuperGrip Sign Holders

In the early 1980s, a new product began appearing in the accessory market. FFr recognized this product's superior holding ability—it was able to hold paper signs in place more securely than existing technology. It represented a threat to FFr's product line, so the company tracked down the patent and began trying to develop its own version of the clip. At almost the same time, the clip's Canadian inventor, unhappy with his distributor, negotiated with FFr to distribute the product. FFr began distributing the clip and eventually purchased the patent from its Canadian partner. FFr renamed the clip and applied the technology to its existing products, thus expanding the product line. SuperGrip products were very successful with both retailers and consumer goods companies and, at one point, accounted for almost 20% of sales.

For years FFr's marketing thrust was proprietary products. Recent efforts focused on developing an increasing number of custom products, designed to meet specific customer needs. New products were introduced as they were designed, without concern for cannibalizing sales of existing products. FFr encouraged the development of both custom and proprietary products, promoting internal competition within the organization.

FFr typically offered customers more than 100 new products every year. New product ideas came from FFr personnel, from customers, and from the acquisition of new product concepts. New product development statistics were impressive. In a niche known for commodity products, FFr had almost 75 patents and patents pending. Patented products accounted for 20% of all products offered and represented a significant competitive advantage. On average, products that had been developed in the last 5 years accounted for 30% of sales. FFr valued and actively protected its designs.

SERVICE

FFr's products and superior service separated it from its competition. Independent audits repeatedly found that customers rated FFr's customer service as superior. An early hire recalled:

> When I began working here, we weren't quite sure who we were or what market we were in, so we looked around at other organizations and emulated what was best about them. Through that process, we became leaders. Following Gerry's lead, we never took things for granted. As a family-owned company, we were able to respond quickly to opportunities and customer needs.

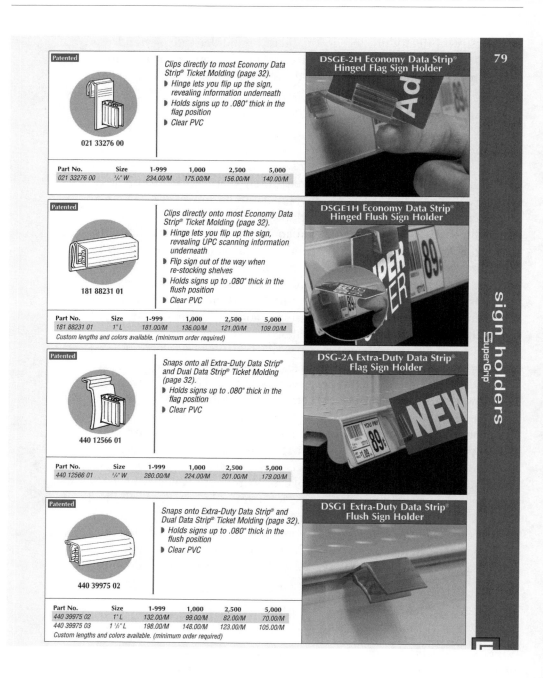

Figure 4   SuperGrip Sign Holders

While its competitors maintained limited inventories and dictated shipment terms to customers, FFr offered a complete line of products, kept a well-stocked inventory, bagged products to meet the customer's specifications, and shipped products as requested. Other vendors offered better prices but poorer service. FFr came to dominate its market by offering both service and selection. Conway recalled:

> We created our competitors. After a few years, they looked at us and said, "We can do that too." We had a broad product line and did custom work; others began adopting those programs. Our success in branding is evident from the widescale copycatting of our colors, style, and product line.

FFr was both a direct sales and a marketing sales company. It relied on its salesforce, direct mail catalogue, trade media advertising, trade shows, and sample department to promote its products. The company's unique product catalogue, the FFR Yellow Pages®, set a new standard for the industry and helped establish FFr as a first-look supplier within the industry. The sales organization consisted of a direct salesforce, international distributors, a customer service group, and a telemarketing staff.

CULTURE

From its first hire on, FFr was a company whose employees, from designers to warehouse staff, focused on customer satisfaction (see Figure 5). As a 16-year veteran recalled:

> Gerry had the ability to hire people who would work independently but in a common direction and for a common goal. He was fortunate to have surrounded himself with people who had the sense of urgency and good work ethic to make things happen. This was true even of outsourced services. . . . Employees of our service center treated our clients as if they [the service center employees] were actually FFr.

FFr's customer-first focus extended to the company newsletter, which told tales of employees going above and beyond expectations to deliver superior customer service. It offered hints for achieving customer satisfaction, solicited new product ideas, and reported on product development. The newsletter also filled a more traditional communication role, introducing new hires and announcing promotions, company anniversaries, and birthdays.

Maintaining profit margins was also part of the FFr culture. President Don Kimmel recalled, "When I arrived, the focus on margins was so strong that I occasionally had to take a hammer to break it a bit. We would rather lose an order, if we couldn't beat the hell out of a supplier to get the margin we wanted, than deviate from our margins."

FASTENERS FOR RETAIL

Welcome to FFr!

On behalf of all the employees at FFr, I welcome you to the FFr team and our thriving organization. We realize you may have put significant time and effort into your decision to join FFr, and we are pleased you have made a commitment to further your career with us. It's important we work together to fulfill both your professional goals and our overall company goals.

Since 1962, FFr has been recognized as a leader in custom and stock merchandising systems and accessories, as well as in providing outstanding customer service. We are very proud of this recognition, as well as our long-term customer and employee relationships.

To this end, the following "Statement of Values" guides our daily operations:

- Commit ourselves to excellence in creativity, quality, and service.
- Treat our customers and each other with respect.
- Seek opportunities for continuous improvement, with our goal being 100 percent customer satisfaction.
- Focus on developing and maintaining customers for life by maximizing the value we provide.
- Work as a team to support each other and achieve our goals.

We realize our continued success rests solely on our ability to recruit and retain the best people, like you.

Again, welcome to FFr. I wish you every success in your career with us.

Sincerely,

Donald F. Kimmel
President & COO

Figure 5   FFr's Statement of Values

Growth in the 1980s

FFr grew at a consistent and steady pace. In 1980 the company had five employees and sales of US$3 million. Business began to boom in the early 1980s as a result of an expanding product line and a larger salesforce. FFr grew steadily, adding employees in accounting, customer service, product design, and marketing. Company offices were moved to accommodate additional warehouse and distribution functions. Paul, one of Conway's sons, observed, "Dad managed the business like a football halfback, scanning the horizon looking for an opening and then heading for it. He was never afraid to explore new business possibilities and was always looking for opportunities."

This opportunistic philosophy supported FFr's growth. The business was always profitable, there was no debt, and the company never got tied up in long-term commitments. Production and most warehousing were subcontracted, and office space was leased. The company made quick decisions, and arrangements with vendors were frequently based on handshakes.

The flip side of FFr's opportunism and speed was that it lacked a business plan and strategic discipline. When Conway came across an interesting idea, he wanted to implement it. Company lore had it that when Conway sat next to a consultant on an airplane, the consultant would be onsite the following week to redesign something. This approach led to some important innovations and prevented the company from becoming stagnant, but it also created a sense of confusion and the feeling that priorities were constantly changing.

To keep the company growing, Conway realized that he needed to hire a president with managerial expertise. Although he understood the value of management, he was an entrepreneur, not a traditional manager. The company went through several presidents. FFr, for a time, was a company with an organizational chart but not a lot of organization. That changed in the late 1990s.

Growth in the 1990s and Beyond

In the early 1990s, Conway and his wife, Marty, joined Case Western Reserve University's Partnership for Family Business. Through the program and conversation with other business owners, Conway began to see the need for different points of view regarding the business, and he decided to establish an advisory board:

> One of the things that sprang from the family business program was that we set up a board of advisors. The board consisted of four independent current

and former company CEOs. It included my brother and my son Stuart, who ran his own nonprofit organization. Preparing for these meetings was a great discipline. The board challenged me through a review process and an implied evaluation of my performance. These men had all managed their own businesses. From their advice I learned that entrepreneurship alone isn't enough to generate continued growth. Management and systems become essential once a business reaches a sales volume of $10 million plus or has 50 plus employees.

These advisors helped the family better understand nonfamily management's needs and helped nonfamily managers appreciate the unique aspects of family firms. Most significantly, the board encouraged Conway to professionalize the staff and to build internal controls and an infrastructure (see Figure 6). The board had no statutory power but did provide good advice and served as a valuable sounding board.

After several unsuccessful hires, Conway named Don Kimmel as president. Kimmel was the perfect foil to Conway's creative vision and energy. He introduced a financial system and an organizational structure to complement the creative design and sales energy that had propelled the company for many years. Kimmel's strengths as a manager allowed Conway to shift out of the daily management role and focus on sales and product design, his strengths.

Under Kimmel's leadership and with the support of the advisory board, FFr began a rigorous strategic planning process in 1997. An internal analysis recommended that the company upgrade its management talent, consolidate its sales organization, and focus on selling to the major retail chains. These chains were rapidly expanding and represented a potential US$600 million market. The needs of these retailers were different from

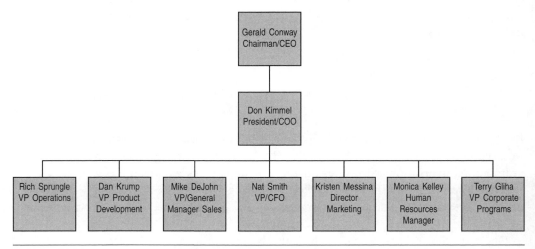

Figure 6   Organizational Chart of Fasteners for Retail, 1999

those of FFr's traditional customers, so FFr created a program selling division and made other internal changes to address those needs. The company expanded its engineering, design, and in-house sales team to meet customer expectations. FFr revisited its previously inviolate margins and adjusted them to be price competitive. It began sharing cost and margin information with its suppliers, partnering with them to meet customer needs for design and price. The company made its first significant sale to Wal-Mart in 1998. A few years later, program sales to retailers accounted for over 20% of sales.

Family Involvement

Family involvement began in the 1970s when the Conway children earned extra money by putting adhesive on the backs of Arrowhead fasteners. They had all done odd jobs for FFr, but of the seven children only three worked in the business as adults (see Figure 7).

Initially, the children did not see joining FFr as a career option. During their formative years, the company was pretty much a one-man operation. In the words of one son, "There was nothing to join." As the company grew, several of the children began to consider joining the firm.

Kevin, the eldest, joined in the early 1980s and became an outstanding salesman. Kevin had Gerry's gift for sales and was frequently on the road, visiting customers and closing orders. Kevin worked at FFr for many years until health problems prompted him to resign.

From an early age, the youngest son, Paul, planned to join FFr. At his father's urging, he began his work career with another employer. It was

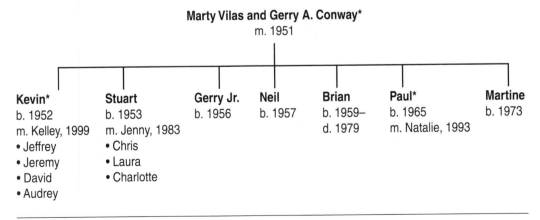

Figure 7   Conway Family Tree

*Family members active in the business

only after he'd been successful there that he joined FFr in 1988; his first job was in the marketing department.

Neil, the fourth son, worked in the warehouse. Neil developed schizophrenia during his first year of college, and the structure of part-time employment in the warehouse worked well for him and for the company. As a result of the positive work experience with Neil, FFr hired other workers with neurobiological disorders.

It wasn't until the early 1990s that Gerry Conway began to focus on succession. His attention was driven by the company's success, his sons' active presence in FFr, and participation in the family business program. Through the program, the Conways were introduced to the components of a well-executed succession process, including strategic planning, communication, and accommodation among family members through family meetings, estate planning for business agility, leveraging family skills with those of nonfamily managers, using outside board members as advisors, and promoting the development of the next generation.

Family meetings were a high point for Gerry's wife, Marty:

> From the family business program, we learned about family meetings. We had an outside facilitator at the first meeting and it was marvelous—he had experiential learning games for us to play and different ways to communicate. By the third meeting, different family members were taking responsibility for planning activities for the meetings. The focus for the meetings shifted to the business of family from family business. Everyone in the family looked forward to the family meetings. They were a chance for us all to be together as a family. We talked about business and caught up with each other as family.

The family meetings were important to Gerry as well:

> Before we had family meetings, I kept pretty much everything to myself. I was not that open. One of the things I learned was the importance of communication. At the first meeting, there was a critical point where I had to remind my family that while this was a family business, I had to make the final operating decisions.

As adults, all seven next-generation members of the Conway family got along well and respected each other and each other's life and career choices. They also respected FFr—the house that Gerry had built—and the family values that Marty continued to nurture. Their sense of family unity was balanced by an appreciation for individual differences.

As part of their estate planning, Gerry and Marty created a trust and transferred the majority of their FFr shares to their children. Gerry retained voting rights, however. Family meetings began around this time and proved to be a useful way for the new owners, particularly those not active in managing the business, to learn more about the business and the estate.

Estate Planning

One of the goals of the Conways' estate plan was to transfer a substantial amount of the value of FFr to their children during their lifetime so as to avoid estate taxes, but to do so without relinquishing control of the company. Gerry and Marty knew that by transferring sizable value while they were alive, they would avoid the 55% estate tax—not only on the value transferred but also on the future growth of the value transferred. To transfer value without relinquishing control, the company's stock was split into voting and nonvoting shares. Nonvoting shares were used for gifting purposes.

In addition, the Conways used a grantor-retained annuity trust (GRAT) for each child. In other words, the nonvoting shares were transferred into a trust for each child, and the trusts required that Gerry and Marty, as grantors, receive an annuity (income stream) from the trusts for a period of years. The per-share value of the shares transferred was reduced by the present value of the annuity interest Gerry and Marty retained, meaning that they could give more shares away.

After a period of years, the GRATs terminated in accordance with the trust provisions. Children who were over 30 took their shares outright; the shares belonging to those who were not over 30 remained in successor trusts. To provide liquidity in the event of the untimely death of a shareholder, the Conways and their children entered into shareholders' agreements for the voting and nonvoting shares. They funded the crosspurchase obligations in the agreements with life insurance policies, held in an insurance trust.

Succession: Paul and Kevin's Stories

Although Kevin was the first child to join FFr, he was never a candidate for CEO. Like so many excellent salesmen, he did not like managerial activities. As the company grew, his interest in it waned, in part because he disliked the increased number of systems that were implemented to support the company's growth.

Paul Conway joined FFr a few years after Kevin did. Paul's earliest memories were of working for FFr. When he was 8 years old, he had put adhesive tape on the backs of 10,000 Arrowhead fasteners and had earned enough money to buy his first bicycle. An entrepreneur was born. Over the next 10 years, he and his friends continued to put adhesive on the backs of fasteners each time they needed spending money.

Paul began seriously imagining his future with FFr while he was in high school. He worked at FFr during college vacations and then joined another business after college graduation to gain additional work experience. After only 1 year, FFr's nonfamily marketing manager encouraged Paul and Gerry to negotiate Paul's entry into the company. Paul began work as a marketing assistant and sales representative and rotated through FFr's business units. Paul had clear ideas about how he wanted to be perceived:

> I admired my dad's knack for success and was happy to be with him in the business. Still, I wanted to make sure that I was not the typical SOB [son of boss]. I didn't want to take advantage of my family relationship or have people perceive that I was, even though I knew that some people would, no matter what I did.

Paul became the international sales manager and built FFr's international business while also maintaining a position in the marketing department. After 7 years he became the marketing manager. Two years after that promotion, Paul was asked to become the assistant to the president, Don Kimmel. The timing of the offer was significant. FFr's rapid expansion had left Don without time for long-range planning. Adding Paul to the executive suite provided needed support and allowed Paul to learn the business from a different vantage point:

> I reached the Peter Principle as marketing manager. I didn't have formal training and the position was getting a little unwieldy for me. I just didn't have the tools, and Don needed help with management. Either I was going to use this new role as a launching pad or I was going to figure out that I didn't want to work at FFr anymore and would move on to something else.

For the first time in his career at FFr, Paul was working directly with his father on a regular basis. With greater access to management's decisions, he came to a realization about his future with FFr:

> I didn't like my dad's management style. I'd always tell him about it, and we'd talk it through. We argued at times, but our arguments were always short-lived. It was as healthy an element of communication within our family as I had. But regardless of that, the disagreements were part of why the experience grew sour. I started to think about the reality of working in a larger corporation. When the business was smaller and a little more family-oriented, it was more enjoyable to me.

Paul worked for over a year to clarify his goals, first to understand what leading FFr would mean and then to explore other career opportunities. In his view, Gerry was able to manage the business because he had grown with it. Paul felt that he was less equipped than his dad to manage the large and growing business (see Table 1). Members of the advisory board felt that Paul could learn the job if he wanted to and that having an experienced management team in place would give him time to learn. One board member recalled: "At the beginning of the succession process, Paul was really the only son who was actively involved in the company. I thought that Paul would become president and believed that he had the capability to do the job well."

At one point, Paul said that he didn't want to be in the position of making some of the tough decisions. Gerry's brother, FFr board member Bill Conway, said:

> Now that is being very honest, but I think he was looking at the responsibilities and the pressures of being the CEO as being more than they needed to be. Gerry was a loner in the way he ran his business. Paul may not have realized that he could do the job differently—probably in a more decentralized and collaborative way. I kept wondering if there was something I might have done with respect to Paul that would have made him feel more comfortable in the potential role.

Bill suggested that Paul give himself more time in the business before he made that decision. Paul thought about his choices for about a year and

Table 1   Annual Revenues for Fasteners for Retail, 1994–2001

Year	Net Sales (millions)
1994	$18
1995	23
1996	29
1997	33
1998	41
1999	47
2000	52
2001	62

ultimately decided that he wanted to leave the company and become a teacher. The decision to leave FFr was not easy:

> I felt like I was the last of the Mohicans—the last possible guy to run the company. When I decided that I didn't want to do it, I felt guilty. . . . My dad deserved a lot of credit. He really wanted to pass the business along to one of his children. After I said that I didn't want to stay in the business, he said OK, and then we met as a family to discuss the implications.

Succession: Marty's Point of View

Marty Conway was one of Gerry's chief advisors. While Gerry was the obvious leader of the company, it was Marty who signed the checks and kept an eye on corporate finances. She had a public role at company functions and was a people booster. She played a more significant role behind the scenes, supporting Gerry as he considered important business changes, such as handing over the administrative reins or making personnel changes. Both family members and outsiders described Marty as the glue that worked behind the scenes to hold the family together through the predictable challenges that families who work together face. She summed up Paul's role at FFr as follows:

> When Paul would come over, Gerry and Paul would talk business all the time, which used to drive me crazy. But that was just part of their life together. The only person I really talked to about the business in terms of succession was Paul. When Paul was young, he said, "Someday, I am going to grow up and I am going to run the company."
>
> After he graduated from college he went to work. . . . Gerry's advice to all of them had been if you want to join the company, you have got to go out in the real world first. Paul worked very hard for an insurance company and won salesman of the year during his first year. At that point, FFr was just starting to grow. I said, "If you really want to get involved in this company, now is the time." So Gerry took him in then.

Succession: Gerry's Dilemma

Gerry Conway was a passionate entrepreneur, a business builder. During the early part of his career, he traveled extensively, meeting customers and serving as chief salesman, marketer, and innovator for the company. Whether he was on the road or in the office, his presence was felt throughout the organization.

Conway's life had been organized around his family and his company. For almost 4 decades, home and work were the center of his life—his passion and his zeal. He had always thought of them as being joined. Suddenly that didn't seem possible anymore:

> Kevin was out of the picture. Stuart had long ago decided that he didn't want to work in the business. Paul recently had decided he didn't want the responsibility. None of the other kids were interested. At the same time, I felt frustrated every day as I tried to handle this big company. I thought it was time to move on.

Then Conway's thoughts shifted to his personal situation, and he said to himself, Oh my God, what am I going to do with the rest of my life? "I hadn't done a tremendous amount of planning on the retirement side. I had done some, but the demands of running a business didn't leave a lot of time."

As Conway contemplated the future of FFr, his management team put the finishing touches on the company's new strategic plan. The plan made a strong and well-supported case for making a significant capital investment to develop fulfillment capabilities, to consider manufacturing selected items, to expand sales internationally, and to increase the product line through strategic acquisitions.

Conway intuitively knew that the time for the business to aggressively explore these growth opportunities had arrived. Funding the plan would take all the cash out of the business and would also require outside financing. A combined advisory board and family council meeting was scheduled for the following week. It was time for Conway to decide what action to take.

Case Questions

1. What was Gerry Conway doing to lead these three key constituencies: (a) nonfamily employees, (b) family members working in the business, and (c) other family shareholders?

2. What managerial and governance best practices was Gerry Conway relying on to promote family business continuity? Discuss each practice and how it was used.

3. What do you predict will happen in this case? Explain your reasoning.

The Vega Food Company

This case was prepared by Professor Ernesto J. Poza as the basis for a class discussion rather than to illustrate the effective or ineffective handling of a family business management situation. For permission to publish this case, grateful acknowledgment is made to the chairman and the executive vice president of the company. Note that while the case is factually and historically accurate, the names have been changed to protect the privacy of the family.

In February 1997 Francisco Valle, Jr., president of Industrias La Vega, organized the first family council meeting in the owning family's history to address problems he was having with his youngest sister, Mari, a shareholder in the company. He felt that the problems were not of his making and were interfering with his management of the company. Francisco, 45, had worked closely with his father, Francisco Sr., since 1976 and had become president of the company in March 1994 when his 72-year-old father was killed in an automobile accident. Industrias La Vega was a Spanish meat processing business that produced hams, sausages, and other delicacies for domestic and export markets. The US$104.8 million-a-year business was demanding, of course, but Francisco Jr. felt most challenged by the family conflicts that often overwhelmed him.

The ownership structure of Industrias La Vega had been updated just months before the tragic accident involving Francisco Sr. At the request of Francisco Jr., who was concerned about the possible loss of control of the enterprise he had co-managed with his father for years, Francisco Sr. and his attorneys had created two classes of stock. The voting A shares did not pay dividends. The nonvoting but dividend-bearing B shares had a par value 10 times higher than that of the A shares.

Except for brief stints, none of the Valle daughters had worked in the business prior to their father's death. Ana, the second eldest daughter, was an artist, and she had been instrumental in designing the image and logo of a new premium product line. Working alongside her father, she had created the look for the Gold Label line of meats and cold cuts; Francisco Jr. had not been particularly enthusiastic about this new line.

Mari, 27, the youngest of the Valle siblings, was concerned about her future and the security of her own young family after her father's death. She worried about how her interests as a shareholder would be protected.

She had trusted her father completely, but she was not sure she had the same faith in Francisco Jr.

She did admit to being a little more optimistic now that Francisco was making an effort to get closer to the lower-level employees and be more of a leader in the company. As it turned out, Francisco was not just his father's successor in the company, but also in politics. His father had won a Senate seat in the last election before his tragic accident. Francisco campaigned for and won the seat and served what would have been his father's term. Mari and his four other sisters would chide Francisco about being so effective in his political campaigning and yet so unable to instill a team spirit among the company's employees. He was, in fact, still spending 3 to 4 days a week on political endeavors.

The farmers and cattle ranchers of whom Francisco Sr. had been a life-long customer trusted him. As a major customer for their products, he had much influence with them. His successful run for the Senate at the age of 72 was evidence of the degree of this influence, even outside of business circles. In the food processing industry, good relations with the government represented an asset for the Valle family from which both generations derived competitive advantage.

The Valle Family

The Valle family was wealthy by the standards of the small town in which they had most of their production facilities. Francisco Valle, Sr., was a self-made entrepreneur. He married Isabel in 1947 and had five daughters and a son (see Figure 1). In 1997 Valle family members included Isabel, 71, Francisco Sr.'s widow; Rosa, 47; Francisco Jr., 45; Ana, 42; María, 38; Tere, 33; and Mari, 27. Of these, only Francisco Jr. and Tere worked in management positions. And Tere had joined the company only 3 years earlier.

Relations between family members were warm, particularly among the women, though several next-generation members had created very different lives for themselves. Rosa and Maria lived overseas but visited Isabel two or three times a year. The only son, Francisco Jr., had studied agribusiness overseas and then returned to run the family business.

In a traditional display of primogeniture, Francisco seemed pre-ordained to be the successor to his father. He took his responsibilities toward his mother and sisters seriously, although they all complained a little about not being involved enough, not being kept sufficiently informed, and not being treated the same way Francisco was treated by the company. Francisco received a reasonable CEO salary, bonus, and benefits package. But the sisters' dividends were nowhere close to his take-home pay, and Francisco, with his expensive tastes, seemed to flaunt the

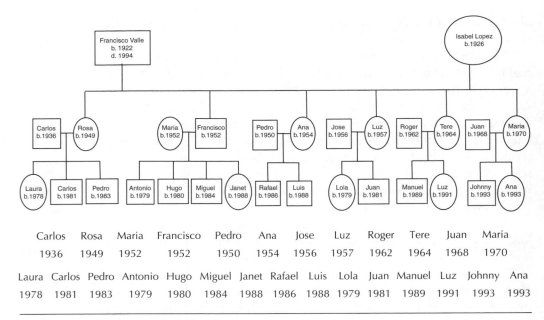

Carlos	Rosa	Maria	Francisco	Pedro	Ana	Jose	Luz	Roger	Tere	Juan	Maria
1936	1949	1952	1952	1950	1954	1956	1957	1962	1964	1968	1970

Laura	Carlos	Pedro	Antonio	Hugo	Miguel	Janet	Rafael	Luis	Lola	Juan	Manuel	Luz	Johnny	Ana
1978	1981	1983	1979	1980	1984	1988	1986	1988	1979	1981	1989	1991	1993	1993

Figure 1   Valle Family Genogram

difference. A palatial home, luxury car, helicopter, boat, and assorted other toys all seemed essential to Francisco in his executive post. A couple of the sisters were divorced and had additional financial responsibilities toward their own children. Even Isabel lived in a more modest house and drove a less expensive car than Francisco did.

Family members characterized themselves as being hermetically sealed, meaning that they were not great communicators. This was particularly true on the subject of money; the few conversations about finances that took place were one-on-one and had the quality of family gossip. Tere remembers one of her sisters saying, "Is it true that you receive 1% of the company's profits and Francisco gets 10%? That is robbery!" Francisco was often the target of the gossip, but mostly he ignored it, except for telling himself and his advisors, "After all, I have been the one working the business for more than 20 years now."

There was plenty of evidence of love, caring, and tenderness in the family. There was less evidence of respect for titles, organizational structure, hard work, reporting relationships, institutions, and formality of any kind. The family seemed ill equipped for financial responsibility. In the past, dividends had been distributed infrequently. Individual family members' needs were brought to the attention of Francisco Sr., who usually granted requests as a generous father would. For Mari, the youngest daughter, who grew up surrounded by evidence of the family's wealth, and for other siblings who needed money for new houses or trips, asking was often akin to receiving.

Family Council Meeting, February 1997

Francisco took the initiative in sponsoring this first family council meeting. It followed a day-long shareholders' meeting, where financial information and the state of the business were discussed with shareholders. The news for shareholders was not great. Although company sales had continued to increase, profits had plummeted in the last couple of years and dividend distributions had been cut (see Table 1).

With Tere's help Francisco had interviewed and selected the family business advisor who facilitated the family council meeting. The consultant had conducted a private meeting with every member of the family. A few days prior to the meeting, Mari told the family business consultant:

> It is important that each of us know what we have, what we don't, and what we can and cannot do as shareholders. We have to speak clearly about these things. Right now, bringing up the subject is taboo. We need more transparency in all of this. We need to recognize that we are all siblings here.

Tere observed, in her meeting with the advisor:

> The reason for these meetings is that we need Industrias La Vega to continue as a family business. In order for that to happen, Francisco needs to be supervised. There has to be more balance between Francisco and the sisters. Those inside the company have to live by corporate rules, manage with transparency, and meet the needs of the inactive shareholders. There has been too much centralization by Francisco. Financial information about the company has to be sent out regularly and explained in such a way that all shareholders understand it. Without this education, there will be no sense of justice. But don't get me wrong; we love each other a lot. We have grown in family unity. My mother is a very strong woman and a very steadying influence.

Table 1   Financial Results for Industrias La Vega, 1992–1999

	1992	**1993**	**1994**	**1995**	**1996**	**1997**	**1998**	**1999**
Sales	42.5	51.7	57.4	69.4	84.1	104.8	112.6	109.7
Cost of Sales	32.1	36.6	41.1	52.6	62.6	78.2	79.6	74.9
Gross Margin	10.4	15.1	16.3	16.8	21.5	26.6	33.0	34.8
Administration Expenses	5.6	10.2	11.9	13.3	19.6	18.8	22.4	22.7
Interest Expenses	0.0	0.0	0.0	0.0	0.0	3.1	4.4	5.6
Net Profit	4.8	4.9	4.4	3.5	1.9	4.7	6.2	6.5

Isabel expressed her own expectations of the meeting this way: "In the interests of the family and the business, everything has to come out well defined and organized. Things have to be clear for everybody, after some discussion and reflection, so that there is no second-guessing later."

The meeting started with the setting of meeting goals and behavioral norms for constructive problem solving and conflict resolution. Feedback from the conversations with the family business consultant was provided for family members to discuss, clarify, and then use to build an agenda that responded to the identified needs, problems, and opportunities. Selected as the top two priority items on the agenda were (1) the lack of clarity and organization in the ownership structure, estate plan, and financial reporting mechanisms for shareholders; and (2) the lack of a well-organized family forum and board of directors. Board meetings existed only on paper, and only family members were on the board. While a mini-family business presentation made by the consultant early in the meeting may have influenced the selection of topics, both Tere and Francisco had attended a family business course for next-generation members and had been convinced of the need for both of these governance bodies. Obviously, their opinions had significant influence in the larger shareholder group. Other topics selected for discussion included the need to define the responsibilities of shareholders toward the business and of managers toward shareholders, the need to define the rules guiding relations between members of the family acting as suppliers or subcontractors to the company, and the third-generation scholarship fund.

By the end of this first family council meeting, an action plan had been drafted that directed various family members to review the ownership structure and the possession of stock certificates, retain a valuation expert to perform a company valuation, review and account for the family benefits that individual members had been granted to make appropriate decisions regarding family benefits in the next shareholder meeting, and continue to schedule open conversations about what shareholders wanted from the business—things like higher dividends, more reinvestment for long-term growth, and liquidity of shareholdings via buy–sell agreements. An agreement was reached among family members that the company hierarchy would be respected, and any information required by shareholders regarding the company and its finances would be directed to Francisco, the president, and not to accounting department personnel. Francisco, in return, agreed to respond to such requests in a timely manner. Shareholders also reached other agreements regarding the expectations they had of management and what management could rightfully expect of shareholders.

Finally, a discussion on family business boards produced a consensus on the desirability of a board with independent outsiders and a list of board responsibilities. These responsibilities were to promote the continuity of the business, review the strategy of the business, review and approve financial reports and budgets, review the compensation of key executives, and provide oversight on large capital investment decisions. The criteria for selecting board members were to be developed by a task force made up of Francisco, Tere, and Rosa. The selection of independent board members themselves and the holding of the first board meeting were deemed to be the responsibilities of Francisco, though shareholders wanted to be consulted.

Family Council Meeting, September 1997

The next family council meeting was held in September 1997. This meeting addressed three new topics: (1) the family foundation (a study of its various projects in the past 5 years had been done), (2) college scholarships for members of the third generation, and (3) the possibility of selling a couple of parcels of company farmland. The bulk of the meeting was focused on following up on the action plans drafted at the February meeting. Although there had been much progress on many fronts, shareholder information, company valuation, and liquidity concerns had not been addressed by the time this second meeting was held. And a new board of directors or advisory board had not been assembled.

Mari Brings in the Attorneys

The semiannual family council meeting was scheduled to take place in May 1998. Mari felt sick and checked herself into a hospital for observation. This precluded her from attending the meeting. Instead, she sent two attorneys whom she and her husband had retained to put pressure on Francisco for fuller disclosure of corporate financial information. The family council meeting was canceled after a brief conversation with the attorneys to determine the nature of their involvement.

Francisco was very upset and quite worried that if the company's accounting and financial records were scrutinized, they would be found lacking and this would create more chaos and family disharmony and possibly even result in legal ramifications. The business, as a result of a very strong entrepreneurial culture and unsophisticated financial and administrative systems, had very unsophisticated accounting procedures. Francisco Sr. had never been very concerned about establishing such systems. Now the responsibility for historical reconstruction of financial information had fallen on Francisco Jr. He said:

> That was the reason that I could not be any clearer with shareholders about the books than I was. I was not hiding anything; they had the same

information I had available to me. But I knew how shrewd those two attorneys that Mari hired were, and I was very worried for the family and the business's reputation.

In the aftermath of the family council meeting, Francisco stayed very close to his mother, Isabel, and consulted her often on what to do. But, of course, all of this was very hard on her, because she did not want this to be the legacy of her very successful late husband. Francisco respected Isabel's wisdom and her ability to influence her daughters. Mari had hired the lawyers, but most of her sisters were secretly rooting for her. They too wanted to better understand what they considered to be rightfully theirs. Isabel talked to her daughters on many occasions during that period about the importance of preserving the family and about the need to give Francisco time to run the company, get things in shape, and show them what he could do. But her arguments did not dissuade Mari, who continued her inquiry through her attorneys.

About this time company and family attorneys finally unraveled the details of the estate plan. It was determined that upon Francisco Sr.'s death, Francisco Jr. held 50% of the voting A shares and 20% of the non-voting dividend-bearing B shares. Each of his five sisters owned 15% of the B shares, and Isabel retained 5% of the B shares and the remaining 50% of the voting shares. Voting control therefore rested in the hands of the founder's surviving spouse and Francisco Jr., the successor president.

Hurt and disillusioned by Mari's actions, Francisco began the process of negotiating with Mari and her attorneys for a buyout of her shares. On the advice of her mother-in-law, an influential banker in town, Mari asked for US$10 million, but she was offered US$4 million instead. During the last round of negotiations, Francisco, concerned about the future of both the family and the business, agreed to US$6 million on an installment basis—a price he considered exorbitant but worth the peace of mind and the ability to move on, both of which he so desperately wanted. Mari agreed to this offer and sold all of her shares to Francisco, who, as a result, now owned 35% of the B shares.

Family Council and Shareholders' Meetings, October 1999

Family council meetings were not held for over a year while the wrangling and negotiations were going on. In October 1999 family members held their next family council and shareholders' meetings. (Mari, who was no longer a shareholder, decided not to attend either meeting.) The agenda for the one-day shareholders' meeting and the additional day for the family council meeting included discussion of a draft of a shareholder buy–sell agreement, discussion of the new dividend distribution policy, and discussion of a draft of a family constitution. The family constitution included an emergency contingency plan naming Tere, the one sister active in management, as the successor if something should happen to Francisco.

The Pruned Family Tree Grows

All this upheaval and animosity did have several positive side effects. Francisco dedicated himself fully to the business. He fired several members of the top management team who were hurting his efforts to professionalize the business, replacing them with competent key managers. Concurrently he began to successfully execute a growth strategy that had been in the planning stages for several years. In 1998 revenues and net profit rose to US$112.6 and US$6.2 million, respectively. Then, in 1999, when revenues went down slightly, to US$109.7 million, net profit rose to US$6.5 million (see Table 1). Starting in 1998 dividends increased significantly, which gained Francisco much respect with shareholders (see Table 2).

Francisco retained a financial consultant as the CFO and, to his delight, found that this CFO knew as much about business as he did about finance and was a great general manager. Francisco now had key nonfamily managers whose skills complemented those that he and Tere brought to the corporation. Together, they turned things around dramatically and increased company profitability.

While Mari achieved her goal of liquidity and personal oversight of her own inheritance, the other family members recommitted themselves to the business and stayed involved. The work of the family foundation continued. The foundation was successful in getting a highway named in memory of Francisco Sr., and all the family members gathered to honor and celebrate the family's proud past. The increased participation by the Valle sisters in committees, task forces, the family council, shareholders' meetings, and the family foundation led to a greater sense of transparency

Table 2   Dividends for Industrias La Vega, 1995–1999

1995	$ 181,000
1996	$ 322,000
1997	$ 639,000
1998	$1,256,000
1999	$1,488,000

and ownership. As they walked to a shareholders' meeting in the spring of 2000, Ana reflected on the changes:

> A long time ago, my father gave one of my siblings $650,000 to buy a house. Francisco has been adjusting distributions to equalize us all with that gift. After that, we will receive our dividends based on our ownership stake and company profitability. Dividends have increased. We receive company information. There is a great effort to be fair. We've come a long way.

Case Questions

1. What are the key facts of this case? List the factors that, in your opinion, led Mari to sell her shares.

2. Would you have called a family council meeting when Francisco Jr. did? Why or why not?

3. To what do you attribute the improvement in Valle family–business relationships over the last couple of years?

4. What major issues should Francisco and the rest of the Valle family continue to address to ensure the survival of the business? Select one to three issues, and support your selections with the facts of the case.

5. What actions should Francisco take next? What should he do to promote shareholder loyalty and the effective governance of the family–business relationship in the future?

Reliance Industries

Research Associate Tracey Eira Messer prepared this case under the supervision of Professor Ernesto J. Poza as the basis for class discussion rather than to illustrate effective or ineffective handling of an administrative situation.

M ore inches of newsprint have been dedicated to telling the story of the Ambani family and Reliance Industries than perhaps any other story in Indian business history. Dhirubhai Ambani, a poor schoolteacher's son from the Indian state of Gujarat, built India's largest industrial empire. Along the way, he rewrote the practices of Indian enterprise. At the time of his death, the conglomerate he founded (the Reliance Group) was so large that it alone accounted for more than 3% of India's total gross domestic product (GDP) and 10% of the country's indirect tax revenue.

Dhirubhai Ambani died suddenly at age 69 without a will or succession plan, leaving two sons in equivalent executive positions within the business. Within 2 years of Dhirubhai's death, his sons began arguing about ownership issues and accused each other of business improprieties. Politicians and financiers, concerned by the instability that this family squabble was having on the financial markets, tried unsuccessfully to broker an agreement between the sons, Mukesh and Anil Ambani. In the end, the sons would only listen to their mother. A settlement has just been announced. Is the settlement fair? What would the founder, Dhirubhai, have to say about it?

Achievement is history. Look ahead.[1]

Dhirajlal Ambani was born on December 29, 1932, into the Modh Bania, a Hindu commercial caste based in the arid Saurashtra peninsula of India's western Gujarat state. Dhirubhai, as he was known, left home at 16 to work as a gas station attendant for Shell Petroleum in Yemen. Within a few years he rose to the position of sales manager.

---

1. Dhirubhai was well-known for mantras about management. This adage reflects his belief that success comes from building on achievement and that achievement becomes history the moment it is achieved.

A successful employee, Dhirubhai had an entrepreneur's ability to identify and take advantage of opportunities not observed by others. While in Yemen Dhirubhai realized that the local currency (the riyal) was worth more for its silver content than its purchasing power. With this insight, he began to melt the coins into silver ingots at a small profit.

Dhirubhai returned to India in 1958 with his pregnant wife and infant son to start his own business. He founded Reliance Commercial Corporation with US$100 in his pocket and approximately US$275 in borrowed capital. The company began as a trading company, exporting spices, nuts, and other commodities to the duty-free Yemeni port of Aden. In Aden Dhirubhai used his many contacts to develop this market. By 1965 Dhirubhai shifted Reliance's focus from trading to textiles to take advantage of another opportunity—government programs designed to promote the export of rayon, which was plentiful in India. Reliance exported rayon at a loss because doing so enabled the company to import nylon, which it sold at a premium.

By 1966 the Indian economy was growing and the demand for better clothing was taking hold. Reliance Corporation opened its first textile mill to take advantage of this new market. In 1978 Reliance began focusing on India's domestic market after its successful IPO and the end of the government-sponsored rayon promotion. The Indian wholesale textile market was crowded and extremely competitive. To gain market share and to bypass the competitive wholesale market, Dhirubhai adopted a competitor's idea and opened company stores. He then expanded the idea by traveling throughout India franchising the store concept and promising advertising support to any outlet that would sell Reliance textiles. In this way he built a national customer base that included previously untapped nonmetropolitan markets. By 1980 Reliance fabrics could be found across India in 2,100 retail stores and franchised outlets. During this period Reliance established the Vimal textile brand (named for Dhirubhai's eldest nephew). Dhirubhai worked to create a strong brand image and was so successful that it took many years for Reliance to have better name recognition than Vimal.

Dhirubhai was known for his many managerial mantras that reflected his philosophy and that provided short heuristics for management success. One of them stated "Growth has no limit—keep revising your vision." Dhirubhai did just that after earning his first million in textiles. He began to backwardly integrate from fabric weaving to establishing plants to make polyester filament yarn in 1981. His philosophy of entrepreneurial growth was evident when he built a factory at Patalganga (a small village outside of Mumbai, formerly Bombay) that could produce 4,000 more tons of polyester yarn than the Indian market required. Soon after the factory was completed, the government issued legislation that limited the use of polyester filament yarn to small textile businesses. To increase demand for Reliance's yarn, Dhiruhai arranged to sell yarn to these small looms and then to buy the fabric that they produced, finishing it and selling it under the Vimal name. Two years later, in 1983, he again moved backward in the supply chain and gained the license to manufacture purified terephthalic acid, one of the chemicals that can produce polyester filament fiber.

From the production of yarn and fiber, Reliance integrated horizontally and began producing products including high- and low-density polyethylenes used by plastics processors. Reliance slowly began the manufacture of petrochemical intermediaries, including mono-ethylene glycol and n-paraffin. Reliance achieved domination in these industries soon after its entry, becoming the world's second-largest producer of polyester fiber and filament yarn, the third-largest producer of paraxylene, and the fourth-largest producer of purified terephalic acid. From chemicals, Reliance entered the oil and gas exploration business and built refineries through Reliance Petroleum Limited, fulfilling a dream Dhirubhai had nourished since he worked for Shell Petroleum in Yemen. Reliance Petroleum went public in 1993 in what was at the time India's largest public offering.

Reliance Industries fully entered the world industrial stage by building Asia's biggest chemical complex in 1991. The Hazira facility, the world's largest single-feed ethylene cracker,[2] was built in Dhirubhai's home state of Gujarat. Building the facility exhausted the local Gujarti resources and required Dhiubhai to create his own infrastructure to support the plant.

A second world-class facility, and the world's largest refinery, was then built in Gujarat at the cost of US\$6 billion. This facility, known as the Jamnagar plant, extends over 31 square kilometers (the size of Manhattan south of Central Park) and represents the single largest investment ever made at a single location in India. Jamnagar is one of only a few refineries in the world that can take thick, high-sulfur, highly acid grades of crude oil and turn them into pure low-polluting gasoline and diesel fuel. Like the Hazira plant, building Jamnagar required the creation of infrastructure including a 350-megawatt power plant, two chemical plants, 105 miles of road, housing for 3,000 families, a seawater desalination plant, and an IT network that connects 50 servers and 2,500 terminals with 200 kilometers of fiber-optic cables.

The decision to build Jamnagar illustrates Reliance's innovative business approach. In 1996, when the project was launched, refineries had a historic return on capital of 6%–8%, while the cost of capital was 12%. To get adequate returns, Reliance focused on developing efficiencies both in constructing and running the facility. According to a family story, Dhirubhai traveled to Jamnagar during construction to check on the

2. Cracking is the name of the process that ethane (a naturally occurring gas) goes through to become ethylene. Ethane is heated to approximately 800 degrees Celsius in a reactor called a cracker.

progress. He went for a walk at night and found that work had ended for the day. He asked his eldest son Mukesh, who was managing the project, why work had stopped and observed that there was no reason they could not run three shifts. Mukesh called in the contractors the following day and made arrangements for them to receive bonuses for meeting or exceeding project deadlines and, in turn, to give bonuses to their employees for meeting or exceeding the deadlines. The Jamnagar complex was completed within 36 months and the refinery's total cost was reduced to the point that it operates at a 30%–50% lower cost than similar refineries in Asia.

While most refineries specialize in a small number of products, the Jamnagar refinery can produce a wide range of petrochemicals. This flexibility enables it to take advantage of market fluctuations and consistently focus on producing high-profit products. Jamnagar is able to change its product mix in response to market demand, which enables it to refine the product with the best profit margin at any given time. From exploration to production to pipelines, Reliance owns a piece of the entire oil and gas value chain, except for gas stations which, in India, have traditionally been government owned.

Financing Growth

Finding sufficient capital is a challenge faced by most enterprises. In India in the 1970s, the challenge was magnified by a government-controlled financial system. The leading sources of capital were slow moving state-owned financial institutions that were not always willing lenders and frequently charged high rates of interest. In 1977 Reliance solved its funding challenge in a unique way. It launched the first initial public offering of company shares in Indian business history. This advance is recorded on the Reliance Web site as " . . . Dhirubhai introduced equity cult in India, a new model of business leadership from a base of the broadest public shareholding."

By selling shares to the public in small lots, Dhirubhai introduced ordinary people who had never owned shares to the financial markets while financing Reliance's growth. In a short time so many individuals owned shares that Reliance was forced to rent football (soccer) stadiums each year to provide a venue large enough for the annual meeting.

Other financial firsts include being the first Indian corporation to raise funds through overseas capital markets and being the first private company in India to be rated by international credit agencies. The ability to finance growth enabled Reliance to enter high-growth sectors outside petroleum and petrochemicals. The Reliance corporate family also includes financial services and insurance, power, telecommunication, and digital communication initiatives. (See Figure 1 and Table 1 for additional

POLYMERS, CHEMICALS, FIBERS, AND FIBER INTERMEDIATES
Location: Hazira, Gujarat state

Repol
- Polypropylene
- Purified Terphthalic Acid
- Ethylene Oxide
- Mono-Ethylene Glycol
- Di-Ethylene Glycol
- Tri-Ethylene Glycol
- Ethylene
- Propylene
- Benzene
- Toluene
- Xylene
- Carbon Black Feed Stock
- Vinyl Chloride Monomer

Reon
- Polyvinyl Chloride
- Recalir
- Linear Low-Density Polyethylene
- Relene
- High-Density Polyethylene
- Recron
- Recron Stable Fiber
- Recron Filament Yarn
- Recron Fiber Fill
- Relpet
- Polyethylene Terephthalate

REFINERY PRODUCTS, POLYMERS, AND FIBER INTERMEDIATES
Location: Jamnagar, Gujarat state

Refinery
- Liquefied Petroleum Gas
- Propylene
- Naphtha
- Reormate
- Motor Spirit
- Middle Distillate Pool
- Suppher
- Coke

Petrochemicals
- Paraxylene
- Polyporpylene
- Port and Terminals
- Power

TEXTILES
Location: Naroda, Gujarat state

Vimal
- Suitings and Shirtings
- Dress Materials and Sarees
- Harmony
- Furnishing Fabrics
- Day Curtains
- Automotive Upholstery
- Slumberel
- Fiberfilled Pillows

Recron
- Texturized Yarn
- Twisted/Dyed Yarns
- Ruerel
- Suitings
- Reance
- Shirts
- Trousers
- Jackets

OIL AND GAS
Location: Panna and Mukta, off Bombay High Tapti—Northwest of Mumbai
- Crude Oil
- Natural Gas
- Exploration and Production

POWER GENERATION
Facilities:
- Dahanu Thermal Power Station
- Jogimatti Wind Farm Project
- BSES Kerla Combined Cycle Station
- Goa Power Station

OTHER INITIATIVES
- Telecommunications—Reliance Telecom
- Financial Services—Reliance Capital
- Engineering, Procurement, Construction
- Infrastructure—Reliance Industrial Infrastructure
- Infocomm—Reliance Infocomm
- Insurance—Reliance General Insurance

Figure 1   Reliance Industries Product Listing by Brand Name and Type

Table 1   The Reliance Family of Companies

Reliance Industries Ltd.	In 2002 Reliance Industries and Reliance Petrochemical merged into Reliance Industries, India's largest petrochemical firm, second-largest company, and largest exporter. Polyesters and polymers account for most of the Reliance Group's sales. The company's leading products are used widely in agriculture, clothing, consumer goods, and electronics. Petrochemical products, including benzene, polypropylene, and polyvinyl chloride are used in packaging, kitchenware, and furniture.
Reliance Capital Ltd.	Reliance Capital is one of India's leading nongovernment-sponsored financial services companies. It focuses on infrastructure projects that offer opportunities for enormous growth and significant tax benefits.
Reliance Energy (formerly BSES Energy)	Reliance Energy generates, transmits, and distributes electricity to more than 5 million customers in portions of India. Its service area covers more than a million square kilometers and includes the cities of Mumbai and Delhi.
Reliance General Insurance	Reliance General Insurance is one of the few companies in the nongovernmental sector to provide a complete insurance solution. It is also one of the first nonlife companies to be licensed to operate.
Reliance Industrial Infrastructure	The company was incorporated in 1988 to serve the Patalganga Plant. It transports petroleum products through product pipelines and raw water through water pipelines. The company boasts that there have been no failures or leakage of the petroleum operation during the last 11 years of operation.
Reliance Infocomm Ltd.	Reliance Infocomm is India's largest mobile service provider with over 7 million customers. Launched in 2003, it has established a pan-India high-capacity integrated and divergent digital network and offers services for enterprises and individuals, applications, and consulting.
Reliance Mutual Fund	Reliance Mutual Fund was established as a trust in 1995 with Reliance Capital Asset Management Ltd. It is among the fastest growing mutual fund companies in India. The company's vision is to be India's largest and most trusted wealth creator.
Reliance Telecom	Reliance Telecom provides cellular services in 10 Indian states. It recently introduced international roaming services throughout India.
Reliance Life Science	Established in 2001, Reliance Life Services is a new initiative of the Reliance Group. The company is developing business opportunities in medical, plant, and industrial biotechnology. It also conducts contract research and clinical trials.

SOURCE: *The Economic Times,* November 23, 2004, and www.hoovers.com

information about Reliance companies and products.) Some entities, such as Reliance Infrastructure and Reliance Capital, were formed primarily to support Reliance Industries. Other units, such as Reliance Telecomm and Reliance Life Science, were created to propel Reliance into new technologies and to take advantage of the opportunities presented by the growing Indian economy. (See Figure 2 for additional details.)

- 1958: Dhirubhai Ambani starts Reliance Commercial Corporation in Mumbai.
- 1966: Reliance enters the textile industry and sets up a mill in Naroda, Ahmedabad.
- 1975: World Bank team visits mill and declares that it is as modern and well managed as those in developed countries.
- 1977: Reliance goes public with India's first IPO.
- 1981: Dhirubhai calls Mukesh home from Stanford University's School of Business after 1 year of study toward his MBA. Mukesh begins working at Reliance and later completes his MBA degree.
- 1983: Anil earns his MBA from the University of Pennsylvania's Wharton School and begins working at Reliance.
- 1985: Mukesh marries Nita.
- 1985: Reliance's total assets equal US$227 million.
- 1986: Reliance Capital, a merchant bank, is created.
- 1986: Dhirubhai suffers his first stroke. He returns as chairman. Mukesh and Anil take on additional responsibilities as co-managing directors of Reliance.
- 1988: Reliance Industrial Infrastructure, a petroleum pipeline provider, comes online.
- 1988: Reliance sales exceed US$404 million.
- 1991: Hazira petrochemical plant commissioned.
- 1991: Anil marries Tina Munim.
- 1992: Reliance is the first Indian corporation to raise capital from international markets through Global Depository Receipts offering. It sets a record with Reliance issue that received over 1 million investor applications.
- 1993: Reliance Petroleum goes public in India's largest public offering to date. Sales exceed US$909 million, making Reliance Petroleum India's largest publicly traded company. Also Reliance offers the first Euro Convertible bond issue.
- 1994: Reliance is awarded Companion Membership of the Textile Institute (UK). Award is limited to 50 members who have substantially advanced the fiber industry.
- 1994: Reliance offers the second Euro issue of Global Depository Receipts.
- 1995: Reliance's net profit exceeds US$242 million.
- 1995: Reliance Mutual Funds, an asset management and mutual fund provider, is launched.
- 1997: Reliance is the first corporation in Asia to issue 50- and 100-year bonds in the United States.
- 1997: World's largest multifeed cracker is commissioned in Hazira.
- 1998: Reliance's revenue tops US$3 billion and total assets approach US$8 billion.
- 1999: World's largest petroleum refinery complex commissioned at Jamnagar.
- 1999: Reliance Infocomm, a mobile service provider, is launched.
- 2000: Reliance's revenues exceed US$4 billion and total assets are US$11.8 billion.
- 2002: Reliance Industries Ltd. and Reliance Petrochemical Ltd. merge into Reliance Industries. The new firm is named to the Forbes Global 500 in 2003, entering at position 306.
- 2002: Dhirubhai Ambani passes away on July 6.

Figure 2   Ambani Family and Reliance Industries Milestones

The Ambani family's shares in these companies were owned by a web of investment firms. These, in turn, were controlled by over 1,000 entities, including offshore trusts in tax haven countries. This complex structure enabled the family to avoid onerous taxes and still retain family control.

The Next Generation

Dhirubhai and Kokilaben Ambani had four children: Mukesh, Anil, Nina, and Dipti (see Figure 3). In the early years, Dhirubhai, Kokilaben, Mukesh, Anil, and Dhirubhai's mother, uncle, and brother lived together in a one bedroom house in a lower middle-class neighborhood in Mumbai. As Reliance flourished, the family moved to more spacious accommodations and most recently to Sea Wind, the family estate. Nina and Dipti moved from Mumbai when each married. Mukesh, Anil, and their families also resided at Sea Wind. While each family had its own living quarters, the extended family usually had dinner together. Dhirubhai was known for quizzing his grandchildren about current events, a practice he began when his own children were young.

Siblings raised together can be as different in their personalities as people from different families. Mukesh and Anil are no exception. Each had an especially close relationship with one parent. Mukesh was reportedly his father's favorite. Father and son were extremely close. It was Mukesh who Dhirubhai consulted first about business matters before asking Anil his opinion. As a child, Anil was closest to his mother and their special relationship has continued over time. To the public eye, Mukesh and Anil were groomed for careers with Reliance and got along well. Disputes were settled in the privacy of the family compound. When mediation failed, Dhirubhai would reprimand Mukesh and Anil and impose a solution. Dhirubhai's goal was to see Reliance succeed and to prove to the world that India was the place to invest. Family disputes were not going to get in the way of these goals; Mukesh and Anil were expected to work together successfully for the benefit of Reliance and all of India.

In 1997 when Mukesh and Anil were jointly honored as "Businessmen of the Year," they commented that they felt like they had built the company with their father rather than simply benefiting from his efforts. In their official corporate biographies both brothers take credit for bringing about financial innovation to the Indian capital market through the introduction of international offerings of Global Depository Receipts, convertible issues, and bonds. Their efforts are credited with raising US$2 billion in the past 12 years to fund Reliance's aggressive growth.

MUKESH AMBANI

Mukesh, the eldest, was born in Yemen in 1957. He is described as analytical and detail-oriented; he is known for taking detailed notes during meetings and conversations. Mukesh is a private person who rarely speaks publicly.

Mukesh earned a bachelor of chemical engineering at the University of Mumbai and continued his graduate studies at Stanford University. After his first year in the MBA program, Dhirubhai called Mukesh home. He was 24 years old. Mukesh recalls, "My father told me 'you will take this over and I will give you one other person from Reliance. Everyone else has to be new.'"

Mukesh's task was to oversee the construction of the petrochemical plant at Patalganga. The technology they selected for the plant came from DuPont. To get DuPont to sell their technology, Dhirubhai sold everything but equity. He later explained, "Technology is available for the asking in the international bazaar. Why should I make a foreign company my partner and give them 51%?" The plant was completed in 14 months, ahead of a competitor who had started building before Reliance. Being first to market gave Reliance a significant advantage in the marketplace.

After the success at Patalganga, Mukesh quickly gained a reputation for building new megaplants under budget and ahead of schedule. He has since directed the creation of over 60 new, world-class manufacturing facilities.

Mukesh happily entered into an arranged marriage at age 28. His mother reportedly saw his future wife, Nita, at a recital and came home and told Dhirubhai that she had found the right match for Mukesh. Dhirubhai interviewed Nita and the match was made. From the start, Nita was a family insider, taking responsibility for family philanthropy. A former teacher, she is responsible for the creation of the Dhirubhai International School, a premiere K–12 private school which opened in 2003. Nita serves as the school's chairperson.

ANIL AMBANI

Anil joined Reliance in 1982, a day after he graduated from Wharton with an MBA. Dhirubhai greeted him saying, "You have got an American MBA, now you must get an Indian MBA," meaning that the American degree provided good theory but could not be applied to Indian realities. Anil's first experience with Reliance was in the textile business, where he stayed for 4 years.

After Dhirubhai's first stroke in 1986, Anil assumed new responsibilities. He handled corporate finances and became Reliance's spokesperson. Anil is considered aggressive and has strong financial and networking skills. Anil likes the limelight. Newspaper accounts about Anil and his family are common—he is frequently featured attending social events or advocating physical fitness. Anil was voted Youth Icon in 2003 in an MTV-sponsored survey. Anil had his own Web page: www.anildambaniforindia.com.

Anil married the former Miss India and film star, Tina Munim. Tina and Anil are said to have met at a party and Anil was immediately smitten.

When the two decided to marry, Dhirubhai opposed the marriage and tried his best to break the alliance. He went so far as to encourage government foreign currency investigations into Tina's accounts. After the marriage Tina was reportedly given the cold shoulder in the Ambani household. Tina is known for support of the Harmony Art Show, an annual event that provides a forum for new artists to showcase their work.

The End of an Era

One of Dhirubhai's last major decisions was to merge Reliance Industries and Reliance Petrochemicals into Reliance Industries Limited. The merger proclaimed Dhirubhai's desire to keep the company, his legacy, together. He did not want Reliance Industries Limited (RIL) to suffer the fate of other Indian firms that were broken into pieces to satisfy the next generation, only to find individuals in that generation fighting each other in the market and destroying the value created by the founder. The merger also created a business that was large enough to be recognized in the Forbes Global 500 listing of the world's largest companies. Reliance Industries was selected for the list in 2003, a year after the merger. It was the first Indian business to qualify for the listing and was ranked the 306th largest business in the world.

At the time of Dhirubhai's death, Reliance Group was India's largest private sector business with total revenues of US$22.6 billion, exports of US$3.6 billion, and net profit of US$1.4 billion. Reliance exported its products to more than 100 countries around the world. The companies of the Reliance Group included oil and gas exploration and production, petrochemicals, textiles, financial services, and insurance.

Reliance Group's revenue is equivalent to approximately 3.5% of India's total GDP. It contributes nearly 10% of India's indirect tax revenues and over 6% of the country's exports. As one of the first private firms to offer shares to the public, it had 3.1 million shareholders, enjoying the largest participation by investors of any company in India. Today, one in every four Indians holds shares in Reliance.

At the time of Dhirubhai's death, the Ambani family directly or indirectly owned 46% of Reliance Industries, including 5% held by the family in the names of individual family members. Additional shares were held by a web of companies controlled by RIL's chairman. Three months after Dhirubhai's death, the four Ambani children relinquished their share of their father's assets and signed those assets over to their mother. This was likely done to take advantage of the Hindu Undivided Family Unit, a tax status that permits families, especially those with family businesses, to pay tax as a single entity.

The Struggle for Control

Mukesh became chairman of RIL after his father's death, gaining management control and, by default, being in a position to review and approve or veto major investments and changes in Reliance's businesses. In the beginning, questions arose about the cohesiveness of Reliance's top leadership. The brothers denied any difficulties, saying that differences of opinion are "constructive tension" of the type that their father encouraged as a way to look at an issue from all angles.

But a series of events in 2003 precipitated a struggle for control. Mukesh had taken an interest-free loan from Reliance Industries Limited to finance the nascent Reliance Telecomm. Anil questioned this financing arrangement, though the practice of making interest-free loans was common. Mukesh, in turn, was annoyed because Anil, as head of Reliance Energy, had made a US$10 billion capital investment without consulting Mukesh or the RIL board.

The brothers' mutual dissatisfaction continued until a July board meeting. At the meeting, the Reliance board passed a resolution giving Mukesh the authority to "vary or revoke" managing director Anil's duties. Anil maintained that the resolution had been introduced in a sneaky way and sent an e-mail expressing his dissatisfaction to Mukesh. This e-mail was obtained and published by a local paper. Anil's dissatisfaction with Mukesh's actions was ironic given that it was Anil who originally performed the ceremonial role of proposing that Mukesh be elevated to the role of chairman. Mukesh in turn had supported Anil for vice chairman and managing director.

In November 2004 Mukesh sent an e-mail to Reliance's 80,000 employees stating, "There is no ambiguity in his (Dhirubhai Ambani's) legacy that the chairman and managing director is the final authority on all matters concerning Reliance." He then announced to the press that his father had settled all ownership issues pertaining to Reliance within his lifetime. Anil and other family members responded to the news by asking Mukesh to provide appropriate details of the steps taken to settle ownership. In a conciliatory move, Anil also said that he would agree to any settlement that his mother proposed.

For the next 7 months, the brother's disagreements were played out in the media. Confidential e-mail messages and internal boardroom documents were regularly leaked to journalists. The press suggested that there was a lack of camaraderie between Mukesh's wife, Nita, and Anil's wife, Tina, which contributed to the disagreement. Anil ran a sustained campaign against Mukesh and his associates, accusing them of misleading the public. As the discord continued, it became clear that a formal split between the two brothers would call for a very complex settlement. The interrelationships between the companies that made up RIL were significant. Reliance Industries, for example, owned portions of gas fields which powered Reliance Energy's electricity production.

Mukesh asserted that his father had intended for him to become the managing chairman. Under Hindu tradition and succession laws, the eldest son becomes the successor. He stated that he was also concerned by Anil's lifestyle. Anil's friendships with film stars and his intention to run as a member of parliament made the family uncomfortable. Mukesh believed that Anil's political involvement had the potential to harm Reliance. Aligning with one political party was against the practices of Dhirubhai, who worked to befriend all politicians and bureaucrats at all levels of government.

From Anil's perspective, he and Mukesh had worked as equals for many years and during that time he had run his own businesses independently. Anil did not believe that his father had intended for that arrangement to change. He did not find primogeniture compelling and felt that he was more capable of leading Reliance than Mukesh was. He also commented at the time that his political activities were not his brother's business.

Kokilaben Ambani Intervenes

For most of her adult life, Kokilaben Ambani stayed out of the limelight, quietly supporting her husband and raising her family. Kokilaben is described in the press as being quiet, poised, and deeply religious. Although not formally educated, she learned conversational English along with her children when her husband hired a tutor for them. With English skills, Kokilaben was able to participate more easily in their frequent business dinners. The Ambani children hold their mother in great esteem and the family is frequently together, especially during religious holidays.

When the disagreement between Mukesh and Anil first became public, Kokilaben stated that she did not want to mediate because she did not know enough about the business. She did observe that both brothers were made managing director in Dhirubhai's lifetime, a decision that did not seem to suggest to her that Anil should be denied a say in running the business.

As the months passed without resolution, Kokilaben ultimately did intervene, but did so with the help of a family friend and respected banker, K.V. Kamath. In March 2005 Mr. Kamath performed a valuation of the company and drafted a suggested settlement. In the months that followed, and at Kokilaben's request, Mr. Kamath continued to broker the settlement while she held almost daily individual meetings with each of her sons. Together, they were able to fashion a settlement that was ultimately agreeable to both Mukesh and Anil. Throughout the process Kokilaben appeared to the outside world as graceful, even-handed, and mindful of her late husband's legacy.

The Settlement

Peace was declared on June 18, 2005, almost exactly 7 months after Anil's public questioning of Mukesh's authority. Peace came with a brief e-mail announcement from Kokilaben invoking her late husband and the name of the Hindu god Krishna and announcing that she had negotiated a settlement between her sons. Her announcement read:

> With the blessings of Srinathji[3], I have today amicably resolved the issues between my two sons, Mukesh and Anil, keeping in mind the proud legacy of my husband, Dhirubhai Ambani.
>
> I am confident that both Mukesh and Anil will resolutely uphold the values of their father and work toward protecting and enhancing value for over 3 million shareholders of the Reliance Group, which has been the foundational principle on which my husband built India's largest private sector enterprise.
>
> Mukesh will have responsibility for Reliance Industries and IPCL, while Anil will have responsibility for Reliance Infocomm, Reliance Energy, and Reliance Capital.
>
> My husband's foresight and vision and the values he stood for combined with my blessings will guide them to scale new heights.

The following day, June 19, 2005, Anil announced his own plans for the businesses he would be leading, Reliance Energy, Reliance Capital, and Reliance Infocomm, to a gathering of journalists and analysts.

A simple formula was used to split the family's 34% ownership in Reliance Group's companies. Kokilaben retained 30%, her daughters Nina Kothari and Dipti Salgocar each received 5%, and Mukesh and Anil each got 30%. The brothers resigned from each other's boards and signed a 10-year noncompete agreement. Both could use the Reliance logo and brand, but Anil's companies would carry the tag line "A Dhirubhai Ambani Enterprise."

Under terms of the agreement, Mukesh kept the flagship petrochemical business, Reliance Industries Limited, and the smaller Indian Petrochemicals. Anil assumed full control of a power company, a telecom and

---

3. A reference to the Hindu god Krishna.

Table 2   Company Ownership and Management After the Settlement

		Sales*	Profits*
MUKESH AMBANI			
Reliance Industries	Petrochemicals, textiles	$16.7 billion	$1.7 billion
Indian Petrochemicals	Petrochemicals	$2.1 billion	$180 million
ANIL AMBANI			
Reliance Energy	Power	$1 billion	$119 million
Reliance Capital	Finance	$67 million	$24 million
Reliance Infocomm	Cellular	$1.2 billion	$11.7 million

* For the year ending March 2005; in U.S. dollars

broadband provider, and a finance company (see Table 2). The brothers agreed to swap shares in each others' companies so that neither owned shares in the others' business, and Anil received an additional payment (estimated at between US$2 and 3 billion) to equalize the value of the divided assets. While Anil's companies are much smaller, they are in industries with much greater growth prospects.

While a divided RIL was not the vision of Dhirubhai Ambani, his legacy may well be sustained. In dividing RIL into logical pieces along industry lines there is no reason to suspect that the parts will not grow to become greater than the original whole.

Think Big, Think Fast, and Think Ahead

"Think big, think fast, and think ahead" was a favorite expression of Dhirubhai Ambani, who brought those words to life during his entrepreneurial career. Mukesh and Anil moved quickly after the settlement to focus on developing their businesses and go on with their lives. The price of Reliance Industry's stock has regained the value it lost during the Ambani brother's dispute and moved even higher. Mukesh recently terminated Reliance Infocomm's service of Reliance Industries and now purchases these services from another provider, rather than from his brother's company. Mukesh and his family have moved from the family estate to a residence of their own.

Anil, while keeping the Reliance name, is actively rebranding each of the companies he received in the settlement. And even though his sons

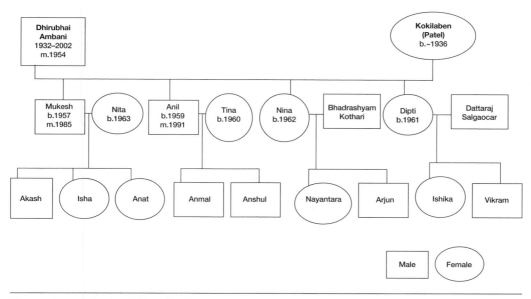

Figure 3   Ambani Family Tree

are still very young, Anil has already written a succession plan for his business.

Case Questions

1. How would you describe the culture and communication style of the Ambani family?

2. Discuss the ways in which Kokilaben used her formal and informal power to influence the settlement between Mukesh and Anil.

3. What role did the outside consultant, K.V. Kamath, play in the ongoing negotiations? What role did company valuations play in the final settlement?

4. From a family perspective, would you characterize this succession as successful or unsuccessful? Why?

5. From a business perspective, would you characterize this succession as successful or unsuccessful? Why?

Buying Office Supplies—Easy!

Sample Business Plan

Presented by

Joseph Naaman

Submitted in

Glendale, AZ, February 13, 2008

Confidential business plan number: _____

Table of Contents

List of Exhibits

Operations Management Exhibits

Common Exhibits

Executive Summary

The Venture and Its Industry

EGYPT'S PROBLEM

Businesses and consumers alike find purchasing office supplies in Egypt a difficult task. There are no product lists or catalogs to facilitate the process, and there are few choices for office supplies. Traditional local office supply stores are the main medium through which to purchase office goods. Usually, there is no delivery system offered and a minimal variety of products, causing businesses and consumers to spend their time either inefficiently looking for the proper office supply or improvising by making the best of what they have.

OUR SOLUTION

Maktabi provides businesses and consumers with an efficient and inexpensive way to order office supplies from a catalog or online—offering a wide variety of products and diverse styles to choose from at the comfort of one's own desk. The person placing the order can either go online or pick up the phone and dial one of the toll free numbers to order whatever they need. Through operational excellence and efficient distribution systems, the customer will receive the order quickly at a minimal cost.

THE INDUSTRY

Maktabi is in the office supplies industry. Included in this industry are wholesalers, distributors, and retailers. Maktabi fits into each of these categories, making classification difficult but allowing for unique positioning in the minds of businesses and consumers.

The Entrepreneur

Joseph Naaman

Mr. Joseph Naaman started his first business as a sophomore at Boston University, where he earned his degree in finance and marketing. He was a partner in a venture exporting Arizona Iced Tea from the United States to Italy, achieving approximately $2.5 million in sales within the first 2 years. Since then he has joined an established multinational pharmaceutical company, Bristol-Myers Squibb, to gain additional experience in global supply chain and logistics. He continued his professional education globally in business development for a luxury motor yacht company based in Egypt, where he started his second venture exporting organic agricultural products worldwide from Egypt. Along the way Mr. Naaman wrote two award-winning business plans, one for consumer products and one in the services industry. Currently, he is attending the Thunderbird School of Global Management, where he is focusing on entrepreneurship and finance. He has used his time at Thunderbird to refine the skills required to ensure the smooth operation of his new passion—providing office supplies to the Egyptian workplace.

The Board of Advisors

Mahmoud Mohieldin

Dr. Mohieldin has been the Minister of Investment in the Arab Republic of Egypt since 2004. This ministry is responsible for administering investment policy; management of state-owned assets, including privatization and restructuring of public enterprises and joint ventures; and nonbanking financial services, including capital market, insurance, and mortgage finance.

Dr. Mohieldin was born in Egypt in 1965. He received his bachelor of science in economics, with highest honors, first in order of merit, from Cairo University, Egypt. In 1989 he received a diploma in quantitative development economics from University of Warwick, England; in 1990 he received a master of science in economic and social policy analysis from University of York, England; and in 1995 he received his PhD in economics from University of Warwick, England.

Dr. Mohieldin has declared that he will provide his support in this venture by ensuring the efficient flow of orders through the bureaucratic red tape that companies in Egypt sometimes face.

Majid Al-Futtaim

Mr. Majid Al-Futtaim is the founder of several large regional shopping malls and hypermarkets throughout the Middle East. His ventures include such giants as the Mall of the Emirates in Dubai, United Arab Emirates; Ski Dubai in Dubai, United Arab Emirates; and Maadi City Center, Cairo, Egypt. Owning the Carrefour chain of stores in Egypt, Mr. Al-Futtaim hopes to share the expertise of his leadership team in creating a business whose products and service would be used throughout Egypt and the rest of the Middle East. His vision for Maktabi is a Staples for the Middle East.

Tarek Ragheb

Mr. Tarek Ragheb owns several businesses throughout the Middle East, the majority of which are located in Egypt. His contacts and expertise in setting up businesses and seeking funding have made him a crucial member of the Board of Advisors. Additionally, due to his American education, Mr. Ragheb brings a Western ideology of doing business to the Middle East. He is excited about the potential of being part of another winning business opportunity such as Maktabi.

The Management Team

Sherif Naaman

Mr. Sherif Naaman has over 35 years of experience in both the United States and the Middle East, leading projects in the fields of marketing and information technology. Fifteen of his 35 years have been spent as Managing Director in Saudi Arabia for various companies: the Alshaya group, a Kuwaiti holding company; Wardeh Al-Salehiya, a Saudi holding company; and Bristol-Myers Squibb, a U.S. corporation and the fifth largest pharmaceutical company worldwide. With his experience and exposure to the Middle East market, Mr. Naaman is confident that he would efficiently manage the company. He is excited about the opportunity to move back to the Middle East to aid companies in doing business the way they should.

Mahmoud Hindi

Mr. Mahmoud Hindi has over 5 years of experience working for SGS, a global transportation and freight forwarding company whose Egyptian offices were founded by his father. With the exposure that he has received at this high level, Mr. Hindi believes that his experience, contacts, and know-how in distribution and transportation will enable him to manage logistics at Maktabi with excellence.

Nancy Sharkawi

Ms. Nancy Sharkawi has worked for several years in the supply chain and as a sales representative for a large pharmaceutical company in the United States. With this background, Ms. Sharkawi will be able to manage the purchasing department of Maktabi. Naturally a people person, Ms. Sharkawi will foster the relationships required with Eastern and Southeastern Asian countries to ensure the smooth flow of product into Egypt. She is excited to be able to use the skills she has developed in the United States in a global setting.

Christine Chami

Ms. Christine Chami has several years of experience working in the marketing departments of large consumer goods companies. With the beginning of her career based in Canada, she knows how marketing departments are run in the west. She has successfully applied the knowledge she gained from this experience as a high performer at the company she currently works for in Dubai. Living in Dubai has enabled her to learn about doing business in the Middle East.

The Market

A SNAPSHOT

Businesses

- Average combined annual revenues of $1.3 million
- Regular use of office supplies

- Two or more departments in each company that order separately

Consumers

- Average annual household income of $12,000
- Regular use of office supplies
- More than two individuals per household who order office supplies

The Bigger Picture

In interviews conducted with executive assistants and secretaries at small and large corporations, the majority expressed that they would probably or definitely use our service to order office supplies for three reasons:

- It would simplify the processes currently in place in their office.
- There is a trend toward accepting already established ways of doing business in more developed countries.
- Some of the products sold will be considered as trendy or new on the market, making consumers happy to try something different.

Further emphasis will be placed on executive assistants, secretaries, and office buyers because it has been proven that this group is more likely to be into innovations in this type of industry.

Overall, focus has been placed on these users because

- Office supplies are a vital component in the workplace.
- There is no need to double sell consumers on office supplies and the service that we offer.
- These consumers are already familiar with the products and current processes used to order them, and would welcome a service that enhanced the process.
- Our interviews show that these users have a high probability of using our service.

Another market of consumers exists that is not part of a business or an organization, but rather is composed of individuals. These are individuals who have a predisposition for purchasing office supplies because of the nature of their education, hobbies, or interests. Included in this group would be school children and their parents—since it is the parents who would actually purchase the products—artists, hobbyists, and individuals who like to own new and innovative office supplies.

	2008	2009	2010	2011	2012
Total Orders	19,500	202,500	702,500	790,000	917,500
Total Dollars	$215,000	$2,149,000	$7,079,000	$7,951,000	$9,215,500

Figure ES1   5-Year Base Case Sales Projection (US$)

Sales and Profits

In 2008 Maktabi sales will exceed $200,000 by completing over 19,500 different orders. By the 5th year, sales are expected to exceed $9 million (see Figure ES1).

A net loss is expected during the 1st year and the venture will break even by the end of year two. By the 3rd year, the net profit margin is expected to level out at approximately 14%—a net margin that should remain stable throughout the life of the company.

Call for Action

Investors can earn an internal rate of return greater than 32% over the life of the project with an investment of $870,000 that is spread over a 2-year period. The capital investment has an approximate net present value of $1,100,000 with a payback period of less than 2 years. This investment offers you the opportunity to better the Egyptian business environment.

The Maktabi Group has the drive and capabilities to become the leading company in the office supplies industry in Egypt because of its fresh and innovative approach. The detailed business proposal presents our step-by-step process for ensuring the financial success of your investment.

Description of the Business

Description of the Venture

EGYPT'S PROBLEM

Businesses and consumers alike find purchasing office supplies in Egypt a difficult task. There are no product lists or catalogs to facilitate the process and there are few choices for purchasing office supplies. Traditional local office supply stores are the main medium to purchase office goods. Usually, there is no delivery service offered or variety of products, causing businesses and consumers to spend their time either inefficiently looking for the proper office supply or improvising by making the best of what they can find.

OUR SOLUTION

Maktabi provides businesses and consumers with an efficient and inexpensive way to order office supplies from a catalog or online—offering a wide variety of products and diverse styles to choose from at the comfort of one's own desk. The person placing the order can either go online or pick up the phone and dial one of the toll free numbers to order whatever they need. Through operational excellence and efficient distribution systems, the customer will receive the order quickly at a minimal cost.

CRITICAL SUCCESS FACTORS

- Educating businesses and consumers on a new, efficient, and inexpensive way to order office supplies

- Motivating consumers and businesses to change their current ordering practice

- Concentrating on operational excellence as a core competency by maintaining the highest quality standards at the lowest operational costs

- Maintaining constantly updated and original product lines and communicating about them through our catalog and Web site

MISSION STATEMENT

Our mission is to help Egypt fulfill its pursuit of improved and modernized business performance. Our objective is to make Maktabi an integral part of the Egyptian business and home, stressing the importance of an easy and fun office supplies purchasing process. To achieve our mission, we affirm our values of performance, quality, leadership, teamwork, and customers focus.

The Business Model

MARKETING

The target market is split into two distinct groups: businesses and consumers. Our target market is composed of approximately 35,000 businesses and 15 million consumers. The businesses and consumers purchase office supply products on average seven times per year. Special emphasis will be placed on forward-thinking businesses that want to do business like those in more developed countries because they tend to understand the cost-savings of an efficient ordering process. We will reach this primary market by creating a team of salesmen who will aggressively approach these companies to offer our services and free catalog—a salesman "blitz."

Our secondary market will be composed of consumers who purchase office supplies on a regular basis. This group will include school children and their parents, hobbyists, and artists. We will target this group by inciting a feeling of necessity for our products. A more traditional advertising approach will be used to reach them, and an elaborate marketing campaign will be used to introduce the company and the products it offers. Maktabi's products will initially only be found in catalogs and online.

OPERATIONS

Maktabi's products will be organized in essentially two categories: local and outsourced. Through an advanced sourcing model, the buyers at

Maktabi will be faced with a myriad of in-house and outsource decisions, with the majority of our products coming from Southeastern Asia due to its product and export quality, growth, and competitive pricing. The products that Egypt has an advantage in producing will be purchased locally. This careful examination of product sourcing, a state of the art distribution facility located near Cairo, a customer-centric customer service team, coupled with an excellent partnership with a global transportation and distribution third-party logistics provider will enable us to ensure our operational excellence critical success factor (see Figure DB1).

INFORMATION SYSTEMS

There are several information systems that must be in operation in order for Maktabi to run efficiently. These systems include customer order processing, inventory management, warehouse management, accounting and sales representative monitoring, and basic software requirements. All of these systems can be purchased as one package through an enterprise resource planning system.

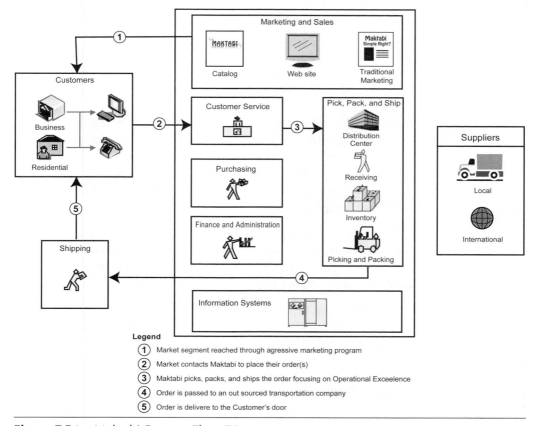

Figure DB1   Maktabi Process Flow Diagram

Competitor, Industry, and Consumer Analysis

Industry Analysis

Maktabi is in the office supplies industry. Included in this industry are wholesalers, distributors, and retailers. Maktabi fits into each of these categories, making classification difficult but allowing for unique positioning in the minds of businesses and consumers.

INDUSTRY AND ENVIRONMENT TRENDS

- Continued economic progress, principally based on Egypt's large, diversified economy, expanding international opportunities, modest external debt levels, fulfillment of debt service requirements, political stability, sustainable GDP growth, and the potential for further economic growth as a result of continued structural reforms.

- A population of over 75 million means a large potential market for investments, particularly in consumer goods and services such as Maktabi's. Demand has kept pace with modernization and is escalating with respect to services and technology.

- Consumer tastes and preferences have evolved with economic liberalization. Egyptian consumers today adapt to change and accept new products far more willingly than was once the case. The younger generations are especially eager to keep up with the latest developments worldwide, and therefore generate a large portion of domestic demand.

- Egyptian middle-income households make up most of Egypt's total household expenditure.

- The middle class is increasingly keen on such equipment as microwaves, stereos, videos, washing machines, and cellular phones, which reflects the change of lifestyle resulting from the recent improvement in the standard of living.

- Egypt offers advantages to multinational companies looking to establish a competitive edge and capitalize on investment decisions. Intermediate goods may be outsourced, and platforms exist for the production and export of goods at different stages of production.

Porter's Five Forces

BARGAINING POWER OF CUSTOMER—MODERATE

- Maktabi's products are sold to businesses large and small as well as consumers. This means that businesses and consumers have some degree of influence on the type of products sold. Though most are standard products, Maktabi will have to follow the patterns of this demand in order to maximize sales.

THREAT OF SUBSTITUTE PRODUCTS—HIGH

- Maktabi's business concept is simple and can easily be copied by any wholesaler, distributor, or retailer already in operation.

- The products that Maktabi sells are standard office supply products that can easily be purchased from local providers or global companies located in regions such as Southeastern Asia.

- The required start-up investment amount is moderate and can be matched by larger competitors who feel their market share is being threatened.

BARGAINING POWER OF SUPPLIERS—VERY LOW

- The products that Maktabi will sell can be purchased from any number of suppliers because the majority are available from other sources and are indistinguishable from one another.

- Global companies, particularly from Asia and Southeastern Asian countries, are hungry for business and will help open barriers to entry.

BARRIERS TO ENTRY—MODERATE TO LOW

- Moderate capital investment paired with a simple business concept allow for development of me-too companies.

CURRENT COMPETITIVE THREAT—MODERATE

- Local office supply stores threaten Maktabi due to their widespread availability throughout Egypt's major areas. The convenience that these stores offer cannot match that of Maktabi because the customer must physically make the purchase and the product variety is limited.

SWOT Analysis

STRENGTHS

- Maktabi is the first company in Egypt to offer office supplies along with their delivery, rendering the process more efficient.

- Beginning a catalog service as well as selling products online will enable Maktabi to sell other products such as furniture and technology related to the office.

- Our core competence is operational excellence. Our sourcing strategy along with our modern distribution facility will enable us to provide products to customers with a minimum error rate in an expected amount of time at little cost.

WEAKNESSES

- No prior experience in the office supplies industry.

- The company's success will depend in large part on an aggressive sales force and a robust marketing and sales promotions plan.

- Ability to find required talent to staff the operation in a forward-thinking, culturally borderless business environment.

OPPORTUNITIES

- Extremely large potential market that is already purchasing the type of product we are offering.
- Introducing a larger variety of products or partnering with companies who would want to use our reputation or our network to sell their own products.
- Expand into other sectors.
- Expand into other countries in the Middle East—borders are less concrete because of the Internet.

THREATS

- Competitors see an opportunity to get into the market using already existing political and economic relations to compete.

Competitive Analysis

Currently, there is one organization and two types of existing business models that directly compete with Maktabi: Speedsend is the former, and traditional office supply stores and hypermarkets are the latter. Consumer perceptions of product attributes are diagramed by Maktabi's positioning matrix in Figure CI1.

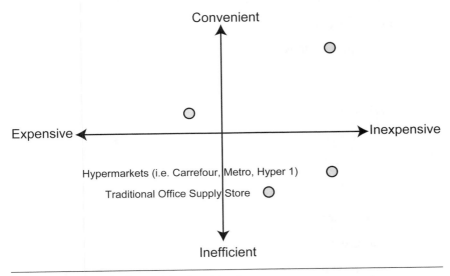

Figure CI1   Maktabi Positioning Matrix

Of the aforementioned competitors, attributes of each are outlined below:

Speedsend (www.speedsend.com)

- In operation since June 2001
- Only offers its services in Cairo
- HP business partner
- Xerox certified corporate reseller
- Make its own brand of paper

Traditional office supply stores (includes high-end stores such as Ali wa Ali and Aswak)

- Located throughout Egypt
- Do deliver locally
- Do not have catalogs
- Do not innovate with the types of product they carry
- Cannot buy in bulk

Hypermarkets

- Increasing in popularity throughout Egypt
- Purchase items in bulk
- Few locations and located primarily outside of the major cities
- Do not innovate with the types of product they carry
- Do not deliver locally
- Do not have catalogs

Target Markets

A SNAPSHOT

Businesses

- Average combined annual revenues of $1.3 million
- Regular use of office supplies
- Two or more departments in each company that order separately

Consumers

- Average annual household income of $12,000

- Regular use of office supplies

- More than two individuals per household who order office supplies

The Bigger Picture

In interviews conducted with executive assistants and secretaries at small and large corporations, the majority expressed that they would probably or definitely use our service to order office supplies for three reasons (see Figure CI2):

- It will simplify the processes currently in place in the office.

- There is a trend toward accepting already established ways of doing business in more developed countries.

- Some of the products sold will be considered as trendy or new on the market, making consumers happy to try something different.

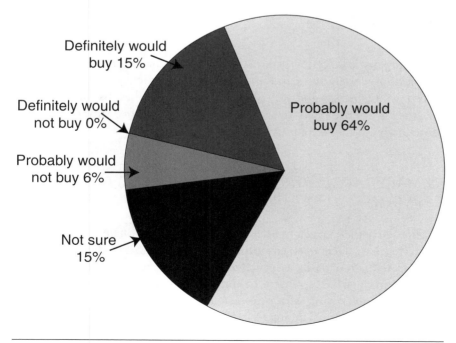

Figure CI2   Usage by Percentage of Population

Further emphasis will be placed on executive assistants, secretaries, and office buyers because it has been proven that this group is more likely to be into innovations in this type of industry.

Overall, focus has been placed on these users because

- Office supplies are a vital component in the workplace.

- There is no need to double sell consumers on office supplies and the service that we offer.

- These consumers are already familiar with the products and current processes used to order them, and would welcome a service that enhanced the process.

- Our interviews show that these users have a high probability of using our service.

Another market of consumers exists that is not part of a business or an organization, but rather is composed of individuals. These are individuals who have a predisposition for purchasing office supplies because of the nature of their education, hobbies, or interests. Included in this group would be school children and their parents—since it is the parents who would actually purchase the products—artists, hobbyists, and individuals who like to own new and innovative office supplies.

Consumer Profiles

Our company is targeting two distinct markets characterized by a combination of psychographics and usage behavior. Particular emphasis will be placed on businesses and we will appeal to women because studies show that they are more likely to use a wide variety of office supplies and are more inclined to make a purchase.

PRIMARY TARGET: TRENDSETTING EXECUTIVE ASSISTANTS, SECRETARIES, AND OFFICE BUYERS

This particular target market is receptive to rationale-based appeals, preferring hard facts over emotional-based motivation. They respond to quick facts that are easily assimilated and applied to their job. This group will be particularly responsive to our sales force strategy and our more traditional advertising strategies, such as billboards, magazines, and advertising. Additional characteristics of these consumers are that they

- are concerned with making their jobs more efficient;

- are aware of the different ways business is being done in more developed countries;

- want to be considered competent and able to make business decisions (no matter the size);

- are influenced by their peers, supervisors, friends, and the media;

- use the Internet often, particularly for work, newsgroups, entertainment, and shopping; and

- value helping the company.

SECONDARY TARGET: OFFICE SUPPLY ENTHUSIASTS

Our secondary target market is less affected by rationale and facts as they are motivated by their hobbies or by their need to own trendy items. This group is not as business-oriented as our primary market, but equally important in our marketing efforts. Catchy advertisements that highlight how trendy our products are and the service that we offer drive them to purchase our product. We assumed less of a consumption rate for this market than the primary target market. Additional characteristics of these consumers are that they

- are excited by new products and new ways of purchasing products;

- are motivated by their hobbies and their emotions;

- are easily influenced by the media, friends, and perceived social leaders; and

- use the Internet for entertainment, online magazines, special interest groups, or gossip columns.

Marketing Strategy

Sales Forecast

In 2008 Maktabi sales will exceed $200,000 by completing over 19,500 different orders (see Figure MK1).

The 5-year sales projection is comprised of several calculations that consider the following (see Exhibits MK1-A, MK1-B, and MK1-C for Base, Best, and Worst Case Sales Projections, page 528–530):

1. Anticipated Demand has been determined by market research through focus groups and surveys (see Exhibits MK2 and MK3). This calculation is contingent upon business and consumer office supply usage (see Figure MK2).

2. Sales Representative Market Penetration determines Maktabi sales with regards to the market awareness created by each of our regional sales representatives (see Figure MK3).

3. Business and Consumer Awareness is a percentage that measures how effective advertising is at making the business user and the consumer aware of the product. Our marketing mix will effectively reach 39% of our target market in year one, with 76% of business

	2008	2009	2010	2011	2012
Total Orders	19,500	202,500	702,500	790,000	917,500
Total Dollars	$215,000	$2,149,000	$7,079,000	$7,951,000	$9,215,500

Figure MK1   5-Year Base Case Sales Projection

users and 2% of consumers becoming fully aware of Maktabi. A lower level of awareness is assigned to the "Office Supply Enthusiasts" group because they do not regularly use office supplies or they are less concerned with office supplies reaching them in an efficient manner; therefore, this group will be less receptive to marketing efforts.

		Purchase Intent	Adjustment	Total Adjusted Trial
Businesses	Definitely Buy	10%	80%	21%
	Probably Buy	62%	20%	
Consumers	Definitely Buy	14%	80%	26%
	Probably Buy	71%	20%	

Figure MK2   Anticipated Demand Calculations

	Year 1	Year 2	Year 3	Year 4	Year 5
Sales Representative 1 (Cairo 1)	2712	2880	2304	2304	2304
Sales Representative 2 (Cairo 2)	2712	2880	2304	2304	2304
Sales Representative 3 (Cairo 3)	2712	2880	2304	2304	2304
Sales Representative 4 (Cairo 4)	2712	2880	2304	2304	2304
Sales Representative 5 (Alexandria and North Coast 1)	2712	2880	2304	2304	2304
Sales Representative 6 (Alexandria and North Coast 2)	2712	2880	2304	2304	2304
Sales Representative 7 (Sinai Peninsula and Red Sea)	2160	2880	2304	2304	2304
Sales Representative 8 (Upper Egypt)	2160	2880	2304	2304	2304
Sales Representative 9 (Upper Egypt)	2160	2880	2304	2304	2304
Total	22,752	25,920	20,736	20,736	20,736
Cumulative	22,752	48,672	69,408	90,144	110,880

Figure MK3   Sales Representative Market Penetration Calculations

Situation Analysis

BEST AND WORST CASE SCENARIOS

Situation analysis considers several internal and external factors that affect sales projection figures. Five-year best case and worst case scenarios have been applied to our sales forecast to anticipate changes in the environment and predict how it could affect the company's performance (see Figure MK4). See Exhibit MK1 for further details.

Factors of Best Case Scenario

- Maktabi earns the support of top companies such as Orascom, ExxonMobil, or EGYPTAIR, increasing business support and awareness by word-of-mouth communication (see Exhibit MK4 for a sample letter of intent to use Maktabi's services, page 538).

- Office supply enthusiasts are more concerned with the efficiency that Maktabi is offering, causing them to be more receptive to the service. This is indicated by 16% of survey respondents that indicated they would definitely buy and 17% that indicated they would probably buy actually purchasing the products, an increase of 6% and 3% respectively from the base case.

Factors of Worst Case Scenario

- Economic downturn equates to less spending by businesses and consumers. This results in a lower adjusted purchase rate with 4% of the consumers who would definitely buy and 11% of the consumers who would probably buy actually purchasing the products.

	Year 1	Year 2	Year 3	Year 4	Year 5
Base	$215,000	$2,149,000	$7,079,000	$7,951,000	$9,215,500
Best	$1,000,000	$5,470,000	$7,990,000	$10,630,000	$10,915,000
Worst	$136,500	$1,875,000	$3,730,000	$2,915,000	$3,000,000

Figure MK4   Anticipated Demand Calculations

- Advertising successfully creates sense of need, but consumers choose to use alternative sources for office supplies. This is represented by lowering awareness.

- After year two's peak of 86% among businesses and year four's peak of 10% among consumers, awareness drops by an average of 18% each year. This decrease in awareness can be attributed to a 13% decrease of consumer reach and 57% lower frequency.

Marketing Strategy

Our promotions and advertising are meant to educate businesses and consumers, which enforces a pull strategy. Heading our marketing efforts, Maktabi's marketing director will focus efforts on informing businesses and consumers about the need to make their work habits more efficient and motivate them to use our services as the solution (see Exhibit MK5 for the curriculum vitae of Maktabi's marketing director candidate, page 539). These marketing strategies support our company's critical success factors. Our marketing efforts must make businesses and consumers aware that they will waste time and money by using traditional office supply ordering habits.

The success of the Maktabi brand is dependent upon how well our marketing efforts align and communicate our companywide strategies and objectives. These objectives manifest themselves as a cohesive theme throughout each level of the marketing and distribution process. Maktabi's marketing strategy can be summarized by a four-stage progression and acronym called REEM:

1. Reason with businesses and consumers about the inefficiencies of current office supply ordering.

2. Educate businesses and consumers about the need to make the office supply ordering process efficient and modern.

3. Empower businesses and consumers to change their office supply ordering habits.

4. Motivate businesses and consumers to use our services.

Market Life Cycle

It will take several years for Maktabi to reach full market saturation. Lack of competitors and high product differentiation indicates that the market is currently in the introduction phase. This will be the longest stage of our market life cycle. This is due to the time and resources it takes to educate businesses and consumers and to motivate them to change their habits, two of our critical success factors. Market growth will occur as our sales increase and businesses and consumers become more aware of the product. We have accounted for this slow growth by taking a more conservative approach in our sales forecasting. We calculated that 80% and 20% of the survey respondents that indicated they will definitely buy and probably buy, respectively, actually purchase the product (see Exhibit MK1-A through MK1-C).

Pricing Strategy

Minimal profit margins will be allocated to each product to undermine the prices set forth by our competitors for similar products. Survey results indicate that the majority of respondents are willing to pay between 5EGP and 9EGP (US$0.87 and US$1.57) for our service (see Exhibit MK2). By providing the business user or the consumer with the choice of several delivery options, the minimum amount will be charged for that service and no gratuity will be required because the delivery will be made by a professional transportation company. Pricing Maktabi's products as competitively or more competitively compared to standard products from other outlets is necessary because consumers consider office supplies low-price commodities. Businesses and consumers will compare the price of our products and service to other alternatives they are familiar with. The more sophisticated consumers will compare Maktabi products to the expensive high-end stores such as Ali wa Ali and Aswak and recognize that we can offer a greater variety of products more efficiently. Similarly, consumers more inclined to make large one-time purchases will compare our products and services to those of the hypermarkets which will have less variety, a less efficient process, and similar or more expensive pricing. We hope that the perception from the beginning will be that Maktabi is the more time- and cost-effective choice.

Product Availability

The large size of our target market requires that our distribution methods ensure that Maktabi's products are available to every potential business and consumer. This is achieved by maintaining accurate forecasts based on historical and analytical data, as well as distributing to all regions of the country. At the beginning of every catalog and on the Web site, a "How to . . ." section will be made available, enabling businesses and consumers to understand how to place orders, how to ask questions, how to complete returns, and more.

Sales Force

During the first 5 years that Maktabi's products and service will be available, the marketing department will employ and train nine sales representatives. All agents will be provided with catalogs, a vehicle, and a laptop computer with access to the Internet from any location for activity tracking and client demonstration purposes. Each representative will earn a base salary of 300EGP (US$52) per month with a 2% increase each year. The nine representatives will earn a 3% commission. The base salary allows the representatives to have a vested interest in the long-term concerns of the company, while the commission motivates them to establish and maintain contacts with businesses. The sales force will be led by a marketing manager who will also be responsible for developing and assessing the marketing mix. For an organizational chart, see Exhibit CM1, page 601.

Advertising Mediums

NEWSPAPER ADVERTISEMENTS

Newspaper advertising will be used as a way to introduce Maktabi to the public. Every newspaper advertisement has a black background and white type that states a bold, high impact, logical statement about better business processes, ending with our recognizable catchphrase "Easy!" These ads act as a stimulant to inform the public about better business practices. This advertising campaign will run for the first 2 years to stir up general awareness about better office supply ordering practices and our products. The advertisement will appear twice a month. Our Web site and our toll free number will be located at the bottom of all newspaper advertisements. Though, based on our analysis, radio, television, and Internet advertising is recognized by businesses and consumers as the medium that will best convey the message about our products and services, we feel newspaper advertising will convey a sense of reliability and urgency to initially create awareness among consumers.

MAGAZINE ADVERTISEMENTS

A continuous magazine advertisement campaign creates awareness among our target consumers. Each magazine selected has been chosen through an extensive cost/reach analysis. Our advertisements will initially be found in *Business Today, Egypt Today, Al-Ahram, Al-Riyadi* and *Kol El-Nas* three times per year per magazine. Our Web site and our toll free number will be located at the bottom of all magazine advertisements.

The advertisements directed at the businesses are meant to create logical relationships to better business practices by using our products and service. These particular advertisements are smart, witty, and filled with images portraying peace and tranquility. The advertisements targeting our consumers are a little less sophisticated in that they demonstrate that every good home must also use our products and services. These advertisements make the consumer feel that they have a problem and that Maktabi is the solution.

RADIO ADVERTISEMENTS

A 30-second radio advertisement will be aired during peak times when our target markets would be tuning in. This will be maintained twice a week after the first 6 months of operation for 6 months to act as a reminder to all businesses and consumers about the company, the free catalogs and where they can be found, as well as the common goal we are both trying to achieve: a more efficient process at no additional cost. After year one, the advertisements will be aired once a week during the programming that best targets our market. The radio advertisement will contain a recognizable tune with lyrics that illustrates, as a message, "This is your office—Easy!"

Other radio advertising will come in the form of free giveaways sponsored by Maktabi during the very same programs that reach our target market.

TELEVISION ADVERTISEMENTS

According to our survey, television advertisement is the number one medium for reaching our potential target market. Television advertisement will come in the form of commercials as well as signage that will be viewable via television (for example on the back of football jerseys of one of Egypt's club teams). The advertisements will include comparisons between Maktabi's process and the traditional office supply ordering process. The commercials will be upbeat and portray a sense of comfort and happiness. The television advertisements will not occur until after year one because it is still necessary for people to know a little about the products that we offer and the service we provide. Coupled with our aggressive sales blitz, the television advertisements will act as support for our marketing strategy. Signage on the football jerseys of one of Egypt's club teams will not occur until after the third year because that is when it will be targeting the business as well as the consumer that already has knowledge about the company.

Promotional Strategy

MAKTABI CLUB CARD AND POINTS

Businesses and consumers will have the ability to sign up for the Maktabi club card (see Exhibit MK6). The idea behind using such a card is to entice businesses and consumers to purchase from Maktabi for two different reasons:

- Special discounts on particular products will be made when the card number is provided.

- The customer will be able to earn points that can be redeemed for any product (predetermined by Maktabi) that the customer needs.

Needless to say, the advantages of providing the club card are numerous:

- Creating repeat customers

- Tracking customer's purchasing trends, and providing them with all the appropriate sales

- Having all customer contact information readily available when an order is placed

- The ability for the card to be used in the future as a credit card on which interest may be charged

GIVEAWAYS AND DISCOUNTS

Maktabi will continually create promotional opportunities by providing free giveaways at contests or when a customer makes a purchase greater than a predetermined amount. Discounts will also be made available during different times of the year to increase sales during slower periods.

Public Relations Efforts

PRESS RELEASES—EDUCATION THROUGH INFORMATION

The following forms of communication are used to create talk within the industries, to sell our products and service to media representatives, and as promotion in the form of word-of-mouth communication and published articles (see Exhibit MK7 for a detailed communication schedule, page 543).

- Press releases to newspapers, magazines, and business journals about Maktabi (see Exhibits MK8-A and MK8-B for sample press releases, pages 547 and 548).

- A sales representative will attend business tradeshows and conferences to solicit endorsements and promote our products and services.

TRADESHOWS AND CONVENTIONS

Tradeshows and conventions are suitable places to promote Maktabi products and services, especially when representatives of businesses in our target market are gathered in one area. Thus, Maktabi participates in the following tradeshows and conventions in Egypt, whether we are exhibiting ourselves or attending to promote the company:

Tradeshows

- Cairo ICT: International telecommunications, information technology, networking, satellite and broadcasting technology trade fair of the Arab World (February)

- APEX: Arab African packaging, paper, and printing exhibition (March)

- Cairo International Fair: General goods and industrials products (March)

- Beem Egypt: Construction and building (June)

- Egypt Invest: International investment and trade forum (November)

Conventions

- International educational conference and exhibition (May)

- Tourism and shopping festival and exhibition (July)

- International exhibition for developing business (November)

- HACE: Hotel supplies and catering equipment (November)

- Office furniture and requirement expo (December)

Catalog Strategy

Though the catalog will be used as a visual aid for customers to see the products that Maktabi is offering, it also serves an important marketing purpose—as a means to communicate with customers to promote new items that have been added to the product line. Market research will determine the products that should be included in the catalog as well as their pricing and the way each item is promoted.

Web Strategy

Maktabi's Web site will be used as an additional outlet for our catalogs as well as an extension of our print media marketing efforts. On the Web site consumers will find all of our available products. They will be able to order them online and find answers to inquiries they may have regarding products, policies, the company, and contacts. Visitors will also be able to give feedback on yet to be released products and advertisements. Banners, links, and online partnerships will be created to ensure maximum exposure to the Web site as well as additional benefits such as support for large customers. Further information about the Maktabi Web site can be found within the Information Systems section of this business plan, page 522.

Company, Product, and Service Presentation

BRAND NAME

After a number of test names, we selected Maktabi as our comany name because it best embodies the qualities of our marketing strategy. Translated into English, the word Maktabi signifies "my office," which carries with it the idea that we are just an extension of the customer's very own office. We want our customers to feel that it is literally that easy to use our service.

POINT OF PURCHASE DISPLAYS

Point-of-purchase (POP) displays are essential, not only to convince business customers to use our service, but also to support our advertising and draw attention to the products in our catalog. Key POP display attributes are

- Displays should be located in businesses where customers who purchase office supplies regularly go, such as shopping malls and grocery stores

- Free catalogs will be made available at the POP displays to encourage consumers to, at a minimum, read about the products and the service that we offer

PACKAGING

The packaging that we will use is an integral element of our marketing mix because it is a visual of our service in action. Just like major brands, such as FedEx or Nike, our brand name and logo must become recognizable upon first glance. Our packaging will come in several different sizes as required by the size of the order (determined by computer systems as discussed in the Organization and Operations Management section).

Our marketing objectives are to educate and motivate consumers, supporting and fulfilling our first two critical success factors. Operations management begins to address our two final critical success factors: operational excellence and original products. Next we review the financial portion of this plan.

Return on Investment

The project yields a 32% return over a 5-year period.

Investment Requirements and Ownership

The launching of Maktabi requires an initial investment of $690,000 in year one (see Exhibit CM2 for a detailed implementation plan, pages 602–605). Although we break even at the end of year two, an additional investment of $180,000 is needed for the acquisition of capital and expenses in year two (see Exhibits FE1-A through FE1-J for base case

Sources		Applications	
Self	$45,000	Vehicles	$74,775
Friends and family	$225,000	Computer system	$643,000
Investor(s)	$600,000	Computers and hardware	$46,130
Bank loan		Furniture and other equipment	—
		Stock/inventory	$84,055
Total	**$870,000**	Working capital	$22,040
		Reserve for contingencies	$45,000
		Other	—
		Total	**$870,000**

Figure FE1 Sources and Uses of Funds

scenario financial statements, pages 549–569). Capital investors will own approximately 70% of all project investments, while the remaining 30% will be owned by management. A breakdown of sources and uses of funds is shown in Figure FE1.

Sensitivity Analysis

A sensitivity analysis was performed to observe the change in IRR when adjusting key variables. In Figure FE2, markup, distribution cost, transportation cost, business orders, and consumer orders were adjusted until the IRR changed to below 20%.

Risk Analysis and Reduction

DECREASE IN MARKUP

Markup can decrease by 5% simultaneously for businesses and consumers before IRR falls below 20%. Key factors that affect markup are supplier relationships and locations.

REDUCING THE RISK

- There is low risk that suppliers will increase their prices due to the abundance of different suppliers.

- To ensure that suppliers do not change their prices, proper, long-lasting relationships with suppliers will be made along with incentives.

Sensitivity Analysis	Percent of Change
Markup	Decrease 5%
Distribution cost	Increase 50%
Transportation cost	Increase 33%
Business orders	Decrease 95%
Consumer orders	Decrease 10%

Figure FE2   Sensitivity Analysis

DISTRIBUTION COST

Distribution cost is based on the quote received from the third-party logistics provider Maktabi will be using. Their costs can increase by 50% before IRR falls below 20%.

REDUCING THE RISK

- A robust contract with the logistics company will provide the fundamental basis for any expected costs related to distribution.

- Providing the sense of partnership between Maktabi and the third-party logistics company will motivate the provider to view Maktabi's success as their own.

TRANSPORTATION COST

Maktabi's orders will be transported to businesses and consumers nationwide; therefore, the variable transportation costs are high and are directly correlated with the fluctuations in fuel prices.

REDUCING THE RISK

- Maktabi's relationship to the transportation company is the same as the one with the distribution company; both services are provided by GSI—Global Structure Industries, precisely to reduce the risk associated with each by managing one company.

BUSINESS AND CONSUMER ORDERS

The sales projections are highly correlated with the accuracy of survey results and the effectiveness of the marketing strategy. Another threat to the company is the introduction of me-too companies.

REDUCING THE RISK

- Each year a portion of the marketing budget is allocated to additional market research. Necessary adjustments on target market, price, and product attributes will be made.

- The marketing director will monitor all elements of the marketing mix and the effect on awareness.

- Strive for continuous improvement. Customer service
  representatives and the Web site will be ways of communicating
  with customers to receive feedback.

Situational Analysis

WORST CASE SCENARIO: IRR = 16% (PROBABILITY OF OCCURRENCE = 10%)

See Exhibits FE2-A through FE2-D for worst case scenario financial
statements, pages 570–573. The worst case scenario is based on the worst
possible occurrences for the aforementioned risks.

Contingency Plan

- Utilize additional communications vehicles, such as press releases
  or television. Better identify Maktabi's target market.

- To help prevent me-too companies from stealing the Maktabi
  concept, Maktabi will establish all necessary documentation to
  protect its interests with the Egyptian government.

BEST CASE SCENARIO: IRR = 69% (PROBABILITY OF OCCURRENCE = 5%)

See Exhibits FE3-A through FE3-D for best case scenario financial
statements, pages 574–577. The best case scenario is based on the best possible outcomes of the opportunities that Maktabi faces.

Plan of Action

- Increase capacity through appropriate communications with
  customers, investors, third-party service providers, and
  management.

Organization

Form of Ownership

Maktabi will incorporate as a limited liability company (LLC) under the Investment Law. Foreign companies prefer to incorporate under the Investment Law to benefit from the privileges that it offers. The Investment Law has one authority that is responsible for investor incentives and guarantees—the General Authority for Investment and Free Zones (GAFI). It also groups over 20 exemptions and incentives under one law, and specifies activities that would automatically accrue benefits to investors. It allows 100% foreign ownership and guarantees the right to remit income earned in Egypt and to repatriate capital.

The LLC itself may be formed with a minimum of 2 shareholders and a maximum of 50 shareholders. The minimum share capital required to form an LLC is 50,000EGP (US$9,078). The capital must be divided into equal shares, either in cash or in kind, and the value of each share must be at least 100EGP (US$18.16). The management of an LLC may be vested in one or more managers. At least one manager must be of Egyptian nationality.

Principals and Management Team

In addition to the Board of Advisors, the principals of Maktabi are key figures on the management team. The Board of Advisors will follow a set of policies that have been predetermined to ensure no conflict of interest. These policies will also ensure that the Board of Advisors, which has a vested interest in the company, makes the right decisions for Maktabi. Both the Chairman and the Chief Executive Officer will participate in board meetings. We feel that with a five-member board, decisions that require a vote will be dealt with efficiently. The credentials of the Board of Advisors are listed here and are followed by the credentials of the principals of the management team. For a breakdown of the organizational structure, refer to Exhibit CM1.

THE BOARD OF ADVISORS

Mahmoud Mohieldin

Dr. Mohieldin has been the Minister of Investment in the Arab Republic of Egypt since 2004. This ministry is responsible for administering investment policy; management of state-owned assets, including privatization and restructuring of public enterprises and joint ventures; and nonbanking financial services, including capital market, insurance, and mortgage finance.

Dr. Mohieldin was born in Egypt in 1965. He received his bachelor of science in economics, with highest honors, first in order of merit, from Cairo University, Egypt. In 1989 he received a diploma in quantitative development economics from University of Warwick, England; in 1990 he received a master of science in economic and social policy analysis from University of York, England; and in 1995 he received his PhD in economics from University of Warwick, England.

Dr. Mohieldin has declared that he will provide his support in this venture by ensuring the efficient flow of orders through the bureaucratic red tape that companies in Egypt sometimes face.

Majid Al-Futtaim

Mr. Majid Al-Futtaim is the founder of several large regional shopping malls and hypermarkets throughout the Middle East. His ventures include such giants as the Mall of the Emirates in Dubai, United Arab Emirates; Ski Dubai in Dubai, United Arab Emirates; and Maadi City Center, Cairo, Egypt. Owning the Carrefour chain of stores in Egypt, Mr. Al-Futtaim hopes to share the expertise of his leadership team in creating a business whose products and service would be used throughout Egypt and the rest of the Middle East. His vision for Maktabi is a Staples for the Middle East.

Tarek Ragheb

Mr. Tarek Ragheb owns several businesses throughout the Middle East, the majority of which are located in Egypt. His contacts and expertise in setting up businesses and seeking funding have made him a crucial member of the Board of Advisors. Additionally, due to his American education, Mr. Ragheb brings a Western ideology of doing business to the Middle East. He is excited about the potential of being part of another winning business opportunity such as Maktabi.

THE MANAGEMENT TEAM

Joseph Naaman—Chairman

Mr. Joseph Naaman started his first business as a sophomore at Boston University, where he earned his degree in finance and marketing. He was a partner in a venture exporting Arizona Iced Tea from the United States to Italy, achieving approximately $2.5 million in sales within the first 2 years. Since then he has joined an established multinational pharmaceutical company, Bristol-Myers Squibb, to gain additional experience in global supply chain and logistics. He continued his professional education globally in business development for a luxury motor yacht company based in Egypt, where he started his second venture exporting organic agricultural products worldwide from Egypt. Along the way Mr. Naaman wrote two award-winning business plans, one for consumer products and one in the services industry. Currently, he is attending the Thunderbird School of Global Management, where he is focusing on entrepreneurship and finance. He has used his time at Thunderbird to refine the skills required to ensure the smooth operation of his new passion—providing office supplies to the Egyptian workplace.

Sherif Naaman—Chief Executive Officer

Mr. Sherif Naaman has over 35 years of experience in both the United States and the Middle East, leading projects in the fields of marketing and information technology. Fifteen of his 35 years have been spent as Managing Director in Saudi Arabia for various companies: the Alshaya group, a Kuwaiti holding company; Wardeh Al-Salehiya, a Saudi holding company; and Bristol-Myers Squibb, a U.S. corporation and the fifth largest pharmaceutical company worldwide. With his experience and exposure to the Middle East market, Mr. Naaman is confident that he would efficiently manage the company. He is excited about the opportunity to move back to the Middle East to aid companies in doing business the way they should.

Mahmoud Hindi—Distribution Director

Mr. Mahmoud Hindi has over 5 years of experience working for SGS, a global transportation and freight forwarding company whose Egyptian offices were founded by his father. With the exposure that he has received at this high level, Mr. Hindi believes that his experience, contacts, and know-how in distribution and transportation will enable him to manage logistics at Maktabi with excellence.

Nancy Sharkawi—Purchasing Director

Ms. Nancy Sharkawi has worked for several years in the supply chain and as a sales representative for a large pharmaceutical company in the United States. With this background, Ms. Sharkawi will be able to manage the purchasing department of Maktabi. Naturally a people person, Ms. Sharkawi will foster the relationships required with Eastern and Southeastern Asian countries to ensure the smooth flow of product into Egypt. She is excited to be able to use the skills she has developed in the United States in a global setting.

Christine Chami—Marketing Director

Ms. Christine Chami has several years of experience working in the marketing departments of large consumer goods companies. With the beginning of her career based in Canada, she knows how marketing departments are run in the west. She has successfully applied the knowledge she gained from this experience as a high performer at the company she currently works for in Dubai. Living in Dubai has enabled her to learn about doing business in the Middle East.

Operations Management

Strategic Value Chain

One of Maktabi's strategic objectives is to focus on operational excellence to provide the customer with the most value at a competitive price while offering a variety of new and original products. To describe the value added at each process, we break down the ordering process into the following areas: purchasing, publications, customer service, distribution and returns,

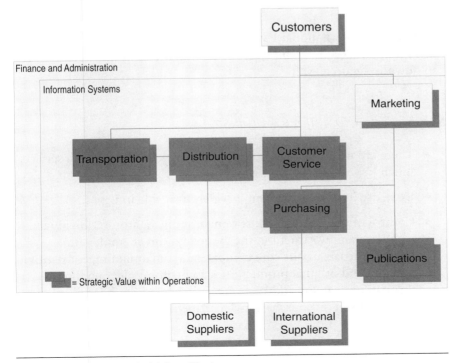

Figure OM1 Strategic Value Chain

513

transportation and accounts receivables, information systems, and finance and administration. The strategic value chain is depicted in Figure OM1.

The following alternatives have been evaluated using make–buy analysis considering quantitative and qualitative factors to determine the ideal combination of processes that make up the value chain.

Purchasing

Initially, purchasing will consist of a team of two local buyers and two foreign market buyers led by the purchasing manager. The buyers are divided into their area of expertise as determined by the type of products that they purchase (see Exhibit OM1 for a product group listing). The objective of the purchasing department is to supervise the day-to-day purchasing activities of all products that Maktabi purchases domestically and internationally, monitor inventory levels to keep the distribution center stocked at required levels, implement a sourcing strategy to investigate new products in the market, and make recommendations based on assessments to reduce costs and improve the quality of the products that we sell.

FINANCIAL CONSIDERATIONS

The costs of running a purchasing department are minimal because all that is required is employee salaries and benefits, overhead, tools for domestic and international communication, and minor travel expenses for training, tradeshows, and conventions. The total of these costs is broken down in Figure OM2.

STRATEGIC CONSIDERATIONS

- There are no companies in Egypt that offer purchasing as a service, much less at the level that is required.

- Expertise in this department is widely available in Egypt.

- Control of the products must remain in the hands of individuals who have an investment in the company (direct employees) because the last of our core competencies, maintaining constantly updated and original product lines and communicating them through our catalog and Web site, will depend on the skills of the individuals in our purchasing department.

Decision: In-house

	Year 1	Year 2	Year 3	Year 4	Year 5
Number of personnel units	4	4	4	4	4
Wages	$8,846.85	$14,508.11	$15,958.92	$17,554.81	$19,310.29
Bonuses	$0.00	$0.00	$0.00	$0.00	$0.00
Social and other personnel costs	$0.00	$0.00	$0.00	$0.00	$0.00
Office material	$104.50	$172.97	$1,470.27	$1,902.70	$1,902.70
Travel and refreshment	$4,180.18	$6,918.92	$6,918.92	$6,918.92	$6,918.92
Communication	$1,567.57	$2,594.59	$2,594.59	$2,594.59	$2,594.59
Depreciation	$1,028.46	$1,702.27	$1,702.27	$686.26	$20.59
Total Purchasing	$15,727.56	$25,896.87	$28,644.98	$29,657.28	$30,747.10
In % of sales	7%	1%	0%	0%	0%

Figure OM2 Purchasing Financial Consideration

Publications

The publications department will consist of creative associates, catalog editors and their assistants, as well as Web editors and their assistants. The entire department will be overseen by a publications manager. The duties of the two creative associates are to choose the photos to be shown, and determine the content and the layout of both the catalog and the Web site. The catalog and the Web editors' roles are to ensure that the catalog and the Web site are updated regularly to reveal the most recent products available at Maktabi along with their description, prices, and specifications.

FINANCIAL CONSIDERATIONS

Costs for the publications department include employee salaries and benefits, overhead, publishing tools, software, and hardware (see Information Systems section, page 522), as well as printing costs. The total costs for the publications department are estimated in Figure OM3.

	5-year Net Present Value (NPV)
In-house	$760,000
Outsource	$181,000

Figure OM3 Present Value of the Cost of Publications

STRATEGIC CONSIDERATIONS

- Creating, editing, and managing a catalog and a Web site are not considered a core competency.

- The publications department will require a high number of employees to ensure that every detail is addressed.

- A link between purchasing and the publications department needs to be available to manage the information flow of new products that should be placed in either the catalog or on the Web site. The link must be from within the company to maintain efficient communication flows.

- Additional printing machinery needs to be purchased and housed and must be able to print catalogs in thousands of copies.

- Web servers must be managed and housed to ensure smooth Web flow based the capacity for the total number of forecasted users.

- Graphic Art Group based in Alexandria is a company with an excellent reputation, good work ethics, and capacity to handle the required quantities while providing quality results that has already demonstrated their capabilities and has provided us with a competitive offer.

Decision: Outsource to Graphic Art Group with the exception of the publications manager

Customer Service

Customer service is perhaps one of the most valuable areas for the company because it will be the face of Maktabi to the customer, be it by phone or by Web. The customer service department's responsibilities will include, but will not be limited to, answering any inquiries the customer has regarding our products or processes (ordering, returns, payment, etc.), placing the orders, and processing and coordinating any returns. Based on the total orders forecast for the first year, 15 customer service representatives need to be hired. Keeping customer-centric focus (customer relationship management), the customer service representatives will be separated based on the client that they are serving. There will be customer service representatives who will handle businesses and will even be assigned to specific accounts. Other representatives will be assigned to the consumers and another set of representatives will focus on returns only. Representatives who focus on taking orders will also be in charge of reviewing and releasing all orders that come in via the Web. At the head of each customer service area will be a team lead. One analyst will be included in this department to continuously provide reports and analysis on the performance of the customer service representatives, to keep track of customers with issues such as nonpayment, and to offer six-star quality customer service to big customers and their orders. The customer service department will be headed by a manager who will oversee the day-to-day activities and by a director whose responsibility will be to align the department with corporate strategies.

FINANCIAL CONSIDERATIONS

Though a complex area to manage, the customer service department is relatively simple for budgeting; in addition to employee salaries and benefits, training and overhead are included. Technology will play a large role in this department because it will all be automated from the telephone queue, to finding the answers to customer inquiries, to placing orders and processing returns. The information systems portion of the analysis is provided in the Information Systems section, page 522. Figure OM4 is an outline of the costs that will be incurred.

	5-year Net Present Value (NPV)
In-house	$651,000
Outsource	$399,000

Figure OM4 Present Value of the Cost of Customer Service

STRATEGIC CONSIDERATIONS

- Customer service is considered part of operational excellence and needs to be closely monitored.

- Customer service requires a large amount of manpower with skills in servicing, computers, and the Arabic and English languages.

- There are no companies in Egypt that specifically offer this service. If this service is offered, it will be in conjunction with distribution and it is not a core competency of the distribution companies that would be required to gain knowledge of our product and services, even if it is technologically automated.

- Customer service is a delicate issue that must be supported by the dedication of employees who have a direct investment in the company.

Decision: In-house customer service

Distribution and Returns

Maktabi's distribution process is the core of its operational excellence. With the distribution center (DC) located near one of Egypt's largest shipping ports for incoming vessels from Eastern shipping points, Maktabi's 7,000 square meter facility is strategically located for easy access to meet the needs of its customers throughout all of Egypt (see Exhibit OM2, page 596). Included as part of distribution are the processes of customs clearance, inventory stocking, order picking and packing, shipping, quality control, and returns collections.

CUSTOMS CLEARANCE AND TRANSPORTATION TO DISTRIBUTION CENTER

Maktabi expects to receive into the country close to 100–200 shipments per month from many different suppliers mainly located in Southeastern Asian countries (predominantly China, Taiwan, and India). With this many incoming shipments, it is critical that a team with an excellent network within the Egyptian government's Department of Commerce is established. This team would include individuals whose primary role would be to follow up with official processes and ensure that the proper documentation is available for smooth importation. Following the clearance from customs, the shipment must be delivered to the DC.

INVENTORY STOCKING

Once the stock is received, it must be registered with the company's store and placed in an organized manner within the confines of the secured DC. Inventory levels must be closely monitored electronically and low-level notifications sent to the purchasing department. The inventory will also be placed in such a way as to facilitate the next step of the process: picking the order.

ORDER PICKING AND PACKING

The customer service department puts the order through to the DC electronically, at which point a picking document (pick doc) is created. When the pick doc is created, personnel at the DC, using radio frequency technology (RFID), will know where and when to pick each item as stated on the pick doc. The items are placed in a package, which is also electronically determined by the system. Once the order picking and packing process is complete, the order is checked manually by quality control and placed on the appropriate shipping dock according to region, ready for shipment.

QUALITY CONTROL—6 SIGMA

Operational excellence as one of our four core competencies can only be measured through quality control. More specifically, from the time that product is ordered by the purchasing department to the time it reaches the customer, quality will be strictly adhered to. In our case quality is a factor of the variety of products offered, the timing by which they enter the DC (just-in-time), the condition of the products upon acceptance at the DC, efficiency of picking the order, accurate order picking, and accurate and safe delivery. To achieve the superior quality standards required, a total quality management (TQM) approach will be utilized with policies and standard operating procedures (SOPs) completed and signed by management. All workers are to be trained and must sign-off on the training for all applicable policies and SOPs. All policies and procedures will be strictly enforced through disciplinary action.

RETURNS

As a matter of courtesy to all our customers, returns will be accepted as long as firm criteria are followed. There are a limited number of reasons why returns will be accepted, such as damaged product, wrong product (though these will be kept at a minimum due to the quality control in place), and nonpayment. Returns will be properly recorded, closely monitored, and analyzed by the analyst in the customer service department. This point is critical because an investigation and action must take place if any trends are discovered, especially in the case of lost orders.

FINANCIAL CONSIDERATIONS

A summary of all financial considerations are outlined in Figure OM5 (for a more detailed analysis, see Exhibit OM3 on page 597).

STRATEGIC CONSIDERATIONS

- Lease and management of a 4,000 square meter distribution center.
- Fleet of trucks required to transport the shipments from Ain Sukhna port to the distribution center.
- Expertise and network in customs clearance and distribution is required.
- There is a considerable amount of inbound shipments to manage.
- Customs clearance must work closely with the purchasing department to estimate arrival times and have all documentation prepared.
- Flexible shelving must be available according to different seasons when inventory will be higher or lower.
- Large number of unskilled and skilled labor is required for picking and packing, as well as the management of these laborers.
- Time will be required to create the entire set up from scratch.
- Quality control managers must be properly trained and independent of the management of the company in order to remove any conflict of interests. However, senior management must have the flexibility to determine where quality control is required.
- Time and effort will be required to establish all the proper policies and SOPs.

	5-year Net Present Value (NPV)
In-house	$3,250,000
Outsource	$725,000

Figure OM5   Present Value of the Cost of Distribution

- The distribution center must by transparent to the company so as to properly manage and communicate the entire operational process.

Decision: Outsource to GSI—Global Structure Industries with the exception of the quality control director (see Exhibit OM4 for GSIs' letter to provide service, page 598)

Transportation and Accounts Receivables

When a package is ready for shipping, it will be loaded onto a truck along with other packages to be delivered to the same region. Depending on the type of delivery that the customer has requested, the transportation company is contacted by the DC and arrives ready for shipment pickup. A customer service representative then returns a phone call to the customer confirming the shipment and any special delivery notes required. At the destination point, the delivery is considered complete when the driver receives cash or a check for the delivery, unless the cutomer has prepaid by bank card. Those customers who do not pay will not receive the requested shipment and it will be returned to the DC to be restocked into inventory.

FINANCIAL CONSIDERATIONS

Financial considerations for basic transportation include the cost of delivering the shipment with regard to location domestically, the transportation manager's salary and bonus, and overhead (see Figure OM6 for a breakdown of in-house transportation versus outsourcing it).

STRATEGIC CONSIDERATIONS

- Fleet of trucks to be maintained is required.

- Reliable drivers who can pick up payments are required.

- An average of over 8,100 estimated deliveries to be completed per month for year one.

	5-year Net Present Value (NPV)
In-house	$14,580,000
Outsource	$830,000

Figure OM6 Present Value of the Cost of Transportation

- Separate delivery options must be offered, such as next day delivery, 2-day delivery, and regular delivery (with according variation in costs).

Decision: Outsource to GSI—Global Structure Industries with the exception of the transportation director (see Exhibit OM4 for GSIs letter to provide service, page 598).

Information Systems

There are three main information systems that will play a decisive role in the profitability of our company and its continued growth. It is important that the foundations of the system are laid appropriately at the launch of the project to properly support the growth of the company. The Order Processing System (OPS), the Inventory Management System (IMS), and the Warehouse Management System (WMS) will be implemented during the first year. Ensuring that orders placed via customer service or the Web are handled in an efficient and timely manner is vital to sustaining a customer-centric focus and lowering costs. The IMS will enable us to manage our inventory to keep inventory holding costs and purchasing costs low. Finally, the WMS will further develop our core competency of operational excellence by ensuring a smooth flow from order to picking and packing. In addition, important systems that are required are a full accounting system for budgeting, accounts payable and receivable, metrics, and employee payroll. A full marketing system will also be required to ensure that the marketing department has the tools required for market analysis and forecasting. Over and above these systems, the essential Microsoft package will be made available to all employees. With the exception of the Microsoft package, all the other software packages can be summed into one Entity Resource Planning (ERP) system that will allow all the separate systems to operate under one umbrella. This umbrella, as well as the Web site and any internal information technology (IT) issues, will be managed by the IT officer.

FINANCIAL CONSIDERATIONS

Figure OM7 is a summary of the costs between using off-the-shelf software and developing our own software rather than completing a make–buy analysis.

STRATEGIC CONSIDERATIONS

- More than one system will be required if purchased separately. In addition, experts in each software program will be required for training and maintenance purposes.

	5-year Net Present Value (NPV)
In-house	$940,000
Outsource	$195,000

Figure OM7 Present Value of the Cost of Developing a System or Purchasing an Off-the-Shelf System

- The functioning of the company will rely on information systems as its main business tool.

- There needs to be quick turnaround for remedies to any issues that arise with the information systems.

- SAP Corporation has ERP software and expertise in consulting that can handle all systems simultaneously, ensuring proper alignment between all systems as well as addressing any issues that arise.

Decision: Develop system with SAP with the exception of the chief information officer and staff

Finance and Administration

The finance and administration department of Maktabi are referred to as the soul of the company. This department includes the chief executive officer (see Exhibit OM5, page 599), the chief financial officer (heading this department), the accounting manager, two administrative associates, company drivers, and janitors. It is from this department that the company vision stems. The company headquarters will be located near Cairo in approximately 300 square meters of office space. The reason for choosing Cairo as the headquarters is that it is the central commercial hub of Egypt.

FINANCIAL CONSIDERATIONS

The costs of running the finance and administration department are relatively low since all that is required is employee salaries and benefits, overhead, and minor travel expenses for training and networking. The total of these costs is broken down in Figure OM8.

	Year 1	Year 2	Year 3	Year 4	Year 5
Number of personnel units	7	7	7	7	7
Wages	$41,621.62	$78,337.84	$86,335.14	$94,968.65	$104,465.51
Bonuses	$0.00	$0.00	$0.00	$0.00	$0.00
Social and other personnel costs	$0.00	$0.00	$0.00	$0.00	$0.00
Office material	$223.42	$299.10	$302.70	$302.70	$302.70
Travel and refreshment	$1,117.12	$1,495.50	$1,513.51	$1,513.51	$1,513.51
Communication	$3,351.35	$4,486.49	$4,540.54	$4,540.54	$4,540.54
Insurance	$1,074.32	$10,745.50	$35,396.12	$39,755.36	$46,076.75
Prof. services (legal, accounting, etc.)	$121,562.65	$80,727.27	$80,000.00	$80,000.00	$80,000.00
Provisions for unpaid invoices	$0.00	$0.00	$0.00	$0.00	$0.00
Office rent	$17,972.97	$22,702.70	$22,702.70	$22,702.70	$22,702.70
Water, electricity	$513.51	$648.65	$648.65	$648.65	$648.65
Maintenance, repairs	$128.38	$162.16	$162.16	$162.16	$162.16
Depreciation	$2,198.77	$2,943.51	$2,978.98	$841.84	$36.04
Total Finance and administration	$189,764.13	$202,548.72	$234,580.51	$245,436.12	$260,448.57
In % of sales	88%	9%	3%	3%	3%

Figure OM8 Finance and Administration Purchasing Considerations

STRATEGIC CONSIDERATIONS

The roles required to fulfill the finance and administration duties cannot be outsourced to an outside entity.

DECISION: IN-HOUSE

Our efficient means of operation and our required quality standards ensure that our critical success factor of operational excellence will be achieved. Moreover, the introduction of the Enterprise Resource Planning system will help the company offer high-quality service at a lower cost by improving efficiencies and productivity.

Conclusion

The Maktabi Group is presenting a simple, effective solution to the Egyptian public. We are addressing their need to use an efficient and inexpensive way to order office supplies from a catalog or online—offering a large variety of products with a diverse array of styles from the comfort of one's own chair! Current alternatives do not address all requirements for providing this service. Trends in the market indicate that Maktabi's potential market is ripe to be provided with an efficient office supplies ordering process. Our unique positioning and thorough analysis of target consumers gives Maktabi the ability to become a household name.

The Maktabi Group's marketing and operations management unify to meet the company's critical success factors of education, motivation, operational excellence, and innovation. This is achieved through our creative marketing strategy and cost-effective and efficient operating methods.

Maktabi is a low-risk project that offers a 32% return on your investment. This investment offers you the opportunity to better the Egyptian business environment. The Maktabi Group looks forward to the launch of our beneficial service. We hope that through our business plan, you have developed the same enthusiasm and confidence about Maktabi that we have.

Joseph Naaman
Partner

Buying Office Supplies—Easy!

Sample Business Plan Exhibits

Exhibit MK1-A: Base Case Sales Projection

	Year 1—Base*	Year 2—Base	Year 3—Base	Year 4—Base	Year 5—Base
Total Egyptian Consumers	2,501,000	2,568,465	2,637,750	2,708,904	2,781,978
Businesses	31,000	31,775	32,569	33,384	34,218
Households	2,470,000	2,536,690	2,605,181	2,675,521	2,747,760
Businesses	31,000	31,775	32,569	33,384	34,218
Businesses—Definitely Buy	10.34%	10.34%	10.34%	10.34%	10.34%
After 80%	8.28%	8.28%	8.28%	8.28%	8.28%
Businesses—Probably Buy	62.07%	62.07%	62.07%	62.07%	62.07%
After 20%	12.41%	12.41%	12.41%	12.41%	12.41%
Average Order per Year	7	7	7	7	7
Awareness (Sales Reps)	76%	86%	69%	69%	69%
Businesses Purchase	4,864	5,680	4,658	4,774	4,893
Total Orders per Year	6,000	39,760	32,604	33,419	34,254
Households	2,470,000	2,536,690	2,605,181	2,675,521	2,747,760
Households—Definitely Buy	14.29%	14.29%	14.29%	14.29%	14.29%
After 80%	11.43%	11.43%	11.43%	11.43%	11.43%
Households—Probably Buy	71.43%	71.43%	71.43%	71.43%	71.43%
After 20%	14.29%	14.29%	14.29%	14.29%	14.29%
Average Order per Year	5	5	5	5	5
Awareness (Advertisement)	2%	5%	20%	22%	25%
Households Purchase	12,703	32,615	133,981	151,358	176,642
Total Orders per Year	13,500	163,073	669,904	756,790	883,208
Combined Total	19,500	202,833	702,507	790,209	917,462

*First year includes initial set-up period when no orders are placed

Exhibit MK1-B: Best Case Sales Projection

	Year 1— Base*	Year 2— Base	Year 3— Base	Year 4— Base	Year 5— Base
Total Egyptian Consumers	2,501,000	2,568,465	2,637,750	2,708,904	2,781,978
Businesses	31,000	31,775	32,569	33,384	34,218
Households	2,470,000	2,536,690	2,605,181	2,675,521	2,747,760
Businesses	31,000	31,775	32,569	33,384	34,218
Businesses— Definitely Buy	15%	15%	15%	15%	15%
After 80%	12%	12%	12%	12%	12%
Businesses— Probably Buy	75%	75%	75%	75%	75%
After 20%	15%	15%	15%	15%	15%
Average Order per Year	9	9	9	9	9
Awareness (Sales Reps)	76%	86%	86%	86%	86%
Businesses Purchase	6,348	7,412	7,598	7,788	7,982
Total Orders per Year	16,755	66,712	68,380	70,090	71,842
Households	2,470,000	2,536,690	2,605,181	2,675,521	2,747,760
Households— Definitely Buy	25%	25%	25%	25%	25%
After 80%	20%	20%	20%	20%	20%
Households— Probably Buy	90%	90%	90%	90%	90%
After 20%	18%	18%	18%	18%	18%
Average Order per Year	5	5	5	5	5
Awareness (Advertisement)	5%	10%	15%	20%	20%
Households Purchase	46,930	96,394	148,495	203,340	208,830
Total Orders per Year	86,820	481,971	742,476	1,016,698	1,044,149
Combined Total	103,575	548,683	810,857	1,086,787	1,115,990

*First year includes initial set-up period when no orders are placed

Exhibit MK1-C: Worst Case Sales Projection

	Year 1—Base*	Year 2—Base	Year 3—Base	Year 4—Base	Year 5—Base
Total Egyptian Consumers	2,501,000	2,568,465	2,637,750	2,708,904	2,781,978
Businesses	31,000	31,775	32,569	33,384	34,218
Households	2,470,000	2,536,690	2,605,181	2,675,521	2,747,760
Businesses	31,000	31,775	32,569	33,384	34,218
Businesses—Definitely Buy	5%	5%	5%	5%	5%
After 75%	3.75%	3.75%	3.75%	3.75%	3.75%
Businesses—Probably Buy	45%	45%	45%	45%	45%
After 25%	11.25%	11.25%	11.25%	11.25%	11.25%
Average Order per Year	4	4	4	4	4
Awareness (Sales Reps)	76%	86%	69%	59%	49%
Businesses Purchase	3,527	4,118	3,377	2,954	2,515
Total Orders per Year	3,100	20,800	26,600	27,900	29,100
Households	2,470,000	2,536,690	2,605,181	2,675,521	2,747,760
Households—Definitely Buy	14.29%	14.29%	14.29%	14.29%	14.29%
After 75%	5%	5%	5%	5%	5%
Households—Probably Buy	71.43%	71.43%	71.43%	71.43%	71.43%
After 25%	10%	10%	10%	10%	10%
Average Order per Year	3	3	3	3	3
Awareness (Advertisement)	2%	10%	8%	5%	5%
Households Purchase	7,410	38,050	31,262	20,066	20,608
Total Orders per Year	8,700	150,000	320,000	240,000	250,000
Combined Total	11,800	170,800	346,600	267,900	279,100

*First year includes initial set-up period when no orders are placed

Exhibit MK2: Survey Results

Thank you for your participation. This study is being conducted by a team of young entrepreneurs and will be used in the development of a business plan for a new service. This study is being distributed to individuals who we feel may benefit from the service's use. All responses will be kept confidential.

PART I

1. What type of office supplies do you purchase? (check all that apply)

   ☐ Batteries, Surge & UPS **29%**   ☐ Filing Supplies **15%**

   ☐ Binders & Accessories **71%**   ☐ General Supplies **38%**

   ☐ Boards & Easels **17%**   ☐ Luggage & Briefcases **23%**

   ☐ Calendars & Planners **46%**   ☐ Mail & Ship/Moving **17%**

   ☐ Cleaning & Break Room **46%**   ☐ Office Machines & Calculators **38%**

   ☐ Desktop Organizers **19%**   ☐ Paper & Pads **44%**

   ☐ Envelopes & Forms **35%**   ☐ Self-stick Notes **19%**

2. On average, how many times do you purchase these office supplies in 1 month? (check one)

   ☐ a. 0–1 **37%**   ☐ b. 2–3 **40%**   ☐ c. 4–5 **12%**

   ☐ d. 6–7 **4%**   ☐ e. 8 or more **8%**

3. How much do you typically spend on office supplies at each purchase? (check one)

   ☐ a. 0–49 EGP **52%**   ☐ b. 50–99 EGP **17%**   ☐ c. 100–199 EGP **13%**

   ☐ d. 200–499 EGP **12%** ☐ e. 500 EGP or more **6%**

4. Where do you primarily purchase your office supply products? (check all that apply)

   ☐ a. Office supply store **75%**   ☐ b. Large department store **27%**

   ☐ c. Supermarket **15%**   ☐ d. Internet **10%**

   ☐ e. Catalog **2%**   ☐ f. Delivery **8%**

   ☐ g. Other _____ **0%**

5. What is your typical method for purchasing office supply products? (check all that apply)

☐ a. Personally purchase the products **77%**

☐ b. Someone else purchases the products **21%**

☐ c. Products delivered **10%**

6. What is your primary reason for using office supplies? (check all that apply)

☐ a. Personal use **67%**   ☐ b. Business use **56%**

7. Please rate how important the following qualities are in relation to purchasing office supplies:

	Not at all Important		Somewhat Important		Very Important
Convenience	☐ a. 1 **4%**	☐ b. 2 **6%**	☐ c. 3 **44%**	☐ d. 4 **10%**	☐ e. 5 **37%**
Variety of Products	☐ a. 1 **8%**	☐ b. 2 **4%**	☐ c. 3 **44%**	☐ d. 4 **17%**	☐ e. 5 **27%**
New Products	☐ a. 1 **6%**	☐ b. 2 **10%**	☐ c. 3 **44%**	☐ d. 4 **15%**	☐ e. 5 **25%**
Time	☐ a. 1 **12%**	☐ b. 2 **2%**	☐ c. 3 **42%**	☐ d. 4 **12%**	☐ e. 5 **33%**
Price	☐ a. 1 **2%**	☐ b. 2 **4%**	☐ c. 3 **58%**	☐ d. 4 **10%**	☐ e. 5 **27%**
Usefulness	☐ a. 1 **6%**	☐ b. 2 **6%**	☐ c. 3 **19%**	☐ d. 4 **21%**	☐ e. 5 **48%**
Quality	☐ a. 1 **6%**	☐ b. 2 **2%**	☐ c. 3 **21%**	☐ d. 4 **12%**	☐ e. 5 **60%**

PART II

A new service will be offered in the market. It is a new method for viewing, ordering, and receiving office supply products. This business will offer office supplies (from pens to paper clips and everything in between), office furniture, and technology products via catalog and an online Web site. Using these catalogs and the Web site, customers can view products they can order via phone or Web site and expect possible next-day delivery. This new process will save time and be more financially efficient.

8. On a 1 to 5 scale, where 1 is strongly disagree and 5 is strongly agree, please rate the business concept on the following characteristics:

	Strongly Disagree		**Somewhat Agree**		**Strongly Agree**
Convenient	a. 1 **4%**	b. 2 **2%**	c. 3 **48%**	d. 4 **10%**	e. 5 **37%**
Expensive	a. 1 **12%**	b. 2 **13%**	c. 3 **54%**	d. 4 **8%**	e. 5 **13%**
Easy to Use	a. 1 **0%**	b. 2 **8%**	c. 3 **44%**	d. 4 **6%**	e. 5 **42%**
Efficient	a. 1 **2%**	b. 2 **4%**	c. 3 **42%**	d. 4 **15%**	e. 5 **37%**
Useful	a. 1 **2%**	b. 2 **4%**	c. 3 **38%**	d. 4 **13%**	e. 5 **42%**
Trendy	a. 1 **17%**	b. 2 **15%**	c. 3 **46%**	d. 4 **4%**	e. 5 **17%**
Modern	a. 1 **0%**	b. 2 **6%**	c. 3 **44%**	d. 4 **12%**	e. 5 **38%**

9. Where would you be most likely to hear about this service? (check all that apply)

a. Office supply store **46%**
b. Television ad **48%**
c. Newspaper ad **44%**
d. Newspaper article **8%**
e. Business magazine ad **15%**
f. Business magazine article **4%**
g. People magazine ad **15%**
h. People magazine article **6%**
i. Radio **17%**
j. Internet **58%**
k. Other _____ **0%**

10. Which name do you think best fits this service?

a. Maktabi **54%**
b. Dabbasa **12%**
c. Maktaba Depot **19%**
d. Other _____ **0%**

11. What is the maximum price you expect to pay, in addition to the office supplies, for this service? **85 EGP**

12. What price, in addition to the office supplies, would you expect to pay for this service?

a. 0–4 EGP **21%**
b. 5–9 EGP **31%**
c. 10–14 EGP **21%**
d. 15–19 EGP **10%**
e. 20 EGP or more **17%**

13. Given your above chosen price, how likely would you be to use our service?

☐ a. Definitely buy **15%**   ☐ b. Probably buy **63%**   ☐ c. Don't know **15%**

☐ d. Probably not buy **6%**   ☐ e. Definitely not buy **0%**

14. Given your answer to the above question, how many times per year would you use our service to purchase office supplies?

☐ a. 0–3 **23%**   ☐ b. 4–6 **33%**   ☐ c. 7–9 **15%**

☐ d. 10–12 **23%**   ☐ e. 13 or more **6%**

PART III

15. What is your gender?

☐ a. Female **42%** ☐ b. Male **58%**

16. What is your age?

☐ a. 18 and under **4%** ☐ b. 19–24 **46%** ☐ c. 25–34 **10%**

☐ d. 35–44 **6%** ☐ e. 45–54 **2%** ☐ f. 55 and above **0%**

17. How many employees are there in your company?

☐ a. 10 and under **27%** ☐ b. 11–19 **13%** ☐ c. 20–49 **7%**

☐ d. 50–99 **20%** ☐ e. 100–499 **13%** ☐ f. 500 and above **20%**

18. What is the approximate annual revenue of your company?

☐ a. 0–49,999 EGP **17%** ☐ b. 50,000–99,999 EGP **0%**

☐ c. 100,000–499,999 EGP **13%** ☐ d. 500,000–999,999 EGP **17%**

☐ e. 1,000,000–9,999,999 EGP **4%** ☐ f. 10,000,000 EGP or more **50%**

19. What is the name of your company? _____

SIDPEC   **TRANSMISR**

HAKETEGP   **CHILDCARE ACADEMY**

STIA   **EXXONMOMBIL**

ORASCOM   **SAUDI ARABIAN AIRLINES**

ABB   **BMW**

SHAVING SYSTEMS   **GT EGYPT**

ALMUTAHIDA GROUP   **DEBIRS YACHTS**

20. What is a telephone number we may be able to reach you at in order to verify any information? _____

21. Your opinion is extremely valuable to us. Please express any additional comments about the service or the survey in the space provided.

_____

_____

_____

_____

Thank you for your time and participation.

Exhibit MK3: Focus Group Results

Moderator: Mahmoud Hindi   **Observer:** Joseph Naaman
Location: Beano's   **Date:** June 5, 2007
          Heliopolis, Cairo, Egypt   **Time:** 21:00 – 22:00

Participants	Age
Mohamad Humeyda	23
Mohamad Medhat	25
Ayman El-Bedihwi	26
Sherif Ezzat	23
Mai El-Ashry	22
Hoda El-Mankabadi	23

Focus Group Description
Office supply enthusiasts

How do you feel about the current office supplies industry in Egypt? Are there any trends that are occurring? Or, do you think they have been pretty similar over the last few years/decades?

Trends recognized: Office supplies in Egypt does not constitute a hot industry mainly because of the lack of variety of products available in the market. Not only is there no variety of products, but part of the reason is the lack of a modern store that offers the latest office supplies. Participants acknowledge that it is a little easier in Cairo, however, it is not enough. They noticed that trends in the office supply industry have been stagnant and there have been no major changes to the industry over the last few decades. Also, most of the time when searching for something specific for a hobby or an interest, they rarely find the products they are looking for. The general feeling is that there is nothing to get excited about when it comes to the office supply industry in Egypt.

The Maktabi concept was then introduced.

What do you think of this new way to purchase office supplies? Do you think it will be useful? More convenient?

Feelings and thoughts: All participants reacted with great enthusiasm about the concept and maintained their enthusiasm throughout the focus group. Once the background of the idea was explained, all participants related the same experiences and said they always wished for something that would enhance the process. They also became very excited by the idea that the variety of products available in different sizes and colors would be greater than what they were actually accustomed to. They thought the process itself would be convenient and simple.

What do you think about the catalog? The Internet? What type of products would you expect to see in the catalog or on the Internet? Talk about variety.

Thoughts: Being that it is a free catalog, the participants loved the idea because they now don't have to waste their time searching for the product they are looking for. They also liked the idea that the products would be delivered to their residence or work as soon as the next day, if that was required. They were interested in the idea of being able to place orders on the Internet because this is now the next logical step for Egypt's Internet industry. They felt it is starting to head in that direction, but needs more support from companies like Maktabi. They did however feel that people need to start trusting the Internet before using it and this might take a few more years.

What is the best way to reach people to advertise this idea? What type of advertisement do you feel would most appropriately target this segment of the market?

How to advertise and promote: All participants felt that the best way to reach the target market would be via television advertising as well as radio, magazine, and Internet promotions. They felt like the advertising would be rather simple because it is only logical that this new concept offers products and service that are better than what most people are used to. They also said that the novelty of the idea would encourage the use of the service.

How much do you expect to pay for Maktabi's products and services compared to other office supplies companies? Would you use this service? At what price?

Pricing: All participants expected to pay a premium for this service, but most did not want to. When they were told that the only increase in price would be the delivery and that this would be kept at a minimum because it can sometimes, depending on location, be equivalent to paying a tip, or "bakshish," they were very excited.

Exhibit MK4: Sample Letter of Intent

 26/07/08

From: xyZyx
         Ibn Jubier Street
         Attarine Alexandria
         ARE
Tel: 203.999.4901
Fax: 203.990.4901
E-mail: xyZyx_egypt@xyZyx.com

To: Maktabi Group

Re: Letter of intent to purchase office materials.

Dear Maktabi Group:

It is our pleasure to inform you of our intent to make Maktabi Group our main supplier of office materials. We believe that the concept the Maktabi Group has presented to xyZyx will offer our company greater efficiency and value.

We hope that the concept presented will be embraced throughout Egypt and the Middle East.

Sincerely,

Sabah Tawil
Vice President of Technical Affairs

Exhibit MK5: Sample Marketing Director Resume

(For more information on this candidate, please contact the Maktabi Group directly.)

Candidate: Louise Cham

Date of birth: October 6, 1978

Citizenship: Canadian and Egyptian

Profile

- Excellent organization and communication skills, strong presentation and negotiating aptitudes, diverse background resulting in the ability to be adaptable and to work well both independently and within a team environment, proven to be resourceful in a variety of fast-paced business environments.

Education

Bachelor of Commerce (International Business), 2002
John Molson School of Business
Concordia University, Montreal, Canada
Semester abroad : "École Superieure de Commerce à Montpellier," France, Fall 2001

Diplôme d'Études Collégiales (DEC) in Social Sciences and Mathematics, 1998
Collège Jean-de-Brébeuf, Montreal, Canada

Professional Experience

ExTech, Pune, India, 2006–Present

Marketing Executive

- Conduct detailed market and trend analysis, identify threats and opportunities, and develop targeted marketing strategies.
- Lead the proposal process for specific clients including pricing development, proposal writing, and contract negotiations.
- Create marketing and financial business plans for the launch of new products.
- Construct innovative promotional programs to ensure market growth.
- Write, edit, and revise content of marketing materials, such as the company Web site, catalogs, and brochures.

Accomplishments:

- Coordinated the launch of a new product line for the company.
- Created a company newsletter informing current and potential customers of the company's business activities and latest industry news.

Barens, Dubai, United Arab Emirates, 2005–2006

Marketing Coordinator

- Developed, designed, and produced marketing collaterals.
- Performed cost and benefit analysis on current market conditions and prepared reports as well as forecasts.
- Organized and attended seminars, board meetings, and conferences.

Accomplishments:

- Created two new databases for the marketing and sales departments.

TRC (Food Supply Specialist), Montreal, Canada, 2003–2005

Buyer/Market Researcher

- Identified and analyzed markets to be developed resulting in new private brand and product labels for goods sold in North America, Europe, and the Caribbean.
- Negotiated prices with multinational suppliers. Negotiated rate quotes with shippers, brokers, and freight forwarders.
- Monitored customers' inventory. Coordinated the logistics and documentation process for local and international transactions.
- Prepared tenders and managed the financials relevant to all new offers.

Accomplishments:

- Earned the position of new business coordinator for the region.

Sports Plus Inc. (Health Centre), Laval, Canada, 2001–2002

Customer Service/Receptionist (part-time)

- Advised clients about various membership plans while managing reception in a fast-paced environment.
- Resolved complaints and solidified continuous customer satisfaction.

Accomplishments:

- Consulted in the development of new internal software.

Life Carrier, Montreal, Canada, Summer 2000

Disability Support Associate—Group Life and Health

- Coordinated medical appointments and carried out follow-ups with the insured after their return to work.

Life Carrier, Montreal, Canada, Summer 1999

Administrative Support Associate—Group Life and Health

- Managed data conversion from in-house software to a new software.
- Provided administrative support to disability analysts.

Davis Promotions, Inc., Montreal, Canada, Summers 1997 and 1998

Administrative Assistant

- Organized U.S. and Canadian promotions.
- Ordered office supplies and insured on-time delivery.
- Prepared and validated accounts payables and receivables.

Linguistic Skills

- French and English: perfectly bilingual; Arabic: fluently spoken; Spanish: basic understanding

Computer Skills

- Microsoft Office: Word, Excel, Access, PowerPoint, Project, Outlook; Paint, Photoshop, Maximizer, SAP, Planosoft
- Expert in navigating and researching the World Wide Web

Other Activities and Interests

Member of Sakaar, April–December 2005, Pune, India

- Social committee bringing aid to the underprivileged in the local community.
- Coordinated events such as the sponsorship of a child's education and tree plantations.

Executive Vice President, 2001–2002, CASA Cares (Commerce & Administration Student Association), Concordia University—mandate of raising funds for different charities

- Organized and planned various social events.
- Raised almost $10,000 for UNICEF, Centraide, and the Cure Foundation.
- Managed task delegation.

Other Activities

- Scuba diving, tennis (participated in multiple amateur tournaments), snowboarding, and physical fitness.
- Travel throughout Europe, North Africa, India, and the United States.

Exhibit MK6: Maktabi Club Card

Buying Office Supplies – Easy!

4290 6239 7922 4350

BMW Egypt   Exp: 01/2009

Front

Authorized
Signature:

Save 10% every time you use your Maktabi Club Card!

Back

Exhibit MK7: Detailed Communication Schedule

Year 1	Jan	Feb	Mar	Apr	May	Jun	Jul	Aug	Sep	Oct	Nov	Dec
Newspaper Advertisements												
Al-Ahram (2x/mos)								X			X	
Akhbar El-Yom (2x/mos)										X		
El-Misri El-Yom (2x/mos)									X			X
Magazine Advertisements												
Business Today									X			
Egypt Today										X		
Al-Ahram Al-Riyadi											X	
Kol El-Nas								X				X
Radio Advertisements								X	X	X	X	X
Television Advertisements												
Tradeshows												
Cairo ICT												
APEX												
Cairo International Fair												
Beem Egypt												
Egypt Invest											X	
Conventions												
International educational conference and exhibition												
Tourism and shopping festival and exhibition												
International exhibition for developing business											X	
HACE—Hotel supplies and catering equipment											X	
Office furniture and requirement expo												X
Sales Rep Visits								X	X	X	X	X
Year 2	Jan	Feb	Mar	Apr	May	Jun	Jul	Aug	Sep	Oct	Nov	Dec
Newspaper Advertisements												
Al-Ahram (2x/mos)		X			X			X			X	
Akhbar El-Yom (2x/mos)	X			X			X			X		
El-Misri El-Yom (2x/mos)			X			X			X			X
Magazine Advertisements												
Business Today	X				X				X			
Egypt Today		X				X				X		
Al-Ahram Al-Riyadi			X				X				X	
Kol El-Nas				X				X				X
Radio Advertisements	X	X	X	X	X	X	X	X	X	X	X	X
Television Advertisements	X	X						X	X			X

(Continued)

Exhibit MK7 (Continued)

Year 2	Jan	Feb	Mar	Apr	May	Jun	Jul	Aug	Sep	Oct	Nov	Dec
Tradeshows												
Cairo ICT		X										
APEX			X									
Cairo International Fair			X									
Beem Egypt						X						
Egypt Invest											X	
Conventions												
International educational conference and exhibition					X							
Tourism and shopping festival and exhibition							X					
International exhibition for developing business											X	
HACE—Hotel supplies and catering equipment											X	
Office furniture and requirement expo												X
Sales Rep Visits	X	X	X	X	X	X	X	X	X	X	X	X
Year 3	Jan	Feb	Mar	Apr	May	Jun	Jul	Aug	Sep	Oct	Nov	Dec
Newspaper Advertisements												
Al-Ahram (2x/mos)		X			X			X			X	
Akhbar El-Yom (2x/mos)	X			X			X			X		
El-Misri El-Yom (2x/mos)			X			X			X			X
Magazine Advertisements												
Business Today	X				X				X			
Egypt Today		X				X				X		
Al-Ahram Al-Riyadi			X				X				X	
Kol El-Nas				X				X				X
Radio Advertisements	X		X		X		X		X		X	
Television Advertisements	X	X						X	X			X
Tradeshows												
Cairo ICT		X										
APEX			X									
Cairo International Fair			X									
Beem Egypt						X						
Egypt Invest											X	
Conventions												
International educational conference and exhibition				X								
Tourism and shopping festival and exhibition							X					
International exhibition for developing business											X	
HACE—Hotel supplies and catering equipment											X	
Office furniture and requirement expo												X
Sales Rep Visits	X	X	X	X	X	X	X	X	X	X	X	X

Year 4	Jan	Feb	Mar	Apr	May	Jun	Jul	Aug	Sep	Oct	Nov	Dec
Newspaper Advertisements												
Al-Ahram (2x/mos)		X			X			X			X	
Akhbar El-Yom (2x/mos)	X			X			X			X		
El-Misri El-Yom (2x/mos)			X			X			X			X
Magazine Advertisements												
Business Today	X				X				X			
Egypt Today		X				X				X		
Al-Ahram Al-Riyadi			X				X				X	
Kol El-Nas				X				X				X
Radio Advertisements	X		X		X		X		X		X	
Television Advertisements	X	X						X	X			X
Tradeshows												
Cairo ICT		X										
APEX			X									
Cairo International Fair			X									
Beem Egypt						X						
Egypt Invest											X	
Conventions												
International educational conference and exhibition					X							
Tourism and shopping festival and exhibition						X						
International exhibition for developing business										X		
HACE—Hotel supplies and catering equipment										X		
Office furniture and requirement expo												X
Sales Rep Visits	X	X	X	X	X	X	X	X	X	X	X	X

Year 5	Jan	Feb	Mar	Apr	May	Jun	Jul	Aug	Sep	Oct	Nov	Dec
Newspaper Advertisements												
Advertise in the two most effective newspapers from the past two years		X		X		X		X		X		X
	X		X		X		X		X		X	
Magazine Advertisements												
Advertise in the two most effective magazines from the past two years	X		X		X		X		X		X	
		X		X		X		X		X		X
Radio Advertisements	X		X		X		X		X		X	
Television Advertisements	X	X						X	X			X
Tradeshows												
Cairo ICT		X										
APEX			X									
Cairo International Fair			X									
Beem Egypt						X						
Egypt Invest											X	

(Continued)

Exhibit MK7 (Continued)

Year 5	Jan	Feb	Mar	Apr	May	Jun	Jul	Aug	Sep	Oct	Nov	Dec
Conventions												
International educational conference and exhibition					X							
Tourism and shopping festival and exhibition							X					
International exhibition for developing business											X	
HACE—Hotel supplies and catering equipment											X	
Office furniture and requirement expo												X
Sales Rep Visits	X	X	X	X	X	X	X	X	X	X	X	X

Exhibit MK8-A: Sample Press Release 1

National Launch of Maktabi

On January 1, 2007, HINA Business & Investment Group will launch MAKTABI, a company that offers a new solution to the traditional way of ordering office supplies.

Maktabi provides businesses and consumers with an effective and inexpensive way to order office supplies from a catalog or online—offering a large variety of products with a diverse array of styles from the comfort of one's own chair! The person placing the order can either order online or pick up the phone and dial one of the toll free numbers to order whatever they require. Through operational excellence and efficient distribution systems, the order will be received quickly at a minimal cost.

The Maktabi Web site is being developed to accommodate all the necessary information for customers to view product information and place orders online.

Exhibit MK8-B: Sample Press Release 2

Helping Egyptian Businesses

December 21, 2007

CAIRO—What do Yasser Refaat, Essam Ali, and Abir Mansour have in common? Their smarts—they have all decided to use Maktabi as the sole source for all their office supply needs.

Yasser Refaat is the General Manager for Guest Relations at the Conrad Hotel located in Mohandiseen, Cairo. He has a staff of over 25 employees who are in constant commotion to ensure that every request a guest has is granted. This seems easier said than done.

Refaat says that he has developed a way of staying organized by creating a color-coded filing system using colored paper and pens. During an interview, he remarked, "It is difficult (work), but, when the shift is over, each employee feels that they have done their utmost to make the guests' experience an unforgettable one." He further comments: "If it were not for the office supplies we purchase from Maktabi, we would be 40%–50% less efficient. Maktabi is so simple to use, I don't know if I would be where I am today without it."

Ali is a Sales Manager for ABX Logistics, whose Egyptian headquarters are in Nasr City, Cairo. He lived in the United States for several years and confesses: "When I first returned to Egypt, I almost got depressed at the process that was in place for ordering office supplies. I often found myself pen-less or paper-less in front of customers—something that never happened to me in the United States!" He then says: "Maktabi is a small piece of the West that has turned business into art. The best part is they are Egyptian!"

Our third interview was with the Executive Assistant for ExxonMobil whose offices are located in Alexandria. Everyday at least 20 (of the 50 or so) employees come to her to ask for specific office supplies. "All I do is have them (the employees) pick what they want from the catalog, mark it down, call Maktabi's call center, place the order, and swish! It's here within 48 hours or less," she exclaims. She says that she orders items about 15 times a month with an average of 100EGP per order.

Although Maktabi sells office supplies, its mission statement is grand and humanitarian to a certain extent: to make business processes in Egypt efficient. More than 30,000 orders have been placed since they first opened their doors in July 2007.

Egypt thanks Maktabi.

Exhibit FE1-A: Base Case—Assumptions

Maktabi

Assumptions for the Financial Plan (Summary)

All figures shown in Egyptian Pounds

SALES	**COSTS OF SERVICES PROVIDED**

SALES
- The first sales will take place in 10/08
- Average order price structure:
  Business orders   14
  Consumer orders   10

COSTS OF SERVICES PROVIDED
- Average material costs per order:
  Business orders   8
  Consumer orders   6

OPERATING COSTS
- Monthly wages reflect current market rates
- Social costs as percentage of wage costs   0.00%
- Annual rise in wages   10.00%
- The model for the number of employees is given in the financial plan
- Import customs and transportation to distribution center   216 / inbound shipment
- Picking and packing   0 / order
- Shipping   1 / order
- Catalog design will be paid at market rates
- Catalog photos   0 / photo
- Catalog printing   2 / catalog
- Information systems will be paid at market rates
- Sales representative commission on sales   3.00%
- Commissions on sales   0.00%
- Advertising media as a percentage of sales   0.25%
- Promotions as a percentage of sales   0.75%
- Public relations as a percentage of sales   0.25%
- Other marketing expenses as a percentage of sales   0.25%
- Consultants for special projects and auditors will be paid at market rates
- Additional costs per person calculated as follows:

Cost per Person/Month	Training	Office Material	Travel	Communication
Customer service	5	7	4	54
Purchasing	0	4	144	54
Distribution	0	4	11	18
Transportation and AR	0	4	4	18
Publications	0	4	4	18
Information Technologies	0	4	4	18
Marketing and Sales*	4	4	4	18
Finance and Administration	0	4	18	54

*Marketing and Sales training for sales representatives only

- Rent per square metre per month   35.00%
- Provisions for unpaid invoices in percentage of sales   0.00%
- Interest income on liquid assets   0.00%
- Returns as a percentage of sales   0.50%
- Income tax   20.00%

BALANCE SHEET
- Debitors are settled within 30 days, creditors within 30 days
- Goods are purchased on average 30 days before the sale of the product/service
- Fixed assets include computers, software, office equipment, and property
- Individual depreciation periods per asset and cost center
- Provisions for wages represent half a monthly salary
- Taxes are paid at the end of the tax period

Exhibit FE1-B: Base Case—Profit and Loss Statement (US$)

Maktabi

Profit and Loss Statement

Sales	2008	2009	2010	2011	2012
Business orders	81,081	533,784	440,541	451,351	462,838
Consumer orders	133,784	1,615,315	6,638,684	7,499,721	8,752,512
Total sales	214,865	2,149,099	7,079,225	7,951,072	9,215,350
Cost of services provided	129,993	1,300,205	4,282,931	4,810,399	5,575,286
Gross margin	84,872	848,894	2,796,294	3,140,673	3,640,063
In % of sales	40%	40%	40%	40%	40%
Operating costs					
Customer Service	18,631	52,157	137,705	179,163	186,520
In % of sales	9%	2%	2%	2%	2%
Purchasing	15,728	25,897	28,645	29,657	30,747
In % of sales	7%	1%	0%	0%	0%
Distribution	33,355	118,051	320,718	363,790	410,644
In % of sales	16%	5%	5%	5%	4%
Transportation and Accounts Receivables	17,397	120,430	391,653	439,572	509,201
In % of sales	8%	6%	6%	6%	6%
Publications	22,875	63,947	52,937	53,099	53,555
In % of sales	11%	3%	1%	1%	1%
Information Technologies	27,661	53,633	60,107	60,531	61,274
In % of sales	13%	2%	1%	1%	1%
Marketing and Sales	41,949	149,718	373,491	417,236	479,376
In % of sales	20%	7%	5%	5%	5%
Finance and Administration	189,764	202,549	234,581	245,436	260,449
In % of sales	88%	9%	3%	3%	3%
Total operating costs	367,359	786,381	1,599,835	1,788,486	1,991,766
In % of sales	171%	37%	23%	22%	22%
Operating profit	-282,488	62,513	1,196,458	1,352,188	1,648,297
In % of sales	-131%	3%	17%	17%	18%
Financing expenditure	0	0	0	0	0
Financing income	0	0	0	0	0
Profit before tax	-282,488	62,513	1,196,458	1,352,188	1,648,297
Income tax	0	0	195,297	270,438	329,659
Net profit	-282,488	62,513	1,001,162	1,081,750	1,318,637
In % of sales	-131%	3%	14%	14%	14%

Exhibit FE1-C: Base Case—Profit and Loss Statement (US$) Details Year 1

Maktabi

Profit and Loss Statement

	Month 1 Jan 08	Month 2 Feb 08	Month 3 Mar 08	Month 4 Apr 08	Month 5 May 08	Month 6 Jun 08	Month 7 Jul 08	Month 8 Aug 08	Month 9 Sep 08	Month 10 Oct 08	Month 11 Nov 08	Month 12 Dec 08	Total 2008
Sales													
Business orders	0	0	0	0	0	0	0	0	6,757	20,270	27,027	27,027	81,081
Consumer orders	0	0	0	0	0	0	0	0	14,865	29,730	39,640	49,550	133,784
Total sales	0	0	0	0	0	0	0	0	21,622	50,000	66,667	76,577	214,865
Expenditure													
Costs of performance													
Material costs	0	0	0	0	0	0	0	0	12,973	30,000	40,000	45,946	128,919
Returns	0	0	0	0	0	0	0	0	108	250	333	383	1,074
Total costs of performance	0	0	0	0	0	0	0	0	13,081	30,250	40,333	46,329	129,993
Gross profit	0	0	0	0	0	0	0	0	8,541	19,750	26,333	30,248	84,872
In % of sales	0%	0%	0%	0%	0%	0%	0%	0%	40%	40%	40%	40%	40%
Operating costs													
Customer Service													
Wages	0	0	0	450	450	901	1,351	1,351	1,351	1,351	1,802	1,802	10,811
Bonuses	0	0	0	0	0	0	0	0	0	0	0	0	0
Social and other personnel costs	0	0	0	0	0	0	0	0	0	0	0	0	0
Training	0	0	0	5	5	9	14	50	50	50	86	86	351
Office material	0	0	0	7	7	14	22	79	79	79	137	137	562
Travel and refreshment	0	0	0	4	4	7	11	40	40	40	68	68	281
Communication	0	0	0	54	54	108	162	595	595	595	1,027	1,027	4,216
Depreciation	0	0	0	31	31	62	93	340	340	340	587	587	2,409

(Continued)

551

Exhibit FE1-C (Continued)

	Month 1 Jan 08	Month 2 Feb 08	Month 3 Mar 08	Month 4 Apr 08	Month 5 May 08	Month 6 Jun 08	Month 7 Jul 08	Month 8 Aug 08	Month 9 Sep 08	Month 10 Oct 08	Month 11 Nov 08	Month 12 Dec 08	Total 2008
Purchasing													
Wages	0	450	450	667	667	667	667	883	1,099	1,099	1,099	1,099	8,847
Bonuses	0	0	0	0	0	0	0	0	0	0	0	0	0
Social and other personnel costs	0	0	0	0	0	0	0	0	0	0	0	0	0
Office material	0	4	4	7	7	7	7	11	14	14	14	14	105
Travel and refreshment	0	144	144	288	288	288	288	432	577	577	577	577	4,180
Communication	0	54	54	108	108	108	108	162	216	216	216	216	1,568
Depreciation	0	35	35	71	71	71	71	106	142	142	142	142	1,028
Distribution													
Wages	0	0	0	818	818	818	818	818	818	818	818	818	7,364
Bonuses	0	0	0	0	0	0	0	0	0	0	0	0	0
Social and other personnel costs	0	0	0	0	0	0	0	0	0	0	0	0	0
Import customs and transportation to distribution center	0	0	0	0	0	9,730	865	1,081	1,081	1,081	1,946	2,162	17,946
Picking and packing	0	0	0	0	0	0	0	0	721	1,622	2,162	2,523	7,027
Office material	0	0	0	4	4	4	7	7	7	7	7	7	54
Travel and refreshment	0	0	0	11	11	11	22	22	22	22	22	22	162
Communication	0	0	0	18	18	18	36	36	36	36	36	36	270
Depreciation	0	0	0	35	35	35	71	71	71	71	71	71	532
Transportation and Accounts Receivables													
Wages	0	0	0	541	541	541	721	721	721	721	721	721	5,946
Bonuses	0	0	0	0	0	0	0	0	0	0	0	0	0
Social and other personnel costs	0	0	0	0	0	0	0	0	0	0	0	0	0

	Month 1 Jan 08	Month 2 Feb 08	Month 3 Mar 08	Month 4 Apr 08	Month 5 May 08	Month 6 Jun 08	Month 7 Jul 08	Month 8 Aug 08	Month 9 Sep 08	Month 10 Oct 08	Month 11 Nov 08	Month 12 Dec 08	Total 2008
Shipping	0	0	0	0	0	0	0	0	1,081	2,432	3,243	3,784	10,541
Office material	0	0	0	4	4	4	7	7	7	7	7	7	54
Travel and refreshment	0	0	0	4	4	4	7	7	7	7	7	7	54
Communication	0	0	0	18	18	18	36	36	36	36	36	36	270
Depreciation	0	0	0	35	35	35	71	71	71	71	71	71	532
Publications													
Wages	0	0	0	360	360	360	360	360	360	360	360	360	3,243
Bonuses	0	0	0	0	0	0	0	0	0	0	0	0	0
Social and other personnel costs	0	0	0	0	0	0	0	0	0	0	0	0	0
Catalog design	0	0	0	0	1,818	0	0	0	0	0	0	0	1,818
Catalog photos	0	0	0	0	721	0	0	0	0	0	0	0	721
Number of catalogs	0	0	0	0	0	0	0	720	1,152	1,440	2,160	2,160	7,632
Catalog printing	0	0	0	0	0	0	0	1,557	2,491	3,114	4,670	4,670	16,502
Office material	0	0	0	4	4	4	4	4	4	4	4	4	32
Travel and refreshment	0	0	0	4	4	4	4	4	4	4	4	4	32
Communication	0	0	0	18	18	18	18	18	18	18	18	18	162
Depreciation	0	0	0	40	40	40	40	40	40	40	40	40	364
Information Technologies													
Wages	0	0	0	270	270	270	270	541	541	541	541	541	3,784
Bonuses	0	0	0	0	0	0	0	0	0	0	0	0	0
Social and other personnel costs	0	0	0	0	0	0	0	0	0	0	0	0	0
Service and maintenance	0	0	0	0	0	0	1,725	1,725	1,725	1,725	1,725	1,725	10,349
Office material	0	0	0	4	4	4	4	4	4	4	4	4	32
Travel and refreshment	0	0	0	4	4	4	4	4	4	4	4	4	32
Communication	0	0	0	18	18	18	18	18	18	18	18	18	162
Depreciation	0	0	0	472	903	1,334	1,765	1,765	1,765	1,765	1,765	1,765	13,301

(Continued)

Exhibit FE1-C (Continued)

	Month 1 Jan 08	Month 2 Feb 08	Month 3 Mar 08	Month 4 Apr 08	Month 5 May 08	Month 6 Jun 08	Month 7 Jul 08	Month 8 Aug 08	Month 9 Sep 08	Month 10 Oct 08	Month 11 Nov 08	Month 12 Dec 08	Total 2008
Marketing and Sales													
Management													
Management wages	0	0	0	2,587	2,858	2,858	2,858	2,858	3,128	3,128	3,128	3,128	26,530
Management bonuses	0	0	0	0	0	0	0	0	0	0	0	0	0
Management social and other personnel costs	0	0	0	0	0	0	0	0	0	0	0	0	0
Office material	0	0	0	4	7	7	7	7	11	11	11	11	76
Travel and refreshment	0	0	0	4	7	7	7	7	11	11	11	11	76
Communication	0	0	0	18	36	36	36	36	54	54	54	54	378
Sales Representatives													
Sales representatives wages	0	0	0	0	0	324	324	324	486	486	486	486	2,919
Sales representatives commissions, bonuses	0	0	0	0	0	0	0	0	649	1,500	2,000	2,297	6,446
Sales representatives social and other personnel costs	0	0	0	0	0	0	0	0	0	0	0	0	0
Training	0	0	0	0	0	22	22	22	32	32	32	32	194
Office material	0	0	0	0	0	22	22	22	32	32	32	32	195
Travel and refreshment	0	0	0	0	0	22	22	22	32	32	32	32	195
Communication	0	0	0	0	0	108	108	108	162	162	162	162	973
Advertising media	0	0	0	0	0	0	0	0	54	125	167	191	537
Promotions	0	0	0	0	0	0	0	0	162	375	500	574	1,611
Public relations	0	0	0	0	0	0	0	0	54	125	167	191	537
Other	0	0	0	0	0	0	0	0	54	125	167	191	537
Consultancy	0	0	0	0	0	0	0	0	0	0	0	0	0
Depreciation	0	0	0	35	71	71	71	71	106	106	106	106	745

	Month 1 Jan 08	Month 2 Feb 08	Month 3 Mar 08	Month 4 Apr 08	Month 5 May 08	Month 6 Jun 08	Month 7 Jul 08	Month 8 Aug 08	Month 9 Sep 08	Month 10 Oct 08	Month 11 Nov 08	Month 12 Dec 08	Total 2008
Finance and Administration													
Wages	0	0	1,171	1,171	1,802	1,802	5,946	5,946	5,946	5,946	5,946	5,946	41,622
Bonuses	0	0	0	0	0	0	0	0	0	0	0	0	0
Social and other personnel costs	0	0	0	0	0	0	0	0	0	0	0	0	0
Office material	0	0	14	14	22	22	25	25	25	25	25	25	223
Travel and refreshment	0	0	72	72	108	108	126	126	126	126	126	126	1,117
Communication	0	0	216	216	324	324	378	378	378	378	378	378	3,351
Insurance	0	0	0	0	0	0	0	0	108	250	333	383	1,074
Professional services (legal, accounting, etc.)	10,811	10,811	10,811	10,811	10,811	10,811	10,811	10,811	10,811	10,811	6,727	6,727	121,563
Provisions for unpaid invoices	0	0	0	0	0	0	0	0	0	0	0	0	0
Office rent	315	315	315	1,892	1,892	1,892	1,892	1,892	1,892	1,892	1,892	1,892	17,973
Water, electricity	9	9	9	54	54	54	54	54	54	54	54	54	514
Maintenance, repairs	2	2	2	14	14	14	14	14	14	14	14	14	128
Depreciation	0	0	142	142	213	213	248	248	248	248	248	248	2,199
Total Finance and Administration	11,137	11,137	12,753	14,386	15,239	15,239	19,494	19,494	19,602	19,744	15,744	15,794	189,764
In % of sales	0%	0%	0%	0%	0%	0%	0%	0%	91%	39%	24%	21%	88%
Total operating costs	11,137	11,825	13,441	21,407	25,561	34,231	32,637	35,935	40,785	45,079	46,855	48,467	367,359
In % of sales	0%	0%	0%	0%	0%	0%	0%	0%	189%	90%	70%	63%	171%
Operating profit (EBIT)	(11,137)	(11,825)	(13,441)	(21,407)	(25,561)	(34,231)	(32,637)	(35,935)	(32,245)	(25,329)	(20,521)	(18,219)	(282,488)
In % of sales	0%	0%	0%	0%	0%	0%	0%	0%	-149%	-51%	-31%	-24%	-131%
Financing expenditure	0	0	0	0	0	0	0	0	0	0	0	0	0
Financing income	0	0	0	0	0	0	0	0	0	0	0	0	0
Profit before tax	(11,137)	(11,825)	(13,441)	(21,407)	(25,561)	(34,231)	(32,637)	(35,935)	(32,245)	(25,329)	(20,521)	(18,219)	(282,488)
Income tax	0	0	0	0	0	0	0	0	0	0	0	0	0
Net profit	(11,137)	(11,825)	(13,441)	(21,407)	(25,561)	(34,231)	(32,637)	(35,935)	(32,245)	(25,329)	(20,521)	(18,219)	(282,488)
In % of sales	0%	0%	0%	0%	0%	0%	0%	0%	-149%	-51%	-31%	-24%	-131%

Exhibit FE1-D: Base Case—Profit and Loss Statement (US$) Details Years 2 and 3

Maktabi

Profit and Loss Statement

	Qtr 1 2009	Qtr 2 2009	Qtr 3 2009	Qtr 4 2009	Total	Qtr 1 2010	Qtr 2 2010	Qtr 3 2010	Qtr 4 2010	Total
Sales										
Business orders	128,378	81,081	175,676	148,649	533,784	110,135	81,081	175,676	148,649	440,541
Consumer orders	267,568	406,306	475,676	465,766	1,615,315	1,659,671	406,306	475,676	465,766	6,638,684
Total sales	395,946	487,387	651,351	614,414	2,149,099	1,769,806	487,387	651,351	614,414	7,079,225
Expenditure										
Costs of performance										
Material costs	237,568	292,432	390,811	368,649	1,289,459	1,061,884	292,432	390,811	368,649	4,247,535
Returns	1,980	2,437	3,257	3,072	10,745	8,849	2,437	3,257	3,072	35,396
Total costs of performance	239,547	294,869	394,068	371,721	1,300,205	1,070,733	294,869	394,068	371,721	4,282,931
Gross profit	156,399	192,518	257,284	242,694	848,894	699,073	192,518	257,284	242,694	2,796,294
In % of sales	40%	40%	40%	40%	40%	40%	40%	40%	40%	40%
Operating costs										
Customer Service										
Wages	5,946	5,946	5,946	5,946	23,784	24,200	5,946	5,946	5,946	96,800
Bonuses	0	0	0	0	0	0	0	0	0	0
Social and other personnel costs	0	0	0	0	0	0	0	0	0	0
Training	302	324	324	324	1,275	459	324	324	324	1,838
Office material	483	519	519	519	2,040	735	519	519	519	2,941
Travel and refreshment	241	259	259	259	1,020	368	259	259	259	1,470
Communication	3,622	3,892	3,892	3,892	15,297	5,514	3,892	3,892	3,892	22,054
Depreciation	2,069	2,224	2,224	2,224	8,741	3,151	2,224	2,224	2,224	12,602

	Qtr 1 2009	Qtr 2 2009	Qtr 3 2009	Qtr 4 2009	Total	Qtr 1 2010	Qtr 2 2010	Qtr 3 2010	Qtr 4 2010	Total
Purchasing										
Wages	3,627	3,627	3,627	3,627	14,508	3,990	3,627	3,627	3,627	15,959
Bonuses	0	0	0	0	0	0	0	0	0	0
Social and other personnel costs	0	0	0	0	0	0	0	0	0	0
Office material	43	43	43	43	173	368	43	43	43	1,470
Travel and refreshment	1,730	1,730	1,730	1,730	6,919	1,730	1,730	1,730	1,730	6,919
Communication	649	649	649	649	2,595	649	649	649	649	2,595
Depreciation	426	426	426	426	1,702	426	426	426	426	1,702
Distribution										
Wages	2,700	2,700	2,700	2,700	10,800	2,970	2,700	2,700	2,700	11,880
Bonuses	0	0	0	0	0	0	0	0	0	0
Social and other personnel costs	0	0	0	0	0	0	0	0	0	0
Import customs and transportation to distribution center	6,486	3,892	10,811	11,459	32,649	13,514	3,892	10,811	11,459	54,054
Picking and packing	13,153	16,937	21,982	20,901	72,973	63,289	16,937	21,982	20,901	253,154
Office material	22	22	22	22	86	22	22	22	22	86
Travel and refreshment	65	65	65	65	259	65	65	65	65	259
Communication	108	108	108	108	432	108	108	108	108	432
Depreciation	213	213	213	213	851	213	213	213	213	851
Transportation and Accounts Receivables										
Wages	2,378	2,378	2,378	2,378	9,514	2,616	2,378	2,378	2,378	10,465
Bonuses	0	0	0	0	0	0	0	0	0	0
Social and other personnel costs	0	0	0	0	0	0	0	0	0	0
Shipping	19,730	25,405	32,973	31,351	109,459	94,933	25,405	32,973	31,351	379,732
Office material	22	22	22	22	86	22	22	22	22	86
Travel and refreshment	22	22	22	22	86	22	22	22	22	86
Communication	108	108	108	108	432	108	108	108	108	432
Depreciation	213	213	213	213	851	213	213	213	213	851

(Continued)

Exhibit FE1-D (Continued)

	Qtr 1 2009	Qtr 2 2009	Qtr 3 2009	Qtr 4 2009	Total	Qtr 1 2010	Qtr 2 2010	Qtr 3 2010	Qtr 4 2010	Total
Publications										
Wages	1,189	1,189	1,189	1,189	4,757	1,308	1,189	1,189	1,189	5,232
Bonuses	0	0	0	0	**0**	0	0	0	0	**0**
Social and other personnel costs	0	0	0	0	**0**	0	0	0	0	**0**
Catalog design	1,818	0	0	0	**1,818**	455	0	0	0	**1,818**
Catalog photos	541	0	0	0	**541**	135	0	0	0	**541**
Number of catalogs	6,480	6,480	6,480	6,480	25,920	5,184	6,480	6,480	6,480	20,736
Catalog printing	14,011	14,011	14,011	14,011	56,043	11,209	14,011	14,011	14,011	44,835
Office material	11	11	11	11	**43**	1	11	11	11	**4**
Travel and refreshment	11	11	11	11	**43**	1	11	11	11	**4**
Communication	54	54	54	54	**216**	5	54	54	54	**18**
Depreciation	121	121	121	121	**486**	121	121	121	121	**486**
Information Technologies										
Wages	1,784	1,784	1,784	1,784	7,135	1,962	1,784	1,784	1,784	7,849
Bonuses	0	0	0	0	**0**	0	0	0	0	**0**
Social and other personnel costs	0	0	0	0	**0**	0	0	0	0	**0**
Service and maintenance	5,175	5,175	5,175	5,175	20,698	5,175	5,175	5,175	5,175	20,698
Office material	11	11	11	11	**43**	1	11	11	11	**4**
Travel and refreshment	11	11	11	11	**43**	1	11	11	11	**4**
Communication	54	54	54	54	**216**	5	54	54	54	**18**
Depreciation	5,296	5,296	7,021	7,884	25,497	7,884	5,296	7,021	7,884	31,534
Marketing and Sales										
Management										
Management wages	10,322	10,322	10,322	10,322	41,289	11,354	10,322	10,322	10,322	45,418
Management bonuses	0	0	0	0	**0**	0	0	0	0	**0**
Management social and other personnel costs	0	0	0	0	**0**	0	0	0	0	**0**

	Qtr 1 2009	Qtr 2 2009	Qtr 3 2009	Qtr 4 2009	Total	Qtr 1 2010	Qtr 2 2010	Qtr 3 2010	Qtr 4 2010	Total
Office material	32	32	32	32	**130**	32	32	32	32	**130**
Travel and refreshment	32	32	32	32	**130**	32	32	32	32	**130**
Communication	162	162	162	162	**649**	162	162	162	162	**649**
Sales Representatives										
Sales representatives wages	1,605	1,605	1,605	1,605	**6,422**	1,766	1,605	1,605	1,605	**7,064**
Sales representatives commissions, bonuses	11,878	14,622	19,541	18,432	**64,473**	53,094	14,622	19,541	18,432	**212,377**
Sales representatives social and other personnel costs	0	0	0	0	**0**	0	0	0	0	**0**
Training	97	97	97	97	**389**	8	97	97	97	**32**
Office material	97	97	97	97	**389**	8	97	97	97	**32**
Travel and refreshment	97	97	97	97	**389**	8	97	97	97	**32**
Communication	486	486	486	486	**1,946**	41	486	486	486	**162**
Advertising media	990	1,218	1,628	1,536	**5,373**	4,425	1,218	1,628	1,536	**17,698**
Promotions	2,970	3,655	4,885	4,608	**16,118**	13,274	3,655	4,885	4,608	**53,094**
Public relations	990	1,218	1,628	1,536	**5,373**	4,425	1,218	1,628	1,536	**17,698**
Other	990	1,218	1,628	1,536	**5,373**	4,425	1,218	1,628	1,536	**17,698**
Consultancy	0	0	0	0	**0**	0	0	0	0	**0**
Depreciation	319	319	319	319	**1,277**	319	319	319	319	**1,277**
Finance and Administration										
Wages	19,622	19,473	19,622	19,622	**78,338**	21,584	19,473	19,622	19,622	**86,335**
Bonuses	0	0	0	0	**0**	0	0	0	0	**0**
Social and other personnel costs	0	0	0	0	**0**	0	0	0	0	**0**
Office material	76	72	76	76	**299**	76	72	76	76	**303**
Travel and refreshment	378	360	378	378	**1,495**	378	360	378	378	**1,514**
Communication	1,135	1,081	1,135	1,135	**4,486**	1,135	1,081	1,135	1,135	**4,541**
Insurance	1,980	2,437	3,257	3,072	**10,745**	8,849	2,437	3,257	3,072	**35,396**
Profesional services (legal, accounting, etc.)	20,182	20,182	20,182	20,182	**80,727**	20,000	20,182	20,182	20,182	**80,000**
Provisions for unpaid invoices	0	0	0	0	**0**	0	0	0	0	**0**

(Continued)

559

Exhibit FE1-D (Continued)

	Qtr 1 2009	Qtr 2 2009	Qtr 3 2009	Qtr 4 2009	Total	Qtr 1 2010	Qtr 2 2010	Qtr 3 2010	Qtr 4 2010	Total
Office rent	5,676	5,676	5,676	5,676	22,703	5,676	5,676	5,676	5,676	22,703
Water, electricity	162	162	162	162	649	162	162	162	162	649
Maintenance, repairs	41	41	41	41	162	41	41	41	41	162
Depreciation	745	709	745	745	2,944	745	709	745	745	2,979
Total Finance and Administration	49,995	50,193	51,273	51,088	**202,549**	58,645	50,193	51,273	51,088	**234,581**
In % of sales	13%	10%	8%	8%	**9%**	13%	10%	8%	8%	**3%**
Total operating costs	175,508	184,828	214,542	211,504	**786,381**	399,959	184,828	214,542	211,504	**1,599,835**
In % of sales	44%	38%	33%	34%	**37%**	44%	38%	33%	34%	**23%**
Operating profit (EBIT)	(19,109)	7,690	42,742	31,190	**62,513**	299,115	7,690	42,742	31,190	**1,196,458**
In % of sales	-5%	1%	6%	5%	**3%**	-5%	1%	6%	5%	**17%**
Financing expenditure	0	0	0	0	**0**	0	0	0	0	**0**
Financing income	0	0	0	0	**0**	0	0	0	0	**0**
Profit before tax	(19,109)	7,690	42,742	31,190	**62,513**	299,115	7,690	42,742	31,190	**1,196,458**
Income tax	0	0	0	0	**0**	0	0	0	0	195,297
Net profit	(19,109)	7,690	42,742	31,190	**62,513**	250,290	7,690	42,742	31,190	**1,001,162**
In % of sales	-5%	1%	6%	5%	**3%**	-5%	1%	6%	5%	**14%**

Exhibit FE1-E: Base Case—Balance Sheet (US$)

Maktabi

Balance sheet at end of accounting year

	2008	2009	2010	2011	2012
Assets					
Liquid assets					
Cash	55,478	124,026	829,547	1,880,907	2,764,140
Net receivables from customers	76,577	199,099	589,935	662,589	767,946
Stock/inventory (30, 60, or 90 days)	84,054	353,961	397,554	460,767	0
Total liquid assets	216,108	677,086	1,817,036	3,004,264	3,532,086
Gross fixed assets	329,982	439,243	450,775	462,306	462,306
Minus cumulated depreciation	21,111	63,459	115,742	157,039	189,300
Net fixed assets	308,871	375,784	335,033	305,267	273,007
Total assets	**524,980**	**1,052,870**	**2,152,070**	**3,309,531**	**3,805,093**
Liabilities					
Debt					
Short-term debt					
Open third-party invoices (creditors)	110,017	394,649	440,100	494,631	525,315
Provisions for wages	7,451	8,196	11,958	14,353	15,789
Provisions for taxes	0	0	48,824	67,609	82,415
Total short-term debt	117,468	402,845	500,883	576,594	623,519
Long-term debt					
Loans and mortgages	0	0	0	0	0
Total long-term debt	0	0	0	0	0
Total debt	**117,468**	**402,845**	**500,883**	**576,594**	**623,519**
Equity					
Share capital	690,000	870,000	870,000	870,000	0
Reserves	0	0	0	0	0
Profit/loss carried forward	-282,488	-219,975	781,187	1,862,937	3,181,574
Total equity	407,512	650,025	1,651,187	2,732,937	3,181,574
Total liabilities	**524,980**	**1,052,870**	**2,152,070**	**3,309,531**	**3,805,093**

Exhibit FE1-F: Base Case—Balance Sheet (US$) Details Year 1

Maktabi

Balance Sheet

	Month 1 Jan 08	Month 2 Feb 08	Month 3 Mar 08	Month 4 Apr 08	Month 5 May 08	Month 6 Jun 08	Month 7 Jul 08	Month 8 Aug 08	Month 9 Sep 08	Month 10 Oct 08	Month 11 Nov 08	Month 12 Dec 08	Total 2008
ASSETS													
Liquid assets													
Cash	54,820	47,160	54,686	56,179	49,544	52,095	50,547	49,575	49,596	51,973	49,310	55,478	55,478
Gross receivables from customers (30, 60, or 90 days)	0	0	0	0	0	0	0	0	21,622	50,000	66,667	76,577	76,577
Provisions for bad debts	0	0	0	0	0	0	0	0	0	0	0	0	0
Net receivables from customers	0	0	0	0	0	0	0	0	21,622	50,000	66,667	76,577	76,577
Stock/inventory (30, 60, or 90 days)	0	0	0	0	0	0	0	12,973	30,000	40,000	45,946	84,054	84,054
Total liquid assets	54,820	47,160	54,686	56,179	49,544	52,095	50,547	62,548	101,217	141,973	161,923	216,108	216,108
Fixed assets													
Vehicle	64,865	64,865	74,775	74,775	74,775	74,775	74,775	74,775	74,775	74,775	74,775	74,775	74,775
Computer system	0	0	0	51,748	103,495	155,243	206,991	206,991	206,991	206,991	206,991	206,991	206,991
Computer hardware and software	0	1,261	6,306	15,315	19,099	20,180	25,045	34,955	37,477	37,477	46,126	46,126	46,126
Furniture and other equipment	0	36	180	468	577	649	829	1,441	1,514	1,514	2,090	2,090	2,090

	Month 1 Jan 08	Month 2 Feb 08	Month 3 Mar 08	Month 4 Apr 08	Month 5 May 08	Month 6 Jun 08	Month 7 Jul 08	Month 8 Aug 08	Month 9 Sep 08	Month 10 Oct 08	Month 11 Nov 08	Month 12 Dec 08	Total 2008
Property, buildings, and plant	0	0	0	0	0	0	0	0	0	0	0	0	0
Total fixed assets	64,865	66,162	81,261	142,306	197,946	250,847	307,640	318,162	320,757	320,757	329,982	329,982	329,982
Cumulated depreciation													
Vehicle	360	721	1,136	1,552	1,967	2,382	2,798	3,213	3,629	4,044	4,459	4,875	4,875
Computer system	0	0	0	431	1,294	2,587	4,312	6,037	7,762	9,487	11,212	12,937	12,937
Computer hardware and software	0	35	210	636	1,166	1,727	2,422	3,393	4,434	5,475	6,757	8,038	8,038
Furniture and other equipment	0	0	3	8	15	23	33	50	68	86	111	136	136
Property, buildings, and plant	0	0	0	0	0	0	0	0	0	0	0	0	0
Total cumulated depreciation	0	35	213	1,075	2,475	4,337	6,767	9,480	12,264	15,048	18,079	21,111	21,111
Net fixed assets	64,865	66,127	81,048	141,231	195,471	246,510	300,872	308,682	308,492	305,708	311,903	308,871	308,871
Total assets	119,685	113,287	135,734	197,410	245,015	298,605	351,419	371,229	409,710	447,681	473,825	524,980	524,980
Liabilities													
Debt													
Short-term debt													
Open third-party invoices (creditors)	10,822	11,024	11,327	11,787	14,503	21,936	14,999	30,501	50,902	64,203	70,643	110,017	110,017
Provisions for wages	0	225	811	3,433	3,883	4,270	6,658	6,901	7,225	7,225	7,451	7,451	7,451
Provisions for taxes	0	0	0	0	0	0	0	0	0	0	0	0	0
Total short-term debt	10,822	11,249	12,137	15,220	18,386	26,206	21,656	37,402	58,127	71,428	78,094	117,468	117,468

(Continued)

Exhibit FE1-F (Continued)

	Month 1 Jan 08	Month 2 Feb 08	Month 3 Mar 08	Month 4 Apr 08	Month 5 May 08	Month 6 Jun 08	Month 7 Jul 08	Month 8 Aug 08	Month 9 Sep 08	Month 10 Oct 08	Month 11 Nov 08	Month 12 Dec 08	Total 2008
Long-term debt													
Loans and mortgages	0	0	0	0	0	0	0	0	0	0	0	0	0
Total long-term debt	0	0	0	0	0	0	0	0	0	0	0	0	0
Total debt	10,822	11,249	12,137	15,220	18,386	26,206	21,656	37,402	58,127	71,428	78,094	117,468	117,468
Equity													
Share capital	120,000	125,000	160,000	240,000	310,000	390,000	480,000	520,000	570,000	620,000	660,000	690,000	690,000
Reserves	0	0	0	0	0	0	0	0	0	0	0	0	0
Profit/loss carried forward	(11,137)	(22,962)	(36,403)	(57,810)	(83,370)	(117,601)	(150,238)	(186,173)	(218,418)	(243,747)	(264,268)	(282,488)	(282,488)
Total equity	108,863	102,038	123,597	182,190	226,630	272,399	329,762	333,827	351,582	376,253	395,732	407,512	407,512
Total liabilities	119,685	113,287	135,734	197,410	245,015	298,605	351,419	371,229	409,710	447,681	473,825	524,980	524,980

Exhibit FE1-G: Base Case—Balance Sheet (US$) Details Years 2 and 3

Maktabi

Balance Sheet

	Qtr 1 2009	Qtr 2 2009	Qtr 3 2009	Qtr 4 2009	Total	Qtr 1 2010	Qtr 2 2010	Qtr 3 2010	Qtr 4 2010	Total
Assets										
Liquid assets										
Cash	142,290	148,342	144,998	316,328	124,026	207,387	207,387	207,387	207,387	829,547
Gross receivables from customers (30, 60, or 90 days)	395,946	487,387	651,351	614,414	199,099	147,484	147,484	147,484	147,484	589,935
Provisions for bad debts	0	0	0	0	0	0	0	0	0	0
Net receivables from customers	395,946	487,387	651,351	614,414	199,099	147,484	147,484	147,484	147,484	589,935
Stock/inventory (30, 60, or 90 days)	241,081	318,378	404,865	595,042	353,961	99,388	99,388	99,388	99,388	397,554
Total liquid assets	779,317	954,108	1,201,214	1,525,785	677,086	454,259	454,259	454,259	454,259	1,817,036
Fixed assets										
Vehicle	224,324	224,324	224,324	224,324	74,775	18,694	18,694	18,694	18,694	74,775
Computer system	620,973	620,973	827,964	931,460	310,487	77,622	77,622	77,622	77,622	310,487
Computer hardware and software	149,189	153,333	154,595	154,595	51,532	15,586	15,586	15,586	15,586	62,342
Furniture and other equipment	6,991	7,315	7,351	7,351	2,450	793	793	793	793	3,171
Property, buildings, and plant	0	0	0	0	0	0	0	0	0	0
Total fixed assets	1,001,477	1,005,946	1,214,235	1,317,730	439,243	112,694	112,694	112,694	112,694	450,775
Cumulated depreciation										
Vehicle	17,117	20,856	24,595	28,333	9,860	3,711	3,711	3,711	3,711	14,845
Computer system	49,160	64,685	83,084	106,083	37,948	17,249	17,249	17,249	17,249	68,997
Computer hardware and software	32,252	45,065	57,913	70,796	25,030	11,453	11,453	11,453	11,453	45,811
Furniture and other equipment	569	831	1,093	1,355	481	233	233	233	233	934
Property, buildings, and plant	0	0	0	0	0	0	0	0	0	0

(Continued)

Exhibit FE1-G (Continued)

	Qtr 1 2009	Qtr 2 2009	Qtr 3 2009	Qtr 4 2009	Total	Qtr 1 2010	Qtr 2 2010	Qtr 3 2010	Qtr 4 2010	Total
Total cumulated depreciation	81,981	110,580	142,089	178,234	63,459	28,935	28,935	28,935	28,935	115,742
Net fixed assets	919,496	895,366	1,072,145	1,139,496	375,784	83,758	83,758	83,758	83,758	335,033
Total assets	1,698,813	1,849,474	2,273,359	2,665,282	1,052,870	538,017	538,017	538,017	538,017	2,152,070
Liabilities										
Debt										
Short-term debt										
Open third-party invoices (creditors)	338,480	421,926	530,479	718,048	394,649	110,025	110,025	110,025	110,025	440,100
Provisions for wages	24,587	24,512	24,587	24,587	8,196	2,990	2,990	2,990	2,990	11,958
Provisions for taxes	0	0	0	0	0	12,206	12,206	12,206	12,206	48,824
Total short-term debt	363,066	446,438	555,066	742,635	402,845	125,221	125,221	125,221	125,221	500,883
Long-term debt										
Loans and mortgages	0	0	0	0	0	0	0	0	0	0
Total long-term debt	0	0	0	0	0	0	0	0	0	0
Total debt					402,845	125,221	125,221	125,221	125,221	500,883
Equity										
Share capital	2,220,000	2,300,000	2,525,000	2,610,000	870,000	217,500	217,500	217,500	217,500	870,000
Reserves	0	0	0	0	0	0	0	0	0	0
Profit/loss carried forward	(884,253)	(896,964)	(806,707)	(687,353)	(219,975)	195,297	195,297	195,297	195,297	781,187
Total equity	1,335,747	1,403,036	1,718,293	1,922,647	650,025	412,797	412,797	412,797	412,797	1,651,187
Total liabilities	1,698,813	1,849,474	2,273,359	2,665,282	1,052,870	538,017	538,017	538,017	538,017	2,152,070

Exhibit FE1-H: Base Case—Cash Flows (US$)

Maktabi

Cash Flow Calculation

	2008	2009	2010	2011	2012
Cash at beginning of year	0	55,478	124,026	829,547	1,880,907
Cash inflow					
Net profit	-282,488	62,513	1,001,162	1,081,750	1,318,637
Plus depreciation/amortization	21,111	42,349	52,282	41,297	32,261
Plus changes in:					
Liabilities from performance	110,017	284,632	45,451	54,531	30,684
Wage provisions	7,451	745	3,763	2,395	1,435
Tax provisions	0	0	48,824	18,785	14,805
Long-term debt/loans	0	0	0	0	0
Total cash inflow	-143,910	390,239	1,151,482	1,198,759	1,397,822
Cash outflow					
Minus changes in:					
Net receivables from performance	76,577	122,523	390,836	72,654	105,356
Stock	84,054	269,907	43,592	63,214	-460,767
Gross fixed assets	329,982	109,261	11,532	11,532	0
Total cash outflow	490,613	501,691	445,960	147,399	-355,411
Cash increase/decrease	-634,522	-111,452	705,522	1,051,360	1,753,233
Financing (increase in equity)	690,000	180,000	0	0	-870,000
Cash at end of year	55,478	124,026	829,547	1,880,907	2,764,140

Exhibit FE1-I: Base Case—Cash Flows (US$) Details Year 1

Maktabi

Cash Flow Calculation (Indirect Calculation)

	Month 1 Jan 08	Month 2 Feb 08	Month 3 Mar-08	Month 4 Apr 08	Month 5 May 08	Month 6 Jun 08	Month 7 Jul 08	Month 8 Aug 08	Month 9 Sep 08	Month 10 Oct 08	Month 11 Nov 08	Month 12 Dec 08	Total 2008
Cash at start of month/year	0	54,820	47,160	54,686	56,179	49,544	52,095	50,547	49,575	49,596	51,973	49,310	0
Cash inflow													
Net profit	(11,137)	(11,825)	(13,441)	(21,407)	(25,561)	(34,231)	(32,637)	(35,935)	(32,245)	(25,329)	(20,521)	(18,219)	(282,488)
Plus depreciation/amortization	0	35	177	862	1,400	1,862	2,430	2,713	2,784	2,784	3,031	3,031	21,111
Plus changes in:													
Liabilities from performance	10,822	202	303	461	2,715	7,433	(6,937)	15,503	20,401	13,301	6,440	39,374	110,017
Wage provisions	0	225	586	2,622	450	387	2,387	243	324	0	225	0	7,451
Tax provisions	0	0	0	0	0	0	0	0	0	0	0	0	0
Long-term debt/loans	0	0	0	0	0	0	0	0	0	0	0	0	0
Total cash inflow	(315)	(11,363)	(12,375)	(17,462)	(20,995)	(24,548)	(34,756)	(17,476)	(8,736)	(9,245)	(10,825)	24,186	(143,910)
Cash deployed													
Minus changes in:													
Net receivables from performance	0	0	0	0	0	0	0	0	21,622	28,378	16,667	9,910	76,577
Stock	0	0	0	0	0	0	0	12,973	17,027	10,000	5,946	38,108	84,054
Gross fixed assets	64,865	1,297	15,099	61,045	55,640	52,901	56,793	10,523	2,595	0	9,225	0	329,982
Total cash deployed	64,865	1,297	15,099	61,045	55,640	52,901	56,793	23,495	41,243	38,378	31,838	48,018	490,613
Increase/decrease in cash	(65,180)	(12,660)	(27,474)	(78,507)	(76,634)	(77,449)	(91,549)	(40,972)	(49,979)	(47,623)	(42,662)	(23,832)	(634,522)
Financing (increase in equity)	120,000	5,000	35,000	80,000	70,000	80,000	90,000	40,000	50,000	50,000	40,000	30,000	690,000
Cash at end of month/year	54,820	47,160	54,686	56,179	49,544	52,095	50,547	49,575	49,596	51,973	49,310	55,478	55,478

Exhibit FE1-J: Base Case—Cash Flows (US$) Details Years 2 and 3

Maktabi

Cash Flow Calculation (Indirect Calculation)

	Qtr 1 2009	Qtr 2 2009	Qtr 3 2009	Qtr 4 2009	Total	Qtr 1 2010	Qtr 2 2010	Qtr 3 2010	Qtr 4 2010	Total
Cash at start of month/year	13,870	13,870	13,870	13,870	**55,478**	31,007	31,007	31,007	31,007	**124,026**
Cash inflow										
Net profit	15,628	15,628	15,628	15,628	**62,513**	250,291	250,291	250,291	250,291	**1,001,162**
Plus depreciation/amortization	10,587	10,587	10,587	10,587	**42,349**	13,071	13,071	13,071	13,071	**52,282**
Plus changes in:										
Liabilities from performance	71,158	71,158	71,158	71,158	**284,632**	11,363	11,363	11,363	11,363	**45,451**
Wage provisions	186	186	186	186	**745**	941	941	941	941	**3,763**
Tax provisions	0	0	0	0	**0**	12,206	12,206	12,206	12,206	**48,824**
Long-term debt/loans	0	0	0	0	**0**	0	0	0	0	**0**
Total cash inflow	97,560	97,560	97,560	97,560	**390,239**	287,871	287,871	287,871	287,871	**1,151,482**
Cash deployed										
Minus changes in:										
Net receivables from performance	19,144	19,144	19,144	19,144	**76,577**	97,709	97,709	97,709	97,709	**390,836**
Stock	21,014	21,014	21,014	21,014	**84,054**	10,898	10,898	10,898	10,898	**43,592**
Gross fixed assets	82,496	82,496	82,496	82,496	**329,982**	2,883	2,883	2,883	2,883	**11,532**
Total cash deployed	122,653	122,653	122,653	122,653	**490,613**	111,490	111,490	111,490	111,490	**445,960**
Increase/decrease in cash	-27,863	-27,863	-27,863	-27,863	**-111,452**	176,381	176,381	176,381	176,381	**705,522**
Financing (increase in equity)	45,000	45,000	45,000	45,000	**180,000**	0	0	0	0	**0**
Cash at end of month/year	31,007	31,007	31,007	31,007	**124,026**	207,387	207,387	207,387	207,387	**829,547**

Exhibit FE2-A: Worst Case—Assumptions

Maktabi

Assumptions for the Financial Plan (Summary)

All figures shown in Egyptian Pounds

SALES
- The first sales will take place in 11/06
- Average order price structure:
  Business orders   15
  Consumer orders   10

COSTS OF SERVICES PROVIDED
- Average material costs per order:
  Business orders   9
  Consumer orders   7

OPERATING COSTS
- Monthly wages reflect current market rates
- Social costs as percentage of wage costs   0.00%
- Annual rise in wages   10.00%
- The model for the number of employees is given in the financial plan
- Import customs and transportation to distribution center   243 / inbound shipment
- Picking and packing   0 / order
- Shipping   1 / order
- Catalog design will be paid at market rates
- Catalog photos   0 / photo
- Catalog printing   2 / catalog
- Information systems will be paid at market rates
- Sales representative commission on sales   2.00%
- Commissions on sales   0.00%
- Advertising media as a percentage of sales   0.25%
- Promotions as a percentage of sales   0.75%
- Public relations as a percentage of sales   0.25%
- Other marketing expenses as a percentage of sales   0.25%
- Consultants for special projects and auditors will be paid at market rates
- Additional costs per person calculated as follows:

Cost per Person/Month	Training	Office Material	Travel	Communication
Customer service	4	7	3	52
Purchasing	0	3	139	52
Distribution	0	3	10	17
Transportation and AR	0	3	3	17
Publications	0	3	3	17
Information Technologies	0	3	3	17
Marketing and Sales*	3	3	3	17
Finance and Administration	0	3	17	52

* Marketing and Sales training for sales representatives only
- Rent per square metre per month   35.00%
- Provisions for unpaid invoices in percentage of sales   0.00%
- Interest income on liquid assets   0.00%
- Returns as a percent of sales   0.50%
- Income tax   20.00%

BALANCE SHEET
- Debitors are settled within 30 days, creditors within 30 days
- Goods are purchased on average 30 days before the sale of the product/service
- Fixed assets include computers, software, office equipment, and property
- Individual depreciation periods per asset and cost center
- Provisions for wages represent half a monthly salary
- Taxes are paid at the end of the tax period

Exhibit FE2-B: Worst Case—Profit and Loss Statement (US$)

Maktabi

Profit and Loss Statement

Sales	2007	2008	2009	2010	2011
Business orders	45,826	307,478	393,217	412,435	430,174
Consumer orders	90,783	1,565,217	3,339,130	2,504,348	2,608,696
Total sales	136,609	1,872,696	3,732,348	2,916,783	3,038,870
Cost of services provided	86,747	1,189,162	2,370,041	1,852,157	1,929,682
Gross margin	49,862	683,534	1,362,307	1,064,626	1,109,187
In % of sales	37%	37%	37%	37%	37%
Operating costs					
Customer Service	12,084	28,695	83,488	104,443	108,942
In % of sales	9%	2%	2%	4%	4%
Purchasing	12,344	17,827	19,596	20,153	21,015
In % of sales	9%	1%	1%	1%	1%
Distribution	32,041	120,977	222,365	200,821	206,458
In % of sales	23%	6%	6%	7%	7%
Transportation and Accounts Receivables	11,579	110,349	217,932	170,398	177,823
In % of sales	8%	6%	6%	6%	6%
Publications	21,629	61,075	50,390	50,528	50,912
In % of sales	16%	3%	1%	2%	2%
Information Technologies	37,563	51,001	56,706	59,959	63,771
In % of sales	27%	3%	2%	2%	2%
Marketing and Sales	31,676	110,526	175,336	150,422	158,923
In % of sales	23%	6%	5%	5%	5%
Finance and Administration	78,101	104,222	118,183	117,369	122,830
In % of sales	57%	6%	3%	4%	4%
Total operating costs	237,017	604,673	943,997	874,094	910,675
In % of sales	174%	32%	25%	30%	30%
Operating profit	-187,155	78,861	418,310	190,532	198,512
In % of sales	-137%	4%	11%	7%	7%
Financing expenditure	0	0	0	0	0
Financing income	0	0	0	0	0
Profit before tax	-187,155	78,861	418,310	190,532	198,512
Income tax	0	0	62,003	38,106	39,702
Net profit	-187,155	78,861	356,307	152,425	158,810
In % of sales	-137%	4%	10%	5%	5%

Exhibit FE2-C: Worst Case—Balance Sheet (US$)

Maktabi

Balance Sheet at End of Accounting Year

	2007	2008	2009	2010	2011
Assets					
Liquid assets					
Cash	169,597	310,272	638,212	817,830	1,136,001
Net receivables from customers	43,826	189,130	311,029	243,065	253,239
Stock/inventory (30, 60, or 90 days)	45,853	195,948	153,131	159,541	0
Total liquid assets	259,276	695,351	1,102,372	1,220,436	1,389,241
Gross fixed assets	180,522	230,296	234,991	239,687	239,687
Minus cumulated depreciation	12,006	34,808	61,951	81,991	96,829
Net fixed assets	168,515	195,488	173,040	157,696	142,858
Total assets	**427,792**	**890,839**	**1,275,412**	**1,378,133**	**1,532,099**
Liabilities					
Debt					
Short-term debt					
Open third-party invoices (creditors)	62,184	231,008	241,135	195,924	189,631
Provisions for wages	5,806	6,386	9,024	10,505	11,555
Provisions for taxes	0	0	15,501	9,527	9,926
Total short-term debt	67,990	237,394	265,660	215,955	211,112
Long-term debt					
Loans and mortgages	0	0	0	0	0
Total long-term debt	0	0	0	0	0
Total debt	**67,990**	**237,394**	**265,660**	**215,955**	**211,112**
Equity					
Share capital	546,957	761,739	761,739	761,739	761,739
Reserves	0	0	0	0	0
Profit/loss carried forward	-187,155	-108,294	248,013	400,438	559,248
Total equity	359,802	653,445	1,009,752	1,162,177	1,320,987
Total liabilities	**427,792**	**890,839**	**1,275,412**	**1,378,133**	**1,532,099**

Exhibit FE2-D: Worst Case—Cash Flows (US$)

Maktabi

Cash Flow Calculation

	2007	2008	2009	2010	2011
Cash at beginning of year	0	169,597	310,272	638,212	817,830
Cash inflow					
Net profit	-187,155	78,861	356,307	152,425	158,810
Plus depreciation/amortization	12,006	22,801	27,144	20,039	14,838
Plus changes in:					
Liabilities from performance	62,184	168,823	10,127	-45,211	-6,293
Wage provisions	5,806	581	2,638	1,481	1,050
Tax provisions	0	0	15,501	-5,974	399
Long-term debt/loans	0	0	0	0	0
Total cash inflow	-107,158	271,066	411,716	122,760	168,804
Cash outflow					
Minus changes in:					
Net receivables from performance	43,826	145,304	121,899	-67,964	10,174
Stock	45,853	150,095	-42,817	6,410	-159,541
Gross fixed assets	180,522	49,774	4,696	4,696	0
Total cash outflow	270,201	345,173	83,777	-56,859	-149,367
Cash increase/decrease	-377,359	-74,108	327,939	179,619	318,171
Financing (increase in equity)	546,957	214,783	0	0	0
Cash at end of year	169,597	310,272	638,212	817,830	1,136,001

Exhibit FE3-A: Best Case—Assumption

Maktabi

Assumptions for the Financial Plan (Summary)

All figures shown in Egyptian Pounds

SALES
- The first sales will take place in 11/06
- Average order price structure:
  Business orders   13
  Consumer orders   10

COSTS OF SERVICES PROVIDED
- Average material costs per order:
  Business orders   8
  Consumer orders   6

OPERATING COSTS
- Monthly wages reflect current market rates
- Social costs as percentage of wage costs   0.00%
- Annual rise in wages   10.00%
- The model for the number of employees is given in the financial plan
- Import customs and transportation to distribution center   174 / inbound shipment
- Picking and packing   0.35 / order
- Shipping   0.35 / order
- Catalog design will be paid at market rates
- Catalog photos   0.09 / photo
- Catalog printing   2 / catalog
- Information systems will be paid at market rates
- Sales representative commission on sales   3.00%
- Commissions on sales   0.00%
- Advertising media as a percentage of sales   0.25%
- Promotions as a percentage of sales   0.75%
- Public relations as a percentage of sales   0.25%
- Other marketing expenses as a percentage of sales   0.25%
- Consultants for special projects and auditors will be paid at market rates
- Additional costs per person calculated as follows:

Cost per Person/Month	Training	Office Material	Travel	Communication
Customer service	4	7	3	52
Purchasing	0	3	139	52
Distribution	0	3	10	17
Transportation and AR	0	3	3	17
Publications	0	3	3	17
Information Technologies	0	3	3	17
Marketing and Sales*	3	3	3	17
Finance and Administration	0	3	17	52

* Marketing and Sales training for sales representatives only

- Rent per square metre per month   35.00%
- Provisions for unpaid invoices in percentage of sales   0.00%
- Interest income on liquid assets   0.00%
- Returns as a percent of sales   0.50%
- Income tax   20.00%

BALANCE SHEET
- Debitors are settled within 30 days, creditors within 30 days
- Goods are purchased on average 30 days before the sale of the product/service
- Fixed assets include computers, software, office equipment, and property
- Individual depreciation periods per asset and cost center
- Provisions for wages represent half a monthly salary
- Taxes are paid at the end of the tax period

Exhibit FE3-B: Best Case—Profit and Loss Statement (US$)

Maktabi

Profit and Loss Statement

Sales	2007	2008	2009	2010	2011
Business orders	218,543	863,674	891,913	914,217	936,522
Consumer orders	830,451	4,610,157	7,101,949	9,724,935	9,987,509
Total sales	1,048,994	5,473,831	7,993,862	10,639,153	10,924,030
Cost of services provided	634,641	3,311,668	4,836,286	6,436,687	6,609,038
Gross margin	414,353	2,162,163	3,157,575	4,202,465	4,314,992
In % of sales	40%	40%	40%	40%	40%
Operating costs					
Customer Service	17,451	50,342	132,915	172,506	179,350
In % of sales	2%	1%	2%	2%	2%
Purchasing	15,181	24,996	27,649	28,626	29,678
In % of sales	1%	0%	0%	0%	0%
Distribution	58,487	228,838	338,452	443,752	454,841
In % of sales	6%	4%	4%	4%	4%
Transportation and Accounts Receivables	42,644	201,262	293,544	390,023	400,972
In % of sales	4%	4%	4%	4%	4%
Publications	18,018	51,430	42,606	42,763	43,203
In % of sales	2%	1%	1%	0%	0%
Information Technologies	87,419	117,699	130,540	138,202	146,897
In % of sales	8%	2%	2%	1%	1%
Marketing and Sales	79,113	298,990	412,864	536,258	554,142
In % of sales	8%	5%	5%	5%	5%
Finance and Administration	135,233	183,191	204,931	225,804	237,274
In % of sales	13%	3%	3%	2%	2%
Total operating costs	453,545	1,156,748	1,583,500	1,977,935	2,046,358
In % of sales	43%	21%	20%	19%	19%
Operating profit	-39,193	1,005,415	1,574,075	2,224,531	2,268,634
In % of sales	-4%	18%	20%	21%	21%
Financing expenditure	0	0	0	0	0
Financing income	0	0	0	0	0
Profit before tax	-39,193	1,005,415	1,574,075	2,224,531	2,268,634
Income tax	0	193,244	314,815	444,906	453,727
Net profit	-39,193	812,171	1,259,260	1,779,625	1,814,907
In % of sales	-4%	15%	16%	17%	17%

Exhibit FE3-C: Best Case—Balance Sheet (US$)

Maktabi

Balance Sheet at End of Accounting Year

	2007	2008	2009	2010	2011
Assets					
Liquid assets					
Cash	31,310	784,897	1,849,392	3,600,926	5,942,327
Net receivables from customers	220,387	518,139	666,155	886,596	910,336
Stock/inventory (30, 60, or 90 days)	194,807	399,693	531,958	546,202	0
Total liquid assets	446,504	1,702,729	3,047,505	5,033,724	6,852,663
Gross fixed assets	318,504	423,965	435,096	446,226	446,226
Minus cumulated depreciation	20,415	61,291	111,755	151,122	181,579
Net fixed assets	298,089	362,675	323,341	295,104	264,647
Total assets	**744,594**	**2,065,404**	**3,370,846**	**5,328,828**	**7,117,311**
Liabilities					
Debt					
Short-term debt					
Open third-party invoices (creditors)	226,647	458,955	483,003	626,164	595,751
Provisions for wages	10,183	11,201	15,162	17,835	19,619
Provisions for taxes	0	60,531	78,704	111,227	113,432
Total short-term debt	236,830	530,687	576,869	755,226	728,801
Long-term debt					
Loans and mortgages	0	0	0	0	0
Total long-term debt	0	0	0	0	0
Total debt	**236,830**	**530,687**	**576,869**	**755,226**	**728,801**
Equity					
Share capital	546,957	761,739	761,739	761,739	761,739
Reserves	0	0	0	0	0
Profit/loss carried forward	-39,193	772,978	2,032,238	3,811,863	5,626,770
Total equity	507,764	1,534,717	2,793,977	4,573,602	6,388,509
Total liabilities	**744,594**	**2,065,404**	**3,370,846**	**5,328,828**	**7,117,311**

Exhibit FE3-D: Best Case—Cash Flows (US$)

Maktabi

Cash Flow Calculation

	2007	2008	2009	2010	2011
Cash at beginning of year	0	31,310	784,897	1,849,392	3,600,926
Cash inflow					
Net profit	-39,193	812,171	1,259,260	1,779,625	1,814,907
Plus depreciation/amortization	20,415	40,876	50,464	39,368	30,456
Plus changes in:					
Liabilities from performance	226,647	232,308	24,048	143,161	-30,413
Wage provisions	10,183	1,018	3,961	2,674	1,784
Tax provisions	0	60,531	18,173	32,523	2,205
Long-term debt/loans	0	0	0	0	0
Total cash inflow	218,052	1,146,904	1,355,906	1,997,350	1,818,939
Cash outflow					
Minus changes in:					
Net receivables from performance	220,387	297,752	148,016	220,441	23,740
Stock	194,807	204,886	132,265	14,244	-546,202
Gross fixed assets	318,504	105,461	11,130	11,130	0
Total cash outflow	733,699	608,099	291,411	245,815	-522,462
Cash increase/decrease	-515,647	538,805	1,064,495	1,751,535	2,341,401
Financing (increase in equity)	546,957	214,783	0	0	0
Cash at end of year	31,310	784,897	1,849,392	3,600,926	5,942,327

Exhibit OM1: Product Group Listing, Phase I

Phase I Beginning at Year 0

Phase I			
Product Group	**Product Category**	**Product Type**	**Product Item**
Office Supplies	Binders and Accessories	Presentation Binders	0.5" Presentation Binders
Office Supplies	Binders and Accessories	Presentation Binders	1.0" Presentation Binders
Office Supplies	Binders and Accessories	Presentation Binders	1.5" Presentation Binders
Office Supplies	Binders and Accessories	Presentation Binders	2.0" Presentation Binders
Office Supplies	Binders and Accessories	Presentation Binders	Easel Binders
Office Supplies	Binders and Accessories	Reference Binders	0.5" Reference Binders
Office Supplies	Binders and Accessories	Reference Binders	1.0" Reference Binders
Office Supplies	Binders and Accessories	Reference Binders	1.5" Reference Binders
Office Supplies	Binders and Accessories	Reference Binders	2.0" Reference Binders
Office Supplies	Binders and Accessories	Reference Binders	3.0" Reference Binders
Office Supplies	Binders and Accessories	Storage Binders	4.0" Storage Binders
Office Supplies	Binders and Accessories	Storage Binders	5.0" Storage Binders
Office Supplies	Binders and Accessories	Storage Binders	Archival and Heavy Duty Storage Binders
Office Supplies	Binders and Accessories	Binder Accessories	Multiple
Office Supplies	Binders and Accessories	Index Dividers	Customizable Tabs
Office Supplies	Binders and Accessories	Index Dividers	Preprinted Tabs
Office Supplies	Binders and Accessories	Index Dividers	Insertable and Write-On Tabs
Office Supplies	Binders and Accessories	Index Dividers	Untabbed Dividers
Office Supplies	Binders and Accessories	Index Dividers	Adhesive Tabs
Office Supplies	Binders and Accessories	Report Covers	Clear Front Report Covers
Office Supplies	Binders and Accessories	Report Covers	Fastener Folders With Pockets
Office Supplies	Binders and Accessories	Report Covers	Fastener Folders Without Pockets
Office Supplies	Binders and Accessories	Report Covers	Presentation Folders
Office Supplies	Binders and Accessories	Sheet Protectors	Presentation Sheet Protectors
Office Supplies	Binders and Accessories	Sheet Protectors	Specialty Sheet Protectors
Office Supplies	Binders and Accessories	Specialty Binders	Data, Post, and Hanging Binders
Office Supplies	Binders and Accessories	Specialty Binders	Specialty-Sized Binders
Office Supplies	Binders and Accessories	Two-Pocket Portfolios	Presentation Folders
Office Supplies	Binders and Accessories	Two-Pocket Portfolios	Two-Pocket Portfolios
Office Supplies	Boards and Easels	Dry-Erase Boards	Dry-Erase Premium Magnetic
Office Supplies	Boards and Easels	Dry-Erase Boards	Dry-Erase Premium Non-Magnetic
Office Supplies	Boards and Easels	Dry-Erase Boards	Dry-Erase Commercial
Office Supplies	Boards and Easels	Dry-Erase Boards	Dry-Erase Economy
Office Supplies	Boards and Easels	Dry-Erase Boards	Electronic Whiteboards
Office Supplies	Boards and Easels	Dry-Erase Boards	1.5 × 2 Boards
Office Supplies	Boards and Easels	Dry-Erase Boards	2 × 3 Boards
Office Supplies	Boards and Easels	Dry-Erase Boards	3 × 4 Boards
Office Supplies	Boards and Easels	Dry-Erase Boards	3 × 5 Boards

Phase I			
Product Group	**Product Category**	**Product Type**	**Product Item**
Office Supplies	Boards and Easels	Dry-Erase Boards	4 × 6 Boards
Office Supplies	Boards and Easels	Dry-Erase Boards	4 × 8 Boards
Office Supplies	Boards and Easels	Bulletin Boards	Bulletin Boards—Premium
Office Supplies	Boards and Easels	Bulletin Boards	Bulletin Boards—Commercial
Office Supplies	Boards and Easels	Bulletin Boards	Bulletin Boards—Economy
Office Supplies	Boards and Easels	Bulletin Boards	1.5 × 2 Boards
Office Supplies	Boards and Easels	Bulletin Boards	2 × 3 Boards
Office Supplies	Boards and Easels	Bulletin Boards	3 × 4 Boards
Office Supplies	Boards and Easels	Bulletin Boards	3 × 5 Boards
Office Supplies	Boards and Easels	Bulletin Boards	4 × 6 Boards
Office Supplies	Boards and Easels	Bulletin Boards	4 × 8 Boards
Office Supplies	Boards and Easels	Bulletin Boards	Bulletin Boards—Stylish
Office Supplies	Boards and Easels	Easels and Easel Pads	Pads Easels
Office Supplies	Boards and Easels	Cubicle and Personal-Size Boards	Cubicle and Personal-Size Bulletin Boards
Office Supplies	Boards and Easels	Cubicle and Personal-Size Boards	Cubicle and Personal-Size Dry-Erase Boards
Office Supplies	Boards and Easels	Chalkboards and Accessories	Chalkboards and Accessories
Office Supplies	Boards and Easels	Letter/Message Boards and Accessories	Letter/Message Boards and Accessories
Office Supplies	Boards and Easels	Cubicle Management Systems	Cubicle Management Systems
Office Supplies	Boards and Easels	Conference Cabinets	Conference Cabinets
Office Supplies	Boards and Easels	Dry-Erase Markers and Accessories	Dry-Erase Accessories
Office Supplies	Boards and Easels	Dry-Erase Markers and Accessories	Dry-Erase Marker Kits
Office Supplies	Boards and Easels	Dry-Erase Markers and Accessories	Dry-Erase Markers
Office Supplies	Boards and Easels	Dry-Erase Magnetic Accessories	Dry-Erase Magnetic Accessories
Office Supplies	Boards and Easels	Presentation Boards	Presentation Boards
Office Supplies	Boards and Easels	Dry-Erase and Bulletin Board Systems	Dry-Erase and Bulletin Board
Office Supplies	Calendars and Planners	Calendars and Planners	2006 Calendars and Planners
Office Supplies	Calendars and Planners	Calendars and Planners	Academic (Aug-Jul)
Office Supplies	Calendars and Planners	Calendars and Planners	Calendars and Planners
Office Supplies	Calendars and Planners	Calendars and Planners	Personal Organizers
Office Supplies	Calendars and Planners	Calendars and Planners	Undated Organizers and Calendars
Office Supplies	Cleaning and Breakroom	Paper Products	Paper Towels
Office Supplies	Cleaning and Breakroom	Paper Products	Facial Tissue
Office Supplies	Cleaning and Breakroom	Paper Products	Bathroom Tissue
Office Supplies	Cleaning and Breakroom	Cleaning Supplies	All-Purpose Cleaners
Office Supplies	Cleaning and Breakroom	Cleaning Supplies	Pre-Moistened Wiped

(Continued)

Exhibit OM1 (Continued)

Phase I			
Product Group	**Product Category**	**Product Type**	**Product Item**
Office Supplies	Cleaning and Breakroom	Cleaning Supplies	Hand Soaps, Sanitizers, and Lotions
Office Supplies	Cleaning and Breakroom	Breakroom Supplies	Cups and Lids
Office Supplies	Cleaning and Breakroom	Breakroom Supplies	Cutlery
Office Supplies	Cleaning and Breakroom	Breakroom Supplies	Plates and Bowls
Office Supplies	Cleaning and Breakroom	Trash Bags and Cans	Trashbags
Office Supplies	Cleaning and Breakroom	Trash Bags and Cans	Plastic Wastebaskets
Office Supplies	Cleaning and Breakroom	Trash Bags and Cans	Fire Safe and Metal
Office Supplies	Cleaning and Breakroom	Trash Bags and Cans	Wastebackets
Office Supplies	Cleaning and Breakroom	Lightbulbs and Extension Cords	Extension Cords
Office Supplies	Cleaning and Breakroom	Lightbulbs and Extension Cords	Light Bulbs
Office Supplies	Cleaning and Breakroom	Equipment, Storage	Padlocks
Office Supplies	Cleaning and Breakroom	Equipment, Storage	Step Stools and Ladders
Office Supplies	Cleaning and Breakroom	Equipment, Storage	Flashlights
Office Supplies	Desktop Organizers	Desktop Organizers, Holders, and Accessories	Business Card Holders
Office Supplies	Desktop Organizers	Desktop Organizers, Holders, and Accessories	Desk Pads
Office Supplies	Desktop Organizers	Desktop Organizers, Holders, and Accessories	Desktop File Sorters
Office Supplies	Desktop Organizers	Desk Sets/Organizers	Desk Organizer Collections— Plastic
Office Supplies	Desktop Organizers	Desk Sets/Organizers	Desk Organizer Collections— Wire Mesh and Metal
Office Supplies	Desktop Organizers	Desk Sets/Organizers	Desk Organizer Collections— Wood and Faux Leather
Office Supplies	Desktop Organizers	Drawer Organizers	Drawer Organizers
Office Supplies	Desktop Organizers	Wall Art	Wall Art
Office Supplies	Desktop Organizers	Wall Organizers and Pockets	Wall File Organizer Systems
Office Supplies	Desktop Organizers	Wall Organizers and Pockets	Wall Files
Office Supplies	Desktop Organizers	Rolodex Card Organizers	Business Card Books
Office Supplies	Desktop Organizers	Rolodex Card Organizers	Card Files and Accessories
Office Supplies	Desktop Organizers	Cubicle and Partition Organizers and Accessories	Cubicle and Partition
Office Supplies	Desktop Organizers	Cubicle and Partition Organizers and Accessories	Organizers and Accessories
Office Supplies	Desktop Organizers	Index Cards, Guides, and Files	Index Card Files
Office Supplies	Desktop Organizers	Index Cards, Guides, and Files	Index Cards Guides

Phase I			
Product Group	**Product Category**	**Product Type**	**Product Item**
Office Supplies	Desktop Organizers	Index Cards, Guides, and Files	Index Cards
Office Supplies	Desktop Organizers	Desktop Computer Accessories	Desktop Copyholders
Office Supplies	Desktop Organizers	Desktop Computer Accessories	Desktop Drawers
Office Supplies	Desktop Organizers	Desktop Computer Accessories	Keyboard Wrist Rests
Office Supplies	Desktop Organizers	Bookends, Book Shelves, and Magazine Files	Bookends and Book Shelves
Office Supplies	Desktop Organizers	Bookends, Book Shelves, and Magazine Files	Magazine Files
Office Supplies	Desktop Organizers	Decorative Accessories	Clocks
Office Supplies	Desktop Organizers	Decorative Accessories	Frames
Office Supplies	Desktop Organizers	Decorative Accessories	Maps, Magnifiers, and Flags
Office Supplies	Desktop Organizers	Supply Closet Organizers	Supply Closet Organizers
Office Supplies	Envelopes and Forms	Business Envelopes	Gummed Closure
Office Supplies	Envelopes and Forms	Business Envelopes	Pull and Seal/Self-Sealing
Office Supplies	Envelopes and Forms	Business Envelopes	Security
Office Supplies	Envelopes and Forms	Mailers and Tubes	Bubble Mailers
Office Supplies	Envelopes and Forms	Mailers and Tubes	Corrugated Mailers
Office Supplies	Envelopes and Forms	Mailers and Tubes	Flat/Media Mailers
Office Supplies	Envelopes and Forms	Large Format/ Catalog Envelopes	Clasp
Office Supplies	Envelopes and Forms	Large Format/ Catalog Envelopes	Gummed Closure
Office Supplies	Envelopes and Forms	Large Format/ Catalog Envelopes	Padded
Office Supplies	Envelopes and Forms	Specialty Envelopes	Coin and Media
Office Supplies	Envelopes and Forms	Specialty Envelopes	Colored and Invitation
Office Supplies	Envelopes and Forms	Specialty Envelopes	Document and Booklet
Office Supplies	Envelopes and Forms	Forms	Pads—Message/Memo
Office Supplies	Envelopes and Forms	Forms	Automotive
Office Supplies	Envelopes and Forms	Forms	Clipboards
Office Supplies	Envelopes and Forms	Columnar Pads, Journal, and Record Keeping	Columnar Pads
Office Supplies	Envelopes and Forms	Columnar Pads, Journal, and Record Keeping	Journals and Record Keeping
Office Supplies	Envelopes and Forms	Tax Forms	Tax Forms
Office Supplies	Filing Supplies	Filing Supplies	File Folders
Office Supplies	Filing Supplies	Filing Supplies	Hanging File Folders
Office Supplies	Filing Supplies	Filing Supplies	File Jackets and Sorters
Office Supplies	Filing Supplies	Filing Supplies	Filing Accessories
Office Supplies	Filing Supplies	Filing Supplies	End Tab Filing
Office Supplies	Filing Supplies	Filing Supplies	Expandable Files
Office Supplies	Filing Supplies	Filing Supplies	Medical Filing
Office Supplies	Filing Supplies	Filing Supplies	100% Recycled Filing

(Continued)

Exhibit OM1 (Continued)

Phase I			
Product Group	**Product Category**	**Product Type**	**Product Item**
Office Supplies	General Supplies	Tape, Glue, and Adhesives	Invisible Tape
Office Supplies	General Supplies	Tape, Glue, and Adhesives	Tape Dispensers
Office Supplies	General Supplies	Tape, Glue, and Adhesives	Mounting and Specialty Tapes
Office Supplies	General Supplies	Tape, Glue, and Adhesives	VELCRO Brand Fasteners
Office Supplies	General Supplies	Tape, Glue, and Adhesives	Glue and Adhesive Products
Office Supplies	General Supplies	Tape, Glue, and Adhesives	Vinyl Numbers and Letters
Office Supplies	General Supplies	Clips, Tacks, and Rubber Bands	Binder Clips
Office Supplies	General Supplies	Clips, Tacks, and Rubber Bands	Paper Clip Holders
Office Supplies	General Supplies	Clips, Tacks, and Rubber Bands	Paper Clips
Office Supplies	General Supplies	Clips, Tacks, and Rubber Bands	Pins and Tacks
Office Supplies	General Supplies	Clips, Tacks, and Rubber Bands	Rubber Bands
Office Supplies	General Supplies	Clips, Tacks, and Rubber Bands	Specialty Clips and Fasteners
Office Supplies	General Supplies	Scissors, Rulers, and Paper Trimmers	Scissors
Office Supplies	General Supplies	Scissors, Rulers, and Paper Trimmers	Scissors for Kids
Office Supplies	General Supplies	Scissors, Rulers, and Paper Trimmers	Paper Trimmers
Office Supplies	General Supplies	Scissors, Rulers, and Paper Trimmers	Paper Trimmer Accessories
Office Supplies	General Supplies	Scissors, Rulers, and Paper Trimmers	Rulers
Office Supplies	General Supplies	Scissors, Rulers, and Paper Trimmers	Letter Openers
Office Supplies	General Supplies	Scissors, Rulers, and Paper Trimmers	X-Acto and Utility Knives
Office Supplies	General Supplies	Scissors, Rulers, and Paper Trimmers	Drafting Supplies
Office Supplies	General Supplies	Scissors, Rulers, and Paper Trimmers	Clipboards
Office Supplies	General Supplies	Staplers and Staples	Desktop Staples
Office Supplies	General Supplies	Staplers and Staples	Electic Staplers
Office Supplies	General Supplies	Staplers and Staples	Heavy-Duty Staplers
Office Supplies	General Supplies	Staplers and Staples	Stapel Removers
Office Supplies	General Supplies	Staplers and Staples	Staples
Office Supplies	General Supplies	Paper Punches	Desktop Paper Punches
Office Supplies	General Supplies	Paper Punches	Heavy-Duty Paper Punches
Office Supplies	General Supplies	Paper Punches	Electric Paper Punches
Office Supplies	General Supplies	Paper Punches	1-Hole Paper Punch
Office Supplies	General Supplies	Paper Punches	2-Hole Paper Punch

Phase I			
Product Group	**Product Category**	**Product Type**	**Product Item**
Office Supplies	General Supplies	Paper Punches	Paper Punch Accessories
Office Supplies	General Supplies	Batteries	Alkaline/Lithium Batteries
Office Supplies	General Supplies	Batteries	AA/AAA/9V Rechargeale
Office Supplies	General Supplies	Batteries	AA/AAA/C/D/9V Chargers
Office Supplies	General Supplies	Batteries	Digital Camera Batteries
Office Supplies	General Supplies	Batteries	Camcorder Batteries
Office Supplies	General Supplies	Batteries	Camcorder/Digital Camera Chargers
Office Supplies	General Supplies	Batteries	Camcorder/Digital Camera Power Supplies
Office Supplies	General Supplies	Batteries	Notebook Batteries
Office Supplies	General Supplies	Batteries	PDA Batteries
Office Supplies	General Supplies	Batteries	MP3 Batteries
Office Supplies	General Supplies	Batteries	Portable DVD Player Batteries
Office Supplies	General Supplies	Batteries	Cordless Phone Batteries
Office Supplies	General Supplies	Batteries	Cell Phone Batteries
Office Supplies	Luggage and Briefcases	Luggage and Briefcases	Briefcases
Office Supplies	Luggage and Briefcases	Luggage and Briefcases	Catalog Cases
Office Supplies	Luggage and Briefcases	Luggage and Briefcases	Computer Backpacks
Office Supplies	Luggage and Briefcases	Luggage and Briefcases	Computer Bags and Accessories
Office Supplies	Luggage and Briefcases	Luggage and Briefcases	Gift Gallery
Office Supplies	Luggage and Briefcases	Luggage and Briefcases	Luggage
Office Supplies	Luggage and Briefcases	Luggage and Briefcases	Messenger Bags
Office Supplies	Luggage and Briefcases	Luggage and Briefcases	Padfolios
Office Supplies	Luggage and Briefcases	Luggage and Briefcases	Presentation Portfolios
Office Supplies	Luggage and Briefcases	Luggage and Briefcases	Travel Accessories
Office Supplies	Luggage and Briefcases	Luggage and Briefcases	Women's Totes
Office Supplies	Mail and Ship/Moving	Mailers and Tubes	Bubble Mailers
Office Supplies	Mail and Ship/Moving	Mailers and Tubes	Corrugated Mailers
Office Supplies	Mail and Ship/Moving	Mailers and Tubes	Flat/Media Mailers
Office Supplies	Mail and Ship/Moving	Shipping and Moving Boxes	Shipping Boxes—Fixed Depth
Office Supplies	Mail and Ship/Moving	Shipping and Moving Boxes	Shipping Boxes—Multi Depth
Office Supplies	Mail and Ship/Moving	Shipping and Moving Boxes	Moving Boxes and Kits
Office Supplies	Mail and Ship/Moving	Bubble Wrap and Packing Material	Bubble Wrap—Adhesive
Office Supplies	Mail and Ship/Moving	Bubble Wrap and Packing Material	Bubble Wrap—Standard
Office Supplies	Mail and Ship/Moving	Bubble Wrap and Packing Material	Foam Rolls
Office Supplies	Mail and Ship/Moving	Packaging Tape and Dispensers	Masking and Duct Tape
Office Supplies	Mail and Ship/Moving	Packaging Tape and Dispensers	Packaging Tape
Office Supplies	Mail and Ship/Moving	Packaging Tape and Dispensers	Packaging Tape Dispensers

(Continued)

Exhibit OM1 (Continued)

Phase I			
Product Group	**Product Category**	**Product Type**	**Product Item**
Office Supplies	Mail and Ship/Moving	Mailroom Equipment and Supplies	Handtrucks and Dollies
Office Supplies	Mail and Ship/Moving	Mailroom Equipment and Supplies	Letter Folders
Office Supplies	Mail and Ship/Moving	Mailroom Equipment and Supplies	Literature Holders— Wall Style
Office Supplies	Mail and Ship/Moving	Poly Bags	Flat Poly Bags
Office Supplies	Mail and Ship/Moving	Poly Bags	Reclosable Poly Bags
Office Supplies	Mail and Ship/Moving	Poly Bags	Reclosable Poly Bags with White Block
Office Supplies	Mail and Ship/Moving	Recycled Mailing Supplies	Recycled Mailers
Office Supplies	Mail and Ship/Moving	Recycled Mailing Supplies	Recycled Mailing Tubes
Office Supplies	Mail and Ship/Moving	Recycled Mailing Supplies	Shipping Boxes—Fixed Depth
Office Supplies	Mail and Ship/Moving	Postal Scales and Meters	Postage Meters
Office Supplies	Mail and Ship/Moving	Postal Scales and Meters	Shipping and Postal Scales
Office Supplies	Mail and Ship/Moving	Shipping and Mailing Labels	Inkjet Address Labels
Office Supplies	Mail and Ship/Moving	Shipping and Mailing Labels	Label Printers
Office Supplies	Mail and Ship/Moving	Shipping and Mailing Labels	Laser Address Labels
Office Supplies	Mail and Ship/Moving	Stretch Wrap and Dispensers	Clear Stretch Wrap
Office Supplies	Mail and Ship/Moving	Stretch Wrap and Dispensers	Goodwrappers Stretch Wrap
Office Supplies	Mail and Ship/Moving	Stretch Wrap and Dispensers	Strapping Kits
Office Supplies	Mail and Ship/Moving	Stamps and Pads	Electronic Stamps
Office Supplies	Mail and Ship/Moving	Stamps and Pads	Pre-Inked Stamps
Office Supplies	Mail and Ship/Moving	Stamps and Pads	Self-Inking Stamps
Office Supplies	Paper and Pads	Paper and Pads	Cards and Badges
Office Supplies	Paper and Pads	Paper and Pads	Brochure and Specialty
Office Supplies	Paper and Pads	Paper and Pads	Colored Paper
Office Supplies	Paper and Pads	Paper and Pads	Computer Paper
Office Supplies	Paper and Pads	Paper and Pads	Cover and Card Stock
Office Supplies	Paper and Pads	Paper and Pads	Fax Paper
Office Supplies	Paper and Pads	Paper and Pads	Inkjet Paper
Office Supplies	Paper and Pads	Paper and Pads	Laser Paper
Office Supplies	Paper and Pads	Paper and Pads	Multiuse and Copy Paper
Office Supplies	Paper and Pads	Paper and Pads	Notebooks, Pads, and Filler Paper
Office Supplies	Paper and Pads	Paper and Pads	Photo Paper
Office Supplies	Paper and Pads	Paper and Pads	Printing Paper
Office Supplies	Paper and Pads	Paper and Pads	Recycled Paper

Phase I			
Product Group	**Product Category**	**Product Type**	**Product Item**
Office Supplies	Paper and Pads	Paper and Pads	Register and Calculator Rolls
Office Supplies	Paper and Pads	Paper and Pads	Stationary
Office Supplies	Paper and Pads	Paper and Pads	Wide Format Paper
Office Supplies	Self-Stick Notes	Super Sticky Notes	Super Sticky Notes
Office Supplies	Self-Stick Notes	Staples Sticky Notes	Flat Notes
Office Supplies	Self-Stick Notes	Staples Sticky Notes	Memo Cubes
Office Supplies	Self-Stick Notes	Staples Sticky Notes	Pop-Up Notes
Office Supplies	Self-Stick Notes	Self-Stick Notes	Flat Notes
Office Supplies	Self-Stick Notes	Self-Stick Notes	Memo Cubes
Office Supplies	Self-Stick Notes	Self-Stick Notes	Pop-Up Notes
Office Supplies	Self-Stick Notes	Recycled Self-Stick Notes	Recycled Flat Notes
Office Supplies	Self-Stick Notes	Recycled Self-Stick Notes	Recycled Pop-Up Notes
Office Supplies	Self-Stick Notes	Self-Stick Note Dispensers	Bonus Packs
Office Supplies	Self-Stick Notes	Self-Stick Note Dispensers	Flat Note Dispensers
Office Supplies	Self-Stick Notes	Self-Stick Note Dispensers	Pop-Up Note Dispensers
Office Supplies	Self-Stick Notes	Self-Stick Flags and Index Tabs	Flags
Office Supplies	Self-Stick Notes	Self-Stick Flags and Index Tabs	Flag Dispensers
Office Supplies	Self-Stick Notes	Self-Stick Flags and Index Tabs	Page Markers and Tabs
Office Supplies	Self-Stick Notes	Index Cards, Guides, and Files	Index Card Files
Office Supplies	Self-Stick Notes	Index Cards, Guides, and Files	Index Card Guides
Office Supplies	Self-Stick Notes	Index Cards, Guides, and Files	Index Cards
Office Supplies	Self-Stick Notes	Message Pads and Memo Slips	Pads—Message/Memo
Office Supplies	Self-Stick Notes	Self-Stick Easel Pads and Self-Stick Boards	Self-Stick Easel Pads
Office Supplies	Self-Stick Notes	Self-Stick Easel Pads and Self-Stick Boards	Self-Stick Accessories
Technology	Batteries, Surge, and UPS	Batteries, Surge, and UPS	Batteries
Technology	Batteries, Surge, and UPS	Batteries, Surge, and UPS	Battery Backups/UPS
Technology	Batteries, Surge, and UPS	Batteries, Surge, and UPS	Surge Protectors
Technology	Office Machines and Calculators	Office Machines and Calculators	Calculators

Exhibit OM1: Product Group Listing, Phase II

Phase II Beginning at Year 2

Phase II			
Product Group	**Product Category**	**Product Type**	**Product Item**
Office Supplies	Cleaning and Breakroom	Food and Beverage	Beverages
Office Supplies	Cleaning and Breakroom	Food and Beverage	Snack
Office Supplies	Cleaning and Breakroom	Food and Beverage	Coffee
Office Supplies	Cleaning and Breakroom	Appliances	Refrigerators
Office Supplies	Cleaning and Breakroom	Appliances	Water Dispensors and Filtration
Office Supplies	Cleaning and Breakroom	Appliances	Heaters
Office Supplies	Cleaning and Breakroom	First Aid and Safety	Aspirin and Pain Relievers
Office Supplies	Cleaning and Breakroom	First Aid and Safety	Band-Aids and Bandages
Office Supplies	Cleaning and Breakroom	First Aid and Safety	First Aid Kits
Office Supplies	Cleaning and Breakroom	Healthcare Products	Bandages, Wraps, and Masks
Office Supplies	Cleaning and Breakroom	Healthcare Products	Cleaners and Sanitizers
Office Supplies	Cleaning and Breakroom	Healthcare Products	Diagnostic Equipment
Technology	Computer Accessories	Notebook Accessories	Adapters, Cords, and Power
Technology	Computer Accessories	Notebook Accessories	Computer Cases—Nonrolling
Technology	Computer Accessories	Notebook Accessories	Keypads and Headphones
Technology	Computer Accessories	Mouse Pads and Wrist Pads	Keyboard Wrist Rests
Technology	Computer Accessories	Mouse Pads and Wrist Pads	Mouse Pads
Technology	Computer Accessories	Mouse Pads and Wrist Pads	Mouse Pads With Wrist Rests
Technology	Computer Accessories	Monitor and Machine Stands	CPU Stands
Technology	Computer Accessories	Monitor and Machine Stands	LCD Monitor/Plasma Mounts
Technology	Computer Accessories	Monitor and Machine Stands	Monitor Arms
Technology	Computer Accessories	Screen Filters/Protectors	CRT 13"–15" Filters
Technology	Computer Accessories	Screen Filters/Protectors	LCD 13"–15" Filters
Technology	Computer Accessories	Screen Filters/Protectors	Notebook Filters
Technology	Computer Accessories	Keyboard Drawers	Articulating Drawers
Technology	Computer Accessories	Keyboard Drawers	Desktop Drawers
Technology	Computer Accessories	Keyboard Drawers	Underdesk Drawers
Technology	Computer Accessories	Copyholders	Desktop Copyholders
Technology	Computer Accessories	Copyholders	Monitor Mount Copyholders
Technology	Computer Accessories	Media Storage	Case Storage
Technology	Computer Accessories	Media Storage	Desktop Storage
Technology	Computer Accessories	Media Storage	Filing/Binder Storage
Technology	Computer Accessories	Cleaning and Maintenance	Air Dusters
Technology	Computer Accessories	Cleaning and Maintenance	CD/DVD Maintenance
Technology	Computer Accessories	Cleaning and Maintenance	Cloths and Wipes
Technology	Computer Accessories	Back and Foot Rests	Back/Seat Rests
Technology	Computer Accessories	Back and Foot Rests	Foot Rests
Technology	Computer Accessories	Keyboards	Corded Keyboard

Phase II			
Product Group	**Product Category**	**Product Type**	**Product Item**
Technology	Computer Accessories	Keyboards	Cordless Keyboard
Technology	Computer Accessories	Keyboards	Keypads and Headphones
Technology	Computer Accessories	Mice	Corded Mice
Technology	Computer Accessories	Mice	Cordless Mice
Technology	Computer Accessories	Mice	Mice and Keyboard Bundles
Technology	Computer Accessories	Speakers and Headsets	Headsets
Technology	Computer Accessories	Speakers and Headsets	Speakers
Technology	Computers and PDAs	Build Your Own Pc	Build Your Own Desktop
Technology	Computers and PDAs	Build Your Own Pc	Build Your Own Notebook
Technology	Computers and PDAs	Pre-Configured PCs	Desktops
Technology	Computers and PDAs	Pre-Configured PCs	Notebooks
Technology	Computers and PDAs	PDAs and Handheld PCs	Palm Powered
Technology	Computers and PDAs	PDAs and Handheld PCs	Pocket PC Based
Technology	Computers and PDAs	Electronic Organizers	Electronic Organizers
Technology	Computers and PDAs	Electronic Organizers	Electronic Reference
Technology	Computers and PDAs	Notebook Accessories	Adapters, Cords, and Power
Technology	Computers and PDAs	Notebook Accessories	Computer Cases— Nonrolling
Technology	Computers and PDAs	Notebook Accessories	Internal Notebok Hard Drives
Technology	Computers and PDAs	Notebook Accessories	Keypads and Headphones
Technology	Computers and PDAs	Notebook Accessories	Locks, Lights, and Fans
Technology	Computers and PDAs	Notebook Accessories	Notebook Batteries
Technology	Computers and PDAs	Notebook Accessories	Notebook Memory
Technology	Computers and PDAs	Notebook Accessories	Notebook Stands and Pads
Technology	Computers and PDAs	Notebook Accessories	Travel Mice
Technology	Computers and PDAs	PDA Accessories	PDA Adapters and Cables
Technology	Computers and PDAs	PDA Accessories	PDA Anti-Virus Software
Technology	Computers and PDAs	PDA Accessories	PDA Cases and Protectors
Technology	Computers and PDAs	PDA Accessories	PDA Cradles and Chargers
Technology	Computers and PDAs	PDA Accessories	PDA Expansion
Technology	Computers and PDAs	PDA Accessories	Cards/Modems
Technology	Computers and PDAs	PDA Accessories	PDA Financial Software
Technology	Computers and PDAs	PDA Accessories	PDA Input Devices
Technology	Computers and PDAs	PDA Accessories	PDA Productivity Software
Technology	Computers and PDAs	PDA Accessories	PDA Reference Software
Technology	Copiers and Fax	Copiers and Fax	All-in-One Machines
Technology	Copiers and Fax	Copiers and Fax	Copiers
Technology	Copiers and Fax	Copiers and Fax	Fax Machines
Technology	Digital Scanners and Scanners	Digital Scanners and Scanners	Digital Cameras
Technology	Digital Scanners and Scanners	Digital Scanners and Scanners	Digital Camera Accessories
Technology	Digital Scanners and Scanners	Digital Scanners and Scanners	Digital Camcorders
Technology	Digital Scanners and Scanners	Digital Scanners and Scanners	PC and Web Cameras

(Continued)

Exhibit OM1 (Continued)

Phase II			
Product Group	**Product Category**	**Product Type**	**Product Item**
Technology	Digital Scanners and Scanners	Digital Scanners and Scanners	Scanners
Technology	Digital Scanners and Scanners	Digital Scanners and Scanners	Flash Memory
Technology	Digital Scanners and Scanners	Digital Scanners and Scanners	Photo Paper
Technology	Digital Scanners and Scanners	Digital Scanners and Scanners	Photo Printers
Technology	Digital Scanners and Scanners	Digital Scanners and Scanners	Security Cameras
Technology	Digital Scanners and Scanners	Digital Scanners and Scanners	Photo Center
Technology	Digital Scanners and Scanners	Digital Scanners and Scanners	Instant Cameras and Film
Technology	Drives and Media	Drives and Media	CD Drives
Technology	Drives and Media	Drives and Media	CD Media
Technology	Drives and Media	Drives and Media	Floppy Drives
Technology	Drives and Media	Drives and Media	Media Labels
Technology	Drives and Media	Drives and Media	Floppy Diskettes
Technology	Drives and Media	Drives and Media	Hard Drives
Technology	Drives and Media	Drives and Media	Media Storage
Technology	Drives and Media	Drives and Media	Tape Backup and Data Cartridges
Technology	Drives and Media	Drives and Media	USB Flash Drives
Technology	Drives and Media	Drives and Media	Zip Drives
Technology	Drives and Media	Drives and Media	Zip Media
Technology	Drives and Media	Drives and Media	REV Media
Technology	GPS and Satellite Radio	GPS and Satellite Radio	Portable Automotive GPS
Technology	GPS and Satellite Radio	GPS and Satellite Radio	PDA and Notebook GPS
Technology	GPS and Satellite Radio	GPS and Satellite Radio	Handheld GPS
Technology	GPS and Satellite Radio	GPS and Satellite Radio	Marine GPS
Technology	GPS and Satellite Radio	GPS and Satellite Radio	GPS Accessories
Technology	GPS and Satellite Radio	GPS and Satellite Radio	XM Satellite Radio
Technology	Ink and Toner Finder	Ink and Toner Finder	All Brands
Technology	MP3 and Media Players	MP3 and Media Players	MP3/Digital Audio Players
Technology	MP3 and Media Players	MP3 and Media Players	MP3 Accessories
Technology	MP3 and Media Players	MP3 and Media Players	Media Players
Technology	Monitors and Digital Projectors	Monitors and Digital Projectors	CRT Monitors
Technology	Monitors and Digital Projectors	Monitors and Digital Projectors	LCD (Flat Panel) Monitors
Technology	Monitors and Digital Projectors	Monitors and Digital Projectors	Plasma and LCD Televisions
Technology	Monitors and Digital Projectors	Monitors and Digital Projectors	Monitor Accessories

Phase II			
Product Group	**Product Category**	**Product Type**	**Product Item**
Technology	Monitors and Digital Projectors	Monitors and Digital Projectors	DVD Players and Televisions
Technology	Monitors and Digital Projectors	Monitors and Digital Projectors	Digital Projectors
Technology	Networking and Cables	Networking and Cables	Wireless-G with MIMO
Technology	Networking and Cables	Networking and Cables	Wireless-G Enhanced
Technology	Networking and Cables	Networking and Cables	Wirless-G
Technology	Networking and Cables	Networking and Cables	Wireless-A/G
Technology	Networking and Cables	Networking and Cables	Accessories
Technology	Networking and Cables	Networking and Cables	Wires (Ethernet)
Technology	Networking and Cables	Networking and Cables	Internet Phone (VoIP)
Technology	Networking and Cables	Networking and Cables	Cables, Hubs, Connectors, and Switches
Technology	Networking and Cables	Networking and Cables	Modems
Technology	Office Machines and Calculators	Office Machines and Calculators	Binding Machines and Supplies
Technology	Office Machines and Calculators	Office Machines and Calculators	Cash Registers and Credit Card Terminals
Technology	Office Machines and Calculators	Office Machines and Calculators	Copiers
Technology	Office Machines and Calculators	Office Machines and Calculators	DVD Players and Televisions
Technology	Office Machines and Calculators	Office Machines and Calculators	Digital Projectors
Technology	Office Machines and Calculators	Office Machines and Calculators	Fax Machines
Technology	Office Machines and Calculators	Office Machines and Calculators	Label Markers and Printers
Technology	Office Machines and Calculators	Office Machines and Calculators	Laminators and Supplies
Technology	Office Machines and Calculators	Office Machines and Calculators	Office Machines Supplies
Technology	Office Machines and Calculators	Office Machines and Calculators	Overhead Projectors and A/V Equipment
Technology	Office Machines and Calculators	Office Machines and Calculators	Paper Folders
Technology	Office Machines and Calculators	Office Machines and Calculators	Printers and All-in-One Machines
Technology	Office Machines and Calculators	Office Machines and Calculators	Recorders and Transcribers
Technology	Office Machines and Calculators	Office Machines and Calculators	Shredders
Technology	Office Machines and Calculators	Office Machines and Calculators	Time Clock and Cards
Technology	Office Machines and Calculators	Office Machines and Calculators	Typewriters
Technology	Peripherals and Memory	Peripherals and Memory	CD Drives
Technology	Peripherals and Memory	Peripherals and Memory	DVD Drives

(Continued)

Exhibit OM1 (Continued)

Phase II			
Product Group	**Product Category**	**Product Type**	**Product Item**
Technology	Peripherals and Memory	Peripherals and Memory	Floppy Drives
Technology	Peripherals and Memory	Peripherals and Memory	PC and Web Cameras
Technology	Peripherals and Memory	Peripherals and Memory	Hard Drives
Technology	Peripherals and Memory	Peripherals and Memory	USB Flash Drives
Technology	Peripherals and Memory	Peripherals and Memory	Zip Drives
Technology	Peripherals and Memory	Peripherals and Memory	Components and Upgrade Equipment
Technology	Peripherals and Memory	Peripherals and Memory	Flash MEmory
Technology	Peripherals and Memory	Peripherals and Memory	Gaming
Technology	Peripherals and Memory	Peripherals and Memory	Keyboards
Technology	Peripherals and Memory	Peripherals and Memory	Mice
Technology	Peripherals and Memory	Peripherals and Memory	Modems
Technology	Peripherals and Memory	Peripherals and Memory	PC Memory
Technology	Peripherals and Memory	Peripherals and Memory	Sound, Video, and Upgrade Cards
Technology	Peripherals and Memory	Peripherals and Memory	Speakers and Headets
Technology	Peripherals and Memory	Peripherals and Memory	Touchpads and Pens
Technology	Printers and All-in-Ones	Printers and All-in-Ones	All-in-One Machines
Technology	Printers and All-in-Ones	Printers and All-in-Ones	Dot Matrix Printers
Technology	Printers and All-in-Ones	Printers and All-in-Ones	Inkjet Printers
Technology	Printers and All-in-Ones	Printers and All-in-Ones	Label Printers
Technology	Printers and All-in-Ones	Printers and All-in-Ones	Laser Printers
Technology	Printers and All-in-Ones	Printers and All-in-Ones	Photo Printers
Technology	Printers and All-in-Ones	Printers and All-in-Ones	Portable Printers
Technology	Printers and All-in-Ones	Printers and All-in-Ones	Printer Accessories Finder
Technology	Printers and All-in-Ones	Printers and All-in-Ones	Wide Format Printers and Plotters
Technology	Shredders	Cross-Cut Shredders	Light/Med Duty Cross-Cut
Technology	Shredders	Cross-Cut Shredders	Heavy-Duty Cross-Cut
Technology	Shredders	Cross-Cut Shredders	Commercial Cross-Cut
Technology	Shredders	Strip-Cut Shredders	Light/Med Duty Strip-Cut
Technology	Shredders	Strip-Cut Shredders	Heavy-Duty Strip-Cut
Technology	Shredders	Strip-Cut Shredders	Commercial Strip-Cut
Technology	Shredders	Micro-Cut Shredders	Micro-Cut Shredders
Technology	Shredders	Media Destroyers	Media Destroyers
Technology	Shredders	All Shredders	All Shredders
Technology	Shredders	Shredder Oil and Bags	Shredder Oil
Technology	Shredders	Shredder Oil and Bags	Shredder Bags
Technology	Software	Software	Accounting and Finance
Technology	Software	Software	Anti-Virus and Internet Security
Technology	Software	Software	Business Productivity
Technology	Software	Software	Communications

Phase II			
Product Group	**Product Category**	**Product Type**	**Product Item**
Technology	Software	Software	Digital Media
Technology	Software	Software	Graphics and Design
Technology	Software	Software	Learning and Reference
Technology	Software	Software	Macintosh
Technology	Software	Software	Microsoft
Technology	Software	Software	Operating Systems
Technology	Software	Software	System Utilities
Technology	Software	Software	Tax Software
Technology	Telephone and Communications	Corded Phones	Multi-Line Phones—Corded
Technology	Telephone and Communications	Corded Phones	Single-Line Phones—Corded
Technology	Telephone and Communications	Cordless Phones	Single-Line Phones—Cordless
Technology	Telephone and Communications	Cordless Phones	Multi-Line Phones—Cordless
Technology	Telephone and Communications	Cordless Phones	Expandable Phone Systems—Cordless
Technology	Telephone and Communications	Headset Telephone Systems	Headset Telephone Systems
Technology	Telephone and Communications	Mobile Headsets	Mobile Headsets
Technology	Telephone and Communications	Office Headsets	Office Headsets
Technology	Telephone and Communications	Answering Machines and Caller ID Devices	Answering Machines
Technology	Telephone and Communications	Answering Machines and Caller ID Devices	Caller ID Devices
Technology	Telephone and Communications	Telephone Accessories	Cordless Phone Batteries
Technology	Telephone and Communications	Telephone Accessories	Cords, Couplers, Amplifiers, and Adapters
Technology	Telephone and Communications	Telephone Accessories	Stands, Shoulder Rests
Technology	Telephone and Communications	Wireless Accessories	All Brands
Technology	Telephone and Communications	Two-Way Radios	Two-Way Radios
Technology	Telephone and Communications	Two-Way Radios	Accessories Two-Way Radios Accessories
Technology	Telephone and Communications	Internet Phone (VoIP)	Internet Phone (VoIP)
Technology	Telephone and Communications	Broadband and Internet Services	Broadband Services
Technology	Telephone and Communications	Broadband and Internet Services	Dial-Up Services
Technology	Telephone and Communications	Weather/Alert Radios	Weather/Alert Radios

(Continued)

Exhibit OM1 (Continued)

Phase II			
Product Group	**Product Category**	**Product Type**	**Product Item**
Technology	Telephone and Communications	Wireless and Cellular	Wireless and Cellular
Furniture	Armoires	Armoires	Armoires
Furniture	Bookcases	Bookcases	Commercial Wooden Bookcases and Systems
Furniture	Bookcases	Bookcases	Small Office/Home Wooden Bookcases
Furniture	Bookcases	Bookcases	Commercial Metal Bookcases
Furniture	Bookcases	Bookcases	Small Office/Home MetalBookcases
Furniture	Bookcases	Bookcases	Furniture Collection Bookcases
Furniture	Bookcases	Bookcases	Literature Holders
Furniture	Carts and Stands	Carts and Stands	Audio/Visual Carts
Furniture	Carts and Stands	Carts and Stands	Computer Carts
Furniture	Carts and Stands	Carts and Stands	Craft Stands
Furniture	Carts and Stands	Carts and Stands	Lecterns
Furniture	Carts and Stands	Carts and Stands	Mail Carts
Furniture	Carts and Stands	Carts and Stands	Mobile Workstations
Furniture	Carts and Stands	Carts and Stands	Printer/Machine Carts
Furniture	Carts and Stands	Carts and Stands	Utility Carts
Furniture	Chairmats and Floormats	Chairmats and Floormats	Chairmats—Anti-Static
Furniture	Chairmats and Floormats	Chairmats and Floormats	Chairmats—Carpet
Furniture	Chairmats and Floormats	Chairmats and Floormats	Chairmats—Hard Floor
Furniture	Chairmats and Floormats	Chairmats and Floormats	Floormats—Anti-Fatigue
Furniture	Chairmats and Floormats	Chairmats and Floormats	Floormats—Carpeted
Furniture	Chairmats and Floormats	Chairmats and Floormats	Floormats—Industrial
Furniture	Chairmats and Floormats	Chairmats and Floormats	Floormats—Outdoor
Furniture	Chairs	Executive Chairs	Fabric Executive
Furniture	Chairs	Executive Chairs	Leather and Chrome
Furniture	Chairs	Executive Chairs	Leather and Wood
Furniture	Chairs	Executive Chairs	Leather Executive
Furniture	Chairs	Executive Chairs	Mesh Fabric
Furniture	Chairs	Management Chairs	Big and Tall
Furniture	Chairs	Management Chairs	Ergonomic
Furniture	Chairs	Management Chairs	Fabric Executive
Furniture	Chairs	Management Chairs	Leather
Furniture	Chairs	Management Chairs	Mesh Fabric
Furniture	Chairs	Commercial Chairs	Commercial
Furniture	Chairs	Task and Drafting Chairs/Stools	Fabric Task
Furniture	Chairs	Task and Drafting Chairs/Stools	Leather Task
Furniture	Chairs	Task and Drafting Chairs/Stools	Drafting Supplies

Phase II			
Product Group	**Product Category**	**Product Type**	**Product Item**
Furniture	Chairs	Task and Drafting Chairs/Stools	Stools
Furniture	Chairs	Reception and Guest Chairs	Fabric
Furniture	Chairs	Reception and Guest Chairs	Rception
Furniture	Chairs	Reception and Guest Chairs	Guest
Furniture	Chairs	Reception and Guest Chairs	Futons
Furniture	Chairs	Wood Chairs	Bankers
Furniture	Chairs	Wood Chairs	Side
Furniture	Chairs	Stacking and Folding Chairs	Stacking
Furniture	Chairs	Stacking and Folding Chairs	Folding
Furniture	Chairs	Educational Furniture	Chairs and Desks
Furniture	Chairs	Accessories	Casters
Furniture	Chairs	Accessories	Chair Arms
Furniture	Chairs	Accessories	Chair Carts
Furniture	Chairs	Accessories	Ottomans
Furniture	Desks	Desks	Compact and Student Desks
Furniture	Desks	Desks	Computer Desks
Furniture	Desks	Desks	Corner Desks
Furniture	Desks	Desks	Writing Desks
Furniture	Desks	Desks	"L" Shaped Desks
Furniture	Desks	Desks	Mobile Workstations
Furniture	File Cabinets	File Cabinets—Vertical	All Vertical File Cabinets
Furniture	File Cabinets	File Cabinets—Vertical	Commercial Metal
Furniture	File Cabinets	File Cabinets—Vertical	Small Office/Home Metal
Furniture	File Cabinets	File Cabinets—Vertical	Wood Vertical File Cabinets
Furniture	File Cabinets	File Cabinets—Lateral	All Lateral File Cabinets
Furniture	File Cabinets	File Cabinets—Lateral	Commercial Metal
Furniture	File Cabinets	File Cabinets—Lateral	Small Office/Home Metal
Furniture	File Cabinets	File Cabinets—Lateral	Wood Lateral File Cabinets
Furniture	File Cabinets	File Cabinets—Lateral	Open File Shelves
Furniture	File Cabinets	File Cabinets— Wood Lateral	Wood File Cabinets
Furniture	File Cabinets	File Cabinets— Wood Vertical	Wood File Cabinets
Furniture	File Cabinets	Fire Resistant	Fire Proof
Furniture	File Cabinets	Flat and Roll Files	Drafting and Printout File Systems
Furniture	File Cabinets	Flat and Roll Files	Flat File Systems
Furniture	File Cabinets	Storage Cabinets	Metal Storage Cabinets
Furniture	File Cabinets	Storage Cabinets	Lockers
Furniture	File Cabinets	Storage Cabinets	Storage Cubes
Furniture	File Cabinets	Mobile File Cabinets and Carts	Mobile File Cabinets
Furniture	File Cabinets	Mobile File Cabinets and Carts	Mobile File Carts
Furniture	File Cabinets	Locks and Accessories	Locks and Accessories

(Continued)

Exhibit OM1 (Continued)

Phase II			
Product Group	**Product Category**	**Product Type**	**Product Item**
Furniture	File Cabinets	Safes Sentry	Fire-Safe Chests
Furniture	File Cabinets	Safes Sentry	Fire-Safe Files
Furniture	File Cabinets	Safes Sentry	Fire-Safe Safes
Furniture	File Cabinets	Safes Sentry	Security Safes
Furniture	File Cabinets	Safes Sentry	Waterproof Fire-Safe Safes
Furniture	Furniture Accessories	Furniture Accessories	Chairrmats and Floormats
Furniture	Furniture Accessories	Furniture Accessories	Ottomans
Furniture	Furniture Accessories	Furniture Accessories	Clocks
Furniture	Furniture Accessories	Furniture Accessories	Desk Sets/Organizers
Furniture	Furniture Accessories	Furniture Accessories	Pads and Protectors
Furniture	Furniture Accessories	Furniture Accessories	Coat Hangers
Furniture	Furniture Accessories	Furniture Accessories	Coat Racks and Hooks
Furniture	Furniture Accessories	Furniture Accessories	Costumers/Garnment Racks
Furniture	Furniture Accessories	Furniture Accessories	Chair Arms
Furniture	Furniture Accessories	Furniture Accessories	Frames
Furniture	Furniture Accessories	Furniture Accessories	Maps, Magnifiers, and Flags
Furniture	Furniture Accessories	Furniture Accessories	Door Stops
Furniture	Furniture Accessories	Furniture Accessories	Casters
Furniture	Furniture Collections	Furniture Collections	Commercial Grade Collections
Furniture	Furniture Collections	Furniture Collections	Small Office/Home Office Collections
Furniture	Home and Office Furnishings	Home and Office Furnishings	Accent Furniture
Furniture	Home and Office Furnishings	Home and Office Furnishings	Area Rugs
Furniture	Home and Office Furnishings	Home and Office Furnishings	Audio Towers
Furniture	Home and Office Furnishings	Home and Office Furnishings	Breakroom and Kitchen
Furniture	Home and Office Furnishings	Home and Office Furnishings	Contemporary Seating
Furniture	Home and Office Furnishings	Home and Office Furnishings	Entertainment Centers
Furniture	Home and Office Furnishings	Home and Office Furnishings	Entertainment Furniture
Furniture	Home and Office Furnishings	Home and Office Furnishings	Entertainment Stands
Furniture	Home and Office Furnishings	Home and Office Furnishings	Folding Screens
Furniture	Home and Office Furnishings	Home and Office Furnishings	Futons
Furniture	Home and Office Furnishings	Home and Office Furnishings	Media Storage
Furniture	Lamps and Lighting	Desk Lamps	Contemporary—Desk Lamps

Phase II			
Product Group	**Product Category**	**Product Type**	**Product Item**
Furniture	Lamps and Lighting	Desk Lamps	Functional—Desk Lamps
Furniture	Lamps and Lighting	Desk Lamps	Traditional—Desk Lamps
Furniture	Lamps and Lighting	Floor Lamps	Contemporary—Floor Lamps
Furniture	Lamps and Lighting	Floor Lamps	Tasks—Floor Lamps
Furniture	Lamps and Lighting	Table Lamps	Contemporary—Table Lamps
Furniture	Lamps and Lighting	Table Lamps	Traditional—Table Lamps
Furniture	Lamps and Lighting	Magnifying Lamps	Magnifying Lamps
Furniture	Lamps and Lighting	Under-Cabinet and Panel Lamps	Under-Cabinet and Panel Lamps
Furniture	Lamps and Lighting	Light Bulbs	Light Bulbs
Furniture	Office Décor and Plants	Office Décor and Plants	Desk Sets/Organizers
Furniture	Office Décor and Plants	Office Décor and Plants	Wall Art
Furniture	Office Décor and Plants	Office Décor and Plants	Accent/Coffee Tables
Furniture	Office Décor and Plants	Office Décor and Plants	Decorative Chalkboards
Furniture	Office Décor and Plants	Office Décor and Plants	Decorative Corkboards
Furniture	Office Décor and Plants	Office Décor and Plants	Mirrors
Furniture	Office Décor and Plants	Office Décor and Plants	Plants
Furniture	Office Décor and Plants	Office Décor and Plants	Privacy Screens
Furniture	Office Décor and Plants	Office Décor and Plants	Rugs
Furniture	Office Décor and Plants	Office Décor and Plants	Umbrella Stands/Coat Racks
Furniture	Panel Systems/ Accessories	Panel Systems/Accessories	Panel Systems
Furniture	Panel Systems/ Accessories	Panel Systems/Accessories	Panel Systems Hardware
Furniture	Panel Systems/ Accessories	Panel Systems/Accessories	Cubicle and Parition Organizers/Accessories
Furniture	Panel Systems/ Accessories	Panel Systems/Accessories	Panel Accessories
Furniture	Panel Systems/ Accessories	Panel Systems/Accessories	Under-Cabinet and Panel Lamps
Furniture	Shelving	Shelving	Literature Holders
Furniture	Shelving	Shelving	Metal Shelving
Furniture	Shelving	Shelving	Plastic Shelving
Furniture	Storage Cabinets	Storage Cabinets	Lockers
Furniture	Storage Cabinets	Storage Cabinets	Media Storage Cabinets
Furniture	Storage Cabinets	Storage Cabinets	Metal Storage Cabinets
Furniture	Storage Cabinets	Storage Cabinets	Storage Cubes
Furniture	Storage Cabinets	Storage Cabinets	Wood, Resin, and Laminate
Furniture	Storage Cabinets	Storage Cabinets	Storage Cabinets
Furniture	Tables	Tables	Folding and Banquet Tables
Furniture	Tables	Tables	Utility and Special Tables
Furniture	Tables	Tables	Meeting/Conference Room Tables
Furniture	Tables	Tables	Drafting Tables
Furniture	Tables	Tables	Training Room Tables
Furniture	Tables	Tables	Reception Area Tables

Exhibit OM2: Location in Egypt

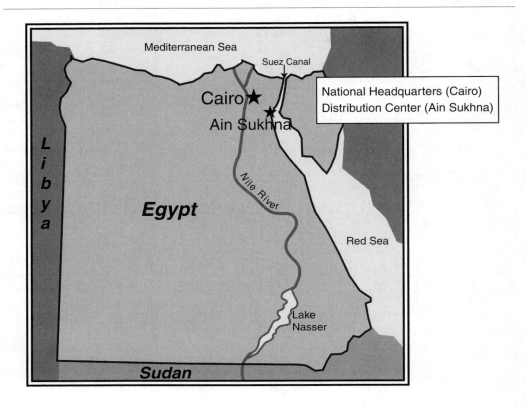

Egyptian Transportation

Railways: total: 5,063 km standard gauge: 5,063 km 1.435-m gauge (62 km electrified) (2004)

Highways: total: 64,000 km paved: 49,984 km unpaved: 14,016 km (1999 est.)

Waterways: 3,500 km note: includes Nile River, Lake Nasser, Alexandria-Cairo Waterway, and numerous smaller canals in delta; Suez Canal (193.5 km including approaches) navigable by oceangoing vessels drawing up to 17.68 m (2004)

Pipelines: condensate 289 km; condensate/gas 94 km; gas 6,115 km; liquid petroleum gas 852 km; oil 5,032 km; oil/gas/water 36 km; refined products 246 km (2004)

Ports and harbors: Alexandria, Damietta, El Dekheila, Port Said, Suez, Sukhna, Zeit

Merchant marine: total: 77 ships (1,000 GRT or over) 1,194,696 GRT/1,754,815 DWT by type: bulk carrier 14, cargo 34, container 2, passenger/cargo 5, petroleum tanker 14, roll on/roll off 8 foreign-owned: 10 (Denmark 1, Greece 6, Lebanon 2, Turkey 1) registered in other countries: 34 (2005)

Airports: 87 (2004 est.)

Heliports: 2 (2004 est.)

Exhibit OM3: Detailed Analysis of Distribution Costs (US$)

	Year 1	Year 2	Year 3	Year 4	Year 5
Number of personnel units	2	2	2	2	2
Wages	$7,363.64	$10,800.00	$11,880.00	$13,068.00	$14,374.80
Bonuses	$0.00	$0.00	$0.00	$0.00	$0.00
Social and other personnel costs	$0.00	$0.00	$0.00	$0.00	$0.00
Number of inbound shipments	$83.00	$151.00	$250.00	$300.00	$300.00
Import customs and transportation to distribution center	$17,945.95	$32,648.65	$54,054.05	$64,864.86	$64,864.86
Number of orders	$19,500.00	$202,500.00	$702,503.59	$790,190.00	$917,458.00
Picking and packing	$7,027.03	$72,972.97	$253,154.45	$284,753.15	$330,615.50
Office material	$54.05	$86.49	$86.49	$86.49	$86.49
Travel and refreshment	$162.16	$259.46	$259.46	$259.46	$259.46
Communication	$270.27	$432.43	$432.43	$432.43	$432.43
Depreciation	$531.96	$851.14	$851.14	$325.61	$10.30
Total distribution	**$33,355.06**	**$118,051.14**	**$320,718.02**	**$363,790.01**	**$410,643.83**
In % of sales	16%	5%	5%	5%	4%

Exhibit OM4: GSI—Global Structure Industries
Letter to Provide Services

 GSI—Global Structure Industries
221 Hafaz Badwy
Nasar City
Seventh District
Cairo, Egypt
Telephone: +2 0105853129
Fax: +2 0105853137

August 19, 2008

To: Mr. Stephan Shar
    Vice President, Maktabi

Re: Service Agreement

Dear Mr. Shar,

I am pleased to confirm GSI's agreement with Maktabi to provide third-party services to your company. These services are to include, but are not limited to:

- Freight forwarding and customs clearance
- Renting or construction of a distribution center near Cairo
- Transportation to distribution center
- Management of distribution center
- Picking and packing
- Order fulfillment
- Customer tracking

The details of services to be rendered will be discussed at the meeting scheduled during the second week of October and the final contract will drawn up for approval and signature in December.

We are looking forward to developing a close relationship with you and the Maktabi Group.

Sincerely,

A.M. Mahmood

A. M. Mahmood
Sales Manager
GSI

Exhibit OM5: Sample Chief Executive Officer (CEO) Resume

(For more information on this candidate, please contact the Maktabi Group directly.)

Objective

To obtain a challenging position that utilizes my diverse experience in the U.S. and international market including, but not limited to, sales, technical operations, supply chain, and financial analysis.

Experience

June, 2004–Present, InterMed

Pharmaceutical Sales Representative and Associate Territory Business Manager

Pharmaceutical Sales Representative for assigned medicines in a territory that includes greater New York. Sales goals have been exceeded every quarter, with an annual sales volume of over $10 million.

- Overall sales portfolio and goal attainment is above 110%, exceeding sales quota and achieving top ten ranking nationwide.
- Currently ranked in the top 2% of sales in the neuroscience group.
- Ranked top sales representative for numerous contests.
- Converted targeted physicians to 100% market share expansion.

September, 2002–June, 2004, InterMed

Senior Analyst, U.S. Market Planning

Responsibilities included the detailed analysis and the production of reports concerning product demand, management of the Materials Planning System, organization of logistical fulfillment, and coordinaton of production efforts with third-party manufacturers.

- Coordinated with marketing, finance, and sales departments, production operations, customer service, and the regulatory group to develop overall marketing strategies.
- Evaluated market trends to ensure inventory and manufacturing goals were on target.
- Responsible for the rollout of the company's new central planning system, which will be used for the global coordination and execution of materials replenishment and logistical delivery.
- Managed a global inventory that supported over $10 billion in sales revenue.
- Provided direction to site production planners to ensure adequate production to meet market demand.

August, 2000–September, 2002, Baya Cosmetics

Supply Chain Analyst

Responsible for ensuring the integrity of the global supply chain.

- Resolved capacity issues and ensured the balance of supply across regions and manufacturing plants.
- Achieved a significant reduction in backorders within 6 months.
- Improved Customer Service fill rates from 65% in 2000 to 96% in 2002.

February, 1995–May, 2000, Best Cleaners (Family Business)

Manager

- Hired, trained, and managed a staff of five.
- Initiated a new automation process by computerizing the establishment and training the staff in the new mode of operation, resulting in increased productivity.
- Performed all financial aspects including payroll, income tax, billing, and charge accounts.

Education

Rutgers University, New Brunswick, New Jersey

Bachelor of Arts in Political Science with Economics Minor, May 2000

- Graduated with Departmental Honors—GPA in Major 3.60/4.00
- Dean's list from 1997 to 2000
- Volunteer/Teaching Assistant, Paul Robinson Community School of the Arts: taught grammar, reading, and math to over 20 students with learning disabilities for academic year 1999/2000.

Skills

Advanced skills in SAP, MRP I/II, Business Warehouse, Dendrite, and Microsoft Office

Other

- Languages: Arabic and basic understanding of Spanish
- Member, Toastmasters International; received many speech awards
- Completed the Dale Carnegie Seminar
- Occupational Safety & Health Association (OSHA) Certified for Hazardous Materials Emergency Response
- Member of Minority Pharmaceutical Sales Representative Organization

Exhibit CM1: Organization Chart

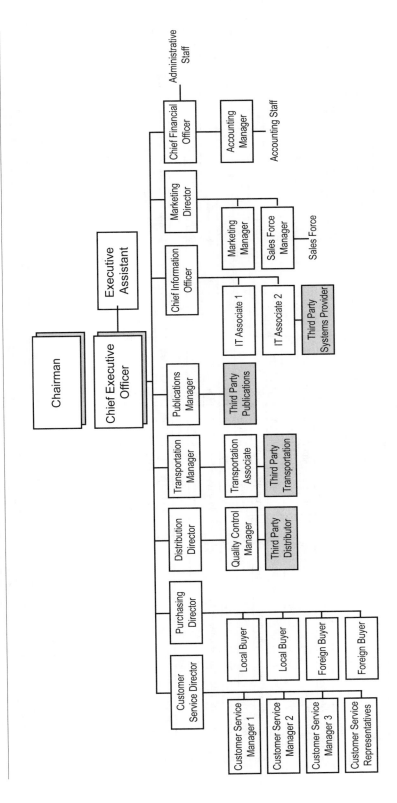

Exhibit CM2: Implementation Plan

ID	Task Name	Duration	Start	Finish	Predecessors	Gantt (resources)
1	Maktabi Implementation	183 days	Sun 2/3/08	Tue 8/5/08		
2	**Phase I: Business setup and sourcing**	**40 days**	**Sun 2/3/08**	**Thu 3/27/08**		
3	**Initial setup**	**10 days**	**Sun 2/3/08**	**Thu 2/14/08**		
4	Office space search and move-in	1 week	Sun 2/3/08	Thu 2/7/08		CEO, CIO
5	Computer hardware and software purchase	1 week	Sun 2/3/08	Thu 2/7/08		CIO
6	Furniture and other equipment purchase	1 week	Sun 2/10/08	Thu 2/14/08	4	CEO, CIO
7	Office material purchase	2 days	Sun 2/10/08	Mon 2/11/08	4	CEO, CIO
8	Telephone and mobile line purchase	1 day	Sun 2/10/08	Sun 2/10/08	4	CIO
9	**Legal and financial business setup**	**40 days**	**Sun 2/3/08**	**Thu 3/27/08**		
10	Required legal formalities setup	2 months	Sun 2/3/08	Thu 3/27/08		CEO, CIO
11	Open small business bank account	1 week	Sun 2/3/08	Thu 2/7/08		CEO, CIO
12	**Phase II: Pre-sales setup**	**159 days**	**Thu 2/7/08**	**Tue 9/16/08**		
13	**Administration setup**	**71 days**	**Thu 2/28/08**	**Thu 6/5/08**		
14	Directive, policy and procedure creation	3 months	Thu 2/28/08	Wed 5/21/08	31	CEO
15	CFO search and hire	3 weeks	Sun 5/4/08	Thu 5/22/08	4FS + 60 days	CEO, CIO
16	Insurance purchase	2 weeks	Sun 5/25/08	Thu 6/5/08	15	CFO
17	Executive assistant search and hire	2 weeks	Sun 5/25/08	Thu 6/5/08	15	CEO
18	**Customer service setup**	**90 days**	**Sun 5/4/08**	**Tue 9/1608**		
19	Customer service director search and hire	3 weeks	Sun 5/4/08	Thu 5/22/08	4FS+ 60 days	CEO, CIO, CFO
20	Customer service setup plan creation	1 month	Sun 5/25/08	Thu 6/19/08	19	Customer service director
21	Customer service setup plan approval	0 days	Thu 6/19/08	Thu 6/19/08	20	6/19
22	Customer service manager search and hire	3 weeks	Thu 6/12/08	Thu 7/2/08	19FS + 14 days	Customer service director
23	Computer hardware and software purchase	1 week	Wed 9/10/08	Tue 9/16/08	95FF	CIO
24	Furniture and other equipment purchase	1 week	Wed 9/10/08	Tue 9/16/08	95FF	CFO
25	Office material purchase	2 days	Mon 9/15/08	Tue 9/16/08	95FF	CFO
26	Telephone and mobile line purchase	1 day	Tue 9/16/08	Tue 9/16/08	95FF	CFO

ID	Task Name	Duration	Start	Finish	Predecessors
27	**Purchasing setup**	**90 days**	**Thu 2/7/08**	**Wed 6/11/08**	
28	**Sourcing initiation**	**55 days**	**Thu 2/7/08**	**Wed 4/23/08**	
29	Purchasing director search and hire	3 weeks	Sun 2/10/08	Thu 2/28/08	4
30	Final product selection	3 weeks	Thu 2/7/08	Wed 2/27/08	29SF+ 14 days
31	Final product selection approval	0 days	Wed 2/27/08	Wed 2/27/08	30
32	Local supplier search	1 month	Thu 2/28/08	Wed 3/26/08	31
33	Foreign market supplier search	2 months	Thu 2/28/08	Wed 4/23/08	31
34	Purchasing department setup	35 days	Thu 4/24/08	Wed 6/11/08	
35	Purchasing manager search and hire	3 weeks	Thu 4/24/08	Wed 5/14/08	33
36	Product order and purchase plan	1 month	Thu 5/15/08	Wed 6/11/08	35
37	Product order and purchase plan approval	0 days	Wed 6/11/08	Wed 6/11/08	36
38	Computer hardware and software purchase	1 week	Thu 5/8/08	Wed 5/14/08	35FF
39	Furniture and other equipment purchase	1 week	Thu 5/8/08	Wed 5/14/08	35FF
40	Office material purchase	2 days	Tue 5/13/08	Wed 5/14/08	35FF
41	Telephone and mobile line purchase	1 day	Wed 5/14/08	Wed 5/14/08	35FF
42	**Distribution setup**	**57 days**	**Sun 5/4/08**	**Mon 7/21/08**	
43	Distribution director search and hire	3 weeks	Sun 5/4/08	Thu 5/22/08	4FS+ 60 days
44	Contract with distribution provider	3 weeks	Thu 6/12/08	Wed 7/2/08	43FS+ 14 days
45	Quality control manager search and hire	3 weeks	Tue 6/3/08	Mon 6/23/08	43FS+ 7 days
46	Quality control policy creation	1 month	Tue 6/24/08	Mon 7/23/08	45
47	Quality control plan approval	0 days	Mon 7/21/08	Mon 7/21/08	46
48	Computer hardware and software purchase	1 week	Sun 5/18/08	Thu 5/22/08	43FF
49	Furniture and other equipment purchase	1 week	Sun 5/18/08	Thu 5/22/08	43FF
50	Office material purchase	2 days	Wed 5/21/08	Thu 5/22/08	43FF
51	Telephone and mobile line purchase	1 day	Thu 5/22/08	Thu 5/22/08	43FF

(Continued)

Task ▢   Milestone ◆

Split ·············   Summary I——I

603

Exhibit CM2 (Continued)

ID	Task Name	Duration	Start	Finish	Predecessors
52	**Transportation setup**	**57 days**	**Sun 5/4/08**	**Mon 7/21/08**	
53	Transportation director search and hire	3 weeks	Sun 5/4/08	Thu 5/22/08	4FS+ 60 days
54	Contract with transportation provider	3 weeks	Thu 6/12/08	Wed 7/2/08	53FS+ 14 days
55	Transportation associate search and hire	3 weeks	Tue 6/3/08	Mon 6/23/08	53FS+ 7 days
56	Transportation plan policy creation	1 month	Tue 6/24/08	Mon 7/21/08	55
57	Transportation plan approval	0 days	Mon 7/21/08	Mon 7/21/08	56
58	Computer hardware and software purchase	1 week	Sun 5/18/08	Thu 5/22/08	53FF
59	Furniture and other equipment purchase	1 week	Sun 5/18/08	Thu 5/22/08	53FF
60	Office material purchase	2 days	Wed 5/21/08	Thu 5/22/08	53FF
61	Telephone and mobile line purchase	1 day	Thu 5/22/08	Thu 5/22/08	53FF
62	**Publications setup**	**37 days**	**Sun 5/4/08**	**Mon 6/23/08**	
63	Publications manager search and hire	3 weeks	Sun 5/4/08	Thu 5/22/08	4FS+ 60 days
64	Contract with publisher	3 weeks	Tue 6/3/08	Mon 6/23/08	63FS+ 7 days
65	Computer hardware and software purchase	1 week	Tue 5/13/08	Mon 5/19/08	63FS+ 7 days
66	Furniture and other equipment purchase	1 week	Tue 5/13/08	Mon 5/19/08	63FS+ 7 days
67	Office material purchase	2 days	Tue 5/13/08	Wed 5/14/08	63FS+ 7 days
68	Telephone and mobile line purchase	1 day	Tue 5/13/08	Tue 5/13/08	63FS+ 7 days
69	**Information technologies setup**	**57 days**	**Sun 5/4/08**	**Mon 7/21/08**	
70	IT associate search and hire	3 weeks	Sun 5/4/08	Thu 5/22/08	4FS+ 60 days
71	IT requirements draft	1 month	Tue 6/3/08	Mon 6/30/08	70FS+ 7 days
72	IT requirements approval	6 days	Mon 6/30/08	Mon 6/30/08	71
73	Contract with IT service provider	3 weeks	Tue 7/1/08	Mon 7/21/08	72
74	Computer hardware and software purchase	1 week	Sun 5/18/08	Thu 5/22/08	70FF
75	Furniture and other equipment purchase	1 week	Sun 5/18/08	Thu 5/22/08	70FF
76	Office material purchase	2 days	Wed 5/21/08	Thu 5/22/08	70FF
77	Telephone and mobile line purchase	1 day	Thu 5/22/08	Thu 5/22/08	70FF

Gantt chart timeline columns (1st Half: Jan, Feb, Mar, Apr; 2nd Half: May, Jun, Jul, Aug, Sep, Oct, Nov, Dec) with resource annotations:

- 53: CEO; CIO
- 54: Distribution director
- 55: Distribution director
- 56: Quality control manager
- 57: 7/21
- 58: CIO
- 59: CFO
- 60: CFO
- 61: CFO
- 63: CEO; CIO
- 64: Publications director
- 65: CIO
- 66: CFO
- 67: CFO
- 68: CFO
- 70: CIO
- 71: IT associates
- 72: 6/30
- 73: CIO
- 74: CIO
- 75: CFO
- 76: CFO

ID	Task Name	Duration	Start	Finish	Predecessors	Timeline label
78	**Marketing and sales setup**	**49 days**	**Sun 5/4/08**	**Wed 7/9/08**		
79	Marketing director search and hire	3 weeks	Sun 5/4/08	Thu 5/22/08	4FS+ 60 days	CEO, CIO
80	Marketing promotions and advertising sales creation	1 month	Thu 6/12/08	Wed 7/9/08	79FS+ 14 days	Marketing director
81	Marketing promotions and advertising sales approval	0 days	Wed 7/9/08	Wed 7/9/08	80	7/9
82	Marketing manager search and hire	3 weeks	Tue 6/3/08	Mon 6/23/08	79FS+ 7 days	Marketing director
83	Computer hardware and software purchase	1 week	Sun 5/18/08	Thu 5/22/08	79FF	CIO
84	Furniture and other equipment purchase	1 week	Sun 5/18/08	Thu 5/22/08	79FF	CFO
85	Office material purchase	2 days	Wed 521/08	Thu 5/22/08	79FF	CFO
86	Telephone and mobile line purchase	1 day	Thu 5/22/08	Thu 5/22/08	79FF	CFO
87	**Phase III: Pre-sales operations**	**164 days**	**Thu 2/28/08**	**Mon 8/11/08**		
88	**Administration operation**	**15 days**	**Sun 5/4/08**	**Thu 5/22/08**		
89	New office search and move in	3 weeks	Sun 5/4/08	Thu 5/22/08	4FS+ 60 days	CFO
90	New office approval	0 days	Thu 5/22/08	Thu 5/22/08	89	5/22
91	Accounting manager search and hire	3 weeks	Sun 5/4/08	Thu 5/22/08	4FS+ 60 days	CFO
92	Personnel (drivers, janitors, etc.) search and hire	3 weeks	Sun 5/4/08	Thu 5/22/08	89FF	CFO, Executive assitant
93	**Customer service operation**	**60 days**	**Wed 7/23/08**	**Mon 9/22/08**		
94	Customer service training preparation	1 month	Wed 7/23/08	Tue 8/19/08	22FS+ 14 days	Customer service manager (CSM)
95	Customer service representatives search and hire	1 month	Wed 8/20/08	Tue 9/16/08	94	CSM
96	Customer service representatives training	1 month	Wed 9/17/08	Tue 10/14/08	95	CSM
97	**Purchasing operation**	**185 days**	**Thu 2/28/08**	**Wed 8/6/08**		
98	**Sourcing operation**	**117 days**	**Thu 2/28/08**	**Tue 6/10/08**		
99	Local supplier visits	1 month	Mon 3/10/08	Sun 4/6/08	32SS+ 7 days	CEO, CIO, Purchasing director
100	Foreign supplier market visits	2 months	Wed 3/19/08	Tue 5/11/08	33SS+ 14 days	CEO, CIO, Purchasing director
101	Temporary warehouse space search and rent	1 week	Thu 2/28/08	Wen 3/5/08	31	Purchasing director;
102	Purchase/receipt of local supply samples	1 month	Mon 3/10/08	Sun 4/6/08	32SS+ 7 days	CEO, CIO, Purchasing director
103	Purchase/receipt of foreign supply samples	3 months	Wed 3/19/08	Tue 6/10/08	33SS+ 14 days	CEO, CIO, Purchasing director

Timeline headers: 1st Half (Jan, Feb, Mar, Apr, May, Jun) | 2nd Half (Jul, Aug, Sep, Oct, Nov, Dec)

Legend: Task ▮ | Milestone ◆ | Split ·········· | Summary

(Continued)

Exhibit CM2 (Continued)

ID	Task Name	Duration	Start	Finish	Predecessors	Gantt / Resources
104	**Purchasing department operation**	**40 days**	**Thu 6/12/08**	**Wed 8/6/08**		
105	Pre-sales product orders and purchase plan execution	2 months	Thu 6/12/08	Wed 8/6/08	37	Purchasing director, Purchasing manager
106	**Distribution operation**	**60 days**	**Thu 7/3/08**	**Wed 9/24/08**		
107	Operations setup with distribution provider	3 months	Thu 7/3/08	Wed 9/24/08	94	Distribution director
108	**Transportation operation**	**60 days**	**Thu 7/3/08**	**Wed 9/24/08**		
109	Operations setup with transportation provider	3 months	Thu 7/3/08	Wed 9/24/08	54	Transportation provider
110	**Publications operation**	**40 days**	**Tue 6/24/08**	**Mon 8/18/08**		
111	Initial catalog design	1 month	Tue 6/24/08	Mon 7/21/08	64	Publications director (PD), Publications manager (PM)
112	Photos of sample products	3 weeks	Tue 7/22/08	Mon 8/11/08	113SS	PD, PM
113	Initial catalog design	1 month	Tue 7/22/08	Mon 8/18/08	111	PD, PM
114	Final catalog approval	0 days	Mon 8/18/08	Mon 8/18/08	113	8/18
115	**Information technologies operation**	**60 days**	**Tue 7/22/08**	**Sun 9/21/08**		
116	Operations setup with IT service provider	3 months	Tue 7/22/08	Mon 10/13/08	73	CIO, IT service provider
117	**Marketing and sales operation**	**60 days**	**Thu 7/10/08**	**Wed 10/1/08**		
118	Pre-sales marketing promotions and advertising plan execution	3 months	Thu 7/10/08	Wed 10/1/08	81	Marketing director
119	Sales representative training preparation	1 month	Mon 7/14/08	Sun 8/10/08	82FS+ 14 days	Marketing manager
120	Sales representative search and hire	1 month	Mon 8/11/08	Sun 9/7/08	119	Marketing manager
121	Sales representative training	3 weeks	Mon 9/8/08	Sun 9/28/08	120	Marketing manager
122	Sales representative visits execution	0 days	Sun 9/28/08	Sun 9/28/08	121	9/28
123	**Phase IV: Operations kickoff**	**0 days**	**Wed 10/1/08**	**Wed 10/1/08**		10/1

Task ▮   Milestone ◆

Split ·············   Summary I——I

Index

About the Author

Robert D. Hisrich is the Garvin Professor of Global Entrepreneurship and Director of the Walker Center for Global Entrepreneurship at Thunderbird School of Global Management. He holds an MBA and a doctorate from the University of Cincinnati.

Professor Hisrich's research pursuits are focused on entrepreneurship and venture creation: entrepreneurial ethics, intrapreneurship, women and minority entrepreneurs, venture financing, and global venture creation. He teaches courses and seminars in these areas, as well as in marketing management and product planning and development. His interest in global management and entrepreneurship resulted in two Fulbright Fellowships in Budapest, Hungary; honorary degrees from universities in Russia and Hungary; and visiting faculty positions in universities in Austria, Australia, Ireland, and Slovenia. Professor Hisrich serves on the editorial boards of several prominent journals in entrepreneurial scholarship, is on several boards of directors, and is author or coauthor of over 300 research articles appearing in such journals as *Journal of Marketing, Journal of Marketing Research, Journal of Business Venturing, Journal of Small Business Finance, Small Business Economics, Journal of Developmental Entrepreneurship,* and *Entrepreneurship Theory and Practice.* Professor Hisrich has authored or coauthored 25 books, including *Entrepreneurship: Starting, Developing, and Managing a New Enterprise* (translated into nine languages), *The 13 Biggest Mistakes that Derail Small Businesses and How to Avoid Them,* and *Marketing: A Practical Management Approach.*